ORACLES OF (

THE ROMAN CATHOLIC CHURCH
AND IRISH POLITICS, 1922–37

David McNeve.

Dublin

Dec 2011.

ORACLES OF GOD

THE ROMAN CATHOLIC CHURCH
AND IRISH POLITICS 1922–37

Patrick Murray

University College Dublin Press
Preas Choláiste Ollscoile Bhaile Átha Cliath

First published 2000 by University College Dublin Press
Newman House, St Stephen's Green, Dublin 2, Ireland

© Patrick Murray 2000

ISBN 1 900621 27 4 hardback
1 900621 28 2 paperback

Cataloguing in Publication data available from the British Library

Typeset in Baskerville in Ireland by Elaine Shiels, Bantry, County Cork
Printed in Ireland by ColourBooks Ltd

CONTENTS

PREFACE

THE PERIOD BETWEEN the Treaty and the 1937 Constitution saw the active involvement in politics of a considerable body of Roman Catholic clergymen. A substantial majority of these strongly supported the Treaty settlement and helped in a variety of ways to sustain the Provisional and Free State Governments. Led by the bishops, they also deployed the spiritual and moral resources of the Church to counteract Republican resistance to the Treaty. A minority of clergymen, whose numerical and political strength it has been one of my principal aims to assess, rendered material and spiritual assistance to the anti-Treaty cause throughout the Civil War period and beyond. The great majority of these, together with some previously pro-Treaty border clergy disappointed by the 1925 Boundary settlement and others disillusioned by aspects of Free State policy, transferred their allegiance to Fianna Fáil from 1926 onwards.

A notable feature of de Valera's strategy as leader of Fianna Fáil was his firm identification of the party with specifically Roman Catholic interests, which were also generally served by Cumann na nGaedheal administrations. In both instances, there was a widespread congruence between religious conviction and political expediency on the part of politicians. From the late twenties on, almost the only anti-clerical notes were sounded by those Republicans whose radicalism brought them into conflict with the moral and social teaching of the Church.

I have examined the political activities, as well as the outlook and motives of Irish churchmen, at home and abroad, in the light of a wide range of archival material, mainly diocesan, much of this previously unexplored. I have drawn on the expertise of many scholars and historians, specialists in Canon Law, ecclesiastical history and theology, and many individuals throughout the country, including survivors of the period and their relatives.

I considered it essential to include a survey of developments in Northern Ireland during the period in order to illustrate, among other things, the impact of the Civil War in the South on the concerns and destinies of the Northern minority.

PATRICK MURRAY
Athlone, May 1999

ACKNOWLEDGEMENTS

This book has its origins in my doctoral dissertation presented at Trinity College, Dublin in 1998. I would like to record my thanks to Professor David Fitzpatrick, Department of Modern History, Trinity College, for suggesting my topic and for his stimulating guidance and criticism at every stage. Professor Tom Garvin of University College Dublin and Professor David Dickson of Trinity College provided valuable advice and encouragement. Over the years the late Cardinal Tomás Ó Fiach maintained and intensified my interest in ecclesiastical politics, while I gained much enlightenment from conversations with the late Professor T.P. O'Neill, who had an intimate knowledge of the period covered in this book, and an unrivalled command of local detail.

I have been able to make use of the papers of Monsignor John Hagan and Monsignor M.J. Curran in the Irish College, Rome, through the courtesy of the Archivist, Monsignor John Hanly. I am also grateful to Mr Séamus Helferty, Archives Department, University College Dublin, and to the staffs of the National Library of Ireland, the National Archives of Ireland, the TCD libraries and the county libraries of Galway, Longford–Westmeath, Roscommon and Sligo. I owe a special debt to Gearóid O'Brien, Librarian, Athlone, and to his helpful and courteous staff. I am also grateful to Margaret Grennan, Editor, *Westmeath Independent*, for giving me access to the valuable archives of her newspaper, and to the late Senator Liam Naughton, Cathaoirleach of Seanad Éireann, for suppying me with useful source material. Philip Hannon facilitated my research in the Fianna Fáil archive. My sister, Seosaimhín Ní Mhuirí, was always willing to place her considerable knowledge and expertise in several fields at my disposal. My niece, Helena Grenham, typed this manuscript with skill, intelligence and patience. The maps were drawn by Stephen Hannon.

This work would not have been possible without the generosity and kindness of many bishops, diocesan archivists and members of religious orders and congregations. I am especially grateful to the following bishops who provided me with access to diocesan archives: Bishop Brooks, Dromore; Bishop Duffy, Clogher; Bishop Jones, Elphin; Bishop Kirby, Clonfert; Bishop McKiernan, Kilmore; Bishop McLoughlin, Galway; Bishop Murphy, Kerry; Bishop O'Reilly, Ardagh and Clonmacnois; Bishop Ryan, Kildare and Leighlin; Bishop Walsh, Killaloe. Father Michael Wall guided me through the Limerick diocesan archive. My work in the Dublin Archdiocesan Archive was made easier by David Sheehy, Archivist, while Father Brendan Kilcoyne, Archdiocesan Secretary, made arrangements for me to inspect material in the Tuam Archdiocesan Archive. Father John Gates was a helpful guide to the Armagh Archdiocesan Archive. Father Stephen Redmond gave me access to useful material in the Jesuit Archive. Father Ignatius Fennessy was extremely helpful during my visits to the Franciscan Archive, Killiney. Deirdre Quinn of the Central Catholic Library, Dublin, went to considerable trouble to find whatever material I sought.

The names of those who generously shared their knowledge of the subject with me are recorded in the Bibliography. The following helped me in various ways: Father Gerald Dolan; Father Michael Duignan; William Fraher; Father Anthony Griffin; Mary Guinan-Darmody; Sr Maureen Keogh; John Mansfield; Tom May; Aubrey Murphy; Sean Murphy; Paul Murray. In common with other historians of twentieth-century church–state relations in Ireland, I am conscious of a strong general obligation to the pioneering research done by Professor Dermot Keogh in this area. His work has provided an indispensable frame of reference for many of my explorations of detail, although my focus and direction differ in essentials from his.

It has been a pleasure to work with Barbara Mennell, the Executive Editor of UCD Press. I am grateful for her encouragement and support, and impressed by her professionalism and efficiency.

KEY TO ABBREVIATIONS

AAA	Armagh Archdiocesan Archive
ARCDA	Ardagh and Clonmacnois Diocesan Archive
CLDA	Clonfert Diocesan Archive
CLRDA	Clogher Diocesan Archive
CLYDA	Cloyne Diocesan Archive
DAA	Dublin Archdiocesan Archive
DRDA	Dromore Diocesan Archive
ELDA	Elphin Diocesan Archive
FAK	Franciscan Archives, Killiney
GDA	Galway Diocesan Archive
ICD	*Irish Catholic Directory and Almanac*
IER	*The Irish Ecclesiastical Record*
IHS	*Irish Historical Studies*
IRA	Irish Republican Army
IRB	Irish Republican Brotherhood
KILLDA	Killaloe Diocesan Archive
KLDA	Kildare and Leighlin Diocesan Archive
KYDA	Kerry Diocesan Archive
LKDA	Limerick Diocesan Archive
NAI	National Archives of Ireland
NLI	National Library of Ireland
RIC	Royal Irish Constabulary
TAA	Tuam Archdiocesan Archive
TCD	Trinity College Dublin
TCDA	Trinity College Dublin Archive
UCD	University College Dublin
UCDA	Archives Department, University College Dublin
UIP	United Ireland Party

For my wife Patricia and our son Paul

CHAPTER ONE

=====

INTRODUCTION

THE PASSIONATE ENGAGEMENT of many of the Roman Catholic clergy in Irish politics following independence in 1922, together with the troublesome issues arising from this engagement, are best seen as part of a process having its origins in the third decade of the nineteenth century, when Daniel O'Connell marshalled a considerable number of priests as agents in the struggle for Catholic Emancipation. Having thus acquired a taste and talent for political activity, and for the exercise of political power, priests soon came to regard these as their right, and even their duty. The energetic political activity of the Irish clergy was greatly facilitated by the absence of effective secular leadership, particularly from the Catholic professional classes, between the death of O'Connell and the rise of Charles Stewart Parnell. In several respects priests were well qualified to fill this void. Their educational attainments and middle-class status marked them out for the social and political leadership of communities less educated and less socially privileged than they were. Their superior administrative talents, their intimate acquaintance with the people of their localities, the prestige they derived from their spiritual functions, and their fund-raising capacities, uniquely qualified them as officers and organisers of political parties and movements favoured by the Church from time to time: the Irish Parliamentary Party in the nineteenth century, and Sinn Féin and pro-Treaty groups in the twentieth. The extent of priestly involvement was often massive. In Tipperary, for example, 79 per cent of the priests between 1879 and 1891 lent active support to the agrarian revolution.[1]

[1] J. O'Shea, *Priests, Politics and Society in Post-Famine Ireland* (Dublin 1983), p. 117. For an outstanding account of the political involvement of priests from the seventeenth century to recent times, see J.A. Murphy, 'Priests and People in Modern Irish History', *Christus Rex*, vol. xiii, October, 1969.

The encouragement offered by the decrees of the National Council of Bishops in 1854 was also significant. While the bishops forbade the clergy to discuss politics inside churches or to engage in political controversy with each other in the press or at public meetings, priests were nevertheless instructed to secure the election of 'men of integrity and favourable to the Catholic religion'.[2] Large numbers of Catholic priests gave practical expression to this injunction at critical times throughout the nineteenth century, almost always on behalf of constitutional candidates. Their more moderate political activities included canvassing, resolutions of support for candidates, conveying voters to the polls, addressing meetings, and being present at the booths as personation agents, to help illiterate voters to express their preferences. Less worthy clerical interventions included the hiring of intimidatory mobs and, somewhat more rarely, the supply of intoxicating drink to the electors. Both of these activities, however, could lead to the unseating of their successful candidates in cases where petitioners succeeded in having them adjudged guilty of corrupt practices.[3]

Priestly involvement in politics throughout the period from Catholic Emancipation to the mid-1930s varied in its intensity. The period from the mid-1880s to the fracture of the Irish Parliamentary Party, when under Parnell's unquestioned leadership the Party enjoyed the support, as Archbishop Croke put it, 'of the bishops as a body and the priests almost universally'[4], marked a temporary decline in effective clerical involvement in political action. The creation of a powerful, centralised party machine, which the priests supported, had the paradoxical effect of reducing the power and influence of clerical politicians. The abolition of the convention system, for example, meant the disappearance of priestly influence on the promotion and selection of candidates. The split in the Party and the consequent severe damage to its political apparatus opened the way for a renewed clerical involvement in parliamentary politics, to the extent that the post-Parnellite era marked a golden age in the political ascendancy of the clergy, despite the often bitter anti-clerical sentiment engendered by the vehement priestly condemnation of Parnell. The principal motives behind the sometimes savage episcopal and priestly assaults on Parnell and his supporters during the post-divorce period, apart from a sense of betrayal, were the fears of churchmen that his continued leadership would mean the

[2] J.H. Whyte, in P.J. Corish (ed.), *A History of Irish Catholicism*, vol. 5, part 2, 1970, p. 31. Priests could be members of local authorities until 1898.
[3] See E. Larkin, *The Consolidation of the Roman Catholic Church in Ireland, 1860–70* (Dublin, 1987), p. 665, and O'Shea, *Priests, Politics and Society*, pp. 50–1, 162–4.
[4] M. Tierney, *Croke of Cashel. The Life of Archbishop Thomas William Croke, 1823–1902* (Dublin, 1976), p. 181.

frustration of Home Rule and undermine public morality. The vigorous anti-Parnellite rhetoric of the priests had a further, more subtle origin: a desire to see a political movement which had been dominated by laymen returned to a greater measure of clerical control. Soon after the Parnell split, Archbishop Logue of Armagh reminded Archbishop Walsh of Dublin how much the Parliamentary Party MPs owed to the clergy. They had 'climbed to their present influential positions on the shoulders of Irish priests and Irish bishops'. The priests had worked up the electoral registers for them, fought the elections, and contributed to 'the sinews of war'.[5] It seemed, therefore, that some political debt was owing to them, in the form of renewed influence.

The by-elections in Kilkenny and Carlow in 1890 and 1891, which followed the fall of Parnell, provided the local priests with a welcome opportunity to display their political talents once more. In the struggle with Parnellism, now tinged with radicalism, the priests were the leaders of the cause of conservative Catholic nationalism. Their effectiveness in this role was saluted by Bishop Brownrigg of Ossory, who encouraged them to go 'off canvassing in all directions' and on election day to 'head their men and march to the polling place'. The Kilkenny priests also addressed after-Mass meetings, and acted as election agents. Brownrigg pictured the humiliated Parnellites, 'like spaniels at the feet of the priests, watching for a token of forgiveness'.[6] Brownrigg felt able to assert that the anti-Parnellite victory in Kilkenny would not come from the exploitation of the moral issue, but 'purely and utterly' from the 'family, personal and material' influence 'of the priesthood of Ossory'.[7] Elsewhere, priests involved themselves enthusiastically in anti-Parnellite activity, although not always with the same success. In Athlone, in December 1890, hundreds of artisans and labourers of the town, members of the League of the Cross, a Catholic temperance society, whose President was a priest, demonstrated in favour of Parnell and sent a telegram of support to him in Kilkenny. This was done without the permission of the President and contrary to the wishes of the Bishop of Ardagh and Clonmacnois and the local clergy, all of them devoutly anti-Parnellite. The priests retaliated by locking the members of the League out of their own hall. The Administrator of the parish, Dr Langan, later a spirited defender of the Free State, had already visited the boardroom of the workhouse to get a resolution passed condemning Parnell. In this case, public opinion defied clerical wishes and sanctions. In January 1891, Parnell

[5] F.S.L. Lyons, *Charles Stewart Parnell* (London, 1977), p. 471.
[6] Ibid., p. 544.
[7] O'Shea, *Priests, Politics and Society*, p. 225.

addressed a wildly enthusiastic crowd, estimated at 10,000, outside St Mary's Church, Athlone.[8]

In his account of Irish life in his *Ireland in the New Century* (1904), Horace Plunkett asserted that the two most potent influences on the thought and action of the Irish people were the political leaders and the Catholic clergy. Plunkett had his reservations about the nature and extent of the power exercised by the priests in purely political questions 'and by the unrivalled organisation of the Roman Catholic Church', but he had no doubt about the pervasiveness of that power in political and social affairs. The three thousand Irish Catholic clergymen, he believed, 'exercise an influence over their flocks not merely in religious matters, but in almost every phase of their lives and conduct', a phenomenon, he considered, that had no parallel in other Catholic countries. For decades to come, churchmen would continue to wield the exceptional political power noted by Plunkett. In the 1918 by-elections in South Armagh and East Tyrone, Archbishop Logue used his influence to defeat the Sinn Féin candidates. In the December 1918 General Election, amid clerical fears that Catholics would be unrepresented in parliament, Sinn Féin and the Parliamentary Party agreed to an equal division of the eight marginal Ulster seats, leaving the allocation of specific seats to Cardinal Logue, whose efforts helped to return agreed candidates in seven of the eight constituencies.[9]

The popular campaign to resist the conscription of Irishmen in the British forces, which came to a head in April 1918, offers a compelling illustration of the political power of Catholic churchmen, particularly when the leadership of the Church was willing to place itself at the head of a popular movement. The determined episcopal opposition to conscription marked a significant change in the bishops' attitude to legitimate government in Ireland. In principle, they had long recognised the Imperial Parliament as having the legal and moral right to legislate for Ireland, but in 1918, by encouraging Catholics to resist conscription, they were advocating resistance to a law passed by that parliament. Although conscription was defeated by an alliance of churchmen and politicians expressing the popular will, it is probable that the outcome would have been different without episcopal intervention.[10] The genuflection of the bishops to the popular will in 1918, rather than to the traditional theological imperative of support for the law of the land,

---

[8] See 'Athlone Miscellany', by 'Oisín', *Westmeath Independent*, 5.2.1999.
[9] The Earl of Longford and T. P. O'Neill, *Eamon de Valera* (Dublin, 1970), p.71; E. Phoenix, *Northern Irish Nationalism, Nationalist Politics, Partition and the Catholic Minority in Northern Ireland, 1890–1940* (Belfast, 1994), pp. 51–4.
[10] T. Ó Fiaich, 'The Irish Bishops and the Conscription Issue', *Capuchin Annual*, 1968, p. 365.

has an instructive parallel in episcopal rejection of the Papal decree against the Plan of Campaign in 1888. In that year, fearing massive public hostility and consequent loss of public authority and political power, the bishops chose to follow the people rather than the Pope.[11]

The rise of nationalist movements dedicated to the violent overthrow of British rule became a major problem for the Church in the nineteenth century and an even more acute one after 1916. In the nineteenth century, even popular democracy, especially if this had a socialist character, was frequently condemned in Papal pronouncements, on the basis that democratic civil government would represent a threat to the rights of the Church and undermine Christian values. The outlook of the Church on the moral legitimacy of revolt against existing governments was strongly influenced by the experiences of the Papacy and of European churches at the hands of revolutionary movements and regimes. These movements, deriving their ideological inspiration from the French Revolution, were frankly anti-religious and anticlerical. During the Communard Revolution in France in May 1848, the Archbishop of Paris and several priests were butchered, while in clerical eyes the Papal States, where revolutionaries proclaimed the Roman Republic in February 1849, became a celebrated case of legitimate authority overthrown by unlawful force.

The Irish bishops saw the Young Irelanders and the Fenians as posing similar threats to the system of constitutional politics in Ireland and to the position of the Catholic Church. In 1850, the Synod of Thurles condemned those leaders who tried to persuade the Irish people to sympathise with 'the apostles of socialism and infidelity', who in other countries had undermined the foundations of government and infringed the rights of the Holy See. The standard theological response to revolution was to regard existing governments as *ipso facto* legitimate, thus making the theological justification of rebellion impossible for Catholics. An influential and patriotic Maynooth theologian, Patrick Murray, held that acceptance of a government over a short span of years made it, irreversibly, the legitimate government.[12] In 1870, when all but two of the Irish bishops, MacHale of Tuam and Derry of Clonfert, asked the Holy See to condemn Fenianism, they were rejecting rebellion and affirming the necessity of obedience to established authority. They were also striving to preserve their political

[11] See E. Larkin, *The Roman Catholic Church and the Plan of Campaign, 1886–1888* (Cork, 1978), pp. 308–10.
[12] See P.J. Corish (ed.), *History of Irish Catholicism*, part 3, p. 18. See also Walter McDonald, *Some Ethical Questions of Peace and War with Special Reference to Ireland* (London, 1920).

power and influence and their control over their clergy: episcopal authority in these areas was clearly threatened by an oath-bound secret society like the Fenians. The 1867 Fenian Rising had taken place against a background of growing friendship between some of the country clergy and members of the Irish Republican Brotherhood. In Kerry, there was much clerical disapproval of Bishop Moriarity's celebrated condemnation of the Fenians and in 1872 many priests worked for an election candidate opposed to Moriarity's choice.[13]

Until 1916 and the ensuing War of Independence, when violent nationalism replaced constitutional action as the dominant mode of resistance to British rule, the Church had worked with considerable success in the promotion of non-violent methods of settling Irish grievances. The 1916 Rising and the subsequent armed struggle inspired by its republican principles confronted the many churchmen anxious to uphold the traditional teaching on rebellion with serious challenges. The Rising itself met none of the theological requirements for a just revolt: it lacked popular consent, had no reasonable chance of success and did not appear to be directed against an intolerable and manifest tyranny. The War of Independence similarly contravened traditional theological teaching on rebellion. The acute moral questions it raised in the minds of many of the bishops and clergy are illustrated in a letter from the elderly Jesuit William Delany to Archbishop Walsh of Dublin in November 1920. In his days in Rome, Delany had experienced the dire consequences for religion and society of armed revolution. He could not see how cold-blooded killings by such groups as Collins's 'squad' could be justified in the light of traditional Church teaching. He had come to the view that the British administration was unfit to govern any country but was convinced that the controlling 'inner gang', the authors of 'abominable assassinations' and those who had sworn to obey without question orders from 'unknown chiefs' in that gang, automatically incurred the penalty of excommunication from the Church.[14]

The rigorous theological position on just rebellion began to appear less and less credible when, in 1916, churchmen were confronted with the spectacle of Catholic mystics and idealists invoking the imagery of Christianity, particularly its sacrificial aspects, to justify a rebellion which clearly contravened explicit Catholic teaching on the subject. The distinctively Catholic republicanism of the Easter rebels, the popular

[13] T. Ó Fiaich, 'The Clergy and Fenianism', *Irish Ecclesiastical Record*, February, 1968, p. 90.
[14] T.J. Morrissey, *Towards a National University. William Delany, S.J. 1835–1924* (Dublin, 1979), 378–9.

cult of martyrdom generated by the execution of their leaders, stories of whose exemplary courage, piety and even sanctity, were widely publicised, earned the active good will of large numbers of the clergy. By early 1917, it was being reported that the great majority of priests 'showed open sympathy with, or approval of, the action taken by the rebels'. Whatever ecclesiastical opposition there still was to the War of Independence was articulated by strong-minded, traditionalist bishops such as Logue and Coholan. This opposition, when publicly expressed, tended to focus on the methods employed to achieve freedom from British rule rather than on the desirability or otherwise of independence as the ultimate goal of the struggle. It was left to the Church of Ireland to make the case for continuing British control, and for the legitimacy of violent and repressive expedients for maintaining it. In May 1920, Dr D'Arcy, the Church of Ireland Archbishop of Armagh, publicly advised the British Government to prosecute the war in Ireland 'with the ruthlessness of fate' by substantially increasing the number of troops, and to show 'an excess of firmness rather than weak yielding to disorder' in the vital task of preserving British rule in Ireland. An early British response to D'Arcy's call was the inauguration by the new Chief Secretary, Sir Hamar Greenwood, of a campaign of ruthless reprisals, including the murder of suspected insurgents. Of D'Arcy's intervention, the Jesuit Patrick Gannon remarked that 'perhaps only in Ireland could one find a Primate of a National Church clamouring for the invasion of his country'.[15]

To understand the changing clerical perspectives on violent revolt against established authority, one must also take account of the capacity of the Church to accommodate itself to successful or popular revolt. Ancient patriots, however violent their methods, had long enjoyed retrospective priestly benediction. Between 1916 and 1921, approval for violent patriotism was much more speedily forthcoming. The clerical tendency to welcome *post factum* the positive effects of violence and terror used in the cause of freedom can be discerned in the comments of Cardinal Logue in 1920 and again in 1922. In 1920, Logue made clear his resolute opposition to the terror organised by Collins and his circle. 'No object', he declared, 'would excuse them, no hearts, unless hardened and steeled against pity, would tolerate their cruelty'. Two years later, the death of Collins, the organiser of much of this terror, transformed him, in Logue's eyes, into 'a young

[15] For clerical sympathy with the 1916 rebels, see David Fitzpatrick, *Politics and Irish Life, 1913–1921. Provincial Experiences of War and Revolution* (Dublin, 1977), p. 140. For D'Arcy's statement, see *Catholic Herald*, London, 22.5.20. See also Patrick J. Gannon, 'An Amazing Document', *IER*, July 1922, pp. 1–12.

patriot brave and wise'.[16] The juxtaposition of such contradictory verdicts might well give the unfortunate impression that Logue was suggesting that while the horrors perpetrated by Collins and his associates were morally indefensible, these same horrors, once they succeeded in their aim, were capable of being interpreted as acts of bravery and wisdom. A standard Catholic handbook of ethics published in 1917 described rebellion as 'always a violation of natural law . . . a grave violation of the Divine law, and a grave sin'.[17] This was the point of view of the Pastoral Letter of the Irish bishops in October 1922, which defended a régime recently born out of violent rebellion. A cynical interpreter might suggest that the bishops were in effect saying that while rebellion might be morally evil, it had, nevertheless, been the indispensable means of giving Ireland the freedom from alien rule in which churchmen, and Irish people in general, might justifiably rejoice.

The support of the bishops and a big majority of the clergy for the Treaty settlement thus brought into sharp focus the moral ambiguities and inconsistencies inherent in the general political attitudes of the Irish Church throughout the century since Emancipation. Many opponents of the Treaty, including priests, saw episcopal enthusiasm for it as part of a well-defined and long-established pattern of opposition to full Irish independence. One of the most forthright priestly critics of the warm episcopal defence of the Free State regarded the Bishops' Pastoral of October 1922, which provided a theological defence of the Cosgrave government and excommunicated those who opposed it in arms, as the logical extension of what the Irish episcopacy had always stood for. The Carmelite Bernard Ó Maoiléidigh argued that 'the Pastoral just issued by the bishops is the culmination of their ignominy', suggesting that they had outdone all their predecessors. In 1798 and 1867 they had 'backed up our tyrannous and murderous oppressors', but in 1922, they 'gave their solemn benediction to a murderous and traitorous usurpation'.[18] Republican discourse featured many such extremely partisan verdicts on the long-standing commitment of the Church to social stability based on orderly government.

The acrimonious post-Treaty debate about the source of civil authority in Ireland, and the legitimacy or otherwise of the Free State Government, involved the bishops and some pro-Treaty theologians in proposing a relatively novel theory of legitimate government as if it were the constant teaching of the Church. This was the theory,

[16] See the valuable article by P. Donnelly, 'Violence and Catholic Theology', *Studies*, Autumn 1994, pp. 331ff.
[17] Ibid.
[18] B. Ó Maoiléidigh, ODC, 'Reply to the Pastoral Issued by the Irish Hierarchy, October 1922'. MacSwiney Papers, UCDA, P48a/223.

notoriously contested by some Republicans, that the consent of the majority of the people was the sole criterion on which the legitimacy of a government could be judged. This conflicted with the teaching of Pope Leo XIII, who in his encyclical *Diuturnum illud* (1881) had accorded a grudging recognition to democracy, and affirmed that popular consent was only one of many possible legitimating agencies. The majority rule theory also represented a major departure from the common nineteenth-century view that government based on the will of the majority could be a menace to the rights of the Church and to social harmony. This evolution of episcopal thought on civil authority provoked some cynical reflections from Republicans, one of whom suggested that some bishops probably believed that such authority came down straight from the Almighty into the hands of King George. Other bishops, however, believed that 'God sends down to the Irish people direct, as he does with every other nation, the power to govern themselves, although it may be that they did not think so until Woodrow Wilson came on the scene'.[19]

In most essentials, there is a marked continuity between the nature and scope of clerical involvement from 1922 to 1937 and what went before. The one notable break with nineteenth-century tradition is the willingness of the Church in the twenties to come to terms with popular democracy, even to become its champion, and to accommodate itself to the fruits of violent revolution. Apart from this, there is little to distinguish post-Treaty clerical activity in political affairs from that which prevailed in the nineteenth century. There is the same extensive involvement in electoral politics, the same minority dissent from official Church teaching, the same passionate, partisan, and often violent rhetoric. There is also the same acceptance by the majority of the people of the right of the Church to sustain a political role based on the notion of harmony between Church and people, the priests deriving their political power from their being 'of the people and with the people'.[20] The anti-Treaty minority attempt to keep unsympathetic clergymen out of politics is in the Fenian tradition.

The social origins of the clergy had significant political consequences in both periods. Most secular priests were sons of tenant-farmers, while some had middle-class backgrounds. The majority had to fund their own studies. The social backgrounds of the priests undoubtedly influenced the attitudes of many of them to the Fenians, who were predominantly urban labourers, artisans and agricultural labourers,[21]

[19] Ibid.
[20] See F. Callanan, *T.M. Healy* (Cork, 1996), pp. 372–3.
[21] See O'Shea, *Priests, Politics and Society*, p. 151 and G. Moran, *Patrick Lavelle. A Radical Priest in Mayo.* (Dublin, 1994), p. 1.

and to Parnell's followers after the split, most of whom were artisans and non-farming labourers. To many clerical minds, low social status was identified with unhealthy attitudes to the Church and religion and with undesirable political views. In 1891, Archbishop Croke told a correspondent that 'the lower stratum of society', consisting of 'corner-boys, blackguards of every hue, discontented labourers, lazy and drunken artisans . . . all irreligious and anti-clerical scoundrels' were almost entirely for Parnell, while his opponents comprised 'every thoughtful, intelligent, and industrious Christian man'.[22] Bishop Brownrigg charac-terised Parnell's followers as 'the lowest dregs of the people . . . the Fenian element and the working-classes'.[23]

The social status of post-Treaty Republicans was not a matter of much public comment by the clergy, mainly, perhaps, because of the absence of a clear class-distinction between supporters and opponents of the Treaty. In the 1920s and 1930s, however, the social backgrounds of the great majority of priests made it difficult for them to identify themselves with working people, with working-class organisations, or with political movements operating outside the direct influence of the Church for the reform of the social system. The nineteenth-century ecclesiastical hostility to radical social action found one of its twentieth-century counterparts in the severe censure of Republican socialist activity in the late 1920s and early 1930s.

Whatever the political issues and the political movements from Catholic Emancipation to the end of the 1930s, the attitude of the Church to these was characterised by one fundamental feature: vigorous opposition to ideas and organisations it could not control, Fenianism and its ideological successors being the most notable of these. The kind of absolute, oath-bound commitment required by such groupings was bound to undermine the loyalty the Church considered was due to its teaching, irreconcilable as this was with revolutionary principles. The Church, as the 1922 Bishops' Pastoral reminded its people, saw itself as the divinely appointed guardian not only of faith, but of political morality.

ke of Cashel, pp. 241–2.
p. 543.

CHAPTER TWO

THE FORCES DISPLAYED

I

THE ROMAN CATHOLIC CHURCH, whose political ideas and activities between 1922 and 1937 are the subject of this book, is not the body of the faithful, but the bishops and clergy, secular and regular. When either clergymen or laymen referred to the Church, this was almost invariably the meaning they had in mind. In 1921, there were four Archbishops, 23 bishops, 3,082 secular priests and 754 members of male religious orders, societies and congregations. There was no significant alteration in these numbers between 1922 and 1937.[1] According to the 1911 Census, 89.6 per cent of the population of the future Free State was Catholic. By 1926, the percentage had risen to 92.6. In the Six Counties, the census taken in the latter year shows that Catholicism, at 33.5 per cent, was the largest single religious denomination.[2] Before 1916, the great majority of the Catholic clergy were committed supporters of the Home Rule policy of Redmond's Parliamentary Party. Many of these were leaders and organisers of the United Irish League on which the Party depended for its support. Disappointment at Redmond's failure to win Home Rule, and his agreement in June 1916 to the exclusion of the six North-Eastern counties from the Home Rule Bill, seriously weakened clerical support for his cause. By 1916 also, the general hostility of churchmen to the physical force tradition, which had marked their dealings with Fenianism, had moderated.[3] Young priests who had been Maynooth students in the first decade of

---

[1] The *Irish Catholic Directory* for the period gives annual returns for the numbers of the clergy.
[2] See G.E. Maguire, 'The Political and Military causes of the Divisions in the Nationalist Movement, January 1921 to August 1923'. DPhil thesis, Oxford, 1985, p. 204; D. Harkness, *Northern Ireland since 1920* (Dublin, 1983), p. 48.
[3] See T. Ó Fiaich, 'The Clergy and Fenianism, 1860–70', *Irish Ecclesiastical Record*, February 1968, pp. 81 ff.

the century came under influences, both cultural and political, which 'had turned several of the ablest among them into ardent Gaelic Leaguers and advanced Nationalists'.[4] After the 1916 Rising, as an ill-defined revolutionary ideology gained a dominant influence over Catholic Ireland, considerable numbers of clergymen, especially younger ones, abandoned the cause of Home Rule and gave their support to the more radical courses advocated by Sinn Féin. The treatment of the 1916 leaders, the contrast between this and the tolerance shown to Protestant sedition in the North, and the attempt to impose conscription in 1918, all aroused widespread clerical hostility.[5]

The War of Independence placed considerable strains on the relationship between many bishops and their clergy and Catholics actively involved in acts of violence against the government. Ó Fiaich points out that such factors as their theological training, the statements of the bishops and concern for the welfare of their people, caused a great number of the clergy to entertain the gravest objections to the use of physical force.[6] Ecclesiastical condemnation of violent IRA activity, often matched by equally vigorous public disapproval of the retaliatory actions of the authorities,[7] was not as great a problem of conscience for IRA members as it might have been had they not enjoyed the moral support of a growing number of sympathetic priests. Most, perhaps a very large majority, of the Volunteers appear to have experienced no great difficulty in reconciling their loyalty to the Church with engagement in violence, and many tended to ignore

[4] T. Ó Fiaich, 'The Catholic Clergy and the Independence Movement', *Capuchin Annual*, 1970, p. 480.
[5] See P. McKevitt, 'The Church since Emancipation', in P. Corish (ed.), *A History of Irish Catholicism*, vol. v, chapter 10, pp. 1–6; L. de Paor, 'The Rebel Mind: Republicans and Loyalists' in R. Kearney (ed.), *The Irish Mind* (Dublin, 1984), p. 185.
[6] Ó Fiaich, 'The Catholic Clergy', p. 501.
[7] The following, from a letter written by Bishop O'Doherty of Clonfert, who had profound reservations about IRA activity, to Archbishop Gilmartin of Tuam, suggests that even in such quarters, government counter-measures were seen as much the greater of two evils. 'You will remember', O'Doherty wrote, 'the recommendation made in Maynooth that each bishop should have compiled a list of outrages committed in his diocese, parish by parish, by the agents of the British government. Curiously enough, the very same idea comes to me this morning from a friendly foreign correspondent [who] suggests that something more is wanted – a full list, together with details of the worst cases, names, dates, localities, authors (certain or presumed) . . . the English Government [*sic*] is publishing broadcast every outrage committed by Irishmen, while concealing or denying or explaining away their own evil deeds. Could Your Grace get this work done for Tuam? I am writing to the other bishops of the Province and also to the members of the Publication committee in the other Provinces. Your 'Truce of God' is most desirable, but you know how it is being violated by one party [the British] in Tuam diocese'. O'Doherty to Gilmartin, 1.2.20, TDA.

clerical denunciations as if these were merely biased political comments. Some abandoned full religious practice as a result of personal condemnation by individual priests or the refusal of absolution, but Ó Fiaich, who had conversations with many veterans both of the War of Independence and the Civil War, concludes that this was not at all as great a problem during the War of Independence as it became later for those fighting on the Republican side in the Civil War.[8]

Strong episcopal claims to the leadership of the Catholic people of Ireland in political affairs were characteristic of the period both before and after the Treaty. The vigour with which such claims were prosecuted intensified during the period immediately following the Treaty, when Republicans alleged that the bishops, in condemning anti-Treaty activity, denouncing individual Republicans from the altar, denying them the sacraments, placing the full weight of their spiritual and moral authority at the disposal of the pro-Treaty cause, and allowing priests whose political views coincided with their own to take an active political role while denying a similar right to Republican priests,[9] were acting from party bias rather than from spiritual zeal, refusing to be pastors of all their people. No Republican was likely to question the doctrine that Catholics owed loyalty to the bishops as successors to the Apostles or as their divinely appointed teachers in faith or morals. As Emmet Larkin has pointed out, Fenians, Parnellites and Republicans 'have all complained that the Church was exceeding the limits of its legitimate power and influence in condemning them, but they have never dared to go so far as to maintain [that] the Church had no claim to power and influence in Ireland'.[10] The real difficulty for many of those who opposed the Treaty, whether politically or in arms, was in accepting the view that episcopal inerrancy prevailed in political and constitutional matters which were, in the Republican view, in legitimate dispute.

Episcopal attitudes on this issue and on the general question of their own authority tended to be uncompromising.[11] Underlying much

---

[8] Ó Fiaich, 'The Catholic Clergy', p. 501.

[9] See a Republican letter of complaint to the Vatican, dating from late 1923. Todd Andrews Papers, P. 91/99, UCDA.

[10] 'Church, State and Nation in Modern Ireland', *American Historical Review*, vol. 80, 1975, p. 1276.

[11] 'The bishops', according to John Hagan, the strongly Republican Rector of the Irish College in Rome, 'don't want to listen to arguments about their political partisanship and the damage it has done to religion. The bishops will not listen to any such view. They are persuaded that they are right – and are inclined to tolerate no doubt. Indeed, I am inclined to gather that they regard doubts of the kind as a sort of personal affront. Naturally, the main body of the priests in a diocese think as the bishop thinks, and thus we have a vicious circle, which bounds the horizon all round'. Hagan to Archbishop Mannix, 5.10.23, Hagan Papers.

opal discourse during the post-Treaty period was the principle
it was the exclusive right and duty of the bishops themselves to
determine what issues, political or otherwise, came within the sphere
of their authority. There was the further principle that once the
episcopal body, or indeed an individual bishop, had decided that a
pronouncement was justified, anybody wishing to remain a Catholic
was obliged to accept and act upon the teaching mediated in the
pronouncement. The first of these principles was to remain a fundamental feature of the Irish episcopal outlook long after the Civil War.
In 1951, Archbishop Kinane of Cashel was still asserting it. 'Bishops',
he declared at a prize-giving ceremony at Rockwell College, 'are the
authentic teachers of faith and morals in their own diocese and their
authority includes the right to determine the boundaries of their
jurisdiction – in other words to determine in case of doubt whether
faith or morals are involved'.[12] The teaching that bishops could decide
infallibly whether they were entitled, for example, to pronounce definitively on the morality of the Republican struggle against the Treaty
settlement enjoyed the support of such prominent theologians as the
Jesuit Peter Finlay, who seemed to place the matter beyond dispute by
pronouncing that 'local bishops were divinely-appointed teachers of the
flocks with the Holy Ghost committed to their care', that their
authority was delegated to them not by their people, their clergy, or
even the Pope, but by God, and that there was 'no authority on earth'
which might gainsay their teaching or 'defy their commands'.[13]

In the eyes of the bishops, then, their pronouncements, even on
the political issues of the day, were not matters for debate but for
uncritical acceptance by the faithful to whom they were addressed.
Bishop Cohalan of Cork made this clear in September 1922 when he
declared that 'one who is a Catholic, who already believes in the
Catholic Church, in the teaching office of the Catholic Church, does
not set up his own subjective speculations or judgments in opposition
to the teaching of the Church or of its pastors, whom he is bound to
obey'.[14] In 1888, a celebrated pronouncement of Leo XIII in condemnation of the Boycott and Plan of Campaign was received by Bishop

[12] *Irish Independent*, 2.6.51. Sixteen years earlier, as Bishop of Waterford and Lismore,
Kinane had made the same claim for episcopal authority. This authority, he
held, gave him the right to 'determine the boundaries of his jurisdiction, in other
words to determine in case of doubt whether faith or morals are involved, so that
one cannot evade his authority on the pretext that he has gone outside his own
sphere'. It therefore followed that 'his teaching is binding and that his subjects
must obey it even under pain of mortal sin'. *Irish Press*, 4.3.35.
[13] *Irish Independent*, 12.10.22.
[14] Pastoral Letter, 25.9.22, *Irish Independent*, 26.9.22.

O'Dwyer of Limerick as definitive, and binding on Irish Catholics. 'It is', O'Dwyer claimed, 'no longer a matter of opinion. *Roma locuta est. Causa finita est*, and I am no more now than the mouthpiece of the Pope to his subjects in this diocese'.[15] In August 1922, Bishop Hackett of Waterford asserted that he himself held in his own diocese 'that power which the Pope has for the whole world' subject to unspecified limitations. He acknowledged that there was 'liberty of discussion' before the bishops spoke on the state of the country in June, but the bishops having spoken, 'all room for doubt is hereby removed'. Hackett was not prepared to tolerate further opposition to episcopal decrees, and was ready to enforce obedience to these. He hoped it would not be necessary for him to employ 'every weapon that my position as a bishop gives me'.[16] At the Catholic Truth Society conference at the Mansion House in October 1922, after the bishops had collectively condemned the Republican cause in a pastoral letter,[17] Bishop O'Doherty of Clonfert asserted that 'they could not but regard their present [Provisional Government] rulers as lawful'.[18] The clear implication of this was that the bishops' 'subjects' must regard the Provisional Government in the same light. As a means of ensuring this, the episcopal bench adopted a policy, described somewhat oddly to one of its members by John Hagan of the Irish College in Rome, of 'making absolution depend on one's ability to see in the body that calls itself the Irish government the one and only lawful government of the country'.[19]

After the Civil War had formally ended, O'Doherty, preaching from the text, 'Obey your prelates and be subject to them', emphasised the obligation of his hearers 'to submit to his advice and guidance' and prophesied that 'even those who disregarded the teachings of their spiritual superiors would recognise the unwisdom of their ways when passion had died down'.[20] Taken collectively, episcopal pronouncements on the state of the nation in the post-Treaty period constitute a powerful affirmation of the bishops' sense of the immense power their divinely sanctioned authority had placed in their hands and their determination to wield this as their judgment directed. The same pronouncements offer a clear sense that the bishops regarded their relationship with the laity as resembling that between master and servant, their function being to order and direct, that of the laity to

[15] Emmet Larkin, *The Roman Catholic Church and the Plan of Campaign, 1886–1888* (Cork, 1978), p. 255.
[16] *Freeman's Journal*, 17.8.22.
[17] See Appendix One for the text of this letter.
[18] *Irish Independent*, 12.10.22.
[19] Hagan to Bishop O'Dea, 22.8.22, GDA.
[20] *Irish Independent*, 30.6.23; *ICD*, 1924, p. 579.

listen and obey. The language of power, mastery, subjection and unfailing obedience is the distinguishing mark of episcopal discourse, particularly in 1922 and 1923. In September 1922, Bishop O'Sullivan of Kerry pronounced that every Catholic was bound to 'acquiesce' in considered statements of the 'United Irish episcopate'; no statement of an individual priest or layman could lessen the 'binding force' of such statements of the bishops 'on the consciences of all their subjects', since the Holy Spirit had appointed the bishops and no one else 'to rule the Church of Christ'.[21] In 1927, the Synod of Maynooth issued decrees affecting the Catholic laity; among these was one which enjoined them to demonstrate 'obedience and respect' to their bishops, especially to 'their particular pastor with authority over, and responsibility for, them', since they are his 'subjects'.[22]

Not everybody, even within the clerical body, was prepared to concede to the bishops the degree of authority in the political affairs of the twenties that they reserved to themselves. Many of the lower clergy believed that enthusiastic episcopal support for the Treaty and denunciation of its opponents were ill-judged and ultimately harmful to the interests of the Church and religion. A significant number of secular and regular priests ignored the bishops' views and openly or covertly sustained the spiritually embattled republicans.[23] A number of clerical polemicists questioned the right of the bishops to condemn the Republican cause as fiercely and as absolutely as they did in their October Pastoral of 1922. The most memorable of the clerical replies to the Pastoral was written by Berthold Meleady, a Discalced Carmelite. Meleady described as blasphemous the bishops' invocation of divine law in support of those 'whom a short time ago they denounced as murderers and plunderers and who have since become traitors to their people'. He accused them of 'robbing our bravest and holiest of the sacraments', and of trying to suspend 'the few noble priests who have not forgotten their theology and who are still faithful to the land that bore them', of being 'callously and wilfully blind to the torturing and murdering of Irish Republicans by Free State forces'. He charged

[21] *Westmeath Independent*, 2.9.22. Such views enjoyed the general support of those who controlled the Press. An editorial in the *Irish Independent* on the day of the publication of the October 1922 Pastoral declared that 'upon moral and religious questions, Catholics are bound to accept the teaching of their divinely-appointed guides, and it is to be hoped that no section of Irish Catholics will cause disedification by dissent from the principles definitively laid down in this Pastoral by the bishops, who have interfered only out of true charity to the young men themselves specially concerned'. *Irish Independent*, 11.10.22.
[22] *The Synod of Maynooth. 1927. Decrees which affect the Catholic Laity. Translated with some notes by M.J. Browne, DD, DCL.* CTS Pamphlet, 1927.
[23] For numerous examples, see Chapter Three and Appendix Two.

them with having 'arrogated to themselves a power which the Pope himself does not possess' by pretending to pronounce definitively on the right of the Provisional Government to rule Ireland, a political question which was, as Republicans argued, a matter of legitimate dispute. In declaring that Catholics were bound in conscience to abide by their latest teaching, on the ground that it was morally impossible for them to teach false doctrine, the bishops and such apologists as Peter Finlay were 'on the high road to rank heresy'. History, Meleady suggested, was 'littered with the errors of bishops and benches of bishops and the indiscreet and mistaken actions of Councils and Popes'.[24] Peter Yorke, a Republican priest who edited the San Francisco *Leader*, issued another pamphlet whose main argument was that by pronouncing judgment on the Irish political question, a judgment which only the Pope could properly deliver, the Irish bishops 'had been guilty of grievous rebellion against the Pope' and that it was they and not the Republicans 'that are cast out of the Church while living and to be deprived of Christian burial when they die'.[25] While Republican controversialists like Meleady and Yorke marshalled some impressive theological, legal and constitutional arguments against episcopal intervention in the post-Treaty conflict, they avoided examining the morality of the Republican struggle in the light of the Catholic teaching setting out the requirements for a justifiable rebellion, in particular that 'there should be good hope of success so that resistance by armed force will not entail greater evils than it seeks to remedy'.[26] Probably not many defenders of Republicanism thought this necessary in view of the fact that Pearse and his fellow-insurrectionists had effectively abandoned traditional Catholic principles and devised a new moral code for Republicans which laid down that a rebellion against established authority might be militarily futile and at the same time morally justifiable provided that the bloodshed involved could be regarded as purifying, sanctifying or stimulating the Irish nation.[27]

The hazards inherent in the political pronouncements of bishops had already been illustrated in the episcopal statement of 18 April 1918 on attempts being made by the British Government to impose conscription on Ireland. In the key passage of this statement the bishops

[24] Reply to the Pastoral Issued by the Irish Hierarchy, October 1922. January 1923. Signed B. Ó Maoiléidigh. MacSwiney Papers, UCDA, P48a/223.
[25] *Irish Bishops Usurp Papal Rights*, by V. Rev. Dr Yorke, DD of the San Francisco *Leader*, Glasgow, 1923.
[26] See Archbishop Gilmartin's summary of these requirements in *The Irish Catholic* 10.11.17. See also G. Vann, o.p. *Morality and War* (London, 1939), p. 35.
[27] D.W. Miller, *Church, State and Nation in Ireland, 1898–1921* (Dublin, 1973), pp. 319–20; 398.

declared that 'conscription forced in this way upon Ireland is an oppressive and inhuman law, which the Irish people have a right to resist by all means that are consonant with the law of God'.[28] The position taken here by the bishops was open to the obvious objection that while as a body they acknowledged that the Imperial Parliament was the legitimate civil authority for Ireland, they were at the same time claiming that Irish Catholics could refuse to obey a law enacted by that Parliament. In 1919, the episcopal statement was analysed with destructive effect by Walter McDonald, Professor of Theology at Maynooth and editor of the *Irish Theological Quarterly*, who pointed out that after the Roman Inquisition had pronounced that membership of the Fenian Brotherhood incurred excommunication *ipso facto*, the Irish Church authorities taught officially, 'enforcing the teaching with the severest penalties at their disposal, that the government against which the Fenians plotted was legitimate'. The bishops, McDonald argued, by encouraging the passive resistance of Irish Catholics to their legitimate government, had left that government 'exposed to a powerful foreign enemy with whom it was engaged in a life and death struggle at the time'.[29]

For most anti-Treaty Republicans, the great evil of the Treaty was that its acceptance would involve the violation of the oath to the Republic which they had taken in 1919. It became a standard anti-Treaty argument that once the members of the Republican government and army had sworn allegiance to the Republic, they could not in conscience betray this allegiance by pledging loyalty to the King. Their hostility to this line of conduct was quickly converted to disapproval of the bishops for condoning it and urging them to follow it.

[28] Quoted in T. Ó Fiaich, 'The Irish Bishops and the Conscription Issue, 1918', *Capuchin Annual*, 1968, p. 356.

[29] W. McDonald, *Some Ethical Questions of Peace and War With Special Reference to Ireland* (London, 1919), p. 48. McDonald believed that Australian resistance to conscription was open to the same objection as that promoted by the Irish bishops. Had France and Great Britain acted similarly, 'the German armies would now be in London, and a German fleet in Botany Bay'. Ibid., p. 150. Ó Fiaich, who writes from a Republican standpoint, acknowledges the inconsistency of the bishops' position in 'using the legitimacy of the Westminster Government in order to condemn Irish revolutionary movements and then rejecting the right of that Government to pass a law which is to be applied to Ireland', 'The Irish Bishops', p. 366. Those Republicans who, in 1922, deplored the intervention of the bishops and many of the clergy in politics could also be accused of double standards, as Bishop Foley was to point out in 1925. Many of these same Republicans, Foley recalled, 'were among those who in 1918 had welcomed their interference most warmly' during the conscription controversy. *Nationalist and Leinster Times*, 4.4.25.

As one of their apologists put it, 'it was a shock to the ordinary lay mind that they [the bishops] should approve the breaking, by the Plenipotentiaries, of their pledged word and the violation by the Teachtaí of their solemn oaths'.[30] The oath had originated with Cathal Brugha who, in a move to reinforce the official jurisdiction of the Dáil over the IRA, decided in the summer of 1919 to administer to all members of the Republican government and army an oath of allegiance to the Dáil. This project was discouraged by Michael Collins and Richard Mulcahy, but supported by W.T Cosgrave and Arthur Griffith.[31] On 20 August 1919, Brugha proposed a motion to the effect that every deputy, officer and clerk of the Dáil and every member of the Irish Volunteers 'must swear allegiance to the Irish Republic and to the Dáil'. The oath committed those who took it 'to support and defend the Irish Republic and the government of the Irish Republic which is Dáil Éireann, against all enemies, foreign and domestic'.[32]

Criticism of the bishops for their indifference to the violation of the Republican oath by those who supported the Treaty settlement was, in episcopal eyes at least, beside the point. Bishop Cohalan argued that the Dáil oath of 1919 was 'not an oath for the establishment of an Irish Republic', but 'an oath of fidelity to the Republic as already existing'; for this reason it was clear to him that the deputies' promise of fidelity, 'even confirmed by oath, to a non-existent government, is an invalid promise'.[33] Like Cohalan, the other bishops could not bring themselves to recognise Dáil Éireann as the legitimate government of Ireland, or the declared Republic as anything more than an abstraction. As late as June 1921, when de Valera visited Maynooth to urge the bishops to give formal recognition to the Republican Government set up by Dáil Éireann and given a strong mandate in the General Election of the previous month, they felt unable to accede to his request. A few months earlier, Cohalan had explained why. To the question, 'Was the proclamation of the Irish Republic by the Sinn Féin members of parliament after the last General Election sufficient to constitute Ireland a Republic according to our Church teaching?', he answered that it was not.[34] If this line of argument was valid, there could be no moral or legal objection to the so-called 'disestablishment of the Republic' involved in the establishment of the Free State, since

[30] Columban na mBanban, *False Pastors*, n.d. p. 39.
[31] Mulcahy Papers, UCDA, P70 67, Vol. 1, p. 20.
[32] The text of the oath is reproduced in D. Macardle, *The Irish Republic*, 4th edn (Dublin, 1951), p. 304.
[33] Pastoral Letter, 25.9.22. Reprinted in *Irish Independent*, 26.9.22.
[34] See T. Ó Fiaich, 'The Catholic Clergy and the Independence Movement', *Capuchin Annual*, 1970, p. 490.

the Republic was no more than a notional thing and the oath taken to defend it an absurdity.

During the War of Independence, the bishops and many of their clergy acted on the assumption that since the Republican Government lacked legitimacy, the IRA lacked moral sanction for its activities, that the killing of soldiers and policemen in any circumstances was murder.[35] The attitude of the bishops to the post-Treaty Republican movement was based on the belief that the Provisional government had replaced the Imperial one as the *de jure* and *de facto* government of the Twenty-Six Counties, and that the 'Republic' on behalf of which the anti-Treaty forces had taken arms had no claim to legitimacy or allegiance. Some of the politicians who acquiesced in the Treaty settlement did not, however, appear to think as the bishops did about the implications of the oath to the Republic which they had taken in 1919. Patrick McCartan argued that to vote for the Treaty would be 'violating my oath which I took to the Republic, that I took to the IRB.' On the other hand, to vote against it would be to 'vote for chaos', which he was not willing to do.[36] Kevin O'Higgins believed that the ratification of the Treaty was 'technically a breach of the mandate of the Dáil' and 'technically *ultra vires*'. Against this, since the alternative appeared to be war 'on an extensive and grand scale', he considered it better that deputies should 'commit a technical breach of our mandate' than to commit the people to war.[37] Bishops, however appealing some of them might have found such arguments, could scarcely have rehearsed them in their public pronouncements by teaching that there were circumstances in which a solemn oath could be set aside. They were instead compelled to assert that those who took this oath did not realise that an oath taken to uphold or defend a non-entity such as the Irish Republic of 1919 had no validity.

Republicanism, whether before or after the Treaty, was not, in any case, a political doctrine especially congenial to the Irish bishops and senior clergy. The twentieth-century Church was heir to a strong tradition of clerical antipathy to all forms of radical political thought and revolutionary movements. There is an ample Republican literature of complaint against this, featuring such claims as John O'Leary's that priests expressed their opposition to Fenianism by pronouncing it a

[35] See Fr Colmcille, o. cist. 'Tipperary's Fight in 1920', *Capuchin Annual*, 1970, p. 261.
[36] Treaty Debate, Public Session, 20.12.21, p. 81. McCartan voted to approve of the Treaty. He declared that 'You cannot go to the Secretary of State of any foreign government and ask him to recognise the Republic of Ireland, because I submit it is dead'.
[37] Treaty Debate, Private Session, p. 223.

mortal sin 'even to wish that Ireland should be free' and by 'doing the work of the enemy',[38] that of Mellows who held that the members of the Irish Hierarchy were 'invariably wrong' in their political outlook from the time they took sides 'against the people' in 1798,[39] and that of de Valera who felt impelled to protest to the Pope in 1925 at 'incitements by priests to physical violence on Republicans during election times'.[40] Clerical commentators since the late eighteenth century had associated revolutionary and democratic creeds in general and Republicanism in particular with secularism, anti-clericalism and irreligion. Irish Catholic bishops were among the stoutest champions of monarchy. In 1793, Archbishop Troy of Dublin, in his exposition of Church teaching on the relationship between Irish Catholic subjects and their Protestant English King, 'dismissed accusations of Catholic disloyalty by showing the very nature of the Catholic faith as Royalist'.[41] In 1798, Edmund Ffrench, Bishop of Elphin, devoted a Pastoral Letter to outlining the duties of 'fealty and allegiance' owed by Catholics to King George, the strict observance of which, he claimed, 'has for centuries back marked the character of Irish Catholics'. He urged his flock to reflect that they would have no share 'in the great merits of redemption' should they prove 'regardless of the unshaken fidelity' they owed to 'the best of kings and benign legislature which have extended to us immunities and conferred on us favours in reward for the fidelity of our ancestors'. The law of God, he affirmed, clearly prescribed allegiance to King George as an indispensable duty and should deter Catholics from having their royalist principles 'poisoned by the infectious influence' of those 'evil agents' promoting the rebellion of 1798.[42] Cardinal Cullen was convinced that even an Irish Home Rule Parliament would launch the first attack 'on the liberty of the Church and on the interest of religion', by passing laws 'to weaken and destroy the Church's action', because the moving spirit in the agitation for Home Rule was identical with the revolutionary one which had undermined the Catholic religion on France and Italy.

[38] John O'Leary, *Recollections of Fenians and Fenianism* (London, 1896), p. 199.

[39] Correspondence of Eamon de Valera and others. Published by the Stationery Office for Dáil Éireann. 1922, p. 20. Compare Stack's comments following the October Pastoral of 1922: 'Adrian's Bull, Edward Bruce's War, the Union, '48, the Pope's Bras Band (Sadlier and Keogh), the Fenians, the Plan of Campaign, the Irish Volunteers and 1916, the Republic itself when functioning – the stories of all these periods were simply the telling of how the Church's heads helped the oppressor against the people'. Stack to McGarrity, 18.10.22. S. Cronin, *The McGarrity Papers*, Tralee, 1972, p. 122.

[40] De Valera to Pope Pius XI, 9.5.25, FAK, AMI, 1452.

[41] Marianne Elliott, *Wolfe Tone. Prophet of Irish Independence* (Dublin, 1989), p. 204.

[42] Pastoral of Bishop Edmund Ffrench, Elphin, 1.4.1798, ed. B. Ó Cuív, *Éigse*, XI.

Cullen's sentiments may help to explain why such Tory opponents of Home Rule as Lord Randolph Churchill felt they could regard the Irish bishops as potential allies. In a letter written in 1885, on the eve of Gladstone's first Home Rule Bill, Churchill declared that 'it is the bishops entirely to whom I look in the future to turn, to mitigate or to postpone the Home Rule onset. . . . The Bishops, who in their hearts hate Parnell and don't give a snap for Home Rule, having safely acquired control of education, will, according to my calculation, complete the rout. That is my policy, and I know that it is sound and good and the only possible Tory policy. It hinges on obtaining the confidence and friendship of the bishops.'[43] In 1917, Cardinal Logue described agitation for a Republic as a thing that would be 'ludicrous if it were not so mischievous' and wondered if what emerged would be 'the Bolshevik Republic of Russia glorified at a Sinn Féin meeting in the Dublin Mansion House'. In the same year, the Catholic bishops issued a statement declaring that 'forms of government that are popular at the moment [Republics] have been and are associated with the worst forms of civil tyranny and religious persecution'.[44]

In many twentieth-century clerical eyes, Pearse's promotion of Tone as the father and guiding spirit of Irish Republican nationalism inevitably compromised the modern Republican movement. In a speech at Bodenstown on 22 June 1913, Pearse blasphemously transformed Tone's secular Republicanism into a religious creed by ignoring all its essential features. Conor Cruise O'Brien points out that Tone and his friends were 'militant secularists, deists and atheists, contemptuous of superstition and especially Roman Catholic superstition', seeing themselves as 'leading their backward fellow-countrymen towards enfranchisement, both from material despotism and from their Romish superstitions'.[45] Even in his days as spokesman of the Catholic Committee, Tone held to the fundamental Irish Protestant belief that Catholicism was 'a dying superstition'.[46] Such considerations did not inhibit Pearse from telling his Bodenstown listeners in 1913 that they had 'come to the holiest place in Ireland, holier to us even than the place where Patrick sleeps in Down'. To become part of the cult of

[43] For Cullen's statement, see *The Tablet*, 27.3.1886. Reprinted in pamphlet form by the Irish Loyal and Patriotic Union, 109, Grafton Street, Dublin. Lord Randolph Churchill's letter was published by his son Winston Churchill in his *Life* of his father. The excerpt quoted was published in *Sinn Féin*, 13.10.23.

[44] Logue's statement and that of the bishops were used by the British authorities in an anti-Republican leaflet published in 1918. There is a copy in the MacSwiney Papers P48a/222. For Logue's anti-Republicanism, see Miller, *Church, State and Nation*, pp. 398–9.

[45] *Passion and Cunning and Other Essays* (New York, 1988), p. 202.

[46] R.F. Foster, *Modern Ireland 1600–1972* (London, 1988), pp. 268–9.

'the greatest of all that have died for Ireland' was, according to Pearse, to come 'unto a new baptism, unto a new regeneration and cleansing'.[47] Post-Treaty churchmen were not deceived by Pearse's distortion of Tone's ideas and significance. A number of these proclaimed their abhorrence of him and his fellow United Irishmen, Bishop O'Doherty of Galway denouncing them as 'exemplars of conduct unfitting for Catholics, young or old, to imitate'.[48] In 1925, Bishop Downey of Ossory sent Cosgrave a polemic in which Tone is denounced as a frightful swearer, a shameful drunkard and a liar, possessed by an unchristian hatred of England, a blasphemer who rejoiced in the dethronement and exile of the Pope, events he compared to the fall of Lucifer, and the hero of modern Bolsheviks as well as Republicans.[49] Apologists for Tone, anxious to preserve his spurious status as a model for Catholic Republicans, tried to counter this kind of disapproval by stressing the part he played in the emancipation of Catholics at a time when many of the Catholic bishops were hostile or indifferent to that enterprise. In 1932, Richard Hayes wrote of Tone, 'the first Republican as Catholic champion', whose 'tireless labours, more than those of others . . . first led Catholic Ireland out of bondage and placed her in 1793 . . . on the roadway to full religious freedom'.[50] A Cumann na mBan statement reminded O'Doherty of what 'every student of history knows': that eighteenth-century bishops in Ireland were, with few exceptions, 'as much opposed to the campaign in favour of Catholic emancipation as they are to-day to political freedom'.[51]

II

In 1923, Bishop Hallinan of Limerick asserted that it was perfectly acceptable for bishops and priests to exert their dominance in political affairs. In no country, he argued, had the political power of the clergy been more manifest than in Ireland, and 'for very evident and unassailable reasons': over the years the clergy had earned their right to such power through their active leadership of the people, 'when natural [political] leaders failed them, through imprisonment or exile,

[47] Elliott, *Wolfe Tone*, p. 416. Elliott points out that Tone was not the democrat of popular tradition. 'While he had considerable compassion for the poor, he had no intention whatsoever of involving them directly in politics. His men of no property were the middle classes who composed the Catholic and United Irish leadership alike. Irish Republicanism started out as a campaign to secure political power for the middle classes'. Ibid., p. 418.
[48] *The Irish Times*, 24.5.33.
[49] James Downey to Cosgrave, 19.9.25, NAI S 4127.
[50] *Irish Press*, 20.6.32.
[51] Ibid., 12.6.33.

through death or perhaps through treachery'.[52] During the post-Treaty period, and particularly from 1922 to the September General Election of 1927, active ecclesiastical leadership of the people meant, in practice, that pro-Treaty and anti-Treaty clergy became political partisans, freely used their pulpits to denounce political opponents, frequently identified these by name, in the course of sermons, at the altar rails or at political meetings; engaged in electioneering as platform speakers, election and publicity agents, proposers of candidates and subscribers to their funds. The relevant provisions of ecclesiastical law had the practical effect of facilitating the political activities of pro-Treaty clergymen while discouraging, and even preventing, many of those who opposed the Treaty from participating in the public debate. Anti-Treaty curates were forbidden by the terms of statutes drawn up by the Synod of Maynooth in 1882 from being present at public meetings in their own parishes without the consent of their parish priests. Priests who wished to attend meetings outside their parishes required the formal consent of the local parish priests. The experience of Thomas Burbage, CC Geashill, Co. Offaly, was a common one. He could not participate in a de Valera rally in Tullamore in April in 1922 because the local parish priest would not permit the attendance of priests at a Republican event. The same parish priest, however, had, only a week before, raised no objection when a priest presided at a pro-Treaty meeting.[53] The ardent political commitment of many post-Treaty clergy represented an intensification of what had gone before; from 1917 on, Sinn Féin and the Irish Parliamentary Party each had among its active supporters a considerable clerical faction. In some places, at least, the excitement generated by post-Treaty clerical politicians can scarcely have been greater than that which attended the pronouncements of many of the same men a few years before, when the partisan enthusiasm of what David Fitzpatrick calls 'the wild curates' of Clare found expression in such outbursts as that of Daniel Flynn against 'the bloody old peelers', the assertion of Patrick Gaynor that if conscription were attempted 'the fit resting-place for an Irish bullet is in an English heart', and the prediction of Stephen Slattery,

---

[52] *Limerick Herald*, 26.2.23. In 1935, Bishop Kinane of Waterford and Lismore answered the common argument that the church had 'no right of interference or guidance in political or social activities' by asserting that such activities, 'quite as much as those which are purely personal and private, are subject to God's moral law, of which the Church is the divinely-constituted interpreter and guardian'. *Irish Press*, 4.3.35.

[53] For the implications of the 1882 statutes see Rev. P. Finlay, SJ in *The Irish Catholic*, 4.3.22. For Burbage's experience, see *Midland Tribune*, 22.4.22. See also p. 140, note 13.

PP Quin, defending the older political tradition, that Sinn Féin would bring 'red ruin and revolution'.[54]

Among the decrees of the Plenary Synod of Maynooth in 1900 was one forbidding priests 'from entering into disputes and squabbling among themselves concerning political matters at public meetings and even more so in journals and daily newspapers'. The object of this decree was to induce the clergy to 'avoid brawls and disputes with others, to preserve the dignity of the priesthood from damage, to ensure that the charity which is the strength of the Church may not be violated in the slightest degree'.[55] The record of subsequent clerical dealings with political affairs suggests a marked unwillingness on the part of Irish priests, North or South, to comply with either the letter or the spirit of this decree or of other episcopal or even Papal pronouncements delivered from time to time on the subject.[56] On 28 June 1917, the Irish Hierarchy issued a reminder to priests that it was 'strictly forbidden by the statutes of the National Synod to speak of political or kindred affairs in the church', where 'nothing should fall from the lips of God's ministers that could wound the queenly virtue of charity or give reasonable cause for offence to any member of his [the priest's] flock'.[57] In February 1924, a circular letter from the relevant Vatican Congregation to the heads of religious orders reminded clergy, both secular and regular, 'to keep themselves completely aloof from the struggles of political parties and above every competition merely political'. The Cardinal Prefect responsible for the circular might have been thinking of recent Irish events when he noted that one priest or another had 'incautiously thrown himself into the political struggle, assuming even at times the pose of a tribune with the applause of one party or the other . . . always with harm to the Church'. It was the 'express will' of the Pope that the clergy absolutely avoid partiality

[54] 'De Valera in 1917: The Undoing of the Easter Rising', in J.P. O'Carroll and J.A. Murphy (eds), *De Valera and His Times* (Cork, 1983), p. 110.

[55] The decree, Number 193, reads: 'Prohibemus quominus lites et iurga inter se de rebus politicis in conventibus publicis et magis adhuc in foliis seu epheremeridibus, ineant sacerdotes, ita ut rixas et contentiones cum aliis evitent, ut dignitas sacerdotalis nihil detrimenti capiat, utque caritas illa quae robur est Ecclesiae minime violetur'. *Acta et Decreta Synodi Plenariae Episcoporum Hiberniae. Habitae Apud Maynutiam*, MDCCC (Dublin, 1906), p. 85.

[56] Intelligence notes compiled by officers of the RIC in 1915 contain the names of 50 priests, from all the provinces of Ireland, who came to notice, some on several occasions, for 'disloyal language or conduct'. Examples of disloyalty included the use of strong pro-German and anti-recruiting language from the pulpit, support for the Irish Volunteers, encouragement for their efforts to recruit and get arms, and incitement to break the connection with England. B. Mac Giolla Chiolle (ed.) *Chief Secretary's Intelligence Notes, 1913–16* (Dublin, 1966).

[57] *Freeman's Journal*, 29.6.17.

towards any political party.[58] A similar papal attitude was discreetly expressed to Logue and the Irish bishops in August 1922.[59]

Striking evidence of clerical defiance of ecclesiastical authority in these matters was provided by Bishop O'Brien of Kerry on the eve of the 1933 General Election. Conscious of the disedification caused by priestly abuses of ecclesiastical law during the 1932 campaign, O'Brien found it necessary to issue a circular letter[60] prohibiting the clergy of his diocese from repeating such misdemeanours as canvassing for votes for party candidates, transporting voters to the polling booths, remaining 'in or near the polling booths for the purpose of influencing or interfering with the free choice of the electors'. He drew attention to a statute promulgated at the Maynooth Synod of 1927, which had been introduced in an effort to curb a practice common during the two General Elections of that year.[61] This statute laid it down that 'political addresses, election harangues and all such discourses in church' were forbidden 'under pain of suspension'. O'Brien's general instruction to the diocesan priests of Kerry encouraged a code of conduct widely different from that tolerated in the diocese under his predecessor Bishop O'Sullivan.[62] The parochial clergy were now to act as 'spiritual guides and fathers of all their people, irrespective of their political affiliations', and to avoid 'political quarrels, party politics and local party disputes'. Also in 1933, Mgr McCaffrey, President of Maynooth College, warned newly ordained priests that interference by the clergy in political matters was forbidden by the law of the Church in Ireland, especially where it tended to bring the sacred ministry into contempt. McCaffrey, however, was careful to provide an opening for clerical intervention. Priests would be well advised to leave secular and political

---

[58] Donal Hales, 'Republican Consul in Rome', sent a copy of the circular to Dublin. It was published in Sinn Féin, 1.3.24.

[59] See p. 185, note 205.

[60] A copy of this document, dated 3.1.33 will be found in the Kerry Diocesan Archive. De Valera, who had felt himself and the parties with which he had been associated since 1922 injured by clerical politicians, declared in March 1934 that 'every Irishman and every Catholic knows full well that it would be a bad day for the Church and a bad day for religion that it identified itself with political parties'. He made his pronouncement following an address by Lord Muskerry to the labourers of Limerick, in which he declared that the Blueshirts were associated with St Patrick and Fianna Fáil with 'a thinly disguised policy of Communism'. See Fianna Fáil pamphlet, The Way to Peace, 1934, p.9.

[61] For a notorious example, see the address from the altar of Patrick Neary, PP Ballyforan, in which de Valera was compared to 'Lucifer, head of the Ku Klux Klan', referred to in note 388, p. 127.

[62] O'Brien himself had nominated John Marcus O'Sullivan, a Cumann na nGaedheal candidate and relative of the bishop, in the September 1927 General Election. The Kerryman, 10.9.27.

matters, 'when faith and morals are not concerned', to those 'who care to undertake such responsibilities'. By holding aloof from 'political wrangles and factions', Churchmen would then be 'in a stronger position to intervene in case political programmes and policies deviated from sound Catholic principles'.[63]

The partisanship engendered by the political divisions following the Treaty involved not only conflicts between clergymen and politicians, but also between bishops and those of their clergy who took political positions opposed to theirs. It was relatively safe for priests during the twenties to act as defenders and agents of the Free State government, since almost all their bishops were actively engaged in the same work. When bishops condemned priests for political activity prejudicial to the spiritual influence of the Church, to the reputation of the priestly ministry and to clerical discipline, they invariably had Republican priests in mind. The nature of episcopal dealings with such troublesome priests varied considerably from diocese to diocese, depending on the character and behaviour of the priest as well as the temperament and political outlook of his bishop. Two examples will illustrate this. The severest penalty a bishop could inflict on a refractory diocesan priest short of formal reduction to the lay state was *suspensio a divinis*, which meant that the offender could not say mass publicly, hear confession or administer any of the other sacraments of the Church. In 1918, Bishop Coyne of Elphin imposed this kind of suspension on Michael O'Flanagan, then Vice-President of Sinn Féin, who had defied his instruction not to engage in political controversy. In the post-Treaty period, during which his bishop was a warm supporter of the Free State, O'Flanagan persisted in delivering anti-episcopal Republican harangues in Ireland and abroad, and in 1925 was suspended from his priestly ministry.[64] John Fahy, CC Bullaun, Loughrea, an even more radical Republican than O'Flanagan, was, during the 1920s and 1930s, able to break the criminal law, serve a term in prison, deliver speeches denying the legitimacy of the State, and openly involve himself in IRA activity, without incurring any penalty more severe than a transfer to an inhospitable curacy where he persisted in his defiance of the Free State regime. The relative leniency with which Fahy was treated may

[63] *Irish Press*, 21.6.33. The application of this principle was a feature of episcopal conduct in the 1930s, when Cardinal MacRory, as well as Bishops Cohalan, Fogarty and Morrisroe commented unfavourably on some acts and policies of de Valera's administration. See Chapter Five for examples.

[64] See D. Carroll, *They have fooled you again. Michael O'Flanagan (1876–1942). Priest, Republican and Social Critic* (Dublin, 1993), pp. 83, 151. Carroll gives details of the partial reinstatement of O'Flanagan by Paschal Robinson, the Papal Nuncio.

be attributed to the fact that John Dignan, Bishop of Clonfert since 1924, was an avowed Republican.[65]

Thomas Burbage, CC Geashill, Co. Offaly, was an early platform speaker for the anti-Treaty party. In the presence of national troops, he vigorously condemned the Free State government from the altar in 1922 and 1923 for its execution of Republicans and was reported to his bishop by the military authorities for inciting his parishioners to rebellion.[66] He answered the latter accusation to the satisfaction of his bishop while justifying the former. Burbage's considerable reputation as a patriot, his impressive prison record during the War of Independence and his sturdy defence of his attitude to the Free State government which he castigated for executing a mentally unstable prisoner, influenced the bishop to refrain from action against him. Other less determined diocesan priests than Burbage could suffer sanctions involving the temporary withdrawal of faculties to preach or hear confession, or transfer to another parish. They could also find that promotion was unduly slow, especially when the bishop was a determined opponent of Republicanism.[67] Episcopal jurisdiction also extended to members of religious orders. If a regular priest contravened diocesan regulations governing the conduct of the clergy, the bishop could withdraw faculties. The imposition of more stringent penalties was a matter for the major superior or provincial.[68] In extreme cases, such as those of the Capuchin priests Albert and Dominic, whose Republican activities in 1922 met with the stern disapproval of the Provisional Government and of the Bishop of Cork, who suggested that Father Dominic renew his theological studies, the Provincial of the Order resolved an embarrassing problem by encouraging the two to volunteer for the American mission.[69]

---

[65] See pp. 314–17, notes 50–9.

[66] See pp. 147–8, notes 43–6. In April 1922, after Burbage had denounced the Treaty and those who supported it at a public meeting in Maryboro', his bishop reprimanded him and another priest in the hope that this might 'prevent the random talking of clergymen at public meetings'. He also submitted forms for the priests to sign. Foley to Mgr M.J. Murphy, 13.5.22, KLDA. Almost a year later, however, Burbage was still condemning the Free State Government from the altar. Murphy to Foley, 2.2.23, KLDA.

[67] Mgr. Daniel Long, PP Emeritus, Kenmare, in correspondence with the author, cited the case of one Kerry priest, Robert O'Reilly, as an example.

[68] I am grateful to Patrick Conlan, o.f.m. for elucidating these matters.

[69] Information from Father Nessan, o.f.m. Cap. Cork.

III

At an ideological level, the Republican enterprise, from the Fenians through 1916 to anti-Treaty Sinn Féin and Fianna Fáil, was fraught with significant contradictions and ambiguities, some of which were to have tragic consequences for many of those who took seriously the fundamentalist version of the Republican creed which the anti-Treaty leaders found it opportune to propagate in the aftermath of the Treaty. The defining elements of the pure Republican gospel on which post-Treaty leaders and their followers took their inflexible stand after de Valera's attempts at compromise had failed were the complete political separation of Ireland from Great Britain, the lawfulness of violent methods to achieve this, and an absolute refusal to compromise. It was to this version of Republicanism that Brugha had contrived to commit the members of the Dáil, the 'Republican Government' and the IRA under oath on 20 August 1919. Following the ratification of the Treaty, strict adherence to the same uncompromising doctrine was presented by opponents of the settlement as the single test of true patriotism: those, including the bishops, who had deviated from its principles by accepting the Treaty were now to be regarded as traitors and agents of the British government. The absolute attachment of anti-Treaty leaders to the fundamentalist Republican position sits uneasily with their much more flexible attitude before the settlement. His part in the proceedings of the first Ard Fheis of the new Sinn Féin in October 1917 makes it clear that de Valera, who stamped his authority on the event, regarded the promotion of the Republican ideal as a means to an end, not as the end in itself which he and others caused it to appear from early January 1922 onwards. He explained to the 1917 Ard Fheis that while the primary aim of the new Sinn Féin constitution was 'to get international recognition for our Irish Republic'; the Irish people might, following the achievement of that status, choose by referendum their own form of government, and, if they wished, disestablish the Republic and decide for example on a monarchy. The only restriction here would be that the monarch could not be of the House of Windsor.[70] For the present, he asserted, the Republican

---

[70] The views of some heroes of Republican folklore suggest that Republicanism needs to be regarded as a generously inclusive term. John O'Leary, the Fenian, is an interesting case. As a youth of 19, he had formed a secret society whose members bound themselves by oath to establish an Irish Republic, but he did not conceal his preference for a form of constitutional monarchy for Ireland. In later years he was in favour of an Irish Republic because that was the aim of the I.R.B. and there was no prospect of an Irish monarchy. 'I am not a doctrinaire', he declared in 1871, 'and would have no objection to a moderate Republic, either in

banner was the only one 'under which our liberty can be won', and it was as an Irish Republic that they would have 'a chance of getting international recognition'.[71]

When the second Dáil assembled in August 1921, de Valera made it clear that his espousal of Republicanism was pragmatic rather than principled, that he was not a doctrinaire Republican, that he was interested in Republicanism not as a political doctrine or as a form of government but as a useful descriptive term for Irish independence.[72] During his negotiations with Lloyd George in 1921, de Valera recognised that the achievement of an isolated and independent Irish Republic was impossible and that 'the Republic, in the sense of a government with no connection with Britain and no limits as to its sovereignty, had to be sacrificed'.[73] In his speech at the close of the Sinn Féin Ard Fheis on 28 October 1921, conscious of the problems which any settlement would pose, involving as it must a compromise of the full Republican position, de Valera was careful not to mention the Republic, either in its isolated or associated form. Instead he urged a spirit of compromise, open-mindedness and tolerance of honest differences of opinion, arguing that 'if such differences of opinion arose and were carried to the country, it would mean disaster to our hopes'.[74] At about the same time, de

(70 cont.) Ireland or elsewhere'. See Marcus Bourke, *John O'Leary. A Study in Irish Separatism* (Tralee, 1967), pp. 165–6. In the GPO in 1916, Pearse and Plunkett, according to Desmond FitzGerald who was present, solemnly discussed the nomination of a German prince to the Irish throne following the establishment of the Irish Republic. Ernest Blythe recalled that the proposal to have a German King of Ireland was discussed with approval by Plunkett and MacDonagh at a meeting in Volunteer H.Q. in January 1915. See 'The 1916 Rising – a Coup d'État or a "Bloody Protest"'. *Studia Hibernica*, vol. 8, 1968, p. 106. D.H. Akenson points out that from 1916 onwards most Irish nationalists called themselves Republicans, 'but beneath the Republican banner marched an array of persons who held viewpoints ranging from strict Republicanism to a willingness to accept dominion status for Ireland'. 'Was de Valera a Republican?' *Review of Politics*, vol. 33, no. 2, 1972, p. 233. R.F. Foster argues that 'Republican' could stand for 'anything merely anti-British to agrarian-syndicalist-revolutionary, not to mention exclusivist-Gaelic Catholic; it was a moral stance rather than a political affiliation'. *Modern Ireland*, p. 542.

[71] Verbatim report of the Sinn Féin Ard Fheis, 1917, probably of Sinn Féin provenance. NLI MS 21523.

[72] Dáil Éireann. Official report for the period 16 August 1921 to 26 August 1921 and 28 February 1922 to 8 June 1922, p. 9. In 1929, a pamphlet commemorating Austin Stack asserted that 'the name Republican in Ireland bears no political meaning. It stands for the devout lover of his country, trying with might and main for his country's freedom'. Foster, *Modern Ireland*, p. 542.

[73] Akenson, 'Was de Valera a Republican?', p. 243.

[74] M. Moynihan, ed. *Speeches and Statements of Eamon de Valera, 1917–73* (Dublin, 1980), p. 75. As soon as the Treaty was signed, he himself was the first to bring such differences of opinion before the country in a proclamation denouncing the agreement. See Macardle, *Irish Republic*, p. 596.

Valera was able to persuade Brugha, whose ideal was 'the Republic, one and undivided', and who had for a long time prevented calm debate on anything less than complete autonomy,[75] to consider and agree to accept something less than the undivided, isolated Republic: Brugha declared himself satisfied to recommend External Association to the Cabinet.[76] Following the approval of the Treaty by the Dáil, de Valera addressed the membership of Sinn Féin in a very different tone from that which marked his pre-Treaty pronouncement. He moved a resolution for the Ard Fheis of 7 February 1922 calling on the organisation to abide by the spirit of its constitution, 'in which it is laid down that the main objective of the movement is to secure inter-national recognition of the Irish Republic, maintain the independence of Ireland and subvert . . . British authority in this country'.[77] The need to have the Republic recognised, now that this prospect was more remote than ever, took on a new urgency in his discourse, and that of fellow-opponents of the Treaty, and became its central theme.

The conflict between the Church leadership and post-Treaty Republicans was not simply a matter of episcopal support for the Sinn Féin pragmatists who accepted the Treaty as the alternative to national ruin and a rejection of the Republican idealists who were prepared to continue the struggle. The tendency of much contem-porary Republican comment was to blame the Church authorities for condoning the disestablishment of the Irish Republic by many of those who had recently been at war to uphold that Republic and who were now prepared to take the most drastic measures against men they had encouraged to fight for it. A straightforward answer to this line of argument was given by Bishop Cohalan, who declared that 'if Ireland was a Republic from 1916 to 1921, I would be a Republican to-day. No one who believed that Ireland was a Republic from 1919 to 1921 would be so base as to surrender the Republican position in 1922.'[78] There was also the consideration that in May 1922, the anti-Treaty leadership was effectively prepared to compromise whatever Republican position there was at the time. The Collins–de Valera pact of May 1922, which Collins described as a final attempt on the part of both men 'to

.[75] Desmond FitzGerald, 'Mr Pakenham and the Anglo-Irish Treaty', *Studies*, vol. xxiv, September 1935, p. 407.
[76] In October 1921, Brugha, at de Valera's request, submitted a formal signed memorandum to him which confirmed his acquiescence in External Association. 'All other matters being satisfactorily settled', Brugha wrote, 'we are prepared to recommend to our people that the accepted head of Great Britain would be recognised as head of the new association.' Memorandum given to the President by Cathal Brugha between 20 and 25 October 1921. FAK, 1315.
[77] *Poblacht na h-Éireann*, No. 5, 21.1.22.
[78] *Irish Independent*, 26.9.22.

prevent the use of force by Irishmen against Irishmen', and which was designed to cover the election to the Provisional Parliament or Third Dáil, committed Republicans to the recognition of a parliament which would inevitably refuse to function as the Government of the Republic because the pact made provision for a pro-Treaty Dáil and Cabinet majority.[79] The contrast between de Valera's frequent public espousal of uncompromising Republicanism and his real views on the subject is clear in a letter he addressed to Mary MacSwiney in September 1922. Here he suggested that her stand for fundamentalist Republicanism placed her 'on the plane of Faith and Unreason'; his own flexibility and willingness to compromise, so uncharacteristic of classical Irish Republicanism, set him apart from Plunkett, Mellows, Brugha and MacSwiney herself, and, as he put it, 'unfitted me to be the leader of the Republican Party'. He had, for the sake of the cause, allowed himself to be put in a position which it was impossible for one of his 'outlook and personal bias' to fill effectively. 'I must', he told MacSwiney, 'be the heir to generations of conservatism. Every instinct of mine would indicate that I was meant to be a dyed-in-the-wool Tory or even a bishop, rather than the leader of a Revolution'.[80] The Republican *persona* assumed with such apparent conviction by de Valera in his post-Treaty days displayed few if any of the elements of the deeply conservative self revealed to MacSwiney.

In 1922, had the bishops and the majority of the clergy been privy to de Valera's judgment of his own essentially moderate temper and outlook, they might have felt reassured, and been less inclined to denounce him as an irresponsible extremist. They might, perhaps, also have appreciated the significance of his engagement in extreme

[79] Ronan Fanning, *Independent Ireland* (Dublin, 1983), p. 13. It might be urged, in fairness to de Valera, that he subscribed to the pact with Collins in the assurance that the constitution being proposed by the latter, but soon to be dismissed as unacceptable by the British government, was in fundamental conflict with the main provisions of the Treaty. The constitution Collins wanted would have given Ireland a degree of independence and sovereignty beyond even what de Valera would have settled for. There was to be no provision for an oath to the Crown, and all powers of government were to be 'derived from the people of Ireland' and 'based on their consent'. In May 1922, when the pact with de Valera was signed, Collins was determined that the constitution should assert Irish independence in ways the Treaty did not permit, and be republican in spirit. See Macardle, *Irish Republic*, pp. 717–27; D.H. Akenson and J.F. Fallin, 'The Irish Civil War and the Drafting of the Free State Constitution', *Éire-Ireland*, vol. v, no. 4, pp. 28–70; T. Towey, 'The Reaction of the British Government to the 1922 Collins–de Valera Pact', *IHS*, vol. xxii, 1985, pp. 65–76.

[80] De Valera to Mary MacSwiney, 11.9.22. FAK, 1444. David Fitzpatrick draws attention to 'de Valera's peculiar blend of superficial inflexibility with profound opportunism'. *The Two Irelands* (Oxford, 1998), p. 105.

bouts of verbal Republicanism when he was away from the centres of power, and his more temperate and responsible form of utterance as he moved closer to these. Just as he sensed in 1917 that the Republican path to independence was a surer one than any other, he was equally conscious in the post-Treaty period that an uncompromising stand for the republic was the course most likely to facilitate his emergence from the political darkness. Once he had emerged, he could afford to compromise once more. His talent for ridding himself and those who followed him of the uncomfortable associations and legacies of the past gradually ensured his restoration to the favour of a large body of the clergy, including a number of bishops. Less than six years after he had rejected the Treaty, he submitted to its exigencies, and swallowed the hated oath, to the relief of some of the clergy and the disedification of others. Fianna Fáil Republicanism was, in Catholic terms, unexceptionable, perpetually striving to make visible its robust religious orthodoxy. The fire of the Church was now turned on those fundamentalist Republicans, of the left and right, whom de Valera had left behind, deadly fulminations being directed against one group whose socialism was seen as a challenge to Catholic teaching, and against another for its violent rejection of legitimate government.[81] By 1937, however, the Church had the satisfaction of knowing that great numbers of its former Republican antagonists, now enlisted in the ranks of Fianna Fáil, were among its most loyal members.

---

[81] In the mid-thirties, Bishop Kinane of Waterford and Lismore was careful to exempt Fianna Fáil from the ranks of Republican groups disapproved of by the Church. The Republic at which Fianna Fáil was aiming, he declared, one in which all classes of society are represented and have their rights, was 'a perfectly legitimate form of government', and the principles upon which it was based were 'in complete accord with God's law'. A socialist Republic, on the other hand, was not a legitimate form of government, and one who professed the principles on which it was based by that very fact put himself 'in opposition to God's law and to the teaching of His Church'. *Irish Press*, 7.1.35.

CHAPTER THREE

SUSTAINING THE STATE

I

THE OPENING OF the Anglo-Irish Peace Conference in London on 11 October 1921 coincided with the annual meeting of the Irish Hierarchy at Maynooth. The resolution passed by the bishops at this meeting extended far more than a perfunctory welcome to the conference. They hoped for a peace 'which will satisfy the National rights and aspirations of the Irish people'; they looked to the British for 'a great act of National freedom untrammelled by limitations and free from the hateful spirit of partition, which could never be anything but a perennial source of discord and fratricidal strife', and they urged the immediate liberation of the internees.[1] Some of the bishops had already made a contribution to the Treaty negotiations through the Committee of Information on the Case of Ulster, which had been set up in September 1921 to gather evidence on the Ulster question for the use of the Irish delegates. MacRory of Down and Connor, Mulhern of Dromore, McHugh of Derry, McKenna of Clogher and O'Donnell of Raphoe were consulted on the likely effects of partition in the six north-eastern counties, with particular emphasis on education and gerrymandering.[2]

A week after the Treaty was signed, the bishops held a special meeting on 13 December to consider its terms. In a statement issued after this meeting they recorded their appreciation of the 'patriotism, ability, and honesty of purpose in which the Irish representatives have conducted the struggle for national freedom'. They did not pronounce on the merits or defects of the Treaty, merely suggesting that the members of Dáil Éireann 'will be sure to have before their minds the

---

[1] *ICD*, 1922, p. 600.
[2] Mary Harris, *The Catholic Church and the Foundation of the Northern Irish State* (Cork, 1993), p. 103. See also Childers Papers, TCD, 7784/66/4;7784/66/8.

best interests of the country and the wishes of the people'.[3] The caution underlying the statement was welcomed by the two senior representatives of Irish episcopal interests in Rome: John Hagan, Rector of the Irish College and M. J. Curran, the Vice-Rector, both of whom were soon to be vigorous opponents of the Treaty Settlement. Curran congratulated Archbishop Byrne of Dublin 'on the excellent declaration of the bishops of yesterday'. The moment the settlement was published, Curran reported, 'the Rector sent a message to the Under-Secretary of State [at the Vatican] that the settlement was not definite until accepted by the Irish and English Parliaments and not to take it for granted that all was over'.[4]

The prudent reticence which marked the joint episcopal statement of 13 December was absent from the responses of many individual bishops who made their strongly pro-Treaty views known to the press in advance of the bishops' meeting. As soon as the news of the agreement was made public, six prelates, Cardinal Logue, Archbishop Gilmartin of Tuam, Bishops McKenna of Clogher, Hackett of Waterford, Gaughran of Meath and Hallinan of Limerick made public statements welcoming it.[5] Bishop Fogarty of Killaloe soon added his distinctive voice to the debate. On 8 December he communicated his enthusiasm for the Treaty to Childers, describing it as 'marvellous' and congratulating all those involved.[6] On the same day, Fogarty issued a fulsome statement of approval, predicting that the men who made the Treaty 'will be immortal', suggesting that the moral effect of the settlement 'will be worth half a navy to England' and expressing confidence that the Irish Free State 'will soon have the cordial allegiance of every Irishman'.[7] Four days after the signature of the Treaty in London, five other bishops publicly indicated their support for it. These were Browne of Cloyne, Foley of Kildare and Leighlin, Cohalan of Cork, Finegan of Kilmore and O'Doherty of Clonfert.[8] Thus, before the episcopal body met to consider their joint response, almost half its members had signified their warm approval of the Treaty, thereby depriving the collective statement of 13 December of much of its meaning. The situation created by the instant responses of so many bishops troubled at least one thoughtful Parish Priest with Republican leanings, Robert Egan of Mullahoran in the diocese of Ardagh, who

---

[3] *ICD*, 1922, p. 538.
[4] M.J. Curran to Byrne, 14.12.21, DAA.
[5] *Freeman's Journal*, 8.12.21.
[6] Fogarty to Childers, 8.12.21, Childers Papers, TCD, 7848.
[7] *Freeman's Journal*, 9.12.21. On the same day that Fogarty issued his statement of welcome for the Treaty, de Valera denounced it.
[8] *Irish Independent* 10.12.21.

noted in his diary: 'The *Independent*, always rotten, stampeded the country; wired the Bishops for their opinions'.[9]

In the case of some of the bishops, public acclaim for the Treaty was supplemented by efforts to persuade declared and potential opponents of the merits of the settlement. Fogarty and O'Doherty, commonly regarded as being sympathetic to Sinn Féin, told de Valera privately of their support for the Treaty at an early stage.[10] Much more significant was Archbishop Byrne's attempt, during the second half of December 1921, to persuade de Valera to accept the evident will of the people and let the Treaty go through the Dáil unopposed. Byrne represented himself to de Valera as occupying 'a more or less detached position' and as a man free from 'any hostile or even partisan feelings'. He saw the Dáil as a representative assembly, having no other *locus standi* apart from this. He pointed out that the country 'so far as it has spoken . . . seems overwhelmingly in favour of the Treaty'. He went on to argue that a Dáil vote on the agreement, whatever the result, would lead to a disastrous split. 'If the Treaty is rejected', he maintained, 'the Dáil will be acting against the will of the Nation'. To avoid 'a miserable split in the National forces when all should unite', Byrne suggested that de Valera 'avoid provoking matters to a division'. This course would be of ultimate benefit to de Valera and his supporters: 'A magnificent gesture such as I suggest will enshrine you in the hearts of the Irish people . . . Those who act with you will, if not at present obviously, be thankful to you that you have not cut them off from public life.'[11]

Byrne was not quite the detached, non-partisan arbitrator of national affairs that this letter suggests. Towards the end of January 1922, three weeks after the approval of the Treaty by the Dáil, Viscount FitzAlan, the Viceroy, who was a Catholic, intimated to the Administrator of the pro-Cathedral that he proposed to be present at a mass in the Cathedral for the late Pope Benedict. Byrne was impressed by FitzAlan's motives, but feared that the Viceroy's official presence at such an event might jeopardise the Treaty settlement when it was still by no means out of danger. In his reply to MacMahon, the Under-Secretary, who had made the initial approach on behalf of FitzAlan, Byrne made it clear that his fundamental concern was to ensure that no opportunity be afforded to opponents of the Treaty to undermine the position of

[9] Diary of Father Robert Egan, P.P. Mullahoran. I am grateful to Father Owen Devanney for making this available to me.
[10] T.P. Ó Néill agus P. Ó Fiannachta, *De Valera*, Vol. II (Dublin, 1970), p. 36.
[11] Byrne to de Valera, n.d. DAA. The letter appears to have been written soon after 13.12.21. It may be significant that Byrne altered his initial relatively cordial mode of address, 'My dear President', to the more formal 'a cara' [*sic*].

the new government or to strengthen their own position. 'National affairs', Byrne argued, 'are passing through an acute crisis, and in the present delicate conditions comparatively small things may sway the balance one way or the other'. Byrne's great fear was that the Treaty 'with its bright promise of lasting friendship between the two peoples' could be endangered were the symbols of British rule again to be made prominent. This would provide valuable propaganda for the anti-Treaty party in the coming election. 'Just at present', Byrne advised, 'the less emphasis is laid on the authority of the Viceroy the better for the Treaty . . . just at the moment, until the Free State is well started on its normal course, public displays, such as appearing officially . . . can do nothing but harm, the magnitude of which I fear to estimate'.[12] FitzAlan, though hurt and offended by Byrne's letter, acquiesced.[13]

Between the signing of the Treaty on December 6th 1921 and its approval by Dáil Éireann on 7 January 1922, bishops and many of their clergy exerted considerable influence on public opinion generally and on the Dáil deputies in particular to secure the passage of the agreement through the Dáil. Dorothy Macardle has pointed out that many Christmas sermons became pro-Treaty speeches.[14] Fogarty used his Christmas Day sermon to express his displeasure that 'differences had developed amongst their public representatives in the Dáil' and at 'the callous disregard openly avowed by some Deputies for the National will and the wishes of their constituents on this awful question'. Fogarty characterised the position taken by the Republican deputies in the pre-Christmas debates as 'wholly indefensible and morally wrong', since it was 'the negation of representative government'. Fogarty's conclusion might have given pause to those who had come to terms, on moral grounds, with the 1916 rising and the War of Independence: 'No man or group of men has a right to lead the country into a ruinous war against the considered judgement of the Nation'.[15] Fogarty's anxiety that Dáil deputies give effect to the wishes of the majority of those who elected them was deeply felt, as was his fear that Republican intransigence might result not only in civil war, but in the return of the

[12] Letter from Under-Secretary's Lodge to Fr. Bowden, 28.1.22: Byrne to MacMahon 29.1.22, DAA.
[13] 'As a Catholic, to be absent on purely political grounds seems to me not only an act of cowardice but an insult to the memory of the late Pontiff and to the Church . . . I cannot believe that my behaving as a Catholic and a gentleman on such an occasion can add one single vote to the anti-Treaty party'. FitzAlan to Byrne, 29.1.22, DAA.
[14] D. Macardle, *The Irish Republic*, 4th edn (Dublin, 1951), p. 624.
[15] *The Saturday Record*, Ennis, 31.12.21.

British. Writing to Hagan at the end of 1921, he expressed the almost universal view that 'the great bulk of the nation want acceptance' of the Treaty and to make the most of it 'as the shortest way to the final acquisition of all their rights'. The problem, as Fogarty saw it, was that a Republican majority in the Dáil seemed likely to reject the Treaty 'and then chaos, war, civil and international'.[16] It was characteristic of Fogarty to personalise his political preoccupations. Early in 1922 he developed an obsessive dislike of de Valera's role in national life, and soon focused on him as the source of all Ireland's political ills. 'De Valera', he told Hagan, 'has a new treaty every other day. He now wants to get over to Lloyd George with a new document to be turned down of course, and then to say the nation was insulted and then on with the war.'[17] His tendency to overestimate de Valera's importance in post-Treaty Republican politics and to attribute sinister or malicious motives to him in almost everything he did was a common one.[18] Fogarty's fear that the activities of Republican extremists might provoke a renewal of the Anglo-Irish war was not entirely baseless. It seems to have been shared by IRA men like Liam Archer who decided to support the Treaty when he realised that Rory O'Connor's objective after 6 December 1922 'was to create a situation wherein the British would have reason to return in force for the purpose of establishing "Law and Order" and we would be plunged into complete submission again, or complete anarchy'. [19]

During the Christmas recess, many pro-Treaty clergymen publicly argued, as Fogarty did, that 'If a Deputy finds himself in such a decision as is now at stake conscientiously in conflict with what he knows to be the national will, his duty is very plain'.[20] In other words, he was morally obliged to resign. Dean Gearty of Strokestown, Co. Roscommon told a public meeting held under the auspices of the Sinn Féin Executive that deputies 'who were not prepared to carry out the wishes of the people' should retire.[21] Eugene Coyle, CC Clontibret, Co. Monaghan, whose faith in the possibilities for Irish unity offered by the Boundary Clause induced him to champion the Treaty, wrote to the press about a decision taken by the Sinn Féin organisation in

[16] Fogarty to Hagan 31.12.21, Hagan Papers.
[17] Ibid.
[18] For an extreme example, see Mulhern's frank letter to de Valera at the height of the Belfast pogrom: 'My own opinion and that of my colleagues in the North, and indeed of anyone I have met, is that you, and you alone, are responsible for the recrudescence of the troubles in the N. East, and of all the disturbances elsewhere'. Mulhern to de Valera, 23.3.22, DRDA.
[19] Michael Hayes Papers UCDA P53/344.
[20] The Saturday Record, Ennis, 31.12.21.
[21] Roscommon Herald, 7.1.22.

Monaghan.[22] A resolution was passed 'that they, voicing the wishes of 99 per cent of the people of County Monaghan, called upon their representatives in the Dáil to vote for ratification of the Treaty . . . Seeing that Mr Seán MacEntee had already in the public meeting of the Dáil expressed opinions entirely at variance with this opinion of his constituents, Mr O'Rourke of Inniskeen and myself were asked to go to Mr MacEntee and point out to him that if he wished to represent his constituents he must vote for ratification of the Treaty'.[23] Priests took a leading part in seeking to influence Sean O'Mahony, TD for Fermanagh, to vote for the Treaty. The argument was the same as that used in the case of MacEntee: the Treaty represented the will of the people to which Deputies were morally obliged to submit. It was in this spirit that James McCabe, CC Derrylin wrote to O'Mahony. 'A rumour has reached me', he told O'Mahony, 'that you are opposed to the Treaty and intend voting against it. You will pardon me for telling you that the people of this district want the Treaty – in fact I don't think there is even one who would oppose it . . . I don't know how the other parts would go. But I know in Co. Cavan a few, but very few, would continue on for a full republic in every sense, but not for [Document] No. 2'.[24] McCabe bluntly asserted that 'Any TD that opposes the Treaty must go and the fear is that worthless fellows like the Parliamentary Party will get in.' If O'Mahony wished to go on representing his constituents, he should, McCabe believed, 'use his influence to have the Dáil unanimous in accepting the Treaty'.[25] O'Mahony got a similar letter from the Thomas Ashe Sinn Féin Club signed by its President, Peter Treacy, CC Strabane. 'All the nationalists in your constituency', O'Mahony was informed, 'favour ratification and by voting against it you are not representing their views'. O'Mahony was given two strong reasons for supporting the Treaty: it secured the essentials of freedom for the Irish nation, and the Orange and ascendancy party would welcome its rejection, since this would destroy Nationalist unity and leave the Unionists masters of Ulster.[26]

[22] Disappointed by the failure of the Boundary Commission to meet his expectations, Father Coyle became a bitter critic of the Free State Government, and an active member of Fianna Fáil.

[23] *Freeman's Journal*, 5.1.22.

[24] James McCabe to O'Mahony, 29.12.21, O'Mahony Papers, NLI 24468. Document No. 2 incorporated de Valera's alternative to the Treaty, and was first put forward by its author at a private session of the Dáil on 14.12.21. Its central provision was that Ireland should be externally associated with the States of the British Commonwealth, with the King as head of the association.

[25] Ibid.

[26] M. Magovern and Rev. P. Treacy to O'Mahony, January 1922, O'Mahony Papers NLI 24468.

MacEntee and O'Mahony resisted these local pressures and voted against approval of the Treaty.

At the beginning of January 1922, the national and provincial press was reporting meetings of Sinn Féin units called to consider the Treaty. All these reports suggest a significant clerical involvement. This was inevitable since in almost all cases the senior Sinn Féin Club and Comhairle officers were priests. On 3 January, the *Freeman's Journal* mentioned that 'hundreds of parish meetings have been held during the week-end all over the country, and without exception ratification was demanded'. When priests made their views known at these meetings, as they almost invariably did, they argued strongly for ratification. Philip O'Doherty, PP VF presided at the Omagh Comhairle Ceanntair meeting, at which the resolution in favour of ratification was proposed by J.H. McKenna CC Knockmoyle. The unanimous support for the resolution to approve was influenced by the belief that the Treaty would safeguard 'our interests in the North'.[27] Patrick O'Donovan, PP Caheragh, presided at the West Cork Sinn Féin Executive meeting; Martin Murphy, the Parish Priest of Durras and Glengarrif, wrote expressing approval of the Treaty.[28] At the meeting of the South Longford Comhairle Ceanntair, Canon Joseph Guinan PP Ardagh seconded the motion for ratification.[29] In the diocese of Killala, the Bishop, Dr Naughton, an ardent advocate of the Treaty, directed that meetings be held in every parish to ascertain the views of the people. The Bishop evidently hoped that these meetings would constitute pro-Treaty lobby groups. Writing to William Greaney Adm. Ballina, in advance of the meetings, Naughton was confident of the outcome: 'From what I know of the feeling in this district, and through-out the diocese generally, I am certain that the people are practically unanimous in their desire to accept the present offer of freedom'.[30] At parish meetings throughout County Roscommon, priests were vigilant upholders of the Treaty cause. At Elphin, the Parish Priest, John McDermott, dealt with the arguments of an opponent of the Treaty who believed that the people generally were not the best judges of what was good for the country. Canon McDermott, 'in a genial way, pointed out the weakness of [this] position', and told his adversary that 'in such matters, authority, to be lawful, must come from the people'.[31] At the North Roscommon Comhairle Ceanntair meeting in Croghan, Malachy Mac Branain, CC Mantua, proposed that the

[27] *Freeman's Journal*, 3.1.22.
[28] *Weekly Freeman*, 7.1.22
[29] Ibid.
[30] Ibid.
[31] *Roscommon Herald*, 7.1.22.

Treaty be approved, even though it contained clauses 'not in harmony with National aspirations'. Another resolution expressed the view that 95 per cent of the people favoured the agreement.[32] In a letter to the West Clare Comhairle Ceanntair, Canon O'Kennedy, President of St Flannan's College, argued that the question of ratification or non-ratification 'is principally a matter for our Irish army', but believed that 'after the public statement of the Chief of Staff' there was no way out of the present crux but ratification.[33] Thomas Dunne, PP Kiltulla, president of the South Galway Comhairle Ceanntair, was joined by three other priests in supporting a pro-Treaty resolution at a meeting in Loughrea.[34]

Bishops and priests continued to exert spiritual, moral and political pressure on public opinion and on the Dáil Deputies. The common themes of episcopal discourse on the subject were the sacredness of the principle of majority rule and the duty of public representatives to vote on the Treaty in accordance with the will of the majority. One Bishop, Hallinan of Limerick, made a passing reference to the need to make 'all due allowance for the personal discretion vested in Parliamentary representatives of the people', but seemed to believe that 'in a supreme crisis like the present' such discretion must be set aside in favour of 'the ascertained wishes of their constituencies as revealed through the ordinary organs of public opinion'. Hallinan warned Deputies that in no case should they misrepresent their constituents 'by voting against their wishes'.[35] Bishop Browne of Cloyne argued in his Christmas Day Sermon that 'the people are the fountain of National authority', and urged supporters of the Treaty to express their point of view publicly, 'and call on their members to obey the mandate of their constituencies'.[36] Archbishop Harty of Cashel asserted that 'The people of Ireland by a vast majority are in favour of the Treaty, and in a democratic country the will of the people is the final court of appeal'.[37]

Spiritual weapons were also deployed in aid of the Treaty. Speaking at Mass in Mullingar Cathedral, Bishop Gaughran of Meath asked the congregation 'to pray that the Treaty might be ratified on Tuesday'.[38] At all the masses in Tralee parish church on the same day, 'the prayers of the congregation were asked for the ratification of

[32] Ibid.
[33] *Freeman's Journal*, 3.1.22.
[34] *The Connaught Tribune*, 7.1.22.
[35] *ICD*, 1923, p. 541.
[36] Ibid. p. 540.
[37] Ibid. p. 542.
[38] *Freeman's Journal*, 3.1.22.

the Treaty'.[39] Telegrams were freely used by priests to remind Deputies of their duty, particularly those who were thought to be wavering. Paul Murphy PP Edenderry wired the newspapers that a pro-Treaty petition had been signed 'by all classes and creeds' for immediate presentation to their Deputy Dr McCartan. The people of 'Edenderry and surrounding districts' felt gravely apprehensive, they told McCartan, 'lest your not voting for the ratification of the Treaty might possibly affect its rejection'.[40] Franics McDermott PP Ballinlough, Co. Roscommon sent a telegram to the *Freeman's Journal* announcing that 'Priests and people and all Sinn Féin Clubs in the parish of Kiltullagh strongly favour ratification and unanimously request our member Mr Harry Boland to vote for ratification'.[41] Many priests used the newspapers to signify their approval of the Treaty.[42] Others appeared at non-political gatherings. John D'Arcy, PP Borrisokane, Co. Tipperary, told a meeting of farmers that while he would not force his views on anyone, he would never consent to see the young men of Ireland slaughtered, 'when they had the opportunity of securing a settlement that would enable the country to have control of its own destiny'. A resolution was adopted urging on the Dáil Deputies 'the advisability of voting for ratification'.[43]

Some clergymen were prepared to employ more direct methods to influence Deputies. Tom Maguire has left an account of his experiences at the hands of Mayo priests at the end of 1921. His own Parish Priest, Martin Henry, PP Kilmovee, disturbed by rumours that he intended to vote against the Treaty, advised him by letter that if he could not see his way to vote in favour he should at least abstain. When Maguire indicated that he could not abstain, Canon Henry explained that he would not have written had he not been requested by Archbishop Gilmartin to use all his influence to secure Maguire's vote for the Treaty.[44] Maguire also received 'an offensive letter' from Dean D'Alton of Ballinrobe ordering him to vote for the Treaty, and was approached in the Gresham Hotel by D'Alton and Father Martin Healy, Parish Priest of Kilmaine, as part of a pro-Treaty lobbying exercise. Even the Chinese Mission at Dalgan Park near Shrule got in touch with Maguire with the same end in view.[45] Maguire claimed that the Treaty was

---

[39] Ibid.
[40] *Limerick Weekly and District Advertiser*, 31.12.22. McCartan's speech in the Dáil debate had suggested that he intended to abstain on the Treaty vote.
[41] *Freeman's Journal*, 3.1.22.
[42] The list in the *Freeman's Journal*, 3.1.22 provides examples.
[43] *Clonmel Chronicle*, 4.1.22.
[44] See U. MacEoin (ed), *Survivors* (Dublin, 1981), p. 289.
[45] Ibid. There is a well-authenticated story that Martin Healy refused to accept Church dues tendered by his Republican parishioners. I owe this information to Father Brendan Kilcoyne, Tuam.

approved only because of clerical pressure. 'Without the priests', he believed, 'the Treaty would never have been put across'.[46] A Limerick Republican, Liam Monaghan, asserted that his Dáil Deputy Bill Hayes was opposed to the Treaty 'until their PP convinced him otherwise'.[47] Tom Maguire recalled that 'the pressure was strong and concerted upon every TD and those who returned home over Christmas were the most exposed' to clerical influence. In his opinion, this accounted for a significant change of heart in a number of Deputies; it facilitated an outcome to the vote in January that did not seem likely before Christmas. Maguire also noted a significant aspect of clerical influence over the general membership of Sinn Féin: many were teachers who depended upon their Parish Priests for the security of their jobs.[48]

It is difficult to establish with certainty that had churchmen not intervened the Treaty would have been rejected by the Dáil. Some Deputies who were subjected to clerical pressure, Harry Boland, Seán MacEntee, Seán O'Mahony and Tom Maguire, for example, voted against the Treaty. Dan O'Rourke, who represented South Roscommon in the Dáil, and who was initially against the Treaty, changed his mind when he returned to his constituency during the Christmas recess, but this new attitude seems to have had little to do with clerical influence. Just before the vote, O'Rourke told the Dáil that when he returned to his constituency at Christmas, he had returned to 'the people – not the resolution passers – to the people who had been with me in the fight . . . the people who are, I believe, Die-Hards . . . and I must say that unanimously they said to me that there was no alternative but to accept the Treaty'.[49] On 5 January, Frank Drohan, Deputy for Waterford and Tipperary East, resigned from the Dáil because he could not conscientiously follow the directive of his Comhairle Ceanntair to vote for the Treaty.[50] To the extent that clerical influence operated in this Comhairle Ceanntair as elsewhere, it might be argued that churchmen played a part in depriving the anti-Treaty party of Drohan's vote.

[46] O'Malley Papers UCDA P176/100, p. 153.
[47] Ibid. P176/117, p. 35.
[48] MacEoin (ed.), *Survivors*, p. 289.
[49] *Dáil Éireann. Official Report. Debate on the Treaty between Great Britain and Ireland. Session December 1921-January 1922*, p. 316. In November 1922, O'Rourke, returned in the June 1922 election as a pro-Treaty deputy, resigned his membership of the Dáil on two grounds: the failure of the Provisional Government to honour the Collins–de Valera pact of May 1922, and the government's recent execution of prisoners, including Childers. O'Rourke argued that 'When Irishmen make a bargain with their own countrymen, they should be at least as careful to fulfil it as a bargain made with Englishmen'. *Irish Independent*, 30.11.22.
[50] Ibid. p. 269.

There is clear evidence that churchmen of all ranks were striving to lead public opinion in a pro-Treaty direction between 6 December 1921 and 7 January 1922. It is also true that when these same churchmen proclaimed that the great majority of the Irish people supported the settlement, they were, to some extent, projecting their own firm convictions and interpreting these as the general will. One must also bear in mind that the strong moral and political influence enjoyed by the Church inevitably affected public opinion on the issue, once the great body of churchmen declared themselves in favour of accepting the Treaty. In the absence of any obvious alternative, bishops and priests were in a particularly strong position to influence local views. Reports of the hundreds of meetings of Sinn Féin units held in late December 1921 suggest that in many cases the priests who were present influenced, and often directed, the course of the proceedings. Against this, however, it might be argued that people wanted to be led on such a central issue as the Treaty, and that a significant majority of Sinn Féin members regarded the parish meetings convened by priests as welcome opportunities for expressing their pro-Treaty views. It is difficult to believe that had a majority of those who were active in Sinn Féin in late 1921 been strongly opposed to the Treaty, clerical influence would have been decisive in the opposite direction. In the course of the Treaty Debate after Christmas, Brian O'Higgins implied that the four pro-Treaty resolutions 'from the whole County of Clare' were passed as a result of unfair and underhand pressure.[51] The reply of a pro-Treaty priest, Alfred Molony of Kilrush, explains how the West Clare Sinn Féin resolution was passed, and throws light on the part played by a typical country priest in political affairs. Molony pointed out that 'People were constantly asking me to do something in order that their views in the present crisis might be made known'. Molony arranged meetings of Sinn Féin clubs, delegates from which, when they attended the Executive meeting, 'were unanimously in favour of the Treaty'. Public opinion in the constituency, he was certain, was firmly in favour of approval; he assured O'Higgins that had he gone around the constituency during Christmas week 'the sad fact would be brought home to his mind that were he to stand an election tomorrow he would find a difficulty in filling up a single nomination paper'.[52] In the absence of contemporary opinion surveys, the General Election of 1922 offers the only guide to popular support for the Treaty. The anti-Treaty vote of just over 20 per cent in that election is in excess of the estimates current among proponents of the Treaty in the first months of 1922.[53]

[51] Ibid. p.191.
[52] *Freeman's Journal*, 3.1.22.
[53] See Map and Table of Results, pp. 45–7.

The General Election, 1922

Table 1: Votes won by parties in each contested constituency, 1922

	Pro-treaty	Anti-treaty	Labour	Farmers	Independents	Total
Carlow–Kilkenny	9,752	4,478	10,875	7,122		31,227
Cavan	18,473			5,620		24,093
Cork Borough	11,388	5,812	6,836		6,311	30,347
Cork E & NE		11,697		6,989	5,029	23,814
Cork N, S, Mid, SE & W	25,070	12,623	10,737	6,372		54,802
Dublin Mid.	4,295	5,670			19,164	29,129
Dublin NW	22,582		5,195			27,777
Dublin S	9,884	5,259	4,734		6,431	26,308
Dublin County	18,434	4,826	8,220	3,697	16,700	51,877
Galway	19,896	11,780	4,821			36,497
Kildare–Wicklow	9,170	6,568	12,515	6,261		34,514
Laois–Offaly	17,425		15,167			32,592
Longford–Westmeath	14,428	5,022	7,073		2,258	28,781
Louth–Meath	16,774	5,733	13,994			36,501
Monaghan	11,792	5,046			3,681	20,519
Sligo–Mayo E.	10,193	19,457			4,849	34,499
Tipperary N, S, Mid	9,309	11,508	7,819			28,636
Waterford–Tipp. E.	6,778	7,039	10,658	5,871	583	34,077*
Wexford	2,370	8,882	13,923	7,786		32,691
National University	1,182	663			791	2,636
Ireland	239,195	132,162	132,567	48,718	65,797	621,587*
(%)	(38.48)	(21.26)	(21.33)	(7.84)	(10.59)	(100.0)
Candidates	65	58	18	13	21	176*
Seats	58	36	17	7	10	128

*including the 3,148 votes of Dan Breen, joint panel candidate
Note: 17 Pro-Treaty candidates, 17 Anti-Treaty and 4 independents were returned unopposed.
Source: provincial and national newspapers.

Table 2: Seats and votes won by Sinn Féin in contested constituencies, by province, 1922

	seats	Pro-Treaty candidates	votes, in %	seats	Anti-Treaty candidates	votes in %
Dublin	10	(12)	40.9	1	(6)	14.7
Rest of Leinster	11	(15)	35.6	4	(11)	18.7
Munster	7	(8)	35.5	7	(15)	28.4
Connacht	6	(6)	42.4	5	(6)	44.0
Ulster	5	(5)	67.8	1	(1)	24.6

Source: M. Gallagher, 'The Pact General Election of 1922', *IHS*, vol. xxi, 1979.

The enthusiastic support given by the bishops and the generality of priests to the Treaty settlement and the emerging Free State was predictable. A major consideration in episcopal minds was the surprising generosity of the settlement. As Logue expressed it to Hagan, 'I don't think there is a man alive who ever expected [that] such favourable terms could be squeezed out of the British government in our time'.[54] MacRory was happy that Ireland, 'for all practical purposes will be mistress of her own destiny', that the country would have the power 'to make and administer its own laws, power over taxation, power over education to shape the national mind in an Irish mould'.[55] McKenna rejoiced that Britain had abandoned all claim to govern Ireland, now 'acknowledged mistress of her own destiny with practically untrammelled power to shape it according to her own ideals. Her Parliament with her own executive subject to it will be freely elected by the people and will be subject to their will alone'.[56] Both Byrne and Harty were equally conscious of the value of having Irish administration and legislation in the hands of Irishmen; as Byrne put it, 'in place of the unsympathetic, wasteful and unintelligent rule of men alien to us in blood and traditions, we see in process of being evolved an Irish Government which will have knowledge of our people's needs and may be expected to take a real interest in solving the many problems that concern our people's well-being'.[57] O'Sullivan argued that under the terms of the Treaty Ireland had gained 'a measure of freedom that, in all the essentials of liberty, falls little short of complete

[54] Logue to Hagan, 10.12.21, Hagan Papers.
[55] *Sligo Champion*, 25.3.22.
[56] Pastoral Letter, 24.2.22. CLRDA.
[57] *ICD*, 1923, pp. 551–2.

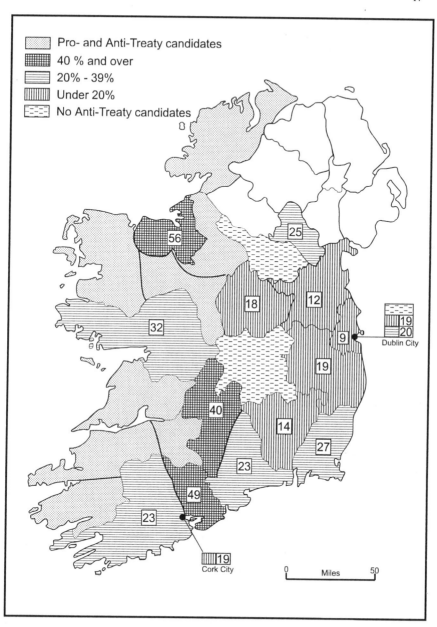

The Anti-Treaty Vote, 1922

The map shows the percentage of first-preference votes cast for Republican candidates in the 1922 General Election.
Adapted from: E. Rumpf and A.C. Hepburn, *Nationalism and Socialism in Twentieth Century Ireland* (Liverpool, 1977).

independence'.[58] Doctrinaire Republicans regarded as absurd such reiterated episcopal claims that the Treaty had conferred a substantial measure of freedom on Ireland. In their view, the fundamental aim of the War of Independence, the removal of British control over Ireland, had been utterly frustrated by the Treaty. This control, instead of being exercised directly, was instead now enforced by the Free State administration, the new agent of British policy.

While some bishops were critical of what Harty called the 'manifest limitations of the Treaty'[59], many were concerned that the merits of the settlement had been, as McKenna charitably put it, 'somewhat obscured by the controversy or rather the friendly difference of opinion which has arisen as to whether a greater might not and should not have been reached'.[60] A matter of much deeper concern to all the bishops was that the demonstrable benefits conferred by the Treaty were being placed in jeopardy by Republicans who were seeking its rejection, and thus risking a renewal of armed conflict with the British, on relatively trivial grounds. This was the theme of much episcopal discourse. MacRory was conscious of the immense risks involved in overthrowing the settlement. In March 1922, he warned that if the Irish people declared for a Republic in the coming election, there could be no plausible reason for saying that Britain would grant it, with the probable consequence that a much weaker Ireland would once more find itself involved in war. It was no longer a question, he pointed out, between having a Free State and complete independence; the choice was between the Free State 'and an Ireland torn by dissensions and immensely weakened in power of resistance'.[61] Gilmartin spoke for his fellow-bishops and the great majority of his clergy when he told Hagan that they did not consider the difference between the Treaty and External Association, the Republican alternative, 'of a sufficiently substantial character to warrant the risk of a renewal of the war'.[62] Fogarty, as usual, was much more forthright. Rejection of the Treaty would inevitably mean war, and such a war would be waged, not for any advance on the powers conferred on Ireland by the Treaty, but to gratify Republicans who wanted to write 'External Association over the door'.[63] To many episcopal minds, Republican

[58] Pastoral Letter, Lent, 1922. KYDA.

[59] *ICD*, 1923, p. 552.

[60] McKenna, Pastoral Letter, 24.2.22.

[61] *Irish Independent*, 17.3.22.

[62] Gilmartin to Hagan, 19.1.22. Hagan Papers.

[63] *Saturday Record*, Ennis, 31.12.21 By describing the position outlined by de Valera in Document No. 2 in these terms, Fogarty and others tended to trivialise it, and to suggest that de Valera and those who promoted External Association

opponents of the Treaty had divorced themselves from political realities to the extent that rational argument would be wasted on them. Logue believed that all 'the de Valera party' wanted to do was to 'talk and wrangle for days about their shadowy Republic and their obligations to it',[64] while Mulhern found that during his interviews with de Valera, the latter 'speculated too much and looked forward to what was impracticable'; to such 'practical minds' as Mulhern's own, 'the question of internal or External Association had little attraction'.[65] Logue warned of the 'terrible calamity' in store for Ireland if the Treaty were to be rejected 'on account of mere verbal quibbles'.[66]

That the Treaty marked the beginning, not the end, of a political process was a persuasive episcopal argument. Bishop O'Sullivan was conscious of 'the short distance to be travelled' before Ireland attained 'the goal of formal independence'. Only irresponsible political leaders would resort to war, or even risk it, 'in the attempt to pluck the fruit' of independence 'before the peaceful and inevitable evolution of events yields it to us'.[67] MacRory, addressing the argument that acceptance of the Treaty involved 'renouncing Ireland's birthright for ever', suggested that if 'in the evolution of things complete independence ever became possible, the present settlement would neither preclude nor impede it but, rather, serve as a great stepping-stone'.[68] To the bishops, the case for patient, intelligent use of the provisions of the Treaty to extend the boundaries of Irish independence, and the enjoyment of the substantial immediate benefits of the settlement, had a compulsive force when weighed in the balance with the probable consequences of its rejection. One such consequence present to the minds of many of the clergy was what MacRory called 'the millstone of foreign government still round our neck',[69] or in the words of an Offaly curate, 'the renewal of Black and Tan ruffianism in a more aggravated form'.[70] It would, MacRory argued, be foolish to imagine

were prepared to divide the Irish people, and even to lead them into war, over the insubstantial difference between it and what the Treaty offered. Anti-Treaty Republicans, however, were not the only people prepared to take an unflinching stand on symbols and their significance. The British Treaty negotiators and the British government considered the position accorded to the monarch in the Treaty of such profound symbolic importance that they could not contemplate any limitation of the kind suggested by Document No. 2. See J. McColgan, 'Lionel Curtis and constitutional procedures', *IHS*, March 1977, p. 333.

[64] Logue to Byrne, 5.4.22.
[65] Mulhern to Hagan, 6.1.22.
[66] *Freeman's Journal*, 3.1.22.
[67] *Irish Independent*, 17.3.22.
[68] Ibid.
[69] *Irish Independent*, 27.12.21.
[70] James Lynam, CC Tullamore, *Westmeath Independent*, 22.4.22.

that Ireland would be no worse off following the rejection of the Treaty than it was before the Truce. He foresaw loss of sympathy abroad, a divided army, a divided people, 'with a swelling tide of emigration of young men all over the country'.[71]

II

Following the approval of the Treaty by the Dáil on 7 January 1922, the new administration needed all the support it could get from the Church in the face of multiple threats to its survival. The permanence of the Treaty settlement, and the stability of the new state, depended on the success of the Treaty Party in the coming General Election. The Bishops devoted considerable attention in their Lenten Pastorals of 1922 to the problems facing the infant government and the need to support it. Archbishop Gilmartin of Tuam directed that prayers be offered 'that God may guide their native Government in the discharge of their onerous duties'.[72] Archbishop Byrne of Dublin affirmed the new Government's right to public support, since it would have 'knowledge of our people's needs and may be expected to take a real interest in solving the many problems that concern our people's well-being'.[73] Archbishop Harty of Cashel dealt with the practical politics of the post-Treaty situation in the most partisan and forthright of all the Lenten Pastorals. The people would have an opportunity of approving or rejecting the Treaty at the polls, but as Harty saw it, there could really be only one morally justifiable outcome to the elections: the return of the Pro-Treaty Party. If this Party were to be rejected at the polls, there would be a real prospect of a renewal of war with little hope of success. The aim of the anti-Treaty party, an Irish Republic, even one externally associated with the British Commonwealth, Harty regarded as unrealistic. In such circumstances, 'it would be criminal folly to reject the Treaty'. Moreover, he pointed out, 'the people will have to judge whether the difference between external association and internal association with the British Empire is so substantial as to justify the risk of renewed terrorism'.[74]

Harty's Pastoral might well have served as a Treaty Party election manifesto. When electoral activity began in the Spring of 1922, Bishops and significant numbers of their clergy involved themselves as platform speakers, organisers and publicists on behalf of the Treaty

[71] *Irish Independent*, 17.3.22; 27.12.21.
[72] *ICD* 1923, p. 552
[73] Ibid. p. 551.
[74] *Freeman's Journal*, 3.1.22

Party. At many pro-Treaty meetings, messages of support from bishops and priests were read from the platforms. The organisers of a rally in Tullamore in April 1922 canvassed the opinions of local clergy, some of whom were anxious to record their warm approval of the new order. Thomas Norris, Parish Priest of Rhode was 'heart and soul in favour of the Treaty', and intended to support it 'in every way'. Michael Kennedy PP Shannonbridge, who was an equally firm advocate of the settlement, and a strong critic of the tactics of some of its Republican opponents, drew attention to the 'hooliganism and barbarism which have characterised recent meetings'. The rights of free speech, he declared, along with 'majority rule and the due subordination of the military to the civil power' must be upheld 'at all costs'. James Lynam of Tullamore emphasised 'the visible benefits' of accepting the Treaty.[75] Archbishop Gilmartin of Tuam sent a message of support and encouragement to a pro-Treaty meeting in the town on 19 March.[76] At the same meeting, a senior clergyman, Charles Cunningham, presided, while the Dean of the Archdiocese, the President of the Diocesan Seminary and two other priests were on the platform.[77] When the election campaign in support of Free State candidates was launched in Carrick-on-Shannon on St Patrick's Day, eleven priests were on the platform, and Malachy Brennan [Mac Bránáin] CC Mantua, Elphin, explained why North Roscommon was in favour of the Treaty.[78] 'Whom could they trust more than Arthur Griffith?', Canon Thomas Langan asked when he presided at a pro-Treaty meeting in Moate. It was through Griffith's 'activity, genius and ability, and in the face of many difficulties that it had been possible to bring the national movement to its present great success'. Langan hoped that 'the people of Westmeath would support the men who brought back freedom to their shores'.[79] At a meeting in Loughrea, John Heagney, PP Abbey explained his presence on the platform by declaring that 'as there were moral questions involved' in the election contest, 'priests would be wanting in their duty if they stayed away from such meetings'. He saw the central moral issue of the election as the choice people would have to make between the unrealistic dreams of the Republicans and the 'large measure of liberty' to be enjoyed under the 'practical' rulers of the new state.[80] At a pro-Treaty rally in Tralee addressed by Michael Collins at the end of April, there were fifteen priests on the

[75] *Westmeath Independent*, 22.4.22.
[76] *ICD*, 1923, p. 558
[77] *Freeman's Journal*, 21.3.22.
[78] *Roscommon Herald*, 25.3.22.
[79] *Freeman's Journal* 21.3.22.
[80] Ibid.

platform.[81] Many Kerry priests were lively and imaginative speakers. Patrick Brennan, Parish Priest of Castlemaine, 'did not believe in letting people starve while they were waiting for de Valera's nebulous Republic'. William Ferris, CC Rathmore, referred to de Valera and Stack as Don Quixote and Sancho Panza and called Cathal Brugha Alexander the Great, 'sighing for fresh barracks to conquer'. Jeremiah Casey, CC Killorglin, said that their Republican opponents 'went into spasms over the oath of fidelity, but the Oath in Document No. 2 would bring people more under the power of the English than the Oath in the Treaty.'[82]

Some of the clergy appearing in support of the Treaty party had to risk serious personal danger in doing so. In Charleville, Co. Cork a pro-Treaty meeting at which a local curate, John Burke, presided, was dispersed by rifle fire. Notices were displayed in the town signed by the local IRA to the effect that anyone found removing obstructions before 6 o'clock would be severely dealt with. This did not deter Burke from addressing a meeting; he was accompanied on the platform by T.C. Mannix, brother of the anti-Treaty Archbishop of Melbourne, whose mother was also present. Burke had read about the efforts of IRA gunmen in Cork 'trying to stampede a crowd of tens of thousands of people'. He believed that the purpose of such activity was 'to suppress public opinion and personal liberty, and he as an Irishman had a right to personal liberty and he was there to challenge that right even at the point of a revolver'.[83] A Kerry priest, Jeremiah O'Connor PP Tarbert, described as being 'prominently identified with the Free State', had shots fired over his head.[84] At a meeting in support of the Treaty in Bandon, violence was directed against Jeremiah Cohalan the Parish Priest of the town who was presiding; he was interrupted 'by the rowdy conduct of an organised mob'. Later at the height of the Civil War, Alexander O'Sullivan, curate of Milltown, Co. Kerry, a former British Army chaplain and strong supporter of the Government, was fired on by Republicans on his way to Castlemaine. He vaulted the wall of Sir John Godfrey's demesne, from where the shots had come, and pursued his assailants.[85]

Priests were also active in helping to organise the pro-Treaty election campaign. Thomas Macken, PP Claremorris, and Michael O'Donnell, CC Castlerea were appointed to the Executive of the organisation for

---

[81] *Kerry People*, 29.4.22.
[82] Ibid.
[83] *Freeman's Journal*, 21.3.22.
[84] *Kerry People*, 6.5.22.
[85] *Freeman's Journal*, 18.3.22. For the O'Sullivan episode, see *Freeman's Journal*, 8.9.22.

South Mayo and North Roscommon.[86] In Kerry, Eugene O'Connor CC Kenmare was made president of the Free State Election Committee and David Breen CC Kilgarvin was also appointed.[87] Charles Culligan, CC Kilkee, President of the West Clare Executive of Sinn Féin, presided at a conference in Ennis to select pro-Treaty election candidates. A letter from James Clancy, PP Killballyowen was read in which he undertook to do all he could to secure the return of the Free State candidates 'in spite of the atrocious threats of sanguinary war to whom [sic] one of the present representatives of Co. Clare has treated us as his contribution to the feast of the national Apostle'.[88] Bishop Fogarty enlivened a pro-Treaty demonstration in Ennis on 30 April with another broadside at de Valera. 'The people of Clare', he promised, 'have no notion of going another round for the difference between the Treaty and Document No. 2 merely to secure the applause of the gallery'.[89] Two Limerick priests, Jeremiah O'Connor of St Mary's, a member of the Treaty Election Committee, and Patrick Thornhill, St Michael's, solicited donations to the Treaty Fund Appeal.[90] Some of the priests approached by the pro-Treaty Party refused to allow themselves to be used for political purposes. A number of priests in the neighbourhood of Tullamore gave their blessing to a pro-Treaty rally in the town.[91] Others were determined to preserve political neutrality, out of a desire not to cause offence. Thomas O'Keeffe CC Tullamore wrote that 'when Catholics are pitted against one another in bitter controversy, I am a firm believer, where we priests are concerned, in the policy of St Paul to be all things to all men in order to save all'. James Flynn, PP Rahan, seemed to have equally strong reservations about the intervention of his clerical colleagues in political affairs. He hoped 'that the people of Offaly will have the opportunity of free choice in the voting, for or against the Treaty, that they will not allow themselves to be bullied by anyone no matter what position he occupies and that they will be accorded a little of the freedom for which so many have fought and died'. A Tullamore priest, Eugene Daly, was determined 'not to take part in the present political contest that has so sadly divided our people'.[92]

[86] Ibid. 15.3.22.

[87] *Kerry People*, 29.4.22.

[88] The reference is to de Valera's 'rivers of blood' speech in Thurles on 17.3.22. See K. Sheedy, *The Clare Elections* (Dublin, 1993), p. 348.

[89] *Clare Champion*, 30.4.22.

[90] *Limerick Echo*, 16.5.22

[91] See p. 51, note 75.

[92] *Westmeath Independent*, 22.4.22.

By early March, there was growing evidence throughout the country of social disorganisation associated with a widespread rejection of the authority of the Provisional Government. Outrages on life and property became commonplace. In Limerick, an outbreak of serious fighting was prevented only by the strenuous efforts of army leaders on both sides of the fractured IRA.[93] De Valera's inflammatory rhetoric suggested the inevitability of Civil War. His notorious speech at Thurles on St Patrick's Day 1922 was widely publicised and promoted widespread belief he had abandoned the constitutional method of settling differences. In the presence of armed IRA units, he told the Thurles meeting that if the Volunteers of the future tried to complete the work the Volunteers of the previous four years had been attempting, they 'would have to wade through Irish blood, through the blood of the soldiers of the Irish government, and through, perhaps, the blood of some of the members of the Government in order to get Irish freedom'.[94] A development with even more disturbing implications for peace and order was the Army Convention of 26 March. This convention, summoned by anti-Treaty officers, had earlier been authorised and then prohibited by the Dáil cabinet, whose members feared a military dictatorship; the Provisional Government knew that a Republican majority would prevail at any IRA convention, no matter who summoned it. The outcome of the March convention was that a substantial section of the IRA removed itself from the control of whatever government might be elected in June.[95] After 26 March there were two armies in the state: the pro-Treaty IRA, under the authority of Dáil Éireann, soon to become the Free State Army, and the Republican IRA with its own executive. A few days before the IRA convention, Rory O'Connor had given a press interview in which he repudiated the authority of the Dáil, declared that the army would have the power to prevent an election being held, and did not discountenance the idea that what he had in mind was a military

---

[93] M. Hopkinson, *Green Against Green. The Irish Civil War* (Dublin, 1988), pp. 62–5.

[94] *Irish Independent*, 18.3.22. See Moynihan, *Speeches and Statements of Eamon de Valera, 1917–73*, 1980, pp. 97–105, for a relatively benign view of the speech. See also Desmond Ryan: 'He had the defence . . . that as a National leader he had the right to utter a warning and that further he was not necessarily responsible for what fools or knaves might read into his words, but he certainly gave fools and knaves most ample opportunities'. *Unique Dictator* (Dublin, 1936), p. 168.

[95] See Childers Diary, TCD for 28 March: 'IRA Convention – 217 present – Traynor, Lynch, Mellows, O'Connor, Moylan, Barry, O'Malley . . . Resolution: Declaration of a Dictatorship – ordering dissolution of all pretended Governments in Ireland by prohibition of parliamentary elections until such time as an election without threat of war from Britain can be held on adult suffrage.'

dictatorship: in other countries armies had overthrown governments.[96] On 13 April, members of the Republican Army Council, including Rory O'Connor and Liam Mellows, ignoring the views of Liam Lynch, set up their headquarters at the Four Courts. The Army Council also decided to raid banks throughout the country to maintain their forces; bank raids took place simultaneously in many areas. Later, other buildings in Dublin were taken over: the Ballast Office, the Masonic Hall and the Kildare Street Club among them.[97] On 16 April, de Valera hailed the occupation of the Four Courts, which had occurred without his knowledge or approval,[98] in an emotional proclamation addressed to the Youth of Ireland.[99] In several places, the IRA tried to prevent pro-Treaty meetings from being held. On 16 April, Griffith, escorted by Seán Mac Eoin and a contingent of the National Army, held a meeting in Sligo despite an 'Irregular' proclamation; a car in which Collins was travelling back from Naas was attacked in a Dublin Street.[100] On 14 April, when an Irish Labour Party delegation met with de Valera to intercede with him to use his influence to avert Civil War, he told them that the majority had no right to do wrong.[101]

During this troubled period, a number of bishops, while firmly committed to the Treaty settlement, did what they could to avert disaster, but clearly without much hope of success. Many bishops were in regular correspondence with John Hagan, Rector of the Irish College in Rome, a man deeply immersed in Irish political affairs, sympathetic to the anti-Treaty point of view and a close friend of Seán T. O'Kelly.[102] Hagan persuaded a number of the bishops to have discussions with O'Kelly, whom he appears to have regarded, at this time at least, as more moderate and clear-headed than de Valera.

[96] *Irish Independent*, 23.3.22. See Ó Néill agus Ó Fiannachta, *De Valera*, Vol. II, p. 15; M. Hopkinson, *Green Against Green*, p. 67.

[97] Hopkinson, *Green Against Green*, p. 72.

[98] 'How well I remember the day shortly after occupying the Four Courts when R. O'Connor told Erskine and me that he had acted without consulting you or even informing you of what was planned . . . He and his staff had decided to act independently of political leaders thenceforward and this although he held you in respect and trust'. M.A. Childers to de Valera, 28.11.40, Childers Papers TCD, 299.

[99] *The Times*, London, 17.4.22, quoted from de Valera's proclamation, which contained the following: 'Young men and women of Ireland, the goal is at last in sight. Steady all together; forward, Ireland is yours for the taking. Take it.'

[100] Leon Ó Broin (ed.), *In Great Haste, The Letters of Michael Collins and Kitty Kiernan* (Dublin, 1983), p. 145.

[101] D. O'Sullivan, *The Irish Free State and its Senate* (Dublin, 1940), p. 59.

[102] See *Seán T. Scéal a bheatha ó 1916 go 1923 á insint ag Seán T. Ó Ceallaigh in eagar ag Padraig Ó Fiannachta*, 1972, pp. 89-93.

Hagan and his Vice-Rector M.J. Curran were anxious to press, on any bishop who would listen, the claims of O'Kelly as an ideal representative of moderate republicanism, one who might be in a position to 'exercise soothing influences and thus prevent asperities from becoming more intense'. In early April, O'Kelly, who was leaving Paris where he had been representing 'The Irish Republican Government', was invited by Hagan to visit him in Rome where the two 'discussed the situation and outlook in all directions'. In a letter to Archbishop Byrne, marked 'Confidential', Hagan insisted that O'Kelly 'is not out for bloodshed nor is he either unreasonable or irreconcilable. On the contrary he is out for a constitutional policy which, if carried through should, I think, be of advantage to the country in general'. Hagan, unlike some of the bishops, had a clear understanding of difficulties faced by both de Valera and O'Kelly. The latter, he believed, while loyal to de Valera, 'is not one prepared to swear unthinkingly *in verba magistri*'. Hagan suggested that should de Valera 'exceed the bounds of what is right and proper', O'Kelly would have no hesitation 'in turning him down'. On the other hand, Hagan believed that de Valera was 'for the present at least, the best man to control and keep in order various unruly elements which must be expected to accompany great revolutions'. Hagan showed an admirable grasp of what de Valera was attempting to do in the months leading to the civil war. He found much to commend O'Kelly's view 'that it will be easier to control these [unruly Republican] elements from within than to constrain them from without'. If Byrne would meet O'Kelly, Hagan had no doubt that the latter could outline the policy by which militaristic republicans would subject themselves to constitutional procedures. O'Kelly, he concluded, 'is no anarchist'.[103] Hagan's Vice-Rector, Curran, writing to Byrne about the same time, suggested that if the Archbishop was anxious to learn 'the inner history of the various elements of the anti-treaty opposition and their movements or indeed of the treaty people', he could find 'no better informant or go-between than Seán T.' Curran had been O'Kelly's friend since school days. He tellingly remarked that 'he is, as Your Grace knows, an excellent Catholic'. He was also 'level-headed and absolutely trustworthy', with 'hosts of friends outside his own camp'. Above all, O'Kelly's 'moderation in the expression of his advanced views, his moral courage and above all his rare tact eminently fit him for helping in the solution of political differences'.[104]

The correspondence between Hagan and a number of the Irish bishops during April and May 1922 throws light on episcopal attitudes

[103] Hagan to Byrne, 3.4.22, DAA.
[104] M.J. Curran to Byrne, 3.4.22, DAA.

and activities. Early in April, Hagan advised Bishop Fogarty to talk to O'Kelly about the deteriorating political and military situation. Fogarty promised to try and see O'Kelly at Easter, but had come to the conclusion that de Valera's public behaviour had made conciliation impossible: 'You have only to read today's *Independent* [105] to see that de Valera has now identified himself with the army junta and has given his benediction to their scheme of suppressing elections by force'. Fogarty also believed that the country was facing a military *coup d'état* with de Valera to be 'proclaimed dictator at the proper time'. Fogarty held out little hope for the peace efforts being made by Archbishop Byrne; de Valera, he believed, wanted 'no peace but his own', and having lost public sympathy and support was relying on intimidation 'as his last resource'.[106] About the same time Fogarty, writing to Bishop O'Doherty of Clonfert, believed that a meeting of the Bishops might help to 'effect peace between the warring factions', although he was by then convinced that 'the de Valera crowd are wrecking everything'.[107]

In April, Byrne and the Lord Mayor of Dublin, Laurence O'Neill, made a major effort to bring about peace between the contending factions. Byrne acted as chairman of a conference at the Mansion House representative of all the interests involved. The Conference, which began on 13 April, broke up on the 29th, without achieving Byrne's objective. Byrne told the delegates that he had no intention of interfering with political principles or dictating political beliefs to anyone on either side. He was not acting in the interests of any party or any faction. He shared 'the well-founded fear that the nation is heading straight for Civil War', and found it strange that 'we should use the first instalment of anything like freedom to engage in fratricidal strife'.[108] 'As you may have seen', Byrne ruefully told Hagan, 'I have made an effort to secure that the pro- and anti-Treatyites might at least keep their hands off each other. The effort, as I more or less anticipated, has resulted in failure'.[109] Other bishops who became involved in peace efforts at this time were MacRory of Down and Connor and Archbishop Gilmartin of Tuam. Kathleen O'Connell records in her diary for 7 April that 'Bishop MacRory called and spent about two hours in office with Chief'. A memorandum by Father Joseph Walsh, Archbishop Gilmartin's secretary, drawn up on April 21st, refers to a meeting which a Mr Martin, BE had arranged

[105] *Irish Independent*, 11.4.22.
[106] Fogarty to Hagan 11.4.22, Hagan Papers.
[107] Fogarty to O'Doherty 6.4.22, CLDA.
[108] Byrne's notes on the Mansion House Conference, DAA.
[109] Byrne to Hagan, 1.5.22, Hagan Papers.

between de Valera and the Archbishop for 22 April. The Archbishop 'would be very glad to see Mr de Valera and to have dinner with him and Mr Martin after the meeting finishes . . . If Mr de Valera wishes to bring any friends with him, his Grace the Archbishop will be pleased to see them also and to entertain them'. A post-script delicately affirms that 'this invitation is of course devoid of all political significance'.[110]

Hagan was also in correspondence with Bishop O'Donnell of Raphoe and Bishop Mulhern of Dromore, pressing the claims of Seán T. O'Kelly as the man most likely to facilitate a political solution to the problems confronting the nation. Hagan was still confident in early April 1922 that Republican leaders could be persuaded to take the political road, although O'Donnell pointed out to him that 'the violence in act and word seems to be all on one [the Republican] side'. O'Kelly had convinced Hagan that Republican leaders recognised the value of 'a vigorous opposition that did not rely on violence'. O'Donnell was sceptical: 'If what Mr O'Kelly has told you be his policy, the sooner there is evidence of it the better'. Meanwhile, all O'Donnell could see was evidence of Republican intransigence. He told Hagan that 'the line now pursued by many of these fellows could scarcely serve the cause of the Republic even if it did not seriously endanger Irish liberty'. O'Donnell professed himself willing to see O'Kelly 'or anyone through whom I can hope to be of the least service' but at the same time thought it strange if 'the men on both sides did not understand one another's position' and required inter-mediaries to enlighten them. O'Donnell made a telling point against Republican attacks, especially those of de Valera, on the Treaty delegation. 'If logic counted for anything', he suggested, 'any charge which the men who selected the Treaty delegates bring against them they bring against themselves for sending them'. O'Donnell, the former mainstay of the Irish Parliamentary Party, found the origins of the present conflict in the evolution of physical force nationalism during the immediate past. The real difficulty between the contending parties, he told Hagan, 'arises from the prestige of physical force as a remedy in recent years and from impatience over delay . . . on the part of many who keep before their eyes the public commitments to a republic and the bitter sacrifices endured to achieve it'.[111]

In April, Edward Mulhern, Bishop of Dromore, had a letter from Hagan suggesting that a meeting with Seán T. O'Kelly might well help to open the way to peace. It was Mulhern who, on 25 June 1921,

[110] Tuam Archdiocesan Archive. I am grateful to Fr Brendan Kilcoyne, Tuam for showing me this item.
[111] O'Donnell to Hagan, 10.4.22, Hagan Papers.

had handed de Valera a letter from Lloyd George suggesting a conference between the British Government and representatives from Southern and Northern Ireland to explore the possibility of a settlement of the Irish question.[112] By April 1922, Mulhern had become thoroughly disillusioned with de Valera, and regarded him and the militant republicans as obstacles to peace, harmony and progress in Ireland, North and South. Mulhern was one of the most politically conscious of all the bishops. Early in April he told Hagan that he had been informed before the Truce that de Valera was to be 'set aside in favour of your friend Seán T'. He could now see little hope of peace as long as de Valera held sway, as he believed he did, over the Republican ranks. 'The cry in everyone's mouth', he wrote, 'is why isn't there someone to bring the leaders together and the only reason one can give is that the task is hopeless'. He believed that the Treaty Party would welcome 'an advance of this kind'; he also knew that friends of de Valera had tried to get him to see that the Treaty gave Ireland 'if not all that one could desire, at the very least a broad basis of freedom and puts us in the way of working towards the ultimate object'. Mulhern pointed out that Fogarty had argued with de Valera along these lines, and that Archbishop Byrne 'more than once spoke to him but told me his efforts were useless'. He took a jaundiced view of de Valera's futile attempts to circumscribe the conflict by publicly assuming a responsibility he did not actually have. Mulhern exaggerated de Valera's part in the genesis of the civil war, not realising that the evolution of events had condemned him to playing an ineffectual role which was quite at odds with his fiery rhetoric. All he could discern was de Valera's weakness, moral as well as political: 'De Valera', he observed, 'publicly supported the Republican side, but exercised no leadership among them. Many of them despised what he stood for, and especially Document No. 2, with its implicit acquiescence in Partition'. He also remarked, perceptively enough, that most Republican extremists 'would have thought of de Valera's own loyalty to the republic as a rather dubious article, especially in the light of Document No. 2'.[113]

Early in April, Mulhern, in response to Hagan's suggestion, wrote to O'Kelly to say that he would be glad to receive him in Newry 'were it not that the arrival of a suspicious stranger' might lead to his being shot.[114] Instead, he met O'Kelly at his home in Dublin. He thought O'Kelly had a reasonable plan, 'that of a constitutional opposition

[112] The Earl of Longford and T.P. O'Neill, *Eamon De Valera* (Dublin, 1970), p. 128.
[113] Mulhern to Hagan, 7.4.22, DRDA.
[114] Mulhern to Hagan, 18.4.22, DRDA.

within the Irish Free State, if the new constitution meets with approval'. The problem with O'Kelly's 'somewhat relaxed views on the whole situation' according to Mulhern, was that 'so long as there is in his mind any idea of having the terms of the Treaty even slightly changed' the rest of his projects would be nullified. Mulhern argued that the Treaty was 'a substantial unchangeable fact and it must be dealt with as such for the benefit of the country'. Again, he showed his contempt for de Valera's failure to deal with 'the secessionists from the regular army' who were 'playing at militarism' and who refused to recognise his authority: 'If de Valera had the manliness to openly repudiate them instead of approving of them, we might have some confidence in the efforts of His Grace of Dublin and the Lord Mayor to secure peace'. At this stage, Mulhern believed that 'mutual understanding' of the points of view of the Free Staters and their opponents was 'a useless method of reaching peace'. He believed the Provisional Government should stand absolutely for the Treaty: the Republicans 'wish to destroy the Treaty and have no alternative except a return to war and resultant occupation by British forces'.[115]

In the months following the signing of the Treaty, the Provisional Government looked to the Church to reinforce its authority. In return, the bishops were involved in the preparation of the new Constitution and were consulted, for example, on 10 April about the Article providing for free elementary education as a right.[116] When the Government decided to form an Advisory Committee to consider the Northern Question, prominent northern Churchmen were invited to become members.[117] By the beginning of April, some politically active bishops, among them Cardinal Logue, Browne of Cloyne, O'Doherty of Clonfert and Fogarty of Killaloe had concluded that it was time for the bishops as a body to make a statement on the critical situation facing the country. Some of his colleagues had been sufficiently impressed by O'Doherty's Lenten pastoral, with its emphasis on the need for obedience to lawful authority, to write letters of encouragement to him and to seek to persuade him to join in formulating a general episcopal statement. Fogarty took the initiative on 6 April, writing a congratulatory letter to O'Doherty on his 'admirable pronouncement', which he considered 'perfect in phrase and teaching' and 'timely as well as excellent'. The real point of Fogarty's letter was to suggest to O'Doherty that 'the general body of bishops are called

---

[115] Ibid.
[116] See Ronan Fanning, *Independent Ireland* (Dublin, 1983), pp. 18ff. See also D.H. Akenson and J.F. Fallin, 'The Irish Civil War and the Drafting of the Free State Constitution'. *Éire-Ireland*, vol. v, no. 2, 4. 1970 and p. 141, note 18.
[117] Collins to Mulhern, 8.3.22, DRDA.

upon to speak in their corporate capacity on the new doctrines now formulated by the military junta. Instead of the Standing Committee meeting on the 25th April there should be a general meeting'. Fogarty asked O'Doherty to get Gilmartin, Archbishop of Tuam, to communicate with the Cardinal.[118] Fogarty's suggestion bore fruit. On 15 April Logue told O'Doherty that he had been forced, 'by appeals from all sides', to summon a general meeting of the bishops for 26 April. Logue thought this meeting should issue a 'strong pronouncement'. To this end he was asking O'Doherty and Fogarty 'both of you having already made admirable pronouncements, to form a committee under the presidency of the Archbishop of Dublin, to draw up a statement'.[119] Soon afterwards, Browne of Cloyne, Secretary to Episcopal meetings, wrote to O'Doherty urging him to help draft a 'very strong pronouncement, full and clear' on 'the deplorable – the awful – condition of the country at the present time'. Browne believed that 'the people are most anxiously awaiting the Bishops' pronouncement in the hope that it will bring order and peace'.[120]

At their meeting on 26 April the bishops saw themselves confronted by two issues, one political, the other moral. In their statement, they argued that 'the great question of the Treaty is a legitimate question for national discussion and debate', although they pointed out that 'like the great bulk of the nation we think that the best and wisest course for Ireland is to accept the Treaty, and make the most of the freedom it undoubtedly brings us, freedom for the first time in 700 years'. The bishops were more decisive on the moral questions arising from the claim by extreme Republicans that 'the Army, or a part of it, can, without any authority from the nation as a whole, declare itself independent of all civil authority in the country'. Such a claim to 'military despotism' would amount to 'an immoral usurpation and confiscation of the people's rights'. The bishops recognised that 'speculative views were being entertained', presumably by Republican theorists, 'as to the organ of supreme authority in this country at present', but in practice there could be only one legitimate national authority: the Dáil and the provisional Government acting in unison.[121]

[118] Fogarty to O'Doherty, 6.4.22, GDA.
[119] Logue to O'Doherty, 15.4.22, GDA.
[120] Browne to O'Doherty, 19.4.22, GDA.
[121] *ICD*, 1923, pp. 598-602. According to Childers, Canon Hackett of Killaney, Co. Monaghan, a Republican sympathiser, told him that 'a Vatican message was sent calling on Bishops not to express anti-Republican message'. This [Vatican message] arrived 'evening before Maynooth meeting – delivered to Archbishop of Dublin'. Childers Diary, TCD, 26.4.22.

In the April Pastoral, the Bishops appealed to the leaders on both sides, civilian and military, 'to meet again, to remember old fellowship in danger and suffering' and even if they failed to agree upon the main question, to announce to the world that 'the use of the revolver must cease' and that elections be 'allowed to be held, free from all violence'.[122] This emotional appeal found an echo, though not a demonstrable response, a few weeks later in the Collins–de Valera pact, an agreement signed by the two leaders on 19 May, unanimously approved by the Dáil and by the Sinn Féin Ard Fheis of 20 May. The essential feature of the Pact was that it provided for an election in which 66 pro-Treaty and 58 anti-Treaty Sinn Féin candidates would form an agreed panel, each voter being expected to give votes to candidates of the opposing party as well as to those representing his own.[123] The many Churchmen who, like Bishop Mulhern, regarded the Treaty as 'a substantial unchangeable fact', to be upheld intact at all costs by the Provisional Government, must have been startled when Collins, the head of that government, told the Sinn Féin Ard Fheis amid wild cheering that 'unity at home is more important than any Treaty with the foreigner, and if unity could be got at the expense of the Treaty, the Treaty would have to go'.[124] Against this, Mulhern might have found sad confirmation of his scepticism about Republican bona fides in another of Rory O'Connor's press conferences. O'Connor underlined the fragility of the Collins–de Valera Pact at the end of May when he told reporters that the popular will should not be expressed through parliamentary channels. He claimed that Republicans controlled three-quarters of the arms in Ireland and that it was the seizure of the Four Courts that had compelled Collins and de Valera to make peace moves.[125]

III

The Collins–de Valera Pact inhibited the great majority of bishops and priests from making political comments in advance of the June election. Some of the bishops, however, had grave objections to an election fought on the terms envisaged in the Pact. Bishop Foley of Kildare and

[122] *ICD*, 1923, p .601.
[123] See Hopkinson, *Green Against Green*, pp. 97 ff and D.H Akenson and J.F. Fallin, 'The Irish Civil War and the Drafting of the Free State Constitution', *Éire-Ireland*, vol. v, no. 4, pp. 35ff.
[124] Hopkinson, *Green Against Green*, p. 98. See also Childers Diary, 7816, p. 14, 23.5.22: 'Ard Fheis. Collins a remarkable speech – stressing value of unity greater than value of Treaty'.
[125] *Cork Examiner*, 29.5.22.

Leighlin was one of these; he told his Vicar-General that 'the Coalition Panel is a horrible fraud'. He could not imagine men like Séamus Lennon, a former Dáil Deputy, 'who robbed the Bank of Ireland in Bagenalstown at the head of an armed band of brigands put on the Panel for Counties Carlow and Kilkenny, and one of the great objects of the Coalition is to stop brigandage of this very character'. Foley hoped that the electors of Carlow–Kilkenny 'will not mind the panel men'.[126] A week later, Foley wondered about Fogarty's support for the Panel candidates in Clare, especially since 'he was very strongly opposed to de Valera and declared to me that he was a desperate fellow who would stop at nothing'. Foley could only surmise that Fogarty must have altered his opinion 'or have got some information from Collins which induced him to support the Panel candidates'.[127] After the Pact had been agreed in May, Foley was 'greatly afraid that the extraordinary concessions made by Collins to de Valera will land us ultimately in war with England. It cannot but immeasurably strengthen the Republicans. The Election will not reveal the true sentiments of the people'.[128]

The available evidence suggests that the bishops generally felt about the Pact as Foley did. In September 1922, Bishop Cohalan of Cork argued that the will of the country 'would have been declared much more emphatically' in the June Election 'had not the freedom of election been seriously restricted by the Pact which the country did not approve of or welcome'.[129] Both Foley and Cohalan correctly drew attention to the limitation on genuine electoral choice imposed by the Panel system. While it was true that a saving clause in the pact stipulated that 'Every and any interest is free to go and contest the election equally with the National-Sinn Féin Panel',[130] this freedom was restricted in several constituencies by the intimidation of prospective non-panel candidates and by the heavy moral pressure brought to bear on others.[131] Of the 28 constituencies, there was no contest in eight,

---

[126] Foley to M.J. Murphy, 2.6.22, KLDA. Lennon, brother of Father John Lennon CC Mountmellick, suffered a humiliating defeat in the 1922 Election, getting only 1113 first preferences, the quota being 6246. In 1924 he was tried in the Central Criminal Court for the bank robbery described by Bishop Foley. He refused to recognise the Court and claimed that he had acted under orders as a soldier of the Irish Republic when he raided the bank in May 1922. The jury disagreed in Lennon's case. *Roscommon Herald*, 5.7.24.

[127] Foley to M.J. Murphy, 9.6.22, KLDA.

[128] Foley to M.J. Murphy, 23.5.22, KLDA. On the other side, Foley acknowledged, 'there is the staving off of Civil War and perhaps the cessation of the horrible onslaughts in Ulster'.

[129] Cohalan's pastoral letter, 25.9.22. Quoted from *The Westmeath Independent*, 30.9.22.

[130] *Irish Independent*, 22.5.22.

[131] M. Gallagher, 'The Pact General Election of 1922', *IHS*, vol. xxi (1979), pp. 408–9.

representing 38 seats out of 128.[132] Two other members of the Hierarchy, Archbishop Byrne and Bishop Browne of Cloyne, clearly disapproved of the electoral arrangements promoted by the Pact. Archbishop Byrne was reliably reported to have voted for Independents and pro-Treaty candidates only.[133] Browne took a public stand against the Panel system. He told the press that he regarded it as one of his first duties to subscribe to a fund being raised to meet the election expenses of Michael Hennessy and John Dinneen, two Independent pro-Treaty candidates for East and North-East Cork,[134] a gesture described by J.J. O'Kelly as a 'flagrant violation of the Pact issued as a Dáil decree'.[135]

Many bishops and priests proclaimed their political allegiance by nominating pro- or anti-Treaty candidates for the 1922 election. In the Galway constituency, for example, the Bishop of Clonfert, Thomas O'Doherty, and four priests nominated the pro-Treaty Panel candidates; the Republican Panel candidates were nominated by twelve priests including Dr John Dignan, the future Bishop of Clonfert.[136] In no case did a Galway clergyman nominate candidates from both sides of the panel. When Michael Bolger, PP presided at a pro-Treaty panel meeting at Graigue, he declared that he viewed the Collins–de Valera Pact with suspicion, calling on Sinn Féin clubs 'not to submit to muzzling and enslavement of the race but to be Sinn Féin in truth, in fact as well as in name'. This was another way of telling his listeners to ignore the Republican members of the Carlow–Kilkenny panel, which was what the great majority of the electors did.[137] In some areas, priests made attempts to preserve the spirit of the Pact. On the last day of the election campaign, Matt Ryan, PP Knockavilla, pre-siding at Cathal Brugha's meetings in the Cashel area, strongly endorsed Brugha's appeal for unity.[138] In Wexford, where many priests endorsed candidates, a few proposed those from both sides of the Panel.[139]

[132] The uncontested constituencies were Clare, Donegal, Dublin University, Kerry–Limerick West, Leitrim–North Roscommon, Limerick City–Limerick East, Mayo North and West, Mayo South–Roscommon South. See B.M. Walker, *Parliamentary Election Results in Ireland, 1918–92* (Dublin, 1992).
[133] M.J. Curran to Hagan, 20.6.22, Hagan Papers.
[134] *Freeman's Journal*, 14.6.22. Both Hennessy and Dinneen were elected.
[135] Sceilg [J.J. O'Kelly], *A Trinity of Martyrs* (Dublin, 1941), p. 86.
[136] *Connaught Tribune*, 10.6.22.
[137] The two Republican panel candidates between them got 14.3 per cent of the first-preference votes, and neither was elected.
[138] Sceilg, *Trinity of Martyrs*, p. 85.
[139] *The Free Press Wexford*, 10.6.22. James Furlong, CC Skreen, proposed both James Ryan, an anti-Treaty candidate, and J.J. O'Byrne, a pro-Treaty one. O'Byrne was also proposed by a leading Republican, P.F. Keogh, PP Cloughbawn, who also nominated Séamus Doyle, an anti-Treaty candidate.

The involvement of the clergy in the 1922 Election campaign was largely confined to nominating candidates and giving financial support. Before nominations closed, Collins and de Valera issued a joint manifesto suggesting that non-Panel candidates, representing Labour, Farmers and Independents, should have refrained from exercising their right to contest the election, since electoral contests 'could not fail at present to engender bitterness and promote discord and turmoil'.[140] On election day, 40 per cent of the voters expressed their dissent from that view, by giving their first preferences to non-Panel candidates.[141] M.J. Curran told Monsignor Hagan that Father Joe McArdle of the Pro-Cathedral had boasted to him that he had voted for Bernardo, a unionist candidate in Mid-Dublin, to keep Seán T. O'Kelly out. Curran also told Hagan that 'Numbers of the younger Maynooth graduates saved the situation for the anti-Treaty party at this election'.[142] While one of the aims of the Pact had been to postpone a decision on the Treaty, most of the priests who publicly identified themselves with individual candidates seem to have regarded the election as a vote for or against the Treaty, an affirmation of the Republican position or a rejection of it. In Galway, the twelve priests who nominated Republican Panel candidates all subsequently supported anti-Treaty Sinn Féin and Fianna Fáil; the five supporters of the pro-Treaty Panel gave their allegiance to Cumann na nGaedheal.[143]

Table 3: Recorded numbers of clerical nominators of candidates in the Pact Election, 1922

Pro-Treaty Sinn Féin candidates	Independents and Farmers supporting the Treaty	Anti-Treaty Sinn Féin candidates
20	7	25

[140] *Irish Independent*, 6.6.22.

[141] See Gallagher, 'The Pact General Election', for a detailed analysis of the voting patterns.

[142] Curran to Hagan, 20.6.22.

[143] Those who nominated pro-Treaty candidates in the Galway constituency were: Bishop O'Doherty of Clonfert; Francis Barry, ODC Loughrea; James Craddock, PP Oughterard; M. Farragher, PP Athenry; M. Healy, Athenry. Republican Panel candidates were nominated by: T. O'Kelly, University College Galway; R.F. O'Reilly, CC Galway; H.J. Feeney, Galway; J. O'Dea, Bishop's Secretary, Galway; S. Considine, Oughterard; S.T. O'Kelly, PP Kilbecanty; T. Cawley, PP; P. O'Dea, Gort; J. Considine, Gort; J. Dignan, DD; P. Moran PP Claregalway; T. Dempsey, Ballinasloe. See *Connaught Tribune*, 10.6.22. For a survey of recorded clerical nominators of 1922 candidates, see accompanying table.

While the 1922 Election Campaign was in progress, the Provisional Government was modifying the Draft Constitution, which in its original form went a long way towards satisfying Republican aspirations, in compliance with British demands that it be amended 'in any particular in which it was shown to infringe the Treaty'.[144] The form of the Constitution to which the Irish government representatives agreed was, as Churchill noted, 'such as to preclude Mr de Valera and his followers from sharing in the Government'.[145] Prior to the election, the Irish electorate was largely uninformed about these vital matters. Almost on the eve of the poll, Collins repudiated his own Pact with de Valera; the revised Constitution was published in the Dublin newspapers on 16 June, which was polling day.[146] Following Collins's disavowal of the pact and the publication of the British-inspired Constitution, the anti-Treaty IRA disowned its own political leadership and held a convention on 18 June. The Four Courts garrison had been pressing for an immediate attack against the British, believing that such a move would unite the divided Irish forces in the event of a British counter-attack and lead to national reconciliation and rejection of the Treaty. The majority at the Convention rejected this idea; the minority walked out of the meeting, returned to the Four Courts and prepared for military action against both the Provisional Government and the British.[147] The assassination of Sir Henry Wilson in London on that 22 June led to strong British demands that the Provisional Government act decisively against the Republican extremists believed to be responsible.[148] On 28 June, when the Four Courts garrison refused to comply with a government order to surrender, the

---

[144] *The Times* (London), 9.6.22.

[145] Winston S. Churchill, *The World Crisis, 1918–1928: The Aftermath* (New York, 1929, pp. 358–9. Quoted in Akenson and Fallin, 'Irish civil war', *Éire-Ireland*, vol. v, no. 4, p. 66.

[146] Collins made use of a meeting in Cork on 14 June to repudiate the Pact and to redefine the question before the electors as one of choice between supporting the Treaty and rejecting it. See Akenson and Fallin, 'Irish civil war', vol. v, no. 4, pp. 66–7. Macardle, *Irish Republic*, p. 721, quotes Collins' speech repudiating the Pact, but gives no source.

[147] See Akenson and Fallin, 'Irish civil war', vol. v, no. 4, p. 68; Hopkinson, *Green Against Green*, pp. 115ff.

[148] Hopkinson, *Green Against Green*, p. 112 points out that 'The testimony of many of those who were involved in the events surrounding the affair suggests strongly that Collins was directly implicated' in the assassination of Wilson. See, however, Peter Hart, 'Michael Collins and the assassination of Sir Henry Wilson', *IHS* XXVIII, November, 1992, pp. 150–70. Having reviewed the literature to date, Hart concludes that 'There is no solid evidence to support a conspiracy theory linking Michael Collins or anyone else to the murder. In the absence of such evidence, we must accept the assertions of the murderers that they acted alone, in the (grossly mistaken) belief that Wilson was responsible for Catholic deaths in Belfast'.

building was shelled with guns borrowed from the British, and the Civil War began.

While the members of the Four Courts garrison were preparing for military action, the Bishops were meeting in Maynooth to consider the worsening political situation, North and South. They deplored the humiliation of Cardinal Logue by the Ulster Specials, suggested that 'the deadly effect of Partition has been to ruin Ireland', drew attention to the campaign of terror against Catholics in the North, and condemned the 'comparatively few' instances of 'barbarous treatment of our Protestant countrymen' in the South. With the Four Courts Republicans clearly in mind, they described as 'miscreants and murderers' all those 'belonging to any military body acting independently of civil authority'. They stopped just short of naming the individuals they deemed most responsible for the present trouble when they wondered who could measure 'the responsibility of any man, who, in his folly, would take his own blind course and engulf the future of Ireland in chaos, in defiance of the known sense and measured judgment of his people'. The Bishops' solution to the problems of Ireland, North and South, was an administration that would 'put down crime and ensure the reign of law and justice'.[149]

IV

The outbreak of full-scale Civil War prompted priests throughout the country to render moral and material help to the beleaguered government. Even before this, however, many of the clergy had been indicating their approval of the new administration and its agencies in a variety of ways. In February 1922, a young man, alleged to have disobeyed an order given to him by an officer of the republican IRA, was chained to the railings of the Catholic church in Westport, but liberated by a priest.[150] When, in March 1922, the Athlone Military Barracks were handed over to a pro-Treaty force under Seán Mac Eoin, the local Administrator, John Crowe, presided at a function to honour the occasion, and proposed the health of the Irish Army 'with which he associated the name of Commandant-General Seán Mac Eoin'.[151]

[149] *ICD*, 1923, pp. 604–7. In their statement of 20 June, the bishops complained that Logue had three times been held up and rudely searched by the Ulster Specials. On one of these occasions, they alleged, 'His Eminence was covered with revolver and rifle at close range, while his correpondence was examined and the box containing the sacred oils opened'.
[150] *Freeman's Journal*, 2.2.22.
[151] *Roscommon Herald*, 4.3.22. John Crowe, Adm. Athlone (1921–55) was a celebrated fund-raiser for ecclesiastical purposes. In 1923, he wrote to the

Also in March, priests were prominent in organising a temporary police force for Drogheda and outlying districts, since it was not possible for the Provisional Government to establish a full-time police force immediately. Patrick Segrave PP and John Nulty, PP were associated in this project with property owners and businessmen.[152] In Kerry, Jeremiah O'Connor, PP Tarbert, called at the local barrack and Coast Guard Station, which were being held by the Republican IRA, and demanded the surrender of both buildings 'in the name of the Irish Free State'. The men in charge were reluctant to show any opposition to the priest, and walked quietly out, permitting their arms to be taken by him. Eamon Dee, Commandant of the Republican forces in the area, complained to the Bishop of Kerry that the action of Father O'Connor had resulted in a serious breach of the peace in Tarbert; it was all the more grave coming as it did 'when the tension on both sides was very high, and every effort was being made to unite the Army'.[153] In Sligo, Canon P.A. Butler told members of the local Temperance Insurance Society that they could look forward to a better state of things when the new government 'which has the unanimous will of the majority of the Irish people has swept out of its way the artificial barriers that are being raised to prevent its functioning'. The enemies of the country, he warned, were men ambitious to become 'leaders and dictators' ready to 'spill the blood of their brothers in the pursuit of a phantom republic'.[154]

In many parts of the country, priests led their parishioners in repairing damage done to public utilities by anti-Treaty forces. In North Offaly, priests and people cooperated in removing trees and road obstructions.[155] T. Meehan, CC Borrisokane led 'upwards of 100 young men' who cleared all the roads of felled trees in the district.[156]

---

[151] *cont.* Minister for Home Affairs for permission to organise a Sweepstake to raise funds for the erection of a church in Athlone. The Executive Council decided not to make an exception in his case 'to a decision already made not to permit the holding of Sweepstakes in Saorstát Éireann'. NAI F 2/2, 8.5.23. Despite this refusal, he organised a Sweepstake on the Derby of 1924, with a prize-fund of £12,500, for which tickets were sold throughout the world. Among the patrons of this enterprise were the Earl of Granard, Baron de Freyne, Sir Thomas Stafford and General Seán Mac Eoin. When the case came to court, Canon Crowe's counsel claimed that among the purchasers of tickets were the Governor-General and John A. Costello, the state's prosecuting counsel in the case. Crowe was ordered by the judge to refrain from taking part in a lottery for two years. See *Westmeath Independent*, 18.6.93.

[152] *Freeman's Journal*, 13.3.22.

[153] Eamon Dee to Bishop Charles O'Sullivan, 9.5.22, KYDA.

[154] *Roscommon Herald*, 6.5.22.

[155] *Freeman's Journal*, 7.7.22.

[156] Ibid. 12.7.22.

In Sligo in mid-July, the Courthouse was occupied by Provisional Government troops. The leader of the Republican forces in the town threatened to fire on the building unless Republican prisoners were released from the local jail. Two priests failed to bring about a settlement, and the Provisional commander was determined to hold the courthouse to the last man. Bishop Coyne of Elphin tried to persuade the Republicans to leave the town, but they refused, demanding the surrender of the courthouse. The Bishop then joined the Provisional garrison in the courthouse, determined to remain, whatever happened, correctly assuming, however, that the Republicans would not fire on the building while he was there. He stayed in the Courthouse overnight despite being unwell and the besiegers left the town before morning.[157] This kind of moral support was afforded to the forces of the government by numerous other bishops and priests. When, on 21 July a detachment of National troops took possession of the Tuam workhouse, the local Administrator, Charles Cunningham, presided at a function organised in their honour. He told them 'how honoured the people were by their presence' and that 'ninety-nine per cent of the people' were delighted that 'by the presence of the National troops, there would be a more settled order of things'.[158] When John Dillon's house in Ballaghadereen was occupied by Republican forces, Bishop Morrisroe of Achonry denounced 'the activities of the Irregulars' declaring that 'the wilful destruction of bridges etc. would be treated as a reserved sin in the diocese'.[159]

In early August 1922, W.T. Cosgrave, Acting Chairman of the Provisional Government, addressed a letter to each Irish Parish Priest suggesting what the people should do to help the government and the Army in the present crisis. 'The Government', he wrote, 'urges that all clergy and public men throughout the country should impress upon their neighbours the importance of taking immediate steps to clear the roads wherever they have been obstructed, to repair bridges where possible, and to give any assistance in their power to workmen engaged in the repair of railways'.[160] The response to this request

[157] Ibid. 19.7.22. At Kilcormac in Offaly, 'the National troops got a splendid welcome from Edward O'Reilly, PP and the people, without exception'. *Freeman's Journal* 7.7.22.
[158] Ibid. 22.7.22. On 22 July, after the fall of Limerick to the National forces, Bishop Hallinan 'paid an official visit to the headquarters of the National Command in Cruise's Hotel, and offered congratulations to Commandant-General Michael Brennan on the success of the National Army in Limerick'. *ICD*, 1923, p. 578.
[159] *Roscommon Herald*, 22.7.22.
[160] *Westmeath Independent*, 5.8.22.

appears to have been swift and enthusiastic. In several parts of Offaly
and Tipperary, 'the people, led by their priests, have been actively
engaged in the task of removing the obstructions to roads and did so
in spite of the threats of the Irregulars'.[161] There were reports from
Mayo of a Volunteer Civilian Guard which the young men of town
and country were joining in large numbers. The Treaty Election
Committees had taken control of this force and in many places were
being assisted by the clergy.[162]

The vast majority of Irish clergymen who took a public stand on the
matter clearly regarded the military activities of the Republicans
during the Civil War as crimes against the State and against individuals. The pulpit was constantly used to enforce this point of view.
The sacredness of the principle of majority rule, the unquestionable
status of the Provisional Government as the sole legitimate ruling
authority in the South and the wickedness of armed rebellion against
it, were the central themes of Sunday sermons throughout the period.
For Archdeacon John Fallon of Castlebar, the political choice was
simple: the Provisional Government or a 'Revolver Government'
backed by bullies 'determined to thrust their own opinions down the
throats of the people'.[163] Some pulpit rhetoric was much more fiery
than this. Even before the death of Collins had ushered in a more
barbaric phase in the Civil War, some preachers were denying the
right of those under the Republican IRA Executive to receive the
Sacraments. Eamon Dee, Commandant of the Kerry No. 1 Brigade,
reported his Parish Priest to the Bishop for using a sermon on 30
April as a vehicle for personal abuse. Dee claimed that the priest had
described him as a hooligan who had cravenly submitted to the Black
and Tans to save his life while his comrades were being murdered; he
also accused him of expressing delight as some young Republicans
walked out during Mass, saying 'he hoped all such men would leave
the House of God'. Through the Bishop, Dee wanted 'a public withdrawal of those base statements'.[164] In many churches, Republicans in
the congregations memorised and recorded those sermons in which
their motives and conduct were impugned. In one such sermon delivered
soon after the death of Collins, Patrick Fitzgerald PP Killarney,
described the IRA men who had recently taken possession of the town
as 'scoundrels' and 'bandits'. The people of Killarney, he believed,
should have found some means of hounding the Republicans out of

---

[161] Ibid.
[162] Ibid.
[163] *Roscommon Journal*, 5.8.22.
[164] Eamon Dee to Bishop O'Sullivan, 9.5.22, KYDA.

the town, 'instead of, as a foreign paper described them, holding down their heads like sheep while the highwaymen did the work of destruction'. He contrasted Collins 'their grand leader of Irish blood' with de Valera and Childers, men of 'alien blood, leading them along the path of murder and above all leading them away from God'.[165] This kind of comment sounds relatively urbane when compared with some of what came later. In Cork Cathedral, Michael O'Sullivan Adm. was reported as describing Republicans as 'human vermin to be crushed out of existence by all decent people', while Canon Tracy of Kilmurry, Cork, declared that 'Republicans would burn in the hottest part of hell'. Maurice Costello CC Listowel described Cumann na mBan women as immoral. A priest at Cuff's Grange, Kilkenny, was reported to Mary MacSwiney as having said 'vile things about Cumann na mBan from the altar'.[166] In Kerry, clerical militancy sometimes went beyond such colourful depictions of the Republican enemy. Towards the end of 1922, John McDonnell, Parish Priest of Dingle, informed the Bishop that the officer commanding the National troops had begged him to permit the placing of a machine gun on the tower of his church and that he had given permission for this to be done. Canon McDonnell was told that 'this had been done in Killorglin and has prevented raids and so saved lives'. It seems to have had the same result in Dingle as 'we had no raid since the troops arrived. There is a machine gun in the tower of the Protestant church also'.[167] If we are to accept the veracity of some of the material in the Mary MacSwiney papers, not all the violence during this troubled period was perpetrated by Republicans. Here we find reference to a Father O'Connell who, in 'the district round Kinsale openly carried arms. Held up and searched passers-by at the point of revolver. Had officer's rank in the English Free State Army'.[168] A letter from the secretary of

---

[165] Father Fitzgerald's sermon was delivered on 27.8.22. MacSwiney Papers, UCDA, P48a/204 (1).
[166] Éire, 23.6.23; M. MacSwiney to Miss Gaffney 28.3.23. Desmond FitzGerald Papers, P80/797, UCDA.
[167] Canon McDonnell, PP Dingle to Bishop O'Sullivan, 28.12.22, KYDA.
[168] MacSwiney Papers P48a/213, UCDA. The priest here identified may have been Patrick O'Connell. C.C. Clonakilty, or Patrick O'Connell, PP Enniskean. MacSwiney provides no date, but the following item in Éire, 31.3.23, refers to the same priest: 'At present, the Free State Military Commandant of Kinsale District is a Catholic Priest, Rev. Fr O'Connell. By his orders, peaceful homes are broken into and raided, little children and women terrorised. Under his command, Paddy Duggan (Capt.) operates [as a] well-known torturer of prisoners. All known to ecclesiastical authorities. [Duggan is] now known as Topcliffe Duggan after the villain who tortured Catholics during the reign of Queen Elizabeth . . . O'Connell says Mass daily in Bishop Cohalan's diocese.'

the Skibbereen Sinn Féin club gives details of the violent intervention of two priests when local Republicans held a function in aid of the Prisoners' Dependants' fund. Two priests of the parish, Edward Lambe and John Collins, entered the Parish Hall and ordered those attending the function to leave. When one of them refused to leave, 'the two priests beat him, giving him a black eye'. After this the priests, having scattered the food to be consumed by those attending the function all over the wet road, threw tea and paraffin oil on it.[169]

By October 1922, the bishops had come to the conclusion that the moral, as well as the political, authority of the government should be affirmed by them in the most decisive way possible. Government ministers were acutely conscious of the need to impose political and social order if democratic institutions were to survive in the Free State. The Executive Council, aware that a meeting of the bishops was imminent, decided on 4 October to invoke the support of the Hierarchy. Ministers considered it 'desirable that a pronouncement should be made by the Bishops at their forthcoming meeting regarding the low moral standard prevailing throughout the country. A draft letter has been submitted to the Government for approval.'[170] On the day before the Executive Council meeting, a Government Proclamation offered an amnesty to 'Every person who is engaged in . . . insurrection and rebellion against the State' and who 'on or before the 15th day of October 1922 voluntarily delivers into the possession of the national forces all firearms, arms, weapons, bombs, ammunition and explosives, and all public and private property now unlawfully in his possession'.[171] Those who failed to avail of this amnesty, who continued to engage in armed activity against the National forces and who abetted such activity or were found in possession of war materials, faced trial before Military Courts which had the power to impose the death penalty.[172]

The Church–State alliance in October 1922 was inspired by the well-grounded fears of Government Ministers and churchmen that without strong, determined action on the part of the Government enjoying the moral sanction of the Church at the highest level, anarchy would prevail. Until 25 October, when de Valera proclaimed his Republican 'Emergency Government', the Republican IRA, whose self-imposed mission was the defence of the Republic against those who had betrayed it, was independent of any semblance of civil

---

[169] Ibid, P48a/196 (25). The report on Lambe and Collins is dated 30.12.23.
[170] NAI S1792, 4.10.22.
[171] *Irish Independent*, 4.10.22.
[172] The proclamation announcing the establishment of the Military Courts was published in the provincial and national press. See, for example, *Roscommon Herald*, 14.10.22.

control. It was a heavily armed force; many of its units and individual members engaged in 'looting, house-burnings, land-grabbing, murder and, occasionally, rape'. The country was unpoliced, and 'uncontrollable gangs of young men roamed at will and burned out unionists, shopkeepers, and those they regarded as either political anathema or agrarian enemies. Post offices and banks were raided for enormous sums'.[173] As Tom Garvin points out, 'A Hobbesian state of nature seemed in prospect, not only in the eyes of the rich and privileged, but also in the eyes of the poor and vulnerable'.[174] In the course of a raid on a licensed premises in Dublin in early October, P.J. Cosgrave, uncle of President Cosgrave, was shot dead by a gunman.[175] Episcopal thinking on the situation was soon afterwards expressed by Bishop Hallinan of Limerick, when he told a huge Arch-Confraternity demonstration in the city that continued IRA militancy would be 'a usurpation of the people's right and subversive of all civil liberty'. The Bishops, he argued, felt compelled to denounce 'the disastrous consequences' of armed Republican activity, divorced as this was from the control of 'the civil authority in the country'. He dwelt on 'the assassinations, the campaign of plunder and incendiarism, the general demoralisation, especially of the young, and the campaign by a section against the bishops, whose pastoral office they would silence by calumny and intimidation'.[176]

During the War of Independence, Church leaders, whatever their reservations about the moral aspects of the military struggle, could support the forces of opposition to the government because most of them regarded it as an alien one. However, now that an Irish government had popular approval, 'the church could enthusiastically support the established order'.[177] There is strong evidence that by October 1922 the Provisional Government was seen by a large majority of people as the only defender of their lives, liberties and interests. The wholesale atrocities perpetrated by Republicans and others acting in their name had the effect, as Garvin argues, of 'making people end up being indifferent to Free State ruthlessness'. Support for the

---

[173] Tom Garvin, *1922: The Birth of Irish Democracy* (Dublin, 1996), pp. 54, 105.

[174] Ibid. p. 105. In October, following the wholesale rejection by Republicans of the conditional amnesty, Father Dominic impressed on Republican leaders like Ernie O'Malley the urgency of establishing a Republican government, since without a formally established civil authority, he argued, Republicans were 'nothing more in the eyes of the world than murderers and looters'. C. D. Greaves, *Liam Mellows and the Irish Revolution*, 1971, p. 377.

[175] *Westmeath Independent* 7.10.22.

[176] *Limerick Herald*, 26.2.23.

[177] Hopkinson, *Green Against Green*, p. 182.

government was reflected in the popular enthusiasm which marked the arrival of National Army units in towns evacuated by Republican forces. 'There were night-long celebrations', Garvin remarks, 'when the IRA were driven out of Claremorris, County Mayo, on 24 July. At the end of July the Free State Army was welcomed by huge crowds in Tipperary town. This was in part due to the fact that the IRA had burned down such factories as the town possessed, thereby throwing many out of work.' Popular attitudes were also influenced by the weighty consideration that 'unlike the IRA the Free State Army was relatively controllable by its hierarchy, and the IRA had, in the absence of payment, maintained themselves at the expense of the local people'.[178] Popular attitudes were, however, soon influenced in contrary directions. Enthusiasm for the Free State troops among the 'liberated' populations gave way to justified criticism of the indiscipline and heavy drinking of many of them. The behaviour of soldiers of the Western Command under Seán Mac Eoin and Tony Lawlor attracted widespread opprobrium. Lawlor boasted to his mother, in a letter intercepted by Republicans, that 'a wonderful shot' of his had fatally wounded Patrick Mulrennan, a Republican prisoner in Athlone jail, during a riot on 6 October 1922. His action was defended by Mac Eoin. The killing of Republican prisoners on the slopes of Ben Bulben, Co. Sligo in September 1922, by two Free State officers and four former British soldiers serving in the Western Command, involved the use of machine-guns. One of the prisoners was Brigadier-General Seamus Devins; another was Brian MacNeill, one of the sons of Eoin MacNeill, Minister for Education in the Provisional Government. A Free State army witness to the shootings recalled that the officers and former British soldiers carried them out because the rank and file soldiers of the Free State unit refused to form a firing party to shoot prisoners.[179]

Government propaganda and episcopal pronouncements during the Civil War and its immediate aftermath understandably placed their emphasis on Republican atrocities. There is no record of a specific episcopal condemnation of Free State misdemeanours during the period. There is compelling evidence, however, that many members of the armed forces of the state were involved not only in major infractions of the rules of war, but in all forms of criminal activity against civilians. In December 1923, the Executive Council considered a report from the Ministry for Home Affairs on 'Returns of Serious Crime in Ireland with particular reference to responsibility of Members of the Army'. These returns had been compiled by the Garda

[178] Garvin, *1922*, p. 103.
[179] Hopkinson, *Green Against Green*, pp. 212–20.

Siochána and the Dublin Metropolitan Police, referred to 'serving or demobilised' members of the Army, and covered the six months from 1 July to 31 December 1923. They showed that members of the National Army 'were guilty or suspected of being guilty' of 60 per cent of murders; 28 per cent of raids, hold-ups, robberies and larcenies involving the use of guns; 43 per cent of manslaughters; 21 per cent of attempted murders; 31 per cent of armed attacks on houses; 20 per cent of robberies with arms and 50 per cent of rapes, indecent assaults and other sexual offences.[180] When, early in 1924, Kevin O'Higgins alleged in the Dáil that two Republican deputies in County Sligo were leading armed gangs of robbers, Frank Carty, TD, one of the deputies in question, denying the allegation, claimed that 'the people have abundant evidence from the reports published in the local press that several Free State soldiers are awaiting trial on charges of attempted murder and armed robbery, and how in one case recently a member of the Free State Army has been sent to penal servitude for an unmentionable crime'.[181]

The Pastoral Letter issued by the Bishops at Maynooth on 10 October 1922 was timed to coincide with the government amnesty offer to Republicans and with the application of the Public Safety Bill.[182] In the Pastoral, the bishops hoped and prayed that those still opposing the state in arms would 'take advantage of the Government's present offer, and make peace with their own country'.[183] The Provisional Government could scarcely have expected more enthusiastic or more powerful support than that afforded by the October Pastoral. The bishops declared it a matter of 'divine law' that 'the legitimate authority in Ireland just now' was the Provisional Government; that there was 'no other Government, and cannot be, outside the body of the people'; that 'the guerrilla warfare now being carried on by the Irregulars is without moral sanction; and therefore the killing of National Soldiers in the course of it is murder before God'. Other forms of Republican IRA activity such as the seizure of property and damage to roads, railways and bridges were deemed to be 'robbery' and 'criminal destruction'.[184] From the point of view of active Republicans who

---

[180] Meeting of the Executive Council, 22.12.23. Extract from Minutes C 2/355. Crime in Saorstát Éireann, July-December 1923. NAI S 3527. I would like to thank Professor David Fitzpatrick, TCD for drawing my attention to this source.
[181] Letter of Frank Carty TD to the *Irish Independent*, 27.2.24.
[182] See Hopkinson, *Green Against Green*, p. 182. For the 'official' and 'unofficial' versions of the October Pastoral see Appendix One. It is interesting, and possibly significant, that Archbishop O'Donnell did not sign the document.
[183] *ICD*, 1923, p. 612.
[184] Ibid., p. 610.

regarded themselves as conscientious Catholics, the most disturbing, perhaps alarming, aspect of the October Pastoral was a penal section which pronounced that those who contravened the bishops' teaching would 'not be absolved in Confession, nor admitted to Holy Communion, if they purpose to persevere in such evil courses'.[185] The bishops also attempted to ensure that Catholic Republicans would not enjoy the moral support of sympathetic priests. Such priests, they declared, 'are guilty of the gravest scandal, and will not be allowed to retain the faculties they hold from us'. They threatened to suspend any priest who dared to 'advocate or encourage this revolt, publicly or privately'.[186]

Many of those against whom the Pastoral was directed professed astonishment at its lack of balance and its partisan tone. The fundamental Republican objection was that the bishops were pretending to pronounce definitively on a major constitutional issue then the subject of acrimonious debate: the legitimacy or otherwise of the Provisional Government. When the bishops described this government as having been 'set up by the nation', the general Republican response was that in the June election a considerable majority had supported the idea of a coalition government. When they accused Republicans of having 'chosen to attack their own country', a plausible reply was that it was the Provisional Government which had attacked the Four Courts. The Pastoral appears to have been put together in haste; in places it is contradictory and even absurd.[187] The bishops warn 'our Catholic people' that the teaching of the Pastoral is 'authoritative' and that they are 'conscientiously bound to abide by it, subject, of course, to an appeal to the Holy See'.[188] This saving clause may represent an effort on the part of the bishops to avoid the imputation of Gallicanism,[189] but it is difficult to imagine, given the claim made elsewhere in the Pastoral that their teaching on the central issues represented 'divine law', what difference they believed an appeal to the Holy See might make.[190] Soon

[185] Ibid., p. 610-11.
[186] Ibid.
[187] For the most egregious example, see the discussion of 'unauthorised murders' in Appendix One.
[188] *ICD*, 1923, p. 610.
[189] Gallicanism was originally a complex of French ecclesiastical and political doctrines advocating the restriction of papal power, involving the union of clergy and King to limit the intervention of the pope within France. The word was commonly used in the nineteenth century to identify the position opposing Ultramontism, which emphasised papal authority. The First Vatican Council dealt a final blow to Gallicanism by formally declaring for Ultramontism.
[190] A group of Republicans drew up an appeal to the Pope at the end of December 1922, and Professor Arthur Clery and Dr Conn Murphy presented it to him. The document setting out the terms of the appeal is in the Hagan Papers, Irish College, Rome and is discussed in Chapter 4, pp. 180-3.

after the Pastoral was issued, the Jesuit Peter Finlay, a respected apologist for both the bishops and the government, tried to clarify these matters. He explained that 'when the Bishops, with all the authority which God had conferred upon them, declared that definite acts were specific sins of murder, robbery and other injustices, when the Holy See had approved it, and when no one appealed against it, then if anyone a subject of the Bishops would remain a Catholic, he must accept that teaching'.[191] This exposition seems to give the teaching and sanctions promulgated in the October Pastoral a decidedly provisional status, all the more so since the Vatican made no public statement approving of its contents and, indeed, seemed anxious to avoid doing so. Writing to Archbishop Byrne in November 1922, Cardinal Logue was all too conscious of the need for Vatican support for the stand taken by the Irish episcopal body. 'The authority of the Bishops is impeached, vilified and condemned', he complained, urging that 'it is the part of the Holy See to support and maintain the authority of the Bishops'. Acknowledging that he had written to Cardinal Gasparri, Vatican Secretary of State, urging a fulmination from Rome, he told Byrne that he had supported his demand for such a course by reminding Gasparri that fulminations were issued 'frequently by the late Popes when any of the Italian bishops were opposed'.[192] Whatever the Vatican authorities may have thought of the sagacity or otherwise of the bishops in committing themselves so energetically and so exclusively to one side in a murderous dispute which deeply divided the country, the October Pastoral emboldened the Provisional Government and many of the clergy to take a sterner stand than they had previously felt able to against militant Republicans.[193]

The reference in the Pastoral to crimes against property seems to have inspired a new determination not to let these go unpunished, even to the extent of excommunicating the perpetrators. It is true that before the Pastoral was issued, Cardinal Logue, outraged by the looting of oil from a boat owned by the Carlingford Lough Commissioners, promised that anyone 'aiding or abetting' those who did such things

[191] *Irish Independent*, 12.10.22.
[192] Logue to Byrne, 22.11.22, DAA.
[193] There is evidence that the Vatican authorities maintained a more even-handed attitude to the conflict than the Irish bishops did. In April 1923, the Pope, much to the annoyance of the government, granted his Apostolic Benediction to Conn Murphy, who was on hunger-strike against his arrest by the Free State forces. *Éire*, 24.4.23. About the same time, a Free State diplomat complained that the Vatican 'was inclined to give undue consideration to the Irregulars' claims'. NAI D/FA 52. In a letter to Logue and the other Irish bishops in August 1922, the Pope urged the Irish bishops to reconcile the warring sides. Pius XI to Logue, 2.8.22, AAA.
[194] *Freeman's Journal*, 19.7.22.

'would, by that very fact, be excommunicated'.[194] After October, looting and damage to property attracted the most vigorous denunciations. Early in 1923, Archdeacon Langan of Moate referred to the destruction of railway engines at Streamstown. The property destroyed, he declared, 'belonged to religious institutions that had their money invested in railway shares' and the destruction of the carriages 'cried to Heaven for vengeance'. In January 1923, Bishop Foley of Kildare and Leighlin heard it rumoured that a motor belonging to Christopher Coyne PP Mountrath 'had been taken from him by the Irregulars', the occasion being his denunciation of a raid which had occurred a short time previously. Foley believed that the theft 'would deserve excommunication if it were done in the knowledge that the machine was the chief means of enabling Father Coyne to discharge his spiritual duties'.[195] It does not appear to have occurred to Bishop Foley that excommunication in this case would have been supererogatory, since the perpetrators, if they were republicans, were already excommunicated by the terms of the October Pastoral.

Excommunication for theft was a relatively minor consequence of the Pastoral. In general, priests throughout the country seem to have obeyed, often with enthusiasm, its injunction that Republicans who persisted in their 'evil courses' should be deprived of the sacraments. A Kerry Republican, Timothy O'Carroll, who claimed he had never been a gunman, but who acknowledged that he held anti-Treaty views, complained that in November 1922 he had been 'refused Holy Communion at the altar rails' by the Parish Priest . . . 'thereby holding me up to the ridicule and opprobrium of the congregation'. When O'Carroll challenged the priest to explain his action, the reply was that 'he'd expose himself to suspension by giving me Holy Communion'.[196] Anna O'Rahilly, sister of The O'Rahilly who had been killed in 1916, complained to the Head of the Congregation of the Council at the Vatican that when she approached the altar at her Parish church in Donnybrook in early December, the priest refused to administer communion to her. She alleged defamation of character and public humiliation. She considered the October Pastoral *ultra vires*, and even if it were not, pointed out that its strictures could not apply to her, as she had been employed in purely humanitarian work since 1916.[197] Mary MacSwiney recorded numerous items of evidence in support of her claim that 'Priests in every village in Ireland refuse the Sacraments to those whose allegiance is given to an Independent

---

[195] Foley to M.J. Murphy, 10.1.23, KLDA.
[196] Timothy O'Carroll to Bishop Charles O'Sullivan, 4.11.22, KYDA.
[197] MacSwiney Papers, UCDA, P48a/205 (1)

Ireland'. A young girl, she noted, was told by a priest that 'if any priest gave her absolution knowing her to be a Republican, she and the priest would burn in hell fire for all eternity'.[198] Eithne Nic Suibhne claimed that in Cork jail Father Scannell refused absolution to the men on hunger-strike 'on the grounds that they were committing suicide', but pointed out that all the girls in the North Dublin Union on hunger-strike received Holy Communion. She wondered why hunger-striking 'was considered suicide by Bishops and priests in Cork', and at the same time considered a 'justifiable weapon in Dublin, where the Sacraments are given'.[199] In October 1923, Austin Stack and nine other Republican TDs signed a letter which was forwarded to the Archbishop of Dublin complaining that a hospital chaplain, John Fennelly, refused to give absolution to a gravely ill Republican TD who was on hunger-strike.[200]

In Republican eyes, episcopal efforts to sustain the Provisional Government, reaching their climax in the ordinances of the October Pastoral, inaugurated a regime of spiritual terrorism, with the sacraments and rites of the Church freely deployed as weapons. The bishops having anathematised militarily active Republicans and their collaborators and excluded them from the body of the Church, the clergy had a genuine difficulty, not only in the matter of Confession and Communion, but in giving Christian burial to those Republicans who died on active service or on hunger-strike. Towards the end of the Civil War, two Republican soldiers were killed in Waterford. Local members of Cumann na mBan were obliged to take charge of the funeral arrangements when the Parish Priest, on the orders of the Bishop, failed to appear.[201] Michael Mansfield was a prominent Waterford Republican. When his father died early in 1923, the local priest refused to allow his body to lie in the church, 'even though the deceased had a son a priest and two daughters in religious orders. The active service unit descended on Grange, took over the church, and carried out the funeral service and burial'.[202] The Republican journal *Éire* printed many stories of similar happenings. A prisoner in Kilkenny jail reported that when a Republican prisoner died there in January 1923, neither the chaplain nor his assistants could be persuaded to visit his cell.[203] C.S. Andrews recalled that when a member

---

[198] Ibid., P48a/213.
[199] Ibid., P48a/196 (21)
[200] NAI S 1859
[201] *Éire*, 21.4.23.
[202] Seán and Síle Murphy, *The Comeraghs. Refuge of Rebels, Story of the Deise Brigade IRA, 1914–1924* (n.d.).
[203] *Éire*, 27.1.23.

of Cumann na mBan and a member of an IRA brigade wanted to marry, the local priest refused to administer the Sacrament because of the Bishops' Pastoral.[204]

The case of Denis Barry illustrates the determination of churchmen to enforce the doctrines outlined in the October Pastoral long after the formal ending of the Civil War. Barry was one among thousands of Republican prisoners on hunger-strike late in 1923. When he became very ill, C.S. Andrews approached the prison chaplain to request attendance on Barry, 'but was met by a blast of abuse against Republicans in general supported by quotations from the Bishops' Pastoral'. The chaplain, Andrews remembered, 'was particularly scathing about the men who were prolonging the hunger-strike to the point of committing suicide; they had put themselves outside the Church'.[205] Barry was removed from prison to the Curragh Hospital where he died, still refusing to take food. When his body arrived in Cork on 27 November for interment in the Republican plot, arrangements had been made that it should lie in state in St Finbarr's Catholic Church overnight. Bishop Cohalan, however, would not permit the body to be taken to any church and it was instead taken to the rooms of the Sinn Féin Executive. Cohalan explained his decision in a letter. He was not allowing 'religious exercises which constitute Christian burial to take place at the burial of Denis Barry', since, 'anyone who deliberately takes his own life is deprived of Christian burial, and I shall interpret the law of the Church and refuse a Christian burial'.[206] Cohalan and other leading Churchmen had given qualified moral support to Terence MacSwiney during his hunger-strike in 1920. From Cohalan's perspective, however, a hunger-strike undertaken in the cause of national independence was of a different moral order from one undertaken in an unjustified rebellion against a lawful government. Privately, Cohalan was much less assured of the moral rectitude of his treatment of Barry than his stern public utterance suggested. Two days before the body arrived in Cork, we find him writing to Bishop Foley of Kildare and Leighlin, in whose diocese Barry had died. He wanted to know whether Barry had received the last Sacraments, as he felt unable to trust a Republican statement that he had. Although he had made up his mind not to permit a Catholic

[204] C.S. Andrews, *Dublin Made Me* (Dublin, 1979), p. 267.
[205] Ibid., pp. 301–2.
[206] *ICD*, 1924, p. 600. Professor Corish describes Cohalan, who became senior Professor of Theology in Maynooth in 1894, as 'a guardian of orthodoxy, a man of the manuals' who, before his lectures, 'distributed lithographed notes to his students so that there might be no occasion for error'. *Maynooth College 1795–1995* (Dublin, 1995), p. 251.

funeral service even if the last Sacraments had been administered, he still wondered how a confessor might deal with such a case as Barry's. His letter to Foley is a splendid piece of casuistry. As the bishop of Barry's diocese he had to deal with the matter '*in foro externo* in relation to the public life of the Church'. He believed that, objectively, the hunger-striking of Barry ended in suicide, that from the nature of the case there was no repentance, since there was 'persistence to the end'. There was also no proof of mental aberration. Subjectively, Barry might have been in good faith, but *in foro externo* Cohalan had to assume that he 'ought to have been guided by his ecclesiastical teachers', whereas in fact the strike was continued 'in defiance of Bishops and priests'. In 'a non-essential thing like Christian burial', Cohalan was tempted to 'adhere to the letter of the law that in the absence of repentance', he should not allow such burial. But, he concluded, 'if Barry got the last Sacraments, and as the strike is ended, I might reconsider the question'.[207]

V

The bishops who, in their October Pastoral, committed themselves heart and soul to the Provisional Government and placed unrepentant Republicans beyond the pale of tolerance, could scarcely have foreseen what spiritual and moral problems they would encounter in November and December. On 10 November, Erskine Childers was arrested in possession of a pistol which had been given to him by Michael Collins. He was executed on 24 November before the legal procedures involved in his appeal to the courts had been exhausted.[208] On 7 December Seán Hales, a pro-Treaty TD, was murdered by

---

[207] Cohalan to Foley 24.11.23, KLDA. 'I would be surprised, C.S. Andrews wrote of Barry, 'if he did not die in the arms of the Church as I think it unlikely that many priests faced with this situation were prepared to see the terms of the Bishops' Pastoral through to the ultimate conclusion'. Andrews, *Dublin Made Me*, p. 302. Judging by Cohalan's subsequent action, Andrews may have been mistaken in this case. The problems faced by prison chaplains in dealing with political prisoners are discussed by Bishop Foley in a letter to his Vicar-General. Pointing out that the application of agreed principles must be left to the judgment of the confessor, he adds that this will depend on the 'psychical state' of confessor as well as penitent. 'Hence', he believes, 'uniformity in the application of these principles is undesirable and even if it were not, it seems to me morally impossible'. Foley mentions 'the principle that *per exceptionem* it may be lawful for the confessor to keep silent, that is if he is morally certain that the penitent is *bona fide* and he has grave reason to fear that admonition would be injurious'. Foley to M.J. Murphy, 25.9.22, KLDA.

[208] Macardle, *Irish Republic*, pp. 811 ff.

Republican gunmen who were implementing an IRA decision to use reprisals against members of the Dáil who had voted for the Resolution giving the National army powers to execute. On the following morning, four Republican leaders, Rory O'Connor, Liam Mellows, Joseph McKelvey and Richard Barrett, were shot in the prison yard at Mountjoy after a cabinet meeting 'had explicitly authorised their deaths as a reprisal'.[209] The government could not argue that the executions had the protection of the Public Safety Act, since all four men had been captured in July during the Four Courts attack and had been in Mountjoy ever since. None of the executed men had been brought to trial. It is difficult to dispute Macardle's assertion that 'no cover of legality could, at that time or any other, be adduced' for these executions.[210]

It soon became a commonplace of Republican discourse that church leaders bore a moral responsibility for the executions, which many commentators, other than Republican sympathisers at home and abroad, found abhorrent.[211] C.S. Andrews records the common Republican attitude: 'By any, except some metaphysical or occult standards, these executions were murder. We found it hard to accept that Mulcahy, pietist that he was, would have outraged his conscience unless he had some advice that would justify, for him, his action in the sight of God.'[212] Some commentators believed that the first, unrevised, version of the Pastoral, published in the national newspapers on 11 October, had provided the government with all the moral backing it needed to execute Republicans, tried or untried. Sean O'Casey, writing less from a Republican than from an anti-episcopal standpoint, gives a heightened account of the Pastoral, 'fresh with dieu, condemning Unauthorised

---

[209] Hopkinson, *Green Against Green*, p. 191. The reprisal execution without trial of the four Mountjoy prisoners as a deterrent against the further assassination of elected representatives provides an instructive contrast to the methods adopted by the Northern Ireland government in dealing with Republican militancy. Legislation passed by the Free State parliament provided for internment, flogging and the establishment of military courts with the power to execute prisoners. In Northern Ireland, as Bryan Follis points out, although the government established special non-jury courts to try subversives, it did not empower these courts to impose the death penalty. B. Follis, *A State Under Siege. The Establishment of Northern Irealnd, 1920–1925* (Oxford, 1995), p. 110. Tom Wilson justifiably speculates on the 'horrified reaction' and 'outrage' that would have been provoked had the 'hard-pressed Ulster Government' executed Republican prisoners without trial as a reprisal for the crimes of others. See *Ulster, Conflict and Consent* (Oxford, 1989), p. 63.

[210] Macardle, *Irish Republic*, p. 822.

[211] The New York *Nation* called the executions 'murder foul and despicable and nothing else'. Those who sanctioned the deed were described by Gavan Duffy as 'not in a normal frame of mind'. See Macardle, *Irish Republic*, p. 823.

[212] Andrews, *Dublin Made Me*, p. 252.

Murder on the part of the Republicans, implying to many minds that the same kind of progressive activity on the part of the Free State followers, came within, according to the clergy, the shadow of canonical condonation. They seemed to be investing it with a kind of legal validity'.[213] In the immediate aftermath of the executions, Republican apologists were freely suggesting that the Pastoral was a licence to kill Republicans. On 12 December, Seán T. O'Kelly's wife Cáit told Hagan that she and some other Republicans had 'collected a number of representative people here to go to see the Archbishop [Byrne] as a story got round that quite a number of other [Republican prisoners] were to be executed . . . For would they have dared to execute only for the Pastoral. I wonder how the pastoralers like the shooting of prisoners for a reprisal by an established government.'[214] Byrne's response suggested that the bishops had less power as advocates of clemency than as facilitators of what Cosgrave called the terror that his government would strike into Republicans.[215] Byrne, Mrs. O'Kelly reported, 'received our people courteously, made himself charming, said he was glad they came but he was powerless: he already made representations in vain'.[216]

Republican insistence on seeing the executions as the logical outcome of the October Pastoral exposed some of the bishops to stern rebukes, many of them involving moral blackmail. The role of bishops as moral arbiters now seemed less and less sustainable; many high-minded Republicans felt that they had a warrant to lecture those who had so recently been castigating them. Mary MacSwiney, whose discourse was usually marked by a strong ethical bent, evidently found her censorial function especially congenial. 'May I ask', she wrote to the Archbishops and bishops of Ireland on 8 December 1922, 'if the base murder of four men in Mountjoy this morning has your ecclesiastical approval as an authorised murder? . . . We can draw no other conclusion than that you do approve if you do not openly condemn, and we count you guilty of this blood.'[217] The twin notions that

[213] *Autobiographies*, 2, (Dublin, 1963), p. 92.
[214] Cáit O'Kelly to Hagan, 12.12.22, Hagan Papers.
[215] Macardle, *Irish Republic*, p. 823.
[216] Cáit O'Kelly to Hagan 12.12.22, Hagan Papers. Mrs O'Kelly added that she had heard 'rather indirectly, that those people who went to see the Archbishop on Tuesday learned that he was broken-hearted . . . Perhaps he tried and even succeeded in staying certain executions. I hardly think so, however.'
[217] Mary MacSwiney to Archbishops and Bishops of Ireland, 8.12.22. Byrne Papers, DAA. MacSwiney asked the bishops 'if further murders of helpless prisoners are committed in this barbarous and inhuman manner . . . murders of men who, because of their long imprisonment, can have had nothing to do with any recent developments arising out of your Government's murder Bill; and if the Irish Hierarchy have not lifted their voices against the murders already carried out, what do Your Lordships think will be the effect on lovers of justice in this country?'

episcopal support had been a direct influence on what Republicans saw as a reign of terror, and that episcopal silence on extra-legal state activity implied consent if not complicity in this, were freely expressed by angry victims and their relatives. The executions of 8 December 1922 inaugurated a long campaign of Republican complaints to senior churchmen. Writing to Archbishop O'Donnell in the Spring of 1923, Hagan claimed that he was still getting many letters 'to the effect that the executions would never have been possible had the Bishops not given their official corporate sanction by the October Pastoral'. He pointed out that 'great stress is laid on the silence observed [by the bishops] with regard to the execution of Mellows and his companions'. Hagan felt that 'in all justice it is a pity that there was not some public expression of what I believe to be the episcopal mind on the Mellows incident'.[218] Conn Murphy, a committed Catholic who had experienced some of the rigours of Free State militancy, wrote to each of the bishops, sternly admonishing them for the effects of their intervention in national affairs. 'Your public espousal of the Free State cause', he wrote to Bishop O'Dea of Galway, 'has enabled its Government to illegally and unjustly seize and imprison tens of thousands of Irish Catholic boys and men and hundreds of Irish Catholic women; to torture habitually defenceless prisoners . . . to murder them . . . You are very directly and specifically responsible for these injustices [through] your failure to utter a single word of protest or disapproval of murders, tortures [and] raids.'[219]

No member of the Irish hierarchy seems to have publicly condemned, or even publicly commented on, the November and December executions. To this extent, the complaints of Mary MacSwiney, Hagan and Murphy are justified. Archbishop Byrne and Archbishop O'Donnell, however, intervened privately in efforts to prevent the killing of Childers in November and the Four Courts leaders in December. On the day following the execution of Childers, O'Donnell wrote movingly to Hagan of his admiration for Childers and of his effort to save his life. 'Much as I dislike intervening in any way', he told Hagan, 'when I saw a few days ago that he was in jeopardy, I wrote to the law adviser suggesting that he should be spared. Plainly I had nothing for my pains'. O'Donnell's view was that all the executions were 'most deplorable', especially that of Childers; he also claimed that both Logue and Archbishop Byrne were opposed to what the Government was doing.[220] Byrne had also

---

[218] Hagan to O' Donnell, 26.3.23, AAA.
[219] Conn Murphy to Bishop O'Dea, 28.2.23, GDA.
[220] O'Donnell to Hagan, 25.11.22, Hagan Papers.

intervened with the authorities on behalf of Childers, a gesture which prompted Hagan to congratulate and thank him. 'Your action to have him spared', he wrote, 'does honour to you and him; and I am glad to know that even one voice was raised on the side of mercy'.[221] On the eve of the 8 December executions, Byrne visited Cosgrave to plead with him not to put into effect the decision of the Executive Council taken earlier that day to execute four prisoners as a reprisal for the murder of Seán Hales. Cosgrave stood firm.[222] After the executions had taken place, Byrne took advantage of Cosgrave's earlier assurance to him that he would not consider a letter from him 'on a public matter as anything like undue interference', to condemn the executions. Byrne told Cosgrave that 'it was with something like dismay' that he had read in the newspapers that the men had been executed as reprisals for the death of Hales. Byrne regarded the policy of reprisals as 'not only unwise but entirely unjustifiable from the moral point of view', finding it 'absolutely unjust' that one man should be punished for another's crime. There was the further consideration, according to Byrne, that the policy was bound to alienate many friends of a government that needed 'all the sympathy' it could get. Byrne pleaded that the 'road to clemency' be kept open, and that if any Republicans were to suffer, this should be 'after a fair trial and without the appearance of haste'.[223] It does not appear that all the bishops shared the concerns of Byrne and O'Donnell about the morality of executing imprisoned opponents of the government without trial as reprisals. While Byrne saw the government action as a crime as well as a blunder, Bishop Foley took a more benign and tolerant view. He does not seem to have been unduly troubled about the moral aspect of the affair, but was worried that the executions might have been politically inopportune. Writing to his Vicar-General, Foley suggested that 'The procedure in connection with the last executions was, to say the least, inexpedient in that it is calculated to evoke opposition to the government and even to alienate a certain type of supporter. I thought the defence made by the Minister unsatisfactory, but they [the Government] have a terrible task before them, and flesh and blood could not but assert itself under the strain of the last few months.'[224]

[221] Hagan to Byrne, 2.12.22, Byrne Papers, DAA.
[222] See Dermot Keogh, *The Vatican, the Bishops and Irish Politics* (Cambridge, 1986), pp. 97–8. Keogh derived his information about Byrne's intervention from Professor T. Desmond Williams, who had interviewed Cosgrave.
[223] Byrne to Cosgrave, 10.12.22, Byrne Papers, DAA. Keogh, *The Vatican, the Bishops*, p. 98, refers to a meeting between Byrne and Cosgrave following the 8 December executions, which, according to Bishop Dunne who accompanied Byrne, 'was effective in moderating government policy'.
[224] Foley to M.J. Murphy, 14.12.22, KLDA. 2.12.22.

Writing to Byrne after the execution of Childers, Hagan warned that 'deeds like this are bound to awaken deadly echoes'.[225] Within months, O'Donnell was to be an innocent victim of the cruel processes in which the October Pastoral had helped to involve the Irish bishops. In March 1923, four Republican prisoners held at Drumboe Castle in Donegal were sentenced to death. When O'Donnell was informed, he convened a meeting of Raphoe diocesan clergy and as a result two messages were sent to the Government in Dublin pleading for clemency for the prisoners. His efforts were not known to Donegal Republicans, a small group of whom victimised him and members of his family after the Drumboe prisoners were executed on 14 March. 'My native home and everything in it', he wrote to Hagan, 'was burned down on the night of St Patrick's Day with considerable harshness or cruelty to the inmates as a reprisal for Drumboe on the score that the Bishops cared little how many were executed'. O'Donnell's account of the wrong inflicted on his family illustrates his characteristic charity and forbearance: 'I suppose the poor fellows [the arsonists] little knew that when the news [of the imminence of the Drumboe executions] reached me late the evening before, I managed after hours to make telegraphic communication with Dublin, and I sent the most earnest representations against the executions.' He also sent priests to Drumboe to see if anything could be done.[226] When T.M. Healy, the Governor General, sympathised with him on the burning of his home, O'Donnell could not conceal his disapproval of the executions. 'The burning of my native home' he replied to Healy, 'is, indeed, a bad business. In my opinion, the executions at Drumboe, for which it was a reprisal, should not, to say the very least, have taken place.'[227]

On 17 November 1922, four Dublin youths found in possession of arms and ammunition were the first to be executed in accordance with the provisions of the emergency legislation. On the day before, Byrne asked Cosgrave to facilitate the release from Mountjoy of Mary MacSwiney, on the ground that 'her death, by her voluntary abstention from food' would have a more harmful effect than her release. Cosgrave refused: if the prisoner persisted 'in her present indefensible attitude until death', the Government might regret it, but she would do so 'of her own volition'. Cosgrave's reply to Byrne is dated 18 November. He warned the Archbishop that other tough measures like the

[225] Hagan to Byrne, 2.12.22, Byrne Papers, DAA.
[226] O'Donnell to Hagan, 21.3.23, Hagan Papers.
[227] D. Ó Doibhlin, eag. *Ón Chreagán go Ceann Dubhrann. Aistí le Tomás Ó Fiaich* (An Clócomhar, 1992), pp. 142–3.

executions of the day before were being planned. The Government, he wrote, with the security of the nation in jeopardy, 'have most reluctantly and painfully been forced to a decision which may involve the carrying out of many stern but, we hope, just actions'.[228] A good deal more disturbing, from Byrne's point of view, must have been Cosgrave's firm, and somewhat cynical, declaration that he believed the October Pastoral had given his Government an unexceptionable moral basis on which to proceed with those 'stern' actions which Byrne was soon to find morally reprehensible. With an irony which may have been unintended by him but which must have struck Byrne quite forcibly, Cosgrave proceeded to use the Pastoral to enlighten one of its chief authors on the issues of the day. He was sure that in taking responsibility for 'all these actions' now in contemplation, his government would be acting 'in the spirit of the solemn teaching of our highest moral authority and recalling in the grave words of the Pastoral Letter of the 11th October that in all this there is no question of mere politics but what is morally right or wrong according to the Divine Law'.[229] The notion that the Divine Law might sanction the shooting of Childers while awaiting a Court appeal or that of Mellows, a prisoner not charged with any crime, almost certainly was not the kind of one that the bishops had in mind when composing their Pastoral. Secure in the general support of the bishops, however, Cosgrave clearly felt that he could disregard the finer shades of meaning or intention in their document. He and his government could also respond to many episcopal appeals for clemency in the last six months of the Civil War with polite but firm rebuffs. In April, Cáit O'Kelly appealed to Archbishop Byrne to intervene on behalf of three women on hunger-strike for 25 days. Byrne promised to do what he could, admitting at the same time that 'my power in these matters is very small'.[230]

In February 1923, incensed by allegations that agents of the Government had ill-treated Republican girls, Mary MacSwiney sought 'a public episcopal denunciation of this outrage'. She blamed Cardinal Logue, whose 'unstinted support' for the government 'encourages these people [military personnel] in their crimes'.[231] At this point, however, the Free State authorities do not appear to have required episcopal backing for what Tom Garvin calls their 'determined and

---

[228] Cosgrave to Byrne, 18.11.22.

[229] Ibid.

[230] M.K. O'Kelly to Byrne, 16.4.23; Byrne to M.K. O'Kelly, 17.4.23, Byrne Papers, DAA.

[231] Mary MacSwiney to Cardinal Logue, 21.2.23. There is a copy of the letter in the Dromore Diocesan Archive.

occasionally bloody defence of the new electoral democracy'.[232] Already in August 1922, Hugh Kennedy, the Government's law adviser, was pointing to the need for 'prompt, effective, vigorous and utterly ruthless action' against the forces of disorder, citing with approval the recent action by the Reichswehr and the paramilitary Freikorps in crushing the pro-Soviet Spartakus uprising in Germany. This had involved the murder of Karl Liebknecht and Rosa Luxemburg and the dumping of their bodies in the Landswehrkanal in Berlin. Kennedy believed that such ruthlessness should not be tempered by 'a mistaken idea of humanity'.[233] In January 1923, Kevin O'Higgins was urging that the desirable end of the preservation of the infant state justified the most horrifying means, including the killing of several prominent anti-Treatyites without trial.[234] In February 1923, Cosgrave went even further, telling a delegation of peacemakers that he was prepared to employ mass killing in defence of the Free State. He was encouraged by 'the remarkable effect' produced by the executions to date, even though these had involved 'unfortunate dupes' rather than 'the responsible people'. He was not going to hesitate, 'and if the country is to live and if we have to exterminate ten thousand Republicans, the three millions of our people are bigger than this ten thousand.'[235] In such a climate, the moderating voices of those bishops who were willing to intervene had little chance of being heard.

For most senior churchmen, as for Cosgrave, the stark choice appeared to lie between exterminating militant Republicans and being overwhelmed by them. One immediate effect of the October Pastoral had been to precipitate the formation of an 'Emergency Government' by de Valera with the motive of giving legal and moral sanction to the activities of the IRA and giving concrete expression to the Republican view that the Provisional Government was an illegal junta.[236] This move did nothing to moderate episcopal hostility to militant Republicanism. If anything, it made some bishops more uneasy, as O'Doherty's letter to Hagan suggests. 'De Valera', O'Doherty wrote, 'has allowed himself to be hoisted into the "presidency" on the remaining bayonets of Rory O'Connor's squad. It is not a very dignified or comfortable position now. The Republic is now out for a victory or extermination and the women are screaming or fasting.'[237]

[232] Garvin, *1922*, p. 162.
[233] Ibid. p. 162.
[234] Ibid, p. 140.
[235] Ibid. p. 163.
[236] See Longford and O'Neill, *de Valera*, p. 203; Hopkinson, *Green Against Green*, pp. 186–8.
[237] O'Doherty to Hagan, 11.11.22, Hagan Papers.

At this stage of the Civil War, when Republican women were becoming prominent as agitators, propagandists and hunger-strikers, a number of bishops began to be concerned at the consequences of such activity for society. What these women were doing was clearly not in conformity with their proper role as the bishops understood it. While Logue was troubled by the thought that young male Republican activists would when they grew into men, 'be very undesirable members of society', he feared even more for the moral welfare of Republican women. 'What is perhaps worse still', he declared in his Lenten Pastoral for 1923, 'a number of young women and girls have become involved in this wild orgy of violence, if not as active agents at least as abettors and fomentors of strife'.[238] Bishop Coyne of Elphin was even less temperate. 'Half-crazed, hysterical women', he wrote, 'who know not what they want, devote a large portion of their time to the circulation of calumnies and misleading statements about Bishops and priests. They assist, by carrying despatches and arms, in the slaughter of some of the best and bravest of Ireland's sons. They glory in the destruction of the property and in the continued crucifixion of the plain people of the country.' Coyne was unconvinced by the expressions of outrage on the part of many female Republicans at being denied the Sacraments, and could not conceal his contempt for them and for the cause they were upholding. 'With pretended piety and brazen effrontery', he claimed, 'they kneel in prayer to God, and heedless of Our Lord's warning that "His pearls were not for swine" they assert a right to the Sacraments and to the other ministrations of the Catholic Church'.[239] With apparently unconscious irony, Bishop Coyne added that 'The brotherly charity which Christ commanded and of which St Paul speaks in such glowing terms, is completely ignored'.[240] Here he was attributing to Republicans an outlook that they seemed to find characteristic of the bishops and many of the clergy. One such Republican, Jim Coffey, who had survived the Free State killing of his comrades at Countess Bridge, complained that when he was a prisoner in

---

[238] *Westmeath Independent*, 17.2.23. Many clergymen in the twenties did not want to see women involved in political activity, particularly of a militant Republican variety. Bishop Doorly of Elphin told children before he confirmed them at Castlerea that 'Women who go around taking despatches from one place to another are furies. Who respects them or who would marry one of them? Never join Cumann na mBan or Cumann na Saoirse or anything else. Do your work as your grandmothers did before you'. *Roscommon Journal*, 23.5.25.

[239] Bishop Coyne's Lenten Pastoral for 1923, ELDA.

[240] Ibid. 'We have reason to fear', Coyne added, 'that the attractions of the wild life and more especially the craze for intoxicating drink are more responsible than any passionate devotion to an ideal, for the present campaign of national destruction'.

Killarney Barracks, he and other prisoners were taunted by Father Fidelis, the Franciscan chaplain. Coffey alleged that the chaplain 'had asked us how much nearer to a Republic we were than when we started. He also stated that we had the country destroyed; our leaders had cleared off to America and left us fools to fight for them.'[241] There are, however, numerous accounts of sympathetic chaplains. In December 1922, Bryan Moore, on the eve of his execution, wrote to his brother: 'I have just had the priest. He says we are to be envied the deaths we are about to meet . . . we shall go straight to Heaven . . . we will die like men anyway'.[242]

The overwhelming impression conveyed by the public and private discourse of bishops and clergy is one of firm attachment to the Government and institutions of the new state, a willingness to excuse or ignore the atrocities perpetrated by its agents as inevitable consequences of intolerable provocation by the other side, a tendency to blame Republicans exclusively for what Archbishop Harty called 'the evils accompanying this unholy civil war'[243] and, above all, a longing for peace which, as Harty hoped, would bring 'spiritual and temporal prosperity to a harassed nation'.[244] Widespread material ruin and moral chaos inspired such apocalyptic visions as Logue's. To him it seemed 'as if the powers of darkness were, from day to day, inspiring with fresh ingenuity' the Republican 'agents of destruction'.[245] Logue, at any rate, had no doubt that 'the wild and destructive hurricane' of civil war had originated in the 'thin, insubstantial vapour' created by de Valera: 'the difference between some equivocal words in an oath: the difference between external and internal connection with the British Commonwealth'. Logue also found it possible to attribute the foundations of the civil war to 'pride, jealousy, ambition, self-interest, even mere sentimentality', qualities notoriously associated in many minds with de Valera.[246] It is easy to appreciate Fogarty's sense of

[241] *Éire*, 28.7.23.

[242] Ibid., 31.3.23. There is evidence that many Republicans experienced hostility and insensitivity from prison chaplains. Ernie O'Malley claimed that 'the only Republican that the Prison Chaplain voluntarily visited was Bob Barton, a Protestant and therefore a possible convert'. *The Singing Flame*, Tralee, 1978, p. 206. O'Malley also reports that Fr MacMahon, Prison Chaplain in Mountjoy, told a prisoner in great pain from rheumatic fever that he would give him the sacraments if he signed a form promising not to make war on the Free State. The prisoner refused, and 'asked the other men in the ward to prevent the priest annoying him'. Ibid., p. 215.

[243] *ICD*, 1924, p. 555

[244] Ibid.

[245] *Westmeath Independent*, 17.2.23.

[246] Ibid.

relief early in 1923 as the struggle appeared to be nearing its end. 'The Irregulars', he told Hagan in January, 'as far as the rank and file are concerned, are fast breaking up, and they are dwindling into a mere assassination club, with a few clumps of desperadoes scattered through the country. The rank and file are most anxious for peace, but their leaders are holding out for some trick of their own, which they are hardly likely to get. We may have some troubled months ahead of us, but the worst is over in my opinion'.[247]

With the worst over, the bishops and clergy could gradually desist from the more vigorous anti-Republican rhetoric and champion the cause of the Free State, emphasising above all the virtue of whole-hearted loyalty to the new government. This kind of loyalty, as Bishop Browne of Cloyne explained, 'supposes that we extend to our Government a large share of trust and forbearance'.[248] Browne's own Pastorals for the early twenties, like those of many other bishops, are frankly political in content, unequivocal in their support for the government, and intolerant of alternative points of view. 'It is not', Browne declares in 1923, 'consistent with whole-hearted loyalty to try to force our government to take to its bosom the unrepentant forces of disorder. In dealing with this very grave matter our Government has to its credit candour, prudence and commendable firmness.' Browne often adopted the *persona* of a Government apologist and spokesman, as, for example, when he advised that 'The door of the Free State is wide open, with a genuine welcome for every Irishman who is pre-pared to work for the ordered peace and prosperity of Ireland', and when he rejoiced that 'numbers of young men who had been led astray by evil counsellors are daily returning to allegiance to their mother and her Government'.[249] Browne's 1924 Pastoral is an optimistic review of the condition of the country now that 'the impetuous brave young men, who for a time fell under the spell of mischievous guides, are fast returning to work hand in hand with their brothers for the common welfare of the country, and we bid them a hundred thousand welcomes'. Browne takes an almost utopian view of the achievements of 'our young legislators' who 'bravely shouldered the heavy burden, trusting to their honesty of purpose, indomitable energy, intelligence and freedom from mere party politics to win the confidence and support of all the people'. Browne is overwhelmed by the response to the appeal by the Government for a National Loan of ten million pounds, which

[247] Fogarty to Hagan, 10.1.23.
[248] Browne's Lenten Pastoral for 1922. I am grateful to Sr M. Cabrini, Archivist of the Cloyne diocese for making this document available to me.
[249] Browne's Lenten Pastoral for 1923, CLYDA.

he regards as the practical testimony of the people 'to their unshaken confidence that our Irish Parliament will continue to give an example of intelligent, honest and pure administration, seeking the greater good of all the people, unbiased by personal or class prejudice or party politics and untainted by even a suspicion of corruption'.[250]

Browne's account of a happily inclusive political system and of a nation uniting under a benevolent, enlightened, non-partisan administration may not have reflected all the facts as they might have appeared, for example, to those Republicans like de Valera and Stack still in jail. Browne did reflect, however, a widespread clerical determination to identify the Church and its interests with the welfare of the Free State. Public and private gestures of Church support and encouragement helped to foster and extend the moral authority of the government; well publicised electoral support proved to be particularly significant. When T.M. Healy was made Governor-General, Cardinal Logue and some of his episcopal colleagues were entrusted by the bishops at their meeting at Maynooth with the duty of conveying to him cordial good wishes for 'his success and happiness in the high office which his devotion to the cause of the country had induced him to accept'.[251] Logue used the occasion of his visit to the Viceregal Lodge to express his gratification and that of the bishops 'that the Free State Government, notwithstanding its want of experience, was working so efficiently in the face of many difficulties and obstacles'.[252] Such warm affirmations of the Free State regime were well publicised. Private tokens of support were also common. In December 1922, Patrick Lyons, Parish Priest of Ardee, congratulated Healy, now that he was 'firmly fixed on the throne as uncrowned King of Ireland, in fact as well as in name' and assured him that before long he would be 'prayed for officially in the Church's liturgy'.[253]

VI

A number of bishops and priests in Australia and the USA, most of them Irish or of Irish descent, lent valuable moral and political support to the Free State. The most outspoken of the Free State publicists among the American clergy was Archbishop Curley of Baltimore, who was always ready to express his approval of Cosgrave's government and his contempt for its opponents, whether these were

---

[250] Browne's Lenten Pastoral for 1924, CLYDA.
[251] *ICD*, 1923, p. 578.
[252] Ibid.
[253] P. Lyons PP to T.M. Healy, Healy/O'Sullivan Papers P6/C/18, UCDA.

Irish or American. He frequently insisted that his relatively simple view of the Irish conflict was shared by the great majority of Americans and Irish-Americans. When the *Freeman's Journal* asked him to comment on the Irish situation in December 1922, he replied that 'One hundred and ten million Americans, with the exception of a few Irregulars [are] delighted with Ireland's forward step in the establishment of the Free State. No doubt of American good wishes for the present Government's success. De Valera's campaign of riotous destruction is a sad spectacle to all of us.'[254] During a visit to Ireland in August 1922, Curley was appalled 'to see the senseless stupidity of the de Valera people' who seemed to him 'to be bent on murder and destruction and nothing else'.[255] By February 1923, however, he was happy that 'the substantial people of Massachusetts are with the Irish people in their attempt to settle down to real living and are not with the few in the country [the USA] who are aiding the continuation of the most horrible system of destruction I ever witnessed'.[256] Curley blamed de Valera and his followers for making Ireland 'the laughing stock for the Nations of the World', for 'advancing to all intents and purposes the regime of the hated Black and Tans', and for making Americans indifferent to Irish affairs.[257]

Bishop Turner of Buffalo was another influential apologist for the Free State. During de Valera's extended visit to America in 1919–20, Turner formed an unfavourable impression of his attitude and personality. When de Valera declared that the country was not big enough for Judge Cohalan and himself, Turner remarked that the judge could hardly be expected 'to leave his native land just because the President had decided to come in'.[258] Like Curley, Turner visited Ireland at the height of the Civil War; he too proclaimed his allegiance to the Free State and his hostility to the Irish Republican cause, particularly its leadership. In August 1922, he delivered an outspoken

[254] *Freeman's Journal*, 1.1.23.
[255] Letter from Curley to Matthew Cummings, 2.2.23. Quoted in T.D. Tansill, *America and the Fight for Irish Freedom, 1886–1922.* New York, 1957.
[256] Ibid.
[257] *Freeman's Journal*, 21.8.22. Archbishop Curley continued to affirm the achievements of the Free State Government in the years following the Civil War. On a visit to Dublin in August 1925, he declared that 'The Government of the Saorstát has succeeded better than any other Government in the world has done in aiding the Nation's progress and in developing the country's resources'. *Catholic Bulletin*, 1925, p. 859. During the same visit, from his Dublin hotel, Curley announced 'that he had never seen such prosperous crowds – this in the middle of Dublin's fashionable Horse Show Week. Meanwhile, there were reports of children starving in Clonmel and Waterford'. See *An Phoblacht*, 14.8.25.
[258] T. Ryle Dwyer, *De Valera: The Man and the Myths* (Dublin, 1991), p. 39.

address to members of the Redemptorist Arch-Confraternity in Limerick, basing his remarks on the impressions he had gained during a tour of some southern counties. He was troubled by what he called 'the underlying forces of Bolshevism in the Irregular campaign', as well as by evidence of 'radical labour discontent'. Fine young Republicans, he believed, had been misdirected by their leaders. From the point of view of the Free State authorities and the Irish bishops, however, the significant part of Turner's address was his strongly expressed determination to educate American public opinion and to counteract the efforts of Republican propagandists and fundraisers who had been touring America since the Spring of 1922. A Republican mission composed of Michael O'Flanagan, Austin Stack, J.J. O'Kelly, Countess Markievicz, Peter Golden and Kathleen Barry had enjoyed considerable success; Stack was able to return to Ireland in May bringing eighty thousand dollars for Cumann na Poblachta, the anti-Treaty political group formed by de Valera in early 1922.[259] Turner told his Limerick audience that he would not spare the Republican leaders when he got back to America. 'De Valera was my friend in America', he declared, 'and I did all in my power to help him; but when I go back, if I can use my influence as I intend to do, he will not get another dollar from America. I am ashamed that it is Irish-American money [that] is supporting them in this campaign'. He would also tell the Irish in America that 'all the annoyance, loss and destruction they are causing the people of Ireland is simply due to their own feelings of revenge, because they lost the elections'.[260]

Many Irish bishops, perhaps a majority, tried to enlist members of the American episcopate as agents of the Free State. Archbishop Curley publicly acknowledged that he had received letters from 'most of the bishops in Ireland asking him to use his influence on behalf of the Free State and peace in Ireland'.[261] The Lenten Pastorals of Cardinal Logue and Bishop Coyne of Elphin were being used early in 1923 in America as propaganda for the Free State.[262] Bishops appear to have been in touch throughout the period with sympathetic Americans, lay as well as clerical, in an effort to enlighten them on the Irish situation. In May 1922, we find Fogarty replying to a pro-Treaty correspondent in New York, thanking him for his assurance 'that the

---

[259] Denis Carroll, *They have fooled you again. Michael O'Flanagan (1876–1942). Priest, Republican, Social Critic* (Dublin, 1993), p. 142
[260] *Freeman's Journal*, 9.8.22. Turner told the Dublin newspapers of his satisfaction with conditions in Ireland in 1925. He was especially pleased that the Free State 'was being rendered more attractive to tourists from America'. Ibid., 20.7.25.
[261] See Carroll, *They have fooled you*, p. 141.
[262] Ibid., pp. 143–4

bulk of the people in America, like our people at home, are for peace and working the 'Treaty', and warning him that 'if the Americans proceed to finance Civil War in Ireland, they will be doing the Orangemen's work better than the Orangemen themselves'. Fogarty thought it advisable to warn his correspondent about the dangers posed by de Valera, whose 'revolt has thrown everything into confusion', with the result that 'we are in imminent danger, after all the sacrifices, of seeing everything carried off like a wreck in a flood'.[263] Irish episcopal archives contain material suggesting that during the more turbulent phase of the struggle at home, Irish bishops were in the habit of sending copies of their Pastoral Letters to those of their American counterparts whose dioceses had significant numbers of Irish-Americans. The replies from the American recipients must not have appeared greatly encouraging. They are bland and perfunctory, and offer no promise of anything more than sympathy and prayers. Bishop Cantwell of Los Angeles and San Diego found in Hallinan's Lenten Pastoral for 1923 'a most hopeful commentary on conditions in the Emerald Isle', and hoped God would give its author 'many years to see Ireland settled down to work out its destiny in peace and in faith and love'.[264] The Archbishop of San Francisco, who had received a copy of the April 1922 Joint Pastoral from Mulhern, regretted 'very much, as everyone does, that the condition of affairs in Ireland is far from satisfactory' and was 'hoping from day to day for a permanent settlement'.[265] Cardinal O'Connell of Boston read the same Pastoral 'with much interest', and told Mulhern that he hoped and prayed 'that an era of peace and happiness will soon succeed these sad and troubled days'.[266] Some letters from America were more positive than these. In May 1922, P.W. Russell, a Massachusetts merchant, assured Fogarty that 'the de Valera support is weakening, and his followers are few, but they are led on by politicians'. He enclosed some excerpts from newspapers to 'show the feelings of 95 per cent of the American public and what is being done to counteract the influence of a leader [de Valera] who has brought disgrace on the Irish people and the good name of Ireland and you are at liberty to use it for publication if you so desire.' Russell suggested that 'the people of Ireland write to their friends in all parts of the world and call on them to support the Free State and beware of treacherous leadership'.[267]

---

[263] *Limerick Weekly and District Advertiser*, 13.5.22.
[264] Bishop Cantwell to Hallinan, 16.4.23, LKDA.
[265] Chancellor of the Archdiocese of San Francisco to Mulhern, 29.5.22, DRDA.
[266] Cardinal O'Connell to Mulhern, 2.6.22, DRDA.
[267] P.W. Russell to Fogarty, 20.5.22, KILLDA.

Following the ratification of the Treaty, Australia became another battleground for Free State and Republican propagandists. The Australian bishops, with the important exception of Mannix, were enthusiastic supporters of the Free State. In August 1922, Archbishop Kelly of Sydney telegraphed Logue to indicate that 'Nineteen Archbishops and Bishops of Australia strongly deprecate National dissension. They look for practical union of action according to majority vote.'[268] Logue asked the Irish newspapers to publish Kelly's message 'as one of the many proofs of how deeply lovers of Ireland in every land are afflicted by the very distracted state of the country'.[269] In March 1923, Father O'Flanagan and J.J. O'Kelly arrived in Australia as Republican envoys, their self-imposed mission being 'to refute current propaganda inimical to the Irish Republic'. As part of this propaganda, generous use was made of Pastoral letters of Cardinal Logue and Bishop Coyne of Elphin, both of which documents were remarkable for their vehement denunciations of the motives and actions of Republican men and women.[270] The Republican envoys concentrated their efforts on Melbourne, Sydney and Brisbane. In Melbourne, Archbishop Mannix not only welcomed them and introduced them to sympathetic audiences; he also delivered a St Patrick's Day oration with a strongly Republican colouring. 'A free untrammelled vote of the whole Irish people', he argued, 'would cause partition to be wiped off the map of Ireland and there would be not a vestige left of British rule in Ireland'.[271]

In Brisbane and Sydney, O'Flanagan and O'Kelly had to contend with two hostile prelates, Archbishop Duhig and Archbishop Kelly. Duhig used the local press to counteract the arguments of the envoys, claiming that 95 to 98 per cent of the Irish people supported the Free State, and making it clear that such Republican emissaries as O'Flanagan and O'Kelly were unwelcome.[272] If they were, O'Kelly, at any rate, does not seem to have noticed; he was later to describe one of their outdoor meetings in Brisbane as 'one of the greatest and most

[268] Archbishop Kelly to Logue, 29.8.22, *ICD*, 1923, p. 584.
[269] Ibid.
[270] Carroll, *They have fooled you*, pp 143 ff. See p. 89, notes 238 and 239.
[271] Ibid., p. 145.
[272] Ibid., p. 144. It was common for supporters of the Free State to assert that Republicans did not represent more than five per cent of the people; in the Dáil, Griffith has suggested a figure of two per cent. 'In Griffith's fantastic statement', J.J. O'Kelly later claimed, 'we clearly have the origin of the fable circulated abroad by men like Archbishop Curley of Baltimore, Rev. Dr Ryan of Washington and Archbishop Duhig of Brisbane to the effect that 95 to 98 per cent of the people were for the Treaty – a fable Father O'Flanagan and I had to correct in the Antipodes'. Sceilg, *Trinity of Martyrs*, p. 79.

enthusiastic in the history of the city'.[273] The public utterances of the Irish bishops on the political question provoked intemperate language from the envoys, who spared neither Duhig nor the bishops at home, characterising them as traitors. Duhig wrote a letter to the *Catholic Advocate* denouncing O'Kelly and O'Flanagan, declaring that he had met bishops in Ireland 'who through love of their country were practically driven from their own dioceses', and that the bishops he had met with at the funeral of Collins 'were idolised by the young men of Ireland'.[274] Duhig could speak with some authority on the Irish situation. He had been in Ireland during the Civil War, and had immediate experience of its horrors. Like many ecclesiastics of the period, however, he attributed a degree of importance and a depth of malevolence to de Valera disproportionate to what the evidence would seem to warrant. Duhig's biographer reports that he regarded de Valera as guilty of the murder of Michael Collins and as 'that black figure of Ireland's historic curse, the man who betrays the chief'.[275]

Duhig was a friend and admirer of W.T. Cosgrave. During the Civil War period and well beyond it, he remained constantly alert to the dangers posed by Republican activists in Australia to the interests of the Free State Government. Late in 1923, a Republican appeal for funds in aid of prisoners' dependants was circulated in Australia. Duhig responded with a cablegram to Cosgrave: 'Is Irish Distress Appeal Australia necessary and approved?'[276] Cosgrave replied immediately, telling Duhig that 'the appeal for help to Australia is made only on behalf of those responsible for destruction here and for their dependants', and that there was 'more propaganda than charity' in the appeal, which was not approved by the government.[277] Cosgrave's principal fear in the matter was that subscriptions received would be 'translated by unscrupulous propagandists here as evidence of hostility towards the established government on the part of the Irish in Australia'.[278] In a belated reply, Duhig did not disclose details of whatever efforts he might have made to undermine the success of the Republican appeal. He did, however, express astonishment and admiration that Cosgrave

---

[273] *Catholic Bulletin*, 1925, pp. 317–21.
[274] Quoted in *The Sligo Champion*, 11.8.23.
[275] Quoted by Dermot Keogh, 'Mannix, de Valera and Irish Nationalism', in J. O'Brien and P. Travers (eds), *The Irish Emigrant Experience in Australia* (Dublin, 1991).
[276] NAI S 1369/21. The appeal was signed by Kevin Barry's sister Kathleen and accompanied by a letter signed by P.J. Ruttledge, who was 'Acting President of the Irish Republic' while de Valera was in jail.
[277] Cosgrave to Duhig, 27.12.23, NAI S 1369/21.
[278] Ibid.

did not break down 'under the terrific and lengthy strain of mind and body' during the Civil War. Cosgrave could take encouragement from Duhig's news that every Australian priest who had been to Ireland had come back 'a convert to the Free State', and that 'Australia was being, slowly but surely, permeated with a favourable impression regarding all of you who have stood out against the extremists'.[279]

During the visit of O'Flanagan and O'Kelly to Australia in 1923, by no means all the priests there were well disposed towards the Free State. Archbishop Kelly of Sydney felt it necessary to rebuke several of his priests who had welcomed the Republican envoys.[280] On the other hand, not even the influence of Archbishop Mannix could prevent the editor of one of Melbourne's two Catholic papers, Father William Mangan, from excoriating the envoys throughout the course of their mission. Mangan accused O'Flanagan of bringing his priestly office into disrepute. 'The good people in their Catholic halls' he wrote 'are being asked to contribute to propagating the work of extremists. The burnings and shootings, the stab in the back, the looting of houses and the sacking of defenceless villages . . . these are the gentle aims and objects of Father O'Flanagan.'[281] A friend of Mannix, who had rendered 'invaluable service' to 'every Catholic cause in Melbourne',[282] told Hagan that 'at least 95 per cent of Irish Australians are completely satisfied with the present settlement and would not approve of a Republic'.[283] In the Summer of 1922, a Clonfert priest ministering in New South Wales told Bishop O'Doherty that 'the vast majority of Irish descent in these counties are in favour of the Treaty and it staggered them to learn that Mr de Valera and his following rejected it'.[284]

With the possible exception of Mannix, the most effective and influential clerical apologist for the Republican cause abroad was Monsignor John Hagan who was Rector of the Irish College in Rome

---

[279] Duhig to Cosgrave, 22.7.24, NAI S 1369/21. In the same letter, Duhig reported that 'Father O'Flanagan and Mr. O'Kelly created a good deal of trouble here. Brisbane proved to be their Waterloo. They were soon afterwards deported'. At Brisbane, O'Kelly had made derogatory personal remarks about the Governor Sir Matthew Nathan, who had earlier been Under-Secretary in the Dublin Castle administration. These remarks were later used to secure the envoys' deportation. Carroll, *They have fooled you*, pp. 144–5.

[280] See Patrick O'Farrell, 'Archbishop Kelly and the Irish Question', *Journal of the Australian Catholic Historical Society*. In 1916, Kelly had prepared a telegram denouncing the rising as 'anti-patriotic, irrational and wickedly irreligious'. Carroll, *They have fooled you*, p. 144.

[281] *The Melbourne Tribune*, 29.3.23.

[282] Mannix to Hagan, 29.1.23, Hagan Papers.

[283] C. Ahern to Hagan, 22.9.23, Hagan Papers.

[284] Father John J. Irwin to O'Doherty, 22.5.22. CLDA.

throughout the twenties. Rome had a large population of Irish ecclesiastics, mainly drawn from the major religious orders and congregations: Franciscans, Dominicans, Carmelites, Augustinians, Redemptorists and Jesuits. Apart from Hagan and his Vice-Rector Curran, the Irish clergy in Rome did not manifest Republican sympathies; many, indeed, strongly upheld the cause of the Free State. In January 1924 Hagan addressed a very long, detailed report to O'Donnell on the attitudes of Irish churchmen in Rome to the major political questions of the day. One of Hagan's constant themes is the danger which British influence at the Vatican posed for Irish political and ecclesiastical interests. His contempt for Irish clergymen in Rome, who as he saw it sacrificed their nationality to the cause of imperial harmony, is undisguised. From Hagan's point of view, 'Imperialist' Irish clergymen are, by definition, supporters of the Free State, so that when he condemns individuals and groups for their pro-British outlook, he is ascribing Free State sympathies to them. The Redemptorists, apart from their Superior-General, Patrick Murray, who has been 'most correct all these many years', are described by Hagan as 'the most active of pro-British propagandists', while 'in a field all to himself stands a Dominican named Nolan [285] who has been and is a good friend of the Empire and who is anything but scrupulous in the methods he adopts towards its foes'. Hagan notes with disapproval that Father Nolan, when the British established an embassy at the Vatican, 'went out of his way to welcome the first minister whom he even invited to a special dinner'. Among other Roman apologists for the Free State, Hagan identifies Canice O'Gorman, a leading Augustinian, and his 'two chief satellites', Angelus Irwin, a Discalced Carmelite, and Edmund Power, SJ, a Professor at the Biblical Institute.[286]

VII

The General Election held in August 1923 afforded an opportunity for clergymen of all ranks to give practical expression to their support for the Free State. Cosgrave reconstituted the pro-Treaty Party under the name of Cumann na nGaedheal; throughout the country, priests were active as organisers and senior officers of the new party. In Clare, for example, where the selection convention was held on 30 July, Eoin MacNeill's nomination as a candidate was supported by three priests, two of whom, Canon O'Kennedy and James Monaghan PP Crusheen, were asked to visit him to secure his consent to stand. Of the 46 mem-

[285] Fr Louis Nolan, Via S. Vitale.
[286] Hagan to O'Donnell, 10.1.24, O'Donnell Papers, AAA.

bers elected to regional constituency committees, twelve were priests, as
were three of the five senior election organisers; Canon O'Kennedy
was appointed director of elections.[287] In most constituencies, Cumann
na nGaedheal conventions were presided over by priests.

A striking feature of the 1923 election was the enthusiastic
involvement on the Cumann na nGaedheal side of many of the
bishops. The commonest method of episcopal intervention was
through the medium of letters read from platforms at party rallies.
Some bishops were clearly worried that the election of large numbers
of Labour Party candidates, Farmers and Independents would lead
to an unstable political situation. Cardinal Logue, in a letter addressed
to a meeting in Dundalk, which was in his archdiocese, expressed
unease at the fact that 'numbers who thoroughly agree on the main
issue are putting forward candidates to advocate particular interests'.
There was, he believed, 'a class of candidate of which the electorate
would do well to be on their guard, so-called Independent candidates'.
Logue then proceeded to explain to those present how they should
vote. 'I am convinced', he wrote, 'that the safe course for the electors
is neither to follow too many particular interests, nor to run after
Independents . . . but to go forward in a body in support of the
Ministry, who may have made some mistakes, but have done wonders
during the past year to reorganise the country, establish order, secure
peace and lay a solid foundation to build up the future prosperity of
the country.'[288]

In a letter welcoming Cosgrave to Tralee, Bishop O'Sullivan
suggested that the continued existence of a 'stable and national
government was an essential condition of the country's welfare'.
O'Sullivan argued that the new government would have to be
sufficiently strong and independent to be able to refuse to subordinate
national interests to sectional demands. 'As far as those sectional
interests are concerned', O'Sullivan wrote, 'men should put themselves
the question whether the risk of their suffering through any weakening
of the Government is not much greater than any hope there might be
of a gain'. Like Logue, O'Sullivan was prepared to tell his people
how they should vote. 'By ability, courage and patriotic zeal', he
argued, 'President Cosgrave and his colleagues have proved their
worth in the past; we on our part ought to show that the men who
manned and have unflinchingly held the Bearna Baol [gap of danger]
for Ireland have in no way forfeited our confidence'.[289] Archbishop

[287] K. Sheedy, *The Clare Elections* (Dublin, 1993), pp. 351–2.
[288] *The Irish Times*, 11.8.23.
[289] *Westmeath Independent*, 28.7.23.

Gilmartin of Tuam declared in a message to the electorate that 'in the best interests of the country the people should vote solidly for the present Government' if they wanted to suppress disorder and protect life and property. The Republican revolt, he believed, was a crime; the people had a duty to make the repetition of such a crime impossible. Gilmartin could see no point in voting for the Sinn Féin minority which instead of forming a constitutional opposition had organised an armed revolt.[290] Archbishop Harty of Cashel wrote to a Cumann na nGaedheal rally in Thurles that 'the good of the country demands the return to power of the present government', although he would not mind seeing 'all important interests' obtain due representation.[291]

Cardinal Logue's plea that the electors should not 'follow too many particular interests' was taken to heart by Patrick Howley PP Belmullet. At a North Mayo Farmers' Union election meeting in the town, as the candidates Charles Flynn and Timothy O'Sullivan were about to speak, Howley asked them 'to go forward on the Cumann na nGaedheal ticket as it was the only one on which they would be elected'. The candidates refused, the crowd became excited, and the meeting was abandoned. When Canon Howley attempted to address the crowd on behalf of Cumann na nGaedheal, 'he was met with boohs and hisses and asked why he did not allow the Farmers' candidates to speak'. Howley called on the Army and the Civic Guards to remove the protesting supporters of the Farmers' candidates. A riot ensued, the soldiers and the Guards charged, using belts and batons, the people retaliating with 'sticks, stones, wooden boxes and hammers'. The soldiers were beaten back, with many casualties on both sides; several revolver shots had to be fired before the crowd dispersed.[292] In Mullingar, J.C. Macken, CC, Chairman of the local branch of Cumann na nGaedheal, was less concerned with the dangers posed by Independent and minority party candidates than with ensuring the electoral annihilation of Sinn Féin. He regarded Cumann na nGaedheal as the Nation, 'in deadly grips with the enemies of the Nation'; the Government must win at this election if the Nation was to be saved. He told his listeners that 'when they had ensured that not one of the anti-Treaty candidates would get a seat, then they could say that the future of Ireland was safe'.[293] In a supporting statement read to the meeting, Bishop Gaughran of Meath stopped short of advocating such extreme courses, suggesting instead that it would be 'folly as well as

[290] Ibid., 25.8.23.
[291] Ibid., 4.8.23.
[292] *The Irish Times*, 17.8.23. Neither of the Farmers' Union candidates was elected.
[293] *The Irish Times*, 23.8.23.

ingratitude to take out of the hands of men so capable the destinies of the country that they have so safely guarded', and wishing 'that the Free State will be returned with a substantial majority'.[294] In a statement to the newspapers, Countess Markievicz wondered how Gaughran or any of the clergy 'should have a word to say in favour of a Government which includes in its machinery a Senate which contains thirty Freemasons; for Freemasons, as every Catholic knows, are under the ban of our Holy Father the Pope'.[295]

Several other bishops composed election messages strongly affirming the right of Cumann na nGaedheal to hold power. Bishop Foley warmly commended 'the candidature of President Cosgrave and his colleague, my old school fellow Tom Bolger'; he believed that the extraordinary achievements to date of Cosgrave and his government had provided 'a guarantee of future success which no other group of politicians who are seeking the suffrages of the electors can furnish'.[296] Bishop Naughton of Killala hoped to see representatives returned to the Dáil for Mayo 'who will be not only willing and able to conserve our local interests, but be also active supporters of our present Government'.[297] While Bishop Cohalan of Cork did not give so explicit an endorsement to Cumann na nGaedheal, the advice he did give to the electors amounted to substantially the same thing. He asked that people should vote for 'those who would co-operate in establishing good and stable government in the country, for those who would give security to life and home'.[298] Bishop Hallinan's message to Cosgrave's meeting in Limerick conveyed his admiration for the 'clear vision, undaunted courage, unfailing patience and perseverance' of the Government in going about its task of reconstruction in the face of 'unparalleled difficulties'; its members, he suggested, 'deserve well of the Irish Nation'.[299] In the course of the election campaign Bishop Finegan of Kilmore was an enthusiastic spokesman for Cumann na nGaedheal. Sending the party organiser Martin Comey, Adm. Cavan, a second subscription of £5 for the election fund, Finegan 'emphasised that to save the country from a possible renewal of the terror, to

---

[294] Ibid.
[295] *The Irish Times*, 24.8.23. Donal O'Sullivan, in his history of the Free State Senate, refers to allegations 'dishonestly made by some, and ignorantly repeated by others, to the effect that it was predominantly a Protestant and Freemason body'. He points out that the first Senate consisted of thirty-six Catholics and twenty-four non-Catholics, and that not all of the non-Catholics were Protestants. See *The Irish Free State and its Senate* (London, 1940), p. 95.
[296] *Nationalist and Leinster Times*, 25.8.23.
[297] *The Irish Times*, 23.2.23
[298] *The Irish Times*, 27.8.23.
[299] *ICD*, 1924, p. 576.

protect the people in the coming adjustment of the financial relations with Great Britain and to bring to a satisfactory issue the Boundary Question, there is need for an able, experienced and fearless Government. The government of President Cosgrave was this.'[300]

In the 1923 election campaign, where the bishops led, great numbers of their clergy followed. Clerical participation in the electoral process in all its aspects was considerably greater than it had been in 1922. Only a very small number of priests proclaimed public allegiance to Sinn Féin; the bishops appeared unanimous in their support of Cumann na nGaedheal, the majority of them so firmly committed to its cause that the Church almost appeared like an agency or organ of the State. At a time when the legitimacy of the state was in dispute, the government was fortunate in being able to draw on what Garvin calls 'the superabundant reserves of political legitimacy enjoyed by the Catholic Church at that period'.[301] It would be difficult to over-estimate the political benefit conferred on the Free State by the Church's thoroughgoing commitment to democratic politics, and the willingness of so many of its clergy to work for the only political party that seemed either able or willing to uphold the rule of law, or to offer the prospect of stability and security. This was the central theme of most priestly contributions to the election debate in 1923. Many of the clergy felt as Albert Boylan of Castleblayney did, that Cosgrave had 'saved the country from a great disaster' and that if he 'had not stepped in when Michael Collins was shot the country would long since have been in a worse state than Russia and the cause of freedom set back for centuries'.[302] There was undoubtedly a common feeling among the clergy that Cumann na nGaedheal in 1923 was not a mere political party but also a national movement like the pre-Truce Sinn Féin, standing, as Dr Richard Hayes put it at a meeting in his Limerick constituency, 'for no class interest or political party, but for

---

[300] *Irish Independent*, 27.8.23.
[301] Garvin, *1922*, p. 180. Clerical supporters of the Free State sometimes took a strong public stand against colleagues who identified themselves with the Republican cause. When Thomas Wall, CC Foynes, nominated a Republican candidate in 1923, he was asked by Monsignor O'Donnell, PP Rathkeale, what right he had to do so. O'Donnell also rebuked four priests for convening a public meeting in Limerick in 1923 to demand the release of Republican prisoners. *Éire*, 22.9.23; 29.9.23. Political differences between priests did not necessarily involve personal estrangement. Patrick Marshall, PP Kenmare, was a vigorous and unflinching upholder of the Free State; his curate in the mid-twenties, Joseph Breen, was a fiery Republican. When Breen became seriously ill, Marshall, who cared for him with exemplary devotion, was described as 'a prince among men' by one of Breen's Republican relatives. Information from Sr Philomena, St Clare's convent, Kenmare.
[302] *Irish Independent*, 6.8.23.

the Irish nation, above all private or class interest'.[303] It was in this
spirit that Father Boylan of Castleblayney argued that in supporting
Cumann na nGaedheal 'they were not taking part in party politics but
in the National question'.[304] Malachy Brennan, CC Mantua, a Cumann
na nGaedheal organiser in Roscommon, saw his party as the sole
defender of the Nation 'against external and internal enemies', the
upholder of 'the best interests of the nation as a whole irrespective of
class or creed'.[305]

Garvin has argued that 'the greatest advantage the Free State had
was the utter incoherence of the republican opposition, an unlikely
collection of ultra-Catholics, socialists, Bolshevists, agrarians and
gunmen'.[306] Clerical apologists for Cumann na nGaedheal in 1923
tended to contrast the constructive achievements of their Government
with the anarchist impulses of their opponents. Canon Cummins told
the electors of Roscommon that Cosgrave's Government stood for
'the gospel of peace, protection and progress'; on the other side 'you
have a body of men calling themselves Republicans, who advocated
principles calculated to destroy this infant state, to strangle it in its
early youth'.[307] Canon Lyons reminded the people of Ardee that the
Government had given them money to build a terrace of houses while
anti-Treaty elements 'were coming there to blow their little town to
smithereens'.[308] Edward O'Reilly of Kilcormac told Offaly Cumann na
nGaedheal delegates that it was 'in the interest of all to guard against
and check, as far as possible, the Bolshevistic methods beginning to be
practised even in Holy Ireland'.[309] One Cumann na nGaedheal
platform speaker, John O'Malley PP Turloughmore, had experienced
such methods at first hand. 'You are the man,' he told an interrupter,
'that held me up and tried to rob me'.[310] Pierse Hearne CC Cahir,

[303] *The Irish Times*, 24.8.23.
[304] *Irish Independent*, 6.8.23.
[305] *Roscommon Herald*, 25.8.23.
[306] Garvin, *1922*, p. 182. Another strong advantage enjoyed by the Free State in
the 1923 election was outlined by Macardle: 'Now in almost every town and village,
Sinn Féin found itself deprived, by death or imprisonment, of its experienced
organisers, speakers and writers. Boys and girls took up the work. Until a few days
before the polling they were unable to obtain copies of the registers and these
were found to be grossly inaccurate. Police, Military and Intelligence agents were
used to dislocate the election work of Sinn Féin. Election offices were raided;
literature was seized at the printing works or removed from speakers' cars; boys
engaged in bill posting were beaten . . . many chairmen and speakers were
arrested', *Irish Republic*, p. 863.
[307] *Roscommon Messenger*, 11.8.23.
[308] *Irish Independent*, 17.8.23.
[309] *Westmeath Independent*, 4.8.23.
[310] *The Irish Times*, 21.8.23.

who declared that it was the duty of the electors to cast their first preference votes for the Government candidates, reminded his listeners
that 'President Cosgrave and his gallant Ministers, undeterred by the
revolvers, torches and petrol tins of the disruptionists had carried on
heroically, and had laid the foundations of a strong Government'.[311]
Canon Thomas Barrett of Blarney told a Cumann na nGaedheal
meeting that he would not have participated in the election campaign
were it not for 'the distressing scenes which he witnessed during the
turmoil last year when the mills were shut down and the whole district
was threatened with starvation'.[312] Fearing that the absence of a strong
Government could easily bring about such conditions again, he asked
families and workers to support Cumann na nGaedheal. In Youghal,
the Sinn Féin candidate David Kent was severely heckled by a local
clergyman, 'who referred to the promise of reconstruction before the
country if the Republicans were returned and suggested a visit should
be made to Crompane, Enisk and Killeagh bridges which would furnish
typical examples of Republican methods'.[313] Archbishop Gilmartin of
Tuam hoped for the return of a strong Cumann na nGaedheal government which would rescue the country from the effects of Republican
'anarchy, terrorism and commercial ruin'.[314] One of the few priests
who campaigned for Sinn Féin, John O'Keeffe CC Castletown, Co.
Wexford, blamed the Treaty for 'the lamentable condition of the
country', criticised the government for giving money to Trinity College,
'the training ground for snobbery', and sought votes for the Republican
candidates 'out of respect for the murder of Mellows'.[315]

The intensely partisan nature of the clerical contribution to the
election campaign, particularly the repeated suggestion by bishops and
priest that voters had a moral obligation to support Cumann na
nGaedheal, inevitably provoked a reaction. One thoughtful Republican
layman, P.F. Little, suggested in a letter to Archbishop Byrne that
'Christ never commissioned any of His apostles or disciples to go forth
as election agents'. Little was especially troubled by Bishop Morrisroe's

[311] *The Irish Times*, 27.8.23.
[312] Ibid., 22.8.23.
[313] *Irish Independent*, 20.8.23.
[314] Ibid., 6.8.23. The anxiety of Churchmen to ensure the return of the Government
to power is suggested in the lists of nominators and seconders of candidates. In
Cavan, for example, the three Cumann na nGaedheal candidates and one
Independent were proposed by priests, one of whom also proposed the Labour
Party candidate. The Republican candidate had no priest among his sixty
proposers. *Anglo Celt*, 25.8.23. In Leitrim-Sligo, one of the Cumann na nGaedheal
candidates was proposed by eight priests. No priest appears among the list of
those who proposed the five Republican candidates. *Roscommon Herald*, 25.8.23.
[315] *The Irish Times*, 14.8.23.

claim that if a Sinn Féin majority were to be returned in 1923 the country would face a repetition of 1922. Little wondered, whether, in the event of a Republican victory, the Free Staters would, 'repudiating all democratic doctrine, denounce the electorate, the very electorate they themselves had appealed to as justifying their war upon the Republic'. Would the Free State, he enquired, 'then turn upon the electorate, if it give preference to the Republic and rise in blood and fire against the Republican electorate?' Little feared that if 'the electorate is to be rolled round in a bath-chair by Dr Morrisroe and such', the will of the people would be in danger of being extinguished.[316] He need not have worried. The Republicans, at any rate, were not extinguished, winning 44 seats against 63 for Cumann na nGaedheal, a result which must have disappointed many Churchmen as much as it did Duhig of Brisbane, who told Cosgrave that 'it gave us rather a shock'. Duhig saw it as 'proof of the unreliability of the people as a whole in matters of national concern'.[317]

Table 4: Percentage of total vote won by parties in 1923. Seats won in brackets

Cumann na nGaedheal	Sinn Féin	Labour	Farmers	Independents
39.0 (63)	27.4 (44)	10.6 (14)	12.1 (15)	10.9 (14)

Table 5: Clerical involvement in Elections 1923–1933: Declared Clerical support for candidates

	Cumann na nGaedheal	Sinn Féin	Fianna Fáil	Pro-Treaty Independents/ Farmers	Independent Republicans
1923	113	6	–	–	–
1925 By-Elections	59	2	–	–	–
1927 June and September	188	–	22	4	2
1932	81	–	29	1	–
1933	99	–	100	4	–

[316] P.F. Little to Byrne, August 1923, DAA. Byrne may not have taken the letter very seriously. The Archbishop's secretary wrote a marginal comment on Little: 'Son of Judge Little – poet, eccentric – a well-known figure in Dublin – wore a sack over his clothes for penance.' He was a brother of P.J. Little, a Civil War Republican who became a Fianna Fáil cabinet minister.

[317] Duhig to Cosgrave, 23.7.24, NAI, S 1369/21. For an analysis of the results of the 1923 General Election, see map and tables 4 and 5.

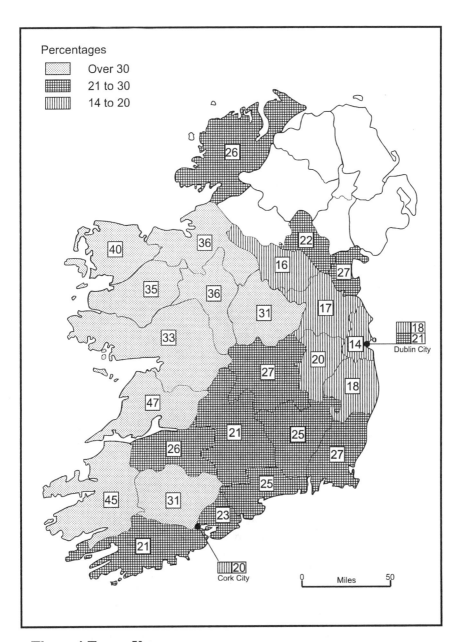

The anti-Treaty Vote, 1923

Percentage of first-preference votes cast for Sinn Féin candidates in the 1923 General Election

Adapted from: E. Rumpf and A.C. Hepburn, *Nationalism and Socialism in Twentieth-Century Ireland* (Liverpool, 1977)

VIII

Cosgrave's tenure of office from 1922 to 1932 was marked by a generally comfortable relationship with the Church leadership and a considerable body of the politically active clergy. He and his party could rely on the same level of clerical support during election campaigns as they had enjoyed in 1923; episcopal and priestly hostility to republicans and other opponents of Cumann na nGaedheal remained strong throughout the period and was slow to diminish although the twenties saw a change of heart on the part of a few disillusioned clergymen in the South and a considerable number in the North. On the whole, the Free State authorities had good reason to be pleased with the attitude of the Church, which in turn could feel well satisfied at the way in which successive administrations headed by Cosgrave showed themselves willing, even eager, to seek Church advice on 'Catholic' issues and to enforce Catholic moral and social teaching by means of legislation. Episcopal preoccupation with influences subversive of personal and social morality was strongly evident in Lenten pastorals during the twenties: late dancing, pornography, gambling and intemperance were frequently denounced. The Cosgrave Governments of the 'twenties responded to these episcopal concerns. The 1923 Censorship of Films Act made provision for a film censor with power to cut or ban films which he deemed harmful to public morality; the Intoxicating Liquor Act of 1924 reduced opening hours for public houses, while in 1927 another such Act made provision for reducing the excessive number of licensed premises in the state. The government set up a Committee on Evil Literature which reported in 1927; the Censorship of Publications Act of 1929 derived from this.[318] In educational matters, church concerns were also addressed. J.H. Whyte has claimed, on good authority, that the then Minister for Education, Professor John Marcus O'Sullivan, 'gave the bishops a written assurance that the vocational education system would stick strictly to its authorised field, and would not be allowed to develop so as to impinge upon the field covered by the denominationally-run secondary schools'.[319]

It would almost certainly be erroneous to argue that in giving legislative force to distinctively Catholic positions on such a variety of issues, Cosgrave and his party were submitting to episcopal dictation or bowing to political necessity. As Whyte points out, 'Ministers were products of the same culture as the bishops, and shared the same values.

[318] See J.H. Whyte, *Church and State in Modern Ireland*, 1923–1979 (Dublin, 1980), pp. 24–39.
[319] Ibid., p. 38.

There was only one Protestant in the government, Ernest Blythe, and his austere Ulster outlook seems to have fitted in well enough with the Catholic puritanism of his colleagues. All the other members of the government were Catholics – several of them, including Cosgrave himself, known as fervent Catholics – and they were probably just as ready as any bishop to see that traditional standards were maintained.'[320] Kevin O'Higgins, Minister for Home Affairs, was, perhaps, the most vigilant member of the Executive Council in this regard. He was described by Compton Mackenzie as a Savanarola, by his biographer, Terence de Vere White, as 'a man to whom religion was the inspiration of life'[321] and by himself as a crusader 'against greed and envy and lust and drunkenness and irresponsibility'.[322] He was prepared to incur widespread unpopularity in attempting to restrict opportunities for drunkenness. The moral and social evils associated with the excessive availability and consumption of alcohol were regularly emphasised by Churchmen throughout the 'twenties in Pastorals and sermons. O'Higgins was as responsive as any churchman to the dangers with which a liberal drinking regime confronted Irish society. He needed no ecclesiastical prompting to take stern legislative action. He was alarmed to discover that there was a publicans' licence in the Free State for every 200 persons, men, women and children.[323] His 1927 Intoxicating Liquor Bill, which 'caused more commotion in the country than did Mr de Valera's agitation about the Oath', reduced the number of public houses and the hours of opening.[324]

In his personal life, Cosgrave manifested many signs of Catholic piety. In 1925, we find him writing to Archbishop Byrne that 'It is with deep joy and gratitude that I received Your Grace's kind letter enclosing the Apostolic Brief according me the cherished privilege of maintaining a private oratory in my house at Beechpark'.[325] In the

[320] Ibid., p. 36.
[321] *Kevin O'Higgins* (Dublin, 1966), p. 175.
[322] O'Higgins to Army Inquiry Committee, 12.5.24, Mulcahy Papers UCDA, PT/C/21. Recent research has established that O'Higgins succeeded in combining the role of public champion of strict Catholic morality with a less exacting view of conventional moral standards as these might have applied in his own case. During the final three years of his life, although married with a young family, he had an intense, obsessive affair with Lady Lavery, the record of which has survived in a number of frank, uninhibited letters, See Sinéad McCoole, *Hazel, A life of Lady Lavery, 1880–1935* (Dublin, 1996), pp. 118–35. It was perhaps fortunate for the Cumann na nGaedheal administration that this relationship did not come under the notice of the Irish bishops at a time when adherence to the Catholic teaching on marriage was a token of political, as well as religious, orthodoxy.
[323] O'Higgins Memo, 24.1.25, NAI S4251A.
[324] D. O'Sullivan, *Irish Free State*, p. 189.
[325] Cosgrave to Byrne, 12.2.25, Byrne Paper DAA.

same year, the *Irish Catholic Directory* announced, following the visit of the Irish Pilgrimage to Rome, that 'the Holy Father has been pleased to confer upon Mr Cosgrave . . . a Knighthood of the Order of Pius IX. The Holy Father was also pleased to send a magnificent autographic photograph of himself to Mr Cosgrave along with the decoration'.[326] More mundane manifestations of the close bonds subsisting between the representatives of religion and those of the State are to be found in surviving correspondence between bishops and government representatives. In early 1923, Bishop O'Sullivan wrote to the Minister for Home Affairs, Kevin O'Higgins, recommending a friend of his, a former Crown Solicitor, as State Solicitor for County Kerry. While O'Higgins pointed out in a reply signed by Patrick McGilligan, then his Secretary, that 'political considerations leave open no other course than to dispense with the services of all Crown Solicitors', he forwarded the Bishop's recommendation to the Law Officer 'for his consideration when filling the resulting vacancies'.[327]

Other correspondence suggests an intimacy and identity of interest between bishops and statesmen. In 1923, Bishop Hallinan of Limerick was troubled by rumours, subsequently acknowledged by him to have been unfounded, that Catholic Primary School teachers might no longer be trained in Catholic Teacher Training Colleges, and would instead be obliged to attend university. Hallinan believed that Professor Timothy Corcoran of UCD and Professor Alfred O'Rahilly of UCC were advocates of the proposal which would, as he and other bishops saw it, have consequences detrimental to the religious formation of Primary School teachers. Hallinan confided his concerns to T.M. Healy, the Governor-General, who immediately took steps to allay his worst fears. Healy had been reliably assured that Corcoran and O'Rahilly were 'such profound Catholics that neither would pursue any educational policy which they thought prejudicial to religion'. He believed that 'nothing which can largely overturn or prejudice the position favoured by Your Lordship is likely to occur'. A recent issue of the *Catholic Bulletin* had dealt with the teacher-training issue, taking a stand which reflected the same concerns as Hallinan felt. Healy's comment on the *Bulletin*, a journal strongly supportive of the anti-Treaty cause, is that of one committed defender of the Free State to another. 'The curious zeal', he remarks, 'to assert the bishops' position as regards Catholic educational rights in the *Bulletin*, compared with its complete disregard for their teachings re the present disorder, makes an instructive contrast and for me shrills a note of insincerity in

[326] *ICD*, 1926, p. 592.
[327] P. McGilligan to O'Sullivan, 19.1.23, KYDA.

that organ's position'.[328] Close personal collaboration between a bishop and a government minister is apparent in a letter written in 1925 by Patrick Hogan, Minister for Agriculture, to Bishop O'Doherty of Galway.[329] 'Please do not thank me', Hogan tells O'Doherty, 'for any trouble I have taken regarding your brother's case'. O'Doherty had also written to congratulate Hogan on the recent Boundary Settlement. The latter provided the bishop, an outspoken adversary of anti-Treaty politicians, with a reasoned defence of the financial aspects of the Agreement and made a slighting reference to de Valera's discomfiture which can only have pleased O'Doherty: 'It was the first time he condescended to come down from patriotism to economics and the results are not exactly satisfactory from his point of view'.[330]

In general, bishops and government ministers wrote to each other in tones of mutual encouragement in their common pursuit of the consolidation and advancement of Cumann na nGaedheal. In 1929, when Seán Mac Eoin contested the Leitrim–Sligo by-election, Bishop Fogarty, whose disapproval of de Valera and all he stood for was reinforced by the passage of time, wrote to congratulate him on his success. Mac Eoin's reply might have been written to a party organiser. He draws attention to what he sees as dishonest campaigning on the part of Fianna Fáil. He tells Fogarty that thirty TDs of that party were sent to Leitrim to promise that 'if their candidate was elected the farmers of Sligo–Leitrim would get a three years moratorium on their land annuities. This was promised in the personal canvass but not publicly off any platform and was most difficult to answer or contend with.' Notwithstanding this, he was happy to report, 'the poor farmers of Leitrim gave us a majority. They were splendid. The towns of Sligo, Mohill and Carrick-on-Shannon were bad for us.'[331] Fogarty

[328] T.M. Healy to Hallinan, 25.3.23, LKDA. Healy found Hallinan's strongly pro-Treaty 1923 Pastoral 'most consoling and finely expressed'.
[329] O'Doherty had been translated to Galway following the death of Bishop O'Dea in 1923.
[330] Patrick Hogan to O'Doherty, 17.12.25, GDA. 'The real advantage of course', Hogan wrote, 'is the removal of Clause 5. We had undertaken liability, subject to a set-off, for a debt which increased between the years 1914 and 1920 from £800,000,000 to £8,000,000,000, and I think it was quite on the cards that we would have been let in for £40,000,000 or £50,000,000 under Arbitration. Moreover, we were in the very awkward position that any reduction in taxation which we might arrange here would make our case worse under Clause 5. We are now the only country in Europe without a substantial National Debt . . . Now that these two clauses [5 and 12] are out of the way the Free State is absolutely safe, and we have got a chance at last. On the other hand, Craig's difficulties are only beginning'.
[331] Seán Mac Eoin to Fogarty, 13.6.29, KILLDA.

must have been more pleased with a letter he got from Hogan, who, apart from providing a sensible analysis of rural population trends, indulged Fogarty with comments on de Valera and Lemass of the kind he himself was fond of making. Hogan was amused that at the 1928 Ard Fheis of Fianna Fáil de Valera was no longer talking about blasting the North out of the way but had adopted the new policy of 'forgetting the North and joining Fianna Fáil'. Lemass was also 'learning sense': when a delegate urged large expenditure for the relief unemployment, Lemass replied that the people could not afford the extra taxation necessary. Fogarty no doubt allowed himself an ironical smile when he read that 'There was not a word about a Republic' at the Ard Fheis.[332]

Keeping bishops fully informed in this way about government thinking on policy matters and doing them the honour of entering into these matters in such detail were ways of ensuring their continuing support. Another was to ask their advice when confronted with urgent legislative issues in which both Church and State might properly be thought to share an interest. One such issue was divorce, which presented acute difficulties for Cosgrave soon after independence. Before independence, Irish residents could obtain a divorce by means of a private member's bill enacted by the Parliament at Westminster. In post-Treaty Ireland, the sovereign power in this matter, as far as Free State residents were concerned, passed to the Parliament in Dublin.[333] Cosgrave's AttorneyGeneral, Hugh Kennedy, believed that 'we should make provision for divorce bills for those who approve of that sort of thing'.[334] Cosgrave wrote to the Archbishop of Dublin asking him to bring the matter before the bishops at their Maynooth meeting on 9 October 1923; the episcopal response was unambiguous.

[332] Patrick Hogan to Fogarty, 5.1..28, KILLDA. Hogan answered the Fianna Fáil argument that many more people should be settled on the land: 'They [Dr Ryan and others] pretend to think that the conditions here in the country in 1840 were ideal, and they point out that in 1840 we had a population of seven or eight millions. We could of course have the same population living again in the 1840 conditions, that is to say, conditions that exist today in Carraroe, Connemara or in Belmullet, County Mayo. The land of this country will not support more than ten or twelve per cent in addition to the people who are on it, but if properly worked will support them at a far higher standard of comfort and they will have money to spare which will go back into circulation to help industry and distribution. The hope for a big increase in population should not be based on a policy of reverting agriculturally to the 1840 standards but rather on a policy aimed at finding non-agricultural industry for the population which is surplus to the present requirements of agriculture and distribution'.
[333] See D. O'Sullivan, *Irish Free State*, pp. 161 ff.
[334] Hugh Kennedy to E.J. Duggan, 12.3.23, NAI S 4127.

A resolution passed by the hierarchy declared that 'it would be altogether unworthy of an Irish legislative body to sanction concession of such divorce [with a right to remarry] no matter who the petitioners may be'.[335] The divorce problem became an urgent one when three private bills for divorce came before the Oireachtas Joint Committee on Standing Orders. The Committee propounded no solution, and the matter was shelved until February 1925 when Cosgrave carried a motion in the Dáil preventing even the introduction of Bills of Divorce *a vinculo matrimonii* and asking the Senate to concur in this. The Chairman of the Senate, Lord Glenavy, ruled that a motion such as that carried in the Dáil could not be moved in the Senate, since it would be a violation of the Constitution and of the Standing Orders. In an effort to avoid a serious conflict between Dáil and Senate and to achieve the object desired by the Dáil, Senator Douglas tabled a motion which provided that Bills of Divorce would have to be read a first time in each House before they were further proceeded with in the Senate.[336] The motion was carried by fifteen votes to thirteen; ten Senators did not vote, eight of these being Catholics. Theoretically, there was provision for Divorce Bills as a result of the Douglas motion, but its practical effect would be to make their passage impossible, given the Catholic majority in the Senate and the overwhelming Catholic majority in the Dáil.

Before taking up a position on divorce, Cosgrave had been careful to seek enlightenment from Byrne whom he interviewed on 7 February 1924. Cosgrave endearingly confessed to Bishop Downey, the Coadjutor of Ossory, that before he received Byrne's document, his knowledge of the subject was slight.[337] Byrne informed him that 'the marriage of baptised persons is governed not only by Divine law . . . but also by Canon Law' and that baptised persons include heretics, schismatics and apostates, indeed all Christians, as well as Catholics. 'The Church', Byrne pointed out, 'claims that every baptised person, by the very fact of receiving baptism, becomes subject to her laws'. He also told Cosgrave that the Church 'claims for herself the sole and exclusive right to deal with all questions . . . concerning Christian marriages', and that a valid Christian marriage cannot be dissolved.[338]

---

[335] Quoted in Fanning, *Independent Ireland*, pp. 55–6.

[336] O'Sullivan, *Irish Free State*, p. 166. For Senator Douglas's own account of the divorce controversy, see J.A. Gaughan (ed.), *Memoirs of Senator James G. Douglas (1884–1954): Concerned Citizen* (Dublin, 1998), pp. 111–22.

[337] 'I was a child', he told Downey, 'so far as my information and knowledge of the subject was concerned'. Cosgrave to Downey, 21.9.25, NAI S 4127.

[338] The document, headed 'Catholic Teaching on Marriage', is in the Byrne Papers, DAA. It is undated, but Cosgrave acknowledged its receipt on 4.3.24. 'I

When Cosgrave spoke in the Dáil in February 1925 on his own motion to prevent the introduction of Divorce Bills in the future, his comments reflected what he had learned about the divorce question from Byrne's document. 'The majority of people of this country', he declared, 'regard the bond of marriage as a sacramental bond which is incapable of being dissolved. I personally hold this view. I consider that the whole fabric of our social organisation is based upon the sanctity of the marriage bond and that anything that tends to weaken the binding efficacy of that bond to that extent strikes at the root of our social life'.[339]

The management of the divorce problem by Cosgrave illustrates the nature of the relationship between the Church and the Free State government. Here the Church was the mentor and Cosgrave the willing pupil, and one of the most significant policy decisions of the decade was made on foot of advice confidentially supplied by a senior member of the hierarchy and accepted without question. Cosgrave's unimpeachable Catholic orthodoxy in the matter of divorce did not, however, preserve him and his party from the wrath of some clergymen. A serious problem arose for Cumann na nGaedheal when one of its Senators, Peter de Loughrey, failed to vote in the division on the Douglas motion. Although the purpose of this motion was to make it impossible in practice for anyone to obtain a divorce in Ireland, some churchmen interpreted it as a sinister move in a game to introduce divorce gradually and by stealth. In a letter to the *Kilkenny People*, de Loughrey's local newspaper, James Doyle, Vicar-General of the diocese of Ossory, claimed that 'according to the opinion of those best qualified to form a correct estimate of its purport, the Freemasons devised this insidious motion in order to have an opportunity of again raising a divorce question when, as they have declared, they have sufficiently educated public opinion and created a favourable atmosphere in the Senate'.[340] In Doyle's eyes this was bad enough, but worse still was the fact that Senator de Loughrey, although present in the precincts of the House, did not cast his vote against the Douglas motion. Archbishop Harty of Cashel was also displeased, accusing de

[338] *cont.* do not', he told Byrne, 'anticipate any difficulty whatever in the matter of a correct interpretation [i.e. the one Byrne had provided] or action by Catholic members of the Oireachtas. The crux of the whole business is how the Committee [the joint Committee on Standing Orders] can best decide to put the matter before the two houses. It is on this that we are all experiencing the real difficulty'. For an incisive account of the 1925 controversy and other aspects of divorce in Ireland, see David Fitzpatrick, 'Divorce and Separation in Modern Irish History', *Past and Present*, no. 114, February 1987, pp. 172–96.
[339] *Dáil Debates*, 1925, 10, 155–9.
[340] *Kilkenny People*, 8.9.25.

Loughrey 'of having abstained without urgent reason from voting against the Douglas resolution'.[341]

Bishop Downey of Ossory had come to the conclusion that de Loughrey was a less than satisfactory Catholic who did not deserve Cumann na nGaedheal endorsement in the Triennial Senate election of 1925. Downey was aware that Cosgrave had written a letter in support of the de Loughrey's candidacy and that this letter had been freely circulated in Kilkenny. Realising that Cosgrave's recommendation was bound to exercise a significant influence on the electors, Downey wrote to him to convey the surprise of the bishop and priests of Ossory at the support so publicly given by him to a candidate who had failed to cast his vote on so important and issue of Catholic principle as divorce.[342] In his letter to Cosgrave, Downey did not advert to the fact that de Loughrey has earlier written to a local newspaper pointing out that he regarded divorce as 'utterly out of the question and quite foreign . . . to Irish notions', and the Douglas motion, far from advancing the cause of divorce, as 'rendering the passing of the Divorce Bills more difficult'.[343] In his reply to Downey, Cosgrave declared himself satisfied that de Loughrey would oppose divorce and would vote against affording facilities for it; he too believed that the Douglas motion was not conceived with a view to facilitating divorce. 'I am very much pained', he told Downey, 'that the Bishops [344] and priests of Ossory should be surprised at my action in recommending Mr de Loughrey as a candidate. I value most highly their good opinions. I should very much like to retain their confidence. My knowledge of the circumstances of the case satisfies me that I was justified in making the recommendation to the electorate to support Senator de Loughrey's candidature'.[345] Harty and the bishops and priests of Ossory were not the only clergymen troubled by the implication of the Douglas motion. In a letter read in the churches of the Cork diocese of 13 September 1925, Bishop Cohalan invoked the treatment of the divorce issue by the Senate as a reason for urging Catholics not to vote 'for any candidate who is likely to support an un-Catholic measure or proposal in the Senate.' Cohalan claimed that 'a

[341] Harty's comment is quoted by Bishop Downey in a letter to Cosgrave, 19.9.25. NAI S 4127.
[342] Downey to Cosgrave, 17.9.25, NAI S 4127. At the Triennial Election of 1925, de Loughrey was one of eleven outgoing Senators who failed to secure re-election. O'Sullivan, *Irish Free State*, p. 598. He was, however, elected to the Dáil in September 1927.
[343] *Kilkenny Journal*, 3.9.25.
[344] He was referring to Bishop Brownrigg and his Co-Adjutor, Downey.
[345] Cosgrave to Downey, 21.9.25, NAI 4127.

certain number of Protestants' had been 'endeavouring, in the name of civil right, to force on us Catholics legislation or permission of divorce with the right to re-marry'.[346]

IX

In 1925, apart from the Senate elections, there were local elections and several by-elections. In all of the campaigns associated with these, clergymen played a significant part. Following the resignation of nine Cumann na nGaedheal TDs in protest at the Government's handling of the Army Mutiny, by-elections were held on 11 March in seven constituencies: Carlow–Kilkenny, Cavan, Dublin North, Dublin South, Leitrim–Sligo, Mayo North and Roscommon. In these contests, Cumann na nGaedheal enjoyed considerable success; seven of their candidates were returned as against two Republicans.[347] In some constituencies, priestly election workers were numerous and their contributions often lively. Roscommon afforded a notable instance of the mobilisation of formidable clerical forces on the Cumann na nGaedheal side. Six priests were present at the Selection Convention at Strokestown; very many more acted as Chairmen of meetings and as platform speakers. Intemperate language and personal abuse were features of many speeches. Canon Cummins, 'the esteemed and patriotic pastor of Roscommon' argued that Cumann na nGaedheal offered the only hope for 'peace and order and security and less taxes and more prosperity and honest, Christian, and God-fearing living'. On the other side were 'de Valera and his crowd of Republican fanatics'. Cummins urged his listeners to 'Vote out those pests. Vote out the vanity of the biggest political criminal whose baneful shadow ever crossed the face of Ireland. Put a silencer on the Spaniard. Does anyone deny that de Valera is out for himself and not for Ireland?'[348] Bishop Morrisroe sent a statement to a Cumann na nGaedheal meeting in Ballaghadareen suggesting that the defeat of the Government would be 'a suicidal act' on the part of the electors, as it would mean that 'the country would return to a state of confusion with a repetition

---

[346] *ICD*, 1926, pp. 584-5.
[347] The successful Cumann na nGaedheal candidates were: T. Bolger, Carlow–Kilkenny; J.J. O'Reilly, Cavan; P. Leonard, Dublin North; T.P. Hennessy, Dublin South; M. Roddy, Leitrim–Sligo; M. Tierney, Mayo North; M. Conlon, Roscommon. The successful Republican candidates were: O. Traynor, Dublin North and S. Holt, Leitrim–Sligo.
[348] *Roscommon Herald*, 7.3.25. Cummins referred to J.J. O'Kelly the Republican candidate as 'the man who, when the fight was on, ran away', the man 'who went through Australia and America maligning the priests and bishops of Ireland'. Ibid.

of the horrors through which the people had recently passed'.[349] At
Four Roads, there was an interesting clash between Republican
idealism and priestly pragmatism. The local curate, John Keane,
played the role of heckler at a meeting addressed by Jack O'Sheehan
of Dublin, who had been stressing the need to uphold the Republic. 'I
tell you', Keane remarked, 'it doesn't matter one halfpenny what flag
is above us as long as we are prosperous . . . Why would we be worrying
about the flags and the rest of it. Give us plenty of money'. O'Sheehan
professed to be shocked by such a basely materialistic view of politics:
'The most virulent anti-clerical agitator that ever stood on a platform
in France never uttered anything so damning against the clergy as that
which has issued from your lips just now . . . You, their pastor, whose
duty is to teach them the higher things in life. You ought to be heartily
ashamed of yourself.' A newspaperman observed that at this point
'the audience burst into cheers that lasted fully a minute'.[350] The
Republican candidate J.J. O'Kelly protested that Canon McDermott of
Elphin had debased the pulpit 'to the level of a political platform for
the purpose of denouncing me as an enemy of the Church'.[351] While
O'Kelly was addressing a meeting, Canon Cummins shouted that he
was there 'to face the lies of the speaker'. 'He [O'Kelly] is a liar',
said Cummins . . . 'He said I owned 400 acres of grabbed land and I
say he is a liar'.[352]

Father Michael O'Flanagan, the single clerical participant in the by-
election campaigns on the Republican side, readily matched Canon
McDermott and Canon Cummins in abusive rhetoric, much of it
directed against bishops and fellow priests for their extreme political
partisanship. O'Flanagan deplored attempts 'that were being made in
Sligo and Leitrim to turn churches into political meeting places by
making stupid, ill-informed political speeches from the altar'. He
believed that 'the rank and file of the Irish people could easily drive
politics out of the Church and until they drive them out of the Church
they would never be a happy or a free people'.[353] O'Flanagan's uncompromising speeches understandably attracted the wrath of politically
motivated Western priests working in the Cumann na nGaedheal
interest. During the North Mayo campaign there was a dramatic
interlude at Callow, where Father Walter Henry, the Parish Priest of
Swinford, told O'Flanagan to remove his clerical collar and advised

[349] *Westmeath Independent*, 14.2.25.
[350] *Roscommon Journal*, 28.2.25.
[351] Ibid.
[352] Ibid.
[353] *Westmeath Independent*, 28.2.25.

the people not to listen to him; he also referred to him as 'a priest without a bishop'. O'Flanagan retorted that it was men such as Henry who were responsible for the loss of 80,000 Irish lives in the Great War.[354] O'Flanagan and the two anti-Treaty candidates for Leitrim–Sligo, Holt and O'Beirne, were addressing a meeting in Cliffoney when five carloads of Cumann na nGaedheal supporters from Sligo town attempted to stop the proceedings. They were routed by Republicans who were present. It was later claimed that the intruders from Sligo had been paid five shillings each by a prominent Sligo priest, whose brother, a policeman in Cork, had been shot by the IRA.[355] Several meetings presided over by priests in the West of Ireland ended in violence. Michael Connolly PP told a Cumann na nGaedheal meeting at Curry that 'Judas Iscariot did great work and then went wrong. So did Frank Carty [Republican TD for Leitrim–Sligo]'. The priest's hint that Carty might have been implicated in two murders led to clashes between rival factions.[356] When John McGauran, CC Ballintrillick, was emphasising how much was at stake in the election, a man in the crowd called him a traitor; a supporter of Cumann na nGaedheal struck the man a blow in the face.[357] Charles O'Donoghue, CC Kinlough, claimed that people from Sligo and Donegal had to come to a Cumann na nGaedheal meeting in North Leitrim armed with sticks hoping to send government supporters home 'with broken heads'.[358]

In the three West of Ireland constituencies, Leitrim–Sligo, Mayo North and Roscommon, priests had an overwhelming influence on the conduct and tone of the Cumann na nGaedheal campaigns. In Ballymote, Co. Sligo, Thomas Quinn, PP Ballymote, one of the leading organisers for the party, made a case for the priesthood as the authentic voice of the people in public affairs. He believed that 'the unswerving, unpurchasable, fidelity of the Irish priest to the Irish people' had won for the clergy the right to be their political advisers. He believed that the historians of the present crisis would applaud the electors in 'following the lead of your duly accredited guides who are true to the trust reposed in them, and in not allowing yourselves to be led astray by renegades and traitors, knaves and tricksters, who are false to every trust, law, and honour'. Following the guidance of the priests meant choosing Cumann na nGaedheal, representing 'ordered, settled, stable government' and rejecting Republicanism with

[354] *Irish Independent*, 2.3.25.
[355] J. McGowan, *In the Shadow of Ben Bulben* (Manorhamilton, n.d.), p. 276.
[356] *Irish Independent*, 21.2.25
[357] Ibid., 2.3.25.
[358] Ibid. 14.3.25.

its 'anarchy, red ruin, and destruction'.[359] Supporting Cumann na nGaedheal was also an affirmation on the part of the electors that they wished to reinforce their traditional attachment to the clergy, the great majority of whom regarded voting for the government candidate as a moral duty. In Carlow–Kilkenny, Bishop Foley nominated the Cumann na nGaedheal candidate, priests presided at all the principal meetings, and six priests accompanied the Countess of Desart, the Earl of Ossory, and the Mayor at Cosgrave's rally in Kilkenny.[360]

The Senate election campaign in 1925 gave many Western priests an opportunity to display their loyalty to Cumann na nGaedheal and at the same time to demonstrate their political power and manipulative skills. On 23 August, a convention was held in Sligo at which representatives of all the major pro-Treaty groups were represented: Cumann na nGaedheal, the Farmer's Union, the Licensed Vintners, the Transport Union, the National Foresters and the Hibernians. The eight priests present were regarded as ex-officio delegates. The purpose of the Convention was to draw up a panel of Senate candidates for Connaught who would be deemed worthy of recommendation to the electors of the province. One of the leading candidates before the Convention was Alec McCabe, one of the nine deputies who had earlier resigned from the Dáil on the Army issue. The eight Sligo priests at the Convention were determined that McCabe should not be endorsed. To accomplish their aim they took control of the machinery of the convention. Canon Butler, seconded by Anthony Timlin, PP Skreen, proposed Canon Quinn as chairman. Standing orders were drawn up by a group headed by another priest; the same group decided on the list of Senatorial candidates to be approved by the Convention. When McCabe's name was proposed and seconded Canon Quinn declared that 'Mr Alec McCabe was not a supporter of the Government and therefore could not be allowed to be put forward at that meeting'; Quinn also ruled that further discussion of the matter was out of order, despite the fact that many of the delegates admired McCabe 'as a man who did everything possible to defend the Treaty when it was menaced'. In the eyes of the priests, however, McCabe had challenged the principle of majority rule and betrayed those who had elected him to the Dáil as a pro-Treaty deputy. As Canon Quinn put it, 'not to use the Constitution for the ends for which it was designed would be folly. To try to overthrow it would be treachery of the deepest dye, and to put revolutionaries [like the Army Mutineers] in power would be establishing a tyranny which – in the interests of

[359] *Roscommon Herald*, 14.3.25.
[360] *Nationalist and Leinster Times*, 28.2.25; *Irish Independent*, 9.3.25.

the general public – God forbid.' This, he told the Convention, was why the priests were asking the delegates to nominate only supporters of the Treaty and the Government for the Senate.[361]

Many priests in positions of power and influence acted in defence of the Government and the Treaty whenever these were challenged. Education Committees throughout the country were largely subject to clerical control. Teachers employed by Technical Education Committees were obliged to take the Oath of fidelity and allegiance to the Constitution of the Irish Free State and of fidelity to the British monarch, as required by Article 4 of the Treaty. Many of these teachers had conscientious objections to doing this. The refusal of Republican teachers to fulfil the requirement brought them into conflict with clerical members of the Committees. In Mayo, the struggle between refractory teachers and clerical upholders of the laws of the Free State was particularly intense. Canon D'Alton regarded the conduct of such teachers as a challenge to the authority of the State. When one of the teachers' unions urged that teachers should not be required to take the oath, D'Alton interpreted this as meaning that 'we should be asked to do away with the Government'.[362] Clerical members of the Mayo Committee penalised Republican teachers by refusing to sign orders authorising the payment of salaries, in the belief that on the issue of the Oath, as D'Alton put it, 'these fellows will not be in a hurry to challenge our authority in the future'.[363] The resolution of the problem involved the payment of arrears due to teachers on condition that they promised to take the Oath for future payments. Another clerical grievance was that Republicans were lowering the moral tone of co-educational night classes by their attendance.[364]

At Ballinamuck, Co. Longford, in September 1928, a memorial was unveiled to mark the 130th anniversary of the battle fought at that place between the Irish insurgents with their allies the remnants of the French Killala expedition, and Government forces. Two leading Longford clergymen, John Keville, PP Drumlish, and Joseph Guinan, PP Ardagh, used on occasion to celebrate the achievements of the Free State. The Battle of Ballinamuck, Keville suggested, 'was fought in defence of Faith and Fatherland . . . to retrieve a lost cause – lost in 1798, but triumphant in 1928'. Canon Guinan, in the course of 'a

---

[361] There is a detailed report of proceedings at the Sligo Convention in the *Roscommon Herald*, 29.8.25. In the election for the Senate, neither McCabe nor Professor Mac Einrí of University College Galway, the candidate most favoured by the priests, was successful.
[362] *An Phoblacht*, 26.3.26.
[363] Ibid.
[364] *An Phoblacht*, 19.3.26.

scholarly memorial oration' declared that the celebration of the battle was to be free of 'political significance or political propaganda', by which he meant that he did not want those Republicans who were present to exploit Rebellion of 1798 as a Republican event. When J. J. Killane, a Fianna Fáil TD, asked the people present to renew their 'Republican pledges', Keville ordered him to sit down. Another Fianna Fáil TD, M.J. Kennedy, pointed out that the official clerical and Cumann na nGaedheal position was that the country was free, that what Tone died for has been achieved and that 'now there was peace for ever more in a free and independent Ireland'. Keville did not silence Lord Longford who made the most Republican speech of all. 'It was the motto of Wolfe Tone' he declared, 'to break the connection of the English execrable Government, and the people united in the name of Ireland in the cause. In honouring the memory of those who died, let us take a lesson from their sacrifice. They were not afraid to give up all for their country and it is for us to use our every effort to make it a great nation. Dia Saor Éire.'[365]

In April 1927, with an Irish General Election pending, Austen Chamberlain, British Secretary of State for Foreign Affairs, received a report from Odo Russell, British representative at the Vatican, outlining details of Papal policy on the involvement of priests in politics. Early in June, a copy of this report was transmitted to the Irish Minister for External Affairs 'for the information of His Majesty's Government in the Irish Free State'. Russell's report was based in an article in the Vatican official journal *Acta Apostolicae Sedis*. In the article, affirmative answers were given to two questions: whether the chief local ecclesiastical authority had the right and duty of forbidding political activity to ecclessiastics who did not conform to the instruction of the Holy See, and whether any ecclesiastics who did not obey could be proceeded against in accordance with the provisions of Canon Law of the Church. Russell conceived this to be consistent with the policy of Pius XI, 'namely to withdraw the Church as far as possible from the political arena so that Catholics shall unite on a religious and moral basis and cast their voting strength in favour of whichever of the existing political parties seems most likely to advance the aims of the Church'. Russell thought it certain that 'any tendencies on the part of the clergy to mingle politics and religion beyond the prudent limits laid down by the Holy See will be severely suppressed'. The Vatican

---

[365] *Roscommon Herald*, 15.9.28. M.J. Kennedy complained that such control as the clergy were able to exert at events such as that at Ballinamuck ensured that the word 'Republican' was banned 'even when commemorating the memory of the greatest Republicans in Irish history'.

formula with respect to those limits, he explained, 'is that the Church only comes into direct contact with politics when politics threaten the altar or the family, and the present Pope seems to be particularly desirous that this rule shall be universally enforced'.[366]

In 1927 neither Fianna Fáil, founded by de Valera on 26 May 1926 as a vehicle for constitutional republicanism, nor what remained of Sinn Féin, was likely to pose a threat to the altar or the family, and Cumann na nGaedheal and Labour were soundly Catholic in outlook. There seemed no pressing need, then, in the light of the Vatican formula, for the Church as a body, or the clergy as individuals, to engage in political activity. The two General Election campaigns of 1927, however, suggest either that the mass of Irish Clergy and their bishops were unaware of the Pope's thinking on the subject of the clergy in politics or that they chose to disregard it. In the constituency of Galway alone, at least 33 priests played an active part in the June campaign, all but five of them supporting Cumann na nGaedheal.[367] The great majority of those participating acted as platform orators, presided at meetings or nominated candidates. A striking feature of the election was the number of clergymen in every constituency who proposed candidates, the great majority of these belonging to Cumann na nGaedheal. Bishop Morrisroe of Achonry and Bishop Keane of Limerick nominated their local Cumann na nGaedheal candidates.[368] The priests who participated in the June 1927 campaign were generally more restrained in their language than most of them had been in 1925. Canon Cummins, the most colourful campaigner in the Roscommon constituency in 1925, refused to take part in the June 1927 campaign because the Cumann na nGaedheal Selection Convention at Strokestown had not nominated Michael Brennan, the candidate who most enjoyed the confidence of the priests of the county.[369]

The Strokestown Convention showed that the role of priests as leaders of the Cumann na nGaedheal party could be a thankless one. The editorial writer in the *Roscommon Herald* believed that Canon Cummins 'and a number of other priests in the county had made possible the victory of the Government candidate in the by-election two years ago'. In 1927, however, the same writer pointed out, 'respected priests in this county were denounced as political acrobats and glugger-headed administrators, and these were only the mildest of the epithets slung about'.[370] At the Strokestown Convention, Cumann

[366] Odo Russell to Austen Chamberlain, 18.4.27. S 5463 NAI.
[367] *Connaught Tribune*, 23.4.27; 30.4.27; 21.5.27; 28.5.27; 4.6.27.
[368] *Irish Independent*, 2.6.27.
[369] *Roscommon Herald*, 21.5.27.
[370] Ibid.

na nGaedheal opponents of priestly paternalism had their way, but many of the offended clergymen retaliated by supporting Brennan, their Convention nominee, as an Independent candidate at the General Election. This meant that some of the bitterest exchanges of the Roscommon campaign were not between the government and Fianna Fáil candidates, but between rival groups supporting the government. One angry priest, B.J. Neilan, declared that the Strokestown Convention was 'not only rigged but rotten'. Such practices, he argued, had killed the Irish Party 'and to-day, unless steps are taken to prevent the nominees of such Conventions being elected, the Cumann na nGaedheal organisation will be destroyed for the same reason'.[371] The active support of the clergy helped to secure Brennan's election. Another priest of the Elphin diocese, Canon Butler of Sligo, was less worried about Republicanism, already, to his mind, 'a spent force' than about 'the unwarranted attacks that are being made on the Government by its own supporters', in particular Thomas Johnson, Leader of the Labour Party. Johnson, Canon Butler declared, 'should not forget that in his addresses to Labour he is speaking to a crowd that does not usually go to the trouble of thinking and therefore are apt to take him literally, and come away with the idea that the Government has been a failure and should not receive further support from them'.[372] Elsewhere, however, the clergy tended to concentrate their attacks on de Valera and what they saw as the baneful legacy of Civil War Republicanism. John Crowe, Adm. Athlone, believed that if the country was in a bad way 'with no money in the Banks', this was not the fault of the Government; all had been spent repairing buildings, bridges, and railways destroyed by the Republicans.[373] Republican abstentionism and fondness for political abstractions were common themes. When de Valera spoke at a meeting in Ennis, Canon O'Kennedy remarked, 'the hungry sheep attended and looked up and were not fed . . . the sheep got nothing but a discussion of oaths . . . It was time for de Valera to come down from the clouds and get behind the plough'.[374] Dean Innocent Ryan of Cashel wondered why people should vote for men 'who would not enter the Parliament of the State to help the farmer, the labourer, and the artisan'.[375]

[371] Ibid., 4.6.27.
[372] Ibid., 5.2.27.
[373] *Westmeath Independent*, 4.6.27.
[374] *Irish Independent*, 6.6.27.
[375] Ibid. The Fianna Fáil policy of abstentionism also worried Bishop Cohalan. In a letter to the press he urged that voters should ask themselves how peace and public order might be maintained. 'Would it contribute to public order', he asked, 'if a number of elected members were to continue the policy of abstention from the Dáil?' *Irish Independent*, 9.6.27.

X
==

The results of the June 1927 election were bitterly disappointing for
Cumann na nGaedheal, which lost 16 seats. Fianna Fáil won 44, Sinn
Féin five, and Independent Republicans two. This meant that the
combined Republican groups had four seats more than Cumann na
nGaedheal. The 55 deputies representing Labour, Farmers, National
League and Independents held the balance of power. On the first day
of the new Dáil, Fianna Fáil deputies were denied admission because
they refused to take the Oath. This led de Valera to prepare a petition
which, if signed by 75,000 people, would force the government to
hold a referendum on the abolition of the Oath in accordance with
Article 48 of the Constitution. The assassination of Kevin O'Higgins
on 10 July as he walked to Mass provoked the Government to introduce
three Bills: a Public Safety Bill establishing non-jury courts with military
members; an Electoral Amendment Bill requiring all parliamentary
candidates to declare their willingness to take the Oath if elected, and
a Constitution Amendment Bill, removing from the Constitution the
provision for the kind of referendum envisaged by de Valera. The
latter now decided that if his Party was to survive politically he would
have to lead it into the Dáil. Neither the Government nor the Clerk of
the Dáil presented major obstacles to this move; the Fianna Fáil TDs
were allowed to sign the register without reading or repeating the
words of the Oath or without having these read to them. De Valera
argued that the declaration he had to sign had 'no binding
significance in conscience or in law', that it was merely 'an empty
political formula which deputies could conscientiously sign without
becoming involved, or without involving their nation, in obligation of
loyalty to the English Crown'.[376] De Valera's dealings with the Oath
left him open to serious criticism. As Ronan Fanning points out,
opponents as well as neutral observers 'might well ask why what could
be treated as an empty formula in 1927 could not have been so
treated in 1922'. But, as Fanning also observes, 'however tortuous the
reasoning, it enabled Fianna Fáil to save face . . . What mattered was
not the ritual of reservation but the reality of participation'.[377]

---

[376] Longford and O'Neill, *de Valera*, p. 255. The implication in de Valera's
comment, that the Oath was exclusively a matter of 'loyalty to the English
Crown', is misleading. The Oath prescribed for members of the Dáil in Article 4
of the Treaty required that they swear 'true faith and allegiance to the
constitution of the Irish Free State', and fidelity to the British monarch 'in virtue
of the common citizenship of Ireland with Great Britain'.

[377] Fanning, *Independent Ireland*, p. 98. When circumstances forced de Valera to
     n his abstentionist policy and subscribe the Oath, or, as he himself would

On 16 August, a motion of No Confidence in the Government, moved by the leader of the Labour Party, Thomas Johnson, was defeated only on the casting vote of the Ceann Comhairle. The Dáil was dissolved and another election called for 15 September. In this campaign, the clergy were, if anything, more active than ever, and most of those who spoke or issued statements concentrated their fire on de Valera and his party for what they regarded as their unethical behaviour with regard to the Oath. They were not alone in finding de Valera's conduct unacceptable. Ten days before the Election, an *Irish Times* editorial made a stern moral pronouncement on the matter. 'A moral issue', the writer declared, 'confronts the electors. Mr de Valera and his party entered Dáil Éireann at the price of a perjury which took the country by surprise. We must presume that the successful candidates of Fianna Fáil will repeat the perjury when the new Dáil meets in October.'[378] Speaking in Limerick a few days before the poll, Cosgrave suggested that 'in a Christian country there can be no countenance for organised perjury . . . There is no moral difference between political oath-breaking and any other sort of oath-breaking – an oath dishonoured in Dáil Éireann and an oath dishonoured in a police court or in the conduct of private business'.[379]

In 1926, a few months after the foundation of Fianna Fáil, Bishop Cohalan hinted that the party should embrace parliamentary politics, since 'there would never be a sense of stability while a considerable number of deputies remained out of the Dáil'.[380] The events surrounding the process of entry into the Dáil and de Valera's glosses on this deeply shocked some priests, and seemed to confirm many others in their reservations about the moral credentials of Republicans. In 1922, the Bishops had taken a strong moral stand against what was being done in the name of Republicanism; in 1927 a great number of clergymen revived the moral issue, placing it at the centre of the

have it, sign the book, he was obliged to make the embarrassing admission that what he and his colleagues did was 'contrary to all our former actions and to everything we stood for – contrary to our declared policy and to the explicit pledges we gave at the time of our election'. *The Nation*, 27.8.27.

[378] *The Irish Times*, 5.9.27. In April 1948, giving evidence in the Sinn Féin Funds Case, de Valera placed on record his version of the events surrounding the Oath. He was annoyed that Mr Casey, Counsel for the plaintiffs, had declared that the members of Fianna Fáil, on entering Dáil Éireann in 1927, had taken the Oath. De Valera wanted the Court to understand that this was a gross misrepresentation. 'I want to say', he told the Judge, 'that no such oath was taken'. He gave the Court an account, running to about two thousand words, of how he and his followers contrived to enter the Dáil without taking the Oath. *Sinn Féin Funds Case*. De Valera's evidence 21.4.48. Sections C3–C5. NAI.

[379] *The Irish Times*, 12.9.27.

[380] *ICD*, 1927, p. 610.

election debate. Dean Ryan of Cashel argued that by staying out of the Dáil de Valera and his followers had disenfranchised one-third of the electorate for five years, but they had used 'unholy means' to redress that situation. He wondered if Ireland had become 'so blasphemous and so irreligious that it would permit any party to prostitute a sacred oath in order to get into the Dáil'.[381] Monsignor John O'Doherty, addressing a Cumann na nGaedheal meeting at Murlog, Donegal, declared that 'men who took an oath to Almighty God, meaning to break it, told a lie to Almighty God and are guilty of perjury and blasphemy', and that 'the conduct of Mr de Valera and the Fianna Fáil deputies is therefore a grave breach of the moral law.' No good, he believed, could come to a party which has been guilty of such a grave public scandal'.[382] Addressing Cosgrave's meeting a Kilkenny, James Doyle, Dean of Ossory, claimed that 'whoever aims a blow at sanctity of the oath aims a terrible stroke at the foundations of the State'.[383] Patrick Fitzgerald, PP Clogheen, Co. Tipperary, thought it would be a serious thing for the people of the country if they voted for men 'who will for the second time go into the Dáil and take a false oath'.[384] Patrick Murray, CC Caltra, Co. Galway, said it was sad to think that they had in Catholic Ireland as leader of a political party a man 'declaring a solemn oath to be an empty formula',[385] while Michael Scanlan, PP The Spa at Churchill, Co. Kerry, 'warned his hearers of the danger to morals of such a pernicious doctrine'.[386] Some priests advised their parishioners that it would be morally unsafe to vote for Fianna Fáil. Thomas O'Hara, PP Ballycroy, Co. Mayo, addressed his congregation from the steps of the altar. Having reminded his listeners of 'the destruction caused by Republicans during the civil strife', he claimed that prior to the assembly of the Dáil after the June election, 'Mr de Valera objected to the Fianna Fáil party attending the Votive Mass which was celebrated in Dublin'.[387] Patrick Neary, PP Ballyforan, Co. Roscommon,

---

[381] *The Irish Times*, 13.9.27.

[382] *Irish Independent*, 13.9.27. A clerical apologist for de Valera, P.J. Dunning C.C. Woodford, Co. Galway, said that Fianna Fáil 'had taken an oath that was odious and distasteful, but they had done so to save the country'. He assured his listeners that 'if Mr. de Valera and his party had not taken the Oath, the people, instead of listening to speeches, would now be listening to the rattle of rifles'. *Irish Independent*, 13.9.27. It is unlikely that de Valera would have approved of Father Dunning's statement that he had actually taken the Oath.

[383] *The Irish Times*, 31.8.27.

[384] *Irish Independent*, 12.9.27.

[385] *Irish Independent*, 14.9.27.

[386] *The Kerryman*, 10.9.27.

[387] *The Irish Times*, 13.9.27. When O'Hara made this claim, Michael Kilroy, an election candidate for Mayo, 'rose from his seat in the body of the church and

was a good deal less flattering about the religious and moral standing of de Valera and his party. In an election speech from the altar of his church, he said that a vote for Cosgrave's party was 'a vote for Almighty God' while de Valera was 'Lucifer head of the Ku Klux Klan and for the destruction of religion'. When Gerald Boland, the local Fianna Fáil TD, was making a victory speech, Canon Neary called him a coward, a perjurer and a 'Dublin corner-boy'.[388]

As well as characterising the Fianna Fáil party as morally disreputable and as an enemy of religion, clerical speakers stressed the destructive role played by its leading members in the history of the recent past, with the clear implication that those responsible for 'five years of turmoil and ruin', as a Kerry priest put it,[389] might well pursue the same course in the future. Patrick McAlpine, PP Clifden, believed that de Valera's policy 'was now the same as it was in the past – plunder, devastation, and ruin'.[390] James Monaghan, PP Crusheen, Co. Clare, wondered what the people had gained by the robbery of banks, the hundreds of early graves, the broken roads and bridges; the way to 'prevent the repetition of such horrors, in this generation at least', was to vote for the Government candidates.[391] Stephen Slattery PP Quin, Co. Clare, believed that 'the people have to decide whether they will entrust Mr Cosgrave's government with completing the work of building up the nation or hand over the country to be destroyed by the destroyers'.[392] P.J. O'Beirne, Adm., speaking to a Cosgrave rally in Sligo, pictured Kevin O'Higgins, 'from his home in high heaven', looking down on the Irish people 'with hopes that rise and fall according as they ascend the mountain of righteousness and truth, or according as they follow the delusive trail that leads to moral degeneracy

said that the statement made by the Rev. Father O'Hara was incorrect, adding that he, as a member of the Fianna Fáil party, was present at all the private meetings at which Mr de Valera presided in Dublin prior to the celebration of the Votive Mass, and that no such thing had occurred as had been stated by Father O'Hara'. However, Patrick Belton, TD, who had severed his connection with de Valera, claimed that he had forced de Valera to have the Fianna Fáil TDs at the Votive Mass after his former leader had at first opposed the idea. See *Irish Independent*, 1.8.27.

[388] See *An Phoblacht*, 8.10.27; *Westmeath Independent*, 1.10.27.
[389] P.J. Brennan, PP Castlemaine, at a Cumann na nGaedheal meeting in Tralee, said that 'the so-called Fianna Fáil party had swallowed the oath and it did not choke them. If de Valera had taken that course five and a half years ago many a mother would have been spared from weeping over the loss of her son, and many a man whose career had been blasted would now be a contented citizen of the Free State'. *The Irish Times*, 8.9.27.
[390] *Irish Independent*, 10.9.27.
[391] *The Irish Times*, 14.9.27.
[392] *Irish Independent*, 7.9.27.

and national dishonour'.[393] Some priests found a continuity between
what they conceived to be the infamous Republican past and its
dishonourable present. Patrick Tracy of Kilmurray, Co. Cork, implied
that de Valera was implicated in the death of Collins, and suggested
that he 'has to his credit all the long list of outrages perpetrated by his
followers . . . Moreover, he has crowned it all by teaching his
followers to trample on the sacred character of an oath.'[394] Jeremiah
Cohalan, PP Bandon, told a meeting of Government supporters that
de Valera's claim to be 'for peace' might well be 'like an oath, an
empty formula', and wondered where 'the dark man' was when
Collins was killed.[395] Cornelius McNamara, PP Castlecomer, Co.
Kilkenny, believed that de Valera's abuse of the Oath was an even
more serious crime than those committed by him and his followers
during the Civil War. 'Great through the destruction was . . . [it] was
merely material destruction, which can be built up, but the teaching
that a solemn act of worship is only an empty formula has a million
times more destructive effect on Ireland.'[396]

It does not appear that such profound misgivings about Fianna Fáil
and its leader were shared by all churchmen, especially the more
senior ones. Dermot Keogh has pointed out, for example, that
Cardinal O' Donnell was considerably relieved at the decision of
Fianna Fáil to become a fully constitutional party.[397] Members of the
hierarchy refrained from public comment on de Valera's activities

[393] *Roscommon Herald*, 10.9.27.

[394] *Cork Examiner*, 14.9.27.

[395] *An Phoblacht*, 17.9.27. Cohalan answered his own question. 'Ask the people of
Béalnabláth and they will tell you. There was a scowling face at a window
looking out over that lonely valley and de Valera could tell you who it was.'
Ibid. Cohalan's attempt to link de Valera with the killing of Collins in an ambush
at Béalnabláth on 22 August 1922 may be seen as part of the popular demonisation
of de Valera as the evil genius of Irish politics. The tradition that de Valera had
some part, shadowy or substantial, in the death of Collins had a recent airing in
Jordan's film on Collins. It has no basis in fact. Hopkinson (*Green Against Green*, p.
176) points out that at the same time Collins was making his fateful journey
through West Cork, de Varera was meeting the Cork Republican leader Liam
Deasy near Béalnabláth and urging peace negotiations.

[396] *Irish Independent*, 12.9.27. There is little evidence of responses from Fianna Fáil
candidates, either during or after the elections of 1927, to the widespread and vehement clerical denunciations of the party as a vessel of unrighteousness. Thomas
Mullins, the West Cork TD, declared that Fianna Fáil candidates 'did not object
to honourable statements on the platforms by clergy of any denomination, but they
did object to the unfair methods used in this campaign on and off the pulpit'.
Southern Star, 24.9.27. The relative temperance of this comment may have reflected
Fianna Fáil anxiety to avoid unproductive controversy with the Church.

[397] D. Keogh, *The Vatican, the Bishops*, p. 113.

in relation to the Oath, despite attempts to influence them in this direction.[398] With the emergence of Fianna Fáil as a democratic party advocating such unexceptionable ideas as the development of a social system affording to every Irish citizen the opportunity ' to live a noble and useful Christian life',[399] and as a possible future government, Church leaders began to reappraise and adjust their attitudes to Republicanism and to become less publicly involved in party politics. The Cumann na nGaedheal administration that emerged from the September 1927 election was not a strong one, depending as it did on minority support for its survival.[400]

There were times when the Cosgrave administration during the later twenties might have hoped for more emphatic support from the hierarchy on important public issues than it actually received. Joseph Walshe, the Secretary of the Department of External Affairs, expressed official disappointment at the episcopal response to the murder of Kevin O'Higgins. In a memorandum, Walshe complained that Archbishop Byrne's denunciation of the murder was inadequate, making it appear that it was merely 'a crime against Catholic piety'. Byrne, Walshe believed, 'had a magnificent opportunity to use all the weight and majesty of the Church to uphold the supreme power of the State, and he has left the people believing that there is no difference between murdering a man set up by the people as one of their rulers and murdering a private citizen'.[401] Two years later, Cosgrave's minister for Justice, James Fitzgerald-Kenney, tried to get the bishops to condemn the perpetrators of a number of murders, one of them of a policeman in Co. Clare. He wrote letters to the bishops in whose dioceses the crimes had occurred. He was worried that there were people who said that these killings were not murders and others who

---

[398] Ibid. See p. 248, note 15.

[399] For this and other aims of Fianna Fáil, see Moynihan, *Speeches*, p. 131.

[400] See Cornelius O'Leary, *Irish Elections, 1918-1977* (Dublin, 1979), p. 25. Although Cumann na nGaedheal had increased its share of the vote from 27.4 to 38.7 per cent and won 61 seats, Fianna Fáil's share increased from 26.1 to 35.2 per cent, and the party won 57 seats.

[401] Walshe Memorandum, 18.7.27. Patrick McGilligan Papers, C5(B) UCDA. Walshe would have found the condemnation of O'Higgins's murderers by Father McInerny, the Dublin Dominican publicist and historian, much more satisfactory. McInerny argued that the slaughter of O'Higgins was in keeping with 'the criminal methods of an uncivilised age' which Irish people had never outgrown. 'For nearly 2,000 years', he wrote, 'we have been a lawless people, strangely and perversely addicted to crimes of bloodshed and rapine'. The question, as he saw it, was 'how to rid ourselves of this infamous tradition'. 'The answer', he believed, 'is that Church and State must co-operate, firmly and perseveringly, in the endeavour to Christianise and civilise us'. *The Irish Rosary*, August 1927.

sought to find 'excuses and palliations' for them. He was disappointed not to have noticed by way of response 'that universal expression of horror and detestation which one might naturally expect to find'. He was convinced 'that a denunciation of this class of crime by an entire bench of bishops would go far to check a recurrence of them and might possibly prevent entirely such a recurrence'. Other such crimes, he had reason to suspect, were in contemplation. Fitzgerald-Kenney clearly believed that he might move Bishop Fogarty to action by suggesting that one of the murders was 'all the worse coming upon the eve of our centenary of Catholic Emancipation'. This, as it turned out, was one of the circumstances that influenced the bishops to avoid commenting on the 'dangerous conspiracy to murder in the State' which so worried Fitzgerald-Kenney. Archbishop Byrne wrote the comment on his copy of the Minister's letter that at 'just this time of national joy and religious fervour', the kind of condemnatory pronouncement sought by Fitzgerald-Kenney 'would come badly from the Bishops'.[402] In 1931, the bishops proved much more accommodating when the government asked them to condemn the activities of left-wing Republicans, who could of course be represented as subversive of both Church and State. In this matter, the bishops realised that they and the government shared a common interest and a common concern, as their Pastoral Letter of 18 October 1931 made clear. They condemned the IRA explicitly and Saor Éire by implication; they were convinced by the 'growing evidence of a campaign of revolution and communism which, if allowed to run unchecked, must end in the ruin of Ireland, both soul and body'.[403]

On several issues, such as divorce and pornography, the Government responded positively to Church appeals that it support Catholic doctrine and Catholic moral values. Tardiness on the part of Cosgrave's government in meeting Church demands could sometimes provoke rebukes from clerical publicists. One such was the Dominican Father McInerny, who imagined the Pope, during a private interview, asking Cosgrave why he permitted the minds of Irish people 'to be poisoned, and their morals to be degraded, by all kinds of pernicious publications'. McInerny imagined Cosgrave telling the Pope that his government had done nothing 'to save the Irish people from the mental and moral poison of pestilent journalism and prurient novels', that they had failed 'grievously' in their moral duty to do so, but promising to deal urgently with the matter. McInerny was pained that

---

[402] Fitzgerald-Kenney to Byrne, 17.6.29. DAA. Fitzgerald-Kenney wrote similar letters to Fogarty and Archbishop Gilmartin.
[403] *Irish Independent*, 19.10.31.

after six years in office, the government had not acted to discharge a grave moral obligation; this, he held, had serious implications 'for the individual conscience of each member of the Ministry, as well as for the individual conscience of each of their supporters'.[404] The Censorship of Publications Act of 1929 met most of the McInerny's concerns.

Towards the end of 1930, the Mayo Library controversy involved Cosgrave in a dispute, not of his making, with powerful clerical forces in the West of Ireland. The Local Appointments Commission appointed Letitia Dunbar-Harrison, a Protestant and a graduate of Trinity College, Dublin, to be County Librarian of Mayo. The Commission had been established in 1926 with the task of making most of the appointments to the local government service with the object of eliminating the corruption and favouritism traditionally associated with such appointments. Local authorities were obliged by law to implement the recommendations of the Commission. The Mayo Library Committee, consisting of a Catholic Bishop, five Catholic priests, a Christian Brother, a Protestant rector, and four laymen,[405] decided by ten votes to two not to accept Miss Dunbar-Harrison, because her Protestant background and education rendered her unfit to know, as Dean D'Alton put it, 'what books to put into the hands of the Catholic boys and girls of this country'.[406] Mayo County Council refused to repudiate the decision of its Library Committee; one member of the Council referred to 'Trinity culture' as not being 'the culture of the Gael' but as 'poison gas to the kindly Celtic people'. He also suggested that with the appointment of a Protestant librarian 'at the command of the bigoted and Freemason press, Catholic rights are ignored'.[407] The government dissolved the County Council and appointed a Commissioner in its stead; he installed Miss Dunbar-Harrison as librarian. Several priests in Mayo, among them the Chancellor of the diocese of Killala, made it clear that they would not tolerate a Protestant librarian; the cause of an unsuccessful Catholic candidate for the post was championed by Dean D'Alton.[408] Charges of corruption were levelled at the Local Appointments Commission for failing to appoint this candidate, Ellen Burke, who according to her clerical advocates, had the double advantage of not being a Protestant and of knowing Irish, unlike Miss Dunbar-Harrison. Cosgrave felt obliged to meet the charges of corruption against the Commission by

---

[404] *The Irish Rosary*, August 1927.
[405] Details of the proceedings may be found in *The Catholic Bulletin*, January 1931, pp. 1–18.
[406] Ibid.
[407] *Connaught Telegraph*, 3.1.31.
[408] *The Standard*, 13.11.30; *Irish Independent*, 31.12.30.

sending an emissary, Sir Joseph Glynn, to Archbishop Gilmartin of Tuam; inspection of the confidential report of the Commissioners by Cosgrave on the advice of the Attorney General revealed that Miss Burke knew very little Irish and that Miss Dunbar-Harrison had been fairly chosen. The Archbishop was made aware of these facts by Glynn.[409] Cosgrave appeared to take a firm stand on the library issue when he told the Archbishop of Tuam that 'to discriminate against any citizen – or exercise a preference for any citizen – on account of religious belief would be to conflict with some of fundamental principles on which this state is founded'.[410] A month after he wrote this, however, Cosgrave conceded to Gilmartin that Miss Dunbar-Harrison would be transferred from Mayo 'within a certain time' and that the Mayo County Library would again be allowed to function.[411] The library episode shows the lengths to which Cosgrave was prepared to go to allay ecclesiastical misgivings about him or his government on matters of common concern to Church and State. A comment he made at the time on his experiences at the hands of the bishops suggests what J.J. Lee calls 'the somewhat distant relationship between government and hierarchy.'[412] Cosgrave found it 'embarrassing for the government to learn the bishops' views for the first time through a condemnatory pastoral letter, or a chance conversation between a bishop and a minister. The government feels it has a grievance here.'[413]

There is evidence, however, that not all of the bishops, nor even the Mayo priests, felt as Archbishop Gilmartin or Dean D'Alton did about the operations of the Appointments Commission. Archbishop Harty of Cashel advised the Government to maintain the integrity of the Commission, while Bishop Fogarty's position was that the government had behaved quite properly in the Mayo library affair, merely acting

---

[409] NAI S 2547 A.

[410] Cosgrave to Gilmartin, 11.3.31, NAI S 2547 B.

[411] See report of meeting between Cosgrave, John Marcus O'Sullivan and Archbishop Gilmartin, 15.4.31, NAI S 2547B. Cosgrave's assurance to Gilmartin was to remain confidential; this was to avoid embarrassing the government. Early in 1932, Miss Dunbar-Harrison took up duty at the Military Library in Dublin. *The Irish Times*, 7.1.32.

[412] *Ireland, 1912–1985. Politics and Society* (Cambridge, 1989), p. 166.

[413] Memo, 'returned by Professor O'Sullivan', 34.3.31 NAI S 2547B. The Pastoral letter to which Cosgrave referred was Gilmartin's Lenten Pastoral for 1931, in which the Archbishop discussed the qualifications needed by the person in charge of 'a public library for Catholic readers'. This 'onerous position', he believed, 'should be assigned to an educated Catholic who would be as remarkable for his loyalty to his religion as for his literary and intellectual attainments'. Gilmartin dismissed the notion that librarians should be chosen from among those 'who are alien to our Faith'. TAA.

in accordance with the law. Perhaps more significantly, three priests, one of them a member of the Tuam Diocesan Chapter, attended the Cumann na nGaedheal Convention in January 1931 and spoke in favour of the Mayo appointment; their speeches could be interpreted as the repudiation of those clergymen who had been critical of the government. Father Brennan regarded the Mayo agitation as a 'storm in a teacup'; Canon McHugh called it a 'misrepresentation', and on the motion of Father Keane, seconded by Canon McHugh, the Convention gave its blessing to the Appointments Commission system as a whole and to the Mayo library appointment in particular.[414]

With echoes of the Mayo library controversy still resounding, a second, related, issue posed a more serious threat to the hitherto stable relationship between Cosgrave's government and the Church. During an interview with a government Minister, the Archbishop of Cashel told him that if the Appointments Commission chose a Protestant as a dispensary doctor in his Archdiocese, he would denounce the government, and no bishop would say a word in its support.[415] Here the Archbishop was expressing an attitude shared by many of the clergy and by those who wrote for such journals as *The Catholic Bulletin*, one of whose contributors argued in 1931 that the appointment of even a Catholic medical graduate of Trinity College to a dispensary post would represent a 'danger for the morality of our Catholic population, rich and poor'.[416] A similar outlook was even more strongly reflected by Father Malachy Brennan, CC Mantua, at a meeting of the Roscommon County Committee of Agriculture and Technical Instruction in 1929. Brennan argued that is was wrong for the government to have taken from the local Councils the power to appoint officials, since 'there were people on the Appointments Commission who belonged to . . . the freemason gang'. He mentioned the recent appointment of two non-Catholic doctors in the County. 'I am not a bigot', he declared, 'but our Church objects to non-Catholic doctors attending the sick. For that reason, in a Catholic county, it is a disgrace for anybody to send us a Protestant doctor.'[417] Some of the

---

[414] There is an account of the Mayo Convention in *The Nation*, 31.1.31.

[415] NAI S 2547 A.

[416] *Catholic Bulletin*, vol. 21, no. 2, 1931, p. 143. Dermot Keogh suggests that the author of this piece might have been Father Edward Cahill, S.J. (*The Vatican, the Bishops* pp. 270–1). Professor Keogh gives a detailed, authoritative account of Cosgrave's dealings with the Church on the issue of medical appointments.

[417] *Roscommon Messenger*, 12.1.29. Canon Cummins, Chairman of the Committee, agreed with Father Brennan's reference to Protestant doctors. Canon Butler, however, could not see 'how any man could rise to condemn the Appointn Commissioners'.

pertinent Maynooth statutes of 1927 were invoked by members of the hierarchy in support of the position taken by Father Brennan; one of these statutes imposed an obligation on the clergy to ensure that positions in the public health service should be filled only by doctors trained in conformity with Catholic ethical principles. As Cosgrave pointed out to Archbishop Gilmartin, 'we are faced with a problem arising from an apparent conflict between the discipline of the Catholic Church and the constitutional position of the state'.[418] In the end, Cosgrave rejected the notion that the Maynooth statutes should govern public appointments, or that the State should discriminate against medical graduates of 'non-Catholic' universities, whether these graduates were Catholics or not. Cosgrave contrived to enforce his view on the bishops without having to endure any further disturbance of the generally, although not uniformly, harmonious relations between this government and the Church which had been so strong a feature of his years in office.[419]

Given the traditional identity between Cumann na nGaedheal and the leadership of the Church and many of its clergy, and the trials they had endured together, it was perhaps fitting that the party should approach the 1932 General Election in a Catholic frame of mind. Its programme stressed the bonds history had created between Irish Catholicism and Irish Nationality. 'No other nation', it claimed, 'has such a tradition of suffering and sacrifice in the cause of Religion as our nation'. The people were warned that a victory for Fianna Fáil might well make Ireland 'a field for the cultivation of those doctrines of materialism and Communism which can so effectively poison the wells of religion and National traditions', while the recognition that the State had received 'from the Holy Father and the principal powers of this world'[420] would be set at naught with the collapse of that State. Cumann na nGaedheal publicists, in their anxiety to identify the party with the Church, simultaneously and injudiciously strove to create the impression that to vote for their opponents was to be seriously deficient in Catholic commitment. An extreme, though by no means unique, manifestation of this tendency is to be found in an election advertisement published in Dundalk. Here, de Valera, whose policy was

---

[418] Cosgrave to Gilmartin, 2.3.31. NAI S 2547 A.
[419] Keogh, *The Vatican, the Bishops*, pp. 168ff. explores the ways in which Cosgrave was able to induce the hierarchy to refrain from further debate on the medical appointments issue. In correspondence with MacRory, he was not above using blackmail, as, for example when he raised the possibility of attention being drawn to marriage dispensations granted by the Church and not notified to the civil authorities.
[420] *Irish Independent*, 7.2.32.

described as 'un-Irish and un-Catholic' was censured for having on more than one occasion ignored the solemn teaching of the Bishops 'on a matter within their Lordships' competency', as well as for propounding a theory on the State ownership of land opposed to Catholic teaching. To vote for Cumann na nGaedheal, on the other hand, the advertisement proclaimed, was to support the maintenance of 'Catholic principles'.[421] At this point, however, many of those committed to upholding Catholic principles seem to have believed that these would be upheld at least as effectively by Fianna Fáil. Defeat at the polls in 1932 deprived Cosgrave and his party of the ultimate formal approval for their steadfast loyalty to the Church which the Eucharistic Congress might have afforded.

While much of its propaganda in 1932 betrayed the anxiety of the Cumann na nGaedheal leadership to benefit electorally from its reputation as a Catholic party, there is some evidence that it could no longer rely on the almost unconditional support accorded to it by the generality of churchmen up to 1925 and even in most places, outside the border counties, up to 1927. In his pioneering exploration of Church-State relations during the period, Dermot Keogh has drawn attention to significant tensions between the Cumann na nGaedheal government and the hierarchy during the late twenties.[422] Fianna Fáil, vigorously projecting itself as the zealous guardian of Irish Catholic, and even episcopal, interests, cleverly exploited the awkward, and from the episcopal point of view, indelicate, arrangements made by the government to establish diplomatic relations with the Vatican. The principal motivation here was to enhance the claims of the Free State to legitimacy and to win for it the kind of prestige a papal nunciature in Dublin would undoubtedly confer. Such a policy was contrary to what many of the Irish bishops saw as their own interests and those of the Church; for many of them, Archbishop Byrne being perhaps the most adamant, the notion that a Papal Nuncio in Dublin would be an unwelcome intruder into Irish ecclesiastical affairs had almost been an article of faith since the establishment of the Free State.[423] When, in 1929, Patrick McGilligan, Minister for External Affairs, told the Dáil that the government had arranged for an exchange of diplomatic representatives with the Vatican, it transpired that he had done this without taking the advice of the Irish bishops or informing them in advance. Seán T. O'Kelly welcomed the opportunity to act as vehicle

---

[421] *Dundalk Democrat*, 13.2.32
[422] *The Vatican, the Bishops.* See especially, pp. 159–84
[423] D. Keogh, *Ireland and the Vatican. The Politics and Diplomacy of Church-State Relations, 1922–1960* (Cork, 1995), pp. 59ff

for the offended sensibilities of the bishops.[424] Other contentious matters imposed strains on Cosgrave's relations with churchmen in the early thirties. One of these arose from frustrated attempts by the Revenue Commissioners to exact what they regarded as properly due taxes from Catholic clergymen, some of whom, according to Cosgrave, were making absurdly low returns of income.[425] Cosgrave eventually resolved the problem to the total satisfaction of the clergy by suggesting that all should return a maximum income just below that on which they would begin to become liable for tax. At one point the prosecution of a priest as a tax defaulter was in prospect; Keogh suggests that the episode was unhelpful to Cumann na nGaedheal in clerical circles.[426] The Mayo Library controversy placed further considerable strain on the Church-State relations in 1930–31. Cosgrave's ultimately unsuccessful attempt to uphold a non-sectarian public appointments system led to some loss of previously warm clerical support, particularly in Mayo.[427] Fianna Fáil showed itself remarkably vigilant in taking advantage of any diminution in the enthusiasm of churchmen for Cumann na nGaedheal, offering itself as the acceptable alternative, 'a party which has behind it over half a million Catholic voters, whose personnel is almost exclusively Catholic'.[428] As Fianna Fáil and large elements of the clergy moved closer together in sympathy, the use of the 'red scare' in late 1931 may, perhaps, best be interpreted as a Cumann na nGaedheal attempt to restore its flagging relationship with the Church and to resurrect the spirit of the early twenties, when Church and Party struggled side by side against the common enemy.

[424] Dáil Debates, XXX, Cols., 820–1. 5.6.29. For further detail on this issue, see pp. 253–4, note 35.
[425] D. Keogh, *The Vatican, the Bishops*, p. 162
[426] Ibid., p. 163
[427] *Irish Press*, 2.1.32
[428] Ibid., 1.2.32

CHAPTER FOUR

AFFIRMING THE REPUBLIC

I

DESPITE THE ENTHUSIASM for the Treaty among the bishops and most of the senior clergy, a minority of secular and regular priests were not convinced of its merits. Some of these expressed their opposition from political platforms; others, working abroad as well as in Ireland, quietly afforded moral support to militant Republicans in conflict with the Free State, while others were actively involved in the Civil War as chaplains to IRA units or even as auxiliary members of such units. Thomas Browne, CC Dromore West, in the diocese of Killala, was one of the latter. A member of a Sligo Irregular Column, Matt Kilcawley of Enniscrone, told Ernie O'Malley that Browne 'at one stage came out with us and he remained out for a while. He wouldn't read the Bishops' Pastoral but he went back again [to his parish after October 1922]. He was always a staunch'.[1] Some of the circumstances of the time make it likely, perhaps inevitable, that even the most diligent enquirer will underestimate the number of clergy involved on the anti-Treaty side or sympathetic to it in various ways. The newspapers, local and national, were almost uniformly hostile to the anti-Treaty position, and were less inclined to publicise the views of Republican priests than those of their pro-Treaty colleagues. Stern episcopal hostility to Republicanism certainly inhibited many priests with Republican views from expressing these in public, but in some cases their political attitudes can be divined from diaries and private correspondence. Scattered pieces of evidence abound. In June 1922, we find M.J. Curran writing to Monsignor Hagan, Rector of the Irish College in Rome, reporting that 'a large number of the younger Maynooth graduates saved the situation for the anti-Treaty party at this election'.[2] In July 1922, Aodh de Blacam, a Republican living in

---

[1] O'Malley Notebooks, UCDA, P17C/136.
[2] Curran to Hagan, 16.6.22, Hagan Papers.

Donegal, told a Capuchin priest who held strong anti-Treaty views that 'we have only four pro-Republican priests in all the diocese [of Raphoe] and of course they are silenced while our lads are denied the Sacraments'.[3] A letter from William Kelly, CC Ballyconneely, Clifden, to Professor Michael Browne of Maynooth suggests a large concentration of Republicans among the younger clergy of West Galway. 'A big combing out among the Connemara curates is on the cards', Kelly writes in February 1923. He has heard that he is among those about to be moved for his political views, but 'would much prefer to remain entrenched in . . . the only Republican barrack in the country'.[4] What even the most extreme among the anti-Republican bishops felt, said and tried to enforce on his priests was not always reflected in their behaviour. A member of the Cork No. 1 Brigade claimed that priests in his area were 'alright in the Civil War, and some of them were quite good . . . of course they had a long history there of defying Cohalan's earlier excommunication order'.[5] On the other hand, one brigade member in North Mayo claimed that all the priests in the area were hostile to the Republican cause.[6] In July 1922, over a hundred priests attended Cathal Brugha's funeral.[7] In more settled times, following de Valera's release from jail in 1924, 'over fifty priests and at least two hundred other visitors invaded Roundstone [in Connemara] and insisted on seeing him'.[8] The largest public manifestation of clerical enthusiasm for the Republican cause was 'The Night of the Priests' at the Rotunda, Dublin, in October 1925 where on the platform to welcome Archbishop Mannix 'were eighty of the sturdy priests who have remained faithful to the indestructible cause of

[3] Aodh de Blacam to Father Canice, o.f.m. cap. 27.7.22, Desmond FitzGerald Papers, UCDA P80/736.
[4] Father William Kelly to M.J. Browne, 6.2.23, GDA.
[5] O'Malley Papers, UCDA P176/111 p.9. Seán Ó Faoláin, who was a Republican activist during the Civil War, recalls an incident from early 1923: 'One evening, somewhere in the hills, I am with a young man who is so deeply troubled by some thought or deed of commission or omission that he insists on visiting the local parish priest in his isolated presbytery. As the young man is carrying a rifle and a bandolier, and is patently an Irregular, the old priest at once refers him to his bishop's command and refuses to have anything whatever to do with him. The young man imploringly persists, until in the end the old priest relents so far as to say: "Well, *I* cannot give you absolution! But if you go down there to my curate's house . . . he might be a bit easier on you. He has a brother in the Irregulars".' *Vive Moi!*, (London, 1965), p. 162.
[6] G.E. Maguire, 'The Political and Military Causes of the Division in the National Movement. January 1921 to August 1923'. Unpublished DPhil thesis, Oxford, 1985, p. 255.
[7] *Catholic Bulletin*, September, 1922.
[8] William Kelly, CC to M.J. Browne, 11.8.24, GDA.

Irish liberty; messages of greeting from some three hundred others were piled high in front of the Secretary, Fr Thomas Burbage'.[9] Maynooth was not a headquarters of Republican sentiment. Curran, generally an accurate observer, reported to Hagan in June 1922 that 'the only anti-Treaty professors in Maynooth are the two Brownes and G. Pierse'.[10] The following table, necessarily incomplete and crude in its assumptions, records the number of clergy variously reported for their active involvement in pro- and anti-Treaty politics in 1922.

Pro-Treaty Secular Clergy	Pro-Treaty Regular Clergy	Anti-Treaty Secular Clergy	Anti-Treaty Regular Clergy
540	42	142	34

Between the approval of the Treaty in January 1922 and the outbreak of Civil War at the end of June, several priests braved episcopal hostility by appearing on Republican platforms and, in some cases, making strong anti-Treaty speeches. When de Valera and Harry Boland addressed a rally at Portlaoise in April, Thomas Burbage, CC Geashill, Co. Offaly and Peter Kavanagh, CC Mountmellick, were among the supporting speakers, both of them denouncing the Treaty, the Free State and the British connection. The Treaty, Kavanagh declared, 'would not bring them peace . . . they were assured by their leaders whom they all loved, that the Republic would come out unscathed, and De Valera would be heard of when Collins and Griffith would not'. Burbage claimed that Lloyd George was 'leading the Free Staters of to-day to smash the Republic . . . The Free Staters were not trying to make Ireland strong and England weak, but were directing all their venom and animosity against their own countrymen'.[11] Reports of these speeches troubled the local bishop, Foley, who took steps to ensure that Burbage and Kavanagh would not further pursue their careers as platform orators. He drew up a document for them to sign, the effect of which, he hoped, would be 'to prevent random talking of clergymen at public meetings'.[12] When

[9] *Catholic Bulletin*, December, 1925.
[10] The two Brownes were Michael J., Professor of Moral and Dogmatic Theology and later Bishop of Galway, and Patrick (Pádraig de Brún) Professor of Mathematics, later President of University College Galway. Garret Pierse had been Professor of Theology since 1914 and was Prefect of the Dunboyne in 1923. This was the Maynooth postgraduate school.
[11] *Nationalist and Leinster Times*, 9.4.22.
[12] Foley to M.J. Murphy, 13.5.22, KLDA. Foley was annoyed that Kavanagh had 'misrepresented the Bishops' declaration of October 1921 and even

de Valera spoke earlier in Tullamore, Burbage had also been on hand. The local Parish Priest made it clear that he did not want to see priests taking part in Republican meetings, although he did not object to their participation in Free State ones. Burbage, however, circumvented the Parish Priest's ruling by accompanying de Valera and Boland to the platform in a car driven by Patrick Smith, a Curate in Tullamore. Like Burbage, Smith had been a Republican Court Judge during the War of Independence, and was a resolute opponent of the Treaty.[13] Three priests holding strongly Republican views appeared with de Valera at a huge rally in Tralee in March 1922: Charles Brennan, CC and Joseph Breen, CC Millstreet, and W.S. Behan, CC Tralee. In a vigorous speech, Brennan declared that 'the magnitude of the meeting was proof to the world that the people of Kerry, at least, were faithful to the Irish Republic and Eamon de Valera'.[14]

Some clerical opponents of the Treaty were slower to declare their opinions publicly. Canon Robert Egan of Mullahoran in the diocese of Ardagh preferred to record his responses in his diary. He considered the Treaty 'the most tragic event in Irish history . . . the beginning of a fresh split after a glorious fight'. Two days before ratification, it appeared to him that 'The Treaty satisfied all who were opposed to Sinn Féin, the cowardly, the older section, Bishops, PPs, old men. It looked everything – just big enough to satisfy peace lovers, and too defective to satisfy those who ventured all, including life, for the cause. Probably it was meant by Lloyd George and Co. to split the people. It just did. The two that people wonder to see backing it are Mac Eoin and Mulcahy'.[15] James O'Dea, Galway Diocesan Secretary, had not welcomed the Treaty or the Provisional Government. His hostility to both intensified with the progress of the Civil War. 'A Government that murders its prisoners', he wrote to

[12] *cont.* misquoted it'. Kavanagh interpreted the 1921 declaration as an appeal from the Bishops to the British government to grant Ireland freedom 'untrammelled by any limits whatsoever'. After this, Burbage seems to have confined his political utterances to the church.

[13] *Westmeath Independent*, 22.4.22. Burbage did not take part in de Valera's meeting, but submitted a letter which was read from the platform. 'As the parish priest of Tullamore', Burbage wrote, 'has refused permission to priests to attend the Republican meeting, I am reluctantly compelled to be absent from your meeting on Sunday. Seeing that a priest presided at the Free State meeting on Sunday last, the refusal of permission is very regrettable . . . I am standing as uncompromisingly for the Republicans as I always did'. *Midland Tribune*, 22.4.22.

[14] *Kerry People*, 24.3.22. Brennan's brother, Patrick, was also a priest, and as extreme in his support of the Treaty as his brother was in his opposition to it. Information derived from Mgr Daniel Long, Tralee.

[15] Diary of Father Robert Egan, PP Mullahoran for 13.12.21 and 5.1.22. The diary was made available to me by Father Owen Devanney, Mullahoran.

Professor Michael Browne of Maynooth, who shared his Republican views, 'deserves no support, not, indeed, that it ever got much support from some of us. The last executions [of 8 December 1922] are an outrage on civilisation'. Like other priests, he was particularly sorry for Mellows. 'After Childers', he felt, 'he was the ablest of the Republicans' and 'had the clearest vision of any of them'. O'Dea did not believe that any of the four executed on 8 December would have been capable of executing a political prisoner opposed to them. Mellows, he pointed out, 'was very religious and would have become a Carmelite . . . only that Dr Magennis advised him not to give up the IRA.'[16] O'Dea was expressing a view common in the aftermath of the executions when he suggested that 'We have come to a nice pass when a gang of ex-British tommies are to be allowed without a word of protest to execute the old IRA.'[17] O'Dea, presumably, would have expected some protest from senior churchmen. Some priests with Republican leanings were worried not only about political developments in the Free State, but also about its spiritual temper. One of Browne's friends, William Kelly, CC Ballyconneely, believed that it bore a distinctly pagan complexion, and that its close ally the Church had much to answer for in this regard. 'That the name of God', Kelly wrote to Browne, 'was inserted grudgingly and even then in the most casual fashion in the Free State Constitution; that it remained for an English Methodist to protest in the name of Christianity against the immorality of reprisals;[18]

[16] James O'Dea to M.J. Browne, 15.12.22, GDA. The Dr Magennis referred to by O'Dea was Father Peter Magennis, Superior of the Calced Carmelites, and a close friend of Mellows.

[17] Ibid.

[18] The English Methodist who protested against the execution by the Free State of Republican prisoners was William Wedgwood Benn, a Liberal MP. I owe this information to Mr Tony Benn, MP. Between March and May 1922, the period of consultation and governmental consideration, Catholic bishops and Unionist leaders were consulted on the provisions of the Constitution. Only one the nine members of the Constitutional Committee, Professor Alfred O'Rahilly of University College Cork, was anxious to give the Constitution a distinctively Christian colouring, and wanted a more vigorous assertion of Catholic principles, for example an acknowledgement that 'political authority comes from God to the people', than the others were prepared to concede. Brian Farrell comments that 'O'Rahilly's attachment to a more specifically Christian concept of the State was obviously out of tune with the strongly secularist tone of the committee'. Farrell suggests that a draft supported by O'Rahilly and James Murnaghan, Professor of Roman Law and Jurisprudence at University College Dublin, but not seriously considered by the government, 'appears to have had some influence on de Valera's thinking' in the planning of the 1937 Constitution. See B. Farrell, 'The Drafting of the Irish Free State Constitution', *The Irish Jurist*, 1970, vol. v, no. 1, pp. 115–40; vol. v, no. 2, pp. 343–56; vol. v, no. 3, 111–35

that a Protestant peer was the first public man to demand that Divine assistance be invoked in the Twenty-Six County Parliament;[19] that the only people who appear to realise what the charity of Christ stands for are the laity – all these are facts which force one to the conclusion that there is a criminal lack of vigilance and duty somewhere in this Catholic land'.[20]

II

With the outbreak of Civil War, several bishops were obliged to deal with government complaints that priests were actively involved in the hostilities in the Republican side, and not always merely as confessors. During the fighting in Dublin which followed the government attack on the Four Courts, Dominic O'Connor of the Capuchin order brought spiritual aid to the Republican garrison there. According to an official complaint made by Cosgrave to Archbishop Byrne, he did much more than this. After the surrender of the Four Courts, he was allowed by the Free State troops to go free. Cosgrave claimed that he availed of this freedom 'to join another group of Irregulars in the Hammam Hotel, thus openly encouraging, and associating himself with, the outbreak of disorder . . . he abused this privileged immunity by conveying information to the Irregulars, and otherwise assisting them in their campaign of brigandage'.[21] With the collapse of Republican resistance in Dublin, Father Dominic ministered to both sides in the Wicklow mountains.[22] Kathleen Clarke recalled that when Republican forces reached Blessington, 'it seemed occupied with a large force of IRA with some members of Cumann na mBan and Father Dominic'.[23] As a further instance of 'the abuse of sacred office for the encouragement of the forces of anarchy' Cosgrave mentioned the publication of the Diary issued from the Four Courts in the name of Father Albert, another Capuchin friar.[24] Cosgrave clearly regarded the diary

---

[19] The Protestant Peer was the Earl of Wicklow. See Donal O'Sullivan, *The Irish Free State and its Senate* (London, 1940), p. 565.

[20] W. Kelly to M.J. Browne, 6.2.23, GDA

[21] Cosgrave to Byrne, 21.7.22, DAA. Father Dominic had been a chaplain to the Allied forces in Greece, returned to Ireland in 1917 and was appointed Brigade Chaplain to the Cork Volunteers by Terence MacSwiney. He was arrested in January 1921 in Dublin and sentenced to five years' penal servitude for being in possession of seditious documents, but was released in January 1922 under the General Amnesty after the signing of the Treaty. See T. Ó Fiaich, 'The Catholic Clergy and the Independence Movement', *Capuchin Annual*, 1970, pp. 497–8.

[22] Obituary notice of Father Dominic, *Irish Press*, 19.10.35.

[23] *Revolutionary Woman*, 1991, p. 198.

[24] Ernie O'Malley, an officer in the Four Courts at the time, describes Father Albert's involvement: 'Underneath the dome, the garrison had gathered. A

as a seriously subversive document, particularly since it identified Republican anarchy with Catholic piety. 'After the Ultimatum was delivered to the Irish Republican soldiers', one entry read, 'the boys all knelt down and recited a decade of the Rosary in Irish, placing themselves and their cause under the protection of the Blessed Virgin and all the patriot martyrs of the Irish Republic'.[25] Father Albert, Cosgrave informed Byrne, also visited the Republicans in the Hammam Hotel, 'with the obvious purpose of encouraging them by his presence and approval'.[26] Both Father Dominic and Father Albert were to pay a heavy price for their intimate involvement with Republican militarism. When Father Dominic returned to Cork at the end of the Civil War, Bishop Cohalan decided that he would need to revise his theology before hearing confession again; he was asked to prepare himself for an examination in the subject before having his faculties renewed. He avoided this humiliation by going to the Capuchin Mission in America at the end of 1922.[27] Father Albert left for America in June 1924, but died in 1925.[28]

Cosgrave also drew Byrne's attention to the case of John Costello, CC St Michael and John's Church, Dublin, whom he described as

Franciscan [*sic*], Father Albert, in his brown habit . . . spoke to us. "I am going to give you general absolution boys" . . . We all knelt down. Some of the men gripped their rifles instead of joining hands: others held their revolvers. We were dedicating our weapons as well as our lives. Then he made the sign of the cross over us . . . "We'll place ourselves under the protection of the Mother of God and under the mantle of Brigid". Father Albert said then, "God bless you boys". The tears were running down his cheeks. Men stood up slowly. Some were still on their knees.' E. O' Malley, *The Singing Flame* (Tralee, 1978), p. 96.

[25] Father Albert's Diary appeared in *Poblacht na hÉireann*, 28.6.22.

[26] Cosgrave to Byrne, 21.7.22, DAA.

[27] Information given to the author by Father Nessan, o.f.m. cap., Cork. During the War of Independence, Cohalan and Father Dominic had entertained radically differing views on the theology of rebellion. In December 1920, Cohalan issued a decree of excommunication against anyone who, in the diocese of Cork 'shall organise or take part in ambushes or kidnappings'. *Freeman's Journal*, 12.12.20. According to Father Dominic, however, if such deeds were performed by the Irish Volunteers as private persons, they would, indeed, rightly incur excommunication, but since they were performing them with the authority of the Republic of Ireland, they were doing something meritorious'. See D.W. Miller, *Church, State and Nation in Ireland, 1898–1921* (Dublin, 1973), pp. 20–1. During the Civil War, Father Dominic believed that he and his fellow-Republicans were still defending the Republic, but against a new enemy.

[28] Father Albert's last letter to de Valera dated 24.1.25 is a celebrated piece of Republican piety: 'To our Beloved Chief, Eamon de Valera, President of the Republic of Ireland. From my death-bed I salute you and wish you to know that I die a citizen of the Irish Republic, unchanged and unchangeable and uncompromising in my allegiance to that Republic and to you its President'. Childers Papers, TCD, 304.

'Republican Justice of the Peace for the South City'. The Army authorities claimed that on 8 July Costello had tried to induce a detachment of government troops to lay down their arms, called them murderers, said he was ashamed of them, told them 'that they were damned for all eternity because they were shooting down men in the Four Courts fighting for a principle', and that they were doing work 'that the Tans refused to do for the British Government.' Cosgrave believed that such statements, in the circumstances in which they were made, 'were bound to have a very serious effect on the minds of young Catholic soldiers who naturally treat the words of their priests with the greatest respect'. When Father Costello was interviewed by an Army officer he acknowledged that he had paid two young men to put up posters 'to inform Republicans of facts useful to the Republic'.[29] Eugene Doyle, from an Australian diocese, but using temporary faculties in the Archdiocese of Dublin, was also reported to Byrne for giving active encouragement to Republican forces during the early stages of the fighting, insisting for example, that priests in the Pro-Cathedral 'should hear the confessions of the Irregulars in occupation of that district'.[30] In his account of the fatal wounding of Cathal Brugha, J.J. O'Kelly recalled that 'Father Eugene Doyle rushed from the street corner to render spiritual aid'.[31] Following the 8 December executions at Mountjoy, Joseph Smith, a Passionist priest at Mount Argus, was so incensed that he accused the authorities of having arranged to have Seán Hales TD murdered by the CID on the previous day in order to provide an excuse 'to murder the men who are fighting for the Republic'. He made this claim in the course of reading the Dead List and praying for Hales. When a member of the congregation interviewed the Rector, he told her he was powerless to stop Smith from having his say. The incident was reported to Byrne by Kevin O'Higgins.[32]

During the fighting in Dublin, the outstanding clerical figure on the Republican side was Patrick Browne, who had held the Chair of Mathematics in Maynooth since 1913. At the Maynooth prize-giving in June 1916, Browne had caused offence to the authorities by encouraging students in their loud cheering 'for the rather unlikely nationalist

[29] Cosgrave to Byrne, 12.7.22, DAA. Acknowledging Cosgrave's letter, Byrne promised that 'the matters you have brought under my notice will receive my most serious consideration'. Byrne to Cosgrave, 23.7.22. Byrne appears to have rusticated Father Costello, who soon appeared as Curate in Ashford, Co. Wicklow.
[30] Ibid.
[31] *A Trinity of Martyrs* (Tralee, n.d.), p 90.
[32] O'Higgins to Byrne, 20.12.22, DAA.

hero', Bishop O'Dwyer of Limerick.[33] As a result of his activities in the East Cavan by-election in 1918, the Trustees felt it necessary to issue a special mandate to the Maynooth staff: they needed the permission of the College President as well as the local bishop before taking an active political role.[34] The terms of this mandate do not seem to have had an effect on Browne's behaviour during the post-Treaty period. In July 1922 Cosgrave complained that he had 'visited the Irregulars in the Swan Public House, York Street, for the purpose of hearing their confessions' and that 'this action could not fail to be interpreted by them as implying complete approval of their unlawful activities'.[35] Browne would certainly not have objected to Cosgrave's suggestion that he approved of the activities of the Republicans, although he would not have considered these activities 'unlawful'. Whatever action Byrne may have taken in response to Cosgrave's complaint did not deter Browne from causing further serious embarrassment to the government in February 1923, when, in the course of an army raid on Sinn Féin headquarters in Suffolk Street, he was arrested in the company of Mary MacSwiney, Mrs Tom Clarke and Kathleen Barry. The circumstances of the raid were communicated by Army Headquarters to Monsignor MacCaffrey, President of Maynooth College, who in turn reported them to Cardinal Logue and the other College Visitors. The arresting party searched Browne, who 'styled himself Father Perry of Maynooth', and the three women, and claimed to have found an assortment of subversive documents, one of these 'inciting to the murder of the Governor-General' in retaliation for having 'confirmed the sentences of execution' of Republicans. The soldiers also found a copy of a poem by Browne signed Pádraig de Brún 'apparently extolling the action of five deserters from the National Forces who took a machine gun and rifles

[33] See P.J. Corish, *Maynooth College, 1795–1995*, 1995, p. 304. Browne (1889–1960) born in Grangemockler, Co. Tipperary; studied at Rockwell, Clonliffe (MA and travelling Studentship, Royal University 1908) at Paris (DSc Sorbonne 1912); ordained priest of diocese of Dublin 1913; Professor of Mathematics and Natural Philosophy in Maynooth, 1913; studied at Göttingen 1913–14; a brilliant mathematician, but with deep literary interests; translated classic works from Greek, French and Italian into Irish; for many years chairman Dublin Institute for Advanced Studies; resigned 1945 to become President University College Galway.

[34] Ibid. Corish reports that Browne was reprimanded by the College Visitors for his part in Griffith's East Cavan campaign. In reply, 'he said he had attended no meeting without the permission of the local parish priest, and had at once obeyed the bishop's ruling to desist, but that he nevertheless admitted the impropriety of what he had done, and promised it would not happen again'.

[35] Cosgrave to Byrne, 21.7.22, DAA.

from Baldonnell camp'. The Army authorities also alleged that Browne gave the officers 'a considerable amount of very unpriestly abuse', and that it was this fact that led to his being detained. He also embarrassed the authorities even further by refusing to sign the undertaking normally required of all suspected prisoners before being released.[36] In the circumstances, the Maynooth authorities felt obliged to take action against Browne. The College Visitors instructed the President to draw his attention to the Statute which forbade any official of the College 'to take public part in politics by presence, word or writing without the approbation of the President'. He was also told to comply strictly with the statutes 'as long as he remained an official' of Maynooth. This caution, issued in June 1923, had, however, a diminished significance for Browne since the formal end of the Civil War had come on 24 May.[37] The ending of the Civil War did not mark the end of Browne's active association with Republicans and Republicanism. In September 1924, along with Mary MacSwiney and young Erskine Childers, he kept vigil all night outside the walls of Beggars Bush Barracks following a rumour that the Free State authorities had decided to exhume the body of Childers and take it to a secret destination.[38] Browne was justifiably regarded by Republicans as a valuable accretion to their cause. He wrote a stirring commemorative poem on the executions of 8 December which enjoyed a wide circulation,[39] while his fame as a scholar and obvious intellectual distinction carried their own weight. C.S. Andrews regarded his open adherence to the Republican side as 'a great help to our morale'. He

[36] McCaffrey to Logue, 2.3.23, DAA. The undertaking Browne refused to sign involved a promise 'not to take up arms against the Parliament elected by the Irish people or the Government responsible to that Parliament, nor support in any way such action, nor interfere with the property or persons of others'. Ibid. Dermot Keogh, in his account of the incident, derives his information about the subversive documents and the 'very unpriestly abuse' from a letter written by a Dublin priest to Hagan. Keogh concludes that since one of his informants, Col. Dan Bryan, who was in the arresting party, was unaware of either the documents or the abuse, this would indicate that reference to these was merely 'priestly gossip'. *The Vatican, the Bishops and Irish Politics* (Cambridge, 1986), pp. 107, 260. The army report to McCaffrey, however, makes it clear that the 'priestly gossip' referred to by Keogh was based on solid fact.
[37] Corish, *Maynooth College*, p. 304.
[38] See M.A. Childers to de Valera; de Valera to M.A. Childers, 16.9.24. Childers Papers TCD, 287. According to Mrs Childers, the decision was revoked at the last minute through fear of the effect on the national feeling. De Valera told her that he was watching to see 'whether we can get something effective done through publicity'.
[39] The poem 'December the Eighth', was first published in *Poblacht na h-Éireann*, Christmas 1922. True to Republican tradition, Browne mingles patriotism with Catholic piety.

also drew attention to another purpose priests like Browne served at a time when many Republicans must have felt demoralised in the face of episcopal and priestly disapproval of their cause and their activities. 'His mere presence as a priestly sympathiser with the Republicans', he claimed, 'assuaged any feeling of guilt I might have had as a result of abandoning my allegiance to the Church, although I would not have imagined myself going to him for confession'.[40] The attachment of such notable clerical sympathisers as Browne to their cause inevitably mitigated the Republicans' sense of alienation from the Church. In some Republican accounts, however, the sympathy of a priestly minority in the face of episcopal and general clerical hostility is seen as supererogatory. A Sligo IRA veteran told Ernie O'Malley that in his area, 'Pastorals had very little effect. Refusal of the Sacraments had very little effect on the men'.[41]

Outside Dublin, there were several pockets of committed Republican priests whose activities troubled both the civil and ecclesiastical authorities. The diocese of Kildare and Leighlin was home to several of these. Here, clerical Republicanism seems to have been organised and coordinated, and not simply the composite of individual opinions. The outstanding figure among the Republican clergy of the diocese was Thomas Burbage, Curate in Geashill, Co. Offaly, who had earned the respect and admiration of priests and people over a wide area for his work in the Republican Courts during the War of Independence. On Easter Sunday 1922, 'to mark the occasion of his release from Ballykinlar Internment Camp', he was presented with an address from the Bishop and priests of the diocese, paying tribute to the manner in which his 'character and judgment contributed to make these [Republican] courts respected and obeyed' and celebrating 'his work for the Irish language, the revival of Irish industries and a rebirth of a spirit of self reliance in the people'. The people of his parish presented him with 'a beautiful two-seater Morris Cowley motor car as a token of their esteem'.[42] Even before these presentations were made, however, Burbage was making speeches at Republican meetings vigorously

---

[40] C.S. Andrews, *Dublin Made Me* (Dublin, 1979), pp. 260–1.
[41] O'Malley papers, UCDA, P 17b/136
[42] *Westmeath Independent*, 29.4.22; *Offaly Independent*, 25.3.22. In 1915, Father Burbage had been an enthusiastic supporter of the National Volunteers. In March of that year he was present at a meeting in Carlow Town Hall to assist in arrangements for a review of the Volunteers in Dublin on Easter Sunday. The event, he told the meeting, would show that 'though they were a part of the great British Empire, they were prouder of Ireland than everything else in the whole of the world . . . It was an advantage, of course, to know that their men were reflecting credit on themselves and Ireland in the battlefields of France and Belgium'. *Freeman's Journal* 22.3.15.

denouncing the Treaty settlement.[43] When asked by Bishop Foley to explain, he claimed that the attack he was reported to have made on the Treaty supporters was confined to the leaders of the Treaty party 'and chiefly on the ground of having violated their oath, particular reference being made to J.J. Walsh, who said he would commit a thousand perjuries if he got value for them'. This, Foley acknowledged, was 'a most scandalous statement to be given to the world as expressing the feelings of a leading TD'.[44]

It later appeared to the Military and Church authorities that the activities of Burbage and some other Laois and Offaly curates amounted to more than making Republican speeches. Early in March 1923, Bishop Foley received a formal complaint from Army General Headquarters in Dublin, signed by the Commander-in-Chief of the Army, General Richard Mulcahy, about alleged subversive activities on the part of Burbage and Albert Byrne, a curate at Clonaslee, Co. Laois. Mulcahy enclosed copies of charge sheets 'indicating charges which, if these two priests were ordinary laymen, would be brought against them by a military court'. The charge against Burbage was that he encouraged 'certain people to take part in or aid and abet an attack on the National Forces in that he at the Roman Catholic church, Ballingar, Offaly on the 25th Day of February 1923 encouraged the congregation there assembled to rise against the National Forces'.[45] Byrne was charged with having 'in his possession, disposition or control written and printed documents calculated to be prejudicial to the safety of the State'. Mulcahy explained to Bishop Foley that 'an Irregular document' in Byrne's possession 'discloses the fact that Fr Byrne was in such close association with the Irregulars that he could be trusted to bring a proposed member of an Irregular Court to the place of sitting of that Court – this particular Court being set up to try some of the unfortunate and coerced members of an Irregular Column for mutiny – namely for declining to carry out what was apparently an instruction to ambush our troops going to Mass'.[46] The charges

[43] See p. 139, note 11.
[44] Foley to M.J. Murphy, 23.5.22, KLDA. Foley, however, pointed out that 'Father Burbage made no attempt in any of his letters to me . . . to show that it was not as easy to prove that the parties who pledged themselves by oath to the Republic should not have done so at all, as having taken it they were bound to stick to it come what might'. Ibid.
[45] General Richard Mulcahy to Foley, 23.3.23, KLDA.
[46] Ibid. 'In framing formal charges', Mulcahy added, 'we have confined ourselves to matters of which we have direct and sufficient proof to establish these charges, but from the other enclosures [the detailed reports on which the charges were based] Your Lordship will I am sure understand that it is possible that the more private actions and attitudes of these two priests may be much more serious in

against Burbage were based on a report by an Army Officer who, with some of the men of the Geashill garrison, had attended a Mass said by Burbage on 25 February 1923. The officer claimed that Burbage's sermon 'was more like a political speech'. He had started off by praying for a Republican named Gibson recently executed in Maryboro, then attacked the government and army, 'saying it was a shame for people to allow such things to be done'. The officer heard from people who had been at a later Mass said by Burbage that 'he came out even worse – saying that everyone should rise up against the government'.[47]

When challenged by Matthew Lalor, PP Mountmellick, on behalf of Bishop Foley, Burbage provided a sturdy defence of his conduct, and at the same time supplied the bishop with matter for reflection with regard to the behaviour of the Government of which he was so outspoken a supporter. Burbage pointed out that the man executed in Maryboro had suffered from shell shock while serving with the British Army, that it was generally known that 'he was unbalanced in mind, and that his mother had been a patient in Maryboro Lunatic Asylum'. He explained that 'in the circumstances the news that he had been executed after being held as a prisoner for three months, shocked and disgusted everyone who knew him'. Burbage acknowledged that he had condemned the policy of executions as 'abominable', because he believed that 'it was altogether opposed to the traditions of our people – that even Cromwell's soldiers were not executed when they fell into the hands of the Irish troops'. He pointed out that 'practically the entire parish' had signed 'a solemn protest' against the executions; even the protest against conscription was not 'nearly so general'. Burbage found it incredible that churchmen should have any doubts about the moral criteria which should apply in the case of executions such as that of Gibson. Demanding to know from Lalor who made the complaint against his sermon, he asserted that 'whoever they are, they pay no compliment to the representatives of the Church in Ireland when they suggest that they should declare themselves in favour of the execution of their own countrymen at a time when the civilised world, with the exception of Ireland, is crying out against the threatened execution of those clerics in Russia who have acted against the regulations of the Russian government'.[48] In defending his own position, Burbage was

themselves and in their results than any offences which it might be possible for us to formally establish against them, and I sincerely trust that Your Lordship will be able to influence them against their present line of conduct'.
[47] Lieut. Canning, Geashill Garrison, to Mulcahy, 26.2.23, KLDA.
[48] Burbage to Matthew Lalor, P.P. Mountmellick, 31.3.23, KLDA. Burbage was one of those who believed that by persisting with the execution of imprisoned Republicans in the Spring of 1923, the government had seriously jeopardised the

effectively challenging his bishop and the senior clergymen of the diocese to justify their failure to take a public position on the executions.

A letter to Bishop Foley from Mgr Murphy, PP Maryboro and Vicar-General of the diocese, suggests that priests other than Burbage and Byrne were involved in forms of republican activity which the government might deem subversive. Matthew Lalor, Parish Priest of Mountmellick, who appears to have been well informed on the political attitudes of diocesan priests, had given Murphy grounds for serious concern about some of them. Lalor had discussed the recent ambush of Free State troops at Geashill, and the popular belief that 'a certain cleric was connected with it, at least in sympathy'.[49] He told Murphy that 'there is a *catina vicariorum* [chain of curates] stretching from Clonaslee through Rosenallis, Mountmellick to Geashill – supporting each other . . . He also suggests that Marlboro is preferable to Mountmellick as the locus.' The curates in question were, of course, Republicans. At the time, James Breen was Curate in Rosenallis; John Lennon, brother of the IRA leader Séamus Lennon was curate in Mountmellick along with Peter Kavanagh[50]; Albert Byrne, accused of subversion by Mulcahy, was curate in Clonaslee. Whatever the details, Murphy told the bishop that the matter was 'of supreme importance'.[51] Other active Republican curates in the diocese of Kildare and Leighlin were Father Edward Campion, Tinryland, Co. Carlow[52] and Father John Kelly, Kilbride, Co. Carlow. The latter drove de Valera to Dublin towards the end of the Civil War having sheltered him in his home.[53]

The existence of a large Republican electorate in a diocese was not necessarily reflected by the presence there of a large body of Republican secular clergy. Kerry and Clare are good examples. While the election returns for the period suggest that very large numbers of those holding political views in the diocese of Kerry were Republicans[54],

---

[48] *cont.* prospect of peace. 'The country', he told Lalor, 'wanted peace, but . . . this policy made even the talk of peace absurd . . . it had done incalculable harm . . . to my knowledge priests throughout the country were contemplating a peace move that presented, at the time, considerable hope of success, but the executions had killed that movement and had produced such an atmosphere of distrust and bitterness that there was not the slightest hope of reviving it'. Ibid.

[49] Burbage is clearly the priest hinted at here. 'In any case', Murphy wrote, 'however groundless the popular suspicion is, it must have a most unwholesome effect'. Murphy to Bishop Foley, 2.2.23, KLDA.

[50] See p. 139, note 12.

[51] M.J. Murphy to Bishop Foley, 2.2.23, KLDA.

[52] Information from the late T.P. O'Neill.

[53] T. Ó Néill agus P. Ó Fiannachta, *De Valera*, Vol. II. Dublin, 1970, p. 106.

[54] In the 1923 General Election, Republican candidates polled 24,732 votes; the Cumann na nGaedheal total was 17,808.

the clergy did not, on the whole, share this outlook. During the election campaigns of the twenties, the great majority of Kerry priests strongly supported the Free State, and in the course of their ministry made life difficult for many Republicans. Offended Republicans frequently complained to the Bishop of Kerry about the conduct of his priests. Mrs Rice of Kenmare and her family decided not to attend Mass or to contribute to the support of the Parish Priest, Canon Marshall, whom she accused of making the pulpit into a 'political platform'. Sunday after Sunday she alleged, 'Republicans have to sit there and listen to insulting remarks cast at our men and boys whose only crime is being true to their oath of allegiance to the Republic'.[55] In the period immediately following the Treaty, the relatively few Kerry Republican priests [56] made up in enthusiasm for what they lacked in numbers. Among these were three members of one family: Joseph Breen, a curate in Kenmare; Canon John Breen, President of St Brendan's College, Killarney, and Frank Breen, a curate in Glenflesk. The latter was one of the six priests who experienced the wrath of Mannix over the O'Hickey affair.[57] Joseph Breen remained sufficiently outspoken in his opposition to the Treaty to attract the unfavourable attention of the Free State government; at a Cabinet meeting in October 1924, it was decided 'that a summary of the statements regarding Father [Joseph] Breen, CC Kenmare, be sent to the local bishop for his information'.[58] Charles Brennan, CC Millstreet, an early supporter of Sinn Féin, was an uncompromising opponent of the Treaty, and a prominent speaker at Republican meetings.[59] The case of Charles Troy, a Dunboyne postgraduate student from Listowel, illustrates the dangers confronting priests who displayed too strong an enthusiasm for the Republican cause. When

[55] Ellen Rice to Bishop O'Sullivan, 21.8.22, KYDA.
[56] Father Anthony Gaughan pointed out to the author that in the diocese of Kerry, curates lived with their Parish Priests and they tended to absorb the conservative attitudes of their seniors or, even if they were strong-minded in their views, to refrain from trying to impose these. There were a few brave exceptions.
[57] Michael O'Hickey, a priest of the diocese of Waterford and Professor of Irish Language at Maynooth 1896–1909, was dismissed after he clashed with the College authorities on their refusal to retain compulsory Irish for junior students. Breen got into trouble for supporting the demand for compulsory Irish in the National university. See Corish, *Maynooth College*, p. 288ff.
[58] Minutes of Executive Council G2/4, 6.10.24.
[59] Brennan's brother, Father Patrick, was a staunch upholder of the Treaty. His resentment of de Valera was proverbial. 'I could forgive them all except the Long Fellow' was one of his catch-cries. When Father David O'Connor of Castleisland, a strong supporter of de Valera, introduced Brennan to him, Brennan is said to have remarked: 'The only thing we have in common is bad eyesight'. Information from Mgr Daniel Long, Tralee.

Troy was home on leave from Maynooth in July 1922, he made an inflammatory speech denouncing the Treaty. Troy was a priest of the Dublin Archdiocese, and when the speech was disclosed to Archbishop Byrne, the offender was rusticated for several years in a remote parish near Glendalough. Troy believed that either Cosgrave or a Kerry Parish Priest had reported him to Byrne.[60] One of the most dedicated Republicans among the Kerry priests, Myles Allman, pursued his career as an anti-Treaty publicist without suffering obvious ill effects. Four guards reported him to the Bishop of Kerry in August 1923 for sending a supportive letter to a meeting 'held by the Irregulars' at Ballyheigue. 'The few remaining true soldiers of the Republic', Allman's letter ran, 'have died and shed their blood for Ireland. Why not trample on the Free State now that you have the opportunity and wipe them out once and for all and re-establish yourselves. The true spirit still lives and shall not be quenched'.[61]

The dominant ecclesiastic in Clare, Bishop Fogarty, appears to have imposed his extreme anti-Republican views on the great majority of his clergy. Very few Killaloe priests openly declared themselves Republicans in a diocese with a considerable Republican electorate.[62] One who did was Daniel O'Flynn, a curate in Ballynacally, who voted to amend a pro-Treaty resolution at a meeting in Ennis in January 1922 and presided at the Republican conference in June 1922 which selected de Valera and Brian O'Higgins, of whom O'Flynn said that 'they might go to the ends of the earth and not find better candidates'.[63] A year later, we find him writing to Michael Comyn, a Republican candidate for Clare, from a new parish near Ennis, where he finds himself 'in obedience to the mandate of my bishop . . . a stranger still amongst my own', expressing reluctance to address a Republican meeting in the parish. He still confides his anti-Treaty views to Comyn, deploring 'that strange spectacle, the Irish bishops with the applause of every enemy of Ireland, blessing the boon [the Treaty] for the sake of peace'.[64] At this point, however, whether motivated by discretion or

[60] I would like to thank Father Anthony Gaughan for the information on Father Troy.

[61] Guards Ó Catháin, Ó Ruadháin, Burke and Farrell to Bishop O'Sullivan, August 1923, KYDA.

[62] In the 1923 General Election in Clare, containing the biggest electoral unit in the Killaloe diocese, Republican candidates polled 18,691 votes, with 11,748 for Cumann na nGaedheal and 9,006 for Labour and Farmers.

[63] K. Sheedy, *The Clare Elections* (Dublin, 1993), p. 345.

[64] *Sinn Féin*, 1.9.23. Father John O'Dea, CC Bodyke, refused to support de Valera in the East Clare Election, but did so in the Civil War; his brother, Father Dan, CC Cloughjordan, was a confidant of de Valera's and a supporter of the Republicans in the Civil War, but subsequently became a Republican die-hard. I owe this information to Professor David Fitzpatrick, TCD.

religious conviction, O'Flynn had decided that no political intervention of his 'should uselessly interfere with my one work as a priest, to bring every willing soul . . . no matter what be its political opinion, into more intimate relation with the Severe Majesty of Christ'.[65]

The many priests of the diocese of Cloyne who sympathised with the Republican cause seem, in general, to have taken the same attitude as O'Flynn. Robert Browne, the bishop of the diocese, was, like Fogarty, an enthusiastic upholder of the Treaty and a strong public advocate of the Free State government; he considered post-Treaty Republicanism a gross aberration. Canon Séamus Corkery, Parish Priest Emeritus of Charleville, whose father, Daniel Corkery was a Republican TD for North Cork in the twenties, recalls that many of the priests on the Republican side kept their views to themselves, since the expression of such views would not have been welcomed by the church authorities in the diocese, particularly the bishop; there was also the consideration that by expressing their Republicanism too openly priests would alienate some of their parishioners, although the latter idea does not appear to have influenced the very many priests who espoused the Treaty cause as election agents and organisers.[66] An extreme manifestation of the reluctance of Cloyne Republican priests to proclaim their allegiance publicly was the failure of any priest of the diocese to appear at the funeral of Liam Lynch at Kilcrumper, Fermoy, in April 1923. William Roche, who laid a wreath from the Mallow IRA on Lynch's grave, recalls that the only priests who officiated at Lynch's funeral were two from the Kerry diocese: Father Joseph Breen of Millstreet and Father Charles Brennan of Castleisland.[67] The most prominent clerical sympathisers with Republicanism in Cloyne were Tom Roche, a teacher in the Diocesan Seminary, an officer in the IRA before the Treaty, who had sworn several men into that organisation and who was close to de Valera; Roche's brother Denis who had a less prominent role; Andrew O'Keeffe, who had a brother in the Republican IRA as had Cornelius Brew; John Keating, PP Aghada and Philip Mortell; Michael Harrington who had brothers in the IRA and who repaired guns for its members; James Leonard, who died as PP Aghina; Tom Wilson of Macroom; Francis Flannery, Parish Priest of Castlemartyr 1924–31. The future Bishop of Cloyne,

---

[65] Ibid.

[66] I owe my information on Republican priests in the Cloyne diocese to Canon Corkery, who generously shared his unrivalled knowledge of the subject with me.

[67] Mr Roche, now in his late nineties, gave this information to Canon Corkery, who believes that Father Breen was suspended by his bishop for refusing to read the October 1922 Pastoral. Father Tom Duggan of the Cork diocese was also at Lynch's funeral. See Carthach MacCarthy, *In Peace and in War*. (Dublin, 1994), pp. 50–1.

John Ahern, belonged to a Republican family, and although he and his brother Jerry, also a priest, 'were perceived to sympathise with the Republicans', they were careful to avoid political involvement, 'conscious that they were priests for all their people of whatever political views'.[68]

Aodh de Blacam's claim in July 1922 that there were only four pro-Republican priests in the diocese of Raphoe is probably justified, given that de Blacam was living there at the time and was in close association with the Republican movement.[69] His other suggestion, that these four 'are silenced while our lads are denied the Sacraments' is impossible to verify from existing records. The Raphoe Archivist, Dr John Silke, points out that during the early twenties, Bishop O'Donnell was Bishop of Raphoe and Co-Adjutor Archbishop of Armagh, with the affairs of two dioceses demanding his attention. In his dealings with the Raphoe clergy, he seems to have been somewhat less preoccupied with the political views of his priests than with ensuring that 'a few priests who had drink problems would get back on the tracks'. Dr Silke could discover nothing in O'Donnell's Raphoe correspondence 'about pro-Irregular priests, much less any censure', and suggests that he may have dealt with this matter at Conferences, where, perhaps, he may have made his views known, and so 'silenced' any pro-Republican priests. Canon O'Gara, probably one of de Blacam's four, referred to Protestants as Cromwellians, but, as Dr Silke points out, he was rather close to Bishop O'Donnell and there seems to have been no question of episcopal censure against him. Another of the four was certainly Alphonsus Ward, member of a family publicly identified with Republicanism; his sister walked out of the church in Milford in October 1922 when the priest began to read the Bishops' Pastoral. In 1921 Ward was moved from Ardahey to Newtowncunningham, where he remained only from July of that year until August 1922 when he was transferred to Raphoe. These changes may, as Dr Silke suggests, be significant.[70]

In some dioceses, it was not politic for priests to take a strong Republican line. Cork was one of these, as Father Dominic's experience at the hands of Bishop Cohalan shows.[71] In common with priests elsewhere in the country, many of those in the diocese of Cork, while sharing their Bishop's intense dislike of Republicanism and the activities of its adherents, must still have felt obliged to adopt a liberal view of

[68] Canon Corkery to author, 3.1.96.
[69] See p. 138, note 3.
[70] Rev. Dr John J. Silke, Portnablagh, Donegal to author, 1.8.96.
[71] See p. 143, note 27.

the sanctions laid down in the October 1922 Pastoral.[72] Only one priest of the Cork diocese, however, was prepared to take a public position somewhat at variance with Cohalan's declared views. This was Tom Duggan, who had been a British Army chaplain in the World War and one of Cohalan's secretaries. Initially, he had favoured the Treaty, but as the Civil War grew in bitterness, his political attitude underwent change. Following the death of Collins and the emergence of O'Higgins as the strong man of the government, Duggan, his recent biographer points out, 'began to have grave misgivings about the political outlook and intentions of the Government'. By the end of 1922, he had come to the conclusion that for most members of the Cabinet, 'the Treaty was an end in itself', while the execution of prisoners revolted him.[73] At the end of February 1923, Archbishop Harty of Cashel and Duggan devised a peace formula which would have involved the cessation of hostilities by the IRA and the dumping of Republican arms and munitions which were to be handed over to the government after the 1923 Election.[74] On 12 March, however, Kevin O'Higgins publicly rejected the idea of a peace based on the kind of compromise Harty and Duggan had in mind, and which Tom Barry had agreed to put to the IRA Executive. Liam Lynch, the IRA chief of staff, was opposed to any form of compromise with the Free State, and warned Barry to desist from negotiations.[75] Duggan's task as a peacemaker was made more difficult when the Free State execution of Republican prisoners was resumed in mid-March after a two-week intermission. This prompted Duggan to send an angry telegram to Archbishop Byrne on 15 March: 'Resumption Executions Ruining Peace Prospects which were excellent. Stop them'.[76] Duggan supplemented his telegram with a letter setting out reasons for immediate intervention. 'Up to the resumption of the executions', he wrote, 'there was a very fair chance that Barry would be able to force his own peace proposals through the Republican executive'; he described as 'criminal' the attitude of the government. 'They abstained from executions for six weeks', he told Byrne, 'and now, just at the

---

[72] See p. 138, note 5.
[73] Carthach MacCarthy, *In Peace*, pp. 90–1.
[74] See M. Hopkinson, *Green Against Green, The Irish Civil War* (Dublin, 1988), pp. 232–3. The Dublin Correspondent of the London *Times* wrote that the proposals 'bridge the difficulties of an unconditional surrender in an ingenious manner'. *The Times*, 9.3.23.
[75] Hopkinson, *Green Against Green*, p. 233. O'Higgins's rejection of the Harty-Duggan proposals was reported in the *Cork Examiner*, 12.3.23. 'This is not going to be a draw with a re-play in Autumn', O'Higgins declared.
[76] Duggan to Byrne, 15.3.23, DAA.

critical moment, when the fruits of their forbearance would be realized, they ruin the whole atmosphere'.[77] Duggan met Byrne in Dublin soon afterwards. 'Father Duggan has just been with me', Byrne wrote to Cosgrave, 'he has made such a strong case to me for the stoppage of executions for another week that I have no scruple in saying I should be lacking in duty if I did not recommend this course'.[78] Cosgrave's immediate response reveals the settled determination of his government to persist with the ruthless measures which had brought early victory within its grasp. Captured correspondence, he told Byrne, revealed that 'pressure is felt in most areas now' by the Republicans; he believed that the more such pressure was applied, 'the greater the peace desire is developed'. A real peace, he argued, 'can only come from good military results, and it would be much better that they [the Republicans] should be beaten in the field which they selected'.[79] The clerical peacemakers could only deduce from Cosgrave's answer to Byrne that the executions would continue. 'If there were a reasonable inference or deduction', Cosgrave told him, 'that peace were likely to result, we would certainly stop these extreme measures'.[80] It is possible, however, that Duggan and his associates influenced the government in the direction of clemency, since there were no further executions of prisoners until 11 April, a month after Duggan had made his case to Byrne.[81]

The diocese of Elphin was not a Republican stronghold; many of its senior clergy, including Bishop Coyne, regarded Republicanism with abhorrence and worked energetically against it. However, the most celebrated champion of fundamentalist Republicanism in the twenties and thirties was Father Michael O'Flanagan, an Elphin diocesan priest with an immense appetite for controversy. Soon after the 1916 Rising he contributed a Partitionist letter to the *Freeman's Journal*

---

[77] Duggan to Byrne, 15.3.23, DAA. Duggan was wrong about a six-week lull in Free State executions. The most recent execution, that of Thomas Gibson in Maryboro, took place on 26.2.23. See Dorothy Macardle, *The Irish Republic* 4th edn (Dublin, 1951), p. 985.

[78] Byrne to Cosgrave, 17.3.23, DAA.

[79] Cosgrave to Byrne, 18.3.23, DAA. Cosgrave told Byrne that the executions of four imprisoned Republicans in Drumboe on 14 March were reprisals. As he put it, 'clemency was withdrawn because of the shooting of two of our officers'. Ibid. Archbishop O'Donnell had made strong efforts to prevent these executions, which he deplored. See p. 86, note 227.

[80] Ibid. Compare Cosgrave's rejection of de Valera's peace proposals in May 1923, and de Valera's response which Kathleen O'Connell recorded: 'President [de Valera] very disappointed . . . As he said himself, the voice of the gladiator rings through Cosgrave's reply'. Kathleen O'Connell's Diary, 8.5.23.

[81] See Macardle, *Irish Republic*, p. 985.

in which he backed Asquith's proposal that the twenty-six counties of Ireland should be granted immediate Home Rule with the North-eastern counties excluded. He argued that Ireland was an historic and social duality, that history had worked against the existence of a single Irish nation, and that the freedom nationalists demanded as a right should be conceded to unionists.[82] A hostile commentator later described O'Flanagan as 'having won the first victory in the campaign for the cutting off of Ulster from the rest of Ireland'.[83] In early 1917, O'Flanagan played a decisive part in the election of the imprisoned Count Plunkett as Sinn Féin M.P. for North Roscommon.[84] Following Plunkett's election, which was brought about with the help of many Western priests, three bishops, Coyne of Elphin, Morrisroe of Achonry and Naughton of Killala, still loyal to the Irish Parliamentary Party, made their displeasure known to O'Flanagan and other clerical supporters of Plunkett.[85] Arthur Griffith, President of Sinn Féin, arguing that two thirds of the priests of Ireland were in revolt against the Irish Parliamentary Party, defended O'Flanagan and the other Sinn Féin priests, telling Bishop Coyne that 'whatever a bishop's individual view in politics may be, the use of his authority in support of that view is illegitimate when it tramples on the equal right of any of his priests to hold and express political views with which he is not in sympathy'.[86] Anti-Treaty Republicans might have found matter for ironic contemplation in Griffith's defence of troublesome priests against episcopal sanctions.[87] At the Sinn Féin Convention of October 1917, O'Flanagan and Griffith were elected joint vice-presidents. In May 1918, O'Flanagan campaigned vigorously for Griffith in the East Cavan by-election; Bishop Coyne retaliated by imposing on him *Suspensio a Divinis*, which debarred him from saying Mass publicly, from hearing Confessions or from administring the other sacraments. The official reason for the suspension was that O'Flanagan had addressed public meetings in three parishes in Cavan without the permission of their parish priests;

---

[82] *Freeman's Journal*, 20.6.16. 'After three hundred years', O'Flanagan wrote, 'England has begun to despair of compelling us to love her by force. And so we are anxious to start where England left off and are going to compel Antrim and Down to love us by force'. Ibid.

[83] *Freeman's Journal*, 6.2.17.

[84] For an excellent account of the North Roscommon campaign see D. Carroll, *They have fooled you again. Michael O'Flanagan (1876–1942). Priest, Republican, Social Critic* (Dublin, 1993), pp. 53 ff.

[85] See *Roscommon Herald*, 24.3.17.

[86] Ibid.

[87] 'It is not the Bishops of Ireland', Griffith declared, 'it is three individual Bishops who are thus abusing their authority as Bishops over their priests in the interest of a political party'. Ibid.

Coyne may also have been influenced by a report given to him by the RIC County Inspector for Sligo on the day before the suspension that O'Flanagan had declared in Cootehill that 'the man who goes to fight for England is a traitor to his country and a fool'.[88]

By early 1921, senior members of Sinn Féin were having serious reservations about O'Flanagan's role in the movement and in Irish politics generally. His approaches to Lloyd George in December 1920 and January 1921, without the authority of the Dáil or its Cabinet, caused considerable disquiet at the highest levels of the national movement in Ireland; his intervention was widely believed to have diminished Lloyd George's interest in negotiating an Irish settlement.[89] In February 1921, P.J. Little, a member of the Sinn Féin Standing Committee, urged de Valera to force O'Flanagan to resign as Vice-President. 'The danger which might be involved in putting him out', Little believed, was 'nothing to the danger of keeping him inside'. His expulsion would 'discourage people who are inside the movement from wavering and going in for intrigue'.[90]

The signing of the Treaty gave O'Flanagan a new cause which he took up with his customary enthusiasm. In the Spring of 1922, he accompanied J.J. O'Kelly, Austin Stack and others on an anti-Treaty mission to America, where his celebrated eloquence helped to raise considerable sums of money; in 1923 he went on a similar mission to Australia, and returned to America in 1924. His speaking-tours of Ireland during the by-elections of March 1925 marked the culmination of his career as an apologist for post-Treaty Sinn Féin; in early 1926, his insistence on maintaining Republican fundamentalism in all its fullness and purity encouraged de Valera to break with him and the entrenched, unyielding attitudes he represented, and to induce the great majority of Republicans to accept the more flexible variety of

---

[88] Carroll, *They have fooled you*, pp. 83–6. In 1920, while de Valera was in America, Archbishop Gilmartin intervened with Bishop Coyne to have O'Flanagan's faculties restored, subject to conditions. O'Flanagan was to make a retreat for a fortnight with the Redemptorists at Esker near Athenry, resign as Vice President of Sinn Féin, be subject to the same statutes as governed the political behaviour of other priests, and if offered a political position in the future, seek his bishop's permission before accepting it. He told Gilmartin that his resignation as a senior officer of Sinn Féin would be a blow 'to the interests of Ireland' but accepted the other conditions with reservations, boldly and uncompromisingly expressed. There is a copy of his undated response to Gilmartin in the Galway Diocesan Archive.
[89] See The Earl of Longford and T.P. O'Neill, *Eamon de Valera* (Dublin, 1970), p. 117.
[90] P.J. Little to de Valera, 19.2.21, FAK, 1366. Little suggested that O'Flanagan 'be invited to take an active and prominent part in the eminently Christian and Patriotic work of the White Cross, and to resign quietly from the other organisation [Sinn Féin]'. Ibid.

Republicanism embodied in Fianna Fáil. O'Flanagan's behaviour during the period between the Treaty and his breach with de Valera in March 1926 was a source of embarrassment to many members of Sinn Féin. The importance of his fund-raising ventures abroad on behalf of the party had to be acknowledged, while his spirited denunciation of clerical and lay enemies of Republicanism must have lifted the spirits of many of its downcast adherents. His multiple political speeches were, however, extremist in content and intemperate, even ferocious in tone, and could be used by opponents of his party to its detriment. His preoccupation with episcopal wrongdoing on the national question began to appear obsessive and tiresome. Instead of dealing with the political issues of the day, he freely indulged his grudges against the Irish bishops. At a meeting in Castlerea in February during the Roscommon by-election campaign, while de Valera concentrated on constitutional matters and explained how the British had got 'Irishmen to garrison Ireland for them and hold Ireland for England', O'Flanagan was wondering why the Bishops of Ireland could not be Irishmen. 'We have', he declared, 'tolerated too much ecclesiastical influence in our political affairs, and I say here, as Pope Pius the Tenth told us in Rome, if it is so wrong for the most distinguished preachers in all Italy to speak of politics during their Lenten sermons in Rome, it must be ten times worse for a Bishop to write a political Pastoral and get it read in all the churches over Ireland'. He had read in America that during the Civil War, 'the very Sacraments of the Church were used as a cudgel to bludgeon the people of Ireland into subjection' to the Free State; under such 'degrading conditions', people would be better off without the Sacraments. O'Flanagan's most notorious utterance of the campaign was his rebuke to Bishop Cohalan for refusing Christian burial to Denis Barry, 'the heroic martyr of Irish independence'. He approved of what MacSwiney's cousin Peter Golden had to say about the case: 'that he would rather go to hell with Denis Barry than to heaven with the people who refused him', but wanted to go further, preferring 'to go to Heaven with Denis Barry than to hell at the head of a procession of high ecclesiastics'.[91]

In the light of this, it is not difficult to understand why, in April 1925, Bishop Coyne once again suspended O'Flanagan from his

[91] *Roscommon Herald*, 28.2.25. At Mohill, Co. Leitrim, O'Flanagan declared that 'Those priests who made political speeches were turning the House of God into a den of corrupt political thieves with these Free State ruffians at their head'. *Freeman's Journal*, 23.2.25. Two years earlier, at Carrick-on Shannon, he excused a Republican bank robbery by alleging that 'banks for a long time had robbed the people of Ireland'. *Roscommon Herald*, 14.3.23.

ministry. In doing this he availed of a communication from New York and 'a solemn and scathing denunciation' of O'Flanagan by Archbishop Duhig of Brisbane. These he supplemented with a charge of his own that O'Flanagan had delivered 'disedifying harangues to excited mobs', as Coyne defined Republican election meetings, 'at five places in the diocese of Elphin'.[92] A number of Republicans were appalled at what O'Flanagan was saying at his meetings. Michael Keane, Parish Priest of Cams, Roscommon, wrote to local newspapers to dissociate himself from O'Flanagan's sentiments. Describing himself as 'a supporter of Mr de Valera', Keane could not agree 'with the particular line of argument of Father O'Flanagan'.[93] Mary MacSwiney was in New York when she read reports of what O'Flanagan had said in Castlerea. 'The *New York Times*', she wrote to de Valera, 'carried his [O'Flanagan's] story yesterday – his attack on the Bishops. I doubt if it will do us any good, in fact I have very little doubt it will do us a good deal of harm'. She wondered whether O'Flanagan's denunciation of the bishops was motivated by vindictiveness: 'Had his Bishop refused to accept him back and was his speech the result?'[94] On behalf of the Labour Party, Senator J.T. O'Farrell, in a reference to O'Flanagan's speeches, 'deplored and condemned the latest attempts to stir up religious strife and bring about a schism in the Catholic Church in the interests of a political party'.[95] Two officials of Cumann na nGaedheal in Roscommon felt that O'Flanagan's real target had been not the episcopacy but the Church itself: 'a most unwholesome effort was made by him to turn the people against their priests and even against the Sacraments of the Church'.[96]

In 1925, thoughtful supporters of Sinn Féin had come to see the simplistic, backward-looking Republicanism preached by O'Flanagan as sterile and unlikely to entice the majority of voters. As an election speaker, while he appeared to deal heavy blows to his opponents, he dealt even more crushing one to those whose cause he was supporting. One of these, M.J. O'Mullane, the defeated anti-Treaty candidate for South Dublin City in the by-election and soon to be a founding member of Fianna Fáil, offered some interesting comments to the press on the effect of O'Flanagan's campaigning on the outcome of the 1925 by-elections, in which Sinn Féin won only two of the nine seats contested. O'Mullane was quite sure that 'Father O'Flanagan's speeches contributed to the decrease in the Republican poll', and believed that

[92] Carroll, *They have fooled you*, p. 151.
[93] *Westmeath Independent*, 28.2.25.
[94] Mary MacSwiney to de Valera, 27.2.25, FAK 1444.
[95] *The Irish Times*, 2.3.25.
[96] *Roscommon Herald*, 28.2.25.

he had cost Sinn Féin seats in Mayo, Roscommon and Cavan.[97] Since one of these speeches was made from O'Mullane's own platform, he resented being 'innocently made a party' to sentiments he could not share. He found O'Flanagan's intervention objectionable on several counts. It might well have contributed to a weakening of 'the bonds of religion' in the community, and even have tended to making the people irreligious. O'Flanagan was no doubt inspired by the best of motives, but 'speaking as he did, his words could not but injure the deep religious feeling of the Irish people'. O'Mullane complained that Republicans like himself, 'whose hope is to see the bonds between the Catholic Church and the people drawn closer and faster than ever in Ireland', had found themselves 'pilloried and misrepresented' on account of O'Flanagan's speeches. By engaging in an anti-clerical crusade during the campaign, O'Flanagan had given a powerful weapon to his Free State opponents. Dr Hennessy and the other Cumann na nGaedheal candidates, O'Mullane observed, 'were enabled to assume the role of defenders of the Catholic Faith, though, with true Gilbertian humour, they will have to enter on their new crusade by taking an oath of allegiance to the King of England, who is also the head of the Protestant Church, and whose son, the Prince of Wales is, I believe, head of the Masonic organisation'.[98]

Professor Michael Browne of Maynooth,[99] a well-informed observer of political affairs totally sympathetic to the Republican cause, was glad to tell Hagan in December 1925 that the influence on Sinn Féin policy of fundamentalists like O'Flanagan was waning. Following 'acrimonious discussions' within the Republican movement the air had been cleared and it was evident to Browne 'that the people that count are on the forward side and that those who keep their principles

---

[97] In a by-election in Dublin South on 18.11.24, Seán Lemass, the Republican candidate, defeated Séamus Hughes of Cumann na nGaedheal by 17,297 votes to 16,340; on 11.3.25, Hennessy of Cumann na nGaedheal got 24,075 to O'Mullane's 13,900. Since November 1924, the Republican vote dropped in Mayo North from 14,628 to 13,458. In Cavan and Roscommon, however, the Republican vote increased.

[98] *Irish Independent*, 14.3.25. Michael Keane, Parish Priest of Cams, Roscommon, a committed Republican, expressed his 'strong dissent from the remarks of Father O'Flanagan when touching on the sacred relations of the church and the faithful. Such a line of argument is calculated to produce painful results not intended by the speaker, and certainly not beneficial to the cause so ably championed by him in every clime'. *Roscommon Herald*, 28.2.25.

[99] Browne was born in Westport, ordained priest of the diocese of Tuam in 1920; appointed Professor of Theology and Canon Law 1921; DCL Rome 1924. He resigned in 1937 on being appointed Bishop of Galway. Corish, *Maynooth College*, p. 443.

nursed in swaddling bands will not pull any weight if it comes to a trial'. For Browne, the people on the 'forward side' were those anxious to find a way to participate in constitutional politics without undue loss of honour or sacrifice of principle. Given O'Flanagan's proven capacity for causing dissension, Browne felt that 'it would be a great blessing' if he were 'retired to some safe and distant occupation. He is at present making something by transcribing letters of O'Donovan[100] from the Academy library but at any moment he may precipitate trouble for he is feeling sore'.[101] In 1925, O'Flanagan was causing offence to both friends and enemies of Republicanism. Bishop Foley described his contribution to the 1925 by-elections as 'the Plan of Campaign against the Bishops and indeed the Pope in politics',[102] and in a Pastoral Letter written soon after the elections he had him in mind when he referred to those who 'seemed to have lost hold of principles which lay at the root of all morality, and contented themselves with a misty subjectivism which could supply no real foundation for faith or morals'.[103] Foley also had in mind a letter written by Seán Lemass to the *Irish Independent* in the aftermath of the elections. Lemass, angered by the energetic campaign waged by priests in all nine constituencies on behalf of Cumann na nGaedheal, argued that 'the question of the political influence of the Catholic clergy, an influence that throughout our history has been used with uncanny consistency to defeat the aspiration of Irish nationality, has to be faced sooner or later'.[104] Republican prisoners in Maryboro, believing that Foley's Pastoral referred to them, created a disturbance in the jail and this, it was believed, had brought punishment on themselves. Foley told Monsignor Murphy, his Vicar-General, that he had a letter from Maud Gonne calling on him to get the punishment stopped, but that he had ignored it. A wire from O'Mullane, who had publicly dis-

---

[100] John O'Donovan's *Letters*, which give an account of his work on the Ordnance Survey and deal with matters of antiquarian interest, were edited in 50 volumes by O'Flanagan between 1924 and 1932.

[101] Browne to Hagan, 20.12.25, Hagan Papers. O'Flanagan's Republican solipsism was cruelly, if not totally unfairly, characterised by 'Irish American' in the *Leader* in 1924. Like Don Quixote, O'Flanagan 'saw things not as they were but as they took shape in his inflamed mind. He lived in a world created by himself. Those who lived in the real world and saw things as they were could not, even when he knew them to have been his best friends, convince him of his error. They were deceived. He saw clearly. And when at times in defeat or failure, he got a glimmer of the real world, it was not real to him'. *The Leader*, 2.8.24. I am grateful to Dr Patrick Maume, Queen's University of Belfast, for this reference.

[102] Bishop Foley to M.J. Murphy, 5.5.25, KLDA.

[103] *ICD*, 1926, pp. 566–7. Foley explained to Murphy that these words had been used in reference to O'Flanagan and Seán Lemass. Reference as note 102 above.

[104] *Irish Independent*, 14.3.25.

sociated himself from O'Flanagan's anti-episcopal speeches,[105] was more kindly received by Foley, who wrote to Kevin O'Higgins, only to be told that the stories about the punishment of prisoners was without foundation.[106]

In 1924, the appointment of Dr John Dignan[107] as Bishop of Clonfert was a significant event in the history of post-Treaty Republicanism. Dignan had opposed the Treaty, and nominated a Republican candidate in the Pact Election of 1922.[108] After his consecration in Loughrea on 1 June, Dignan delivered a stirring Republican speech in reply to an address from local Sinn Féin clubs. He commented unfavourably on the state of the country under Cumann na nGaedheal. 'There was no unity, no peace, no progress', he declared, 'and morally, economically, even nationally, they were on an inclined plane, slipping gradually but slowly into the abysmal pit of confusion and disorder'.[109] He believed as strongly as he did in 1918 'in the right of Ireland to complete freedom and in the efficacy of the means then adopted to secure that right'. He regretted that the majority did not vote in 1923 as they did in 1918, but he urged his Sinn Féin listeners to obey, as he did, the rule of the majority; this would not, however, prevent them 'from using moral and peaceful means' to persuade the people to go back to the position they occupied before the Treaty was signed. Predicting that 'the Republican Party is certain to be returned to power in a short time', Dignan advised Republicans to 'prepare for that day' and to do their best 'for its quick approach', in the meantime obeying the laws of the Free State and subordinating their political interests to those of the nation.[110]

[105] See pp. 160–1, notes 97 and 98.
[106] Foley to Murphy, 5.5.25, KLDA.
[107] Dignan was born in 1880 in Ballygar, Co. Galway, and ordained in 1903 for the Clonfert diocese. He was President of Garbally College, Ballinasloe, 1903–15, and later PP of Abbey, Loughrea. As a young priest he was a member of Sinn Féin, and in 1917 became President of its East Galway Executive. He was a central figure in the organisation of Sinn Féin Courts in County Galway. His parochial house in Loughrea was raided and bombed by Black and Tans. See his obituary in the *Irish Press*, 13.4.53.
[108] *Connaught Tribune*, 10.6.22.
[109] At the bottom of his copy of the address presented to him by the Sinn Féin Clubs, Dignan wrote 'Colourless, brainless, Cumann na nGaedheal'. CLDA.
[110] *Connaught Tribune*, 14.6.24. Dignan sensed that Republicanism, because of its emphasis on Irish cultural values, might offer a remedy for the spiritual malaise that seemed to him to pose a threat to Ireland's wellbeing. He told members of the Gaelic League that 'he believed not only in a free Ireland but in a Gaelic Ireland, and it was almost a duty on all Irish people who loved their country and revered their religion to stem the wave of paganism and materialism and sin that now swept the world, by erecting around their coasts the barrier of the language'. Ibid.

When Hagan wrote to him to express concern that his reputation might suffer as a result of his outspokenly Republican remarks, Dignan explained that his comments were motivated by a sense that the anti-Treaty side had been 'badly treated', and 'in all honesty and fair play, I felt bound to say a word on its behalf'. He was not in the least curious to know 'who the anonymous scribes were who were so perturbed' at his remarks, and he saw no reason 'why I should change or withdraw a single word'.[111] Republicans were soon conscious of the moral and propaganda value to their cause of Dignan's unequivocal pronouncement. He was the first Irish bishop to take a Republican position since the Treaty; the firmness he showed in taking it undermined the status of the episcopacy as a Free State monolith. One of de Valera's first acts following his release from prison in July 1924 was to visit Dignan.[112] Donal O'Callaghan, Republican minister for Foreign Affairs, told Aiken: 'Our stock is rising . . . We're getting quite respectable again'.[113] A writer in the New York journal, *The Irish World*, found cause for rejoicing in 'the courageous statement in favour of the Irish Republicans made by Dr Dignan'; it had been 'a severe blow to the Free Staters. In fact it is recognised [by them as being] as bad as a Republican victory in a by-election'.[114] Dignan dealt another blow to the Free State in November 1925, when, as Chairman of the County Homes Committee, he denounced the practice of obliging public officials to sign the declaration of allegiance, supporting an engineer who refused to do so. 'Were it not', he was reported as saying, 'that I am Bishop of this diocese and the poor my principal care, I would resign from this committee rather than interfere with the liberty of individuals by putting this declaration into effect'.[115] His

[111] Dignan to Hagan, 3.12.24, Hagan Papers. Seán T. O'Kelly told Hagan that he had heard from an *Irish Independent* reporter, who was present in Loughrea for Dignan's consecration, that the Archbishop of Tuam, on hearing the new bishop's Republican prophecy, remarked that he was 'finished consecrating Bishops' after that. S.T. O'Kelly to Hagan, 17.6.24, Hagan Papers.

[112] Kathleen O'Connell records the following in her diary: '16.7.24. Chief released – What joy! 22.7.24 P. [de Valera] motors to Roundstone. Calls on Bishop Dignan'.

[113] D. O'Callaghan to Aiken, 2.6.24. Quoted in T.P. O'Neill, 'Towards a Political Path: Irish Republicanism from 1922 to 1927', *IHS*, vol. x, pp. 158–9.

[114] *The Irish World*, New York, 9.8.24. The same writer suggests that Dignan's 'appointment from Rome' was made against the wishes of 'the Free State intriguers'. Dignan's name was not the first on the list of three names (the *terna*) recommended by the bishops of the Province of Tuam and forwarded to Rome. The first name was that of Father Tom Fahy, who had been close to Liam Mellows during the War of Independence, but had supported the Treaty. Information from Bishop John Kirby of Clonfert.

[115] *An Phoblacht*, 13.11.25. Dignan was to exhibit the same sturdy independence of mind throughout his episcopacy. During the term of the first Costello government

stand on this issue impelled a writer in *An Phoblacht* to assimilate Dignan to the noble but spare tradition of nationally minded bishops. 'Catholic Ireland', he declared, 'has usually been fortunate in having one patriotic bishop in each generation, and Most Rev. Dr Dignan, Bishop of Clonfert, seems to occupy that position to-day'. Dignan's significance for Republicans was clearly understood by the writer. Although his was only 'one episcopal voice raised against a rank injustice', his protest 'reminds our people that however much the Irish hierarchy might like it to appear so, the Catholic Church is not indeed on one side of the controversy'.[116] In Republican eyes, Dignan had partially redeemed the episcopacy from the general shame which the October Pastoral of 1922 had brought upon it; it was due to Republican clerics like him that 'permanent injury had not been done to the faith in Ireland'. Their refusal to use the Sacraments as pro-Treaty weapons saved the Church from 'appearing to be a mere wing of Mr Cosgrave's party'.[117] Dignan's Republican rhetoric encouraged one of his more outspoken curates, P.J. O'Loughlin, CC Clostoken, to champion the rights of fellow-Republicans in the matter of public employment. Two weeks after Dignan's consecration, O'Loughlin, presiding at a meeting of East Galway Sinn Féin, deplored the treatment of a Republican soldier by the Asylum Board, arguing that it was because he was a Republican that the RMS had refused to reinstate him, 'while he had taken back others who had joined the British Army and even the Free State'. O'Loughlin endorsed what his Sinn Féin Executive had agreed, namely 'that it was a combination of anti-Republicanism and Orangeism that is working all over the country trying to keep down Republicans in every way, but the Republicans will soon smash the unholy alliance when the opportunity presents itself'.[118]

(1948–51), he showed sympathy for Noel Browne's point of view when the latter was the object of major episcopal disapproval. Among Dignan's 'Notes and Comments on Department of Health Proposals for a mother and child service under part 3 of the Health Act', is the following: 'Personally hold very strongly that there is nothing in the scheme opposed to Catholic teaching'. CLDA. In 1944, Dignan criticised the State's social services as reminiscent in part of the Poor Law, and called for a national health insurance scheme. His intervention aroused the wrath of MacEntee, who tried unsuccessfully to limit radio and newspaper coverage of Dignan's proposals. He then requested the bishop to resign as chairman of the National Health Insurance Society. Dignan wrote to MacEntee that his behaviour imperilled the democratic character of the State. MacEntee Papers, UCDA P 67/257

[116] *An Phoblacht*, 13.11.25.

[117] Ibid.

[118] *Connaught Tribune*, 14.6.24. At a meeting of the Ballinasloe Mental Hospital Committee in June 1924, O'Loughlin proposed 'that this committee of the

During the Civil War, some bishops appear to have remained untroubled by active priestly opposition to the Free State within their dioceses. The dearth or inaccessibility of appropriate diocesan records in some parts of the country – Achonry, Cashel,[119] Cork, Clogher, Cloyne,[120] Ferns, Killala, Kilmore and Meath[121] – makes it difficult to speak with authority on this matter. There does not, however, seem to be any significant public record of clerical Republicanism in Cavan, which forms a large portion of the diocese of Kilmore, or in the diocese of Killala, which embraces part of North Mayo. The priests of the diocese of Ossory, of which County Kilkenny forms the major part, were notably loyal to the Free State, assiduous in their attendance at public meetings on behalf of the Government party and frequent proposers of its candidates. The only notable Kilkenny Republican priest, Patrick Delahunty of Callan, was treated with considerable severity by his bishop, Abraham Brownrigg. During the War of Independence, Delahunty was court-martialled in Waterford for possession of seditious literature and refused to recognise the Court. He was sentenced to two years' hard labour, but escaped in November 1921.[122] Brownrigg suspended him from his priestly duties because of his 'deep and constant estrangement' from the civil authorities of the time. His support for the anti-Treaty side during the Civil War involved indefinite suspension from active priestly ministry. When his mother died in 1924, he was in the body of the church but was not permitted to participate in the funeral ceremonies. Through the influence of an American priest he was able to get a post as a jail chaplain in Kansas.[123]

Many priests of the diocese of Achrony were as active in the service of the Free State as was their bishop, Morrisroe, one of the most

[118] *cont.* Mental Hospital of the counties Galway and Roscommon do hereby request the Free State authorities to demand the immediate release of all political prisoners confined in English and North-Eastern counties prisons; and as a pledge of the Free State's own sincerity and desire for peace in Ireland they themselves forthwith release the political prisoners in Free State jails notwithstanding the callous opposition of Messrs. Blythe and O'Higgins'. *Roscommon Messenger*, 14.6.24.
[119] There is an excellent account of Cashel priests by Walter F. Skehan in *Cashel and Emly Heritage* (Dublin, 1993). Political affiliations are noted in appropriate cases.
[120] The Cloyne diocesan archivist, Sr. M. Cabrini, is working on the papers of several bishops, but has not so far dealt with those of Bishop Robert Browne.
[121] Bishop Gaughran of Meath (1906–28) saw to the destruction of his papers before he died. Information from Bishop Michael Smith.
[122] T. Ó. Fiaich, 'The Catholic Clergy and the Independence Movement', *Capuchin Annual*, 1970, p. 497.
[123] See Jim Maher, *The Flying Column: West Kilkenny, 1916–21* (Dublin, 1987).

determined episcopal opponents of Republicanism.[124] In other parts of Connaught, however, considerable numbers of priests were openly Republican. Several Galway priests nominated Republican candidates in the elections of 1922 and 1923.[125] The southern part of the county and Connemara[126] had a higher concentration of Republican clergy than almost any other part of the country. Lady Gregory records a visit from Father John O'Kelly, curate of Kilbecanty, Gort, 'a strong Republican', around the time of the 1923 General Election. He told her when he was leaving: 'I think if you had voted it would have been for the Republicans'. She replied, 'No, because I have no surety they will cease doing violence'.[127] Not all were as extreme as John Considine, Parish Priest of Ardrahan, who supported the Republican candidates in the Pact Election of 1922 and whose irreconcilable Republicanism was evident as late as 1933, when 'his sermon at Mass consisted of a warning not to listen to any speaker who had not been out in 1916 or 1922'.[128]

In Leinster, there was determined clerical support for Republicanism in the diocese of Ferns. James D'Arcy, CC Ferns nominated Seán Etchingham, an anti-Treaty Panel candidate in 1922.[129] Paul Kehoe, PP Cloughbawn, was a vigorous opponent of the Treaty settlement.[130] Michael Murphy, CC Galbally, Enniscorthy, nominated Dr James Ryan in 1922.[131] Ryan's brother, Martin, brother-in-law of Seán T. O'Kelly and Richard Mulcahy, was an active Republican until his death in 1929.[132] John O'Keeffe, CC Castletown, delivered a fiery anti-treaty speech in 1923.[133] John Sweetman, Abbot of Mount St Benedict's, Gorey, nominated Etchingham in 1922, and represented the Republican point of view to Luzio, the Papal Legate, in 1923.[134]

---

[124] Philip J. Mulligan, Parish Priest of Carracastle, Ballaghadereen, seems to have been the only prominent Republican priest in the diocese. See his obituary in *An Phoblacht*, 5.11.27.
[125] See, for example, *The Connaught Tribune*, 10.6.22. The high concentration of Republican clerical support in County Galway is suggested by the fact that twelve priests nominated Republican Pact candidates, with five supporting pro-Treaty ones.
[126] For Connemara see p. 138, note 4.
[127] Lennox Robinson, ed. *Lady Gregory's Journals, 1916–1930* (London, 1946), entry for 27.8.23.
[128] Patrick Lindsay, *Memories* (Dublin, 1993), p. 146.
[129] *The Free Press Wexford*, 10.6.22.
[130] See his obituary in the *Irish Press*, 24.10.31.
[131] *The Free Press Wexford*, 10.6.22.
[132] Information from Richard Roche, Dublin.
[133] *The Irish Times*, 14.8.23.
[134] Cáit O'Kelly to Hagan, 7.5.23, Hagan Papers.

Nine other priests of the diocese indicated their Republican sympathies by attending receptions in honour of Archbishop Mannix in 1925: Laurence Allen, CC Wexford; Thomas Byrne, PP Piercestown; Nicholas Cardiff, CC Wexford; Sylvester Cullen, CC Gorey; Patrick Kavanagh, CC Rosslare; Matthew Keating and Patrick Murphy of the House of Missions, Enniscorthy; Aidan O'Brien, CC Castleridge and Father Michael, o.f.m. Wexford.[135] In the diocese of Meath, the leading Republican priests were those who had been active in Sinn Féin during the War of Independence. Christopher Casey, PP Ballymore and Patrick Clarke, PP Drumraney, had attended the great Sinn Féin meeting on the Hill of Uisneach in 1918. Both strongly supported post-Treaty Republicanism, ignored episcopal denunciations, and freely ministered to the spiritual needs of Republicans during the Civil War. Another Meath priest, Patrick Smith, CC Tullamore, maintained the active Republicanism of his days as a Sinn Féin Judge in the post-Treaty period.[136] In the Dublin Archdiocese, while the great majority of the secular priests supported Archbishop Byrne's firm, but moderate, pro-Treaty stand, Republicans could rely on the ideological as well as the material support of such outstanding priests as Professor Patrick Browne and his brother Maurice, a curate in Valleymount, Co. Wicklow, in 1923.[137] An anonymous correspondent in the Italian journal *La Voce Republicana*, writing in 1925 about the dealings of the clergy with Irish Republicanism, suggested that in the cities the influence of the clergy was 'less dangerous' to Republicans than elsewhere in the country 'because city people distinguish more easily between the spiritual mission and the political opinions of the priest'.[138] During the Civil War, Republicans had good reason to applaud the attitude of several Dublin priests who felt able to divorce the political status of penitents from their spiritual needs, and did not appear to regard Republican opposition to the political pronouncements of the bishops as a form of heresy. Canon Daniel Downing, Parish Priest of St Joseph's Berkeley Road, was not an advocate of the anti-Treaty position, but he won the admiration of Republicans for never refusing the services of his

[135] *Catholic Bulletin*, 1925, 108, 116.
[136] For Father Smith, see p. 140, note 13. I owe my information about the other Meath priests to Father Joseph Mooney of Tullamore.
[137] Their sister was the wife of Seán MacEntee. Both participated actively in the Civil War. For Patrick Browne, see pp. 144–7, notes 32–9. Father Maurice Browne maintained close contact with Republican units in his area and with de Valera and other Republican leaders. When Neil O'Boyle, a young Republican, was shot through the head after capture by Free State troops in Wicklow, Browne arranged a visit by de Valera, O'Deirg and Aiken to the dead man's family in Donegal. See P. Ó Baoighill, *Óglach na Rosann* (Dublin, 1994).
[138] Article reprinted in English in *An Phoblacht*, 3.7.25.

church on political grounds. The writer of Downing's obituary in *An Phoblacht* remembered that he had opened his church to receive the body of Cathal Brugha when this had been refused elsewhere, 'and though others allowed him to know what they thought, apparently, he felt that the priestly duty in all circumstances was to be just and good'.[139] However energetically bishops and senior ecclesiastics might try to place Republican activists outside the pale of religion and morality and present clerical sympathy for them as a source of scandal, priests like Downing experienced grave problems of conscience when encouraged to withhold pastoral care from people they had come to regard as exemplary Catholics. It was in such a spirit that Downing wrote to Seán T. O'Kelly following Brugha's funeral: 'I did everything that lay in my power to give token of religious sympathy on the occasion. It will always be a comforting memory that it was given me to honour so noble a character, so devout a Catholic and so superlatively brave a man as Cathal Brugha'.[140] Many prison chaplains must have been similarly moved by the traditional piety of Republican prisoners as John Hughes, Military Chaplain at the Curragh Camp, was in 1923. He came to develop respect and sympathy for their point of view, and treated them as friends. They reciprocated with a series of grateful tributes to his understanding of their position.[141]

III

Religious orders and congregations reflected the political and ideological divisions in secular society. The Capuchins have an honoured place in Republican folklore largely because of the publicity that surrounded the activities of Fathers Albert and Dominic during the early days of the Civil War. Other members of the order, Fathers Augustine, Senan, Sebastian and Canice, were deeply, though less obviously, involved in various forms of Republican activity.[142] The

[139] *An Phoblacht*, 26.6.25.
[140] *Catholic Bulletin*, September, 1922.
[141] Father Hughes was the recipient of numerous autographed comments from the prisoners at Christmas 1923, all of these laudatory, all testifying to his kindness of heart and his consolatory role. Copies of these are in the author's possession.
[142] In 1925, Father O'Flanagan referred to Father Augustine's exile in Switzerland, deploring the fact that the Capuchin order had banished from Ireland 'the three beloved priests who consoled the last moments of our Republican martyrs'. *Roscommon Herald*, 21.3.25. For Father Canice see Aodh de Blacam's letter to him in the Desmond FitzGerald Papers, UCDA, P80/736. On 14.9.31, the *Irish Press* referred to Father Sebastian's 'lasting friendships amongst the national element in the city'. Father Senan was a member of de Valera's entourage. Kathleen O'Connell Diary, 18.7.37.

sympathies of contemplative orders like the Cistercians appear to have been divided. A modern historian of the order believes that approximately half the members of the Roscrea community, and a larger proportion of those in Mount Melleray, were Republican in outlook.[143] These monasteries were sometimes places of refuge for Civil War Republicans.[144] Dom Francis Sweetman, Benedictine Abbot of Mount St Benedict, Gorey, a member of a wealthy Catholic family which had been active in nationalist politics for generations, publicly espoused the anti-Treaty cause, nominated the Republican TD Seán Etchingham in the 1922 Election, sheltered Republicans during the Civil War, and continued to support Republican causes long afterwards. Although he found the Free State position untenable, Sweetman was tolerant of those with pro-Treaty views, and contrary to rumour, kept himself at a distance from 'direct action' politics.[145]

In the years following the Treaty, Redemptorists, Franciscans, Dominicans and Jesuits tended to favour the Free State. When Redemptorists make an appearance, this is generally in association with some Free State event like the great demonstration in Limerick in February 1923, promoted by Bishop Hallinan and organised by the Redemptorists of the city through their confraternity. Although the official purpose of the gathering was to affirm the rectitude of the position taken by the bishops on the Civil War, it was in effect a pro-Treaty meeting.[146] The great majority of Irish Franciscans were solid supporters of the Cosgrave government; whatever Franciscan Republican activity there had been largely ended with the Treaty. In the early 'twenties, some of the leading members of the Order were personally close to leaders of the Free State and people identified with it. Among these were two of Arthur Griffith's brothers-in-law, Fathers

[143] Father Ó Saobhaoís of Roscrea, in conversation with author.
[144] Dan Breen recalled that after Liam Lynch's death, 'Austin Stack, Frank Barrett, Dathaí Kent, Seán Gaynor, Maurice Walsh, George Power, Andy Kennedy and I came up from Araglen and made for the Nire Valley. We reached Mount Melleray after midnight. Before daybreak we resumed our journey through the foothills of Knockmealdown.' *My Fight for Irish Freedom* (Tralee, 1964), p. 179.
[145] See D.A. Bellenger, 'An Irish Benedictine Adventure. Dom Francis Sweetman (1872–1953) and Mount St Benedict, Gorey', in W.J. Shiels and Diana Wood (eds), *The Churches, Ireland and the Irish* (London, 1989). C.S. Andrews remembered spending a few days in January 1923 'in the not particularly safe but hospitable Mount St Benedict'. See *Dublin Made Me*, p. 263. For Sweetman's nomination of Etchingham see *Wexford Free Press*, 10.6.22. On 8.12.31 the *Irish Press* reports him speaking at a meeting for the release of Republican prisoners.
[146] See *Limerick Herald*, 26.2.23. The Redemptorist priests present were Fathers Maguire, Robinson, Jones, Hartigan and FitzGerald.

Leo and Peter Sheehan. Nicholas Dillon, an influential Franciscan, was a brother of John Dillon; Seán Mac Eoin enjoyed a close relationship with many Franciscans, as did Cosgrave, who died as an honorary member of the First Order of St Francis. The first Franciscan Provincial after independence, Hubert Quin, was a strong supporter of the Free State. Within the order generally, the tension was between upholders of the Anglo-Irish tradition and Free Staters rather than between Free Staters and Republicans.[147] A young Athlone Franciscan, Vergil Mannion, who was a novice in the Killarney House of Studies in 1922, experienced the hostility of two of his superiors when they became aware of his Republican background. One of them suggested that the hunger-strikers in Tintown Camp in the Curragh should be allowed to die, knowing that Mannion's brother was one of these; the same priest used his weekly talks as vehicles for Free State propaganda and abuse of Republicans.[148] The most prominent Republican member of the order was Ferdinand O'Leary, a Wexfordman; he and Barnabas McGahan reconciled a number of excommunicated IRA members to the Church.[149] When, in February 1922, de Valera paid his first visit to Ennis after the signing of the Treaty, the only priest to greet him publicly was a Franciscan, Leopold O'Neill.[150]

Like the Franciscans, the Dominicans were generally active champions of law and order in the new state.[151] Their best-known public figure was M.H. McInerny, historian of the order and frequent contributor to *The Irish Rosary*. In both capacities he attracted the extreme hostility of Republicans. In the Preface to his *History of the*

[147] I would like to thank the Franciscan historian, Father Patrick Conlan, for providing these details. The order had reason to be grateful to Cosgrave in 1926 when a serious problem arose for it from large-scale development in Rome planned by the Fascist authorities. There was a proposal to confiscate the garden of St Isidore's for building and road-widening. The Franciscan authorities unsuccessfully appealed to Mussolini and then to Cosgrave, who intervened to save the property. As a reward for his efforts, he was affiliated to the First Order of St Francis in 1929. See Patrick Conlan, *St Isidore's College, Rome*, Rome 1982, pp. 215–16. The Franciscan appeal to Mussolini is to be found in the Desmond FitzGerald Papers, UCDA, P80/548C(1)

[148] Vergil Mannion o.f.m. *A Life Recalled: Experiences of an Irish Franciscan* (Dublin, n.d.), pp. 57–60.

[149] See Patrick Conlan, *The Franciscans in Drogheda* (Dublin, 1987), p. 50. During the Civil War, Republicans in County Galway found sympathetic confessors among the Franciscans in Galway city. Information from Mr Tom O'Donoghue, Galway.

[150] Sheedy, *Clare Elections*, p. 347.

[151] Comment of Father Hugh Fenning, o.p., Dominican archivist, to the author. A Republican journal reported that 'a Dominican giving a lenten mission at Sandymount, Dublin, requested Republicans to leave the Church – he said this before the ceremony and waited'. *Éire* 23.6.23.

Irish Dominicans which was published in 1916, he condemned the Rising. 'I have not', he wrote, 'the faintest sympathy with recent insane attempts at insurrection in Ireland . . . In the Ireland of our day, revolutionary movements have neither moral sanction nor hope of success; they are alike opposed to sound reason, real patriotism, and Catholic teaching. The constitutional movement alone bears the fruit of many victories and the promise of final success'.[152] An article of his in *The Irish Rosary* on the death of Kevin O'Higgins drew an angry Republican response.[153] The Dominican order also nurtured two notable Republicans, Thomas Walsh and Raphael Ayres. Walsh was not a priest during the immediate post-Treaty period, and did not join the order until 1929. In 1917 he was a member of the IRB and the Irish Volunteers. He rejected the Treaty and fought on the Republican side in the Civil War. He surrendered in O'Connell Street, was interned in Mountjoy and the Curragh where he went on hunger strike, resumed his teaching career on his release in 1923, but was denied his salary for refusing to recognise the government. Although he gave up political activity on entering the order, he maintained his friendship with his Republican associates. As a priest, he sought out and reconciled many Republicans who had lapsed from Church practice.[154] Ayres was at the centre of Republican activity in Kerry during the Civil War. As Prior in Tralee in 1922, he organised the production of a Republican newsletter in the Priory. He prevented a member of his community, Father Collins, from preaching on the duty of obedience to the Free State government, telling him to leave the pulpit.[155] Ayres's Republican sympathies brought him to the notice of the Bishop of Kerry in September 1922. 'I have heard on reliable authority', David O'Leary, PP Tralee, wrote to the Bishop, 'that Father Ayres read your letter on last Sunday in such a way that not even one word was heard by the congregation. The reading in fact was to himself and was a mere pretence on his part. This is carrying Republicanism very far'.[156]

The Jesuit order did not have a Republican, or even a particularly nationalist tradition, preferring to remain detached from any extreme form of political ideology. In his account of the Irish Jesuit Province, Louis McRedmond ventures the suspicion that 'on the whole, the

[152] M.H. McInerny, *A History of the Irish Dominicans*, Vol. 1 (Dublin, 1916), p. viii.
[153] 'It shows that there are still a few ranting, raving rabid advocates of authorised murders as a method for dealing with the threat of growing Nationalism to the imperial scheme of things in Ireland'. *An Phoblacht*, 12.8.27.
[154] Information from Father Henry Peel, o.p., Dublin.
[155] Information from Father Anselm Moynihan, o.p., Dublin.
[156] Father John O'Leary, St John's Tralee, to Bishop O'Sullivan, 7.9.22, KYDA.

Jesuits would have preferred the implementation of Home Rule without violent severance of the remaining imperial link'.[157] There was, however, no identifiable Jesuit position on the great political questions of either pre-Treaty or post-Treaty Ireland. The Irish Province was generously accommodating to the disparate views of individual Jesuits on the moral, political and ideological issues raised by the Treaty. Within its membership were to be found defenders of the bishops in their role as upholders of the Free State as well as a smaller number of men with Republican leanings. John Hagan, who tended to judge fellow-clerics on the strength or otherwise of their Republican commitment, clearly found the Jesuits as a whole deficient in this quality. Hagan would never have been able to comment on an order even moderately well disposed to Irish Republicanism in the way he does on the Jesuits in a letter to Bishop Dignan of Clonfert in 1928. Commenting on *The Jesuit Enigma*, a book by Father Boyd-Barrett, he tells Dignan that 'it is a singularly able production, and is certainly the most serious indictment of Jesuit tricks which has appeared since the days of Pascal. If it secures anything like a wide circulation amongst the laity it will ruin the society in their eyes'.[158] Following the publication of their Pastoral Letter of October 1922, the Bishops were able to call on the services of the two leading Jesuit theologians of the day, P.J. Gannon and Peter Finlay, to elucidate the issues raised in the document, to defend its content and their right to issue it. Gannon asserted the primacy of the episcopal body as a fount of moral authority, delivering a sidelong blow to purveyors of a rival, Republican ethic. 'We must', he declared, 'get back to the moral law as interpreted for us for our authorised moral guides, not by amateur theologians who have no permission from God to teach and no acquired knowledge to impart'.[159] Finlay suggested that all those who wished to remain within the Church must accept and follow the teaching outlined in the Pastoral.[160] Another Jesuit publicist, Patrick Connolly, editor of *Studies* from 1914 to 1950, made his Free State sympathies clear in his editorial on the death of Collins: 'He has passed into the ranks of our great dead, breathing forgiveness to his enemies, but bequeathing also to them – however reluctantly – the inevitable and unenviable immortality which always comes to the slayers of the great'.[161]

[157] Louis McRedmond, *To the Greater Glory. A History of the Irish Jesuits* (Dublin, 1991), p. 276.
[158] Hagan to Dignan, 29.1.28, CLDA.
[159] *Irish Independent*, 13.10.22.
[160] Ibid.
[161] *Studies*, September, 1922.

Not all Irish Jesuits were as secure in their attachment to the Free State. At the beginning of 1923, the Provincial, John Fahy, felt obliged to ask Edward Cahill to comment on a report that in the course of a conversation on a railway platform he had expressed his 'approval of the Irregular Insurrection' and 'advocated and encouraged the revolt condemned by their Lordships in their conjoint letter'.[162] In his reply, Cahill acknowledged that in July 1922 he had discussed the political situation with a number of people, including Stephen O'Mara, Senior, an advocate of the Treaty settlement. He explained to Fahy that it was then his opinion that 'the Provisional Government had begun the war contrary to the decision given by the Bishops in the previous Joint Pastoral in which they declared that Dáil Éireann was the Legitimate Government and should be obeyed'. Cahill indicated, however, that he now felt bound by the terms of the October 1922 Pastoral. When consulted 'by boys in reference to their brothers and friends, on other occasions by persons more clearly connected with active operations', he had 'always urged obedience to the Bishops' ruling as a duty'.[163] Fahy was satisfied with Cahill's explanation, remarking that Stephen O'Mara, the source of the report, 'is now old and he does not seem to be capable of grasping nuances'.[164] It would be unfair to blame O'Mara for such a failure, given the difficulties experienced by rival theologians, lay and religious, in dealing with the central political issues. Cahill's Republican sympathies were shared by Timothy Corcoran, Professor of Education at University College Dublin who was close to de Valera and in whose election as chancellor of the National University of Ireland he had played a major part.[165] Corcoran's antipathy to the Cosgrave regime found a congenial outlet in his association with the *Catholic Bulletin*, which consistently advocated the anti-Treaty point of view. Another Jesuit, Edward Boyd-Barrett, whose unfavourable account of the society Hagan admired, gave

[162] Father John Fahy to Father Edward Cahill, 5.1.23, Jesuit Archive, Dublin.
[163] Cahill to Fahy, 6.1.23, Jesuit Archive, Dublin. The 'previous joint Pastoral' referred to by Cahill was that issued on 26.4.22. Cahill had in mind the following passage from that Pastoral: 'As to the organ of supreme authority in the country at present, whatever speculative views may be held upon the subject, there can be no doubt as long as the Dáil and the Provisional Government act in unison as they have hitherto done'. *ICD*, 1923, p.599.
[164] Fahy to Cahill, 11.1.23, Jesuit Archive, Dublin. Cahill was not a willing subject of the Free State. Writing to de Valera in 1932, he described its régime as 'a ten-year nightmare'. During the twenties, Cahill was engaged in a vigorous crusade against Freemasonry, which, according to some political opponents of the Free State, had a sinister influence on Cosgrave's government. His book, *Freemasonry and the Anti-Christian Movement*, appeared in 1929.
[165] McRedmond, *Irish Jesuits*, p.278.

moral support to the cause of Republican prisoners in November 1923, when he publicly gave out the Rosary during a Republican procession to the Limerick County Jail. 'No law, human or divine', he told the demonstrators, 'forbids us to pray for those suffering for freedom'.[166] During the War of Independence, three Jesuit priests, Fathers Cahill, Corcoran and McErlean, had helped prepare a historical case for de Valera to be presented to the Peace Conference at Versailles in 1919.[167] In the post-Treaty period, de Valera felt able to enlist the help of another Jesuit, Lambert McKenna, when he was drawing up a 'Democratic Programme' for his Emergency Government.[168]

Apart from the Capuchins, the two religious orders most intimately associated with Republicanism during the post-Treaty period were the Holy Ghost Congregation and the Calced Carmelites. De Valera had close ties with many Holy Ghost priests, having had his early Secondary education at Rockwell and having later studied and taught at Blackrock. When he needed a passport to travel to the Irish Race Congress in Paris in January 1922, Father Patrick Walshe, with whom he had been friendly at Rockwell, allowed him to use the one recently issued to himself; de Valera travelled to Paris in clerical costume supplied by members of the Holy Ghost Congregation.[169] After his return from Paris, de Valera engaged in a countrywide speaking tour to counteract pro-Treaty propaganda. On his way to meetings in the South-West, he enjoyed the hospitality of Rockwell College, where John Kingston, Brugha's brother-in-law, was Bursar.[170] On the outbreak of Civil War hostilities, Father Walshe accompanied de Valera's secretary, Kathleen O'Connell, to Greystones, where they collected two guns to bring back to Mercer Street after de Valera had enlisted as an IRA Volunteer.[171] By 1923, the active sympathy of individual members of the Holy Ghost Congregation for Republicanism had antagonised the ecclesiastical authorities in at least one diocese: a chaplaincy agreement with an order of nuns in County Offaly was cancelled 'because the Holy Ghost Fathers supported de Valera'.[172] This kind of support was still evident in 1925. Before the first revelations by

---

[166] *Éire*, 3.11.23.
[167] McRedmond, *Irish Jesuits*, p.276.
[168] See De Valera to Fr L. McKenna, SJ, 26.12.22. Quoted in Ó Néill agus Ó Fiannachta, *De Valera*, Vol. II, p. 78.
[169] S.P. Farragher, *De Valera and his Alma Mater. Eamon de Valera's long association with Blackrock College, 1898–1975* (Dublin, 1984), p. 136; Ó Néill agus Ó Fiannachta, *De Valera*, p .9.
[170] Farragher, *De Valera*, p.137.
[171] Kathleen O'Connell's Diary, 29.6.22.
[172] Farragher, *De Valera*, p.147.

the *Morning Post* of details of the Boundary Commission Report, a number of pro-Treaty deputies and former Deputies had consultations with some Republican TDs with the purpose of prevailing on them to enter the Dáil. Father Herbert Farrell, a Holy Ghost priest who was present, warned de Valera that the move was really an effort to draw a large number of Republicans away from his leadership. 'The impression created on me', he wrote to de Valera, 'was very unfavourable. I think they are anxious to conciliate Republicans if the latter will desert you'.[173]

Among religious orders, the Calced Carmelites were, perhaps, the most warmly sympathetic to Republicanism both before and after the Treaty. Leading Republicans, among them de Valera, Harry Boland, Seán T. O'Kelly and Liam Mellows, had established close relationships with members of the order in America.[174] When a Republican delegation visited America in the Spring of 1922, its members frequently enjoyed the hospitality of the Carmelite monks in New York.[175] The Carmelite General was Peter Magennis, a lifelong, uncompromising Republican, who was in the confidence of the Irish Republican leadership in 1922–3. Responding to what he regarded as the unjust treatment of Civil War Republicans by both Church and State, Magennis may have been the one most immediately responsible for inducing Pope Pius XI to send Monsignor Luzio to Ireland in March 1923 as papal Envoy with the task of investigating the political situation and trying to restore peace.[176] During the Civil War, Magennis visited Ireland on a peace mission. On 23 August 1922, the day after Collins was killed, Patrick McCartan wrote to inform Joseph McGarrity, an influential Irish-American sympathiser with Irish Republicanism, that Collins 'was to discuss terms with Father Magennis and myself this morning. Our intention was to go South and find de Valera and get him to get all Irregular officers together'.[177] After the Civil War, de Valera maintained close contact with Magennis, writing to him in

[173] Fr H. Farrell to de Valera, 7.11.25. Quoted by T.P. O'Neill in 'Towards a Political Path: Irish Republicanism, 1922 to 1927'. *IHS*, vol. x, pp. 164–5.
[174] See Desmond Greaves, *Liam Mellows and the Irish Revolution* (London, 1971), p. 199.
[175] D. Carroll, *They have fooled you*, p. 142.
[176] The idea that Magennis exerted a direct influence on the Pope's decision to send Luzio to Ireland is canvassed by Dermot Keogh in *The Vatican, the Bishops and Irish Politics, 1919–39* (Cambridge, 1986), pp. 111–12. Keogh owed his version to an interview he had with Seán MacBride in 1978, but could find no independent confirmation.
[177] S. Cronin, The McGarrity Papers (Tralee, 1972), p. 123. Magennis had already tried to visit Seán T. O'Kelly in Kilmainham Detention Prison, but his request was refused by the Prison Commandant, Seán Ó Muirthuile, on 11.8.22. See A. Isaacson (ed.), *Irish Letters in the New York Carmelites' Archives* (Boca Raton, Florida), 1988.

Rome with detailed information on recent Republican history, correcting common errors perpetrated by Free State propagandists concerning such matters as the behaviour of Liam Lynch in July 1922 after his release by Free State forces, and pointing to 'public and notorious instances in which our opponents have broken their undertakings with us'.[178] When Seán T. O'Kelly went to New York to represent Sinn Féin interests there in 1924, he presented himself to the Carmelites, 'and was at once warmly received by them and was hospitably entertained at their table'.[179] Given Peter Magennis's position as worldwide superior of a venerable religious order, and his undoubtedly high standing in Rome, his open identification with Civil War Republicanism, and his willingness to defend it, carried significant weight. His value as a champion of post-Treaty Republicans was recognised by the writer of his obituary in the *Irish Press* in 1937, who, noticing that the Republican Plot at Glasnevin was near the burial-place of the Carmelites, believed that Magennis's friends would be pleased 'that he should lie so near to many of the Republican dead, who had been his friends in life and to whom he had been a defender when, after death, they were maligned by their enemies'.[180] How impassioned a defender of the Republican dead Magennis was may be discovered in his comment to Hagan on the execution of Mellows, O'Connor, Barrett and McKelvey on 8 December 1922. 'Yesterday', he wrote from Ontario to Hagan in Rome, 'I received the news of the shooting of four, amongst which was my dear friend Liam . . . I knew these fellows [the Free State authorities] were contemptible curs, but it never occurred to me that they were such vampires, drunk with their sudden greatness. Their one idea is to revel in human blood.'[181]

IV

In their October Pastoral, although the bishops pronounced that they were merely enunciating Divine law which clergy and laity were obliged to obey if they were to avoid ultimate spiritual sanctions, they

[178] De Valera to Magennis, 20.6.23, Hagan Papers.
[179] Isaacson, *Irish Letters*.
[180] *Irish Press*, 30.8.37. De Valera, always obsessed with the verdict of history on himself and on his actions, wondered in 1963 whether Magennis had approved of the foundation of Fianna Fáil. Writing to Father Lawrence Flanagan, a Carmelite friend in New York, he expressed his doubts on the question: 'What Father Magennis's views were when Fianna Fáil was founded I do not know. I was told by somebody that he was rather opposed to our action at that time'. Flanagan assured him that Magennis 'never wavered in support of your policy'. Isaacson, *Irish Letters*, pp. 40–1.
[181] Magennis to Hagan, 9.12.22, Hagan Papers.

also declared that the obligation to abide by the terms of their pronouncement was 'subject, of course, to an appeal to the Holy See'.[182]
This interpretation was given the almost immediate sanction of the
Jesuit theologian, Father Peter Finlay.[183] It may then seem surprising
to find Cardinal Logue writing to Bishop O'Doherty of Clonfert to
express his displeasure that Republicans had decided to take the only
course left open to them by the Pastoral if they were to avoid the
grave spiritual penalties it imposed. The source of Logue's displeasure
was a document from Republican Headquarters dated 31 October
1922, announcing that the Republican Dáil Éireann had asked de
Valera 'to make representations to the Vatican formally and emphatically protesting as Head of the State against the unwarrantable action
of the Irish Hierarchy in presuming and pretending to pronounce an
authoritative judgment upon the question of constitutional and
political fact now at issue in Ireland.' The Republican version of this
question, as the document put it, was 'whether the so-called Provisional
(Partition) Parliament, set up under threat of unjust war and by a *coup
d'état* was the rightful legislature and Government of the country or
not'. With the October Pastoral in mind, the writer of the document
accused the bishops of 'using the sanction of religion to enforce their
own political views and compel acquiescence by Irish Republicans in
an usurpation'.[184] In general, as he told O'Doherty, Logue took the
most casual view of the large bundles of Republican propaganda he
received but never read through: 'When I see what it is I tear it up
and throw it into the waste-paper basket'. This latest threat of a
Republican appeal against the bishops to the Holy See required more
serious attention, however. When a copy became available, it might
be necessary to counteract its influence at the Vatican by sending
'some choice specimens of their [Republicans'] crimes to the Holy
See'. Logue was going to stand firm against those foolish Republicans
'who seem to have got it into their heads that they can frighten the
bishops and get them to withdraw or explain their condemnation of
evildoers'. He was glad O'Doherty had sent a copy of the October
Pastoral to Cardinal Gasparri, Vatican Secretary of State; it would
'open the eyes of the [Vatican] authorities to the character and doings
of the people we have to deal with.'[185]

[182] *ICD*, 1923, p .610.
[183] At a Catholic Truth Conference in the Mansion House on 13.10.22. See *Irish
Independent*, 14.10.22.
[184] *ICD*, 1923, p. 593.
[185] Logue to O'Doherty, 2.11.22, GDA. O'Doherty brought his papers with him
from Loughrea when he was made Bishop of Galway in succession to O'Dea
in 1923.

The Republican appeal to the Pope took several weeks to prepare, but in the meantime, the Vatican authorities, and even the Pope, were receiving disturbing accounts of the spiritual disabilities being inflicted on Republicans by the Irish ecclesiastical authorities. Logue told Archbishop Byrne that the Vatican was being 'flooded with de Valera's propaganda', which betrayed itself by its intemperance. He himself had felt obliged to counteract the effects of Republican campaign in which 'the authority of the bishops is impeached, vilified and condemned' by asking the Vatican Secretary of State to encourage a Papal pronouncement supporting what the bishops were doing. 'Every real Catholic', he believed, 'would listen to the voice of the Holy Father and yield obedience to his authority'.[186] The Pope, however, was listening to many voices other than Logue's. Hagan reported to Byrne that Republican propaganda was having its effect in Rome. 'I saw the Holy Father this morning', he wrote, two days after Logue had written to Byrne, 'and found him greatly perplexed by telegrams which have been coming, particularly from America, about Miss MacSwiney'.[187] Hagan had other news which would have displeased Logue. Both the Pope and his Secretary of State had told the Bishop of Portsmouth, Dr Cotter, of Logue's request for an anti-Republican fulmination, but Cotter 'gathered that both were anxious to find any decent excuse for not sending anything of the kind'.[188] The Pope also told Hagan that he had discussed the Irish situation on 23 November with Bishop Amigo of Southwark, who would have been able to give him an authoritative account of Republican responses to the October Pastoral. Earlier in the month, de Valera had written to Amigo that 'the good intention which prompted the announcement [the October Pastoral] is not difficult to understand, but that means so calculated to defeat these intentions could have been chosen is almost incomprehensible'.[189] If the Pope was 'perplexed', as Hagan put it, by the complaints constantly reaching him about episcopal misdemeanours in Ireland, Hagan almost certainly was not. The MacSwiney Papers contain an interesting extract from a 'Letter from Rome', unsigned and undated but likely to have been written towards the end of 1922, giving instructions to Republicans in Ireland and abroad on the readiest way to reach the Pope with their complaints. Only someone as close to the Vatican apparatus as Hagan or his Vice-Rector Michael Curran would have been in a position to provide the kind of advice

[186] Logue to Byrne, 22.11.22, DAA.
[187] Hagan to Byrne, 24.11.22, DAA. Mary MacSwiney was on hunger-strike in Mountjoy, and being denied the Sacraments.
[188] Ibid.
[189] Quoted in Longford and O'Neill, *Eamon de Valera* (Dublin, 1970), p. 204.

the letter contains. If Republicans want to ensure that their messages reach the hands of the Pope 'the one and only sure channel is that of the electric wires', since 'not only does every wire reach his own eye, but a wire impresses in a way that no letter or other communication is capable of doing'. The results achieved by the campaign would be in proportion to the number of complaints reaching the Pope. In this regard, the writer advises, 'it is well to bear in mind that while one wire is a good thing, a hundred wires from as many individuals or bodies are a thousand times better than one, and you would do well to make this known to your friends in Ireland and across the ocean'. He is happy to report that 'a profound impression was created in this way quite recently by numerous wires which reached the Pope here from Ireland and America in relation to Miss MacSwiney and the treatment meted out to her, especially by the chaplains'.[190]

Preparation of the official Republican letter to the Pope, which was to be in French, had been put in the hands of Seán T. O'Kelly's wife Cáit, who taught the language at University College Dublin, Patrick Browne of Maynooth who had studied in Paris, Count Plunkett and Dr Conn Murphy, who, with Professor Arthur Clery, was to present the document at the Vatican.[191] The drafting process was fraught with difficulty. Mrs O'Kelly told Hagan that her biggest problem was to safeguard the contents from the 'malign influence' of Plunkett, who had transformed an acceptable original into 'a document that depended mostly for its effect on a general mendaciousness and its overstatements of its Republican delusions'. She could not imagine the Pope taking Plunkett's contribution seriously, prejudiced as he was by the bishops' statements, 'which the Count only countered by *stating* the

[190] MacSwiney Papers, UCDA, P48a/197 (26). Examples of telegrams sent by Republicans to the Pope were sometimes given in the Republican journal *Éire*. The 'Republican Women of Cork' sent the following: 'Holy Father. We claim justice from you in name of God and Catholic Church. Bishop of Cork made four political speeches at Confirmation ceremonies. Openly incited Free Staters to more murders. How long are Catholics to bear injustices?' *Éire*, 7.7.23. Mrs O'Mahony of Cork also complained of Cohalan's actions: 'As a mother, strongly protest against use made of Sacrament of Confirmation. My little boy scandalised by Bishop of Cork's attack on all he was taught to respect. Will Your Holiness stop politics in Church?'
[191] See Cáit O'Kelly to Hagan, 12.12.22, Hagan Papers.
[192] 'Imagine the Count's argument', Mrs O'Kelly wrote. ' "Now that the Republic is gaining force day by day and in a short time will be completely successful". When I said it [this formulation of Plunkett's] could not stand, he went on to talk about his *hopes* for a realisation of this, and I believe I was condemned as a person who did not hope even for the success of the Irish Republic. I prefer to be condemned by some people'. Ibid.

direct opposite'.[192] Father Browne and Murphy, however, joined her in producing what she considered a more sensible draft. Other problems ensued: 'The hitch of the last few days has been owing to Dev thinking it more advisable that he should not sign. Clery disagrees to the extent of not wanting to go with the appeal at all'.[193]

The letter to the Pope, bearing Dr Murphy's address, Garville Avenue, Rathgar, is an eighty-seven page document consisting mainly of appendices which purport to record the history of modern Irish republicanism. It opens with the impressive claim that the 'Committee of Irish Catholics' who have prepared it are speaking in the name of 'more than a million of our co-religionists, supporters of the Government of the Irish Republic'. Having assured the Pope of the traditional fidelity to the Holy See 'of one of the oldest and most Catholic nations in Europe', the writers seek his help in the 'great spiritual trial' they are now undergoing. The purpose of their document, they explain, is to 'appeal respectfully to Your Holiness against certain decisions of the Irish Hierarchy' which had been promulgated at Maynooth on 10 October 1922. The bishops had issued a declaration which had grave spiritual consequences for all Irish Catholics who supported 'the Republic of Ireland and its government'. In an effort to make the Pope familiar with the context in which the October Pastoral was issued, the authors of the document provide him with the standard Republican interpretation of the constitutional position, explaining that, 'at present, there are two rival governments in Ireland who are at war with each other, each of them claiming to be the legitimate government'. They make it clear which of these governments the Pope should prefer. One is the government of the Republic of Ireland, 'created by the votes of the Irish people themselves at two general elections, the first of these in 1918, the second in 1921'. The other government 'calls itself the Provisional Government, and draws its attributes and whatever authority it possesses from the legislative acts of the British Parliament and rests, exclusively, on force'. The Provisional Government has existed 'only since January 1922, while the Government of the Republic of Ireland has been functioning continuously since January 1919'. The writers go on to tell the Pope that the Irish bishops, in their pronouncement on the constitutional question, have made the wrong choice: their Pastoral Letter 'declares that the Provisional Government is the legitimate Government of the country and has been elected by the nation'. Furthermore, 'it stigmatizes all those who wage war against this government and in defence of the Irish Republic as rebels', and inflicts the severest spiritual

[193] Ibid. De Valera did not sign the document.

penalties on them. The Pope is respectfully told that 'to impose such draconian penalties on those Irish Catholics accused only of having defended what they conscientiously believe to be the legitimate government against the violence of what they conscientiously believe to be an illegal and usurping government, is something not only unjustifiable in itself, but prejudicial to the true interests of our holy religion'. The letter ends with a 'humble' prayer to the Holy See to take 'whatever measures it may judge necessary to bring to a speedy end the serious religious burdens which have been imposed on us'.[194]

The two men given the task of delivering the document to the Pope, Arthur Clery and Conn Murphy, were pious Catholics. Clery was a part-time professor of law in University College Dublin, who spent much of his money on his students and on charitable work in the Dublin slums; his work as a journalist with D.P. Moran's *Leader* allowed him to indulge his distrust of Protestants and Freemasons. He regarded the Oath in the Treaty as 'the Devil's Sacrament' and a renunciation of Faith.[195] Murphy, a civil servant, was equally resolutely opposed to the Treaty. He complained to the press in September 1922 that his house had been raided five times in a month.[196] On their way to Rome, Clery and Murphy visited the sympathetic Bishop Amigo at Southwark, who advised them to refrain from complaining to the Pope about the hierarchy, but to press for an end to the penalties imposed by the October Pastoral; Amigo found both of them 'excellent men', anxious for peace.[197] On their arrival in Rome, Hagan reported to Archbishop Byrne, they were 'received once or twice by Cardinal Gasparri [Secretary of State] and apparently with

---

[194] The letter, 22 pages in length with 65 pages of appendices and signed on behalf of 'Le Catholic Appeal Committee', is now in the Hagan Papers. Quotations are in the author's translation. Historians of the period have so far not made use of this essential document. Dermot Keogh writes: 'Two men, Dr Conn Murphy and Professor Arthur Clery, travelled to Rome with a document in French of over eighty pages setting out their case against the Irish hierarchy. Although I have not been able to see this document, Curran commented that it had all the usual drawbacks of a paper amended by too many cooks', *The Vatican, the Bishops*, p. 105.

[195] See Patrick Maume, *D.P. Moran* (Dublin, 1995), pp. 16, 17, 41.

[196] *Freeman's Journal*, 15.9.22. At the Fianna Fáil Ard Fheis in 1933, Murphy referred to the fact that he had been dismissed from the Civil Service in 1922 for political reasons, and reinstated in 1928. The Fianna Fáil government, he complained, had refused to pay his arrears, and its policy seemed to be 'forgive your enemies and forget your friends'. At this point, Seán T. O'Kelly, the Ard Fheis Chairman, told Murphy that many delegates possibly believed that they had greater personal grievances than he had, and that the delegates 'were there to do the nation's work', not to listen to 'personal grievances'. *Irish Press*, 9.11.33.

[197] Amigo to Hagan, 10.12.22.

sufficient courtesy'; Curran told one of the Archbishop's Secretaries that 'The Cardinal Secretary of State told them the matter would be considered when they had the reply of Cardinal Logue', and that 'they certainly fought their corner well and courageously despite all the difficulties, and despite the fact they didn't seem too satisfied with the form of the document they had to present'.[198] Clery and Murphy had good reason to be pleased with their work. They had convinced the Vatican authorities that both the government and the Irish bishops had a case to answer, and that the Holy See should become involved in adjudicating upon the ecclesiastical aspects of the Republican grievances. The extent of their achievement may be judged from press reports following their return. They had three interviews with Cardinal Gasparri, and an audience with the Pope. Their letter of appeal against episcopal sanctions had been 'duly endorsed on the records of the Vatican'. Gasparri assured them that when Logue's response to their remonstrance had been received, 'the case would be duly considered by the Sacred Congregation whose function it was to deal with such matters' and which would forward a report to the Pope. The latter would then be in a position, 'before issuing a decision, to discuss the merits of the case with the delegates at a further Private Audience, the date of which would be forwarded to the Appeal Committee'.[199] This Republican version of the reception accorded by the Pope and his Secretary of State to Clery and Murphy, and of the response to the grievances they outlined, was not challenged by the Vatican, as a Free State diplomat, Seán Murphy, was to point out to Gasparri. In April, during an interview with the Secretary of State, Murphy complained that 'the Holy See unfortunately omitted to contradict' the Republican statement, thus giving the impression that 'the Vatican was inclined to give undue consideration to the Irregulars' claims'.[200] The Holy See could scarcely have contradicted

[198] Hagan to Byrne, 5.1.23; Curran to Archbishop Byrne's Secretary, 4.1.23, DAA. Hagan wanted to give Clery and Murphy all the help he could in their presentation of the Republican case. 'I will assume', he told Byrne before the two met Gasparri, 'that I am free to employ an Advocate should I find that they are taking the case to the Rota or to one of the regular tribunals such as the Congregation of the Council. Indeed, as long as they are here I should prefer to have assistance of this kind, so as to avoid all possibility of mistake or misconstruction'. Hagan to Byrne, 22.12.22, DAA. According to Hagan, the Vatican had reservations about the content of the October Pastoral. 'As far as I can gather', he told Mannix, 'the people in the Secretary of State's office did not think the Bishops had done right; but as what they did was pleasing to England, the Holy See did not interfere'. Hagan to Mannix, 5.10.23, Hagan Papers.
[199] There is a copy of this report in NAI S 1792.
[200] Seán Murphy's report on meeting with Gasparri, 26.4.23, NAI D/FA 52.

the Republican report of the mission, since it gave an accurate account of what had happened during the Roman visit of Clery and Murphy. The Vatican had indeed given serious consideration to the Republican claims, as Logue discovered in January 1923 when he received a copy of the Appeal for his comments.[201]

In January 1923, Logue told Byrne of the kind of response he had in mind. He did not accept that the most serious charge made in the Appeal was justified, that 'we deprived the Republicans of Sacraments'; he would argue that the bishops had merely stated that 'those who persisted in committing crimes which he enumerated were not fit for Sacraments, which is the plain doctrine of the Church'. It seemed to Logue that the only charge which could be brought against the bishops was that they 'warned the people against crime', which was their duty, 'and exhorted the people to obey the present government, and if they wished, work for the Republic by constitutional means, which we had every right to do'.[202] At this stage, Logue was familiar with the contents of the document presented to the Pope by Clery and Murphy or had, at any rate, received a copy from Rome, but his remarks to Byrne do not suggest that he was concerned with addressing the fundamental issues raised in it. In his letter to Byrne, Logue argued that the stand taken by the bishops against the Republicans had nothing to do with political or constitutional matters, 'pacts and first and second Dáil and elections', for example. A central point of the Republican case, however, was that the bishops had based their moral condemnation of Republicans, and the spiritual penalties they imposed, on their dubious interpretation of a disputed question of constitutional law on which they had no right or no competence to adjudicate.

In March 1923, the Pope intervened in the Irish situation in a way that displeased both the bishops and the Free State government, but gave some comfort to Republicans. On 14 March, the *Giornale di Roma* announced the departure of Monsignor Salvatore Luzio, who had been Professor of Canon Law at Maynooth from 1897 to 1910, as Papal Envoy to Ireland. Luzio arrived in Ireland on 19 March. On the same day Bishop Browne of Cloyne wrote to O'Doherty of Clonfert expressing extreme surprise at the development. He found the coming of Luzio 'amazing, without any previous intimation (so far as I know) to Cardinal Logue or the Irish Hierarchy'.[203] Luzio's arrival had, however, been heralded long in advance. On 13 November, 1922, Hagan told Archbishop Byrne that the news of the projected appointment of an Apostolic Delegate was so definite 'that

[201] Logue to Byrne, 21.1.23, Byrne Papers, DAA.
[202] Ibid.
[203] Browne to O'Doherty, 19.3.23, GDA.

the name of Luzio is a matter of gossip in interested circles'. In mid-December 1922, James O'Dea, Galway Diocesan Secretary, was able to tell his friend Professor Michael Browne of Maynooth of rumours that 'we are getting Luzio as a papal nuncio'.[204] Logue had long been seeking something of this kind: since the beginning of the Civil War he had been pressing the Vatican authorities not only for 'a fulmination' against Republicans, but for a direct intervention in the form of a delegate.[205] Two days after his arrival, Luzio called on Logue, presenting him with a letter of introduction from Cardinal Gasparri. The letter informed Logue that Luzio, 'Domestic Prelate of His Holiness and Regent of the Sacred Penitentiary' was in Ireland 'by charge of the Holy Father' to gather 'all news and information that may be useful for the knowledge of the Holy See on the actual condition of affairs in your nation'. His other task was 'to co-operate, as far as he possibly can, in the pacification of minds in the interests of a much-desired and definite settlement of the country'. The letter also asked Logue to facilitate Luzio's 'acquaintanceship with the most prominent and eminent personages'.[206] To Logue's dismay, it soon became clear that among the 'eminent personages' Luzio and Gasparri had in mind were leading Republicans. Indeed, the Pope also appears to have instructed Luzio to talk to Republican leaders. Arthur Clery, who was in frequent communication with Luzio during his visit, made this clear in a letter to de Valera in late March. 'I saw Luzio again', he wrote; 'He said the Pope told him to meet you so that he might convey the Pope's message to you; he was not to write to you because of the state of the country'.[207] Luzio, in his enthusiasm to follow these instructions, suggested that Logue and himself go on a mission to the

[204] Hagan to Archbishop Byrne, 13.11.22, Byrne Papers, DAA; Father James O'Dea to M.J. Browne, 15.12.22, GDA.

[205] Logue's appeal for an anti-Republican 'fulmination' resulted, as Hagan remarked with much satisfaction to Archbishop Byrne 'in something different from what he had been urging and was expecting'. Hagan to Byrne, 13.11.22, Byrne Papers, DAA. The Pope's reply to Logue , far from betraying any anxiety to condemn Republicans, suggests that the Pope wanted the Irish bishops to act as reconcilers, not as political partisans. 'Trusting as we are in your prudence, Venerable Brothers', he tells Logue and the other bishops, 'we are altogether confident that you will discreetly exert every effort in order that all in Ireland, whosoever they may be (*ut omnes, quotquot sint in Hibernia*), may always be led by a spirit of charity and concord. In that way, your country will not only achieve a much desired tranquillity, but also advance towards a most propitious growth'. Pope Pius XI to Logue, 2.8.22, AAA.

[206] Gasparri's letter introducing Luzio is reproduced in *ICD*, 1924, p. 569.

[207] A.E. Clery to de Valera, 29.4.23 (recte 29.3.23). Quoted in Ó Néill agus Ó Fiannachta, *De Valera*, Vol. II, p. 106. Hagan told Byrne that Luzio was believed to have received instructions 'to see Dev soon after his arrival'. Hagan to Byrne, 8.3.23, Byrne Papers, DAA.

Republicans. Logue, who had a settled contempt for Republicans and their activities, seems to have told Luzio that if he could bring back surrender terms from them he would consider these.[208]

Much of Luzio's stay in Ireland was spent in meeting and corresponding with Republicans. Early in April, he was in touch with Joseph Byrne, the new Irish Provincial of the Holy Ghost Congregation, to arrange a meeting with de Valera. On 6 April, one Holy Ghost priest, Herbert Farrell, collected Luzio at the Shelbourne Hotel where he stayed during his Irish visit; another member of the order, disguised as Luzio, headed towards Dun Laoghaire followed by detectives. Meanwhile, Luzio was conveyed to Mount Street where he met de Valera.[209] The meeting was not satisfactory from de Valera's point of view, although he was impressed by Luzio's good will towards Republicans. Writing to Hagan after Luzio had left Ireland, de Valera reported that 'his attitude was so sympathetic that our people thronged to visit him . . . I had one interview with him, in which we discussed matters generally. He came, unfortunately, at a bad time for us. The peacemaker has always an almost irresistible temptation to try to effect his object by bringing pressure on the weaker side to give in. I am afraid our visitor was succumbing to it when he should have stood rigidly for impartial justice. However, his task was almost superhuman, and it is easy to criticise'.[210] During his interview with Luzio, de Valera placed far less emphasis on the political situation than on the moral and spiritual predicament of Republicans troubled like himself by the implications of the episcopal judgment on their cause. This concerned de Valera a great deal more than did the principles on which peace might be established.[211] A week after the interview, Seán T. O'Kelly's wife Cáit told Hagan that 'L'Espagnol [de Valera] and l'Italien [Luzio] have met here without settling the Irish question so far. Monsignor Luzio is most anxious to see peace reign here and then the Sacraments will cease to be a state monopoly'.[212] Luzio's suggestion that a restoration of peace might be the condition on which the religious sanctions on Republicans might be lifted explains why de Valera considered him 'not too satisfactory on the question of the sacraments'.[213]

[208] See Keogh, *The Vatican, the Bishops*, p.113.
[209] Farragher, *De Valera*, p.140.
[210] De Valera to Hagan, 19.5.23, Hagan Papers.
[211] See Ó Néill agus Ó Fiannachta, *De Valera*, p. 107. From October 1922, until the end of the Civil War, de Valera, in deference to the terms of the October Pastoral, did not receive the sacraments. I owe this information to the late Professor T.P. O'Neill.
[212] Cáit O'Kelly to Hagan, 13.4.23, Hagan Papers.
[213] See Ó Néill agus Ó Fiannachta, *De Valera*, p. 107

Following de Valera's single, inconclusive meeting with Luzio, all further contacts between the two were maintained by means of letters passed from one to the other by Father Byrne. In the first of these letters dated 16 April and addressed to Byrne, de Valera suggested that Luzio go to see 'Cosgrave and Co. and point out to them that a truce is necessary in order to get things properly done. They cannot be blind to the fact that they can never, no matter what they or we do, hope to get in all the [Republican] arms.' For his part, de Valera could guarantee that if he gave a Ceasefire Order it would be obeyed, provided that Republican combatants could return unmolested to their homes, prisoners were released and those who had supplied active-service units were compensated. De Valera did not want Cosgrave's government to know that he had made such proposals. He asked Byrne to 'press these views on our visitor [Luzio] as from *yourself*, if you share them, and ask him to press them on Cosg. as from *himself*. If Luzio were to be 'instrumental in securing a peace that will be practical and real' the result would be advantageous to the Church. He concluded by expressing a common Republican view that the Irish episcopacy had become the most deadly of all the enemies of the Republican cause. Luzio, however, could help to redeem the Church in the eyes of Republicans were he to influence Cosgrave in the direction of a just settlement. 'This act of reparation', he told Byrne, 'however inadequate, may soften the bitterness which our people will feel against the Bishops who more than the military forces of our opponents have brought our cause to this pass'.[214] When this letter was written, Luzio had met Cosgrave, who later explained to the press that he could not discuss political questions with the Pope's envoy. He regarded Luzio's visit to him as merely a 'courteous friendly act', devoid of any other significance. Luzio could not have properly

---

[214] De Valera to Father Joseph Byrne, 16.4.23. This and other relevant correspondence may be found in Farragher, *De Valera*, pp. 141 ff. Compare the views of Aodh de Blacam, a convert to Catholicism who served the Republican cause with a religious fervour. 'Every day', de Blacam wrote to his Capuchin friend and fellow-Republican Father Canice, 'I see more clearly that our movement broke on the Bishops, as the cause did many times in history. And there never was a finer spiritual movement in Ireland than when Kevin Barry and MacSwiney were winning for us. The defeat is due to the Bishops siding with perjury and badness against truth and charity, and as the fight was a spiritual one, their causing a schism in the spirit of the nation broke us. We will never be free till either the people revolt against the Bishops as well as England, or the Church gets pure and sides with the right. If the Church had blessed our movement, we could have smashed all the empire's might, just as we beat it in conscription year.' Aodh de Blacam to Fr Canice, 27.7.22. Desmond FitzGerald Papers, UCDA, P80/736.

presented himself 'in a political or diplomatic capacity'; had he wished to do that he would have been obliged to submit his application 'for reception on a political mission' to the Ministry for External Affairs and then await a government decision 'as to whether his intervention in our political affairs should be permitted'. Since Luzio had followed none of these procedures, he could have no status in Cosgrave's eyes as a political mediator.[215] At this point de Valera decided that the Luzio mission had 'not been of much value'. Under pressure from the Free State government, the Pope had agreed to recall him.[216] De Valera sent Luzio a parting note, in which he declared that in fighting the Free State he had been 'fighting a usurpation that got into power by a coup d'état – by fraud and force'. He hoped that Luzio could arrange for a message to Ireland from the Pope 'asking that the dispute between the rival governments be left to an election'.[217] This latter suggestion was in line with what Luzio had told Clery about the Pope's view of the political situation in Ireland. 'The Pope', Clery wrote to de Valera, 'could not settle the political question; but he [the Pope] thought it might be settled by means of an election, although he admitted that it might be difficult to arrange an election given the present state of things'.[218] In his discussions with Republicans, Luzio had found the idea of a plebiscite on the constitutional issue attractive. Cáit O'Kelly found him 'very enthusiastic' about the notion that the people should be asked to decide whether the Free State was a final settlement, whether it was accepted under duress, or whether it was 'accepted at all, with or without duress'.[219]

De Valera may not have found Luzio's mission of 'much value', but other Republicans who met him seem to have been heartened by his openness to their point of view. Mary MacSwiney told Kathleen O'Connell, de Valera's Personal Secretary, that Luzio had 'assured Professor Clery that the Holy Father commissioned him especially to see Mr de Valera and that he was willing to go anywhere and to make any arrangements we desire'.[220] After Luzio's departure on 5 May,

[215] *Freeman's Journal*, 20.4.23.
[216] On 23.4.23, following representations from Cosgrave to the Vatican, the Pope agreed that 'Monsignor Luzio's ecclesiastical business had come to an end and that he would be recalled immediately by wire'. Seán Murphy's report on meeting with Gasparri, 26.4.23. NAI D/FA S2.
[217] Farragher, *De Valera*, pp. 142–3.
[218] Clery to de Valera, 29.3.23. Quoted in Ó Néill agus Ó Fiannachta, *De Valera*, p. 107.
[219] Cáit O'Kelly to Hagan, 13.4.23, Hagan Papers.
[220] Mary MacSwiney to Kathleen O'Connell, 2.4.23, Kathleen O'Connell Papers. MacSwiney added that she would write a full report for the President [de Valera] during the week, of the people on our side who have seen the Nuncio, and any points I think may be useful to him'.

Cáit O'Kelly told Hagan that he had been 'exceedingly nice and patient.' As long as he was in Ireland, 'the ladies, especially, unburdened their hearts to him and came away comforted. Father Sweetman[221] was of the other half of humanity the most constant in attendance. I met some disconsolate women on Sunday, after His Excellency's departure'. Mrs O'Kelly could not imagine that he had 'come to Ireland to console the Republicans and the downtrodden'. She made a significant observation on Luzio's response to his reception by the Free State authorities. 'He was', she reported, 'brutally treated, and said so, by the governing section'. Hagan later confirmed this sense of outrage on Luzio's part at the way he had been dealt with not only by the government, but also by the bishops, who had largely ignored him. Hagan's letters to the Irish bishops following Luzio's return to Rome have many references to Luzio's intense displeasure and disappointment. Hagan told O'Doherty of Clonfert that 'Luzio was glad to have escaped with his whole skin, and where he expected to meet nothing but warm friends he found little but cold looks and no welcome'.[222] Hagan reported to Archbishop Byrne that 'Luzio is disgruntled, feels dissatisfied with everyone including his secretary[223] and the Bishops, and considers that the latter did nothing to promote his enterprise'.[224] A further letter from Hagan to Byrne has a telling comment on the unfavourable impression created by the Irish Bishops and the Free State Government not only on Luzio but on the Pope. Luzio, Hagan claims, 'is very bitter on the Bishops for their coldness and failure to afford help; he has the utmost contempt for the members of the Cabinet, with the exception of Cosgrave; looks on O'Higgins as the incarnation of evil; blames the English for the whole mess; says H.H.[His Holiness] is fit to be tied and is utterly disgusted'.[225] Luzio clearly felt that he had less reason to be displeased with the reception accorded to his mission by the Republican side. On 29 April, after de Valera had published his own peace proposals, Luzio sent him an encouraging letter. 'I congratulate you', he wrote, 'because you have

---

[221] See p. 167, note 134.

[222] Hagan to O'Doherty, 25.5.23, GDA. In another letter, Hagan explained that the 'cold looks' he had received were from the Irish bishops. Hagan to Byrne, 25.5.23, Byrne Papers, DAA.

[223] Canon Conry, an Irish priest resident in Rome, acted as Luzio's secretary in Ireland.

[224] Hagan to Byrne, 25.5.23, Byrne Papers, DAA.

[225] Hagan to Byrne, 25.6.23, Byrne Papers, DAA. In early October 1923, Hagan told Mannix that he believed that the Pope was 'sick and tired of Ireland, and does not want to hear the word mentioned. He has made no reference to the country the last three or four times I have been speaking to him'. Hagan to Mannix, 5.10.23, Hagan Papers.

succeeded in doing something practical in the interests of peace. Now that your proposals have been published, the Government of the Free State is answerable for any delay in achieving peace'.[226]

Before Luzio's departure, de Valera urged him to assure the Pope that Republicans still regarded themselves as belonging to the Church, whatever sanctions the bishops of Ireland might have imposed on them.[227] He continued to correspond with Luzio, to whom he gave advance notice of the Republican Ceasefire order of 24 May. In the interests of the general pacification of the country, he suggested to Luzio that the Church could now lead by example by removing at once the unjust spiritual penalties it had imposed on conscientious Republicans.[228] In the final stages of the Civil War, Luzio wrote to Father Byrne suggesting that de Valera should not allow the Oath to prevent him from making a peace settlement with the Free State, and warning that 'if negotiations are broken off only for that reason by Mr de Valera, he would not have much sympathy or support even from the Vatican'. In Italy, he pointed out, members of the Republican Party take a similar oath in good faith, 'and feel quite sure they remain as Republican as ever – everybody knows what is the meaning of such an oath taken by a Republican'.[229] Luzio also wanted de Valera to go beyond the terms of the Republican Ceasefire order of 24 May and to surrender or destroy arms.[230] De Valera wrote to him on 22 June, rejecting his two suggestions. 'Acceptance of the oath', he told Luzio, 'is of course quite out of the question. That would be a formal act of obeisance and homage to England, and one of national humiliation for Ireland'. Surrender or destruction of arms would imply a recognition of the authority of the Free State Executive, and

---

[226] Luzio to de Valera, 29.4.23. Quoted in Ó Néill agus Ó Fiannachta, *De Valera*, p.112. This letter was delivered to de Valera by Father Joseph Byrne. Kathleen O'Connell's diary for 29.4.23 records that 'Father Byrne called and stayed the night'.

[227] See Longford and O'Neill, *De Valera*, p. 220.

[228] De Valera to Luzio, 23.5.23. See Ó Néill agus Ó Fiannachta, *De Valera*, p.124. Luzio's presence in Ireland seems to have led to an easing of the conditions imposed on at least some Republican penitents. According to the commonly applied interpretation of the October Pastoral, Republicans could not receive the sacraments unless they repudiated the aims and methods of their movement. According to Kathleen O'Connell's sister Teresa, who was a prisoner during the period, circumstances changed following Luzio's arrival. She recalls that on 24 April a Jesuit priest absolved her without the usual insistence on a renunciation of Republican intent. Statement of Teresa O'Connell to author.

[229] Farragher, *De Valera*, p. 243 quotes Luzio's letter.

[230] For details of the IRA attitude to the surrender of arms, see Macardle, *The Irish Republic*, 4th edn (Dublin, 1951) pp. 849ff.

Republicans, de Valera asserted, 'do not and cannot recognise that authority as legitimate'.[231]

Luzio's visit brought into sharp focus the complex and troubled relationship between the Irish bishops and the Free State government on the one hand, and the Vatican on the other. The government and most of the bishops saw the Luzio visit primarily as a Republican event through which the Vatican had given a wholly unacceptable moral respectability and a constitutional status to the forces of anarchy. Cosgrave made angry representations to the Vatican in the third week of April 1923; a senior diplomat complained to the cardinal Secretary of State that Luzio had not got in touch with the government 'until he had first seen the Irregulars', and that he had remained a month in the country 'without in any way informing the government of his presence'.[232] On 21 April, the Executive Council heard details of what ministers must have regarded as an astonishing Vatican intervention in Irish political affairs. The Minister of External Affairs, Desmond FitzGerald, reported that during an interview with Archbishop Byrne on the previous day, the latter had informed him that he had received a telegram from Cardinal Gasparri, Secretary of State to the Vatican, instructing him to approach the Government of the Free State with a view to securing the release of Dr Conn Murphy, 'the impression at the Vatican apparently being that Dr Murphy had been arrested because he had presented a petition to Rome on behalf of the Republicans'.[233] On 19 April, the *Irish Independent* reported that Cardinal Gasparri had sent the following telegram to Mrs Despard[234] for Conn

[231] De Valera to Luzio, 22.6.22. Copy in Hagan Papers.

[232] The diplomat, Seán Murphy, reported to the government on 26.4.23. See NAI D/FA, 52.

[233] Executive Council Minutes, NAI G2/2, 21.4.23, p.8. The following text of Cardinal Gasparri's telegram of 19.4.23 to Byrne was published by the Republican journal *Éire*: 'It has been represented to the Holy See that Dr. Murphy is in prison for having presented to His Holiness an appeal. His Holiness painfully impressed by such news begs Your Lordship to ask the Government in his [Pope's] name to set him − Dr. Murphy − at liberty as this will help very much in the pacification of the Country'. *Éire*, 5.5.23. On 24.4.23, *Éire* reported the granting by the Pope of his Apostolic Benediction to Murphy 'on hunger-strike against his arrest, via Mrs Despard, not through the Archbishop of Dublin' and claimed that Murphy 'was released within a few hours'. The *Éire* reporter believed that through this act, 'the Pope has done much to prevent loss of faith in Ireland'. On 30.4.23, Desmond FitzGerald explained to Gasparri at the Vatican that Murphy had been arrested because a search of his house showed that it was being used as a centre for the distribution of 'Irregular despatches'. See Desmond FitzGerald Papers, UCDA.

[234] Charlotte Despard (1844–1939) was the elder sister of Lord French. During the War of Independence he was Lord Lieutenant while she supported the IRA. Her status as an upper-class convert to Catholicism would have impressed the Vatican authorities.

Murphy who was on hunger-strike: 'Holy Father sends Dr Murphy Papal Benediction'. The Executive Council meeting was told that Murphy had been released before Gasparri's telegram was sent. Since it was obvious to members of the government that 'His Holiness the Pope had no proper knowledge of the true facts of the case', it was decided that 'the Minister of External Affairs should proceed to Rome with full particulars of Dr Conn Murphy's case, but that his departure should be delayed pending the negotiations [with the Vatican] with regard to Monsignor Luzio'.[235] Two days later, these latter negotiations had been successfully concluded; on 23 April the Pope and Gasparri agreed to recall Luzio to Rome.[236] Cosgrave's relieved response was to offer 'sentiments of grateful appreciation of the gracious consideration of His Holiness . . . whereby the embarrassment caused by the manner of the Right Rev. Monsignor Luzio's intervention in our affairs has been brought to an end'.[237] Government resentment towards Luzio and his mission had come to a head following a statement issued on his behalf by his secretary to the press on 17 April that Luzio was 'now free to devote his entire services to the interests of peace and in this capacity he will be directly representing the Holy Father', and that his 'time and services will be at the disposal of all those, no matter what their political convictions may be, who desire the fulfilment of that end'.[238] This led the Executive Council to decide that Luzio was 'now endeavouring to interfere in the domestic affairs of the country', that his action 'was an encouragement to the forces of disorder and anarchy operating against the government and its people', and that the Pope should be apprised of this view.[239]

Luzio's statement to the press, and his free association with Republicans, could plausibly be interpreted as meaning that he was in Ireland to reconcile two disputing factions, neither of which enjoyed a more secure title to legitimacy than the other, either in his own eyes or in those of the Pope. The notion that the Civil War was a struggle between rival governments or rival pretenders to government was central to the Republican case presented at the Vatican by Murphy and Clery in December 1922; in April 1923, Luzio was at least giving the impression that he was operating as if the Vatican favoured the Republican interpretation of the constitutional position in the Free State. Kevin O'Shiel, a legal adviser to the Free State government, prepared a memorandum on the implications of the Luzio visit for

[235] Executive Council Minutes, 21.4.23, NAI G 2/2 p.8
[236] NAI, D/FA, S2.
[237] Cosgrave to Gasparri, 8.5.23, NAI D/FA S2.
[238] *Irish Independent*, 17.4.23.
[239] Executive Council Minutes, 17.4.23, NAI G2/1.

North–South relations in April 1923, for circulation to each member of the Executive Council.[240] O'Shiel was worried that the attitude adopted by Luzio had given Republicans an excuse for inciting public bodies to pass resolutions calling upon him to work for peace, which really meant trying to encourage Cosgrave to negotiate with de Valera. Some Republicans certainly saw Luzio as an authoritative arbiter of the political question at issue in the Civil War. Fr P.J. O'Loughlin of Ballinasloe thought it would be a good idea if representatives of the Free State Government and de Valera could 'lay their respective claims' before the Pope's representative; if they did, he suggested, 'perhaps agreement will come to end the present campaign of blood and murder'.[241] What worried O'Shiel most was the divergence between the views of the Irish bishops and those of the Vatican on the issues underlying the Civil War. The Irish hierarchy, 'the highest moral authority in the land', had, O'Shiel recalled, given the Free State its 'emphatic endorsement and support'. The Government and the bishops might, he implied, have expected a similar response from the Holy See. Given the 'deliberate and unanimous ruling of the bishops, the alleged activities of Mgr Luzio appear all the more extraordinary, and, considering them in conjunction with the reported grant of the Benediction of the Holy Father to one who comes under the bishops' interdict, one would have to draw the conclusion that the Roman authorities were in direct conflict with the grave and considered opinion of the Irish Church'.[242] At the end of April, Desmond FitzGerald told Gasparri that the 'apparent indifference' of the Vatican to 'the express public declaration' of the Irish bishops in favour of the Free State had been 'a source of grave scandal and disedification' to supporters of the government.[243]

O'Shiel's conclusion that the views of the Vatican authorities on the Irish situation conflicted with those of the Irish bishops was justified, but for reasons not entirely discreditable to the Vatican. Unlike the Irish bishops, the Holy See was in no hurry to give formal recognition to the Free State government. This was made clear to those Irish diplomats who sought such recognition in 1922. Count O'Byrne, who represented the government in Rome up to the outbreak of the Civil War, was told by the Vatican Pro-Secretary of State, Monsignor Borgongini Duca, on 28 February 1922 that 'having regard to the present divergence of opinion', it would be premature for the Holy

---

[240] The report was circulated to the members of the Executive Council on 19.4.23, NAI S 2198.
[241] *Roscommon Journal*, 21.4.23.
[242] O'Shiel Memorandum, 19.4.23, NAI S 2198.
[243] Memorandum by Joseph Walsh, 30.4.23, FitzGerald Papers, UCDA.

See to afford recognition until after the Irish people had expressed their wishes at the elections.[244] When O'Byrne again pressed for recognition following the June elections of 1922, which could be interpreted as an emphatic endorsement of the Treaty, he was asked to wait another month.[245] With the supervention of civil war, the negative attitude of the Vatican was even more emphatically expressed. O'Byrne was told on 27 July that 'having regard to the state of affairs at present prevalent in Ireland, and to the fighting that was going on there' the Holy See 'did not consider it opportune' to recognise the Provisional Government. However, 'once peace was restored' and once 'a government could function normally in Ireland', the representative of such a government would be received by the Pope 'with due formality'.[246] In November 1922, we find Hagan advising Borgongini Duca that the Holy See should be extremely cautious in pronouncing on 'Irish political or semi-political affairs'. Hagan, alerting the Vatican Pro-Secretary to the impending arrival in Rome of Murphy and Clery, professed to have 'intimate knowledge' of the 'aims and hopes' of bishops as well as Republicans. He expressed 'the carefully considered opinion that in dealing with this crisis and with protests and appeals arising out of it, a neutral and procrastinating attitude would seem to me to be the most advisable at the present dark hour'. Any action on the part of the Holy See, even a negative one, he told Borgongini Duca, 'may easily lead to developments and complications gravely prejudicial to the interests of religion for many a year to come'.[247]

Hagan did not want the Vatican authorities to fall into the errors he considered the Irish bishops to have made even before October 1922. In August 1922, on the day Collins was killed, Hagan told Bishop O'Dea of Galway that he was particularly depressed at recent episcopal condemnations of Republicans which seemed to him 'calculated to do much harm in the years that lie ahead'. Hagan, a good historian, reminded O'Dea of 'the many souls held aloof for years from the sacraments as a consequence of the attitude of Churchmen towards the Fenian movement'. The bishops, he believed, should frame their conduct in accordance with the distinct possibility that today's rebels might be tomorrow's governors. Indeed, he had 'little hesitation in forming a forecast that in half a dozen years the republican party will command the majority of the country'. In that event, Irish churchmen would not like to be reminded that 'more than one Bishop today was

---

[244] FitzGerald Papers, UCDA P80/410.
[245] Ibid., 102/22, 3.7.22.
[246] Ibid., 27.7.22.
[247] Hagan to Borgongini Duca, 13.11.22, Hagan Papers

responsible for the denying of absolution to those who rightly or wrongly have made up their minds as to the lawfulness of resorting to certain methods for the realisation of the Republican ideal'.[248] Like Hagan, and prompted by him from time to time, the Vatican, in contrast to the Irish bishops, was taking the longer view of Irish affairs. During 1922 and much of 1923, it could not have appeared prudent to the Vatican authorities to make a formal commitment to either side in a struggle whose outcome was uncertain, and in which both of the warring parties professed strict Catholic principles. A benevolent neutrality and the extension of fatherly solicitude to everybody involved was deemed the saner course. In many Republican eyes, the Vatican did a useful service to the cause of Catholicism in Ireland by refusing to compound the sins of the bishops.

V

The most consistent and zealous advocates of Irish Republicanism in Rome were Hagan, Rector of the Irish College there from 1919 until his death in 1930, and Father Michael Curran, Vice-Rector during the same period and Rector in succession to Hagan from 1930 until the outbreak of the Second World War.[249] As Rector of the Irish College, Hagan was the Roman agent of the Irish bishops. It was his duty to interpret their requests and views, and to transmit these to the appropriate Vatican authorities. In the course of his work, Hagan had close contacts with members of the Roman Curia and, as his massive correspondence makes clear, had regular interviews with the Pope and the Vatican Secretary of State. His closeness to the centre of Vatican power gave him considerable prestige and influence at home. He was in regular communication with almost every Irish bishop, and seldom slow to direct episcopal thinking on political affairs towards conclusions favoured by himself. His status as an indispensable, if somewhat biased, source of intelligence on Roman ecclesiastical politics was widely recognised. Writing from Rome in October 1921, Margaret Gavan Duffy advised de Valera that if he asked Hagan's 'opinion of

[248] Hagan to O'Dea, 22.8.22, GDA.
[249] Hagan was born in 1874 near Rathnew, Co. Wicklow, educated at Clonliffe and Rome, and became Vice-Rector of the Irish College in 1903, during the Rectorship of Monsignor Michael O'Riordan. Between 1911 and 1919, he was Roman correspondent for the *Catholic Bulletin*, a Republican journal which, following his death in 1930, devoted almost a whole issue to his life and work for nationalist causes. Curran was born in Dublin in 1880, was educated at Clonliffe and Rome, and was Secretary to Archbishop Walsh before becoming Vice-Rector of the Irish College.

things here', no one could give him 'such inside information'.[250] Hagan deployed his considerable resources of knowledge, influence, intelligence and diplomacy in the interest of Irish independence before the Treaty and of anti-Treaty Republicanism in its aftermath. Curran, whose political outlook was identical with Hagan's, and who, during his Dublin years, had become intimately involved with many of those at the centre of extreme nationalist politics, supplemented Hagan's efforts on behalf of anti-Treaty Republicanism at every opportunity.

In October 1921, Hagan, having formed 'impressions with regard to certain shortcomings' in the Department for Foreign Affairs, appears to have discussed these with fellow-Irishmen in Rome, who brought them to the notice of Arthur Griffith. The latter wrote an insensitive, admonitory letter to Hagan, which was described by Margaret Gavan Duffy, in a letter from the 'Delegation of the Republic of Ireland, Rome' as 'almost insulting in tone and written as from superior to inferior'. Realising that Hagan had been 'deeply wounded', and finding it strange that a man who had 'worked for over eighteen years here in such a wonderful way unrecognised by those at home' should thus be humiliated, she suggested that it would be 'of immense usefulness' for de Valera to conciliate the Rector.[251] De Valera duly wrote to Hagan paying generous tribute to his patriotic work.[252] Hagan's grateful reply casts useful light on his political outlook, his preoccupations and prejudices, and on the role he had created for himself as an apologist for Irish nationalism. His earnest goodwill for de Valera, which never abated, is unconcealed. 'I have and can have only one feeling', he assures him, 'namely a feeling of admiration for the man who, without pomp or parade has been able to hold his own and bring very near to a successful issue the struggle in which so many brilliant Irishmen went down'. Hagan sees himself as a representative of Irish political as well as ecclesiastical interests in Rome, entitled to receive reliable information on political developments at home, and possessing authority to present the Irish case to influential residents of Rome. The inefficiency of the Department for Foreign Affairs has, he complains to de Valera, inhibited him in the performance of his political tasks. From the beginning of the Treaty negotiations, he has had no communication from this Department. Being ignorant of the trend of events, he had to make up his own mind 'as to whether it was wise or otherwise to keep on asserting that nothing less than a republic or something equivalent to complete separation would be

[250] Margaret Gavan Duffy to de Valera, 19.10.21, FAK 1382.
[251] Ibid.
[252] De Valera to Hagan, 31.10.21, Hagan Papers.

considered and accepted'. Hagan's sense of his selfless dedication to important political work for Ireland is a recurring theme of his correspondence. He has, he tells de Valera, 'tried to do his best, irrespective of consequences, and at the cost of much personal trial, to promote in season and out of season the interests of the cause which all honest Irishmen have at heart'. His best efforts, however, are being impeded by an unspecified 'tiny group of pro-English maniacs in this city'.[253] Hagan may well be referring here to some Christian Brothers. Writing to Archbishop O'Donnell in 1924, he mentions 'the principal Irish Christian Brothers' in Rome 'who for the past ten years have been among the most active of pro-British propagandists, and who, when this College was vacant three years ago, are known to have joined earnestly in the English effort to exclude a particular man [Hagan himself] whose presence in Rome they reported as dangerous to imperial harmony'.[254]

Hagan's political outlook was simple and straightforward. His post-Treaty Republicanism was part of a settled conviction that any form of British influence on Irish affairs was necessarily malign, and he regarded the Free State as little more than an imperial appendage. 'The English view of things', he told Archbishop O'Donnell in 1923, 'coincides with the welfare of the Free State'.[255] After his death, his intimate friend Father Magennis found it easy to describe Hagan's view of Ireland's place in the world. He was, Magennis pointed out, utterly dedicated to the notion of 'a free and independent Ireland, completely cut off from foreign domination . . . His historical knowledge forced him to the conclusion that English influence, in any shape or form, was a hindrance to the spiritual development of the Irish people'.[256] Much of his and Curran's energy was expended in attempts to counteract this influence in Rome and elsewhere. In 1923, Curran complained to Archbishop O'Donnell of the dominance of English ecclesiastics in Rome, and the humiliation of the Irish Church as a consequence. 'It is taken for granted', he pointed out, 'that she [the English Church] represents not merely England and Wales but Scotland, Ireland, the USA, Canada and Australasia, etc., in fact the English-speaking world'.[257] Both Curran and Hagan believed that British governments and their Roman ecclesiastical agents exerted an inordinate influence on the thinking of the Holy See with regard to Ireland; Curran described the English Curial officials as 'respectable

[253] Hagan to De Valera, 17.11.21, FAK 1382.
[254] Hagan to O'Donnell, 10.1.24, Hagan Papers.
[255] Hagan to O'Donnell, 26.3.23, AAA.
[256] Peter Magennis, 'Monsignor John Hagan', *Catholic Bulletin*, vol. xx, 1930, p. 303.
[257] Curran to O'Donnell, 14.3.23, AAA.

spies in the camp'.[258] During the Treaty negotiations, Hagan, seeking
to give Archbishop Byrne 'some sort of accurate idea as to the
Vatican outlook on Ireland and things Irish', could offer no hope that
Irish interests would receive fair consideration in Rome as long as the
Pope, Benedict XV, remained immersed in his 'one hobby, that of
extending and consolidating diplomatic relations'. For the success of
this enterprise, Hagan believed, 'a good understanding with England
and the English ambassador is of the utmost consequence, and anything
endangering that understanding has to be trampled underfoot'. At the
Vatican, as Hagan saw it in the closing months of 1921, the Irish cause
was assumed to be a losing one and the Irish struggle 'a foolish and
even a criminal one', regarded 'as nothing more than a needless
disturbance of the harmonious relations which otherwise could exist
undisturbed between the Holy See and the Empire'.[259] Hagan's extreme
preoccupation with the sinister influence of British ecclesiastics on
Irish affairs remained central to his outlook. Towards the end of 1926,
he told Professor Michael Browne of Maynooth that he could not
hold communication with British churchmen he considered hostile to
Irish interests, and 'could not think of attending social functions at
which they were likely to be present'.[260] In 'the worst of the black-
and-tan days', he recalled, he had refused an invitation to dinner at
the English College, telling the Rector, Hinsley, 'that it would be idle
for him to ask me to meet socially those who either warmly supported
or secretly backed up the doings of those gentlemen'.[261]

Although his Republicanism set him apart politically from the Irish
bishops, he shared the common episcopal view that direct Vatican
intervention in Irish affairs, civil or ecclesiastical, was undesirable. On
12 November 1922, he was alarmed when he received information
from a source he had always found reliable that 'a strong Papal
pronouncement on the actual situation in Ireland' was imminent, and
that the appointment of an Apostolic Delegate to Ireland was in contemplation. Hagan assumed that such a pronouncement would be of
the kind Logue had been seeking and had so far failed to get: an

[258] Ibid. Curran pointed out to Archbishop O'Donnell that his opposition to
British influence was a legacy from Archbishop Walsh; he hoped O'Donnell
would 'make allowance for the thirteen years' training I have got, for good or ill,
from a master who was alive to this evil as no other was'. Curran to O'Donnell,
14.3.23, AAA.
[259] Hagan to Byrne, 7.10.21, Byrne Papers, DAA. 'The Irish', Hagan added
ironically, with himself partly in mind, 'were only making themselves ridiculous
by harping on English atrocities which were either justifiable under the
circumstances or more frequently still were grossly exaggerated.'
[260] Hagan to M.J. Browne, 6.12.26, GDA.
[261] Ibid.

unequivocal denunciation of the Republican side.[262] He moved quickly to circumvent what he believed the Vatican had in mind. On 13 November, he advised the Vatican Under-Secretary of State that the intervention of the Holy See in Irish political affairs would prejudice the interests of religion.[263] Remembering that Byrne had recently expressed the same opinion, Hagan suggested that 'an urgent and authoritative' episcopal statement from Ireland would carry sufficient weight at the Vatican to hold up or modify the projected action. Hagan's dealings with Byrne in this affair illustrate the influence he could exert on the Archbishop. He suggested the kind of letter Byrne should write, approved of the result as 'pertinent and useful', translated it into Italian, and handed it in at the Vatican.[264] The letter incorporates some of Hagan's favourite ideas: the appointment of a delegate would 'put a permanent bar to the ultimate union of North and South' and thus 'lay the Holy See open to the charge of placing the unfortunate Catholics of the North permanently under the heels of their Orange oppressors'; there would always be suspicion in Ireland that the Delegate was under English influence; sending a delegate would be inimical to the best interests of religion in Ireland and to the influence of the Holy See.[265] The Republican Hagan must have enjoyed the experience of having a pro-Treaty Archbishop mediate his view of Irish politics to the Holy See. Hagan was happy with what he had helped to accomplish. 'A month ago', he wrote to Bishop Mulhern of Dromore on Christmas Day, 'there was a Papal letter impending, and with this the probable appointment of an Apostolic Delegate. I am glad to be in a position to think that these two dangers are at least postponed'.[266] In October 1923, he told Mannix that 'the Luzio episode was as unfortunate as it was ill-advised'.[267] In March of that year, he had indicated to Archbishop Byrne why he was opposed to the Pope's decision to send an envoy to Ireland. 'There seems to be no doubt', he told Byrne, 'that the mission, which is ostensibly for peace purposes, is really meant to end up in a permanent delegation. Both Achille [Pius XI] and his Secretary [Gasparri] are bent on this'.[268]

[262] See p. 185, note 205. Hagan was unduly suspicious of Papal motives.

[263] Hagan to Borgongini Duca, 13.11.22, Hagan Papers.

[264] Hagan to Byrne, 4.12.22, Byrne Papers, DAA. Hagan also alerted Archbishop O'Donnell. Hagan to O'Donnell, 14.11.22, AAA.

[265] Byrne to Gasparri, 28.11.22, Byrne Papers, DAA.

[266] Hagan to Mulhern, 25.12.22, DRDA.

[267] Hagan to Mannix, 5.10.23, Hagan Papers.

[268] Hagan to Byrne, 8.3.23, Byrne Papers, DAA. As in the case of most other Roman developments of which he disapproved, Hagan believed that the Luzio mission was 'the result of English influence' at the Vatican. Hagan to O'Donnell, 26.3.23, AAA.

The establishment of a permanent Vatican delegation in Ireland would have involved the accreditation of a Free State representative to the Holy See. In the Autumn of 1923, Hagan was aware of many rumours that such a thing was in prospect. Writing to Archbishop O'Donnell in August, he mentioned 'vague but significant hints' indicating that 'Desmond FitzGerald has come to some sort of agreement with the Cardinal Secretary on the score of diplomatic relations'. There was an expectation that shortly after the 1923 General Election, 'a sort of diplomatic representative of the government of Southern Ireland' would have established himself in Rome, with the 'assent and approbation of the British authorities'. This representative, Hagan believed, would be little more than 'a sort of attaché' to the British Embassy. Hagan had to assume that a Papal representative in Ireland would be a consequence of this.[269]

Hagan found such ideas alarming, since they represented a fundamental threat to the Republican position. He communicated them to O'Donnell because he believed that of all the bishops, he had the soundest outlook on national issues. 'Perhaps I may be wrong', he wrote to O'Donnell a few months later, 'but I have a sort of notion that politically or nationally or patriotically or whatever else it may be called, our views are not very far apart'.[270] Hagan could foresee the appalling prospect of an Irish Delegation in Rome 'whose main function will be that of saying no word that can displease England'; worse still, from the Republican point of view, would be the presence of a Papal representative in the Free State, 'whose role must necessarily be that of preserving the status quo in Ireland North and South'.[271] In October, we find Hagan still worried that the Holy See, whose Secretary of State he believed to be 'altogether in the hands of the British', might soon yield to Free State and British promptings and establish diplomatic relations with the twenty-six counties. At a time when many churchmen were expecting the Boundary Commission to transfer large areas of the North to the Free State, formal Vatican recognition of the twenty-six counties as a political entity would deal a serious blow to the hopes not only of Republicans but of tens of thousands of Northern Catholics.[272] Hagan, however, believed that

---

[269] Hagan to O'Donnell, 13.8.23, AAA.

[270] Hagan to O'Donnell, 10.1.24, AAA.

[271] Hagan to O'Donnell, 13.8.23, AAA. Curran believed that the British government saw in Luzio an 'ecclesiastical weapon in Ireland to replace the Irish bishops', since the Conscription crisis had shown them to be no longer loyal to British interests. Curran to O'Donnell, 14.3.23, DAA.

[272] In June 1923, de Valera told Hagan that he believed Partition to be permanent: 'The Merrion St Company will, I fear, give way to England there again,

the Vatican authorities, strongly sympathetic to imperial interests, would show little concern for the position of Catholics in Ulster. Should the Holy See decide to facilitate British schemes by sending a permanent representative to the Free State, there would be little use, Hagan believed, 'in pointing out the hindrance this would do to the cause of union between the North-East and the rest of the country'.[273] All Hagan felt he could do to counteract the sinister possibilities he envisaged was to alert O'Donnell, since he knew of 'no other man in Ireland who has the experience or the courage or the statesmanship to look ahead and examine in to the possibilities of the immediate future'.[274]

As soon as the terms of the Treaty were known, Hagan and Curran took steps to defend what they conceived to be the Republican position. Both were anxious to prevent the Vatican from publishing an enthusiastic endorsement of the Treaty. Hagan sent a message to the Under-Secretary of State warning the Holy See that 'the settlement was not definite until accepted by the Irish and English Parliaments'; this message arrived just in time to prevent the despatch of a telegram from the Pope to King George and Cardinal Logue. Hagan prepared a memorandum on the Irish situation as it affected the Holy See. He explained that the Treaty might yet be rejected on the Irish side, and that those who opposed it were, like de Valera, good Catholics, and not anarchists or 'American gun-men paid by American gold' as the Anglophile Roman press had told their readers.[275] Curran tried to influence Byrne in a Republican direction. He was, he told the Archbishop, disappointed by the settlement, hoped that 'a majority of the Dáil and country' would not accept it, and that it would be worked by a minority, the majority opposing or abstaining. Curran advocated episcopal silence on the Treaty. Hagan and himself were glad that Byrne had not spoken; Curran hoped that it would 'never be in the

and we shall have some miserable bargain between Craig and Cosgrave. If the F.S. were to redeem the people of Tyrone, Fermanagh, South Down and South Armagh, leaving Craig only a fraction of four counties, it would go some distance towards justifying their policy of accepting the Treaty – but I always told Griffith he would be euchred on this boundary scheme, and I wouldn't have, myself, placed a particle of dependence on it'. De Valera to Hagan, 23.6.23, Hagan Papers.

[273] Hagan to O'Donnell, 3.10.23, AAA.

[274] Hagan to O'Donnell, 13.8.23, AAA. In October 1923, Hagan told Mannix: 'At the present moment I fear there is some sort of deal going on having as its object the sending out to Rome, and the official recognition, of a F.S. representation of the 26 counties. Naturally the institution must dance to the tune England whistles, and the Delegation can be nothing more than a sort of special department of the British Delegation to the Vatican'. Hagan to Mannix, 5.10.23, Hagan Papers.

[275] Curran to Byrne, 14.12.21, Byrne Papers, DAA.

power of any man to say that the Irish bishops caused or had anything to do with a second split'.[276] Hagan provided Mulhern, the Bishop of Dromore, with a more thoughtful analysis of the situation. Had he a vote, he would 'certainly give it against ratification of the Treaty in its present shape', but he believed that in a decision of this kind the last word should lie with the fighting men, and these, he understood were 'out for peace at any price'. Now that the country was divided into 'two hostile camps', Hagan could see no sense in continuing the struggle against the British. He would 'greatly deplore' the absence of de Valera and his adherents from the first government and from the framing of the new constitution. This, he believed, would be bad for the Church as well as for the country. 'I have not', he told Mulhern, 'a whole lot of respect for the solidity and high-mindedness of Collins and Griffith, who I am afraid might easily set things going in a direction that could bode great harm to many interests in which we are concerned'. For this reason, Hagan hoped that de Valera and his supporters, whom he clearly regarded as more likely than their opponents to uphold the interests of religion, would see their way, 'if beaten at a vote, to take up office and make the best of a bad case'. Hagan proposed an interesting alternative to this line of action, which Byrne was also to put to de Valera:[277] Republicans might decline to record their votes and allow 'the upholders of the Treaty to carry it through without opposition'; by doing this they would leave themselves 'free for the future' and uncommitted 'to any particular line of future action'.[278] In a further letter to Mulhern, Hagan again warned him about the dangers to the Church posed by some of the leading advocates of the Treaty. 'For the sake of the Church in Ireland', he hoped that 'neither Collins nor Griffith nor Gavan Duffy will be allowed to indulge the luxury of anti-clericalism to which I fear they may have some inclination'.[279]

In their defence of post-Treaty Republicans, Hagan and Curran frequently relied on two lines of argument: that the existence of a militant Republican opposition to the Treaty represented a useful weapon against possible British treachery, and that the Church would be wise not to antagonise decent, God-fearing Republicans who might yet prove to be her staunchest allies. In March 1922, Hagan had an

---

[276] Ibid.

[277] Byrne's proposal to de Valera was made in an undated letter following the Bishops' meeting of 13.12.21. 'Might I make the suggestion', Byrne wrote, 'that to save those who act with you from being placed in the undesirable position of voting against the declared will of the people . . . you should avoid provoking matters to a division'. Byrne to de Valera, [December 1922], Byrne Papers, DAA.

[278] Hagan to Mulhern, 27.12.21, DRDA.

[279] Hagan to Mulhern, 14.1.22, DRDA.

interview with the Pope, in the course of which the latter wanted to know what precisely de Valera's policy was. Hagan replied that considering the unreliability of the British 'tricksters with whom we were supposed to be in treaty', a strong opposition led by de Valera was likely to be beneficial, 'first while the constitution is being set up and subsequently in the new parliament'.[280] In April, Curran expressed his displeasure to Byrne that only 'some of the Bishops' and none of the Free State politicians were able to see the value of 'either a constitutional opposition or of a reserve guard for defence'. He was appalled that bishops and politicians failed 'to see in de Valera a useful check to control the IRA if only for a time' and 'the use of having at hand the menace of the Republican movement to exhibit in negotiations with either England or Belfast'.[281]

In April 1922, Curran was concerned that 'many influential bishops' were anxious to take a stronger anti-Republican position than they had up to then. They were, he believed, no longer content with issuing a manifesto in favour of free elections, but would, at their meeting of 26 April, issue a statement 'in favour of the new constitution and against both de Valera and the IRA'. The wisdom of episcopal interference in politics beyond declaring for freedom of election troubled Curran, who communicated his fears to Byrne. He wondered how the Church would fare 'in fifteen or thirty years' time if the Bishops of today declare against the Separatists of today'. Curran argued that whatever the bishops said, the fight would go on, and that 'even Dr Fogarty and those who think like him admit that the Republic or separation will come in twenty or thirty years' time'. In the light of this, he asked Byrne to consider the consequences for the Church of the future of a partisan, anti-Republican line of conduct by the bishops of the present day. 'Why', he asked Byrne, 'should the Catholic Bishops of the next generation and the Church of Ireland for all future time be under the incubus of an episcopal anti-separation pronouncement, because of the seemingly critical position of the moment'.[282] Hagan tried to enforce a similar point of view on any of

[280] Hagan to Byrne, 22.3.22, Byrne Papers, DAA.
[281] Curran to Byrne, 21.9.22, Byrne Papers DAA.
[282] Curran to Byrne, 22.4.22, Byrne Papers, DAA. Curran was anxious that Byrne and the other bishops treat modern republicans in full consciousness of the lessons of history: 'Nothing is more humiliating to read than the pseudo-history of the O'Donovan Rossas, the Davitts, the T.P. O'Connors – ever harping on the policy of Troy, of Cullen of McCabe, etc. Yet such will be our fate for ever if the Bishops persist in condemning or suppressing every forward movement of Irish nationality. Separation and independence *will* come. It is just and inevitable. Let us remember the countless generations of the future, not that of the moment'. Ibid, Compare note 248, p. 194 above.

the bishops he felt might be amenable to his influence. In a letter to Archbishop O'Donnell in early 1924, he went even further than Curran had with Byrne. Little good, he suggested, could be done by churchmen who kept Republicans at a distance merely because they happened to be opposed to current episcopal political thinking. 'Who knows', he asked, 'but that in a year or two the Church's best friends in Ireland may not be the present Republicans'.[283] A recurring theme in Hagan's correspondence with Irish bishops is the folly of using spiritual weapons to force the consciences of Republicans, and of assuming that there could be only one correct and morally justifiable interpretation of the constitutional position in the Free State. The most forceful presentation of this idea is found in a letter he wrote to Bishop O'Dea of Galway during the Civil War. 'I cannot', he declared, 'but question the wisdom of making absolution depend on one's ability to see in the body that calls itself the Irish Government the one and only lawful government of the country'.[284]

Through the course of the Civil War, Hagan continued to provide the bishops with a generally acerbic commentary on the dealings of both Church and State with Irish Republicans. In September 1922 he visited Ireland in an attempt to arrange a settlement between the contending parties in the Civil War. Having seen Mulcahy, he discussed with Ernie O'Malley the possibility of opening negotiations. O'Malley told him that having taken the Oath of Allegiance, Republicans meant to keep it; they would fight until they wore the Free State down, or were themselves wiped out. As Hagan proposed to visit the Free State Military Headquarters, O'Malley asked him to mention 'the systematic torture of our prisoners and the deliberate murder of men' and to 'tell them to curb their murder gangs'.[285] By Christmas 1922, Hagan had become bitterly disillusioned by the extreme brutality of both sides. 'There is little to choose', he told Mulhern, 'between the shooting of untried prisoners and the burning of innocent children'.[286] What this suggested to foreigners, he pointed out, was that 'after all the English had some reason for their assertion that the Irish were incapable of governing themselves, and they needed the strong hand of a superior race to keep them in due order and subjection'. Given the apparently pro-Unionist complexion of the

[283] Hagan to O'Donnell, 10.1.24.
[284] Hagan to O'Dea, 22.8.22, GDA.
[285] O'Malley, *Singing Flame*, pp. 154–5.
[286] Hagan was referring to the Mountjoy reprisal executions of four Republican prisoners, including Mellows, on 8.12.22, and the burning by Republicans of Seán McGarry's home in Dublin, as a result of which McGarry's seven-year old son died of burns.

Free State, he wondered what the struggle for independence had been all about. Had he dreamt that it was going to end up 'in the appointment of the present Senate with Campbell [Lord Glenavy] at its head', he would never have become involved.[287] He suggested to O'Donnell that the bishops had to share the blame for the reprisal killing of Mellows and the rest; the executions, he believed, would not have been possible had not the bishops given their 'official corporate sanction by the October Pastoral'. He found the episcopal silence in the wake of these executions unjustifiable. He remarked, however, with some justification, that the more notable Free State leaders were not at that stage disposed to listen even to the bishops.[288] Despite his disillusionment, Hagan remained untiring in his efforts on behalf of Republicans. He thanked Archbishop O'Donnell on behalf Mrs Childers for the efforts he had made on behalf of her late husband and for the 'kindly feelings' he had entertained towards his memory. He was anxious to arrange a meeting between her and O'Donnell, and hoped the latter had not been impressed by the campaign of propaganda against her.[289] In June 1924, we find Seán T. O'Kelly paying tribute to Hagan for the 'successful Republican propaganda' a sympathetic visitor had found everywhere in Rome.[290] He observed the evidence of Republican electoral success with satisfaction. In November 1924, Republican candidates won by-elections in Dublin South and Mayo North. 'The result of the elections in Dublin and Mayo', he wrote to Professor Michael Browne, 'must have come as a shock to many. The 98 per cent of which we used to hear is rapidly growing fine by degrees and beautifully less'. He was, however, troubled by the 'slow and even heartbreaking' Republican march towards ultimate victory at the polls, and by 'ominous' evidence of residual British influence in the form of 'the immense demonstration of puppies with poppies'.[291] By November 1924, Hagan felt that he and other Republicans had good reason for hope. Seán T. O'Kelly had told him that they had been anxiously awaiting de Valera's release in order to start organising on a large scale.[292] What the Morning Post had written about de Valera's

[287] Hagan to Mulhern, 25.12.22, DRDA.
[288] Hagan to O'Donnell, 26.3.23, AAA. This, he believed, was particularly the case with O'Higgins, whom Hagan looked upon as 'not the man for the hour, and who evidently is out for a Die-Hard policy in which he has been able to drag a few lesser lights with him. I have much greater confidence in Mulcahy and Cosgrave.'
[289] Ibid.
[290] Seán T. O'Kelly to Hagan, 17.6.24, Hagan Papers.
[291] Hagan to M.J. Browne, 24.11.24, GDA.
[292] Ibid.

new role, and the general enthusiasm evoked by his reappearance, was immensely cheering to Hagan; de Valera, the *Post* had announced as a 'grim fact', spoke for 'the real Southern Ireland', and forecast that 'the negotiations begun with Mr Cosgrave will have to be finished with de Valera', who would be 'the dominating figure in Nationalist Ireland in three months'.[293]

Any consideration of Hagan's role in Republican history must take account of the part he played in encouraging and facilitating the emergence of de Valera as leader of a credible constitutional Republican party, and the abandonment by the mass of Republicans of the abstentionist policy which many had come to see as sterile and self-destructive. It is clear from his correspondence that Hagan gave considerable thought to the future of post-Treaty Republicanism. Following the 1923 General Election, he told Mannix that 'on the whole' he would like to see Republicans enter the Dáil 'even at the price of taking the Oath'. The alternative seemed to be not a resumption of Civil War but 'some sort of passive resistance with the help of such funds as are coming in fairly well from America'.[294] At Christmas 1923, he hinted to Mrs James Ryan that Republican involvement in constitutional politics might usefully be contemplated. He himself, at any rate, was 'not much in love with the possibility of a sojourn in the wilderness for months or even years'.[295] By the Spring and early Summer of 1925, Republicans had little reason for optimism that the sojourn would soon come to an end. After some striking by-election victories in 1924, they suffered a severe electoral reverse in March 1925,[296] when Cumann

---

[293] *Morning Post*, 22.7.24. Hagan's personal relationship with de Valera was a close one, as the following letter from Sinéad Bean de Valera to him indicates: 'I felt very uncomfortable and dissatisfied to-day that I had not an opportunity of thanking you for your great kindness. Both Dev and I are extremely grateful not only for your generous present but for the very thoughtful way it was given. But at present we have no anxiety about financial affairs and it would be selfishness and covetousness on our part to personally accept such a great gift. Many, many thanks. You have been kindness itself to us all along.' Sinéad de Valera to Hagan, 25.4.26, Hagan Papers. On 17.4.26, de Valera had announced the aims of Fianna Fáil at the Gresham Hotel. See M. Moynihan (ed.) *Speeches and Statements by Eamon de Valera, 1917–1973* (Dublin, 1980), p. 131.

[294] Hagan to Mannix, 5.10.23.

[295] Hagan to Mrs James Ryan, 26.12.23, James Ryan Papers, UCDA, P88/92. This letter illustrates the degree to which Hagan's emotional well-being depended on the fortunes of Republicanism. 'Now and again', he asks Mrs Ryan, 'when you think there are good grounds for hope, I should be glad if you would drop me a line, even if there is not much that you can say. The very fact that you are able to write with some optimism will help to dispel my pessimism'. Ibid.

[296] T.P. O'Neill, however, suggests that the encouraging trend of public opinion, from the Sinn Féin point of view, shown in the November 1924 by-elections was 'confirmed' in the nine by-elections in March 1925. 'Towards a Political Path', p. 160.

na nGaedheal candidates won seven of the nine by-elections caused by resignations and defections from that party as a result of the Army Mutiny affair. The massive intervention of priests had helped to defeat Republican candidates, as had the policy of abstentionism, which was leaving hundreds of thousands of Republican voters unrepresented in the Dáil. Many of the voters clearly had little interest in the fundamentalist theology underlying the Republican position, which had been weakened in 1923 when some of the surviving members of the Second Dáil had lost their seats. The rhetoric purporting to justify the continuing existence of a *de jure* Republic sounded increasingly hollow; the 48 Sinn Féin deputies elected since September 1923 had no effective role in public affairs. In the local elections of June 1925, the Republican vote collapsed, although Sinn Féin candidates were supported by a strong organisation. Sensing that political Republicanism now stood no chance of capturing the country, the IRA, at its first convention since the Civil War, decided that it could no longer offer allegiance to de Valera's Republican 'government'.[297] De Valera's frustration around this time is clear in a stern, admonitory letter he addressed to the Pope in May 1925, setting forth the graver misdemeanours of the Irish bishops and of those priests who were political agents of Cumann na nGaedheal. Republicans, he pointed out, keenly resented the unchecked 'abuses of ecclesiastical authority and discipline, whereby the power and influence of the Church is used to further a favoured political policy'; he also warned that the nationwide scandal caused by these abuses would result in 'serious injury to the prestige of the Church and the cause of true religion'. With the 1925 by-elections in mind, he mentioned the use of the pulpit as a Cumann na nGaedheal political rostrum; violent political speeches by priests and defamatory comments made by them against individual Republicans; incitement by priests to physical violence on Republicans and intimidation by priests on electors.[298]

In May 1925, Hagan, interpreting the recent by-election results as depressing evidence that the Free State was managing to consolidate itself and that 'a Republican majority is not to be expected in the near future', pointed out to de Valera that 'numbers of genuine Republicans' were asking whether the time had perhaps come for 'a reconsideration and possibly a reconstruction' of present policies on such central issues

[297] Peter Pyne, 'The New Irish State and the Decline of the Republican Sinn Féin Party', *Éire-Ireland*, vol. XI, no. 3, 1976, pp. 50 ff.
[298] De Valera to Pope Pius XI, 9.5.25. This letter is reproduced in full in the author's 'Voices of de Valera', an unpublished MLitt thesis, TCD. Father Ignatius Fenessy o.f.m., Franciscan House of Studies, Killiney, believes that this letter was not sent.

as the Oath and abstentionism. In his concern for the future direction
of Republicanism, Hagan drew up a paper outlining for de Valera's
benefit his own views of the possibilities open to Republicans in the
aftermath of their electoral disappointments. In his analysis, Hagan
took it for granted that the Free State was 'definitely and decidedly
established', and that Republican efforts to destroy the Free State
machine from without 'have not been, and are not likely to be,
crowned with immediate success'. In the light of this, Republicans
might well be led by force of circumstances to decide that the time had
come to effect the same object from within, 'capturing and controlling
the machinery, somewhat in the same way as the British government
set about destroying a more or less similar machine in 1800'. To
initiate the process of destruction, however, Republicans 'must first
take an oath of allegiance to the English crown'. Hagan somewhat
cynically points out that 'those immediately responsible for the faith
and morals of the Irish people' have suggested that the oath of
allegiance may be 'little, if anything, more than a formality . . . an
overcoat which can be put on or removed with every change of
weather'. Furthermore, Irish history 'is strewn with the withered leaves
of oaths subscribed by chief and leader and ignored the moment it
was safe to do so'.[299] Hagan's conclusion was that de Valera and his
followers could take the oath in a similar spirit.

His conclusion was reinforced by the affirmative opinions of the
small group of Republican priests in Rome with whom he discussed
his document. Father Peter Magennis, a fundamentalist Republican,
was one of these. Hagan told de Valera that 'even Father Magennis,
uncompromising man that he is, went so far as to state that while he
would not go in for recommending the swallowing of the oath, he
would not have a word to say against this being done, provided it
was decided on with unanimity'. Hagan had also discussed the oath
with Archbishop Mannix, who was in Rome on pilgrimage, and while
the latter did not 'commit himself to any expression of opinion',
Hagan was 'inclined to gather that he would not be disposed to balk
at it in the circumstances if there was no danger of a split'. On this,
Hagan shrewdly remarked that 'there was a possibility of a split
arising sooner or later' even if the present abstentionist policy were
maintained.[300] On 7 May 1925, while Hagan was preparing his
document, the Sinn Féin Standing Committee passed a resolution

---

[299] The full text of Hagan's document may be read in the thesis mentioned in
note 298 above. See also D. Keogh, 'Mannix, de Valera and Irish Nationalism'
in J. O'Brien and P. Travers (eds), *The Irish Emigrant Experience in Australia* (Dublin,
1991), pp. 215–16.
[300] Hagan to de Valera, 31.5.25.

giving de Valera power to 'act on the assumption that the question of Republicans entering the Free State Parliament if the oath were removed, is an open question, to be decided on its merits when the question arises as a political issue'.[301] Hagan considered the possibility that the Free State government might abolish the oath, only to dismiss it. It would, he believed, be idle to expect the Free State authorities to cast aside 'the one weapon that has kept them in power and still enables them to enjoy fat salaries and confer lucrative positions on their friends, relatives and followers'.[302] The suggestions in Hagan's document seem to have found favour among Republicans. Professor Michael Browne, who had close links with the Republican leadership, told Hagan in December 1925 that 'things have developed a great deal along the lines you marked out last summer', adding that 'the process could have been much faster, and it was fortunate that the boundary crisis came to give it an impetus'.[303] The Sinn Féin resolution of 7 May suggests that Republicans were ready to contemplate entering a Free State Parliament that did not require an oath; Hagan with at least the tacit support of Mannix and Magennis, had provided de Valera with a theologically and historically respectable case for entering that Parliament even if this involved taking the oath. This gave de Valera, always preoccupied with the ethical aspects of political action, and always needing to justify his own procedures on ethical grounds, a useful new latitude whatever course he might decide to pursue.

In June 1925, de Valera had an opportunity to discuss Hagan's document in detail, not only with its author, but also with Mannix, Magennis and Curran. Knowing that Mannix was planning to visit Ireland, de Valera met Archbishop O'Donnell in Carlingford to ascertain what kind of welcome the assertively Republican Archbishop might expect from the Irish hierarchy. The response was not altogether encouraging.[304] De Valera, disguised as a priest and carrying a false passport, and accompanied by Seán MacBride who acted as his secretary, went to Rome on 30 May 1925, and had discussions in the Irish College with Mannix, Hagan and Magennis. De Valera and MacBride returned to Ireland on 9 June.[305] MacBride later claimed that it was in the course of discussions in the Irish College between de Valera, Hagan, Mannix and Magennis, at which he himself was present 'in a very minor capacity' that 'the policy of entering the Dáil by taking the oath as an empty formula and of proceeding to dis-

[301] Kathleen O'Connell Diary, 7.5.25.
[302] Hagan to de Valera, 31.5.25.
[303] Browne to Hagan, 20.12.25, Hagan Papers.
[304] Ó Néill agus Ó Fiannachta, *De Valera*, p.171.
[305] Kathleen O'Connell Diary, 30.5.25; 9.6.25.

mantle the Constitution of the Free State' was devised. It was at these
meetings, MacBride suggested, that 'the plan of campaign for the
future policy of Fianna Fáil and the dismantling of the Treaty' was
evolved. While no formal decision 'to proceed with the policy outlined
by Monsignor Hagan and Archbishop Mannix was taken', it was clear
to MacBride 'that Mr de Valera had accepted that policy. Dr Peter
Magennis was not so enthusiastic and was somewhat apprehensive.
So was I'.[306]

VI
==

The purpose of de Valera's visit to Rome in May 1925 was to see not
only Hagan but also Archbishop Mannix, his one episcopal supporter
from the signing of the Treaty until June 1924, when Bishop Dignan
of Clonfert declared himself a Republican at his consecration.[307]
Many of those who had known Mannix in his earlier days must have
been surprised at the stridently Republican tone of his post-Treaty
rhetoric. In 1916, he described the events of Easter Week as
'regrettable', and declared that the British Government, 'by its failure
to deal with the treason of the Carsonites, by its shifting policy in
regard to Home Rule', had unwittingly caused the Rising, an event
'that all must deplore'.[308] In October 1920, he was quoted in the
Catholic Bulletin as saying that his object would be 'to keep Ireland
within the Empire', something not possible of achievement, however,
'unless Englishmen give us freely and as generously as they can just as
much Dominion Home Rule as they conceive to be compatible with

---

[306] Seán MacBride, 'Rome Rule?', *Irish Press*, 12.4.86.

[307] Daniel Mannix (1864–1963) was born in Charleville, Co. Cork. Ordained in
Maynooth in 1890. Professor of Philosophy, Maynooth, 1891. Professor of Theology
1894. Vice-President, 1903. President 1903–12. Co-adjutor Archbishop of Melbourne,
1912–17. Archbishop 1917. For Dignan see p. 163, notes 107 and 108.

[308] Quoted by Niall Brennan, *Dr Mannix* (London, 1965). Some Cumann na
nGaedheal propagandists suggested that Mannix's tangential association with
British royal personages called the sincerity of his Republican commitment into
question. In 1927, William Burke, General Secretary of the party, did not believe
that during his Maynooth days Mannix had been impressive as an Irishman:
'He received the late King Edward and his Queen here, and entertained them
sumptuously at Maynooth, and on their departure presented them with a piece of
silver as a token of his allegiance to the British Throne. A short time ago he
presented the Duke and Duchess of York when he received them in Australia
with a piece of silver.' Mr Burke had no quarrel with that but 'he did say that,
being so far away as he is, and carrying on in Australia as he thinks he can do,
it would be better for him to leave the people here to carry out their own business'.
The Irish Times, 13.9.27. For an account of Mannix at Maynooth, see Corish,
Maynooth College, pp. 283–99.

the safety of the Empire'. On Easter Monday 1921, however, when he was received in audience by Benedict XV, he used 'uncompromising and plain language' to the Pope in his account of British misdemeanours in Ireland, conveying 'a general feeling of surprise' that 'the common Father of Christendom who had words of sympathy for Belgium and Poland was silent with regard to worse things in Ireland'.[309]

From the beginning of 1922, Mannix made clear his total opposition to the Treaty. He was a valuable propagandist for Republicanism; his frequent celebrations of the integrity of those who had rejected the Treaty, and his denunciations of the settlement and those who had been involved in it, gained wide publicity at home and abroad. During the grimmest phase of the Civil War, de Valera told him that there had been 'nothing more cheering through these months than the unerring instinct which enabled Your Grace to appreciate the situation truly'.[310] Reports of the Archbishop's stirring speeches in defence of de Valera and the anti-Treaty party reached Ireland regularly. 'Ireland has accepted the Treaty as a whole', he told a meeting at Queen's Cliff in January 1922, 'but deep down in the hearts of Irish people the most popular man in Ireland today was de Valera . . . the one who never turned his country down . . . who never yielded the smallest fraction of an inch, the man who stood out as Ireland's idealist'.[311] On St Patrick's Day, 1923, Mannix encouraged his audience in Melbourne to ask themselves 'why every enemy of Ireland is on the side of Mr Cosgrave and his party'.[312] In August 1922, following the sudden death of Griffith, Mannix opposed the suggestion of Archbishop Kelly of Sydney that a telegram of sympathy be sent to Cardinal Logue on behalf of the Australian bishops. If he were in Ireland, he told Kelly, he would think it his duty 'to remain as nearly neutral as possible and to refrain from antagonising either party'. He had learned lessons from episcopal errors during the Parnell split, and would not 'wish to see the Irish bishops again taking sides politically against any section of their own people'.[313] Mannix himself seemed to find it impossible to detach himself from the conflict. He gave material as well as moral support to Republicans throughout the twenties. In October 1923, we find P.J. Ruttledge, de Valera's deputy, hoping that 'all friends of Ireland in Australia' were pleased with the results of the 1923 Election, making an earnest appeal

---

[309] Hagan's account of the audience with the Pope is found in his papers at the Irish College. For the Pope's response, see Macardle, *Irish Republic*, p. 435.

[310] Moynihan, *Speeches and Statements by de Valera*, p. 108.

[311] *Poblacht na h-Éireann*, 29.3.22.

[312] FAK, AMI, 1450.

[313] Quoted in Keogh, 'Mannix, de Valera and Irish Nationalism', p.210.

to Mannix 'to intensify the efforts you are already making on behalf of the Irish Republican Prisoners Dependents Fund', and begging his 'intercession with the Almighty God to give us His assistance and guidance'.[314] Mannix, at any rate, rendered speedy assistance. In November, Kathleen Barry wrote to tell him that 'our resources were completely used up when the first Australian £1,200 came. It was really the turn of the tide'.[315] Soon afterwards, Mannix, accompanied on the platform by seven priests, addressed a Republican fund-raising meeting in Melbourne which yielded a considerable sum.[316]

Although his discourse often lacked subtlety and finesse, Mannix was not incapable of displaying these qualities, as, for example in his 'defence' of the political conduct of the Irish bishops in Melbourne on 24 June 1923. It was commonly alleged that the Irish Republican envoys to Australia, Father O'Flanagan and J.J. O'Kelly, had spoken critically not only of the Irish bishops but also of the Pope. Mannix told Catholic press reporters that he knew the Irish bishops better than those 'who were said to have criticised them', and they were all men of peace as well as Irish patriots. It was true that when 'the unfortunate Treaty was signed, the bishops threw in their lot against the Republican policy' but this was because they could, at the time, 'see no good issue from an appeal to force' against the Treaty. Mannix then went on to point out that nobody was obliged to agree with the bishops 'on political matters'. Indeed, it was possible that men of peace that they were, the bishops might have made a dubious political decision in damning the Republicans. After all, men of peace 'sometimes leaned too much to peace and made too little allowance for the claims of patriotism'. Perhaps by doing this, the bishops and those who thought like them were grasping 'at a kind of peace for their own day which made inevitably for unrest and strife and war in the future'. Mannix neatly turned his defence of the Pope against 'reported' Republican attacks into the standard Republican argument against ecclesiastical partisanship in politics. The Pope, he was happy to point out, had 'kept himself above all political controversy' and left the Irish people to settle their own political differences. The Irish bishops, Mannix hinted, might also learn from Luzio, whose 'impartial attitude' had been an example to those who might be disposed 'to assume an aggressive or dictatorial line towards those . . . with whom they did not happen to agree'.[317]

[314] P.J. Ruttledge to Mannix, 30.10.23, NAI S 1369/21.
[315] K. Barry to Mannix, 27.11.23, NAI S 1369/21.
[316] *Éire*, 2.2.24.
[317] *Irish Independent*, 13.8.23. Two years before, Hagan had told Mannix that the bishops were unwilling to listen to even moderate Republican views: 'They are

The most significant intervention by Mannix in Irish political affairs came in 1925. In that year, he brought a group of Australian pilgrims to Ireland, and used the visit to conduct an extensive speaking tour of the country. It is sometimes suggested by historians that the main object of de Valera's visit to Rome in May was to dissuade Mannix from using his visit for political purposes, and that his transformation of his tour into a specifically Republican occasion was at odds with what de Valera had advised. Dermot Keogh, for example, claims that Mannix 'had insisted on coming in a semi-public capacity at the head of the Australian pilgrimage, against the advice of Hagan and de Valera'.[318] Such interpretations seem to derive from de Valera's subsequent account of events. He told his biographers that when Archbishop O'Donnell made it clear to him that the Irish bishops would not receive Mannix with enthusiasm, he felt obliged to convey this news to the latter in person.[319] At a ceremony in Charleville in 1962 to mark the golden jubilee of Mannix's consecration, de Valera claimed he had gone to Rome to plead with Mannix not to lead a pilgrimage to Ireland, but to come, if at all, as a private individual, since this is what the Irish hierarchy wanted.[320] De Valera's reconstruction of historical events, particularly those in which he was intimately involved, must sometimes be received with caution. There is evidence that de Valera and those close to him worked hard to make the Mannix visit what it became: an energetic parade of anti-Treaty Republicanism, and an expression of contempt for the Free State and its upholders. De Valera's correspondence with Mannix in the weeks before the visit makes it clear that he saw the Archbishop primarily as a political agent and ally of Republicanism. When he told Hagan that the actions of Mannix in Ireland would have 'considerable influence', he was certainly thinking of what Mannix might do for the Republican cause.[321] Indeed, when he wrote to Mannix enclosing a tentative schedule, he made it clear that the kind of visit he had in mind would be a decidedly public one, affording multiple opportunities for political comment, of which he knew Mannix would not hesitate to avail. He

persuaded that they are right, and are inclined to tolerate no doubt – indeed I am inclined to gather that they regard doubts of the kind as a sort of personal affront'. Hagan to Mannix, 5.10.23, Hagan Papers.

[318] Keogh, *The Vatican, the Bishops*, p. 219. See also J. Broderick, 'De Valera and Archbishop Mannix', *History Ireland*, vol. ii, p. 41. 'De Valera as he revealed late in life, hastened to Rome to persuade Mannix to refrain from public statements; he was anxious to avoid an open breach between the Irish bishops and his sole episcopal supporter'.

[319] Ó Néill agus Ó Fiannachta, *De Valera*, p. 171.

[320] See C. Kiernan, *Daniel Mannix and Ireland* (Dublin, 1984), p. 187; *Irish Press*, 9.10.62.

had arranged formal civic functions for Mannix in Dublin, Cork and Limerick, meetings with TDs, members of local authorities and priests, and with 'the Bishops of Cloyne and Cork, possibly'.[322] De Valera had played a central background role in helping to organise a gathering of Republican priests to welcome Mannix at the Rotunda, making sure that the participating priests met some weeks beforehand.[323] It was as evident to those who contemplated the visit with disfavour as to those who encouraged it that it was bound to be a political event with a Republican colouring. When Sligo Corporation debated conferring the freedom of the borough on Mannix, Government supporters voted the proposal down because they knew that its anti-Treaty advocates would use the ceremony for 'sectional and political purposes' as Councillor O'Connell, father of General O'Connell, put it. Councillor O'Connell traced the hand of de Valera in the proposal to honour Mannix, something they were being asked to do 'at the behest of a hybrid Spaniard'.[324]

De Valera's letter of welcome to Mannix gives the clearest indication that he had no misgivings about the kind of political comment his guest was likely to make. 'I will not attempt', he wrote, 'to describe to Your Grace the exact position here from a political point of view - your public pronouncements in Australia have shown that you were remarkably well in touch with it and a few minutes conversation will bring your information up to date'. That he saw Mannix as a useful political ally is clear from his suggestion that he might use an interview he would have with the Pope as an opportunity to explain 'the Republican position' to him, and by enlightening His Holiness on the anti-Republican activities of the Irish clergy, which 'have gone from bad to worse' and caused 'much havoc', encourage him to undo the damage, presumably by calling the Irish bishops to account.[325] Having urged Mannix to make the Republican case to the Pope, it is difficult to imagine de Valera hoping that Mannix might, having been briefed again on it when he arrived in Ireland, refrain from explaining it to Irish listeners.

In this respect, Mannix did not disappoint. He used every public occasion during his four-month tour to defend de Valera's 'Republican position' and to expose his opponents to ridicule. In Waterford, he assured his listeners that he was as much opposed to the Treaty as

[321] De Valera to Hagan, 19.5.25, Hagan Papers.
[322] De Valera to Mannix, 9.5.25, FAK AMI 1451.
[323] Kathleen O'Connell Diary, 7.10.25.
[324] *Roscommon Herald*, 18.7.25.
[325] De Valera to Mannix, 9.5.25, FAK AMI 1451. What de Valera had in mind here is set out in detail in his letter of 9.5.25 to the Pope. See p. 207, note 298.

ever, and that no man was more anxious than he that 'the Republican idea should to-morrow become an accomplished fact'.[326] In Carrick-on-Shannon he introduced one of his favourite themes: the imperialist, anti-national outlook of Cosgrave and his government. 'It was well known', he told over a thousand people from the window of the Bush Hotel, 'that the real true Irishmen were not ruling in Ireland. Forces and influences were at work controlling Ireland, which were not making for her good, but making permanently for an Ireland settled within the British Empire'.[327] In Sligo, he developed this idea. There was, he believed, evidence to suggest that Ireland might be 'going back into the heart of the British Empire'. The recent Senate Election afforded an illustration. People who had 'given their lives to their country' were at the bottom of the poll. 'Is it not a singular thing', he asked, 'that the first man to come out at the top of the poll was an English General?'[328] In Dublin at the end of his tour, he expressed dismay that those who had hoped that Ireland would have an Independence Day 'now found that Ireland was celebrating, or preparing to celebrate, Poppy Day'.[329]

The climax of the Mannix visit was the 'Night of the Priests'. This afforded an opportunity for the clergy who sympathised with Republicanism to demonstrate their support in a public forum. On 25 October, the Pillar Room of the Rotunda was 'unable to accommodate the huge throng who came to hear His Grace when representatives of the clergy from all over the country presented him with a beautiful chalice and illuminated address'.[330] Mannix was escorted to the

---

[326] *The Irish Times*, 13.8.25.

[327] *Cork Examiner*, 7.10.25.

[328] *Catholic Bulletin*, 1925, p.1125. The *Bulletin* reported as follows on the Senate Election results: 'The first to be elected for his distinguished services to the Irish Nation was General Hickie. This gentleman had a remarkable career in the British Army, during the South African War and in the Great War . . . His outstanding distinction, however, was in rendering service to ex-British Soldiers in Ireland – not Republican Soldiers'. Ibid., p. 1099.

[329] Ibid., p. 1171. Signs of a recrudescence of British influence were apparent in the mid-twenties, as, for example, in the ceremonies to mark the unveiling of a war memorial erected by the ex-British soldiers of Longford. 'The memorial in the Market Square was draped with a large Union Jack, while three other large Union Jacks floated over streamers lined across the Market Square . . . It is a considerable time since the Union Jack has been publicly displayed in Longford, and its appearance in the Square seemed to be welcomed by the people of both town and county. Some of those present were: Right Hon. the Earl of Granard, Right Hon. the Earl of Longford, General Hickie, Major Boyd Rochford, V.C.; Major Bryan Cooper'. *Roscommon Herald*, 29.8.25.

[330] *Speeches of the Most Rev. Dr Mannix, Archbishop of Melbourne at the Rotunda, Dublin*, published by Sinn Féin, n.d., p. 13.

, on foot, 'by a large body of the Catholic clergy'. On the
'flanked by Ireland's most trusted men and women, were
f the sturdy priests who have remained faithful to the
tible cause of Irish liberty: messages of greeting from some
three hundred others were piled high in front of the Secretary, Fr
Thomas Burbage'.[331] Much of the Rotunda address was a reiteration
of old themes: the penetration of the Free State by British influence,
the need to eliminate this in the interest of a free, independent
Ireland, the ultimate triumph of Republicanism. Appropriately, however, in the circumstances, Mannix, reflecting one of de Valera's main
preoccupations, dwelt on the damage done to the Republican enterprise
by bishops and priests who were partisans of the Free State. He
believed that by ranging themselves so decisively on one side of the
'political controversy', the majority of the clergy had made it impossible
for the Republican minority among their colleagues 'to observe
neutrality'. He and the Republican priests who were present, as well
as the hundreds of like-minded ones who were not, had upheld an
important principle: that Catholics were at liberty 'to take either side'
in a political controversy. They had also performed a valuable service
to religion, having demonstrated that the Church was not identified
exclusively with one political party. Mannix could claim, 'without fear
of contradiction', that the stand taken by Republican priests 'has had
a calming and soothing effect upon the religious atmosphere of
Ireland'.[332] The priests gathered around him were not, he suggested,
with a sidelong glance at episcopal claims to political inerrancy, 'the
men to claim that they alone are right, and that they are always
right'. It was heartening for Republicans whom episcopal rigour had
isolated from mainstream Catholicism to hear a former Maynooth
Professor of Theology suggest that the bishops had erred in making

[331] *Catholic Bulletin*, 1925, p. 1125. For Father Burbage, see pp. 147–50, notes 42–8.
Frank Gallagher reported on the event for *An Phoblacht*: 'The platform was full
now, line upon line of priests, secular priests, order priests, Friars minor in their
brown habits. Canon Hackett, Chairman, won all hearts at once. His hard
Northern accent, his humour . . . The presentations were made, that chalice
which sparkled with such golden light, the illuminated address which sparkled
with its thirty-two panels symbolising the thirty-two counties of Ireland'. *An
Phoblacht*, 6.11.25. The author's efforts to trace the names of the eighty priests
who were present on the night and the three hundred who sent messages of
support have not been successful. Father Ian Waters, chairman of the Melbourne
Diocesan Historical Commission, points out that Mannix ordered the destruction
of his papers at his death: 'Sadly, to the amazement and horror of researchers,
his instructions were faithfully observed by his close collaborators'. Letter to
author, 30.9.96.
[332] *Catholic Bulletin*, 1925, pp.1165–6

claim to 'infallible sanction in political matters'.[333] It was gratifying to be assured on such reliable authority as a 'fact' that those Republican laymen 'who have the same political views as those priests here on this platform' were 'as good as the best'. He was, understandably, loudly applauded when he asked: 'Is it not the fact that their faith is as sound as the Vatican and that they are as loyal as the Pope?'[334]

It is scarcely surprising that Mannix was not given public recognition by either Church or State, that he was ignored by the hierarchy, and not invited to visit Maynooth. When he visited the Church of the Holy Cross in Charleville, the place of his birth, the local clergy had ensured that the building was locked and in complete darkness. Early in June, Bishop Browne of Cloyne paid Mannix a furtive visit at the Imperial Hotel in Cork under cover of darkness. 'So you have come at last', Mannix observed, 'like Nicodemus in the night'.[335] There is an echo of his contempt for Browne's behaviour in his address to the Republican priests, whom he congratulated for having presented themselves openly to greet him, 'not like Nicodemus in the night-time'.[336] The Mayor of Limerick complained that the Freedom of the City had been conferred on Mannix subject to an undertaking by 'a leader of the anti-Treaty movement' that the Archbishop would avoid offending the feelings of the pro-Treaty majority; Mannix, however, had described those who differed from him as 'imperialists'.[337] D.P. Moran's *Leader*, which tried to preserve an air of olympian detachment and impartiality by professing disgust with both Republican 'die-hards' and Free State 'jacks-in-office and beggars on horseback', declared that Mannix had 'quite crudely played to the anti-Treaty gallery', and that he had not added to his dignity by allowing his visit to be worked by Republicans 'for all it is worth to them'.[338] Mannix would no doubt have replied that this was an appropriate definition of the purpose of his visit. He said as much at a ceremony in London soon after leaving Ireland. He went to Ireland, he recalled, 'a few months ago, having nailed the Republican flag to the mast and kept it there, and he found wherever he went he was welcomed by thousands, in many cases by tens of thousands, of Irish men and women, who cheered to the echo the statement that Ireland would never be content until she was absolutely undivided and absolutely free'.[339]

[333] Ibid.
[334] Ibid.
[335] Kiernan, *Daniel Mannix*, pp. 142, 190, 191.
[336] See p. 214, note 323.
[337] *The Leader*, 15.8.25.
[338] Ibid.
[339] *Irish Independent*, 9.11.25.

What Dignan had done in 1924 to lift Republican morale and salve Republican consciences, Mannix did on a much grander scale in 1925.

VII

Following the Treaty the Republican leadership in Ireland looked instinctively to Catholic America as a natural source of moral and material help. In 1919 and 1920, much of de Valera's success as a propagandist and fund-raiser in America for the Irish Republic had been attributable to nationwide clerical support.[340] In 1924, Father O'Flanagan claimed that when he and other Republican envoys visited America in 1919, diocesan chancellors had met them with motors at every pier and railroad station, bishops' residences had been thrown open, and every American parish was a Sinn Féin Club. His post-Treaty visits were, by contrast, largely ignored by the clergy. He complained that in some of the large cities of America, 'the poor priests are as much afraid to go to a Republican meeting as they are in Ireland itself'. On the other hand, when the envoys reached the West of America, 'there were always plenty of priests' at their meetings.[341] This relative lack of enthusiasm among the American clergy for the Republican cause was explained by a contributor to D.P. Moran's *Leader*, who signed himself 'Irish-American'. He believed that the hostility of many Americans, lay and clerical, could be blamed on Republicans themselves, whose activities at home and in America had disgraced Ireland in the eyes of the world, revived all the old slanders about Irish barbarism, and covered Irish-Americans with shame. He pointed to the 'evil effects' produced by denunciations of Irish bishops by O'Flanagan and others, the 'dubious' religious views of another Republican advocate Hanna Sheehy-Skeffington, and the support given to Republicans by left-wing groups. The Republican cause was compromised by its association with 'every renegade with a Gaelic name and Red Socialist aims from the Atlantic to the Pacific'. There was also the 'De Valera Church' of Chicago, which spent 'over a thousand dollars to distribute leaflets at the Church doors in New York and elsewhere', calling on the people to break loose from 'the Roman Cabal' and 'the Treasonable Hierarchy', and to form their own 'Irish Church'.[342]

[340] See, for example, Kathleen O'Doherty, *Assignment America* (New York, 1957), passim.
[341] See *The Leader*, Dublin, 2.8.24; *Roscommon Herald*, 28.2.25.
[342] 'American Ignorance and Protestant Principles'. *The Leader*, Dublin, 30.8.24. 'It is significant, and perhaps ominous', Irish-American added, 'that the leaflets were distributed only at the doors of the down-trodden churches, where the congregations

Much Irish-American anti-Treaty propaganda was crude and abu-sive, and not calculated to win the support of American churchmen, however ardent their Republicanism. One pamphlet of the kind described by 'Irish-American', and issued in December 1922, urged Catholics to 'excommunicate' themselves from the Roman Catholic Church, as thousands were already doing 'through the new American and the new Irish Catholic Churches'.[343] The self-excommunication urged by the author of this pamphlet was clearly intended to parody that imposed upon Republicans by the bishops in their October Pastoral. The same Pastoral provoked extreme anti-episcopal comment from Republican organisations in America with more respectable credentials than the ones associated with the De Valera Church in Chicago. One such body was the AARIR [344], which had been launched by de Valera in Washington on 16 November 1920, with the aim of securing, under his guidance, American recognition of the Irish Republic, and which had a membership of half a million.[345] On 14 October 1922, the Patrick H. Pearse Council of the AARIR resolved to 'condemn the Irish Hierarchy for condemning the Republicans of Ireland and their fight for freedom'. The resolution deprecated 'the political leadership' of the bishops of Ireland 'under the guise of spiritual leadership'. The members of AARIR loved Ireland more than they loved the Catholic Church, 'if by the Catholic Church in Ireland is understood that institution which is supposed to be governed by the tyrannous, politically-corrupt and liberty-destroying Bishops of Ireland'.[346] Copies of this resolution were forwarded to the Vatican and to two of the most prominent American episcopal sup-porters of the Treaty, Archbishop Curley of Baltimore and Bishop Turner of Buffalo. On 22 October, the Terence MacSwiney Council of the AARIR deplored the action of the bishops in issuing the Pastoral as 'un-Catholic, anti-patriotic and calculated to subvert their prestige as the moral teachers of the Irish people'. The Council also found reported utterances of Curley and Turner 'at variance with known facts, and with accepted principles of Catholic ethics', and drew attention to 'the British taint in their theologies'.[347]

are more of the immigrant class than they are up-town'. I owe this reference to Dr Patrick Maume, Queen's University of Belfast.
[343] Anon., 'How Popes and Irish Bishops Treated Irish Patriots', December 1922. For the writer of this pamphlet, 'Up with the Republic of Ireland' meant 'Down with Rome, Down with the Bishops of Ireland, Down with the Freak State, and Down with England'. Author's possession.
[344] American Association for the Recognition of the Irish Republic.
[345] T. Ryle Dwyer, *De Valera. The Man and the Myths* (Dublin, 1991), pp. 44–5.
[346] Resolutions of 14 October, 1922, AARIR, Chicago. Author's possession.
[347] Resolutions of 22 October, 1922, AARIR, New York. Author's possession.

Just as the *Irish Independent* had solicited for publication the pro-Treaty views of Irish bishops as soon as the terms of the settlement were published,[348] the New York *Irish World* performed a similar service in the Republican interest by publishing statements of disapproval from American ecclesiastics. Bishop Michael Gallagher of Detroit was quoted as asking, 'Is Ireland not to be free?', and promising that he would 'not be a party to tearing down the green, white and orange flag'. Father Matthew Tierney of Brooklyn declared that 'the Agreement cannot be adopted by the Irish people. The pill is a sugar-coated one which conceals poison.' Father Downing of Clarksdale, Missouri, wanted Griffith and his associates indicted for high treason, suggesting that if the people accepted 'such a bastard instrument of National and racial perfidy' they would have 'fooled a world that thought they were Irish'. Father Merns of New York lamented that Collins and Griffith had fallen 'before the soft words and the flattery', and claimed that de Valera was 'the only Irish patriot left'.[349]

Among the Irish-American clergy, the most energetic advocate of post-Treaty Republicanism following the outbreak of the Civil War was Peter Yorke of San Francisco,[350] State President of the AARIR. The problems he experienced in 1922 were similar to those which confronted the many Irish-American members of an organisation committed to persuading their government to recognise the Irish Republic. Now that the Dáil had abandoned the Republic by approving the Treaty, Yorke found it difficult to see a role for himself and the AARIR. He later complained to Stack and O'Kelly, the Republican envoys, that members of the AARIR had been left in complete ignorance of the trend of the negotiations, and that even after the Treaty was signed, they 'did not get a single word of advice or guidance from Dublin'.[351] When Stack told him that he and the other envoys had come to America to raise three hundred thousand dollars to save the Republic, Yorke showed little enthusiasm for the venture, pointing out that most Americans would think of the struggle as a faction-fight.[352] The shelling of the Four Courts, however, revived

---

[348] See pp. 35–6, note 9.

[349] *The Irish World*, 17.12.21.

[350] Yorke was born in Galway city in 1864. He was educated at Maynooth, where he was a fellow-student of the Irish language enthusiast Father O'Growney. He was ordained in 1887 for the diocese of San Francisco. He became Chancellor of the diocese in 1894, and was editor of the *San Francisco Leader*, which he used to disseminate Irish Republican views. He died in 1925. See B. Murphy, *Patrick Pearse and the Lost Republican Ideal* (Dublin, 1991).

[351] J. S. Brusher, *Consecrated Thunderbolt: Father Yorke of San Francisco* (New Jersey, 1973), p. 233.

[352] Ibid., p. 235.

Yorke's Republican partisanship. He dedicated the resources of his newspaper the *Leader* and his considerable polemical skills to a propaganda war against the Free State and its episcopal allies. For Yorke, the Irish struggle was no longer a faction-fight but a war waged by idealists against continuing English dominance, with Collins and Griffith 'doing England's dirty work in Ireland'. Pearse's idea of patriotic blood-sacrifice commended itself as appropriate to what Republican 'martyrs' were undergoing in the Civil War: 'The blood of Cathal Brugha and the blood of the high-souled and noble youths who chose to follow Pearse to death [rather] than Collins to profitable treason will fructify yet in the young fields of Éire'.[353] As the war intensified, Yorke came increasingly to identify the Republican struggle with the War of Independence; when it was over, his verdict was that 'Four Courts and Easter Week are forever linked, each equalling each, if indeed the domestic treason that caused the Four Courts battle did not make it the harder, the greater battle'.[354]

When Republican militancy was answered by Free State rigour, apologists for Republicanism had a cause which Yorke and many other American clergymen found it difficult to resist. Months after the ending of hostilities on the Republican side, thousands of prisoners were still in jail. In October 1923, Hagan was sad to hear 'the continuous complaints' being sent to Rome in connection with 'the harm being done to the interests of religion by the refusal of the Sacraments, especially to those in prison and more particularly to those on hunger-strike'.[355] The release of Republican prisoners, the removal of their religious disabilities and the relief of their dependants were enterprises with which even senior churchmen felt able to associate their names, among them Archbishop Mundelein of Chicago, Bishop Dunn of New York, Bishop Hoban of Scranton, Pennsylvania, and Bishop Hickey of Rochester.[356] Yorke engaged in successful fund-raising on behalf of the prisoners' dependants, telling the readers of his newspaper that 'thousands of men, women and children' were 'in dire want and distress'.[357]

---

[353] *San Francisco Leader*, 15.7.22.

[354] Ibid., 23.6.23. The deaths of Griffith and Collins evoked the following pitiless response from Yorke: 'The blood of Cathal Brugha and the blood of Harry Boland did not cry in vain from Irish earth to the Most High. The two authors and contrivers of the treason, Griffith and Collins, have entered into eternal judgment.' Ibid., 2.9.22.

[355] Hagan to Mannix, 5.10.23, Hagan Papers.

[356] *The Monitor*, New Jersey, 23.7.23; *Éire*, 11.8.23.

[357] *San Francisco Leader*, 14.7.23. Yorke also raised 10,000 dollars for de Valera's 1923 General Election Appeal, responding to what he considered a gratifying result by telling a clerical friend that 'it was very pleasant to see the 17,000 kicks that the new KKK received, namely Kosgrove, Kohalen [*sic*] and Kurley'. Brusher, *Consecrated Thunderbolt*, p. 243. De Valera had polled 17,762 votes in Clare.

The many other American responses ranged from a pledge of loyalty to the imprisoned de Valera from the priests of San Francisco on St Patrick's Day, 1924,[358] to an angry demand to Cosgrave from Father Eugene Owens of Nelsonville, Ohio, that he 'release all political prisoners at once'.[359]

VIII

Much Irish Republican discourse in the aftermath of the Treaty is preoccupied with ecclesiastical, and more particularly episcopal, intransigence and hostility to the anti-Treaty cause. The copious Republican literature of remonstrance is marked by a constant emphasis on the disillusionment and sense of betrayal felt by those who, regarding themselves as conscientious Catholics, considered that the Church should be sustaining, rather than rejecting, their political ideals. Unlike the members of the de Valera Church in Chicago, however, Irish Republicans did not, in general, feel impelled to retaliate by excommunicating themselves from the Church. On the contrary, the majority continued to insist on the strength of their commitment to the institution and on their sense of the centrality to their lives of Catholic practice. The 'excommunicated' de Valera represented this point of view to the Pope in April 1923 when he asked Luzio to 'give to the Holy Father my dutiful homage'. He also wanted the Pope to know that although Republicans were 'nominally cut away from the body of Holy Church, we are still spiritually and mystically of it, and we refuse to regard ourselves except as his children'.[360] Gearóid O'Holohan was another excommunicated Republican. Following the October Pastoral, he was refused absolution by the prison chaplain in Mountjoy unless he undertook to sever his connection with the IRA. His wife, convinced that he was 'in grave danger spiritually', told Archbishop Byrne that all her husband's spare hours had been 'given to the cause which, in his mind, comes next to love of God – namely love of country'. She believed that his devotion to Republicanism had been 'a help to him rather than a hindrance spiritually as it served to make an ideal, the absence of which tends so much in this life to make one so materialistic'.[361] In the course of a similar letter to Byrne, Mary MacSwiney, on hunger-strike in Mountjoy in November 1922, told him that if he deprived her of the sacraments, he would inflict a

---

[358] *Éire*, 12.4.24.
[359] Ibid., 22.2.24.
[360] Longford and O'Neill, *De Valera*, p. 220.
[361] Mrs G. O'Holohan to Archbishop Byrne, 27.5.23. Byrne Papers, DAA.

suffering on her far greater than her hunger-strike would cause. 'If I were really in a state of sin', she asked him, 'would I care about the deprivation you inflict on me'.[362] Writing to his wife from Mountjoy in April 1923, Count Plunkett thanked her for sending him a volume from Migne's collection of the Fathers of the Latin Church, 'a storehouse of interesting matter', enclosed a poem he had composed on the Passion of Christ, and told her he had prayed for her 'at the altar on Sunday'.[363] When the 72-year-old Plunkett, who spent seventeen weeks in prison, wrote to her again in July, he devoted his entire letter to an anxious consideration of the spiritual plight of his fellow-Republican prisoners. They were now receiving absolution, but the prison chaplain tended to get 'into political arguments' with some penitents, who refused to have their confessions heard as a consequence. Plunkett expressed his annoyance that 'no public announcement of the withdrawal of ecclesiastical penalties against Republicans' had been made, and that chaplains were still insisting 'on the acceptance of the Pastoral as though we had not stopped the war'; the result was a 'painful carelessness among some of the best men here, and among the easy-going sort, many don't go to Mass who previously never missed doing so'. Plunkett, like many Republicans, found it possible to reconcile extreme Catholic piety with recriminatory comment on the bishops for what he saw as their unprincipled conduct. Some prisoners, he reported, 'who were brutally treated by Free State troops or had relatives murdered by Free State troops are very bitter against the bishops who not only condoned such savagery but have countenanced the Free State in everything'.[364]

In Republican eyes, the primary sin of the bishops had been their attempt to disjoin the practice of the Catholic religion from the only version of patriotism to which Republicans could conscientiously subscribe. Most Republicans would not, or could not, accept this disjunction, having learned to regard their Republicanism as central to their religious faith, and sanctioned by it. The frequent affirmation of this principle was one method of maintaining a sense of moral and spiritual imperviousness to episcopal assault. Republicans also tended to convey to those with whom they were in contention, particularly the bishops, a consciousness of their own moral and spiritual superiority. Many appeared convinced that by making themselves allies of Free State politicians who had compromised national ideals, the bishops

---

[362] Mary MacSwiney to Archbishop Byrne, 5.11.22, MacSwiney Papers, UCDA, P48a/194(1). MacSwiney signed herself 'a devoted child of Holy Church'.
[363] Plunkett to Countess Plunkett, 24.4.23, Plunkett Papers NLI, 11,375.
[364] Plunkett to Countess Plunkett, 9.7.23, Plunkett Papers NLI, 11,375

had forfeited much of the moral authority they had earned up to 1921 when many of them had supported, or at least condoned, Republican nationalism. Ernie O'Malley believed that the leaders of the Free State were spiritually inferior to their Republican predecessors. 'Pearse and his group', he wrote in 1923, 'set out to minister to the spiritual side of the nation', while neither Collins nor Mulcahy was 'spiritual'. O'Malley saw himself and his fellow-Republicans as 'always fighting for God and Ireland, for the spread of our spirituality such as it is, to counteract the agnosticism and materialism of our own and other countries'.[365] Mary MacSwiney placed her commitment to anti-Treaty Republicanism on the same kind of footing as her tenacious attachment to her religion, telling Mulcahy that Republicans 'could no more accept the Treaty than they could turn their backs on the Catholic faith', and that people like her held the Republic 'as a living-faith – a spiritual reality stronger than any material benefits' Mulcahy or the new State could offer.[366] A belief in her own political and religious inerrancy gave MacSwiney the strength to reprimand the bishops, individually and collectively, when she felt that they were deviating from the paths of political probity and keeping morally dubious company. When Cardinal Logue wired his opinion to the world that de Valera's precipitate rejection of the Treaty had prejudiced the decision of the Dáil, MacSwiney urged him and the other bishops 'in God's name and for the sake of our Holy Religion to pause before you take sides in this matter'.[367]

In November 1922, while she was on hunger-strike, MacSwiney submitted a remarkable document to Archbishop Byrne which illustrated, perhaps better than anything else from the period, the characteristic notes of Republican fundamentalism: its religious fervour, moralism, self-righteousness and certitude. With God's help, she tells Byrne, she will carry her hunger-strike through 'as bravely as my sainted brother did, for the same cause and with equal justification'. She does not hesitate to accuse Byrne and the other bishops of moral blindness in offering the support of the Church to men who have

---

[365] R. English and C. O'Malley (eds), *Prisoners* (Dublin, 1993), pp. 129, 110.
[366] Mary MacSwiney to Richard Mulcahy, 24.4.22, Mulcahy Papers, UCDA, P7a/175.
[367] Mary MacSwiney to Cardinal Logue and the Irish bishops, 11.12.21, DRDA. She suggested to the bishops that their true role was a spiritual one, in which they should be guided by 'the Spiritual Father of us all, His Holiness'. As a way of 'helping all and embittering none of your flock', she asked the bishops to arrange that 'the Mass of the Holy Ghost be said . . . that God may give us all light to choose what is best for His Glory and the Honour as well as the Peace and Prosperity of our Beloved Land'. Ibid.

declared that 'what is wrong with this country is that we are too damned religious – too much spirituality about us and it is materialism that pays'. Through the October Pastoral, Byrne and his colleagues 'are supporting perjurers, job-hunters, materialists; and driving away those who stand for Truth and Honour and who refuse to take, or sanction others to take, false oaths'. She will offer her death, 'if it comes, for the immediate triumph of the Republic and the conversion of renegade Irishmen'. God, she reminds Byrne, who must have felt included in the latter grouping, does not always favour the strong. Indeed, He may well have it in mind to show to the world, through the example of Ireland, that 'governments can be built up on a basis of truth, justice and honesty – not as heretofore on trickery, meanness, false oaths and the exploitation of the weak'. She is not above exposing Byrne to the ultimate in moral blackmail when she asks him if he is going to take it on his conscience to deprive her of the Sacraments in the days of her suffering and in the event of her death.[368] To this awesome exhortation Byrne could only answer 'in all humility', that he, too, loved his country and his people 'as much as many who make more open profession of patriotism', and that in composing their October Pastoral the Bishops had acted as 'divinely authorised interpreters of the Divine Law'. He refused to yield to her principal demand, telling her bluntly that if anyone in Mountjoy 'openly manifests to the chaplain an intention of contravening this authorised teaching, it is clear that he is not free to do otherwise than to follow the directions set forth in the Pastoral'.[369] A few days later, however, Byrne, fearful of the consequences MacSwiney's death on hunger-strike might provoke, wrote to Cosgrave appealing for her release.[370]

Many other Republican complaints to bishops were informed by feelings of outrage that idealistic Republicans were being denounced by clergymen whose behaviour did not always conform to strict Republican standards. In August 1922, the mother of an IRA officer in the Kenmare district wrote to the Bishop of Kerry advising him that the priests of her parish seemed anxious to 'snub and insult' members of her family into giving up their religious duties. She had

---

[368]Mary MacSwiney to Archbishop Byrne, 5.11.22, MacSwiney Papers, UCDA, P48a/194 (1). Oonagh Walsh's article in the Trinity History Workshop's volume, David Fitzpatrick (ed.), *Revolution? Ireland 1917–1923* (Dublin, 1990), contains the full text of MacSwiney's letter to Byrne.

[369] Byrne to MacSwiney, 8.11.22, MacSwiney Papers, UCDA P48a/194 (2)

[370] Byrne to Cosgrave, 16.11.22, NAI S 1369/9. 'Personally I have little sympathy for this lady and politically none', Byrne wrote, but told Cosgrave that to allow her to die 'would be a thoroughly unwise policy'. She was released on 28 November, without explanation.

walked out of her place of worship when one of the priests began to deliver a 'political oration' in which he called the IRA volunteers 'misguided youths, uneducated boys', led by officers who were 'infinitely worse'. Her son, one of the officers in question, could, she told the bishop, 'stand a better test of character' than the priest, being a total abstainer from alcohol and tobacco. The priest, on the other hand, was accustomed to drinking whiskey at a public house in Kenmare, and knew all the brands of alcohol better than the barmaid did. She could not, she felt, be expected to sit and listen to a man like that abuse her son or any of the IRA. Many Kerry Republicans found it difficult to endure the regular use of the pulpit on Sundays as a forum for castigating them and their cause. Some retaliated with vigour. In September 1922, a pronouncement by the Bishop of Kerry condemning 'the Irregular revolt' and the killing by anti-Treaty forces of two Red Cross men at Innisfallen was read in all the churches of the diocese. In several of these, attempts to read the document to congregations provoked disorderly protests. At Curraheen, when Fr Casey was reading it, a Republican soldier blew a whistle, and in obedience to the signal, 'the Irregulars jumped from their seats and left the Church'. In response, Casey told those who remained that in every civilised country the interruption of a religious service was a crime punishable by a severe penalty, and that the Republicans who left 'were no great loss'. After Mass, the soldier who had initiated the withdrawal addressed a protest meeting outside the church, telling the people that Fr Casey had a defective understanding of the moral law in general and of the obligations of an oath in particular. Republicans also walked out of churches in Clogher, Currow, Ballymacelligott and Abbeydorney during the reading of the bishop's letter.[371] Republicans who felt that the Free State and its clerical allies had fallen into ignoble ways of living and thinking celebrated their own devotion to a higher cause by making this appear a holy one.

The characteristic language of Irish Republicanism is that of Catholic piety. Peter Magennis, who had been close to Mellows, wrote after his death that 'the independence of Ireland was a religion with Liam, as it was with the noble hearts that despised the materialistic inducements that have been in the past and are still being held out to the weak-souled children of Ireland'.[372] In his last letter to his mother Mellows found in a hazy recollection of a passage from the Sermon on the

---

[371] Mrs E. Rice to Bishop O'Sullivan, 21.8.22, KYDA. For a report on the Republican response to the bishop's letter, see *Freeman's Journal*, 8.9.22.
[372] *Irish Press*, 30.8.37. See Peter O'Dwyer, *Father Peter E. Magennis Priest and Patriot, 1863–1937*, 1975.

Mount the appropriate vehicle for the expression of his Republicanism: 'The path the people of Ireland must tread is straight and broad and true, though narrow . . . It is a hard road but it is the road our Saviour followed, the road of sacrifice . . . Ireland must tread the path our Redeemer trod'.[373] The formal commitment made by the hunger-strikers in October 1923 assimilated devotion to the Republican ideal with zeal for religion. Each pledged himself 'in the name of the living Republic' to persist until he was unconditionally released, and offered his sufferings 'to the glory of God and for the freedom of Ireland'.[374] A Republican journal of the 1920s followed Pearse in adapting a traditional definition of the true Church to the Republican ideal, which bore 'the marks of unity, of sanctity, of Catholicity, of apostolic succession'.[375] The literature of Republican martyrdom is distinguished by its fondness for devotional imagery and its association of Republicanism with exemplary Catholicism. 'Dear Mother', James Fisher wrote on 17 November 1922, 'I am perfectly happy because I've seen the priest and I'm going to die a good Catholic and a soldier of the Irish Republic'.[376] Republican speakers instinctively interwove their political and religious themes, expressing the former in images traditionally associated with the latter. De Valera's speech at Wolfe Tone's grave in Bodenstown in 1925 employs distinctively religious imagery to express Republican ideas: his listeners are 'on a pilgrimage of loyalty'; their 'devotion to the cause is unaltered'; they have repeated their Republican 'vows at this shrine' and had 'glimpses of the Land of Promise'; they have not taken part in 'an idle demonstration of a lifeless faith'.[377] The use of devotional language in the service of Republicanism is a convention which Pearse made popular before the Rising, and which writers in the *Catholic Bulletin* propagated after it, when they sought to immortalise the dead as Christian heroes, martyrs for faith as well as for fatherland. The *Bulletin* presented the leaders of the anti-Treaty movement as heirs to this tradition. 'The country', a writer in that journal declared in December 1921, 'will note the names of the Ministers in opposition to the Treaty. We who

---

[373] Greaves, *Liam Mellows*, p. 387. The Douai version of the ill-remembered passage (Matthew, VII, 14) reads: 'How narrow is the Gate and how strait [i.e. narrow] is the way, which leadeth to Life'. Mellows confused this desirable 'way' with the undesirable one described in the previous verse: 'The Gate is wide, and the way is broad, that leadeth to destruction'. Mellows would, on the evidence of this, have made a very unlearned Carmelite. See p. 141, note 16.
[374] Republican Hunger-Strike Pledge, October 1923. P.J. Ruttledge to Presiding Chairman and delegates, Sinn Féin Ard Fheis, 1923, 16.10.23, NLI MS 5815.
[375] *Freedom (Saoirse na h-Éireann)*, February 1927.
[376] Quoted in *The Nation*, 16.11.29.
[377] Moynihan, *Speeches and Statements of De Valera*, pp. 118–19.

know the three men intimately cannot help thinking that it is the very
irony of Fate to have President de Valera, Cathal Brugha and Austin
Stack on one side and possibly the Hierarchy as a whole and the
great bulk of the clergy on the other; for if ever there were three
laymen the embodiment of all our Holy Faith holds dear in Truth,
Sobriety, Honour and Justice, we believe they would be in a pre-
eminent degree Eamon de Valera, Cathal Brugha and Austin Stack.'[378]
The belief that Republicans tended to be finer exemplars of the
Catholic faith than their opponents was reaffirmed by Mannix in
1925, when he told a meeting of Sligo Republicans that the best
Catholics of the town were in his audience. 'I boldly make the
assertion', he added, 'that the best of Catholics of Ireland throughout
the length and breadth of the land are found amongst those who
agree with those who are in this hall'. Mannix looked forward to the
time when Catholic Republicans would be close allies of the Church,
'when the Pastors of Ireland will have to look to you and people like
you to save them from the dangers of the days to come'.[379]

In 1922 and 1923, Republicans looked to the bishops for help in
dealing with urgent political and spiritual problems. As the Civil War
was drawing to a close, Mary MacSwiney wrote a long, relatively
temperate, letter to Hagan which suggested how central the bishops

[378] *Catholic Bulletin*, vol. xi, no. 12, December 1921. Free Supplement. For adverse
comment on the 'semi-religious cults' and the 'cult of martyrs' generated by the
Bulletin see F.S.L. Lyons, *Culture and Anarchy in Ireland, 1890–1939* (Oxford, 1980)
and T. Garvin, *Nationalist Revolutionaries in Ireland, 1858–1928* (Dublin, 1987). For a
more sympathetic account, see B. Murphy, *Patrick Pearse and the Lost Republican
Ideal* (Dublin, 1991), pp. 65–6.
[379] *Catholic Bulletin*, 1925, pp. 1133–4. There is evidence that Republican Catholic
piety was more than a rhetorical device. C.S. Andrews, writing from the
standpoint of a Republican who no longer regarded himself as a member of the
Church following the October Pastoral, wrote of Liam Lynch that 'he was a
simple, uncomplicated man, believing deeply in God, the Blessed Virgin and the
Saints, and loving Ireland as he did, he dedicated his life to her under God'.
Dublin Made Me, p. 272. Emmet Humphreys, a member of the Dublin Brigade at
the time of the shelling of the Four Courts, recalled that the members of the
Brigade, being in Grafton Street, took advantage of this by 'going to confession,
one after another' in Clarendon Street Church. U. MacEoin (ed.), *Survivors* (Dublin,
1980), p. 432. During the Civil War, Peter Golden found de Valera in a house in
West Cork, 'the household saying the rosary in Irish, de Valera kneeling against
the back of a sugán chair, his face buried in his hands. The prayers ended, the
man who was now reviled and denounced, even from the altars, as a fomentor of
civil war, greeted the visitor with his habitual courtesy'. Longford and O'Neill, *De
Valera*, p. 198. Dan Breen remembered bringing a party from the machine-gun
section of his column to the garden of a house in Knocklofty where 'the men knelt
down, and having taken the rosary beads from their pockets, answered very devoutly
the decades which were given out by the man of the house'. *My Fight*, p. 172.

were to Republican thinking on political issues, and how much the prospects of Republicans now seemed to depend on episcopal action. At this point the Republicans had proposed a settlement by consent which had been rejected by the Free State government. MacSwiney felt that such a settlement would have enabled 'all the best elements to work together on a common basis for good of the nation'. Its rejection would lead to the formation of Republican secret societies 'without responsible leadership and with a programme of destruction and even assassination'. Republicans, she pointed out to Hagan, had no means of warning the people of this kind of danger, since 'the press is muzzled as never before' and, worse still, 'the pulpit is either silent or given over to the promulgation of the principles of hatred and rancour'. The bishops, she believed, could have brought powerful influence to bear in the interests of a settlement. Instead, their voices were drowned 'in the chorus of hatred' which they themselves 'have helped to raise and certainly done nothing to quell'. They could, however, now that the Free State Government seemed determined to bar the way to reconciliation, still redeem themselves in Republican eyes, and at the same time perform a vital national task, if they cast aside the political prejudices by which 'they hitherto seem unhappily to have been swayed'. Even now, she told Hagan, 'at the eleventh hour, the bishops, and they alone, have it in their power to reach the people and to teach the people and to lead them back to the principles of charity and good fellowship'. What she wanted was 'a strong joint Pastoral' in which the principles of a free election 'could be indicated and brought home to the people in a way that is not open to any body or agency in Ireland'. In this way, the bishops would be doing something to 'atone for the blunder' they had made when they issued their October Pastoral. She realised that the bishops might not yet have sufficiently overcome their prejudices against Republicans to act as purveyors of Republican policy. In that case they would need to be subjected to 'powerful' influence. If such influence were to be sought anywhere, she suggested, 'it is in Rome' and the only way it could be exercised would be in the form of 'a brief personal letter from the Holy Father to the Irish Archbishops urging them to throw their influence on the side of peace by understanding'. The Pope should also urge the bishops to insist on a cessation of all military activity, a general amnesty, the release of all political prisoners, a complete parliamentary register, a free election with freedom of speech and the removal of spiritual penalties.[380]

[380] Mary MacSwiney to Hagan, n.d. [Spring 1923] Hagan Papers. Compare de Valera's similar suggestion to Luzio. See p. 187, note 214.

In the circumstances, this was expecting more from the Pope and the bishops than they could be expected to give. Many Republicans, however, managed to persuade individual bishops to intervene on their behalf with the government. Archbishop Byrne dealt patiently and conscientiously with the numerous requests he got. In April 1923, it was represented to him that CID men at Oriel House had threatened to murder two republicans if they had not found the son of one of them by the following day. Byrne immediately wrote to Cosgrave telling him that 'nothing could be more reprehensible or more shocking to the public conscience than that crimes such as the two referred to . . . should be committed by individuals belonging to forces under government control'.[381] Two weeks later, Cáit O'Kelly pleaded for the intervention of a number of bishops, including Cardinal Logue and Archbishop Byrne, on behalf of her sister and two other women who had been on hunger-strike for twenty-five days. She told Bishop Mulhern of Dromore that she 'couldn't help feeling that Cardinal Logue would put the matter right and secure the release of the girls'.[382] Mulhern dismissed her plea with the comment that 'His Eminence knows his own business and no letter of mine could change his mind on this question, if I were willing to write to him. The only solution to the girls' trouble is for them to give up this hunger-strike'.[383] Mulhern was, however, more sympathetic to a request from Mrs Quinn of Newry that he intervene on behalf of her imprisoned sons. He approached the Governor-General, T.M. Healy who felt sure that 'in spite of the ruin and destruction wrought by the Quinns as abettors of Aiken, fair consideration will be given to the request'.[384] Three days later, Mulhern learned from Cosgrave's office that one of the Quinns had been released.[385]

Byrne took Cáit O'Kelly's request much more seriously than either Logue or Mulhern did. 'Don't you think', he asked Cosgrave, 'the government has the rebellion sufficiently in hand without allowing them to die even through their own fault?' Byrne was aware of the government view 'as to the machinations of women in the movement' but he 'would put in a strong word for a gesture of clemency' in this case, since their deaths would cause 'a wave of sympathy through the country'. The strength of the government, he suggested, 'and the imminence of peace, give the government no excuse for appearing to

---

[381] Byrne to Cosgrave, 2.4.23. Byrne Papers, DAA. For Byrne's dismay at the killing of untried prisoners as reprisals see p. 85, note 223.
[382] Cáit O'Kelly to Mulhern, 16.4.23, DRDA.
[383] Mulhern to Cáit O'Kelly, n.d., DRDA.
[384] T.M. Healy to Mulhern, 21.8.23, DRDA.
[385] Cosgrave's Secretary to Mulhern, 24.8.23, DRDA.

make war on women'.[386] Cosgrave replied that real success had not attended the government's efforts to crush the rebellion 'until particular attention was turned to women, who operated with impunity in every possible way'. The Executive Council had, however, decided to release them if they signed an undertaking to desist from further activity against the State.[387] Byrne was also involved in attempts to persuade the government to reach an accommodation with those Republicans who, still interned in October 1923, organised a mass hunger-strike in all prisons and detention centres in the State. Sinn Féin Headquarters gave Byrne an alarming account of the predicament of the prisoners. Eight thousand men were involved in the hunger-strike, which had originated in Mountjoy; they had been driven to seek 'freedom or the grave' after months of torture and ill-treatment. The authorities regarded them, not as political prisoners, but as criminals. They saw themselves as 'unnecessary hostages', prisoners of war detained 'without charge or trial six months after the cessation of hostilities'. Almost all were Catholics, 'offering their sufferings for God and the freedom of Ireland'. Sinn Féin called on Byrne 'for the sake of God and of our country' to do all he could to avert a National calamity.[388]

In November 1922, Byrne appealed for Mary MacSwiney's release from Mountjoy only on grounds of expediency.[389] A year later, pleading for thousands of hunger-strikers, he still used this argument: the Government, however strong, could not allow thousands of men to die in a political cause without putting at risk the foundations of the State and antagonising 'moderate' supporters. He has also been sufficiently impressed by the Sinn Féin account of prison conditions to argue 'from the humanitarian point of view' for the release of the prisoners. His third line of argument, however, is more interesting and significant. With the Republican 'reign of violence' over, the leaders of the movement representing the prisoners have decided 'to seek now to spread their views only by the constitutional way of

[386] Byrne to Cosgrave, 17.4.23, Byrne Papers, DAA.
[387] Cosgrave to Byrne, 19.4.23. See Minutes of Executive Council Meeting, 19.4.23, NAI G 2/2 p.3: 'Correspondence relative to the arrest of Miss K.M. Costello who was now on hunger-strike was considered, including letters from the Archbishop of Dublin and Lord Glenavy, Chairman of the Senate, and a communication from her mother, declaring her daughter's innocence. It was decided that if Miss Costello subscribed to a document similar to that signed by Dr Conn Murphy, she should be released.'
[388] Sinn Féin Headquarters to Byrne, 24.10.23, James Ryan Papers, UCDA P 88/100.
[389] See p. 225, note 370.

educating the public'. Thus Byrne implies, without saying so directly, that he regards Republicans as a legitimate political grouping. Their declaration of exclusively political intent, as he puts it, 'makes at least *a priori* their claim to consideration strong before the world'.[390]

Cosgrave dismissed each of Byrne's arguments. He believed that the Archbishop was not properly informed on the likely public response to deaths in the prisons. He thought there would be 'some casualties'; these, however, he correctly predicted, would have 'quite the contrary effect to that expressed by Your Grace'. He was 'perfectly satisfied that generosity or mercy is thrown away on these people and that a change which they claim has taken place is a change of necessity – not conviction or any sense of wrong doing'. He was therefore not impressed by Byrne's idea that the Republicans were to be regarded as constitutionalists: he remained to be convinced 'that there had been a change of heart as well as of label in this matter of armed versus constitutional agitation'. He and his ministers, he declared, would rather 'give up public life altogether' than to permit 'these people to demand and secure release in this manner'. Cosgrave tried to diminish whatever regard Byrne might have had for 'these people' by telling him that 'one woman leading their Rosaries is a notoriously bad character'.[391] On 20 November, Denis Barry died in Newbridge Camp; two days later Andrew Sullivan died in Mountjoy.[392] On the day of Barry's death, Byrne received an offer from the Sinn Féin Standing Committee: if the Government promised to release all prisoners by Christmas, the hunger-strike would cease immediately. Eoin Ó Caoimh, who conveyed this offer, told Byrne that although he was a member of the Standing Committee, he had 'rigidly obeyed the terms of the Pastoral letter of October 1922'.[393] On 21 November, Byrne met Cosgrave, only to be told that the Government could give no promises or undertakings, and that it would not negotiate on the hunger-strike.[394] On 18 November, Cardinal Logue issued a statement hoping the Government would release, before Christmas, all those not guilty of crime, and that the hunger-strike would be abandoned. The strike was called off a few days later.[395] This episode marked the last significant episcopal involvement with the Free State authorities on behalf of Republicans.

[390] Byrne to Cosgrave, 28.10.23, Byrne Papers, DAA.
[391] Cosgrave to Byrne, 28.10.23, Byrne Papers, DAA.
[392] Macardle, *Irish Republic*, p .387. For Cohalan's refusal to accord a Christian burial to Barry, see pp. 80–1, notes 205 –7.
[393] Eoin Ó Caoimh to Byrne, 31.10.23, Byrne Papers, DAA.
[394] Byrne's copy of the Sinn Féin proposals and Cosgrave's answers are in a document in Byrne's papers dated 20.11.23.
[395] Macardle, *Irish Republic*, p. 867.

Once the bishops committed themselves as a body to one side in the post-Treaty conflict, they inevitably assumed responsibility, in Republican eyes, for the acts of the Government whose agents they had become. The Galway Diocesan Secretary, James O'Dea, told Professor Michael Browne of Maynooth in December 1922 that 'every bishop gets bundles of Republican literature every day, mostly disquisitions on theology and the cardinal virtue of prudence', adding that 'one needs to have a mind like the hide of a rhinoceros'.[396] Most of the surviving letters are from laymen and women with a strong ethical bent, preoccupied with establishing the guilt by association of the bishops, and showing them where they have erred both politically and theologically. This tendency is particularly strong in letters written following the October Pastoral, when bishops are increasingly identified as active or silent partners in Free State misdemeanours. In August 1922, we find Count Plunkett pointing out to Bishop O'Sullivan of Kerry that even the Pope claims infallibility 'solely when dealing with dogmatic teaching', and suggesting that the claim of Irish bishops to 'infallibility in politics' represented 'a narrow and extravagant assertion of authority and ignorance of principles accepted in every other country'. He is sorry to see the bishops blunder in attempting to crush Republicanism 'because of the injury to religion that is pretty certain to follow'.[397] In October, after Archbishop Gilmartin had declared that 'if ever there was a legitimate government it was that now sitting in Dublin', Count Plunkett explained to him patiently and at length, why the 'Provisional Parliament' could be nothing other than 'an English agency set up in Ireland by Acts of the English Parliament and based on the Partition Act which the bishops themselves repudiated'.[398] A note of pity for profound episcopal ignorance and blindness to reality was sounded by J.M. O'Daly from County Meath in a document he issued to the episcopal body in November 1922. He prayed that God would give the bishops 'the necessary humility to realise how far they have overstepped the prudence which should temper their actions and restrain their utterance'. By assuming their partisan role, the bishops had, O'Daly told them, 'emboldened those who are against justice and liberty to commit manifold crimes in the name of law and order'. They had condemned the 'pure and holy patriots' of the IRA who were 'sacrificing their ease and well-being for God and their country', while at the same time nurturing a Provisional

[396] J. O'Dea to M.J. Browne, 15.12.22, GDA.
[397] Count Plunkett to Bishop O'Sullivan, 30.8.22, KYDA.
[398] Count Plunkett to Archbishop Gilmartin, 5.10.22, GDA. For Gilmartin's speech see *ICD*, 1923, p. 589.

Parliament in the process of writing a 'Godless' constitution. O'Daly invoked the example of Pope Benedict XV as something the Irish bishops should follow. When his own country was at war and intrigues were on foot to persuade him to denounce its enemies, the Pope had elected to 'embrace all the belligerents in his charity' since, 'having numerous children in both camps, he ought to be solicitous for the salvation of them all'. O'Daly reminded the bishops that 'the Good Shepherd did not upbraid and fulminate anathemas against the wandering sheep. He went seeking it'. The bishops, on the other hand, 'were trying to close heaven to those of us who do not slavishly bow to an illegitimate Parliament, foisted on us by the ancient enemy of our race and religion'.[399] O'Daly's document is a Republican Pastoral, using some of the methods of the October one to make its authors the objects, rather than the perpetrators, of moral and spiritual intimidation.

When Conn Murphy's daughter was arrested in January 1923 and imprisoned in Cork Jail, his immediate response was to write a letter of complaint, not to the Free State authorities, but to a number of bishops, among them Thomas O'Dea of Galway. His first letter elicited a sympathetic response. O'Dea wrote that 'we all ought to be deeply ashamed of not having ended this quarrel long ago', adding that 'little as this is, I feel it ought to be said, in answer to your letter'.[400] Murphy replied that 'a far-reaching effect for good' would result from publication of O'Dea's 'honest admission that all parties concerned, including yourself and other members of the Irish Hierarchy, have cause to be deeply ashamed'. When the bishop refused to have his admission of shame made public, Murphy described this as a 'deplorable' example of 'episcopal clannishness'. The real point of Murphy's letter, as of many others of its kind, was to tell the bishop that the illegal imprisonment he had complained of could be attributed in great measure to 'Your Lordship's public action in issuing your Pastoral letter of October 22nd'. Murphy found O'Dea 'very directly and specifically responsible' for Free State injustices, 'first, positively, because your public support and approval alone has enabled the Free State to perpetrate them; and secondly, negatively, because of your failure to utter a single word of protest or disapproval of murders, tortures, raids, arrests and suppression of all liberty of speech or action by the Government'.[401] A Kerry priest, Father McEnery, serving in

[399] J.M. O'Daly to The Archbishops and Bishops of Ireland, 9.11.22, DAA.
[400] O'Dea's reply is quoted by Murphy in a subsequent letter to the bishop, dated 28.2.23, GDA.
[401] C. Murphy to Bishop O'Dea, 28.2.23.

England, had a more disturbing case to make to the Bishop of Kerry and the priests of his diocese. McEnery's brother was captured after a fight at Clashmealcon Caves. It was widely rumoured that he and other prisoners were beaten almost to death by their captors.[402] Father McEnery returned in haste from England, was not allowed to see his brother, but was told by the authorities that the prisoners would be executed when time became available.[403] He wrote to Bishop O'Sullivan that his brother, 'after being first tortured, was murdered at Ballymullen Barracks, Tralee'. He was writing, 'not to ask Your Lordship how much Christianity is allowed in your diocese, but what is to be done for his widow and little child', and to point out that 'the very priests who made these young fellows swear a solemn oath of fealty to the Republic are now enjoying comfortable incomes as chaplains to the Free State'.[404] O'Sullivan and his clergy might be considered particularly vulnerable to Father McEnery's line of attack, since their enthusiastic denunciation of Republicans was not matched by a willingness to draw attention to the atrocities perpetrated by the other side.[405]

IX

Conn Murphy could scarcely be blamed for attributing a clannish spirit to the Irish episcopacy: despite the reservations of at least a few bishops by the end of 1922 about some activities of the Free State government, even these refrained from open comment. However, although the public solidarity of the bishops as partisans of the Free State was not impaired until Dignan of Clonfert proclaimed himself a Sinn Féin supporter in 1924, it was apparent even in 1922 that there were differences of approach and emphasis among them on the Republican issue, particularly on the methods used by the Government in dealing with captured Republicans. Two of the most influential members of the hierarchy, O'Donnell and Byrne, tried to prevent executions in 1922 and 1923, and protested at the highest levels when these were carried out.[406] In 1923, Archbishop Harty of Cashel lent

[402] D. Macardle, *Tragedies of Kerry* (Dublin, 1924), p. 86.
[403] Ibid.
[404] Fr T. McEnery to Bishop O'Sullivan, 23.5.23, KYDA. Bishop O'Sullivan's cousin, Charles Daly, was one of the four Republicans executed in Drumboe Castle, Stranorlar in March 1923. In February, Aodh de Blacam's wife appealed to the bishop to try to save his cousin's life. M. de Blacam to O'Sullivan, 4.2.23, KYDA. See p. 86, notes 225-7.
[405] For an account of atrocities committed by both sides, see N.C. Harrington, *Kerry Landing August 1922* (Dublin, 1992).
[406] See pp. 84-6, notes 220-7.

his name to peace proposals approved of by a significant element in the IRA.[407] O'Dea of Galway had a reputation among Republicans for his political moderation and conciliatory disposition. His letter to his clergy in August 1922 did not, like many episcopal discourses at the time, denounce Republicans for causing civil war but concentrated instead on warning that untold 'religious as well as temporal' disasters would come if the struggle went on.[408] J.J. O'Kelly found O'Dea's letter 'admirably prudent', being the first statement 'from any member of our Catholic hierarchy calculated to lead all men's thoughts in the direction of the peace everyone must desire'. O'Kelly pointed out that some of the pronouncements of Cardinal Logue and other bishops were regarded by Republicans 'as so lacking in impartiality that they can aid neither the cause of peace nor the interests of religion'.[409]

In most cases, their political attitudes before the Treaty made the responses of individual bishops to the settlement easy to appreciate. Some had always been deeply troubled by revolutionary action, even in the cause of independence. Warning his people in 1919 to 'beware of secret societies and revolution', Bishop Hoare of Ardagh associated these with the irreligion, anarchy, devastation and injustice experienced in France, Russia, Mexico and Portugal.[410] In 1918, Bishop Coyne described an IRA raid on Rockingham House, Boyle, the home of Sir Thomas Stafford, as 'an outrage', both 'disreputable and cowardly', which caused him 'humiliation and pain'. He suspected that many of those who organised such raids were being paid 'for the purpose of promoting disorder and of besmirching, in the eyes of the world, the good name of our country'.[411] Bishop Kelly of Ross referred to the 1916 Rising as 'an unlawful war' in which 'the killing of men was murder pure and simple'.[412] In June 1921, when de Valera tried unsuccessfully to persuade the bishops to accord recognition to the Republic, Kelly was said to have threatened to break the rule of anonymity if this were done.[413] In December 1920, Cohalan of Cork decreed that IRA ambushes were murders; there was no remedy 'except the extreme remedy, excommunication from the Church'.[414] In January 1921, Archbishop Gilmartin of Tuam declared that armed resistance to the British authorities was unlawful, since it had no

[407] See p. 155, note 74.
[408] *Irish Independent*, 10.8.22.
[409] J.J. O'Kelly to Bishop O'Dea, 10.8.22, GDA.
[410] Bishop Hoare's Lenten Pastoral, 27.2.19, ARCLDA.
[411] Bishop Coyne to Father J. Flanagan, PP Cootehall, Boyle, 22.2.18, ELDA.
[412] D.W. Miller, *Church, State and Nation in Ireland, 1898–1921* (Dublin, 1973), p. 329.
[413] D. Keogh, *The Vatican, the Bishops*, p. 74.
[414] *ICD*, 1922, p. 504.

chance of success, and the evils it would cause would be greater than those it proposed to remedy. He also warned, with the IRB in mind, that under the new code of Canon Law, members of secret societies were '*ipso facto*, excommunicated'.[415]

Some of the older bishops had little sympathy with the independence movement or with the aspiration to establish a Republic. A few would probably have been happier with the maintenance of British rule. Logue found the 1916 Rising 'foolish and pernicious'; he 'enjoyed waiting upon royalty, delighted in entertaining visiting British dignitaries with champagne and oysters'.[416] In his 1921 Pastoral, he condemned the IRA actions as 'crimes committed by extremists among the people' and the shooting of policemen and soldiers as 'not an act of war' but 'plain murder'.[417] In 1915, Brownrigg of Ossory sent a letter to a local recruiting meeting 'heartily endorsing the Allied cause, and appealing in the name of fallen and captured Kilkennymen for more Kilkenny recruits'.[418] Browne of Cloyne maintained the friendliest contact with British forces in Cobh both before and after the Treaty.[419] In his Lenten Pastoral for 1917, Morrisroe of Achonry condemned the 1916 Rising as a 'domestic tragedy' but was thankful that the people of his diocese were at any rate 'free from complicity in this hapless enterprise'. He had no doubt that the British administration in Ireland held authority from God; he saw opposition to 'legitimate authority, in whomsoever vested', as 'rebellion against the Divine Will'. Morrisroe gave no quarter to those who argued that the people of Ireland 'owe no allegiance to the powers that rule us in this country because the Union was effected by fraud'. His answer was that 'the seal of our subjection is stamped on the current coin, and except existing rulers, who else defend our persons and property and vindicate our just personal rights?'[420]

The majority of bishops could only reluctantly accommodate themselves to an independence movement based on violence, and then only after it had enjoyed a measure of success. It would therefore have been surprising to find these bishops supporting another movement willing to engage in militant action against fellow-countrymen in pursuit of an extravagant demand which had no apparent chance of being met. There were, however, two bishops, MacRory of Down and Connor and Fogarty of Killaloe, whose pro-

[415] Ibid., p.509.
[416] Miller, *Church, State and Nation*, pp. 11–12.
[417] *ICD*, 1922, p.517.
[418] Miller, *Church, State and Nation*, p. 312.
[419] Information from Canon Séamus Corkery, Charleville.
[420] *Roscommon Herald*, 24.2.17.

nouncements and actions before the Treaty might have encouraged Republicans to expect at least their neutrality if not their qualified support. MacRory had the reputation of being an ardent, even fanatical, nationalist. He embarrassed other, more moderate, nationalists at the Irish Convention of 1917 when, according to Sir Horace Plunkett, he made a speech 'raking up the past', and awaking some bitter memories of the Anglo-Irish conflict in the nineteenth century.[421] MacRory was a reluctant supporter of the Treaty. Soon after it was signed, he declared that there were several things in it that he disliked very much; had his opinions been asked about it before it was signed, 'and before the country was divided', he would have 'objected strongly to some of it', but now that the Treaty had been signed, he felt they ought to make the best of it.[422] Later, he saw its acceptance by the Dáil as 'a victory for moderate opinion which offered a hopeful opportunity of securing a united Ireland',[423] and later still warned that Ireland would be 'weakened and torn by dissensions at home' were the Treaty to be rejected.[424] Even in April 1922, however, de Valera still seems to have entertained hopes that MacRory might take a benevolent view of Republican opposition to the Treaty. When the two met at Sinn Féin headquarters, de Valera 'was disappointed that MacRory was not sympathetic to the Republican position'.[425] MacRory's response to the Treaty was similar to that attributed by Childers to Kevin O'Higgins who, when his opinion was sought at the first Cabinet meeting called to discuss it, 'said Treaty should never have been signed, but being signed should be supported. Absolute necessity for unity and unity only possible on Treaty.'[426]

Fogarty's behaviour in the immediate aftermath of the Treaty might appear in need of explanation. His instant response conveyed the warmest enthusiasm for the settlement, soon to be combined with expressions of extreme contempt for those who were opposed to it, especially de Valera, whom he had admired extravagantly during the previous four-and-a-half years. 'I cannot imagine', he wrote to de Valera in 1917, 'what way Divine Providence will finally turn your course, but Eamon, He does want you to devote yourself to your country at the present time with all the talents and faculties he has given you.'[427] Fogarty was the one bishop to whom Morrisroe's 1917

[421] Miller, *Church, State and Nation*, p. 363.
[422] *Irish Independent*, 27.12.21.
[423] *Freeman's Journal*, 9.1.22.
[424] *Irish Independent*, 17.3.22.
[425] Ó Néill agus Ó Fiannachta, *De Valera*, Vol. II, p. 36.
[426] Childers Papers, TCD, 7814.
[427] Fogarty to de Valera, 1.8.17, FAK.

verdict on the popular response to 1916 might have seemed most appropriate: 'Those who at first abhorred, with all their souls, the rash venture . . . were afterwards turned into active sympathisers with the victims of military despotism and brutality'.[428] Fogarty's earnest good will was enthusiastically invested in de Valera's political career. He was believed to have voted for him in the East Clare by-election of 1917,[429] and afterwards watched his progress with fatherly care. 'Many thanks', de Valera wrote to him towards the end of 1917, 'for St Augustine and for the advice . . . I wish I could make you understand how we all appreciate what your assistance means to the cause at the present moment'.[430] One of de Valera's supporters, in Rome in June 1920 for the Oliver Plunkett Beatification ceremonies, considered Fogarty 'the flower of the flock', being impressed that 'there were tears in his eyes' as she recounted for his benefit 'the strenuous life our beloved Chief is leading and the miracle he has worked as far as public opinion is concerned over here'.[431] Fogarty, too, was leading a strenuous life in 1920. In December of that year, while he was in Dublin to see Archbishop Clune of Perth, his house was raided by a party of Auxiliaries, with blackened faces and drawn revolvers, thinking he was at home. Brigadier Crozier, who resigned as head of the Auxiliaries partly on account of this episode, was told in confidence that instructions had been received to kill Fogarty by drowning him in a sack from the bridge over the Shannon.[432] By September 1921, Fogarty had reached the conclusion that the time had come for the Irish side to reach an accommodation with Britain. He wrote a worried letter to Collins about de Valera's apparent intransigence in dealing with proposals made by Lloyd George. 'Apart from Partition, which may be remedied in whole or in part', Fogarty wrote, 'the people feel that there is in the proposals something very substantial to negotiate and work upon'. The unacceptable alternative was 'a war of devastation without the good will of the people behind it'. Collins responded by telling Fogarty that 'we are not without regard for our responsibilities'.[433]

---

[428] *Roscommon Herald*, 24.2.17.
[429] David Fitzpatrick, 'The Undoing of the Easter Rising', J.P. O'Connell and J.A. Murphy (eds), *De Valera and his Times* (Cork, 1986), p.109.
[430] De Valera to Fogarty, 28.11.17, KILLDA.
[431] Mary McWhorter to Kathleen O'Connell, 5.6.20, Kathleen O'Connell Papers.
[432] *Irish Press*, 13.4.36; F.P. Crozier, *Ireland for Ever* (Dublin, 1932).
[433] Collins to de Valera, 1.9.21, FAK. Collins quotes the relevant part of Fogarty's letter in his report to de Valera. The 'substantial' proposals referred to by Fogarty were made by Lloyd George to de Valera on 20.7.21. They involved 'complete autonomy in taxation and finance . . . [Ireland's] own law-courts and judges . . . her own military forces . . . autonomy of the self-governing Dominions'. On 10.8.21, de Valera rejected the British proposals as 'self-contradictory'. See Macardle, *The Irish Republic*, p. 483.

It was one thing for de Valera to spurn private political advice conveyed to him through Collins, but when Fogarty publicly advertised his own acceptance of the Treaty, and de Valera at the same time publicly and forcibly expressed a contrary view, warm admiration speedily gave way to blatant hostility. This was not the first demonstration of Fogarty's volatility, a characteristic of which was the infliction of pitiless abuse on what he had once flattered. During a period of enthusiasm for the Irish Parliamentary Party, he called it 'Ireland's army and navy'. In 1918, however, he pictured its members returning from Westminster, 'with the leprosy of Anglicisation visibly developed on their persons to the ruin of our national spirit'.[434] Fogarty's post-Treaty anti-Republicanism tended to focus on de Valera to an almost pathological degree. Peadar O'Donnell described him as 'a simple, holy man who was especially simple in his hates . . . To win a place in his Lordship's hate, he must identify you as a devil. De Valera was a great devil'.[435] There is evidence, admittedly from hostile sources, that Fogarty's lack of balance and obsessive partisanship caused him to be taken with less than total seriousness by his episcopal colleagues. Hagan observed that during the Irish pilgrimage to Rome in 1925, when Fogarty was 'pushing himself and Cosgrave forward to the head of everything', Archbishop Harty of Cashel told him bluntly that 'he must not turn a pious pilgrimage into a political demonstration'. When he tried to influence the bishops against Hagan, they consoled the latter by telling him 'that neither they nor anyone else minded anything Killaloe [Fogarty] said or did'.[436]

Archbishop O'Donnell, who succeeded Logue at Armagh in 1924 and became Cardinal in 1925, was the only member of the hierarchy to enjoy the respect and confidence of large elements on both sides of the post-treaty conflict. At the Irish Convention in 1917, his moderation and his talent for softening bitter emotions deeply impressed both unionists and nationalists.[437] In the wake of the 1918 election, which he regarded as a decisive expression of the national will, he transferred his allegiance from the Irish Parliamentary Party to Sinn Féin; according to Seán T. O'Kelly, his decision influenced a number of hitherto uncommitted bishops to do likewise.[438] O'Donnell understood the historical forces behind Republican responses to the Treaty, while at the same time deploring Republican militancy as futile and

---

[434] *Freeman's Journal*, 30.11.18.
[435] Peadar O'Donnell, *There will be another day* (Dublin, 1963), p. 109.
[436] Hagan to M.J. Browne, 31.10.25, GDA.
[437] Miller, *Church, State and Nation*, p. 363.
[438] Ó Ceallaigh, *Seán T.*, 1972, p. 109.

dangerous, and finding de Valera's position contradictory.[439] He believed that the government had done well up to November 1922: his goodwill was severely tested by the execution of four Republicans at Drumboe in 1923.[440] It may not be significant that O'Donnell's name is absent from the version of the October Pastoral given to the press; its absence would, in any case, seem an appropriate indication of his characteristic even-handedness and his anxiety to remain at a remove from what he regarded as a deplorable conflict. He was not tempted, as so many other bishops were, to commit himself irrevocably to either side. His independence of mind and evident fair-mindedness gave weight and authority to his public pronouncements so often lacking in those of his colleagues. Clergymen on both sides might profitably have taken to heart his plea, during his inaugural address as Primate in February 1925, for good will, North and South, 'no matter how keen the political controversy may be', and for an active spirit of tolerance. 'Nourishing strife', he declared, 'is a poor occupation for a gifted race. It embitters, it corrodes, it poisons the finest natures and leads to national nothingness.'[441] Such goodwill was far from evident in the speeches of the many clergymen who were participating in the by-election campaigns at the time.

O'Donnell's support for the campaign to secure the release of political prisoners North and South in the Autumn of 1923 was unequivocal. Such releases were, he declared, 'long due' in the twenty-six counties, since 'in anything like normal times, no government has the right to imprison numbers of men over a long period without trial. It is a great wrong to do so and it can serve no laudable purpose.'[442] It is not surprising that many Republicans came to regard O'Donnell as a benign influence on public life. Some Republican experts on ecclesiastical politics were inclined to go further by promoting him as the bishop with the soundest outlook on national issues, an approach favoured by *An Phoblacht*, which described him after his death in 1927 as 'a great priest and a great Irish Irelander', regretting that 'the bitterness released by the executions found expression in a way that very much hurt him who above all others did his utmost to prevent them'.[443] In 1925, some knowledgeable Republicans regarded the creation of a Cardinal in succession to Logue as a semi-political event, with the leading candidates O'Donnell and Byrne representing Republican and Free State interests respectively. After O'Donnell's

[439] See p. 58, note 111.
[440] See p. 86, notes 225-7.
[441] *ICD*, 1926, p.554.
[442] *ICD*, 1924, p.594.
[443] *An Phoblacht*, 29.10.27.

appointment, Hagan told Professor Michael Browne of British news-paper reports that T.M. Healy had sponsored Byrne's candidacy, while Cosgrave and Oliver St John Gogarty came to Rome 'to back the same horse'. Hagan had no doubt that 'on national grounds', the selection of O'Donnell was 'the best that could have been made', since the new Cardinal 'certainly has no love for the powers that be, and is just as anxious as we [Browne and Hagan] are to see them off bag and baggage'.[444] A comment by Seán T. O'Kelly on the same subject reinforces the impression of Republican enthusiasm for O'Donnell at Byrne's expense. 'I read the announcement about Armagh [O'Donnell's appointment]', he wrote to Hagan, 'and I was very pleased, and doubly pleased that the honour did not go to my own city'.[445] Towards the end of 1925, O'Donnell might, as Hagan believed, have nourished hopes of an early end to Cosgrave's régime, but the prospects of significant episcopal approval, or even tolerance, of the anti-Treaty position were to be dependent on the emergence of Fianna Fáil as an ultimately credible vehicle for constitutional republicanism.

[444] Hagan to M.J. Browne, 31.10.25, GDA. Hagan was in a better position than most people to know O'Donnell's mind, being one of his most regular correspondents and a close friend.
[445] Seán T. O'Kelly to Hagan, 30.11.25, Hagan Papers.

CHAPTER FIVE

CONSTITUTIONAL REPUBLICANISM: FIANNA FÁIL

I

De Valera's rise to prominence in Nationalist politics before the Treaty was greatly facilitated by the moral and practical support of Catholic clergymen of every rank at home as well as abroad. Many of these became his mouthpieces and apologists and helped to disseminate his cult. He was always profoundly conscious of the influence Catholic ecclesiastics could bring to bear on Irish political life. It was his sense of this that led him to persuade Eoin MacNeill to campaign for him in the East Clare by-election of 1917. 'Don't forget', he told Robert Brennan, 'that the clergy are with MacNeill and they are a powerful force'.[1] In the by-election, this force was predominantly on de Valera's side; a historian of the campaign remarks that he was 'surrounded by clergy' as he spoke to a 'huge gathering' in Ennis.[2] He adapted skilfully to the task of leading a revolutionary movement without alienating the sympathies of the largely conservative priests of Clare. His careful cultivation of Eoin MacNeill was only one aspect of his strategy. Others noted by David Fitzpatrick were separation from the proscribed IRB and his quasi-theological justification of rebellion where success was likely, while his campaign leaflets in East Clare stressed the rift between the Parliamentary Party and the Bishop of Limerick.[3] During the years between the East Clare election and the Treaty, he gradually won the support of many influential churchmen. His opposition to the Treaty and his involvement in the Civil War marked a decisive change in this position. He found himself and his

[1] Robert Brennan, *Allegiance* (Dublin, 1950), p. 153.
[2] Kevin J. Browne, *Eamon de Valera and the Banner County* (Dublin, 1982), pp. 34–5.
[3] See David Fitzpatrick, 'The Undoing of the Easter Rising', in J.P. O'Carroll and J.A. Murphy (eds), *De Valera and his Time* (Cork, 1983), p. 106.

cause vigorously condemned in pastoral letters, from innumerable pulpits, and in speeches made by Catholic priests at political meetings. Many of his episcopal friends now became his determined political enemies, and their hostility was mediated to congregations by great numbers of the lower clergy.

This marked change in clerical attitudes had a profound effect on de Valera's political fortunes; it was one of the things that preoccupied him most throughout the decade following the Treaty. Despite the almost uniformly hostile attitude of the Irish hierarchy, he was never bereft of clerical followers. Even while he and his allies, political and military, were officially outside the pale of the Church, many priests and a few higher ecclesiastics living abroad, Mannix and Hagan among them, afforded the moral and spiritual support essential to one who dearly valued his membership of the institution and regarded it as an essential part of his life. During the term of the Free State government, de Valera strove, with the willing help of some well-placed clerical friends and laymen and women with Church connections, to regain his prestige at the centres of Catholic power. His efforts in this direction were pursued with skill and energy and involved a considerable variety of strategies. As the decade wore on, ecclesiastical hostility to de Valera and his associates softened, and became notably less widespread. Many priests and bishops, however, continued to regard him as an enemy of public morality and public order, and proclaimed these views, particularly at election times.

Between 1917 and 1926, de Valera presided over two Sinn Féin parties. When he seized the presidency of Sinn Féin from Griffith in 1917, its disparate elements, ranging from physical force Nationalists to those still yearning for a Dual Monarchy, maintained an unstable alliance which collapsed with the Treaty. In post-Treaty Sinn Féin, heterogeneous elements were also yoked uneasily together: militarists, intransigents and pragmatists. At vital periods, from the outbreak of the Civil War to the death of Liam Lynch, for example, de Valera was able to exercise little personal control over the activities of those he was supposed to be leading, and for which he attracted intemperate and often unjustified criticism from churchmen. While the evidence attesting to his pacific role in Republican circles may be 'overwhelming'[4] few of his ecclesiastical critics in the early twenties recognised the weakness of his position, the efforts he made to circumscribe the conflict, to subvert militarists opposed to political interference in Army affairs, and to focus the minds of Republicans on the advisability of using

---

[4] See John Bowman, *De Valera and the Ulster Question* (Oxford, 1982), p. 79; M. Hopkinson, *Green Against Green. The Irish Civil War* (Dublin, 1988), p. 70.

constitutional methods to undo the Treaty settlement. Many of the same critics may not have taken due account of the fact that during his period in jail from August 1923 to July 1924, Mary MacSwiney and other Republican fundamentalists had undermined his favoured constitutional approach by making it official Sinn Féin policy that Republicans could not, in principle, attend the Dáil.[5] His establishment of Fianna Fáil on 10 May 1926 gave him, for the first time, an opportunity to impose his leadership decisively on a political party. Those who left Sinn Féin to follow him into Fianna Fáil and out of the wilderness did so unconditionally, fully accepting his authority and his interpretation of political realities. Even after he had firmly committed himself to exclusively political action, the legacy of his former association in many clerical minds with militarism and anarchy continued to have an influence. The participating priests gave little thought to the significance of the June 1927 election as a contest between diehard Sinn Féin Republicanism with its Civil War overtones and de Valera's constitutional variety to which, in principle, they might have been expected to extend a modified welcome, if only as a token of gratitude for his conversion to a better way.[6] Instead, the great majority preferred to perpetuate the notion that he and his party represented a threat to stability and ordered government, still only possible under Cumann na nGaedheal.

With his accustomed prescience, de Valera refrained from publicly confronting this evidence of lingering clerical hostility. He had learned one of the lessons of the 1925 by-election campaign: that public criticism of ecclesiastics adversely affected electoral support for parties who engaged in it. He appeared determined from the start to demonstrate that Fianna Fáil was as soundly Catholic as the Church itself, and perhaps somewhat more so than its main political opponents. This

---

[5] De Valera explained to an American correspondent that in 1923, with the Civil War at an end, he had maintained that the Oath was the real obstacle to Republican entry to the Free State parliament. 'Had I not been arrested in Clare on August 15th 1923', he wrote, 'I would have made it my election programme then, and there would have been very little objection to it. The present opposition is due mainly to the fact that Miss MacSwiney and others, who were free to go about speaking through the country at the time, imposed their own ideas on the organisation, and so to speak moulded the official policy – or what was accepted as such – by their utterances'. De Valera to Austin Ford, 27.5.26. Quoted in T.P. O'Neill, 'In Search of a Political Path: Irish Republicanism 1922–1927', *IHS*, vol. x, p. 161.
[6] Of the outgoing Dáil deputies, elected in 1923, 23 of the Republicans remained with Sinn Féin, while 22 joined Fianna Fáil. As a result of the 1927 June election, Fianna Fáil had 44 TDs, while Sinn Féin had five. The 1927 September election was not contested by Sinn Féin.

was done with remarkable success. His deference to Church doctrine on moral questions, his frequent characterisation of Ireland as a Catholic nation, his regular affirmation of the dependence of Fianna Fáil on Catholic social teaching, his public protestations of filial loyalty to the Pope and Church, his framing of a Constitution owing so much to Catholic principles, all served to establish his eventually unassailable standing as a Catholic statesman, and his party as sound on Catholic matters. In many clerical eyes, this position was strengthened by his frequent demonstrations of Catholic piety, his assiduous attendance at Catholic ceremonies, his patronage of episcopal consecrations and pilgrimages, and his known friendships with numerous Catholic clergymen. Despite occasional suggestions to the contrary, there is no need to seek a Machiavellian origin in de Valera's unwavering attachment to the outward forms of religion and his lifelong cultivation of clerical friendships. Whatever evidence there is suggests a fortunate coincidence of personal taste and conviction with expediency in these matters.

Tom Garvin argues that Fianna Fáil's concessions to the Church were 'due to the pious outlook of its electorate rather than to any particularly clericalist tendencies in its leadership'.[7] The 'pious outlook' of the Fianna Fáil electorate may perhaps be reflected in the fact that the party's vote was largest in the most purely Catholic parts of the country, and that the four counties with the highest percentage of Catholics, Clare, Galway, Mayo and Kerry, were the ones in which Fianna Fáil received the highest percentage of votes in the General Elections of June and September 1927.[8] Again, if one can equiparate 'pious' with 'Catholic', Garvin's point about the outlook of the generality of Fianna Fáil voters is reinforced by a remark made by Seán T. O'Kelly, an informed observer of such matters, in 1929. 'We of the Fianna Fáil party', O'Kelly told the Dáil, 'believe that we speak for the big body of Catholic opinion. I think I could say, without qualification of any kind, that we represented the big element of Catholicity'.[9] There was, however, a greater degree of consonance in the matter of 'clericalist tendencies' between leaders in Fianna Fáil and their followers than Garvin seems to suggest here. De Valera was a notably clericalist figure, manifestly at home in the company of ecclesiastics; some of the inspirational speeches in which he adopts the role of teacher of the higher wisdom read like Lenten Pastorals. Dermot Foley, a librarian in Ennis in the 1930s and 1940s, remembered de Valera's visits to Clare as 'being more like a bishop's visitations

---

[7] T. Garvin, *The Evolution of Irish Nationalist Politics* (Dublin, 1981), p. 155.

[8] See E. Rumpf and A.C. Hepburn, *Nationalism and Socialism in Twentieth Century Ireland* (Liverpool, 1977), pp. 67, 127–8.

[9] Dáil Debates, XXX, 821, 5.6.29.

or coming down to give Confirmation, and he was treated like a bishop in that way'.[10]

Seán T. O'Kelly's clericalism was even more pronounced than de Valera's. His diplomatic activity during the War of Independence on behalf of the Republic brought him into contact with many Church dignitaries including the Pope, and gave him the intimate knowledge of ecclesiastical politics of which he later made considerable use to the advantage of Fianna Fáil. In July 1920, he proudly told de Valera of his achievement in getting most of the Irish bishops to attend a reception he gave in Rome 'in the name of the Republic' at which Bishop O'Doherty sang a patriotic song and Cardinal Logue, Bishop O'Donnell and 'other erstwhile opponents' stood for the singing of 'The Soldier's Song'.[11] In October 1920, we find him writing to de Valera from Paris, noting with pleasure that 'the memo I presented to His Holiness met with your approval', and that as a result, 'the semi-official Vatican press has been much more friendly ever since'.[12] After the foundation of Fianna Fáil, O'Kelly had a central role in making the party acceptable to the leadership of the Catholic Church, in Ireland and abroad. His performance of this role was facilitated by his membership of organisations involved in Catholic action, among them the Knights of St Columbanus and the Catholic Truth Society.[13] His enthusiasm for Catholic action was such that during an audience in 1933, the Pope had to restrain him from retelling what extraordinary work Ireland was doing for the foreign missions.[14] O'Kelly's membership of the Catholic Truth Society gave him opportunities to meet its President, Archbishop Harty. In a letter to Hagan, he describes a lengthy meeting in December 1927 with the Archbishop, to whom he had called at the request of the Fianna Fáil National Executive to ask for assistance in having Republican prisoners released before Christmas. O'Kelly's account of the meeting throws interesting light on the attitude of a senior ecclesiastic to Fianna Fáil following the entry of the party to the Dáil. Harty, according to O'Kelly, was pleased with the latter development. Unlike many of the priests who raised the subject in the September 1927 election campaign, Harty, while he did not like the Fianna Fáil statement on the Oath, recognised the 'difficult'

---

[10] J.J. Lee and G. Ó Tuathaigh, *The Age of de Valera* (Dublin, 1982), p. 205.

[11] S.T. O'Kelly to de Valera, 29.7.20, FAK 1471.

[12] S.T. O'Kelly to de Valera, 10.10.20, FAK 1471.

[13] For O'Kelly's membership of the Knights of Columbanus, see Evelyn Bolster, *The Knights of St Columbanus* (Dublin, 1979), p. 48; for his membership of the CTS see D. Keogh, *The Vatican, the Bishops and Irish Politics, 1919–1939* (Cambridge 1986), p. 160.

[14] Keogh, *The Vatican, the Bishops*, p. 202.

circumstances in which the party found itself, understood the intentions of the leadership, and had even 'defended us sometimes when attacked about it'. While acknowledging that 'very strong efforts' had been made to induce the bishops to 'denounce' Fianna Fáil TDs for dealing with the Oath as they had, Harty assured O'Kelly that 'he would not stand for the like'.[15] He did, however, maintain, in the face of O'Kelly's assertion to the contrary, that the October 1922 Pastoral had not been withdrawn by the bishops, although he had 'instructed his priests to be lenient with the boys when they came out of jail'. O'Kelly had good reason to be pleased with his interview with Harty. 'We parted great friends', he told Hagan, Harty 'saying we had done splendidly in the Dáil, and that our time to take charge would surely come, and perhaps soon'.[16]

O'Kelly long continued to function as Fianna Fáil spokesman for ecclesiastical affairs. In January 1930, the General Committee of the party instructed him to call on the new Papal Nuncio, Archbishop Paschal Robinson, after the official Free State ceremonies of welcome were over. Robinson, O'Kelly wrote to de Valera, who was in America raising funds for the *Irish Press*, 'was very happy that he would be able to report to his Chief that he had got that much recognition from our party'. The Nuncio claimed to know 'little or nothing of the recent history of events here', or of the current Irish political situation. To remedy this deficiency, he asked O'Kelly to call again at an early date. 'By the Nuncio's special request', O'Kelly reported to de Valera, 'I had a talk of two hours with him yesterday, and I brought with me a few back numbers of *The Nation*,[17] containing facts and figures

---

[15] *The Catholic Bulletin* drew attention to 'the effort made in Ireland, and in England, to draw from the Irish Hierarchy a pronouncement on the oath'. October, 1927, p. 1021. The *Manchester Guardian* was worried that 'The prestige of the Church is involved, because Archbishop Mannix has wired from Australia in support of de Valera, while in the press a variety of writers purporting to be priests are producing extracts from the works of Roman Catholic theologians which, read apart from their contexts, suggest to the layman that the end will always justify the means'. 5.9.27.

[16] S.T. O'Kelly to Hagan, 21.12.27, Hagan Papers. At the time of O'Kelly's meeting with Harty, Fianna Fáil still had much to do to convince the bishops of its *bona fides*. On 15 August, only five days after members of the party took their seats in the Dáil, the archbishops and bishops of Ireland issued a Pastoral address on the occasion of the Plenary Synod of Maynooth. Fianna Fáil TDs might have felt that they were referred to in the following: 'Like murder, perjury is an awful crime that draws down the vengeance of God upon the offender . . . to call God to witness a lie or a false promise is a terrible outrage on the God of truth . . . Let us ever remember the sanctity of the oaths we take when we invoke the name of God Almighty'.

[17] A Fianna Fáil newspaper established by O'Kelly himself. See the account of his career in FAK, 1471.

relating to the last General Election and the by-elections . . . He said he was glad to get these figures . . . He also said he would be happy to go into the whole question of the situation here in detail when he returned here after his visit to Rome.' O'Kelly was pleased to report that the Nuncio 'has been told by more than one influential friend that it is possible that Fianna Fáil may win out in the next General Election'. O'Kelly observed that Robinson had so far refrained from comment in reference to toasts and addresses of welcome; he attributed the Nuncio's silence on public affairs to the advice he had received that Fianna Fáil might well be the party of the future, a consideration O'Kelly was also concerned to place before him.[18]

O'Kelly and de Valera were by no means the only prominent members of Fianna Fáil to give the party a reassuringly Catholic complexion. Three of Seán MacEntee's brothers-in-law were priests, the most conspicuous being Professor Patrick Browne of Maynooth; another became head of the Dominican order and a Cardinal. James Ryan's brother was a priest as was the brother of Frank Gallagher, first editor of the *Irish Press*. Three members of de Valera's first Cabinet were members of the Knights of St Columbanus: O'Kelly, Lemass and MacEntee. In 1934, an application was made in the High Court on behalf of O'Kelly as Minister for Local Government and Public Health for an order directing Sligo Corporation to desist from trying to appoint a Protestant with Republican views as Town Clerk in preference to the candidate recommended by the Appointments Commissioners. A member of the Corporation suggested that the Protestant candidate was the victim of religious discrimination, which he associated with the Knights of St Columbanus. In an affidavit, the Corporation member described an interview he had with the Minister. 'After Mr O'Kelly came in', he claimed, 'I accused him of being one of the Knights. He did not deny he was a Knight. I had been informed by Mr O'Connell, head of the Knights in Connaught, that Mr O'Kelly, Mr Lemass and Mr MacEntee were in the Order'.[19] The historian of the Order confirms O'Connell's information; 'Seán T. O'Kelly', she writes, 'managed to reach the summit of the political

---

[18] S.T. O'Kelly to de Valera, 27.1.30, FAK, 1471.

[19] *Irish Press*, 12.4.34. De Valera appears to have denied that any member of his Cabinet was a Knight. Frank Carty, TD, gave evidence to the High Court that the members of a deputation of which he was part 'appeared to be satisfied with Mr de Valera's assurance that none of his Ministers was a member of that body'. *Irish Press*, 24.4.34. A few months earlier, de Valera had given a similar assurance, telling the 1933 Ard Fheis of Fianna Fáil, during a debate on allegations of influence in public patronage, that 'no member of the Executive Council is a member of the Knights of [St] Columbanus'. *Irish Press*, 9.11.33.

ladder without severing or even compromising his connection with
the Order. Similarly with Seán Lemass and Seán MacEntee'.[20] As
late as 1933, Fianna Fáil candidates found it expedient to advertise
their connections with the Church or with manifestations of Catholic
piety. Eamonn Kissane, a Kerry Republican who had been interned
during the Civil War, was described in his election literature as 'First
Cousin of the late Bishop Keane of Oaklands, California, first cousin
of Rev. Dr Kissane, Maynooth, nephew of late Mother Provincial,
Loreto Convent, Stephen's Green'.[21] Also in 1933, under the headline,
'Catholic Torch Bearer', Fianna Fáil publicists stressed the achievements of Helena Concannon, one of their NUI Dáil candidates, as the
author of Catholic devotional works, including *Irish Nuns in Penal Days*,
Ireland's Fight for the Mass, and an account of Jesuit martyrs in North
America.[22] A theme of the party's campaign in Kilkenny was its
commitment to 'a united, free and Catholic Ireland'.[23]

The significance of membership of the Knights of St Columbanus
as a profession of Catholic orthodoxy might, perhaps, be called into
question, given the cautious attitude of both Cardinal Logue and
Bishop MacRory during the early days of the order, and the initial
refusal of Archbishop Byrne even to recognise it.[24] The fact that some
bishops showed hostility to the Knights, that others ignored them,
that others merely tolerated them, and that 'hierarchical support for
the order has never been spontaneous'[25] might suggest that ministerial
membership was open to interpretation as an expression of dissent
from episcopal authority rather than as an accepted token of loyalty to
the Church. This argument, however, is difficult to sustain for various
reasons. The official historian of the order points out that some bishops
were Knights of long standing, and draws attention to the large
clerical membership, general episcopal approval and 'the blessing of

---

[20] Bolster, *The Knights*, p. 70. In the course of a libel action taken by the Protestant
candidate for the Sligo post, it became clear that his membership of the IRA
militated at least as much against his appointment as did his religion. At the
Fianna Fáil Ard Fheis in 1943, de Valera argued that it was 'absurd' for Catholics
to seek the 'type of protection' offered by the Knights of St Columbanus 'where
ninety-three per cent of the people are Catholics'. Such organisations, he
suggested, 'do harm to he very cause they are intended to defend'. Bolster, p. 72.
For Gerald Boland's membership of the Knights, see Bolster, p. 48. Boland
(1885–1973) was brother of Harry Boland, and a member of all de Valera's
cabinets from 1933 until 1954.
[21] *Kerry Champion*, 14.1.33.
[22] *Kilkenny Journal*, 21.1.33.
[23] Ibid.
[24] Bolster, *The Knights*, pp. 21, 22, 27, 28.
[25] Ibid., p. 43.

successive popes'.[26] The central impulse of the order, 'to promote and foster the cause of the Catholic faith', was to be pursued 'subject always to the approval of the Catholic Church'.[27] This could scarcely be construed as anything but a respectful submission to episcopal authority.

Two of three clerical delegates who addressed the 1933 Ard Fheis of Fianna Fáil on the subject were Knights of St Columbanus. Both were offended by a resolution that membership of their order 'be a complete bar' to membership of Fianna Fáil. The proposer of this resolution wanted to ensure that Fianna Fáil would not fall into the hands of what he called 'a sectarian secret society',[28] while James Comyn suggested that the Knights and the Freemasons 'were a menace to the State'.[29] James Hackett, PP Donaghmoyne deeply regretted that such a resolution had been put, since, if it were passed, he himself would be the first to be expelled from Fianna Fáil. Speaking 'as a Catholic priest and a member of Fianna Fáil, he was proud to be a member of the Knights' and told the delegates that if some of them had been in the North of Ireland, 'they would realise what they were up against'. James O'Kelly, PP Spiddal, believed that the Knights had been established 'to counter the insidious influence of the Freemasons' and that they had 'got a special sanction from the Holy Father', while Charles White, PP Bekan, claimed that 'the Church was very proud of them' and that the Pope had ruled that the order was not a secret society. For the sake of Fianna Fáil, if the resolution was passed, 'he would leave the Knights, but it would be the breaking of his heart'. De Valera affirmed his own determination not to join the order, suggesting that with a Catholic majority in the South, they should be able 'by open methods to look after our own Catholic interests'.[30] He thus implied that the Knights of St Columbanus might be less than open in their methods, and at the same time confirmed his own status as an essentially confessional politician.

---

[26] Ibid., p. 33.

[27] Ibid., p. 19.

[28] *Irish Press*, 9.11.33. Bolster points out that 'the Order of the Knights of St Columbanus does not belong to the category of secret societies. It never was and is not oath-bound'. *The Knights*, p. 32.

[29] Comyn, a barrister, alleged that patronage in the Courts was the exclusive preserve of the Knights, and that not one brief had been given by the Attorney-General, except to the Knights of St Columbanus, and there was not one of these Knights to whom he gave patronage who had not been an active enemy of the people from 1916–23'. *Irish Press*, 9.11.33.

[30] Ibid.

II

From the beginning, the Fianna Fáil leadership strove to assure the Church authorities that its kind of Republicanism was in every respect compatible with Catholic values, to demonstrate that whatever traces of anti-clericalism might have clung to some members in their Sinn Féin days were now erased, to earn the friendship and good will of the clergy and to keep these in constant repair. In 1925, Lemass, responding angrily to the crushing electoral blows delivered to Sinn Féin by the political power of the Catholic clergy, proclaimed the need for Republicans to destroy that power as a first condition of achieving victory. 'We are', he announced, 'opening the campaign now against the political influence of the Church. If we succeed in destroying that influence we will have done good work for Ireland, and, I believe, for the Catholic religion in Ireland'.[31] This anti-clerical rhetoric was no longer deemed appropriate a year later when most of Sinn Féin emerged as Fianna Fáil. Under the new dispensation, there was now no question of setting out to destroy the political power of the Church. The outcome of the 1925 by-elections had shown how futile an exercise this was likely to be. The wiser course was to work in harmony with the Church, win its confidence, anticipate its wishes and reflect these, and thus experience, as Cumann na nGaedheal had done and was doing, some of the benefits of its political influence. If, given the unhappy course of Republican relations with the Church as a body since 1922, the bishops and their clergy needed reassurance, Fianna Fáil was ready to provide this and provide it abundantly.

Between its foundation in 1926 and its coming to power in 1932, the work of rehabilitation was vigorously pursued. Fianna Fáil was determined to impress on the Church the soundness of its outlook on moral and spiritual matters, indeed on any issue in which the Church might be deemed to have a legitimate interest. Evidence of good intent is already clear in one of the party's official aims, 'the development of a social system in which, as far as possible, equal opportunity will be afforded to every Irish citizen to live a noble and useful Christian life'.[32] When, in advance of the September 1927 General Election, a questionnaire was sent by the Catholic Truth Society on the Evil Literature Report to all candidates, a greater number of 'satisfactory guarantees' were elicited from Fianna Fáil nominees than from those of any other party or grouping. Seán Lemass, 'on behalf of the Fianna

---

[31] *Irish Independent*, 14.3.25.
[32] M. Moynihan (ed.), *Speeches and Statements by Eamon de Valera, 1917–73* (Dublin, 1980), p. 131.

Fáil party', pointed out that it was 'the declared policy of his party to take all necessary legislative action to prevent the importation of immoral literature and also to deal with the home product, which is frequently as bad, if not worse, than the imported variety'.[33] In the late twenties, leading members of Fianna Fáil were particularly active in promoting specifically 'Catholic' issues, giving the impression in the process that theirs was a more Catholic party than Cumann na nGaedheal. In April 1929, Seán T. O'Kelly, perhaps with the centenary of Catholic Emancipation in mind, drafted a private member's bill, the purpose of which was to remove all penalties and disabilities still in force in statute law against Catholics and religious orders. O'Kelly was conscious of a difference of opinion among lawyers as to whether the Government of Ireland Act of 1920 repealed the Penal Laws in Southern Ireland. O'Kelly pointed out to Professor Michael Browne of Maynooth, whose advice he sought on the proposed bill, that it was held by lawyers that Article 8 of the Free State Constitution 'does not remove the disabilities from religious orders, and that both the Act of 1920 and the Constitution of the Free State have failed to repeal the law relating to gifts for Masses said in private'. O'Kelly was anxious to get his bill in as soon as possible, in spite of the view of the government that 'no disabilities or penal laws of any kind are now in force in the Twenty-Six Counties'. He wondered if Browne knew of any recent decisions which would show that some penal laws were in force in the Free State; more significantly for his own purposes, he wondered if ecclesiastical opinion would favour the introduction of such a bill as the one he had in mind.[34]

In the Dáil in 1929, O'Kelly seized another opportunity to show that Fianna Fáil was vigilant in its defence of the rights of the Church against all forms of encroachment. In this case he promoted himself and his party as the champion of the Irish bishops in the face of apparent government indifference to their right to be consulted on a matter which closely concerned them. In 1929, Patrick McGilligan, the Minister for External Affairs, announced that the government had arranged an exchange of diplomatic representatives with the Vatican, without informing the Irish bishops in advance, or even soliciting their advice on the subject. This lapse provided O'Kelly with an opportunity to present himself before the Dáil as a vehicle for the righteous indignation of the offended episcopate and, in effect, as their spokesman. 'I would like to know', he asked McGilligan, 'whether those who are very intimately and seriously concerned in this matter, those whose

---

[33] *Irish Weekly Independent*, 17.9.27.
[34] S.T. O'Kelly to M.J. Browne, 19.4.29, GDA.

views ought to be given very serious consideration in a matter of this kind, were consulted, for instance, the Primate of All Ireland or the Archbishop of Dublin'.[35] In 1930, a Fianna Fáil deputy, P.J. Little, embarrassed the government on another 'Catholic' matter. A deputation of Catholic bishops had seen the Minister for Justice, James Fitzgerald-Kenney on the need to amend the law relating to legitimacy. Fitzgerald-Kenney undertook to prepare a Bill on the subject, which was at an advanced stage when Little introduced his own private member's bill which provided that children born illegitimate should be legitimated if their parents subsequently married. Little was able to point our that his bill was in conformity with Church teaching, being based on Canon Law. It was this measure, rather than the one that the government had been too tardy in promoting, that became the Legitimacy Act of 1930. Thus Fianna Fáil conveyed the impression of being more alert to the concerns of bishops on moral issues than the government was.

March 1929 saw an interesting and instructive Dáil debate on a Fianna Fáil motion, the leading advocates of which were de Valera and Seán T. O'Kelly, that the Dáil should not sit on Catholic holidays of obligation. O'Kelly, in a lengthy speech, the tone and content of which must have appeared to the members more appropriate to a churchman than to a politician, was concerned to make amends for the hitherto pagan atmosphere of the Dáil. 'This house', he declared, 'has ignored so far the existence of God, and I think that is not quite proper'. It was now time, he suggested, that 'some reference to the existence of God, Who directs our minds, and from Whom we expect guidance and assistance . . . be made by the House'. De Valera's contribution to the debate was a disquisition 'on the nature of the Sabbath generally'. He had felt all his life that there had been a growing and unfortunate tendency 'not to give the Sabbath, and holidays, which for Catholics ought to have the same place as the Sabbath . . . which it would be good for the country that it should be given'. He argued that 'encroachment on the Catholic Church holidays was bound to lead to an encroachment on the Sundays'. It became clear during the debate that both de Valera and O'Kelly were anxious to appear as unofficial spokesmen for the Catholic Church on the issue and to explain the doctrinal position to those TDs who might not, perhaps, have fully understood it. 'From a Catholic point of view', de Valera declared, 'at least from my point of view as a Catholic . . . I think we ought not to distinguish between the holidays that are instituted by the Church and the Sabbath'.

[35] Dáil Debates, XXX, 820–1, 5.6.29.

De Valera's and O'Kelly's presentation of themselves as explicators of Catholic doctrine proved too much for some Cumann na nGaedheal TDs. 'When the Deputy [O'Kelly] comes forward . . . as the exponent of Catholic views on the subject', Marcus O'Sullivan asked, 'what authority is there behind that assumption on his part?' Some deputies believed that both O'Kelly and de Valera were enunciating more rigid and exacting interpretations of the demands imposed by the Church holidays and even the Sabbath, than those made by either Christ or the Pope. Desmond FitzGerald reminded the Dáil that 'the Church's first Teacher warned His Disciples very strongly against asserting as dogmas such things as are not dogmas'. He understood the servile work forbidden to Catholics on Church holidays to mean 'such work as was done by servants in Rome', asserting that there was 'nothing further removed from that than the work done here by the Dáil'. O'Sullivan told Seán Lemass that the Pope did his work on Church holidays. What R.S. Anthony of Labour called the 'manifestations of piety on the part of the leaders of Fianna Fáil' made him wonder if he risked 'being labelled a pagan' for opposing the doctrines of 'the very useful lay preachers' representing Fianna Fáil whose gospel seemed to be, 'We are the only Christians in this country and the rest are anti-Christian'. Many deputies no doubt felt as Anthony did that the zeal displayed by Fianna Fáil on the issue amounted to little more than 'cant, humbug and hypocrisy'.[36] The significance of the Fianna Fáil exercise, however, lay in the evidence it provided that once again the party leaders were able to make it appear that their political opponents were less vigilant than they themselves were in promoting Catholic practices.

De Valera's conduct during the Mayo Library controversy in 1930–31[37] affords perhaps the best illustration during this period of his and his party's eagerness to use Catholicism, and to exploit clerical feeling, for party purposes. Whatever the participants in the controversy might have said, Miss Dunbar-Harrison's appointment as County Librarian for Mayo was opposed by local clerical and political interests not because she knew less Irish than the locally 'approved' candidate, but because she was a Protestant. Fianna Fáil members of Mayo County Council adduced her ignorance of Irish as their reason for opposing her, but did not publicly emphasise the religious issue; this

---

[36] Dáil Debates, 8.2.29, cols., 1161–1194. The Fianna Fáil motion that the House should not meet on Church holidays was defeated by 75 votes to 50. Most of the Labour deputies voted with Cumann na nGaedheal against the motion, although Richard Corish and James Everett supported it.
[37] For details of this controversy, see pp. 131–2, notes 405–13.

led *The Standard* to accuse them of 'naked secularism'.[38] In the midst of the controversy, de Valera's weekly *The Nation*, looking at the issue from the high ground of non-sectarian Republicanism, pronounced that 'there can be only one test for the public service, ability to perform the work . . . to declare her [Miss Dunbar-Harrison] unfitted by religion or by the fact that she holds a Trinity degree is to recreate under the cloak of Catholicism the spirit of ascendancy which has cursed this nation for three hundred bitter years'.[39] In his public dealings with the issue, however, de Valera did not act in the spirit of this proclamation. Instead, rightly sensing that the balance of electoral advantage lay with sacrificing the principles of orthodox Republican theory to the more pressing demands of local feeling, clerical agitation and popular religious prejudice, he committed his party to a distinctively 'Catholic' stand. In the Dáil debate on the appointment, he used the same line of argument that the Mayo priests who resisted the candidacy of Miss Dunbar-Harrison had used. The religious beliefs of a librarian would not matter, he suggested, if her position merely involved 'handing down books that are asked for'. On the other hand, if the librarian had to do 'active work of a propagandist educational character, and I believe it to be such if it is to be of any value at all and worth the money spent on it, then I say the people of Mayo, in a county where . . . over 98 per cent of the population is Catholic, are justified in insisting upon a Catholic librarian'.[40] In the same debate, de Valera placed himself firmly in the camp of those churchmen who argued that the Maynooth statutes should govern the appointment of dispensary doctors, so that non-Catholic doctors should not be appointed in Catholic areas. 'The Catholic community', he asserted, 'does want to be assured that the doctors appointed locally to minister to their people, who will be at their sides at the most critical moment, at the time of death, shall be members of the same religious faith as themselves.'[41] J.J. Lee's verdict on the Dunbar-Harrison case is that it gave de Valera 'a providential opportunity to outmanoeuvre Cosgrave and in the process help reconcile Catholicism with republicanism'.[42] What it really signified, however, was that de Valera had decided to make Fianna Fáil republicanism an essentially Catholic thing, reflecting the outlook of the Church on social and ethical issues, thus implicitly defining it as the political creed of a confessional state. This strategy was to prove most efficacious in winning clerical support where it really mattered to

[38] See *The Nation*, 31.1.31; *The Standard*, 3.12.30.
[39] *The Nation*, 7.1.31.
[40] Dáil Debates, XXXIX, 518, 17.6.31.
[41] Ibid., 517.
[42] J.J. Lee, *Ireland 1912–1985. Politics and Society* (Cambridge, 1989), p. 161.

Fianna Fáil: on the eve of the 1932 General Election the *Irish Press* noted with satisfaction that there were 'clear indications that only a very few of the Mayo priests will on this occasion support the government nominees'.[43]

With the approach of the 1932 Election, the Fianna Fáil leadership took considerable care to avoid being identified with the supposedly communistic and anti-clerical tendencies of fellow-Republicans on the left. In the Autumn of 1931, de Valera became aware of the contents of the memorandum sent to the Hierarchy by the government purporting to show the existence of a conspiracy for the violent overthrow of the institutions of the State, involving Republican elements in 'definite contact with the International Communistic organisations'. De Valera's main anxiety was that Fianna Fáil should not be mentioned either explicitly or by implication in the Pastoral Letter on the conspiracy being prepared by the bishops. His visit to Cardinal MacRory at Maynooth seems to have provided the necessary reassurance.[44] He himself used the Dáil debate on the Public Safety Act to insist that his attachment to Catholic principles governing social and political ideologies was absolute. He addressed the House as a defender of the Catholic position. 'The right of private property', he declared, 'is accepted as fundamental and, as far as Catholics are concerned, there has been definite teaching upon it – the right of private property and the right, on the other hand, of society, insofar as the common good is concerned, of dealing in a proper way with the relations between the community and the private individual'. He was just as anxious as either the government or the bishops were that Bolshevism 'should not be preached here or spread here'.[45] Even at humbler levels of Fianna Fáil, members unselfconsciously exhibited their Catholic piety. Richard English, who examined the minute books of the Fintan Lalor Cumann for 1930 and 1931, notes that the membership was 'emphasising the overlap between its Catholicism and its nationalism by proposing a mass for all those who died for Irish freedom', and that while Saor Éire was having to come to terms with harsh episcopal condemnation, 'the Fintan Lalor Cumann was discussing the provision of flags for the forthcoming Eucharistic Congress'.[46]

On the Fianna Fáil side, the 1932 Election Campaign was marked by an assiduous cultivation of Catholic interests and a display of Catholic credentials. This was perhaps necessary in the circumstances.

[43] *Irish Press*, 2.1.32.
[44] Keogh, *The Vatican, the Bishops*, pp. 179–80.
[45] Moynihan, *Speeches of de Valera*, pp. 187–8.
[46] R. English, *Radicals and the Republic* (Oxford, 1994), p. 157.

'In the emotional atmosphere of the campaign', Ryle Dwyer points out, 'it was not long before de Valera was accused of being a communist, or at best a weak Kerensky who would be toppled by communists in Fianna Fáil once the party came to power. Even Cosgrave stooped to such insinuations when he told a public meeting in Tralee that Cumann na nGaedheal was against Communism and Russianism [*sic*], the obvious implication being that Fianna Fáil was not opposed to them'.[47] A number of priests speaking in the Cumann na nGaedheal interest seemed equally troubled by the dangers facing the Church and Catholic values if Fianna Fáil were returned. At the party convention in Elphin, Bernard Keane, CC Lisacul, predicted 'disruption in the country' following a victory for de Valera. 'The best policy', he believed, 'for our social and religious protection is the return of the government'. Describing Fianna Fáil as 'the jackals of Communism', Keane suggested that if the party gained power there would be 'a big minority in Fianna Fáil in sympathy with a Soviet Republic'. He feared that 'the Soviet workers . . . will not be satisfied, but will demand from Mr de Valera a Workers' Soviet Republic for Ireland', for which, he claimed, 'the Constitution is already in print'.[48] At Gurteen, Co. Sligo, James O'Connor, the Parish Priest, asked his parishioners to reject Fianna Fáil if they wanted to 'save the Nation and have the faith and fatherland handed down to them by St Patrick'. Only Cumann na nGaedheal, he believed, could 'save their country and their faith from the dangers of Communism'.[49] Another Western priest, Patrick Neary, PP Ballyforan, who had 'supported the Cumann na nGaedheal party since its inception', suggested that under a Fianna Fáil government, communist influence would thrive. Like many clerical observers in 1932, Neary found it difficult to make a distinction between Fianna Fáil and radical Republican elements. 'They also had an organisation known as Saor Éire', he warned, 'and with Fianna Fáil ruling this country it was quite possible that we would have in holy Ireland happenings similar to those in Spain'.[50] A desire to avert such happenings prompted Joseph Pelly, an elderly Clonfert priest, to declare that 'if he had to be carried out on a stretcher he would vote for the Cumann na nGaedheal candidates'.[51] Many of the priests who had campaigned for Cumann na nGaedheal in 1927 still saw Fianna Fáil as a threat to social, political and economic stability, and harboured doubts about its soundness on religious and moral issues.

[47] T. Ryle Dwyer, *De Valera, The Man and the Myths* (Dublin, 1991), p. 157.
[48] *Westmeath Independent*, 23.1.32.
[49] *Sligo Champion*, 6.2.32.
[50] *Westmeath Independent*, 6.2.32.
[51] *The Irish Times*, 25.1.32.

Patrick Neary's fears were those commonly expressed by priests from platforms throughout the country: the Fianna Fáil tariff policy would end in hunger, the doctrine of non-cooperation with England was pernicious and fraught with danger, as was the pledge to repeal the Public Safety Bill, while the policy on land annuities was irresponsible.[52] Much clerical opposition to Fianna Fáil's populist Republicanism was based on another consideration seldom acknowledged from political platforms. The class bias underlying some priestly reservations about Fianna Fáil came to the surface early in 1933 in a speech by James Mahon, Administrator of Tullow, Co. Carlow, at a Cumann na nGaedheal Convention. Mahon complained that 'the man who is industrious and who pays his way, and who wishes to make himself prosperous by hard work, has no place in the late government's policy. It was a government for the down and outs'.[53] An apologist for Fianna Fáil regarded Father Mahon's comment as the best recommendation the Fianna Fáil administration could have got. 'It was', he acknowledged, 'essentially a poor man's government. The working man and the working farmer, who are the backbone of the country, were well looked after by Fianna Fáil while in power. On the other hand, during their ten years in office, Cumann na nGaedheal gave the plain people no consideration whatever. They were entirely concerned with the big fellows, the graziers, the landed gentlemen and their ilk'.[54] After the September 1927 General Election, Thomas Mullins, a Fianna Fáil TD for Cork West, claimed that the party had been opposed by a combination of big businessmen, merchants and the Catholic clergy.[55] In 1928, Samuel Holt, the Fianna Fáil TD for Leitrim–Sligo, acknowledged that Cumann na nGaedheal had, 'for the time, a monopoly of the Canons', one of whom, he suggested, was more devoted to the interests of members of the professional classes than to those of the deprived. As an example, he mentioned a proposal of the Cumann na nGaedheal activist, Canon Butler of Sligo, to raise the salary of the Medical Superintendent of the Sligo–Leitrim Mental Hospital by £200. This man, Holt declared, 'had £600 per year and a free house,

---

[52] *Westmeath Independent*, 6.2.32.
[53] *Nationalist and Leinster Times*, 14.1.33. Compare the response of a Wexford Cumann na nGaedheal supporter to what he saw as the social profile of Fianna Fáil voters. In the 1932 Election Campaign, he saw 'two Fianna Fáil cars plying to and from the booths, laden with voters, most of them illiterate and well tutored how to vote'. J. Coakley and M. Gallagher (eds), *Politics in the Republic of Ireland* (Dublin, 1993), p. 255.
[54] Ibid., 21.1.33.
[55] *Southern Star*, 24.9.27.
[56] *Roscommon Herald*, 3.4.28.

fuel and light' and Canon Butler's proposal was made at a time 'when the farmer had no food'.[56]

Clerical reservations about Fianna Fáil were still a potent factor in 1932. The majority of the priests who played a prominent part in the election campaign supported Cumann na nGaedheal, which remained the party favoured by the generality of churchmen. It still seemed appropriate that Cosgrave, visiting Limerick, should go 'immediately to the Bishop's Palace where he spent some time with Most Rev. Dr Keane'.[57] Fianna Fáil, however, attracted its own share of clerical warriors, whose theme was the unsoundness of Cumann na nGaedheal on the great national issues. Such nationally minded priests could not share the view of Patrick Hogan, Minister for Agriculture, that 'the Oath was not half so important as the price of pigs'.[58] Malachy Mac Bránáin, PP Ahascragh, who had been a leading member of Cumann na nGaedheal in the twenties, now denounced that party on patriotic grounds. 'Five years ago', he wrote to the *Irish Press*, 'I hoped for a union of the men with Irish ideals in the two biggest political parties to resist West Britishism and Imperialism; but instead we have in 1932 a Government Party amalgamating with the ex-Unionists and West Britons'. Mac Bránáin was appalled at the lack of interest shown by the government in the grave social and economic problems confronting great numbers of rural smallholders, which a proper policy of land distribution might have helped to alleviate. If Father Mahon of Tullow can be considered representative of the large body of clerical supporters of Cumann na nGaedheal and the men of substance, Father Mac Bránáin's was a loud and persistent voice raised on behalf of Fianna Fáil and the prospect it offered for radical agrarian reform. There were, he pointed out, according to the most recent census, 'in County Galway alone 14,409 tenants with less than 15 acres of land, while at the same time there were 612,200 acres in the hands of 1963 people, whose holdings ranged from 100 acres upwards'. He wanted to see land acquired compulsorily from large farmers or graziers for division among those with uneconomic holdings.[59] Nothing more radical than this was advocated by Fianna Fáil politicians during the campaign; indeed a number of these, among them Seán T. O'Kelly, were anxious to allay whatever misgivings more conservative churchmen might have had by pointing out that 'the Fianna Fáil policy was the policy of Pope Pius XI'.[60] At Tralee, de Valera reassuringly declared, with the same elements in mind: 'I am not a Communist. I am quite

[57] *Cork Examiner*, 6.2.32.
[58] *The Irish Times*, 25.1.32.
[59] *Irish Press*, 10.2.32.
[60] *Irish Independent*, 11.2.32.

the reverse'.[61] During the campaign, he gave outward and visible signs of his Catholicism. At Tulla, when the Angelus bell sounded, 'Mr de Valera immediately ceased speaking, blessed himself and silently said the Angelus prayer; the crowd reverently followed his example'.[62]

While the official Cumann na nGaedheal propaganda handbook for the 1932 Election, *Fighting Points*, did not implicate Fianna Fáil directly as an agent of world communism, there were suggestions that the lawless and putatively socialist backgrounds of some of the party's leading members might make them prone to communist influence and to take a tolerant view of the activities of communists. The converse of this was that Cumann na nGaedheal was an eminently sound Catholic party whose record left no doubt about its future intentions. This approach did not enjoy the success Cumann na nGaedheal might have hoped for among committed Catholics. Professor Alfred O'Rahilly of University College Cork, a leading Catholic publicist, who warmly supported the Treaty, was so appalled by attempts to promote an exclusive identification of Catholicism with Cumann na nGaedheal that he threatened to support Fianna Fáil; he denounced the 'red scare' strategy as 'a usurpation of our holy religion in the hustings of Mr Cosgrave'.[63] At the Fianna Fáil pre-election Ard Fheis, in the proceedings of which several priests took an active part as delegates and officials, a member of the National Executive dealt firmly with attempts to identify Republicanism with Communism. It might be, he conceded, that 'a negligible number of people were concerned with Communism', but as far as Republicans were concerned, 'there was absolutely no foundation for the suggestion that any section of them were actively anti-religious'. He then elaborated a favourite Republican theme: 'The time might come when the Catholic Church might be attacked in this country. If that time ever came, in the front ranks of the defenders of the Church would be found the men who were active as Republicans.'[64]

---

[61] *The Kerryman*, 10.2.32.
[62] *The Irish Times*, 4.2.32.
[63] O'Rahilly's protest was conveyed in a letter to the *Irish Press*, 1.2.32. 'Everyone', he complained, 'who has the temerity to disagree with the present Ministers is declared to be an indifferent Catholic . . . Well even at the risk of excommunication, I declare publicly that unless President Cosgrave and the fellow-members of his new-fangled Synod give up their attempt to intimidate us by issuing impertinent Lenten Pastorals . . . I for one am going, for the first time, to vote for Fianna Fáil as the only hope of securing political peace and social progress in this country'.
[64] *Irish Press*, 28.10.31.

III

When he came to power in 1932, de Valera extended the process of reaching an accommodation with the Catholic Church. Before the 1932 election, he advertised his intentions, giving notice that Fianna Fáil policy would be in close conformity with Catholic teaching. At a Dublin election meeting in February, he declared that 'the majority of the people of Ireland are Catholic and we believe in Catholic principles. And as the majority are Catholics, it is right and natural that the principles to be applied by us will be principles consistent with Catholicity.'[65] A Fianna Fáil advertisement issued on the same day promised that the party would govern 'in accordance with the principles enunciated in the encyclicals of Pope Pius XI on the Social Order'.[66] Before setting out to embody Catholic principles in legislation, he was able to avail of a unique opportunity to demonstrate to the Irish nation that he and his party were true exemplars of Catholic piety. The Eucharistic Congress, held in Dublin in June 1932, a few months after he took office, represented one of the most considerable and enduring publicity triumphs of de Valera's career. His ceremonial appearances in the company of Irish bishops and senior churchmen from all over the world in the presence of hundreds of thousands of people marked the symbolic end to the loss of official Church approval from which he and his associates had suffered so badly since 1922, both politically and personally, and his emergence as a Catholic statesman of unexampled orthodoxy. At this most significant moment in the history of his party's relationship with the Church, de Valera invoked the help of Dr J.C. McQuaid, President of Blackrock College, who was closely bound by ties of friendship to him and his family.[67] McQuaid facilitated him by making the grounds of Blackrock College available for a state garden party during the Eucharistic Congress. This, as T.P. O'Neill pointed out, allowed de Valera 'to avoid the embarrassment of the state function being associated with the Vice-Regal Lodge or with the representative of King George V'.[68] In the month before the Congress, Fianna Fáil deputies concerned themselves with the provision of an appropriate token of religious faith for the

---

[65] *Irish Press*, 16.2.32.

[66] Ibid., 16.2.32.

[67] John Charles McQuaid was born in Cootehill, Co. Cavan in 1895. He was educated at Blackrock and Clongowes Wood and became a priest in the Holy Ghost Congregation. As a teacher in Blackrock and as President of the College from 1932 to 1938, he befriended the boys of de Valera's family.

[68] 'Dr J.C. McQuaid and Eamon de Valera. Insights on Church and State', *Breifne*, 1993, p. 327.

Dáil chamber; a Parliamentary Party meeting agreed that Fianna Fáil members of the Dáil committee on procedure and privileges be instructed to vote for the erection of a crucifix in the chamber.[69]

Until his accession to power in 1932, and particularly from the Treaty to the mid-twenties, de Valera was obliged to depend on all the clerical voices he could muster to counteract the deafening chorus of condemnation from churchmen. In 1932, he began to simulate a clerical voice himself, his utterances on the economic, social and educational issues being often indistinguishable in tone and content from episcopal pastorals or even papal encyclicals. He gradually assumed some of the style and functions of a lay cardinal. One of the early signs of his emergence as a semi-ecclesiastical personage was his address to the Papal Legate at St Patrick's Hall, Dublin Castle, where he gave a formal reception for 'distinguished churchmen and laymen'. Here, he unequivocally equated 'Irish' with 'Catholic'; he made it clear to the Pope's representative that he considered Ireland as an essentially Catholic nation. He interpreted post-Reformation Irish history as a series of brutal attempts by a foreign power to impose an alien faith on a devoted race sustained in their fidelity by a benevolent papacy. 'Repeatedly', he declared, 'over more than three hundred years, our people, ever firm in their allegiance to our ancestral faith and unwavering even unto death in their devotion to the See of Peter, endured in full measure unmerited trials by war, by devastation and by confiscation. They saw their most sacred rights set at naught under an unjust domination. But repeatedly also did the successors of Peter most willingly come to our aid.' De Valera's vision of Ireland as a confessional state was clearest when he reminded his hearers of St Patrick's teaching that being a Christian meant being loyal, as the Irish people were, to the See of Rome'.[70] In 1932, his willingness to see Catholicism as the essential mark of Irish nationality did not entirely insulate de Valera from episcopal misgivings about him and his party. C.S. Andrews remembered that he had to endure the 'personal hostility of the bishops, thinly disguised at the time of the Eucharistic Congress, with a patient shrug'.[71] This attitude must have appeared ungrateful in the face of the clear evidence he had been providing since taking office of his determination to establish what Ronan Fanning calls his 'impeccable Catholic credentials'.[72] Such evidence included a favourable Cabinet response in April 1932 to the idea of suspending sittings of the Oireachtas on Church holidays, and the opening of

[69] Fianna Fáil party minutes, 19.5.32, Fianna Fáil Archives. See Reference 73 below.
[70] Moynihan, *Speeches of de Valera*, pp. 218–19.
[71] C.S. Andrews, *Man of No Property: An Autobiography* (Cork, 1982), p. 236.

Dáil sittings 'with an appropriate form of prayer and the display of a crucifix in the Dáil chamber'.[73] De Valera seems to have taken particular care that none of his followers should publicly reciprocate whatever measure of residual clerical hostility they encountered. Andrews, one of the few leading Republicans to harbour long-term anti-clerical sentiments, recalled advocating, in private conversation, the abolition of the system of clerical management of Primary Schools; de Valera did not comment, but his angry look was a sufficient indication to those present that such ideas were not acceptable.[74] At the end of his first administration in January 1933, the *Irish Press* could truthfully celebrate the party's fidelity to its pre-election commitments in 1932 when it commented that 'there is not a social or economic change Fianna Fáil has proposed or brought about which has not its fullest justification in the encyclicals of either Leo XIII or the present Pontiff'.[75]

In its 1932 manifesto, Fianna Fáil had promised to abolish the parliamentary oath which had presented its Dáil members with acute moral dilemmas in 1927. The Land Annuities were to be retained by the Irish State Treasury, and legal opinion was to be taken on the question of obligation to meet other annual payments, including RIC pensions.[76] On 20 April, de Valera introduced the Constitution (Removal of Oath) Bill; he contrived the dismissal by the King of the Governor-General, James McNeill, on 1 November, and had him replaced by Domhnall Ó Buachalla, who connived with him at reducing the office to an absurdity by refusing to live in the vice-regal lodge and instead taking up residence in a modest house in a Dublin suburb.[77] In the 1932 manifesto, it was urged that the British were not entitled to the Land Annuities in law; in July 1932, when de Valera decided to act on this basis, the British imposed a 20 per cent duty on about two-thirds of all Irish exports in order to recoup what

---

[72] R. Fanning, *Independent Ireland* (Dublin, 1983), p. 129.
[73] Ibid. The Church holiday proposal was a long-standing Fianna Fáil one. See p. 255, note 36.
[74] Andrews, *Man of No Property*, p. 236.
[75] *Irish Press*, 11.1.33.
[76] *Irish Independent*, 8.2.32.
[77] Fanning, *Independent Ireland*, p. 111. When a clerical friend wrote to congratulate him on his appointment as Governor-General, Ó Buachalla replied: 'A great honour was conferred on me when I was chosen by the President to fill this post. It [Ó Buachalla's appointment] is a step in the direction of abolishing the post altogether. I would greatly prefer not to have to bother with it, but since it was the President who asked me to take it for the good of the country, I told him I would do what he wished. May God give me the grace and strength of will to perform the functions of the position according to His will [God's] and for the sake of Ireland.' D. Ó Buachalla to An tAthair P.S. Ó Móráin, 3.11.32, TAA.

they would lose on the annuities. This action marked the beginning of the 'economic war' of 1932–38. During the Christmas recess, de Valera decided to dissolve the Dáil and seek a stronger mandate. In 1932, his party had won 72 of the 153 seats in the Dáil. He could not hope to pursue the stern measures he now foresaw as necessary without a stronger hand. For one thing, he felt that the British would not be likely to negotiate with him as long as they hoped his government might fall; in this, as Ronan Fanning points out, they were encouraged by Cumann na nGaedheal messengers to London from Cosgrave and McGilligan who advised them that 'if they presented an unyielding front de Valera's government might crack or his slender parliamentary dissolve with the result that another Cumann na nGaedheal government with which they could quickly resume harmonious relations, would take office'.[78] There was also the consideration that the Labour Party, on whose parliamentary support de Valera depended, was finding his harsh economic policies increasingly distasteful, while Cosgrave was making overtures to the new Centre Party to form a united opposition grouping.

The 1933 General Election was much more contentious than that of 1932. It was fought with passion, anger and bitterness on both sides. British retaliation to the measures de Valera had taken in fulfilment of his 1932 election promises had given him a potent weapon, which he used with deadly effect. While comparatively little emphasis was placed on the abolition of the Oath, the economic war was represented as a national struggle against British aggression in which Cumann na nGaedheal, the Centre Party and the Senate, which was delaying the passage of the Bill to abolish the Oath, were depicted as being on the side of the enemies of the country. In 1932, Fianna Fáil campaigners had striven to brand Cumann na nGaedheal as an imperialist party, prominence being given to the fact that its members had solicited and obtained donations from ex-Unionists.[79] In the heated patriotic atmos-

---

[78] Fanning, *Independent Ireland*, p. 113. Ryle Dwyer argues that 'Cumann na nGaedheal actively resorted to underhanded and, indeed, treacherous if not treasonous methods. In late April 1932, Senator Joe McLaughlin, the leader of the Irish Senate, brought Thomas a secret message from Cosgrave encouraging the British to adopt an intransigent attitude towards de Valera and asked for a firm and early statement from the British government. A couple of days later, Donal O'Sullivan, the clerk of the Senate, told the Dominions Secretary that Cosgrave was anxious for the British to outline the actions they would take if the oath bill was passed'. *De Valera*, p. 132.

[79] See Donal O'Sullivan, *The Irish Free State and its Senate* (London, 1940), p. 284. A Cumann na nGaedheal letter asked ex-Unionists to subscribe because it was 'essential in the interests of the country as a whole that the anti-Treaty forces should be defeated'. The letter continued: 'For this reason, and because they

phere of 1933, the imperialist label, whether merited or not, was bound to be more of a liability than an asset. The austerities of the economic war might be bitterly resented, but de Valera had promised that these would be shared equitably, that 'if there are to be hair shirts at all, it will be hair shirts all round'.[80] Furthermore, Fianna Fáil speakers could argue that it was a national duty to endure whatever economic deprivation was necessary in the cause of political freedom from Britain, under a leader willing to assert Irish rights and to guard Irish interests as no other could.

There was considerably more clerical participation in the 1933 election campaign than there had been in 1932. This was partly a reflection of the enhanced excitement generated nationally by the issues at stake: in spite of the discomforts of a January campaign, 80 per cent of the electorate turned out to vote. All the evidence points to greater clerical enthusiasm for Fianna Fáil than before: de Valera's efforts to demonstrate the soundness of his Catholicism had borne fruit. There was also a clear sense of pride even among clergy not previously committed to de Valera in the quality of his leadership and in the bold political decisions he had made. Priests throughout the country were caught up in the emotion of a patriotic surge not evident since before the Treaty. Matthew Kenny, Parish Priest of Rosmuck, presiding at a Fianna Fáil rally, said that this was the first time he had appeared on any political platform since 1918.[81] De Valera, accompanied on his platform at Ballinasloe by a dozen priests, told his huge audience that 'the enthusiasm he had witnessed at all his meetings reminded him of the enthusiasm of 1918 and 1919'.[82] He had by now revealed himself to many clerical eyes as a messianic figure. On his assumption of power in 1932, his Jesuit friend Edward Cahill had hailed his re-emergence as a saviour of the country.

---

[79] *cont.* realise that there are people in the Free State who are unwilling to be identified with the Cumann na nGaedheal organisation, or to subscribe directly to it, a large representative committee is being formed for the purpose of collecting funds for use in support of candidates pledged to support the Government in the maintenance of the Constitution . . . The names of the subscribers . . . will be treated as confidential'. *Irish Press*, 26.11.32. The following appeared in the *Irish Press*, 11.1.32: 'Sir John Keane, one of the signatories of the recent secret circular signed by leading ex-Unionists and appealing for funds for Mr Cosgrave's party in the General Election, says in yesterday's *Sunday Times*: "One has only to read the new organ [*Irish Press*], a paper surprising in its sources of information, to see that in the eyes of the Opposition [Fianna Fáil] they (the ex-Unionists) are identified up to the hilt with the present Government."'

[80] Moynihan, *Speeches by de Valera*, p. 205. The remark was made on 29.4.32.

[81] *Irish Press*, 23.1.33.

[82] Ibid., 16.1.33.

'I thank God', he wrote to him, 'that the ten-year nightmare is over and I thank God too that you have been spared to take charge of the helm again. I have great hopes that the good God will utilise you to do great things for His glory in building up the destinies of the country you love so well and have served so faithfully. You have suffered calumny as few men have and as far as I know, have borne it with remarkable Christian patience. All this I look upon as an earnest of the blessings with which God will crown the work which is now before you.'[83] In 1933, Eugene Coyle, PP Devenish Co. Fermanagh, an energetic organiser of Fianna Fáil support in Donegal, declared in a letter to one of the party candidates in Sligo–Leitrim that 'the nation will be redeemed, North united with the South, the tribute of millions and England's dictation and domination stopped once and for all, but only by men with clean hands who have never compromised Ireland's rights. The leader of such men stands on this platform: Eamon de Valera, who never . . . hauled down the flag of a national freedom, and never will.'[84] Coyle told a meeting in Bundoran that the people in the Six Counties were basing their hopes of deliverance on the Fianna Fáil government 'under the leadership of one of the greatest leaders Ireland ever had – Mr de Valera'.[85]

A strong anti-British, anti-Unionist note is struck by most of the clerical advocates of Fianna Fáil in 1933. The forces of imperialism are seen as the inevitable allies of Cumann na nGaedheal in the campaign of resistance to the redemptive, patriotic strivings of de Valera and his party. Canon James Hackett, Parish Priest of Donaghmoyne, Co. Monaghan, believed that 'the unholy alliance between the British Cabinet, supported by the whole British Press, and a pro-British party in Ireland backed up by *The Irish Times* and *Independent*' had made an election in Ireland inevitable.[86] Some clergymen saw a continuity between the circumstances of 1918 and those which prevailed in 1933. Patrick Hewson, PP Bangor Erris, County Mayo told a meeting that 'he resisted conscription in 1918 and he stood on the Fianna Fáil platform to-day because the same enemy now threatened us with an economic war'.[87] The British economic counter-terror of the 1930s was clearly having the same kind of effect on some clerical minds as had the military counter-terror of the War of Independence, and de

[83] Father Edward Cahill to de Valera, 22.3.32. FAK, 1095/1.
[84] *Irish Press*, 12.1.33.
[85] Ibid., 24.1.33.
[86] Ibid., 9.1.33. Cosgrave, Father Hackett said, 'who in 1923 signed away five million pounds of Irish money behind the backs of the people, told them he could get, if returned to power, relief in three days'.
[87] *Irish Press*, 23.1.33.

Valera was again their champion against the aggressor. Charles White, PP Bekan, South Mayo, who had formerly presided at Cumann na nGaedheal meetings, admired the Fianna Fáil government for having 'made a manly and courageous effort to build up the country and secure for the people the opportunity to work and live in their own land'. He believed that 'the present fight to rid the country from British domination was the fight which had been carried on from generation to generation by our forefathers'. He argued that 'the fight for our national and economic freedom must go on, and the victory to which Eamon de Valera will see us through is worth a little sacrifice'.[88]

A recurring clerical theme was that Cumann na nGaedheal politicians were traitors to the national cause. Michael McCarville, Parish Priest of Scotshouse, County Monaghan, told a meeting that 'the first man who ever suggested to England to put a tariff on Irish goods was the man whose name appeared first on the ballot paper for Monaghan – Mr E. Blythe, whose government was far worse on the Irish people than Cromwell'.[89] In a letter to the *Irish Press*, Canon Hackett suggested that Cosgrave and his ministers had never been anything but British agents, won over to the enemy's cause by 'force, fraud or flattery'. Their behaviour since the Treaty had been consistently anti-national. 'Mr Cosgrave and his party', he declared, 'began by putting to death the soldiers who fought by their side for freedom, and ended by secretly signing to their old oppressor an annual tribute of £5,000,000'. Canon Hackett found it deplorable that Michael Davitt's son, campaigning for Cumann na nGaedheal, was 'on the side of Mr Cosgrave and the feudal lords in an endeavour to restore the feudal system demolished by his father'.[90] A number of priests found Cumann na nGaedheal guilty by association with anti-National elements. Terence de Vere White was a Cumann na nGaedheal speaker in Leitrim during the campaign. He went to Mass before addressing a meeting. The priest, he recalled, was young. He told his flock that there would be political meetings after Mass when both sides would express their views. They were entitled to do this and to do it in peace. 'But', he added, 'when it was considered that one side favoured the subjection of Ireland to England, to England which had suppressed their country for centuries, which had persecuted the faith, it was hard indeed for any right-minded person to restrain himself when the continuation of such a connection was advocated outside the House of

---

[88] Ibid., 21.1.33.
[89] *Irish Press*, 14.1.33. Blythe lost his seat in the 1933 General Election.
[90] Ibid., 21.1.33. For a more balanced account of Cosgrave's dealings with the Land Annuities, see O'Sullivan, *Irish Free State*, pp. 286 ff.

God'. Outside the Church, after Mass, de Vere White was met with a hail of sods and shouts of 'English agent' and 'We don't want Jimmy Thomas's men here'.[91] Eugene Coyle claimed that the Orange and Freemason Lodges of Donegal had been ordered 'to poll their full strength so that not alone Major Myles, the prominent Freemason and Imperialist, be returned, but that 40,000 of a surplus may be at the disposal of Cumann na nGaedheal'. Father Coyle wanted de Valera judged on the quality of his enemies as much as on his own merits: the English daily press, the Orange Press of the Six Counties, *The Irish Times*, the *Independent* 'that in 1916 called out for the death of James Connolly, as well as every Freemason and Orange Lodge in the country, are denouncing him in as fierce terms as O'Connell and Parnell were denounced in their day'.[92] Speaking in Cavan, Father Coyle was glad that the Unionist and Orange plot to sustain Cumann na nGaedheal had provoked a nationalist reaction: the Ancient Order of Hibernians in Donegal and Monaghan 'had decided to vote Fianna Fáil, and he asked the men of Cavan to do the same and to be on the side of Ireland against England'.[93] Cumann na nGaedheal were seen to lack courage as well as patriotism. Michael O'Mullan, Parish Priest of Fahan, Co. Donegal, said that 'with the memory of the boundary surrender, the 1923 and 1926 secret agreements, and the attempted legal defence of these outrageous injustices, the Free State electors could not jeopardise their supreme interests by entrusting their government to a weakling like Mr Cosgrave'.[94] In the 1933 campaign, Fianna Fáil was able to use the strongly Nationalist statement of Bishop McNeely of Raphoe for party purposes; banners proclaimed his recent promise that 'the land of the O'Donnells will not be the first to cry surrender'.[95] Father O'Mullan told the Fianna Fáil Donegal Convention that the party members were 'standard-bearers' . . . of 'Irish nationality' in an election where the issue appeared simple but of supreme importance: 'whether we are going to allow the Thomases of England to dictate our policy and bludgeon us into its acceptance on

---

[91] T. de Vere White, *A Fretful Midge* (London, 1957), p. 92. 'Jimmy' Thomas (1874–1949) was Rt Hon. J.H. Thomas, Secretary of State for Dominion Affairs from 1930 to 1935. On 11 May 1932, Thomas told the House of Commons that de Valera's Bill to abolish the Oath was a direct breach of the Treaty, and if it became law, the British government could not be expected to negotiate further agreements with the Free State in regard to tariffs.

[92] *Irish Press*, 12.1.33. Father Coyle's estimate of the likely surplus of Major Myles was too generous. With a first-count surplus of 3053, he did however, help to elect two Cumann na nGaedheal candidates, McMenamin and McFadden.

[93] Ibid., 20.1.33.

[94] Ibid., 18.1.33.

[95] Ibid., 13.1.33.

every occasion when Irishmen seek to assert their just rights and economic independence'.[96]

There was considerable clerical enthusiasm for Fianna Fáil in the border counties. Joseph Connellan, Nationalist MP for South Armagh, claimed that in Armagh, Derry, Down, Tyrone, Fermanagh and Antrim, 'priests and people were subscribing handsomely to the Fianna Fáil funds'.[97] Daniel Gormley PP Roslea, whose parish included part of Monaghan, 'supported neither party at the last election, and did not think as much of de Valera as he does now'. The Cosgrave government, he suggested, had betrayed Irish interests at the start; they 'set out to be aristocrats and cultivated Imperialism'.[98] A curate of the same parish, Peter Smyth, 'who never before stood on a political platform', presided at a Fianna Fáil meeting at Smithborough, County Monaghan.[99] Thomas Gallagher, the 'popular and patriotic curate' of Creeslough, County Donegal, quoted the words of support for the Fianna Fáil campaign spoken by Dr McNeely, 'his patriotic bishop', and was proud that Donegal had given a patriotic lead to the nation.[100] Patrick McManus, PP Pettigo, County Donegal, asserted that the last ten months had shown that de Valera 'was the only man'. In the past, the 'foreign foe' represented the greatest danger to Ireland; now the people had to be on their guard against 'the domestic enemy under the cloak of Cumann na nGaedheal'.[101]

In 1932, a Cumann na nGaedheal advertisement had claimed that 'the Communists are voting for Fianna Fáil'.[102] In the party politics of Independent Ireland, Ronan Fanning remarks, 'the green suit out-ranked the red, and Fianna Fáil played a green ace in their 1932 election manifesto'.[103] In the 1933 campaign, some priests again invoked the red menace. Thomas Cummins, PP Roscommon announced his support for the Centre Party because his study of history had led him to conclude that it had always been the object of those planning subversion 'to create poverty in order to carry out certain schemes . . . and it was part of the Fianna Fáil programme to create dissatisfaction in order to create a communist state'.[104] Patrick Segrave PP Drogheda believed that if Fianna Fáil were returned and continued to foster

[96] Ibid., 9.1.33.
[97] *Derry People*, 28.1.33.
[98] Ibid., 21.1.33.
[99] *Irish Press*, 20.1.33.
[100] *Derry People*, 11.2.33.
[101] Ibid., 22.1.33.
[102] Fanning, *Independent Ireland*, p. 105.
[103] Ibid., p. 105.
[104] *Cork Examiner*, 9.1.33.

bankruptcy and unemployment, agents of 'imperious tyrannies waging war on God and man' might do their hidden work all the more effectively.[105] Bishop Fogarty, who detested de Valera and communism in equal measure, seemed in 1933 to have divined an identity of interest between the two, or at any rate an indifference on de Valera's part to the Russian menace. He welcomed a plan to unite Cumann na nGaedheal, the Farmers' Party and Independents as 'the one way to save the country'.[106] In late 1932, Archdeacon O'Connor of Gurteen, Co. Sligo, a prominent member of Cumann na nGaedheal, detected a further dimension to the conspiracy, when he drew attention to 'the action of a Jewish element in the Dáil in attempting to send some Catholic Irishmen out to Russia to get work there to learn the Russian doctrine to destroy the faith of the whole country'.[107] These clerical conspiracy theorists were not speaking in isolation. The Donegal *People's Press*, for example, argued that Cumann na nGaedheal 'has its work cut out' to 'clean up the mess and stave off the menace of Bolshevism' represented by the 'red allies of Fianna Fáil' who had put the party into power'.[108]

In general, however, clerical attempts to identify Fianna Fáil with a Communist conspiracy enjoyed little success. The Catholic *Standard* was satisfied that the leaders of both major political parties were good Catholics in whose hands religion and morality would be safe.[109] Writing from a Catholic standpoint, Professor John Busteed of University College Cork countered clerical arguments against Fianna Fáil on religious grounds by suggesting that it was Cumann na nGaedheal, not Fianna Fáil, that represented whatever threat there was to Christian values. For his part, Busteed would prefer Fianna Fáil, with its policies based on 'Christian social principles' to Cumann na nGaedheal, which was advocating 'materialistic, irreligious capitalism'.[110] A number of de Valera's supporters among the clergy were sufficiently troubled by the charge made by such speakers as James Dillon that Fianna Fáil was 'tainted by Communism'[111] to attempt a refutation. In Monaghan, Thomas Maguire, PP Aghabog, roundly declared that 'if it is

[105] *Irish Independent*, 14.1.33.
[106] Ibid., 7.1.33. The 'plan' welcomed by Fogarty resulted in the merger of Cumann na nGaedheal and the Centre Party on 8 September 1933 to form Fine Gael, whose first leader was Eoin O'Duffy. See Coakley and Gallagher (eds), *Politics in the Republic*, p. 17.
[107] *Strokestown Democrat*, 12.11.32. The 'Jewish element in the Dáil' was presumably the Fianna Fáil TD Robert Briscoe, who had been elected in 1932.
[108] *People's Press*, Donegal, 14.1.33.
[109] *Standard*, 7.1.33.
[110] *Irish Press*, 10.1.33.
[111] *Derry People*, 22.1.33.

Communistic to follow the Catholic teaching of food and work for all, Fianna Fáil is Communistic'.[112] Clerical admirers of Fianna Fáil tended to see party policies not as reflecting the principles of Communism but as a prophylactic against it. Father Mac Branáin of Ahascragh argued that 'as a matter of fact, the general policy of the Fianna Fáil government in making the poor and distressed their first care and consideration is the surest remedy against Communism and Socialism'.[113] James McCooey, CC Clogher Head, Co. Louth, identified the Fianna Fáil doctrine of 'national provision for national needs' as 'the express teaching of St Thomas, the greatest teacher of the Catholic Church'. Nowhere could Father McCooey find the party 'advocating a policy that is not in harmony with the teachings of the great Pope Leo and the present pontiff' who, like Fianna Fáil, were 'the defenders of the rights of the working man'. Indeed, Fianna Fáil was the only truly Christian party, since 'alone of all the parties it has tried to restore man in his economic life to God's likeness, has tried to elevate the home to its proper sphere by giving the bread-winner work, and by making earlier marriage easier to re-establish Ireland's whole culture and civilisation around the family. This is Christianity translated into economics.'[114] Matthew Prendergast of Cappoquin saw Fianna Fáil as the party of social justice. 'As a priest', he declared, 'I would like to stand on the Fianna Fáil platform, because it is the platform of the workers, who are also in a majority'.[115]

In 1933, the populist economics and assertive nationalism of Fianna Fáil were central to the election debate. On both issues, clerical champions of the party carried much greater conviction than priests who argued on the other side. The contrast with the 1927 elections, and even that of 1932, is remarkable. In 1927, the massive body of clerical support favoured Cumann na nGaedheal; denunciations of de Valera were emphatic and decisive. In 1933, it is the priestly supporters of Fianna Fáil who are confident and assertive, particularly in their enthusiasm for de Valera's willingness to confront the British and their contempt for the uninspired leadership given by Cosgrave

---

[112] Ibid., 28.1.33.
[113] *Irish Press*, 13.1.33.
[114] Ibid.
[115] Ibid., 19.1.33. A much more dispiriting view of Fianna Fáil's attractions for the poor and the working class is offered by Oliver MacDonagh: 'Promises of larger and more comprehensive doles, of protection and industrialisation, coupled with repudiation of British debts, constituted a nice amalgam of nationalism and democracy. They clinched the wide and durable support which Fianna Fáil enjoyed among the poorer classes, especially in the ranks of the small farmers and agricultural labourers'. *Ireland: The Union and its Aftermath* (London, 1972), p. 109.

and his ministers. Priests who spoke in the Cumann na nGaedheal interest, when they were not making unconvincing attempts to identify Fianna Fáil with left-wing extremism, tended to tell farmers of the hardships they were enduring as a result of the economic war, as Owen Hannon, the local PP, did at Cummer, Co. Galway: 'It is your solemn duty to use the franchise, you farmers, who have been in such a pitiful way for the last nine months'.[116] This could not compete with the highly charged patriotic rhetoric of priests on the other side, whose object was to consign Cosgrave and his party to a nightmarish past and to herald a new heroic age of Irish nationalism presided over by de Valera. 'Fianna Fáil', Matthew Prendergast declared, 'is the first real Irish government we ever had in Dublin. It is unthinkable that Ireland would go back to the Cosgrave rule; to crowded jails and emigrant ships; to the policy of using the soil of Ireland to grow food for John Bull, instead of using it, as God intended it should be used, for the purpose of growing food for Irish children'.[117] Eugene Coyle thanked God that the 1933 election would permit the people of the Free State to pass 'final and irrevocable judgment on the men who, in conjunction with England and Craigavon, partitioned insofar as they could do so this historic nation, sold the nationalists in the North into chains and slavery, and to add insult to injury, called the sale a good bargain and the seeds of peace'.[118] The Dean of Cashel, Monsignor Innocent Ryan, celebrated for his vituperative speeches in the twenties, told a meeting that 'one thing that seems to distinguish the Fianna Fáil party is their abysmal and ineradicable hatred of England. They live on hate. I tell you, Christian men and women, that no man ever did well on a diet of hate.'[119] The 1933 nationalist crusade did well on at least a modified version of such a diet. Father McCooey's letter to the Fianna Fáil candidates for Louth strikes the characteristic note. In the version of history promoted by Fianna Fáil's 1933 clerical supporters, de Valera has replaced Cosgrave as defender of the faith. Father McCooey hoped for the return of a Fianna Fáil government 'strong enough to meet in a successful manner the menaces of an economic war launched by the age-long enemies of our country and our Faith for the extermination of the people that are the one bulwark against the insidious attacks of Communism and Freemasonry.'[120]

[116] *The Irish Times*, 16.1.33.
[117] *Irish Press*, 19.1.33.
[118] *Kerry Champion*, 14.1.33.
[119] *The Irish Times*, 23.1.33.
[120] *Irish Press*, 13.1.33.

IV

The attempts made by some clerics to identify Fianna Fáil with Communism had their counterpart in Republican, and later Fianna Fáil, suggestions that Cosgrave's government enjoyed the support of Freemasons, and even that it depended for its survival on such support. Since the Catholic Church forbade its members to join the Masonic Order,[121] the accusation that Cumann na nGaedheal received Masonic support might be construed by those who took it seriously as damaging to a party which often made a virtue of its Catholicism and was enthusiastically endorsed by churchmen. Much confusion was generated by the tendency of critics of Cumann na nGaedheal to suggest that all Protestants were Freemasons, and to exaggerate both the number of Freemasons active in centres of power and the extent of their influence. It was perhaps too easy to assume that those Freemasons who supported Cumann na nGaedheal did so for reasons disreputable to either side. In general, as J.H. Whyte points out, 'Cumann na nGaedheal appealed to the propertied elements in the country, and as Freemasons are generally propertied, no doubt they tend to give Cumann na nGaedheal their support'.[122] Nor was it self-evident that all Protestants were Unionists and all Unionists Freemasons. In 1932, for example, Dr O'Dowd, a Fianna Fáil candidate for Roscommon, pointed out that Fraser Browne, a Fianna Fáil candidate for Leitrim–Sligo, was 'not a Freemason. He was a good Protestant, and there were other good Protestants in the national movement'.[123] In 1924, Arthur Clery, who with Conn Murphy had presented a Republican remonstrance to the Pope in 1922, was concerned that Freemasons would use their power to defend British interests in the Free State without having to experience serious opposition from Cosgrave's government. As Clery saw it, 'a government in which

---

[121] In 1884, Pope Leo XIII devoted a lengthy encyclical letter, *Humanum Genus*, to a condemnation of Freemasonry, the chief tenets of which he described as 'so completely and manifestly at variance with human reason that nothing more wicked can be conceived'. He declared that it was 'the height of folly and outrageous impiety', to wish, as he believed Freemasons did, 'to destroy religion and the Church which God himself has founded . . . to strive to bring back, after the lapse of eighteen centuries, the customs and morals of the pagans.' The full text of *Humanum Genus* appears, in an English translation, in D. Fahy, *The Kingship of Christ and Organised Naturalism* (Cork, 1943), pp. 55 ff.

[122] *Church and State in Modern Ireland, 1923–1979*, 2nd edn (Dublin, 1980), p. 42. For the appeal of Cumann na nGaedheal to the propertied elements, see W. Moss, *Political Parties in the Irish Free State* (New York, 1933), pp. 58, 68 and 183. See also E. Rumpf and A.C. Hepburn, *Nationalism and Socialism in Ireland* (Liverpool, 1977), pp. 69–81; T. Garvin, *The Evolution of Irish Nationalist Politics* (Dublin, 1981), p. 168.

Masonic influence prevails means the complete and final victory of England', since, 'no Masonic or philomasonic government is going to preserve compulsory Irish in schools or maintain an army that might be a menace to their English friends and masters'. Clery believed that 'as long as you have Free Staters in power you'll have Freemasons in power'.[124] In 1931, Clery was still confronting the Masonic issue from a Republican perspective, still postulating an unholy alliance between Freemasonry and the Free State. He did not know, or even know of, any Republican who was a Mason,[125] but he suggested that 'Freemasons have at all times avoided patriotism – as Republicans understand it – in this country, and the block of Masonry in the Free State side is, in fact, one of the principal features of the Irish landscape'. He wondered what would be said if Republicans had 'anything like the same relations with the Masonic body as the Free State has'.[126]

Throughout the twenties, Republican propagandists made frequent allusion to the supposed identity of interest between Cosgrave's governments and the Freemasons. The *Catholic Bulletin* was particularly active in exploiting this idea. In February 1927, it charged that the Free State was 'a happy hunting-ground for pension or job-seeking Masons' and claimed that 'nineteen out of the thirty members nominated by the president of the Executive [Council] to the unnecessary, unde-mocratic senatorial body are Freemasons'.[127] At a by-election rally in

[123] *Roscommon Messenger*, 13.2.32.
[124] *The Leader*, Dublin, 19.7.24; 11.10.24. I am grateful to Dr Patrick Maume, Queen's University of Belfast for this reference.
[125] Three strongly Republican priests wrote hostile accounts of Freemasonry. Thomas Burbage contributed a number of lengthy articles on the subject to *The Catholic Bulletin* in 1917; Eugene Coyle published his book *Freemasonry in Ireland* in 1928; Edward Cahill's *Freemasonry and the anti-Christian Movement* appeared in 1929.
[126] *The Leader*, Dublin, 15.8.31. There is some evidence that de Valera was not averse to the idea of accepting Masonic help, at least from America. In 1922, Terence MacSwiney's widow Muriel told him of an unusual offer. 'Bob Briscoe', she wrote, 'is willing to go to America any time to work for us if he got some approval and sanction from Republican headquarters. He is a Jew and Freemason and he would work among these two sets of people. I consider it most essential and important that he should go as I don't think the Freemasons have been touched at all by our people, at any rate not in the way he would be able to do it as one of themselves'. Muriel MacSwiney to de Valera, 21.8.22, FAK, 1441. De Valera showed interest in this proposal. On the letter he wrote an instruction for Kathleen O'Connell to ensure that 'this and all other documents cannot be got by the F.S.' and explaining how she might get in touch with Briscoe. The latter arrived in New York in September 1922. See *For the Life of Me* by Robert Briscoe and Alden Hatch, London 1957, pp. 187-202. Here, however, Briscoe's account refers exclusively to Irish-American contacts, and nowhere refers to Jews or Freemasons.
[127] For a comment on such claims, see D. O'Sullivan, *Irish Free State*, pp. 90–5. 'Sixteen of the thirty', O'Sullivan points out, 'might be described as belonging to the class formerly known as Southern Unionists'. He also points out that not all of the non-Catholics were Protestants.

Roscommon in 1925, the Republican candidate, J.J. O'Kelly, associated 'misrepresentations of him uttered by Canon Cummins, Finian Lynch, Desmond FitzGerald, Richard Mulcahy and Father O'Flynn' with 'the supporters of English and Freemason domination of Ireland'.[128] In 1928, Eugene Coyle, who had become disillusioned with the Free State government on the boundary issue and was now an active campaigner for Fianna Fáil, suggested that there were 'possibly' 100 or 'at least 90 Masonic Lodges in the great Catholic city of Dublin'. He regarded Cosgrave as merely a puppet of Freemasonry only 'nominally at the head of affairs, a practical Imperialist Catholic' whose profession of the Catholic faith provided a convenient cover for the activities of Freemasons. According to Coyle, the 'cardinal facts' of the Irish situation were that Cosgrave's government could not finance an election tomorrow without Freemason money; that it could not hope to be returned without Freemason support, and that 'even at the present time Cosgrave would have to put up the shutters if the Grand Lodge of Masons raised their finger in opposition'. The position of the Free State government, he concluded, was 'the saddest, most humiliating spectacle on the earth to-day – the bond slave of the Grand Masonic Lodge of England on the one hand, and the Grand Lodge of Ireland on the other'.[129] In 1927, Archbishop Mannix evidently shared some of Coyle's views on the strength of Masonic influence on the government of the Free State. In a speech of support for de Valera, to whom he sent a substantial donation for the September General Election campaign, Mannix declared that as a Catholic he intended to do all he could to release Ireland from 'the stranglehold of the Masons'.[130] Not all suggestions of undue Masonic influence in the Free State came from Republicans. During the controversy on the divorce issue in 1925, James Doyle, Vicar-General of Ossory, condemned an attempt by Senator Douglas to deal with the subject, alleging that 'the Freemasons devised this insidious motion in order to have an opportunity of again raising a divorce question when . . . they have sufficiently educated public opinion and created a favourable atmosphere in the Senate'.[131] A similar impulse prompted one of Cumann na nGaedheal's most vociferous clerical supporters, Father Mac Branáin, to denounce the Cosgrave government in 1927 and eventually to

[128] *Roscommon Herald*, 7.3.25.
[129] *Freemasonry in Ireland*, n.d. p. 66. This pamphlet was based on articles contributed by Father Coyle to *Honesty* in 1928. When Coyle made this assertion in 1928, there were 78 lodges in Dublin, and these included a few in rural areas. *Irish Freemasons' Calendar and Directory* (Dublin, 1928), pp. 43–9.
[130] *The Catholic Bulletin*, October 1927, p. 1021.
[131] *Kilkenny People*, 8.9.25.

become an enthusiastic apologist for Fianna Fáil. Mac Branáin was appalled when Major Bryan Cooper, a Unionist, whom Mac Branáin did not, however, identify as a Freemason, was adopted as an official Cumann na nGaedheal candidate in Dublin. This move, according to Mac Branáin, 'implied not only a danger to nationality, but also a danger to the sacred truths that every Catholic holds in reverence'. He referred to Cooper's activity in the Dáil for a divorce law in the Free State. 'Major Cooper', he declared, 'is an expert on divorce. He divorced his wife and she is still alive, and then married the divorced wife of another man, that man being still alive'. He wondered why 'poor Parnell' was treated as he was 'if this outrage on the marriage tie is possible in our Catholic land of to-day'. He also reminded his parishioners at Kilglass, North Roscommon, to whom he conveyed his objections to Cooper at the chapel gates, that 'Cooper when an MP upheld by his vote the King's blasphemous coronation oath'. To Mac Branáin, the comfortable relationship between Cosgrave's government and the ex-Unionists, based on a common hostility to Republicanism, no longer appeared tolerable. 'It is not enough', he asserted, 'for the Cosgrave government to pass coercion laws that would bring a blush to the cheek of Cromwell, but they must take a real Cromwellian like this to their bosom. From the first to the last the Coopers were bigots, allowing no Catholics to get employment inside their demesne'.[132]

While the proposition that Freemasons exercised hidden control of the Free State through their control of Cumann na nGaedheal may be dismissed as another of the conspiracy theories widely popular in the twenties and thirties, there were suggestions that Cumann na nGaedheal enjoyed useful Masonic backing from time to time, although some of those who made them seemed to assume an absolute and inevitable identity between Protestantism and Freemasonry. Under the heading 'Sligo Freemasonry Backs the Government', various newspapers carried a statement issued by W.R. Fenton to Protestant voters pointing out that there were between 6,000 and 7,000 of them in the Leitrim–Sligo constituency, and if they voted as a group, they could make certain of the success of the candidate of their choice: Fenton urged them to vote for Seán Mac Eoin, the government candidate, to save the country 'from again lapsing into chaos and disorder'.[133] In this contest, the Masons had as their allies a formidable group of Catholic

---

[132] *Roscommon Herald*, 10.9.27. Major Cooper's name does not appear in the index of the names of members of the Masonic Order registered between 1895 and 1930. Information from Ms Alex Ward, Curator, Masonic Archives, Dublin.

[133] Ibid., 8.6.29. The original report was carried in the *Irish Independent*, 4.6.29. To judge from the absence of his name from the *Irish Freemasons' Calendar and Directory*, W.R. Fenton does not appear to have held senior office in the order.

clergymen; Mac Eoin's nomination papers were signed by thirteen of these, including Dr Doorly, the Bishop of Elphin.[134] One newspaper correspondent noted that there were 'no sectarian differences' on the Cumann na nGaedheal side: 'the most prominent Freemasons worked hand in hand with the Catholic clergy to bring voters to the poll for Seán Mac Eoin'.[135] The same correspondent claimed that 'it was the solid Freemason vote whipped up publicly by the leading Freemasons' that gave victory to the government in the recent Dublin North by-election as well as in Leitrim–Sligo.[136] An interesting intimation of more significant Masonic support for Cumann na nGaedheal was provided in 1929 by *The Irish Times*, whose leader-writer felt obliged to defend Irish Freemasons against hostile remarks made by a correspondent in *The Star*, a semi-official government organ. The fact that such a publication could declare that many Protestants 'would have nothing to do with Freemasons' and that 'if a Freemason attempted any tricks, the effort would be detected and frustrated' casts considerable doubt on the notion of camaraderie between Cosgrave's government and Irish Freemasonry. *The Star* went even further in its denigration of Masons than even some Republican publicists had done. Freemasonry, it asserted, might have 'abandoned the attempt to indulge in graft in the public service' but it continued 'to do harm to the national interest', causing 'a muddy stream of suspicion to flow over the whole country'. Its correspondent hoped to see the day when Masonry would be abandoned, 'the grips and passwords forgotten and the Lodges turned into clubs and concert halls'. If it had any worthy object to pursue, 'why not in the light of day without any

---

[134] *Roscommon Herald*, 1.6.29.

[135] *Midland Reporter*, Mullingar, 13.6.29. Mac Eoin was a Knight of St Columbanus. Bolster, *The Knights*, p. 57. Not all Protestant electors seem to have followed the advice of W.R. Fenton. One of them complained that the Cumann na nGaedheal candidate Mac Eoin, for whom they were urged to vote for his 'war' services, had not taken part in anything that might be described as a war in 'any civilised country'. If he were to go to the poll, it would be to vote against Mac Eoin. 'My English friends and Protestant neighbours', he added significantly, 'agree with me in this'. *Roscommon Herald*, 1.6.29. The Carrick-on-Shannon branch of the British Legion decided to support Mac Eoin. Ibid., 8.6.29.

[136] *Midland Reporter*, 13.6.29. In the Dublin North by-election, T.F. O'Higgins defeated Oscar Traynor of Fianna Fáil by 151 votes. Father MacBranáin publicly endorsed the Fianna Fáil candidate in Leitrim–Sligo in 1929 partly because of 'the introduction to the Cumann na nGaedheal party of so many members who were on the side of the British during the Anglo-Irish war'. In January 1932, Monsignor M.J. Curran had similar feelings about Unionist support for Cumann na nGaedheal: 'I wonder the decent nationalist supporters of Cumann na nGaedheal don't revolt when they see the sort of allies they have got'. Curran to Bishop Dignan, 24.1.33, CLDA.

mumbo-jumbo mysteries?'[137] The leading article in *The Irish Times* regarded the attack in *The Star* as 'a sorry compound of ignorance and prejudice' which would be 'negligible' if *The Star* were not an organ of the Free State government. If *The Star* indeed spoke for Cosgrave's government, the *The Irish Times* wondered, 'how does the Ministry reconcile its loathing for Masonic principles with its grateful acceptance of Masonic services? The Order's substantial contribution to the two National Loans were not spurned. Some of the Independent members whose votes now keep the government in office are leading Freemasons. What will they think of *The Star's* disclosure that while they are hurrying into the division lobby they are known and watched?'[138] The claim that Freemason Independent deputies helped to keep Cosgrave's government in office was justified: James Sproule Myles, Ernest H. Alton, William E. Thrift and Jasper Travers Wolfe consistently voted with Cumann na nGaedheal.[139] What these TDs might have regarded as a public-spirited exercise, priests who supported Fianna Fáil looked upon as evidence of a sinister plot to undermine Catholic values. Denis Gildea, CC Achonry, was confident that the 'plain commonsense and Catholic instincts of Mayomen' would repeat the lesson taught to Freemasonry in the Mayo librarianship dispute. Eugene Coyle had detected the presence of 43,000 Masons in the Free State in 1925, an increase of 15,000 since 1920.[140] Gildea claimed that the number had increased from 28,000 to 50,000 under the Free State Government, that 'Freemasons and their associates had contributed £40,000 to return that government to office again and that the Freemason Independents who kept it in power 'told the Government that it must recognise its debt to those who kept it in office'.[141]

In its political obituary of Cosgrave following his defeat in 1932, the *Catholic Bulletin* was anxious to record his imagined debt to Freemasonry and its associated groups. He would be remembered by

[137] *The Star*, 12.1.29.
[138] *The Irish Times*, 18.1.29.
[139] In a letter to the author, Ms Alex Ward, Curator of the Grand Lodge of Masons of Ireland, confirmed the membership of these four Independent TDs. She also confirmed that Baron Glenavy, the Earl of Dunraven, the Earl of Wicklow and Arthur Jackson were Freemasons. These were members of the Senate in 1925.
[140] *Freemasonry in Ireland*, p. 65. Coyle derived his figures from the *Revue Internationale des Sociétés Secrètes*, of 18.4.1926 and C. Van Dalen's *Kalender für Freimaurerei*, 1926.
[141] *Irish Press*, 9.2.32. Van Dalen's *Kalender*, quoted in Coyle, *Freemasonry*, p. 36, records 530 Irish lodges in 1920, of which 59 were in Dublin, and an active Irish membership of 28,000. Coyle and Gildea seem to have been confusing Free State figures with those for Ireland as a whole, although the *Irish Freemasons' Calendar and Directory* lists 1009 Lodges in Ireland, North and South, in 1928.

'the Masonic brethren' as one who struggled to make 'Capitalistic Imperialism and English Protestantism acceptable to the Irish people'. On the Sunday morning prior to the election, the *Bulletin* pictured prayers being offered in all Protestant churches for the success at the polls of Cumann na nGaedheal, along with the usual prayers for 'His Majesty, the royal family, the army and navy'. Thus, 'inflated by masonic gas, Mr Cosgrave soared into oblivion'. With heavy irony, the *Bulletin* declared that Cosgrave, 'being a broad-minded man, accommodated himself in a generous way to the requirements of alien institutions'.[142] The *Bulletin's* verdict was almost kind compared to what *An Phoblacht* had to say about Cosgrave in 1926, following a raid by the CID on the Ursuline Convent in Sligo. 'If the news of this convent raid reaches the ears of the Holy Father', the writer wondered, 'will he alter his opinion about Mr Cosgrave being an example to Catholic rulers?' He also wondered 'if Archbishop Byrne will still allow to the ruler of a Masonic Lodge the privilege of having the Blessed Sacrament in his house while he denies it to the saintly mother of Padraig Pearse'.[143] The notion that Ireland in 1926 was a Masonic lodge presided over by a hypocritical Cosgrave is sufficiently absurd not to require serious notice except as a reflection of the propagandist methods of some of the government's opponents. In no case were the conspiracy theories, involving the alleged dependence of Cosgrave's administration for its survival on distinctively Masonic support, sustained by anything more than unwarranted inference, unfounded allegation, accident and coincidence. Nor was any convincing argument advanced to show that Masonic principles had the slightest influence on the policies pursued by Cumann na nGaedheal governments.

The Masonic scares and conspiracy theories so widely promoted in the twenties and early thirties are perhaps best regarded as the outcome of Republican resentment at Cosgrave's efforts to gain the

---

[142] *Catholic Bulletin*, April, 1932, p. 255.
[143] *An Phoblacht*, 22.1.26. The tradition of imputing, without foundation, a masonic link to Cumann na nGaedheal survived well into the thirties. In February 1934, Seán T. O'Kelly introduced a Bill to abolish university representation in the Dáil. Professor Thrift, a TD for Trinity College, argued that this would be a breach of a long-standing agreement with Southern Unionists; he knew there was an understanding, but could not say whether it was on the records. A Fianna Fáil deputy, Hugo Flinn, remarked that the agreement was 'in the [Freemason] Lodge'. O'Sullivan, *Irish Free State*, p. 415. The agreement referred to by Professor Thrift was a matter of public record. University representation in the Senate for Southern Unionists was provided for in a written agreement with the Provisional Government on 14.6.22. In October 1922, a government offer to transfer university representation to the Dáil was gladly accepted by Professor Thrift. Its terms were confirmed by Kevin O'Higgins in the Dáil. Ibid.

loyalty of Unionists to the new state by exhibiting generosity and tolerance that could readily be construed as acquiescence in the Unionist outlook. Patrick O'Farrell points out that the Free State government 'was anxious that its dominant Catholicism be not reflected formally: it sought to win the allegiance of Unionists and, of course, wished to place no religious obstacles in the way of a prompt ending of Partition'.[144] Many Southern Unionists acknowledged this by giving their support to Cumann na nGaedheal; they feared the consequences for themselves of the Republican alternative. Margaret O'Callaghan points out that in the twenties, 'former Unionists and Free State supporters alike consistently analysed republicanism in terms of criminality', and that 'the civil war camaraderie that developed between ex-unionists and the provisional government was essentially a combination of reserved Unionist relief at the good will of the new government and also a collusion in rhetoric that both parties brought to bear on Republican outrage'.[145] In 1933, de Valera's determination to rewrite the Treaty was a major new threat. In January of that year, Charles J. Rowe of Wexford addressed 'An open letter to my Fellow-Protestants' which explains why many of them, whether Masons or not, might have been reluctant to support de Valera's Republicanism and would regard Cumann na nGaedheal as their natural defender and ally. As Rowe saw it, the central issue facing Protestant voters was membership of the Commonwealth. 'If we're out of it', he argued, 'we shall get freedom at the muzzle of a gun. We'll be forcibly fed on freedom. Prepare to say "Thank God" in Irish'.[146] Continued Free State membership of the Commonwealth, underwritten by Cumann na nGaedheal and threatened by Fianna Fáil, would have offered people like Rowe a stable sense of identity which many, even among the Republican intelligentsia, seemed prepared to deny them. In the minds of senior Republican clerics, Catholicism was the only authentic expression of Irishness; Protestants represented an alien force in league with internal and external enemies of Irish nationality. In this regard, a letter from Professor Michael Browne of Maynooth to Hagan at the end of 1927 is instructive. Commenting on the recent Dáil loan, Browne doubted if more than 30 per cent of the subscribers were 'Irish and Catholic', and believed that 'the gang [Cosgrave's government] is more and more dependent on the Protestant crowd', who were 'doing their best to prevent the coalition going to pieces on the rock of

---

[144] *Ireland's English Question* (London, 1971), p. 278.

[145] 'Language, nationality and cultural identity in the Irish Free State, 1922–7: *The Irish Statesman* and the *Catholic Bulletin* reappraised', *IHS*, vol. xxiv, November 1984, p. 231.

[146] *Wexford People*, 31.1.33.

compulsory Irish'.[147] It may perhaps be significant that in 1933, the Republican Bishop of Clonfert should have been the one chosen to warn Catholics against the dangers posed by Trinity College. At the general meeting of the Maynooth Union, Dignan 'warned parents and others of the grave disloyalty and disobedience they committed in sending students to Trinity College, which came under the ban of the Holy See'.[148]

[147] M.J. Browne to Hagan, 31.12.27. Hagan Papers. Compulsory Irish was a serious problem for many Protestants in the 1920s. In 1929, a midland newspaper responded unfavourably to complaints made by senior Protestant churchmen on the matter: 'Within the past week, two bishops of our Protestant church have raised an outcry in which they strive to convey to the English public that a new system of religious persecution is at work against the members of their flocks. It is the agitation about compulsory Irish that furnishes them with the texts for their fulminations. One of them, Dr Patten, declares that it is driving their younger members out of the country. The other, Dr Miller from Waterford, insists that compulsory Irish is meant to deprive all Protestants in future of posts in the Government service and to prevent them entering the professions.' *Midland Reporter*, Mullingar, 13.6.29.

[148] *Irish Press*, 21.6.33. In a paper, 'Catholics and Trinity College' which he read to the Maynooth Union on 20 June 1933, Dignan said that 'Trinity College's atmosphere, traditions and *genius loci* were as hostile to the Catholic Faith as ever'. The *Catholic Directory* reported that 'after a lucid historical sketch of Trinity College, His Lordship said that every act of hers in her recent, as well as in her past history, proved that she was Protestant and anti-Catholic'. *ICD*, 1934. In his reference to the miscalled 'ban' on the attendance of Catholics at Trinity College, Dignan may have had in mind a rescript issued in 1875 by Pope Pius IX which forbade absolution to parents who sent their children to non-Catholic schools or colleges without adequate safeguards, the judge of such safeguards being the local ordinary in accordance with the instructions of the Holy See. R.B. McDowell and D.A. Webb point out that 'what had hitherto been a somewhat indefinite disapproval thus became crystallized' into what later became known as 'the ban'. See *Trinity College Dublin. An Academic History* (Cambridge, 1982), pp. 257–8. D.A. Webb points out that the censure laid on Trinity College by the Episcopal Synod of 1875 was limited to that laid on the Queen's Colleges of Belfast, Cork and Galway – 'that priests must not in any way favour it nor recommend students to attend it, directly or through their parents. Although he was obviously disapproved of, there was no explicit condemnation of a student who entered without taking advice from a priest'. Webb also points out that it was not until the Synod of 1956 'that the discouragement pronounced in 1875 was replaced by a positive prohibition for Catholics to enter Trinity'. See Webb's posthumous article, 'Religious Controversy and Harmony at Trinity College, Dublin over Four Centuries'. *Hermathena*, 1997, pp. 95–114. Protestant sensitivity to public displays of Catholic triumphalism during the Emancipation celebrations in 1929 was expressed by the Rector of Ballinlough, Co. Roscommon. 'The Emancipation celebration', he wrote, 'which we expected to be a civil pageant to memorialize the winning of Parliamentary and other rights, turns out to be a blatant Church display with its focus on an open-air altar, so called. The military, paid out of the common taxes

V

From the time of its foundation, Fianna Fáil had manifested a distinctly clerical complexion. Eugene Coyle, Parish Priest of Garrison, County Fermanagh, was a member of its first National Executive.[149] Many of the delegates to the Ard Fheiseanna were priests, who took an active part in the proceedings. In 1928, James O'Kelly, PP Spiddal, was calling on fellow-delegates to develop a 'more militant policy in conducting their opposition to the Free State'.[150] In 1931, O'Kelly vigorously denounced the Public Safety legislation, winning loud applause when he declared that they had 'seen the acme of coercion a week ago when the Government's solid majority were brought to prison in Dublin, because they were in prison to the extent that they were guarded by gunmen'. At the same Ard Fheis, Canon James Hackett of Monaghan believed that Fianna Fáil in power should claim 'as a right and not as a request that the counties of Tyrone and Fermanagh belonged to Ireland'.[151] In 1933, Charles White, PP Ballyhaunis, was a delegate to the Ard Fheis.[152] In the thirties, it was common for the membership of local units of the party to include priests. in 1934, Father O'Kelly was chairman of the Galway Dáil Ceanntair; in 1935, three of the eight officers of the Monaghan Dáil Ceanntair were priests: Canon Hackett, Michael McCarville, PP Scotshouse, and Thomas Maguire.[153] In 1933, open clerical support for Fianna Fáil was indicated by the considerable number of priests who addressed public meetings and by the even greater number who nominated candidates. In the Galway constituency, 21 proposed Fianna Fáil candidates; 14 did so in Monaghan.[154] Some priests who had been ill-disposed to de Valera a few years back now treated him with civility, if not with acclamation. Two of his most formidable

of the country, furnish on demand a guard of honour for the Roman hierarchy on the occasion . . . One feels that such Church self-display is simply irreverent, savouring of the unsavoury methods of secular business-pushing . . . Does it not seem as if we were fostering, at least by coward connivance or silence, the quiet up-growth of what is, in all but name, a State Church as in Holy Spain, where Protestants cannot show a Church front or ring a Church bell . . . There are more, and even more dangerous ways of evading Treaty or Constitution than by verbal renouncing or denouncing'. Rev. W.H. Colgan in the *Church of Ireland Gazette*, 4.10.29.

[149] Anon, *The Story of Fianna Fáil. First Phase* (Dublin, 1960), p. 13.
[150] *Kerry Champion*, 3.11.28.
[151] *Irish Press*, 28.10.31.
[152] Ibid., 4.6.35.
[153] Ibid., 23.4.34; 2.4.35.
[154] *Connaught Tribune*, 14.1.33; *Dundalk Examiner*, 14.1.33.

adversaries in Mayo throughout the twenties had been Dean D'Alton and Archdeacon Fallon. In his triumphal progress through that county in 1933, he was received by D'Alton and Fallon, and 'had tea with the curates' of the latter's parish.[155] A few priests, including Eugene Coyle and Myles Allman, are alleged to have acted as unofficial Directors of Elections, the former in Donegal and the latter in Kerry. Allman, a skilled political strategist, put his expert knowledge of the PR system to effective use.[156] In 1932, Professor Michael Browne acted as publicity agent for Fianna Fáil in Maynooth at the request of the National University of Ireland General Election Committee of the party. His work bore fruit, as a grateful letter from Conor Maguire, the successful NUI candidate, testifies. Browne also contributed to Seán T. O'Kelly's election expenses in the same year.[157] Archbishop Mannix provided considerable financial support when it was most needed. in 1926 he launched his 'Fund to Assist de Valera in Early Election', which yielded a substantial sum.[158] In 1927 he subscribed a thousand pounds towards the September General Election campaign.[159]

In Rome, Hagan, who had played his part in the evolution of Fianna Fáil from the ruins of Sinn Féin,[160] showed at least as much enthusiasm for the new party as he had for the old. His and Curran's hostility to Cosgrave was as palpable as ever, and was exhibited on various public occasions. In 1925, when Cosgrave was on pilgrimage in Rome, Hagan could not hide his hostility. When Cosgrave arrived for a reception at the Irish College, Hagan 'remembered Mellows and his many companions, and bitter indeed did he find a situation which compelled him to take the President's hand. He took it however, and

---

[155] *Irish Press*, 16.1.33.
[156] Information from Professor Padraig Ó Fiannachta. Allman had been among the earliest Fianna Fáil platform speakers. In 1927, he told an election meeting that 'the people everywhere were sick and tired of the Free State régime and were turning to-day to the Fianna Fáil party who, under the honest and incomparable leadership of Eamon de Valera, presented a programme which combined a certain promise of progress and prosperity in economic affairs with the cause of Irish unity and independence'. *The Kerryman*, 14.5.27.
[157] Conor Maguire to M.J. Browne, 27.2.32, GDA; S.T. O'Kelly to M.J. Browne, 22.4.32, GDA.
[158] C. Kiernan, *Daniel Mannix and Ireland*, 1984, p. 207.
[159] Fianna Fáil Archive, No. 24. '£1,000 recorded in name of Archbishop Mannix (General Election Campaign September 1927. Subs.)'. There is a note that this amount records 'money received through Chief in the form of personal and institutional subscriptions'. The Parish Priest of Claregalway contributed £5 towards Frank Gallagher's legal costs when, as editor of the *Irish Press*, the latter was prosecuted under the Public Safety Act shortly before the 1932 General Election. Maurice Moynihan to Father P.S. Ó Móráin, 23.3.32, TAA.
[160] See pp. 206–10, notes 294–306.

at once turned to Mrs. Cosgrave, whom he already knew, took her under his arm, brought her into the kitchen, presented her to the nuns, and then led her out into the garden, consigned her to the tender care of one of the bishops, and then went his way, rejoicing that he had shown all possible attention to the Free State of Ireland by showing marked respect for the better half of the head of that institution'.[161] It is not surprising that when Hagan invited Cosgrave and his Minister for Education to the Tercentenary celebration of the foundation of the Irish College, even with the assurance that 'the cordiality of the invitation will be unaffected by the personality or political views of those who shall have been called upon to preside over the destinies of the country',[162] Cosgrave replied through Archbishop Byrne that he and the Minister could not leave Dublin and had 'accordingly been obliged to forgo the honour of the invitation'.[163] Charles Bewley, the first Irish Minister to the Holy See, in a memorandum on Irish-Vatican relations which he drew up in 1929, mentioned 'the notorious fact that Monsignor Hagan is in the closest touch with leaders of the Fianna Fáil party',[164] and suggested that the Irish College authorities

[161] Hagan to M.J. Browne, 31.10.25, GDA. Hagan told Browne that one of the students of the Irish College had dined with Cosgrave, adding 'the family is disgraced for ever more'. Ten years after the Free State execution of Republicans, Curran still nourished deep resentment. 'We await with much interest the election news', he wrote to his friend Michael Browne; 'I only hope the executioners of Childers, Mellows etc. will not meet with a worse fate themselves when they are deprived of protection. I really fear we will be disgraced before the [Eucharistic] Congress'. Curran to M.J. Browne, 17.2.32, GDA.
[162] Hagan to the Secretary of the Executive Council, Irish Free State. 7.10.27, NAI S 5915.
[163] Cosgrave to Byrne, 17.10.27, Byrne Papers, DAA.
[164] Hagan was, indeed, in touch with de Valera and with ecclesiastics in sympathy with Fianna Fáil during the period. In 1927, he was telling Bishop Dignan of his happiness that 'contact has been established [by Fianna Fáil] with the Art O'Connor wing [of Sinn Féin] and that discussions which have taken place have led to a better understanding and to cooperation'. Hagan to Dignan, 22.2.27, CLDA. In 1927, he was giving Michael Browne his views on party strategy: 'Something must be done before even a large minority will vote for the Republicans. A declaration that there will be no trouble with England without a previous referendum would perhaps be a step in the right direction'. Hagan to M.J. Browne, 21.1.27, GDA. In the same year, he was advising de Valera that a petition requesting the removal of the Oath as a requirement for entering the Dáil should be drawn up. 'Unless my information is greatly at fault', he told him, 'you could count on the signatures, not only of your own followers, but on a very large part of those who voted F.S. I gather that many supporters of the latter venerable institution would welcome your party into the chamber.' Hagan suggested that 'if the signature of Cardinal O'Donnell could be attached, half the battle would be won'. Hagan to de Valera, 7.7.27, FAK 1382. Three days after Hagan wrote his letter, Kevin O'Higgins was murdered, with political consequences which were to render Hagan's suggestion redundant.

had disseminated the rumour that the Holy See had no intention of sending a representative to Dublin, the sole object of this being 'to injure the prestige of the country in the hope that the government will suffer in the process'. A 'prominent Irish Benedictine' had told Bewley that Hagan's students were 'Bolshevists'; the Minister was alarmed at the prospect of Hagan's 'training of the future priesthood of Ireland in a spirit of active disloyalty to the government'.[165]

When Hagan died in March 1930, Curran told Archbishop Byrne of his own interest in the Rectorship. Byrne's reply clearly reveals the depth of Irish episcopal disquiet at Hagan's Republican activity since the Treaty. Byrne told Curran that he would forward his candidature if he could get reassurance from him 'about certain matters in the College which offended most of the bishops during the reign of the late Rector'. He wondered if, under Curran, the College would be run on 'non-political lines' or, he asked, 'will the old system be continued including the afternoon balm of non-sympathisers with episcopal views'.[166] Curran's appointment suggests that his response was satis-factory. Five years later, Curran had become thoroughly disillusioned with de Valera, whose policy of supporting sanctions against Italy over the Abyssinian issue he considered both unjust and futile. In a letter to the *Irish Press* he protested 'most earnestly' against the policy, claiming that 'all Irishmen in Rome deplore it as unwise and futile at the very least'. He was embarrassed for all Irish residents of Italy. 'In what unfortunate position', he complained, 'ecclesiastics are to be placed. Guests of Italy, our countrymen are to starve her while we receive all she has to give. Such a procedure is neither Christian nor honourable.'[167] Curran gave his friend Michael Browne a much more detailed explanation of his objections to de Valera's stand on Abyssinia. His letter to Browne shows that the lifelong hostility to Britain's influence in the world which Curran had shared with Hagan had not moderated. He saw the action of the League of Nations against Italy as part of a sinister plot. He dated 'the beginning of all this conspiracy against Italy from 7 January 1935 when it was announced that Laval and the Duce had reached an agreement. England saw her reign in *mare nostrum* in danger, had nightmares of a Latin bloc and saw her opportunity to gather imperialists, socialists, Communists, bolshevists, masons, and anti-Catholics in a great combine against Catholic and papist Italy.' He was appalled that de Valera should have 'addressed the League on the morning following the declaration of Italy's aggres-sion demanding that the question of the imposition of sanctions be not

---

[165] NAI D/FA Secretary's Files S 28A.
[166] Byrne to Curran, n.d. but post 12.3.30 (date of Hagan's death) DAA.
[167] *Irish Press*, 9.11.35.

postponed but should be taken up that day as proposed by Eden'. If he had, on the other hand, 'taken a Catholic stand', instead of going out of his way 'to show his zeal for this British tool', he would have been 'hailed here by Fascists and Cardinals alike as a knight *sans peur*'. His action had earned him 'something bordering the contempt of several foreign diplomats', made Ireland appear 'a slave-dupe of Britain', betrayed the spirit of Sinn Féin and set Curran 'definitely adrift from Fianna Fáil'. He could have nothing to do with a party that based its foreign policies on a League of Nations that was 'a British–French–Russian instrument'.[168] Up to the time of de Valera's intervention on behalf of Abyssinia, a country which Curran associated with slavery and oppression, the latter had based his Republican politics on the identification of Irish pro-Treaty groupings with British interests; it was understandably difficult for him to come to terms with this new vision of his hero as an instrument for British imperialism. A more representative clerical view of de Valera's significance in 1935 was probably that of James McGlinchey, PP Draperstown, Co. Derry, who acclaimed him as 'a providential saviour of Irish ideas and ideals'.[169]

If Irish ideas and ideals were the same as Catholic ones, it can be said that de Valera's second administration, from 1933 to 1937, furthered these with enthusiasm. In his broadcast to mark the opening of the Athlone Radio Station in February 1933, remembering that Ireland had once taken the lead in 'christianising and civilising the barbarian hordes that had overrun Britain and the west of Europe', he hoped that the mission of recalling men to 'forgotten truths' would extend into the future.[170] This mission was not to be promoted exclusively by ecclesiastics, as Seán T. O'Kellly demonstrated in September 1933 when he intervened at the Assembly of the League of Nations to take exception to a document circulated by the Health Organisation of the League calculated, as the Secretary of the Department of External Affairs told Bishop Mulhern, 'to encourage the practice of contraception'.[171] O'Kelly protested that the document was 'susceptible of an interpretation which was entirely contrary to the doctrine of the Catholic Church', pointing out that 'the practice of contraception for any purpose was abhorrent to the people of many countries, including Ireland'. To associate such a practice with measures taken for maternal welfare would 'bring health centres into disrepute in the minds of the faithful'. As a result of O'Kelly's intervention, the circulation of the

[168] Curran to M.J. Browne, 28.12.35.
[169] *Irish Press*, 8.5.35.
[170] Moynihan, *Speeches by de Valera*, pp. 231–3.
[171] J.P. Walshe to Bishop Mulhern, 21.10.33, DRDA.

offending document was 'suspended indefinitely'.[172] In September 1934, de Valera, although voting for Russian entry to the League of Nations, nevertheless expressed misgivings about the denial to Russian Christians of liberty of conscience and freedom of worship, and exhorted the Russian government to guarantee these rights. 'To deprive a man of his religion', he told the Assembly of the League, 'is to deprive life of its meaning', adding that 'to exclude religion from the domain of human conduct is to deprive morals and ethics of all the sanctions which support them against the stress of individual and national greed'.[173] Both de Valera and O'Kelly were publicly saluted by Bishop Mageean of Down and Connor in his Lenten Pastoral for 1935 for their solid defence of religious principles. 'When Russia applied for admission to the League of Nations', Mageean wrote, 'the statesmen of the world uttered no word of condemnation against her envenomed attack on the Christian faith. There was one exception, and the Irish Catholics will ever remember it with pride: it was the voice of an Irish statesman. And it is another Irish statesman that we have to thank for his effective intervention when the same League of Nations was about to sponsor a resolution that threatened the decencies of family life'.[174]

The Censorship Act of 1929 had made it an offence to advocate the use of contraceptives; the Criminal Law Amendment Act of 1935 prohibited their sale and importation.[175] In the preparation of the latter piece of legislation, Seán T. O'Kelly worked in close harmony with the bishops. The parliamentary committee responsible for drafting the legislation had inserted a proviso that 'specified doctors might prescribe contraceptives for those who feel they can conscientiously use them, such appliances to be imported under licence'.[176] O'Kelly called twice on Dr Wall, Auxiliary Bishop of Dublin, to tell him that he had impressed on Ruttledge, the Minister for Justice, how anxious the bishops were to get the legislation through. More significantly, O'Kelly told the bishop 'emphatically' that he could not allow the conscience

[172] A copy of O'Kelly's statement to the League will be found with Mulhern's papers in the Dromore Diocesan Archive.
[173] Moynihan, *Speeches of de Valera*, p. 260. Pius XI was so impressed by de Valera's speech that he sent him a congratulatory telegram. See D. Keogh, *Ireland and the Vatican. The Politics and Diplomacy of Church-State Relations, 1922–1960* (Cork, 1995), p. 125.
[174] *Irish Press*, 4.3.35. Mageean was not correct in asserting that de Valera was the only statesman to draw attention to abuses of religious freedom in Russia. See Moynihan, *Speeches of De Valera*, pp. 259–60.
[175] J.H. Whyte, *Church and State*, p. 49.
[176] Dr Wall, Auxiliary Bishop of Dublin to Bishop Keane of Limerick, 18.12.33, LKDA.

clause because he, as a Catholic, believed that 'no Catholic could permit what was intrinsically wrong no matter how much a person might say that they in their conscience saw no wrong in it'.[177] Understandably, Wall told the bishop of Limerick that O'Kelly was 'most orthodox on these Catholic matters'.[178] Fianna Fáil earned the public praise of some bishops for dealing with other 'Catholic matters'. In 1933, Archbishop Harty expressed his 'warm approval' of recent tariffs on English newspapers.[179] In the same year, the party must have been encouraged by the declaration of welcome by Bishop MacNeely of Raphoe for its electoral success and his support of what it stood for. 'Our people', he wrote in his Lenten Pastoral, 'were asked to take a momentous decision in the recent election; it was a real test indeed, and they stood up to it in a disciplined and resolute fashion. Idealism won the day; those who know best the national psychology would say that they were true to themselves'.[180] In March 1934, Bishop Cullen of Kildare and Leighlin, reflecting on the danger of another Civil War and the duty of patriotic people to alleviate bitterness and hatred, told de Valera that a recent speech of his in the Dáil, 'with its touch of peace and earnestness' had given him 'a special delight', and approved of his suggestion that a mixed force should be assembled to keep the peace at meetings. De Valera suggested to Cullen that 'a short course of sermons from our priests' on the subject of social harmony and tolerance, given without bias, would achieve more than the combined powers of the state.[181]

De Valera and his ministers continued to offer many indications, both to the Irish Church and to the Vatican, that Fianna Fáil Republicanism was essentially a Catholic thing, and that they were building a state on Catholic foundations. They showed an exemplary enthusiasm for honouring Catholic occasions. De Valera and O'Kelly attended the centenary celebrations in Paris of the Society of St Vincent de Paul in 1933. In the same year, de Valera made a Holy Year pilgrimage to Rome, while two senior party members, Ruttledge and P.J. Little, accompanied the Irish national pilgrimage to Lourdes.[182] De Valera's St Patrick's Day broadcasts were, in tone and content, at least as appropriate to a bishop as to a statesman. He spoke as a Catholic to Catholics and on behalf of Catholics. In 1935,

[177] Ibid.
[178] Ibid.
[179] *Irish Press*, 22.5.33.
[180] *ICD*, 1934, p. 585.
[181] T.P.Ó Néill agus P. Ó Fiannachta, *De Valera* (Dublin, 1970), p. 278. Cullen wrote to de Valera on 3.3.34; the latter replied on 5.3.34.
[182] Whyte, *Church and State*, pp. 47–8.

he reminded his listeners that for fifteen hundred years, Ireland had been 'a Catholic nation' and 'remains a Catholic nation and as such she sets the eternal destiny of man high above the "isms" and idols of the day'.[183] In the early days of de Valera's administration, the Vatican authorities seem to have been in need of reassurance that his party's republicanism was in full conformity with Catholic principles. Such reassurance was provided by McCauley, the Irish envoy to the Vatican, who told Pacelli, the Secretary of State, in 1934 that 'the Irish people, irrespective of their domestic politics, were most devoted Catholics, none more than the young and ardent Republicans' and 'emphasised that republicanism was entirely compatible with the sincere practice of the Catholic religion'.[184] In 1934, McCauley found at the Vatican 'at least distrust of the republican movement' and 'a little suspicion of our government', based mainly on reservations about de Valera's British policies. Irish diplomats considered it useful to allay Vatican fears by pointing out that Fianna Fáil was 'governing the State according to the Christian principles laid down in *Rerum Novarum* and other Papal encyclicals', and even by 'bringing to the Holy Father's notice that more members of the Irish Free State Government have gone to Rome for the Holy Year than of any other Government in the world'.[185]

When suitable opportunities presented themselves, Fianna Fáil ministers were quick to demonstrate the impeccable Catholic orthodoxy of their government. In October 1933, Seán T. O'Kelly addressed the Cercle Catholique at Geneva in French, in the presence of the local bishop. He paid tribute to the Austrian Chancellor Dolfuss for declaring that his country's economic policy was inspired essentially by 'the principles set forth by the Holy Father for the solutions of the social problems of our time'. There was, however, O'Kelly announced, 'one other Government . . . that is inspired in its every administrative action by Catholic principles and Catholic doctrine, and that Government is the one to which I have the honour to belong – the Government of the Irish Free State'. Referring to 'that most memorable Encyclical on the Restoration of the Social Order' issued by Pius XI, O'Kelly suggested that 'in no country was this inspiring pronouncement read with greater interest and eagerness than in Ireland'. He was proud that 'neither continental socialism nor communism has made any headway' in Ireland; this was because Fianna Fáil was engaged in 'the wise diffusion of property which Pope Leo XIII and the present

[183] *Catholic Bulletin*, April 1935, p. 273.
[184] Keogh, *Ireland and the Vatican*, pp. 117, 107.
[185] Ibid,. p. 102.

occupant of the Holy See recommended to us'.[186] On occasion, de Valera could go further than the Pope was prepared to go in safeguarding the purity and integrity of Catholic belief. In May 1937, he told the Dáil why he could have nothing to do with the Coronation ceremony for George VI: 'I had made it clear that our attitude towards the whole Coronation ceremony must be one of detachment and protest while our country was partitioned and while the Coronation service implied discrimination – as it still does – against the religion to which the majority of our people belong'.[187] A few days later, it was announced from the Vatican that the Pope was to send a Legate to London for the occasion. The ceremonies were in the charge of the Duke of Norfolk, a Catholic.[188] There was evidently a basis in fact for de Valera's assertion to the 1931 Ard Fheis of Fianna Fáil: 'I declared that, if all came to all, I was a Catholic first'.[189]

The 1937 Constitution may be regarded as a formal expression of de Valera's commitment to the principle of a Catholic Republic. The Preamble provides a clear, perhaps unwitting, indication that the document was drafted with Catholics primarily, if not exclusively, in mind. The 'people of Éire' are described as 'Humbly acknowledging all our obligations to Our Divine Lord, Jesus Christ, Who sustained our fathers through centuries of trial'. These 'centuries of trial', given the religious context created in the Preamble, can only suggest the persecutions endured by Catholics at the hands of Protestants; it is difficult to imagine how Protestants could find their history adequately described here, unless, of course, they assumed that the centuries of trial involved a subtle recognition of the sufferings of Irish Protestant martyrs since 1641 and the problems posed for generations of Protestants by supposed Papal aggression and conspiracy, a theme of much Orange propaganda. The social articles of the Constitution reflect specifically Catholic teaching. In Article 41 the Family is

---

[186] English translation of Address delivered by Seán T. O'Kelly, Vice-President, Executive Council, Irish Free State, to the Cercle Catholique, Geneva, on 4 October, 1933. Private Possession.

[187] Dáil Debates, 1937, LXV, 869.

[188] O'Sullivan, *Irish Free State*, p. 489. On his accession to power, de Valera availed of the first opportunity he had of meeting Pius XI face to face to protest most vehemently against the course of action taken by the Irish bishops in 1922, telling him that they had moved beyond their proper sphere in pronouncing political judgements. 'I told the Holy Father', he later recalled, 'that I was as loyal a Catholic as the bishops – even as the Holy Father himself – and he had no answer'. S.P. Farragher, *Dev and his Alma Mater. Eamon de Valera's long association with Blackrock College, 1898–1915* (Dublin, 1984), p. 140.

[189] *Irish Press*, 29.10.31.

recognised, in the familiar Catholic formulation, as 'the natural primary and fundamental unit group of society'. The guarantee that 'no law shall be enacted providing for the grant of a dissolution of marriage' is seen as the means of protecting marriage and the Family 'against attack'. This again is in conformity with a distinctively Catholic doctrinal position. In Article 42, the Catholic teaching on the superior rights of the Family as 'the primary and natural educator of the child' is adequately summarised. Article 43 reflects the principles laid down in successive Papal encyclicals regarding man's right to the ownership of private property. It would be misleading to suggest that these articles represent de Valera's distinctive outlook on social questions, or a set of attitudes peculiar to Fianna Fáil. The specific embodiment of Catholic values in the Constitution can, as Whyte has argued, 'be considered one more instance of the movement which had been going on, regardless of which party was in power, since the establishment of the State to enshrine Catholic principles in the law of the land'.[190]

The drafting of Article 44, which affords recognition to named religious bodies, caused de Valera considerable difficulty. He told T.P. O'Neill in 1972 that his purpose in this Article was to protect religious minorities. 'Majorities', he believed, 'did not need protection: they were strong enough to look after themselves. It was minorities which needed recognition'. De Valera's difficulty then lay 'in the fact that he could not recognise minorities without saying something about the position of the majority'.[191] On these matters, he was not short of religious advisers, among them Dr McQuaid. The latter was worried that de Valera might have fixed on the term 'other Christians' to describe minority Churches, believing that 'as so many in all these Churches

---

[190] Whyte, *Church and State*, p. 52. On the other hand, the 1937 Constitution took little practical account of vocationalism, a political doctrine favoured by Pope Pius XI in his encyclical *Quadragesimo Anno*, (1931), and strongly advocated during the subsequent decade by Catholic political theorists. Article 19 of the Constitution made provision for the election of 43 of the 60 members of the Senate 'by any functional or vocational group or association'. The Seanad Electoral (Panel Members) Act of 1937, however, went a long way towards undermining the vocational concept suggested in Article 19, by making provision for an electoral college of 355 members, all of whom were TDs or County Councillors. Donal O'Sullivan points out that the first Senate election based on the 1937 Constitution 'resulted in a triumph for the politicians and a rout for those who had allowed their names to go forward in the belief that a vocational second chamber would eventuate', *Irish Free State and its Senate*, p. 272. Of the same elections, J.J. Lee remarks that 'genuine vocational representatives were swamped beneath the avalanche of party loyalists'. *Ireland, 1912–1985*, p. 272.
[191] T.P. O'Neill, 'Dr J.C. McQuaid and Eamon de Valera. Insights on Church and State', *Breifne*, 1993, pp. 327–8.

deny the divinity of Christ, unlike their ancestors, they have truly ceased to be Christian'. McQuaid suggested a religious Article in which the Catholic religion would be 'recognised' and the minorities simply 'tolerated'.[192] De Valera, according to O'Neill, resolved the problem of terminology 'by following a suggestion made to him by Dr Gregg, Church of Ireland Archbishop of Dublin, by using the official titles of the religious bodies, and he was always proud of the fact that he had included recognition of the Jewish congregation at a time when they were under attack in many parts of Europe'.[193] However, the use of the description 'Church of Ireland' in the published Constitution met with strong objections, not only from McQuaid, but from Cardinal McRory, who wrote to de Valera that 'it would be a very great mistake to seem to approve or accept such an arrogant assumption'.[194] One of de Valera's Jesuit advisers, Father P.J. Gannon, did not want any differentiation before the law between the Catholic Church and the Protestant 'sects', but felt this could be made clear 'without according a usurped title to a body which is not really a Christian Church at all . . . nor Irish in any true sense'.[195] Archbishop Byrne, on the other hand, was so impressed by the draft Preamble which recognised God as the source of all authority, that he was prepared, if de Valera thought it necessary, to agree to the omission of any specific reference to the Catholic Church in Article 44.[196] Even more welcome from de Valera's point of view were the laudatory comments of the semi-official Vatican journal *Osservatore Romano* which declared that his constitution differed from others 'because it is inspired by respect for the faith of the people, the dignity of the person, the sanctity of the family, of private property and of social democracy. These principles

[192] Ibid., p. 328.
[193] Ibid., p. 328.
[194] Ibid., p. 329.
[195] Rev. P.J. Gannon to de Valera, 7.6.37, NAI S 9903.
[196] Ó Néill and Ó Fiannachta, *De Valera*, p. 334. For useful accounts of the contribution of clergymen to he drafting of the Constitution, see D. Keogh, 'The Jesuits and the 1937 Constitution', *Studies*, Spring 1989; S. Faughnan, 'The Jesuits and the Irish Constitution', *IHS*, vol. xxvi, no. 101, May 1988. In January or February 1937, McQuaid appears to have drafted a religious article, the most important clause of which read: 'The state acknowledges that the true religion is that established by our Divine Lord, Jesus Christ Himself, which He committed to His Church to protect and propagate, as the guardian and protector of true morality. It acknowledges, moreover, that the Church of Christ is the Catholic Church'. In April, de Valera told the Papal Nuncio that such a clause was 'quite impossible'. Faughnan, 'The Jesuits', p. 100. It also appears that the Vatican could only 'approve completely' if the religious article stated that the Catholic Church was the Church founded by Christ. See D. Keogh, *Ireland and the Vatican*, p. 135.

are applied in a unique religious spirit, which animates the whole constitution'.[197] This comment, widely diffused in Ireland, was bound to be construed as implying papal enthusiasm for the constitution, and to have exerted strong influence on clerical doubters. Even MacRory was impressed by the uniformly favourable impression the Constitution had made on priests, and eventually came to the conclusion that it was 'a great Christian document', which provided a solid foundation 'on which to build up a nation that will be, at once, reverent and dutiful to God and just to all men'.[198]

It is one of the many ironies of the period between 1922 and 1937 that the Free State Constitution, formulated by an administration warmly endorsed and sustained by the bishops of Ireland, afforded no recognition to distinctively Catholic values or concerns, or even broadly Christian ones. It is perhaps odd that the leadership of the Church in the twenties acquiesced in this position without venturing public criticism or protest. It is another irony that the political heirs to the anathematised Republicans should have given the state a constitution with so pervasively Catholic a colouring as the 1937 one. Isolated clerical voices deplored the secular, even pagan, character of the 1922 Constitution. Patrick Daly, PP Castlepollard, Co. Westmeath, wondered at 'a Godless Constitution for a Christian land'.[199] A contributor to the *Irish Theological Quarterly* for July 1922 would have pronounced the Constitution 'good without qualification' were Ireland a pagan country. In the *Irish Ecclesiastical Record* for January 1938, a Maynooth historian rejoiced that the 'reproach' had been taken away in 1937.

VI

However hard Fianna Fáil might strive to establish itself as a model Catholic administration, a substantial number of the clergy who had opposed de Valera since the Treaty remained unreconciled, and possibly irreconcilable, throughout the thirties, and used many opportunities to make this known. At the close of the academic year in Maynooth in 1933, the President, Monsignor McCaffrey, warned newly ordained priests that 'any interference by the clergy in political matters was forbidden by the law of the Church in Ireland'. Having, however,

---

[197] *Irish Press*, 17.5.37.
[198] D. Keogh, *The Vatican, the Bishops*, p. 219. Seán MacEntee echoed MacRory's sentiment, telling voters that it required a 'moral courage almost unique in the world today to adopt as part of the Constitution the fundamental teachings of the Holy Father in regard to the Family'. *Irish Press*, 18.6.37.
[199] *Freeman's Journal*, 27.9.22.

advised the clergy 'to hold aloof from political wrangles and factions', McCaffrey suggested that if they did they would 'be in a stronger position to intervene in case political programmes and policies deviated from sound Catholic principles'.[200] De Valera's leading clerical opponents in the thirties seem to have judged some of his policies so unsound as to justify the most energetic intervention. In 1934, he told the Dáil that 'it would be a bad day for the Church and a bad day for religion that it became identified with political parties'.[201] Here he was conscious that McCaffrey's advice to young priests was being widely ignored by their elders. Some senior ecclesiastics had not been able to forgive or forget Republican activity during the Civil War and de Valera's part in it. Well into the thirties these gave open and active support to his political opponents; a number of bishops were notably hostile in their comments on government policies. In many places priests appeared on the platforms of the United Ireland Party (UIP), an amalgamation of Blueshirts, Cumann na nGaedheal and the Centre Party. In January 1934, Bishop Cohalan travelled to Bandon to preside at the obsequies of a murdered Blueshirt. Marching behind the remains 'to the strains of the Dead March, played by the Rosscarbery Blueshirt Band, were about 800 young men wearing blue shirts and berets and about 250 girls in blue blouses'. Cohalan told the mourners that 'it would be a terrible thing if at any time a Government or any of the various parties in the country were more like factions, looking to the interests of factions rather than to the interests of the country',[202] which was another way of saying that the Fianna Fáil Government was no more than a faction protecting another faction, the IRA, in its murderous activity against Blueshirts. In March 1934, Martin Hegarty, the local PP, presiding at Desmond FitzGerald's meeting at Moygownagh, County Mayo, told his listeners: 'If anybody came here to-day to act the blackguard sock him and sock him in style'.[203] In April 1934, Michael Masterson, Parish Priest of Mohill, who wore a UIP emblem on his coat, presided at a Cosgrave meeting which he opened with prayers and greetings from the League of Youth.[204]

Fianna Fáil did not appear as vulnerable to attack on purely religious or moral grounds as it had in the late twenties; its remaining episcopal critics now preferred to concentrate their fire on its foreign and economic policies. In August 1932, Cardinal MacRory used a Patrician

[200] *Irish Press*, 21.6.33.
[201] Eamon de Valera, *The Way to Peace* (Dublin, 1934), p. 9.
[202] *Irish Press*, 1.1.34.
[203] Ibid., 5.3.34.
[204] Ibid., 30.4.34.

ceremony on the Hill of Slane to convey his displeasure in strong language at the hardship de Valera's tariff war with Britain, 'as discreditable as it was deplorable', was causing to the farmers of Meath. He considered it 'a shame and a sin that this fratricidal policy, so injurious to both countries, should be allowed to go on without further attempts towards negotiation or arbitration'.[205] In December 1933, Bishop Fogarty of Killaloe, an active propagandist for the UIP during the Blueshirt period, made a much livelier attack on the government for its treatment of farmers and Blueshirts during a speech at St Flannan's College, Ennis. The farmers he described as being 'kicked about and laughed at as if they were so many serfs or helots', their industry 'wiped out and destroyed by a heartlessness which is almost inconceivable'. He suggested that political opponents were being denied fair play by the government, that liberty was 'stifled', and that decent citizens were 'crushed into silence by tyranny which is always impolitic as well as unchristian'.[206] When the Blueshirt leader General O'Duffy was released from jail in December 1933 having been involved in public disorder, Bishop Morrisroe, in a well-publicised telegram, described his release as the 'victory of justice over shameless partisanship and contemptible tyranny'.[207] The government complained to the Vatican that the comments of Fogarty and Morrisroe could be construed by ill-disposed people as 'incitements to violence against the State' and as 'justifying violence against lawfully-constituted authority'. The initial Vatican response was that the government should try to establish better relations with the bishops. Later, McCauley, the Irish representative to the Holy See, explained to Pizzardo, a senior Vatican official, that the bishops were nearly all old men who had supported the Redmondite Party and then had transferred allegiance to Cosgrave's government. If they could not accept political change, 'they should at least keep quiet and not impugn the authority of the elected representatives of the people'.[208] Whatever action the Vatican might take in consequence of government complaints, Fogarty, for one, would not be silenced. In his 1934 Pastoral Letter he returned to the theme of tyranny, declaring that if a government 'abuses its authority to oppress the people with unjust laws and partisan

---

[205] *Irish Independent*, 16.8.32.
[206] *The Irish Times*, 21.12.33.
[207] *Irish Independent*, 26.12.33.
[208] D. Keogh, *Ireland and the Vatican*, 1995, pp. 111–16. At a Fianna Fáil function in Kilkenny in January 1934, Tomás Ó Deirg, Minister for Education, declared that 'to be consistent, people like Most Rev. Dr Fogarty should . . . go back under the old flag of the Irish Parliamentary Party, which they scoffed at in the past'. *Irish Press*, 8.1.34.

administration, the people are entitled to ventilate their dissatisfaction'. This time, however, he was careful to point out that those oppressed should 'contend for a redress of their grievances' by 'means consistent with the law of God'.[209] He still remained an active critic of the government and a champion of the UIP. In 1935, he recognised in the latter 'the only body now operating in Irish life that holds out any hope for the salvation of the farmers', since Fianna Fáil policies could have 'only one issue, the destruction of rural life in Ireland'.[210]

In July 1934, when cattle seized from farmers who had defaulted on their annuities were being sold in a Cork stockyard, lorry loads of farmers armed with sticks drove through the Gárda ranks and broke through the stockyard gates; a young man was killed and others wounded by police fire. Almost a year later, at a series of Confirmation ceremonies, Bishop Cohalan commented on the incident and on government policies generally, in a way that angered de Valera, who complained to the Papal Nuncio. Cohalan suggested that 'agents of the government fired deliberately' at the young man they killed, and that reparation should be made by the government to his parents.[211] Cohalan also traced the origins of contemporary factionalism and disorder to the refusal of de Valera and others to accept what the bishops had said to them in their Pastoral of October 1922. Like Fogarty, he also suggested that the government was dealing unjustly with farmers.[212] De Valera told Robinson that Cohalan's attitude seemed to imply 'that the State itself, as personified by the government for the time being, is one of several rival political factions, and nothing more'. He wondered how Cohalan, 'or any other person of similar station', could 'voice opinions and use expressions which destroy all respect for law and order in the minds of the people, and thereby encourage the use of violence against the State'. De Valera used the occasion to make more general observations on the relations between his administration and those senior clerics he saw as attempting to discredit it publicly. 'The Christian motives which inspire the policy of my Government', he told Robinson, 'are clear to everybody'. He asked the Nuncio 'not merely to endeavour to prevent certain members of the clergy from making use of their high office to under-mine the authority of the government, but to secure their active co-operation in inculcating in the people that respect for lawful authority without which the continuance of a Christian Church and a

[209] *Irish Press*, 12.2.34.
[210] Ibid., 13.10.35.
[211] *Irish Independent*, 18.6.35.
[212] Ibid., 3.6.33.

Christian State would soon become impossible'. He believed Robinson would agree that the Bishop of Cork should take an early opportunity 'to repair in some public way the evil effects of his recent statements'.[213] Robinson passed the complaint on to Cohalan, whose lengthy reply he sent to de Valera.

Cohalan gave no token of contrition. He told Robinson that 'the policy of the Government – be it right or wrong – is entailing a grave injury and injustice to a considerable number of farmers'. He did not speak of 'injustice in a vague, loose sense; but of injustice in a theological, moral sense, which involves a duty of restitution'. He showed himself as unrelenting as ever in his contempt for Republican activity since the Treaty. He was glad he had drawn attention to the 1922 Pastoral in his confirmation sermon. If that Pastoral had been obeyed then, he argued, 'there would have been substantial unity from the beginning and we should not have established in Ireland the precedent of an unauthorised army in opposition to the army of the Free State.' De Valera must have been disappointed to read Cohalan's verdict that his communication to Robinson was 'a disappointing note, judged by the range of mind, speculative and practical, that one sees in the official communications of other heads of governments'.[214]

Cohalan, Morrisroe and Fogarty remained de Valera's bitterest episcopal critics. Two other bishops, Keane of Limerick and O'Doherty of Galway, were more restrained in their expressions of hostility. In his 1934 Pastoral, Keane was concerned that members of the UIP were subjected to outrageous attacks from which they were not adequately defended by the government. Disorder, he noted, had been directed mainly against 'one political party which, in view of the important political interests it represents and the character of its leaders, must . . .

---

[213] De Valera to Monsignor Paschal Robinson, 9.7.35, FAK 1280. De Valera characterised Cohalan as an influence potentially subversive of both Church and State: 'His Lordship is not ignorant of the existence here of elements which, if encouraged, would create a state of intermittent internal revolution, and he must surely perceive that his statements might be regarded as giving a certain moral justification to the efforts of those who desire to overthrow the State. The example of other countries should warn His Lordship that the danger to the Church and to our whole Catholic tradition would, in such circumstances, be just as great as the danger to the State'. Ibid. De Valera's claim that Cohalan's sermons implied that the State in 1933, as personified by the government, was 'one of several rival political factions', is profoundly ironic. He and his followers had regarded the Free State in much the same light.

[214] Cohalan to Robinson, 24.7.35, FAK 1280. Cohalan was not the only cleric who believed that de Valera was vulnerable on majority rule. Applauding his commitment to it in 1933, Father Connolly, editor of *Studies*, speculated that 'if he had accepted that principle in 1922, how different the history of the last ten years would have been'. P.J. Connolly, SJ to M.J. Browne, 16.10.33, GDA.

seem entitled to the same consideration as any other party'.[215] At Confirmation in Kinvara in 1933, O'Doherty, condemning the IRA, exposed the entire Republican tradition to scornful abuse, describing Tone as 'a cut-throat' and Emmet as one 'who walked the streets of Dublin at the head of a rabble'.[216] In the dioceses of these two bishops, those collecting money for Fianna Fáil seem to have presented particular problems. In 1935, O'Doherty considered it necessary to invoke against such collectors a Maynooth Statute forbidding collections for secular purposes at church doors, within church grounds or at church gates. When his orders were disregarded, he could not 'but come to the conclusion that this abuse of the Church law was deliberately organised by those responsible for the Fianna Fáil collection'.[217] There was a more serious incident in a County Limerick parish in 1934. The local Parish Priest complained to the bishop that when a Fianna Fáil collection was in progress, he had asked the collectors to alter their position. When this request was not complied with, and when the priest attempted to move the table himself, 'he was assaulted with such violence as to be thrown to the ground, and when he had arisen, the assault was repeated with the same result'. The Vicar-General of the diocese told the parishioners that what had occurred was 'the evil fruit of an evil tree', and that those in charge of Fianna Fáil 'must be held responsible' for the events.[218]

One aspect of Fianna Fáil discourse, its occasionally strident anglophobia, was a matter of concern to a number of bishops, who feared that Irish missionary endeavour might somehow suffer as a result. A similar concern may well have motivated Pius XI in October 1932 when he told the Irish representative at the Vatican that 'England has been patient with Ireland' and that it was the duty of all governments to strive for peace.[219] It is unlikely that many of the bishops shared the sentiments expressed by P.J. Little in February 1933: 'We can now say a fond farewell to England. And let us hope that we shall see the British Empire going down amidst the laughter of the Irish people.'[220] Few of them would have rejoiced with Seán T. O'Kelly five years later that Ireland, under Fianna Fáil, had 'whipped John Bull every time'.[221] From an episcopal point of view, the authentic note was that sounded by Richard Mulcahy, who, in response to O'Kelly, argued

[215] *Irish Press*, 12.2.34.
[216] *East Galway Democrat*, 27.5.33.
[217] *Irish Press*, 23.5.35.
[218] Father O'Gorman to Bishop Keane, 18.6.34, LKDA.
[219] See Keogh, *Ireland and the Vatican*, p. 100.
[220] *Waterford News*, 3.2.33.
[221] *The Irish Times*, 9.6.38.

that 'if there was one power in Europe whose strength was important to the maintenance of Christianity, it was Great Britain . . . If Great Britain was injured, not alone European civilisation, but Christianity itself, would be struck a blow from which it would be difficult to recover'.[222] It was in this spirit that Bishop Morrisroe asked 'ultra-Nationalists' to remember that 'Christian missionaries in the past, like traders, have found security beneath the folds of the British flag'. If, perhaps as a result of what men like Little were joyfully predicting, 'protection were not forthcoming from the same source in the future, it was to be hoped that the Free State would arrange with friendly Powers for the safety of its citizens'.[223]

In 1937, the year of his inauguration of an Irish Republic in all but name, de Valera was able to gratify the somewhat un-Republican desires of a Prince of the Church. In February of that year, MacRory, through an intermediary, let de Valera know that in all states where there is a Nuncio, 'Cardinals hold the rank of Prince, ranking second only to the Head of the State'. As an illustration of such status, it was pointed out that Cardinals in Italy travelled without charge of any kind and that two reserved compartments were placed at their disposal with two aides-de-camp, one a soldier in uniform. Furthermore, 'the Vatican regards with special favour privileges given to Cardinals, taking them as shown to the Holy See itself'. MacRory did not seek the status of an Italian Cardinal; he merely wanted to be allowed 'to enter An Saorstát by motor car without the formality of entering into bond, or reporting to the Frontier Posts at entry or exit'.[224] De Valera was glad to tell MacRory that his request 'would receive immediate attention'. Six days after de Valera's receipt of the request, the Revenue Commissioners granted MacRory the desired facilities. He was now free to enter the Free State 'by motor car at all times and by any road', without complying with normal regulations.[225]

De Valera's gesture of respect for the most senior Catholic churchman may be seen as one among many tokens of the strong links he and his party had forged with the Church. By 1937, Fianna Fáil had provided compelling evidence that it was as soundly Catholic, as reliable on national as well as social questions, as Cumann na nGaedheal had ever been. After 1936, it had become as intolerant of IRA militarism as the most outspoken of the bishops. Here the turning-point was the murder at his home in Skibbereen, Co. Cork on 24 March 1936 of

[222] Ibid., 11.6.38.
[223] *Irish Press*, 3.1.35.
[224] Monsignor H. Tohill to the Surveyor of Customs and Excise, Dundalk, 18.2.37. Copy to de Valera, NAI S 9637.
[225] P.S. Ó Muineachán to Tohill, 24.2.37, NAI S 9637.

Vice-Admiral Somerville, who had been helping young men to enlist in the British Navy. A month later, John Egan, a member of the IRA, was shot as a traitor in Dungarvan. De Valera responded by invoking Cosgrave's 1931 legislation to outlaw the IRA and imprison its Chief of Staff, Maurice Twomey.[226] In his denunciation of the murder of Somerville, Bishop Casey of Ross declared that he had 'long been convinced that most of the present troubles of our people are a divine judgment on past crimes'.[227] De Valera was now in a position to redeem himself in clerical eyes for whatever might have been his own share of guilt for these past crimes, which some bishops who commented on the matter in 1922 believed was considerable.[228] In 1936, he answered critics who accused him of treating Republicans much as Cosgrave had during the Civil War by using arguments and language remarkably similar to what had been deployed against him and his fellow-Republicans during that period. His reply to the furious onslaught of Mary MacSwiney was characteristic. 'Do you not admit', he asked her, 'that in every community there must be some authority to prevent and punish murder? Or do you suggest that the protection of life and the prevention of crime must wait until the community is satisfied with its political status?'[229] Some of his public comments at the time, particularly those in his speech at Enniscorthy in August 1936, were reminiscent of the warnings issued to him and his associates in the 1922 Pastoral. 'If any one section of the community', he pointed out, 'could claim the right to build up a political army, so could another, and it would not be long before this country would be rent asunder by rival military factions . . . if a minority tries to have its way by force against the will of the majority, it is inevitable that the majority will resist by force, and this can only mean Civil War'.[230] Those bishops still alive who had signed the 1922 Pastoral must have been gratified by de Valera's perfect acquiescence in their views, however belated.

[226] Dwyer, *De Valera*, p. 190; J. Bowyer Bell, *The Secret Army* (London, 1970), pp. 155–6.
[227] *Irish Independent*, 30.3.36.
[228] For comments in this sense by Bishop Mulhern and Bishop Fogarty, for example, see Chapter Three above.
[229] De Valera to Mary MacSwiney, 22.6.36. MacSwiney Papers, UCDA.
[230] *National Discipline and Majority Rule: Three Speeches by Eamon de Valera*, 1936, p. 3.

CHAPTER SIX

REPUBLICANS LEFT AND RIGHT, 1926-1937

I

On 9 March 1926, five hundred Sinn Féin delegates assembled for a special Ard Fheis in the Rotunda in Dublin to debate an issue which had been increasingly preoccupying the minds of party members: under what circumstances, if any, should Republican deputies attend the Southern and Northern parliaments. De Valera proposed that once the oaths of admission to the two parliaments were removed, it then became a question, 'not of principle, but of policy, whether or not Republican representatives should attend these assemblies'. An amendment proposed by the Vice-President, Michael O'Flanagan, now a suspended priest, asked the delegates to agree that it was 'incompatible with the fundamental principles of Sinn Féin' and 'injurious to the honour of Ireland' to send representatives to 'any usurping legislature set up by English law in Ireland'.[1] It has been plausibly suggested that de Valera encouraged those who had been converted to his point of view in the course of the proceedings to vote for the O'Flanagan amendment as their cumainn had instructed them, and against his own proposal, in order to have a suitable pretext for severing his links with Sinn Féin and founding his own party.[2] The O'Flanagan amendment was carried by five votes; de Valera announced his formal

[1] The texts of de Valera's and O'Flanagan's proposals are reproduced in *An Phoblacht*, 19.2.26.
[2] Peter Pyne, 'The New Irish State and the Decline of the Republican Sinn Féin Party, 1923-1926', *Éire-Ireland*, 1976, p. 59. Pyne suggests that had de Valera obtained majority support at the Ard Fheis, he would have retained the name 'Sinn Féin' for his organisation, while the dissenting minority would have been forced to establish a new party. Pyne based his conclusions on interviews with Lemass, James Ryan and Gerald Boland.

resignation from the Presidency of Sinn Féin at the end of the Ard Fheis on 11 March.[3] Fianna Fáil was formally inaugurated on 16 May.

The great majority of clerics who had helped to sustain de Valera as leader of Sinn Féin seem to have felt no unease at transferring their allegiance to Fianna Fáil. This is not surprising. Favourable clerical sentiment had encouraged him in the move towards constitutional politics which he had been contemplating since 1925. By March 1926, he knew that he had the support of influential churchmen whose opinions he respected, including Mannix, Hagan, Curran and Michael Browne of Maynooth, for his new departure.[4] O'Flanagan, to the relief of many clerical and lay supporters of Fianna Fáil, remained loyal to Sinn Féin.[5] Like many members of Fianna Fáil and of the greatly depleted Sinn Féin party, some of de Valera's clerical supporters hoped for harmony and cooperation between the two elements of the dissevered Republican family.[6] Indeed, some northern priests had entertained hopes that the fracture in Sinn Féin caused by the Treaty would be mended. Thomas Maguire, PP Aghaboy, Co. Monaghan and later of Newtownbutler, was one of these. He told a Fianna Fáil meeting in September 1927 that 'thinking the two wings of Sinn Féin would come together, he had remained silent for six years, but as they had not done so he thought it his duty to support Fianna Fáil'.[7] After his break with Sinn Féin, de Valera encouraged hopes of Republican unity. In a spirit of genuine or feigned magnanimity, he presented himself to the 46 Sinn Féin TDs on 28 March 1926 as one ready to endure the odium he would inevitably attract for compromising on the pure Republican ideal he had championed since the Treaty, while the idealists among them, who chose to stay with Sinn Féin, could continue to march under the flag of the Republic with their reputations and their values intact. He was prepared, he told them, 'to take the risks and go after the people'. If he went 'into the bog, on the bog road or other hard ground', he would expect to find the Sinn Féin faithful 'on the High Road' when he came out.[8] In Ennis in June 1926, at one of his earliest public meetings as leader of Fianna Fáil, he claimed that 'the only difference between what I propose and that to which others [Sinn Féin fundamentalists] are holding

---

[3] *An Phoblacht*, 16.4.26.
[4] See pp. 206–10, notes 294–306.
[5] See pp. 161–3, notes 97–101.
[6] See p. 285, note 164.
[7] *The Irish Times*, 8.9.27.
[8] B. Murphy, *Patrick Pearse and the Lost Republican Ideal* (Dublin, 1991), p. 162. Dr Murphy is quoting from the Minute Book of the Second Dáil, December 1923 to December 1926, in the Mortimer O'Kelly Collection.

on is that I recognise facts'. From his point of view, the essential fact
that Sinn Féin did not recognise was the difference between *de jure*
claims for a continuing Republic and the *de facto* position that the
Republic was dead or that it had ceased to have practical meaning.[9] In
March 1927, however, he was still sensitive to the need for Fianna
Fáil to preserve a united front with Sinn Féin. 'Do your best', he
wrote to Lemass and Boland from America, 'to see that no unnecessary
antagonisms or controversies are developed. Cooperation [with Sinn
Féin] will come when the proper time comes'.[10]

Whatever cooperation with Sinn Féin de Valera had in mind
would be on his own terms. The main purpose of his 1927 visit to
America was to gain control for Fianna Fáil of the funds donated to
the Republic during his tour of 1919–20. He had told members of the
Second Dáil on 23 May 1926 of his fears that American funds were
'going to be distributed to Sinn Féin and the Army' and that Fianna
Fáil was 'going to be cut off'.[11] Seán T. O'Kelly, who since 1924 had
been acting as his envoy in America,[12] worked to ensure that the
AARIR [13] would support de Valera's new party and its policy,
informing Mary MacSwiney in May 1926 that 'the big majority of
rank and file' Irish-Americans would favour Fianna Fáil.[14] O'Kelly's
task of consolidating Irish-American support for Fianna Fáil at the
expense of Sinn Féin was made easier by the arrival of Archbishop
Mannix in Chicago on 16 June 1926 for a Eucharistic Congress. A
Convention of the AARIR was taking place in the city at around the
same time. O'Kelly attended the Congress, met Mannix, and was
host at a reception in the Carnegie Hall, New York, for the
Archbishop, who made stirring speeches in support of de Valera, not
only there but in Boston, Philadelphia and other centres of Irish-
American population.[15] When Art O'Connor, who had replaced de
Valera as 'President of the Republic' arrived in America in July 1926
to put the Sinn Féin case, he found that Mannix and O'Kelly had
made his task futile. The visit of Mannix, he told Mary MacSwiney,

---

[9] De Valera's meeting in Ennis was on 29.6.26. The corrected typescript of his
speech is with Kathleen O'Connell's papers.
[10] De Valera to S. Lemass and G. Boland, 29.3.27. Kathleen O'Connell Papers.
[11] Murphy, *Patrick Pearse*, p. 168.
[12] In a 'Letter of Instructions' to O'Kelly dated 1.9.24, de Valera had given
O'Kelly 'full control of all delegations from Ireland seeking funds', made him his
own 'deputy and substitute' as Trustee of Dáil Éireann and given him the task of
improving the 'general condition' of the AARIR. FAK, 1471.
[13] The American Association for the Recognition of the Irish Republic.
[14] Seán T. O'Kelly to Mary MacSwiney, 26.5.26. MacSwiney Papers, UCDA,
P 48a/136(12).
[15] Murphy, *Patrick Pearse*, p. 169.

now the principal Sinn Féin strategist, 'was more than a godsend to them: its influence on the places he spoke cannot be estimated. The conjunction of a Catholic Congress and a Convention with a useful interval in between for receptions of a very distinguished Churchman is a new trial I suppose for our Catholic souls'.[16]

By the end of 1927, Fianna Fáil had displaced Sinn Féin as the effective voice of post-Treaty Republicanism. Many of the leading adherents of Sinn Féin continued to operate and speak in the tradition of Terence MacSwiney, in whose hunger-strike, as Patrick O'Farrell remarks, 'the most intense religious fervour and sacrificial ardour seemed happily and luminously united with the ultimate in revolutionary dedication'. From prison, O'Farrell reminds us, MacSwiney issued, not political statements but sermons, casting all that was happening in an orthodox Catholic religious mould'.[17] The discourse of Sinn Féin Republicans in the later twenties and in the thirties posited an identity between pure Republicanism and the purest forms of Catholic Christianity. In December 1929, in a letter to the Pope, the Sinn Féin 'government' noted with displeasure that Charles Bewley, the first Free State government representative to the Vatican, had presented papers of credence 'by which His Majesty the King . . . accredits me as Envoy Extraordinary and Minister Plenipotentiary to Your Holiness'. The letter informed the Pope that a properly accredited Irish representative at the Vatican must speak for all of Ireland, and receive his credentials 'from the Government of Ireland alone without reference to any alien or heretical monarch'. The 'government', out of reverence for the Catholic faith, did not want the forthcoming Eucharistic Congress to take place 'till a United Ireland could fittingly join in that great celebration'.[18] In February 1932, Mary MacSwiney wrote to the Pope to advise against the bestowal of Papal honours on Cosgrave. To honour a man who was a traitor to his county and a murderer of his fellow-countrymen would, she suggested, 'make papal honours a laughing-stock in Ireland'.[19] The suggestion that the Pope and the Irish Church authorities might have an

---

[16] 'X' [Art O'Connor] to Mary MacSwiney, 2.8.26. MacSwiney Papers, UCDA, P 48a/136 (11).

[17] *Ireland's English Question, Anglo-Irish Relations, 1534–1970* (New York, 1971), p. 290. O'Farrell quotes part of the prayer issued by MacSwiney from Brixton to his fellow hunger-strikers in Cork jail: 'O my God, I offer my pain for Ireland. She is on the rack. My God, Thou knowest how many times our enemies have put her there to break her spirit, but by Thy mercy, they have always failed'.

[18] Executive Council, Republic of Ireland to Pope Pius XI, 16.12.29. Private Possession.

[19] Mary MacSwiney to Pope Pius XI, 2.2.32, MacSwiney Papers P48a/59.

imperfect grasp of religious proprieties which were better understood by Sinn Féin has its counterpart in the notion that Sinn Féin Republicans were articulating the only authentic Irish political creed. The defect in this approach has been pointed out by Richard English, who suggests that 'for republican zealots in this period, self effectively became confused with nation; when describing the supposed qualities, ideals and aspirations of the Irish nation, they were in fact merely describing their own'.[20] On the other hand, neither majoritarian arguments nor imputations of solipsism could have disturbed the faith of those who lived by the gospel of the Easter Rising and through it had come to feel at best only a qualified respect for democratic majorities.

By the beginning of the thirties, as Fianna Fáil was progressing steadily to power, Sinn Féin had become little more than a marginal grouping, lacking constructive ideas and operating in an increasingly shadowy world. The 1931 Ard Fheis of the party illustrates the extent of its decline since the mid-twenties. While between 400 and 500 delegates had voted on the de Valera–O'Flanagan proposals in 1926, the most important division of 1931, on whether members of the IRA should be eligible for membership of Sinn Féin, was decided by 35 votes to 3. It is significant that much of the time of the Ard Fheis was devoted to the discussion of religious and moral issues, some of these having no practical political import. O'Flanagan, still enduring understandable episcopal displeasure, was surprised that negotiations were going on between the Second Dáil, the Pope, and the Irish bishops in connection with the Eucharistic Congress, mainly on the subject of the possible appointment of Cardinal Bourne of Westminster as Papal Legate to the event. O'Flanagan could see little point in discussing such matters with either the Papacy or the Irish episcopacy. 'The Pope', he suggested, 'was just as much an enemy of Ireland as Cardinal Bourne, and as far as the Irish bishops were concerned, they were still as unrepentant as they were in 1922 when their men were out fighting for a Republic'. The Pope was vigorously defended against this priestly assault by the new President, Brian O'Higgins, in language perhaps odd for a Republican. O'Higgins could not believe that the Pope 'who was the Vicar on earth of the King of Peace and the King of Love, could be the enemy of any country on earth'. He was not prepared to extend either political or personal tolerance to O'Flanagan's anti-clerical oratory. He could not, he declared, 'stand on any platform with Fr O'Flanagan while he made such statements. That would be his attitude in the future. He would refuse, in public and in private, to be

[20] 'Paying no heed to public clamor, Irish Republican solipsism in the 1930s', *IHS*, November 1993, p. 438.

associated with Fr O'Flanagan'. Mary MacSwiney, whose influence over the minds of delegates was evident throughout the proceedings, told the Ard Fheis that the Second Dáil had taken a firm line with the bishops over their possible role in the 'new terror' against Republicans planned by the government. The bishops were being asked if they considered that the government's 'proposed murder campaign' was likely to afford a proper atmosphere for the Eucharistic Congress. The members of the Second Dáil had also suggested to the Hierarchy that the newest offensive against Republicans 'was a deliberate plan on the part of the Freemason masters of the Free State junta to create a state of affairs in which the holding of the Eucharistic Congress would be impossible'.

It is clear from all accounts of the proceedings of the Ard Fheis that both the members of the Second Dáil and the Sinn Féin membership in general were anxious to present themselves as sound Catholics. The Second Dáil members were clearly troubled by the growing radical tendencies of the IRA leadership, and, as Mary MacSwiney told the Ard Fheis, they 'deprecated any attempt to promote class distinctions and class warfare'. It must have been equally reassuring for the bishops to read that 'on the proposal of Mr J. Fowler, seconded by the Hon. Miss Albinia Brodrick, a resolution was adopted in which the Ard Fheis dissociated itself from anti-Christian propaganda'.[21] Senior members of Sinn Féin shared the value-systems of the bishops on spiritual, moral, cultural and social questions. They also had a profound veneration for the institutional Church, as Brian O'Higgins demonstrated at the Ard Fheis, in spite of what they saw as the occasional

---

[21] *Irish Press*, 5.10.31. Bowyer Bell remarks that 'the irreversible decline [of Sinn Féin] began in 1929 with the death of Austin Stack . . . Although there were still seventy-one branches and some good as well as obstinate people, Sinn Féin was clearly a spent force. The government of the Republic still functioned but on such a high plane of moral righteousness that few could see the point. To the cynical it seemed only to provide a platform for the shrill lecturing of Mary MacSwiney and the disgruntled rumbling of J.J. O'Kelly'. *The Secret Army* (London, 1972), p. 99. The Hon. Albinia Brodrick (1861–1955) was daughter of Viscount Midleton and sister of Lord Midleton, the leader of the Southern Unionists. According to Hubert Butler, she considered it her duty to atone for the sins of her ancestors. She dressed as an Irish countrywoman, adopted an Irish version of her name (Gobnait Ní Bhrudair), and built a hospital for the sick poor of Kerry. She vehemently opposed the Treaty, was imprisoned in the North Dublin Union, and released after 15 days on hunger-strike. She nursed wounded Republicans during the Civil War. In the course of this service, she was shot and wounded by Free State troops. She remained loyal to Sinn Féin after the foundation of Fianna Fáil, founding her own newspaper, *Irish Freedom/Saoirse na h-Éireann* in 1926, and editing it from 1933 to 1937, when it ceased publication. See Pádraig Ó Loinsigh, *Gobnait Ní Bhrudair* (Dublin, 1997).

political aberrations of its leaders. They showed themselves just as concerned as any of the bishops to preserve Ireland from the 'floods of immorality poured into this country from England'.[22] Mary MacSwiney's frequent pronouncements on these issues might just as easily have been made by a bishop or a crusading priest. A Republican government, she asserted, would not tolerate a 'new invasion of Ireland' by the indecent literary productions of her decadent neighbour, 'to the detriment of the religion and morals of the rising generation'. In the new Republic, 'being free as well as Catholic, they would scorn the cant that pretends it is broad-minded to admit every unclean thing'.[23] Her anglophobia and her devotion to Catholic principles are happily reconciled in her treatment of these topics. She attacks the 'Baden-Powell Organisation' for corrupting young Irish minds with the 'English pagan idea of Honour' when what they need is 'guidance of conscience and respect for Catholic principles'.[24] She regarded the teachings of Dr Marie Stopes on birth-control as 'not suitable food for Irish Catholic and Christian girls'.[25]

The attitudes of some leading Sinn Féin members to the emergence of a Republican government in Spain and to the subsequent Civil War there illustrate the essentially conservative Catholic outlook of the party. On this question, J.J. O'Kelly and Brian O'Higgins found themselves on the same side as the bishops, General O'Duffy and the *Irish Independent*, while the only senior member of the party to support the Spanish Republic was O'Flanagan. In June 1931, following the recognition by the Free State government of the Spanish Republic, Arthur Clery explained why the great mass of traditional Irish Republicans did not welcome the new Spanish regime. The Republic that Pearse, Brugha, de Valera and the rest had fought for was, he argued, 'in substance a Catholic Republic'. In all the phases of the Irish Civil War and the war of liberation, 'with all its burnings and destruction of property, not a single church was injured, nor even any insult offered to a single monk or nun'. No Irish Republican leader would have sanctioned such proceedings. In Spain, on the other hand, sacrilegious acts were being performed by Republicans under the direction of Freemasons. As Clery saw it, 'the great danger before Ireland was that in some such crisis as the Spanish one, 'it should be dragged in the wake of England and its Press into a situation unfitting to a Catholic people'.[26] On behalf of Irish Republicans, Mary MacSwiney

[22] Mary MacSwiney in *An Phoblacht*, 8.3.30.
[23] Ibid.
[24] MacSwiney Papers, UCDA, P 48a/387 (7).
[25] *An Phoblacht*, 8.3.30.
[26] *The Leader*, Dublin, 6.6.31.

had already assured those who had doubts about their Catholic orthodoxy that even those among them who were demanding 'a complete revolution of the social system' were 'but preaching the recent Encyclical of Pope Pius XI', while Republicans in general 'are as strong and as effective opponents of an anti-God campaign as any section in Ireland or out of it'.[27]

O'Flanagan seemed to revel in taking public positions which were in conflict with orthodox Catholic ones. While clergymen were alerting Irish people to the menace of communism, O'Flanagan was suggesting that the Soviet system might, after all, have something to recommend it. In August 1925, *An Phoblacht* published an article of his in which he wondered whether the Irish Republic might be a Bolshevik Republic. He believed that the communist system was 'one of the most interesting experiments in government in the history of the world', likened communistic principles to those of religious orders, and urged that the Russian people 'get a fair chance to test their theory of government without any unfair or undue influence from any quarter'.[28] In the same year, a large number of people were held up in O'Connell Street, Dublin, by the appearance on a platform of O'Flanagan and James Larkin, both of whom addressed a meeting 'called to support the people of China in their fight against imperialist forces'. O'Flanagan expressed pleasure at being associated for the first time on the same platform with Larkin. 'If', he declared, 'there was one man in their midst who was a true follower of Christ, that man was Jim Larkin'. While he would like to see 'a combination between the people of Ireland and those of China, he would prefer to have a combination between the working classes all over Ireland, in town and country'. There was, he suggested, 'no law of property in front of a starving people . . . because the rights of humanity are higher than the rights of property'. Larkin was gratified 'to have one of the Lord's anointed giving him a blessing', affirmed that 'the hope of the people of the world and the freedom of the human race' rested upon Russia and China, and concluded that the British Empire was 'the curse of the world'.[29] In 1926, O'Flanagan spoke with Peadar O'Donnell, Maud Gonne, Charlotte Despard and Bob Stewart of the Scottish Communist Party in a commemoration of the anniversary of Lenin's death.[30] In December 1936, he told a meeting called in support of the Spanish Republic that the Civil War in Spain was between the

[27] MacSwiney Papers, UCDA, P 48a/44(5)
[28] *An Phoblacht*, 8.3.35.
[29] *Irish Independent*, 21.8.25.
[30] Ibid., 8.2.26.

'rich privileged classes and the rank and file of the poor'; this caused him to be described as one of 'the reds' Irish friends'.[31]

II

The conflict between the Church and the IRA, which had abated in intensity with the ending of the Civil War, revived in the late twenties when significant elements of the IRA began to advocate radical solutions to social and economic problems. They thus incurred a double ecclesiastical censure, compounding the political crimes which had led to their excommunication in 1922 with the new and, in the eyes of many churchmen, more serious one of attempting to promote communism. Peadar O'Donnell [32] was the single greatest inspirational force behind radical Republicanism in the twenties and thirties, and since he came to personify the Republican left, he attracted wide-spread clerical hostility.[33] It was he who successfully proposed the resolution at the November 1925 Convention of the IRA calling on the membership to sever its connection with de Valera's shadow Republican government and with the Second Dáil, and to act under an independent Executive.[34] The main defect of the post-Treaty Republican leadership, as O'Donnell saw it, was its social conservatism: he believed that its failure to produce a radical programme of social and economic reform which might win mass support for the Republic would ensure its ultimate defeat. He worked to make the IRA the social conscience of Republicanism, and through it to transform the Republican movement into a radical revolutionary alliance. The Republican figure from the immediate past to whom O'Donnell looked for inspiration in his enterprise was Mellows, 'the lone socialist within the leadership'.[35] The reputation of Mellows as a Republican radical is largely based on some sketchy notes he made on the political situation during his imprisonment in 1922. In the course of

[31] *Irish Independent*, 4.12.36.
[32] O'Donnell was born in 1893 into a small-farming family near Dungloe, Co. Donegal. He trained as a teacher, but abandoned teaching in 1917 to become a full-time organiser for the Irish Transport and General Workers' Union. He joined the IRA in 1919, and left his union job to involve himself full-time in IRA activities. At the end of the War of Independence he was in command of the 2nd Brigade of the Northern Division of the IRA. He opposed the Treaty, was captured following the battle for the Four Courts in 1922, and remained in jail until he escaped in 1924. He edited *An Phoblacht* from 1926 to 1930.
[33] O'Donnell gives examples of this hostility in *There Will Be Another Day* (Dublin, 1963).
[34] Bowyer Bell, *Secret Army*, pp. 70–1.
[35] Charles Townshend, *Political Violence in Ireland* (Oxford, 1983), p. 363.

these, he expressed an approving interest in what the *Workers' Republic*, the newspaper of the small Communist Party of Ireland, had to say about the future course of Republican economic policy. 'Under the Republic', it suggested, 'all industry will be controlled by the State for the workers' and farmers' benefit. All transport, railways, canals, etc., will be operated by the State – the Republican State – for the benefit of the workers and farmers. All banks will be operated by the State for the benefit of Industry and Agriculture, not for the purposes of profit-making . . . the lands of the aristocracy (who support the Free State and the British Connection) will be seized and divided amongst those who can and will operate it [*sic*] for the Nation's benefit'. Mellows noted that the IRA Executive had already formulated a policy on land which conformed closely to what the Communist Party had in mind; it had adopted a scheme for the 'confiscation and distribution' of 'demesnes and ranches'. Mellows believed that Republicans must exploit unemployment, starvation and the grievances of workers. 'The situation created by all these', he argued, 'must be utilised for the Republic. The position must be defined: Free State – Capitalism and Industrialism – Empire. Republic – Workers – Labour'.[36]

O'Donnell followed Mellows in utilising, if not exploiting, a major social and political issue for Republican purposes when, in 1926, in his native Donegal, he launched a movement against the payment of land annuities to Britain.[37] This was one way of converting Republican idealism to practical uses, and, as O'Donnell hoped, of gaining widespread popular support for a movement which had tended to lose itself in abstractions. 'To talk of nationhood', he argued, 'as something outside the people on which they are to rivet their eyes and struggle towards is wrong'. He was convinced that 'the hard-pressed peasantry and the famishing workless are the point of assembly'.[38] O'Donnell did not see the IRA as the sole vehicle for Republican radicalism. He wanted to influence all Republican groupings, including Fianna Fáil, in the same direction. He explained to Mary MacSwiney, who was anxious to preserve Republicanism from the politics of the class struggle, that the agitation in which he was engaged was bound to encourage Fianna Fáil to take up the same cause as the price of its survival. His method of influencing such an organisation as Fianna Fáil, he told her, was 'to raise issues behind it and force it either to

[36] Mellows's notes, dated 26.8.22 were published by the Provisional Government in 1922 for its own propaganda purposes under the title, *Correspondence of Mr Eamon de Valera and others*. There is another transcription of Mellows's prison notes in C.D. Greaves, *Liam Mellows and the Irish Revolution* (London, 1971), pp. 363ff.
[37] He provides an account of this movement in *Another Day*.
[38] *An Phoblacht*, 25.3.27.

adjust itself so as to ride the tidal wave or get swamped'. If the radical Republicanism of the IRA aroused national enthusiasm, then, he argued, 'Fianna Fáil would either have to rearrange itself to stand for the people's demand or it would be swept as wreckage around the steps of the Viceregal Lodge'.[39] Fianna Fáil did, indeed, rearrange itself in response to the success of O'Donnell's agitation, but de Valera had no intention of compromising his hard-won credit with a Church which was notably conservative on issues of land and property by identifying himself with the extreme agrarian radicalism of elements in the IRA. In parts of the West and South, however, members of Fianna Fáil collaborated with the IRA in the creation of an 'Anti-Tribute League' and in getting County Councils to pass resolutions against the payments of annuities to England.[40]

Such activities inevitably drew the fire of churchmen. O'Donnell recalled that during his anti-annuities campaign in Clare, Bishop Fogarty 'alerted his diocese and for the better protection of his flock he put a new question in the Catechism: Is it a sin not to pay land annuities? Children for Confirmation were warned that the answer must be spoken clearly: It is a sin not to pay land annuities'.[41] O'Donnell also had to contend with the disapproval of his own bishop in 1928. 'It did not help at all', he pointed out, 'that His Lordship, Dr MacNeely, Bishop of Raphoe, took it into his head to add his voice to the voices aimed at me, even though he made a fair enough attack for he did not take the crozier to me; just a bare, hard-knuckle rap'. 'Pay your rents and don't heed Peadar O'Donnell' was the Bishop's slogan.[42] In December 1928, after resolutions had been passed by the County Councils of Clare, Galway, Kerry and Leitrim against the payment of annuities to England and demanding suspension of legal action for arrears, Bishop Fogarty issued a 'stern rebuke' to those public bodies for endorsing the view 'that farmers were neither legally nor morally bound to pay their annuities'. Fogarty remarked that 'it is not for enunciating Bolshevist principles of this kind that the County Councils are maintained by the rates of the people'. He found it 'very regrettable to see men who should know better propounding subversive principles of that kind, which strike at the very basis of social life'.[43]

De Valera took care to assure the Church and those electors who might have been suspicious of his motives in the annuities campaign

---

[39] Ibid., 29.4.27.
[40] H. Patterson, *The Politics of Illusion, Republicanism and Socialism in Modern Ireland* (Dublin, 1989), p. 39.
[41] O'Donnell, *Another Day*, p. 109.
[42] Ibid., p. 66.
[43] *Irish Independent*, 19.12.28.

that his party was not Bolshevist in tendency. In his election address of 1927, he pointed out that 'the sinister design of aiming at bringing about a sudden revolutionary upheaval, with which our opponents choose to credit us, is altogether foreign to our purpose and programme'.[44] It was characteristic of de Valera that he should want to present the issue of non-payment of annuities to Britain as a question of national honour and national grievance, affecting not merely poorer farmers but the great majority of those living on the land. At the Fianna Fáil Ard Fheis in 1927, a Mayo priest proposed a resolution, which was passed, calling on the Land Commission in urgent cases where writs had been issued and seizure or sale was imminent not to take legal action where the farmer was in a position to pay his arrears by instalment.[45] This attitude was bound to be more pleasing to the Church than O'Donnell's 'No Rent' slogans.[46] In the late twenties and early thirties, however, de Valera took a public stand that appeared to be much closer to O'Donnell's position. In this he was influenced by the considerable support Fianna Fáil derived from Western small farmers and landless labourers. In the 1932 General Election campaign in Mayo, de Valera introduced his own class-war element into the debate when he wondered why the rich lands of the large farmers had not been divided in such counties as Meath, where 5 per cent of the farmers owned 41 per cent of the land, and Tipperary where 485 persons owned 200,000 acres.[47] By late 1931, the campaign to withhold land annuities from Britain had become more widely respectable than it had been when O'Donnell launched it in 1926. In November 1931, the *Irish Press* carried a front page report that 'His Grace, the Most Rev. Dr E.J. Hanna, Archbishop of San Francisco, and 362 prelates and secular and regular priests of California, are signatories to a petition to President Hoover requesting the inclusion in a moratorium on inter-Governmental payments of the £5,000,000 a year paid by the Free State Government to Great Britain'. The petition asked that the inclusion be 'without prejudice to the claim of the Irish people that the said payment is not justly due from them to Great Britain'.[48] This latter interpretation of Irish attitudes is substantially the same as that offered by Fianna Fáil in its 1932 election manifesto, which claimed that the British were not entitled to the annuities 'in law'.[49] It must have been encouraging to the Republican

[44] Earl of Longford and T.P.O'Neill, *Eamon de Valera*. Dublin, 1970, p. 261.

[45] *The Nation*, 3.12.27.

[46] See O'Donnell, *Another Day*, p. 92.

[47] *Mayo News*, 6.2.32.

[48] *Irish Press*, 26.11.31.

[49] *Irish Independent*, 11.2.32.

radicals as it was to Fianna Fáil to learn that a substantial body of Californian clergymen believed that they, and not the Free State Government, reflected the wishes of the Irish people on the vital question, and that it might not after all, whatever Bishop Fogarty might say, be a sin not to pay land annuities.

Despite determined episcopal opposition, O'Donnell did not entirely lack clerical support. In the winter of 1928, when his Donegal campaign against the annuities collapsed, he launched a new one in East Galway on the invitation of John Fahy, Curate of Bullaun, near Loughrea. Fahy was, according to O'Donnell, 'a fine propagandist'; he and a group he gathered around him, which included the O.C. of the local IRA unit, composed an anti-rent catechism which O'Donnell published in *An Phoblacht*, and which was also recited in public houses.[50] His real talent as a propagandist lay in his choice of the kind of direct action that was bound to ensure the widest publicity for his cause. On 18 February 1929, he and some of his associates retrieved seized cattle from the pound in Galway. A week later, when a bailiff from Loughrea seized two cattle from a farm near the town to satisfy a decree obtained against the owner by the Land Commission for unpaid annuities, Fahy and some local men rescued the cattle from the bailiff, who was told not to follow the cattle as 'something might happen to him'.[51] When Fahy was served with a summons to appear in court in March, he declared that he would not attend because he was a Republican. In April, he was arrested and brought before Loughrea District Court. Here he conducted his own case, making a long statement in the course of which he declared the State 'guilty of high treason against the Irish nation in bringing him into that unlawful assembly [the court] in Republican territory under the jurisdiction of an Irish Republican government'.[52] The six weeks he spent in Galway Jail brought him to national attention. His bishop, Dr Dignan, made a public statement suggesting that the responsibility for

[50] O'Donnell, *Another Day*, p. 94. The nature of the catechism may be gathered from the following: 'How did England establish a claim to the land of Ireland? By robbery. What is rent? Rent is a tribute of slavery enforced by the arms of the robber-landlord. What is a landlord? A landlord is a descendant of a land-robber. Who pays rent to landlords? Only slaves. What is a bailiff? A bailiff is a land-robber's assistant. What should be done with a bailiff . . . with a landlord?' Ibid.
[51] I owe most of my information on Father Fahy to Dr Brian S. Murphy, who was kind enough to let me see the typescript of his paper, 'The stone of Destiny: Fr John Fahy (1894–1969) and clerical radicalism in Ireland'. Dr Murphy's paper has since been published under the title 'The Stone of Destiny: Father John Fahy (1894–1969), Lia Fáil and Smallholder Radicalism in modern Irish Society', in Gerard Moran (ed.), *Radical Irish Priests, 1660–1970* (Dublin, 1998).
[52] *Roscommon Messenger*, 20.4.29.

the 'scandal and injury to religion' arising from the jailing of a priest rested with 'the Free State Government . . . which has decided to usurp the functions of the Bishop of Clonfert and also to violate Canon Law'.[53] A number of public bodies interested themselves in Fahy's case. Tuam Town Commissioners lodged a protest at his imprisonment.[54] Wicklow County Council called upon the Government 'to reconsider the question of the release of the Rev. Father Fahy', while the Council of the Tipperary South Riding called for his release. Some members of the Galway County Council Finance Committee were reluctant to attend the Catholic Emancipation ceremonies in June as long as he remained in jail. One member, who believed that he had been imprisoned 'for doing his duty', suggested that the episode meant that 'they were not emancipated and the Penal Laws were in force as they were 100 years ago'. A resolution was passed 'that the Council could not officially take part in the procession while Father Fahy is deprived of his faculties', the reference here being to the belief that he was not allowed to say Mass in jail.[55] By the time Fahy appeared in court in July, Bishop Dignan had persuaded him to apologise for his behaviour. As *An Phoblacht* put it, 'an order from his bishop secured his silence'.[56] Even the Republican Dignan found

[53] *An Phoblacht*, 16.5.29. In suggesting that the Free State authorities had violated Canon Law by trying and jailing Fahy, Dignan was invoking a central and ancient ecclesiastical precept. Since the twelfth century, the Church had been claiming that clergymen, by the privilege of their order (*privilegium fori* or 'benefit of clergy') were amenable to the sole jurisdiction of ecclesiastical courts, and that even clergymen arraigned for felony enjoyed the privilege of exemption from trial by a secular court. The medieval *privilegum fori*, prohibiting civil prosecution of a priest without ecclesiastical approval, was still part of the most recent (1917) Code of Canon Law. When Henry O'Friel, Secretary of the Department of Justice, visited Dignan to discuss Fahy's case, the bishop raised the *privilegium fori*, only to be told by O'Friel that this had no status in law under the British régime before 1921. Fahy was pleased to believe that his arrest and imprisonment 'would definitively expose the Free State as a protestant state under English tutelage rather than [as] the Catholic state it claimed to be'. See Dr Brian Murphy's paper referred to at note 51, p. 314 above. Dignan, believing that Fahy's case raised a significant, unresolved issue in Church-State relations, namely whether the Free State was Catholic in law, suggested a Church–State concordat to resolve the matter. See Einrí O'Friel to Minister [of Justice], 9.4.29, NAI D.F.A. S4(a). Two years later, during the Mayo Library controversy, Archbishop Gilmartin, in the course of an interview with Cosgrave's emissary Sir Joseph Glynn, also suggested that a Concordat might help to avoid further Church-State conflicts. Glynn's memorandum, 26.2.31, NAI S 2547 A.

[54] Ibid.

[55] Copies of the Wicklow and Tipperary resolutions are in the Blythe Papers, UCDA P24 /164(1)/164(3).

[56] *An Phoblacht*, 13.7.29.

Fahy's behaviour trying. The embarrassment caused to the Church by his cattle-driving and imprisonment was compounded by his publication of a pamphlet in which he held, 'as all decent Irishmen hold, that instead of buying back their own lands, the Irish people should take them back. To succeed, the people need only cease paying rents for the lands of which our forefathers were deprived by loot and robbery'.[57] Dignan did not, however, silence Fahy. Instead, he gave him written instructions that he must not discuss politics where two other people were present, and he sent him to Closetoken. 'There is', Peadar O'Donnell explains, 'a Closetoken in nearly every diocese, a ragged curacy which is a sort of place of punishment for priests who stumble'. Here, he and O'Donnell took up residence in a thatched cottage.[58]

Two years later, Fahy's career as a radical Republican entered a more extreme phase, when he became an active member of the IRA. At Easter 1931, he tried to recruit an Athenry man, later tried to buy machine guns from an army reservist in Loughrea, and in September 1931 told a clandestine parade of the Loughrea IRA company that he was 'out for overthrowing any Government that would be established in Ireland except the Irish Republican Government'. The Gardaí believed he was one of the most active IRA leaders in East Galway. He constantly associated with prominent IRA members, was frequently seen 'going around on a motor cycle with civilian cap and overcoat apparently organising for the IRA and other illegal movements', and spent time in the company of men allegedly committing serious crimes. The Gardaí were reluctant to act because he was a priest, and they seem to have believed that Dignan's Republican outlook inclined him to turn a blind eye to Fahy's activities. In the early thirties, Fahy became part of the unofficial Republican alliance with Fianna Fáil, appearing on a platform with de Valera in Portumna in January 1933. Like many radical Republicans, however, he gradually came to believe that de Valera had betrayed many of those who helped him to power. He was particularly disturbed by de Valera's firm dealings with IRA terrorism, his recognition of the King in the External Relations Act of 1936, and his failure to prosecute agrarian reform with the zeal that had been expected of him. In 1957, Fahy founded Lia Fáil, a radical smallholders' movement, against the background of the steady growth of large holdings at the expense of smaller ones over the first four decades of independence. His disillusionment with post-war Fianna Fáil governments caused him to regard de Valera and his ministers, particularly 'the Englishman's son,

[57] Quoted from Dr Murphy's article on Fr Fahy. See p. 314, note 51.
[58] O'Donnell, *Another Day*, p. 100.

Protestant Freemason Childers', as treasonable agents of a new generation of colonists who would eventually own Ireland and hold it for the British Empire.[59]

III

In 1931, when the IRA officially adopted a radical social and economic programme, it found itself in its most serious conflict with the combined forces of Church and State since the Civil War. In the course of that year, the IRA substantially increased its membership against a background of mounting agrarian unrest; with tens of thousands of farmers unable to pay annuities, there were widespread seizures of stock and even of land. The IRA paper *An tÓglach* commented in July 1931 on 'an amazing resurgence of feeling throughout the country', with the result that 'several companies and battalions have doubled and trebled their strength'. The IRA also became noticeably more militant, carrying out a number of officially authorised 'executions'. On 30 January, one of its own members was shot as a spy. On 20 March, a Gárda Superintendent who had worked to eliminate IRA drilling in South Tipperary was murdered; on 20 July, one of the witnesses in the Tipperary drilling case was shot.[60] On 15 February 1931, the General Army Convention committed the IRA membership to a new organisation of workers and working farmers, which was to be known as Saor Éire.[61] Those in the IRA who welcomed Saor Éire saw it as a radical alternative to Sinn Féin; it seemed to give a political purpose and direction to a movement which was gaining much of its publicity as an assassination squad. Its establishment also represented an attempt to win Republican support back from Fianna Fáil and to destabilize the Free State. Saor Éire was formally established on 3 May 1931, one of its chief organisers being Peadar O'Donnell. Seán MacBride was a member of the first National Executive. The first party congress, which promulgated a radically socialist constitution, was held in Dublin on 26 and 27 September. The three main objectives

---

[59] See p. 314, note 51.

[60] Bowyer Bell, *Secret Army*, pp. 104–9. These murders were the subject of an interview given by Frank Ryan at the offices of *An Phoblacht* to an English newspaper correspondent. Ryan declared that the shootings 'were not murder; they were acts of war'. He also claimed that the murdered Gárda superintendent had 'exceeded his duty. He went out of his way to persecute the IRA . . . the Civil Guard have no right to interfere in matters that do not concern them. If they ask for trouble they must not be surprised if they get it'. Cosgrave quoted Ryan's interview in the Dáil during the debate on the government's Public Safety Bill. *Dáil Debates*, 1931, XI, 34–6.

[61] T.P. Coogan, *The IRA* (London, 1970) p. 83.

of *Saor Éire* as set out in its draft constitution were to 'break the connection with England and secure for the Republic of Ireland free expression of its National Sovereignty; to vest all political power within the Republic in the working-class and working farmers; to abolish, without compensation, landlordism in land, fisheries and minerals'.[62] Other objectives included 'a State Monopoly in banking and credits' and in 'export and import services', and to have 'all forms of Public Inland Transport taken over by the State'.[63]

From the beginning, a substantial body of IRA members were not enthusiastic about either the aims or the prospects of the new movement. One of its supporters remarked that many right-wing officers, including the great majority of the Battalion commanders, were openly hostile, doing all they could to sabotage its growth.[64] Maurice Twomey, the Chief of Staff, was 'cautious, not only about entering constitutional politics, but also about the possibly damaging effects of any taint of Communism attaching to the movement'.[65] Coogan describes Twomey as 'a dedicated, right-wing Fenian, scrupulous in his religious observance', and suggests that most IRA men shared his 'strong Catholicism', one of the hazards their organisers most frequently encountered being 'identification by the local police, who would immediately notice their strange faces when they attended Mass in some small country village'. They would, however, 'never think of not going to Mass on account of this'.[66] Had the authorities in Church and State who were soon to denounce *Saor Éire* as a communist conspiracy known more about the dispositions of many of those involved in the movement, they might have been less fearful. Michael Price, a member of the National Executive,[67] was a socially conservative Catholic and did not mind saying so. Just before the IRA gave its

[62] Quoted from *Saor Éire: Draft Constitution and Rules*. Copy in the Kerry Diocesan Archive.

[63] A different formulation of the objectives of *Saor Éire* is given by Richard English in *Radicals and the Republic, Socialist Republicanism in the Irish Free State, 1925–1937* (Oxford, 1994), p. 127. English quotes from the Files of the Department of the Taoiseach, NAI S 5864 A.

[64] Bowyer Bell, *Secret Army*, p. 104.

[65] Coogan, *The IRA*, p. 84.

[66] Ibid., p. 85. For an example of similar risks run by conscientious Catholic members of the IRA during the Civil War, see the report on the experience of Volunteer Jack Keogh in the MacSwiney Papers. Here it is claimed that a priest of the Killaloe diocese heard Keogh's confession and then informed the Free State authorities that they might expect Keogh at mass for Communion the next morning. He was arrested when he turned up. The report describes the priest as 'a violent Free Stater' who had given evidence at the trial of another man who was sentenced to death. MacSwiney Papers, UCDA, P 48a/202.

[67] Coogan, *The IRA*, p. 84.

approval for the launching of *Saor Éire*, Price was defending the right to acquire and own property, supporting ecclesiastical insistence that 'the natural law demands the existence of private property', and sharing the vision of society, promoted in Papal Encyclicals, 'in which the greater part of citizens own land and capital in small quantities'.[68] Had churchmen been present at the September Congress, they might have almost found its tone reassuring, just as Frank Edwards, a left-wing IRA man from Waterford, found it thoroughly disappointing as a demonstration of radical intent. The organisers, Edwards recalled, got a County Council member from Clare [Hayes] as chairman . . . He startled everybody by commencing with a religious invocation. Then to cap it all, Fionan Breathnach stood up later and said we should adjourn the meeting as some wished to attend the All-Ireland in Croke Park that afternoon. It showed you how seriously they were taking their socialism'.[69]

The Government, however, took *Saor Éire* much more seriously than some of its own members appear to have done. The Garda Commissioner, Eoin O'Duffy, wanted the law strengthened. On 27 June 1931, he reported to the government that members of 'Irregular organisations and their followers treat the gardaí with absolute contempt; criminal suspects refuse to answer any questions and the ordinary citizen in the affected areas who, under normal conditions, would assist the gardaí to the utmost of his ability is through fear driven into silence.'[70] The Government employed much the same strategy in dealing with *Saor Éire* and the IRA in 1931 as it had in the desperate circumstances of October 1922. A combination of stringent public safety legislation and the enlistment of the bishops on the side of law and order was once more seen as the most effective remedy. On 11 September 1931, Cosgrave supplied Cardinal MacRory with detailed evidence of what he claimed was a conspiracy, on foot since 1929, which had as its object the overthrow of State institutions; the conspirators, he claimed, were in contact with international communist organisations 'which have their headquarters in, and are controlled by, Russia'. Cosgrave hoped that after MacRory had studied the evidence, he would be as concerned as he himself was 'as to the gravity of the situation', and, if he was, he might advise the bishops as a body to consider 'whether the most effective manner of dealing with the pernicious tendencies which are sapping the bases of all authority in this country would not be a joint episcopal action in the form of a

[68] *An Phoblacht*, 7.2.31.
[69] U. MacEoin (ed.), *Survivors* (Dublin, 1980), p. 6.
[70] O'Duffy Memorandum, NAI S 5864 B.

concise statement of the law of the Church in relation to the present issues, and the penalties attached to its violation'.[71] As an inducement to MacRory, Cosgrave underlined the moral dangers with which the conspiracy confronted 'innocent youth', since doctrines were now 'being taught and practised which were never before countenanced'. The influence of the Church alone, he told MacRory, 'will be able to prevail in the struggle'.[72]

On 14 October 1931, on the reassembly of the Dáil after the Summer recess, the Government introduced the Constitution Amendment Bill, which was, in effect, a Public Safety Bill, giving the Government sanction, now that the jury system had broken down, to establish a military tribunal with power to inflict the death penalty as a means of dealing with all political crime. The Executive Council also assumed the power to declare organisations unlawful. The measure became law on 17 October.[73] Three days later, the IRA, Saor Éire and ten other radical organisations were declared unlawful; Sinn Féin was exempted from this ban. The legislation was also used to censor the 'subversive' press: *An Phoblacht, Irish World, Workers' Voice, Irish Worker* and *Republican File* all had issues declared 'seditious' by the Military Tribunal.[74] Before proceeding with his Public Safety legislation, Cosgrave received assurances from a Dominican priest, M.P. Cleary of Tallaght, that the Special Powers tribunal was consonant with canon law.[75]

On 17 September 1931, the Government provided each of the bishops with its evidence for an IRA– Communist conspiracy, and its interpretation of the motives underlying the growing radical trend in Republicanism. This evidence was contained in a report submitted to the government by the Department of Justice under the heading, 'Alliance between the Irish Republican Army and Communists'. In his covering letter, Cosgrave told each bishop that 'a situation without parallel as a threat to the foundations of all authority has arisen'. The threat was directly associated by the Department of Justice with Saor Éire, which 'appears to mark the definite union of the Irish Republican Army with Communism in the State'. The Department could see benefits accruing to both the IRA and the Communists from this alliance: the IRA 'would lend the support of their military organisation

---

[71] Cosgrave to MacRory, 11.9.31, NAI S 5864 B.
[72] Ibid.
[73] Ronan Fanning, *Independent Ireland* (Dublin, 1983), p. 104.
[74] English, *Radicals and the Republic*, p. 144.
[75] Fanning, *Independent Ireland*, p. 104. The Labour Party opposed the measure. Two of its members, Anthony and Morrissey, were expelled for voting with the government. W. Moss, *Political Parties in the Irish Free State* (New York, 1933), p. 176.

to the Communists and in return the Communists supply to the Irish Republican Army as a potential recruit every man, who, whether from poverty or principle or mere love of agitation, is anxious to see the system of private property and private enterprise destroyed in this State'. At this point, the writer of the Department of Justice document seems to have entertained some doubts about the plausibility of an IRA–Communist alliance, and even advances considerations which might be thought to cast doubt on the existence of such an alliance. He correctly points out that 'there are in the Irish Republican Army men who dislike Communism' and is sure that there are, 'in Communistic circles men who regard the Irish Republican Army movement as merely sentimental, old-fashioned patriotism'. In the absence of a better reason for the troublesome alliance of two such doubtfully compatible movements, he is forced to the somewhat lame conclusion that 'a union has evidently been arranged on the basis that both parties will do their best to destroy the present order of things'. The writer is, perhaps, on surer ground when he examines the impulses behind the Republican move to the left. Few Republicans, he believes would, in 1931, imperil their lives and fortunes for the difference between a Republic and the existing Irish State: the motives for which they had fought the Civil War had lost much of their force. In order to perpetuate itself, therefore, the IRA had to look for supporters outside the tradition of Irish independence, and they found that other support 'in the widespread movement against the system of private property and private enterprise, which movement has Soviet Russia for its example, encouragement and assistance'. In 1929, it was observed that 'about six youths' were specially chosen by Peadar O'Donnell and others to go through a course 'in the technique of revolution' at the Lenin College, Moscow. One of these, Nicholas Boran, a worker in a small coal-mine, had, since his return from Moscow, 'formed a Communist club amongst his fellow-workers'.[76]

The government was aware that the surest means of winning wholehearted episcopal support for its suppression of radical elements was to suggest that these threatened the welfare and influence of the Church as much as the security of the State. The Department of Justice document told the bishops that of the four 'most influential leaders' of subversion, 'Bell, Fox and Stewart are atheists', while O'Donnell was 'openly anti-clerical', having in his latest book, *The Knife*, condemned 'in the strongest terms the influence of the Church, particularly the bishops, on Irish political development'. Twenty 'leading Irregulars' were associated with an Englishman named Ward,

[76] W. T. Cosgrave to Archbishop Byrne, 17.9.31, Byrne Papers, DAA.

who owned a Soviet bookshop in Winetavern Street where 'Red literature' was stocked. A great number of the books 'were anti-clerical and contained the most scandalous attacks on the Church and on all churches'. O'Donnell and his associates were trying to 'popularise Soviet rule' while there was reason to believe that Russell, MacBride, T.J. Ryan, Seán O'Farrell and other members of the Irish Republican Executive 'have been gained over to the Communist movement'.[77] Cosgrave also sent the bishops some choice specimens of the anti-clerical comment which had been appearing regularly in *An Phoblacht* during 1931. A letter from Peadar O'Donnell warned any priest backing landlordism that he would 'have to take his share of our attack on his friends'. O'Donnell further asserted that 'the majority of the priests and all the bishops disgraced themselves and us in 1922, and we paid for their shame in many a way-side murder and in the destruction of our movement for freedom'.[78] The writer of another letter complained that 'ecclesiasticism', which had nothing to do with 'spirituality or Christ's simple, beautiful teaching' was 'rampant in this country – has its tentacles fastened in every activity of our country's life . . . Look at Spain, Italy, Ireland, where ecclesiasticism dominates the national life and see its fruits – ignorance, poverty, slavery, tyranny!'[79]

The response of the bishops was in accord with the most favourable expectations of the government. On 18 October, the day after the Public Safety Bill became law, their joint Pastoral Letter was read in all the churches. They accepted Cosgrave's analysis of the motives and intentions of the IRA and Saor Éire without question. The Pastoral reads almost like a paraphrase of some portions of the documentary material furnished by Cosgrave. The IRA, although not mentioned by name, is described as a 'society of a militarist character, whose avowed object is to overthrow the State by force of arms'. Saor Éire is 'frankly Communistic in its aims', working to 'impose upon the Catholic soil of Ireland the same materialistic régime, with its fanatical hatred of God as now dominates Russia and threatens to dominate Spain'. The 'materialistic Communism' advocated by Saor Éire 'means a blasphemous denial of God and the overthrow of Christian civilisation'. It also meant 'class warfare, the abolition of private

---

[77] Ibid.

[78] *An Phoblacht*, 7.2.31.

[79] *An Phoblacht*, 21.2.31. In 1931, *An Phoblacht* was proposing radical solutions to dire social problems. An editorial of 7.2.31, headed 'Get out of the Slums', called on slum-dwellers to 'take over the half-empty houses of the well-to-do and the half-occupied public buildings and let the worse-housed of the workers move into them until decent accommodation has been built for them. If the workers must live six to a room, why not make the parasite class live likewise?'

property and the destruction of family life'. While the bishops did not fully accommodate Cosgrave by imposing ecclesiastical penalties on those who violated Church law by belonging to the IRA and Saor Éire, they declared the methods and principles of the former to be 'in direct opposition to the Law of God', and implicitly placed adherents of the latter outside the Christian fold.[80] In effect, the 1931 Pastoral marked the indefinite renewal of the sanctions imposed on IRA activists by the 1922 Pastoral, although with the passage of time some priests may not have been sure whether these sanctions still applied. In October 1942, the priest of a parish near Dundalk was visited by an IRA leader and asked to get private masses said for a companion killed in action. When the priest made it clear that he did not approve of IRA activities, his visitor explained that the sole object of the existence of his movement was 'to remove the Border and refrain from any damaging acts in the Free State'. The members had instructions from headquarters 'to receive Confession and Communion once per month'. The priest enquired 'tactfully' whether IRA members 'had got any enlightenment from headquarters about the censure of the bishops, banning them from sacraments'. To this the IRA officer replied that 'the ban existed when [Frank] Ryan and Peadar O'Donnell and other communists held sway', but that 'this influence was now removed, and the ban was now in abeyance'.[81] The priest sought the guidance of the Professor of Moral Theology at Maynooth, John McCarthy, who told him that 'active members of the IRA should not be absolved, unless they promise to sever their connection with the activities of that body'. It seemed to Professor McCarthy 'useless, in the face of the facts, to protest that these activities are confined to an attempt to remove the border', nor could he find 'any convincing argument to show that the bishops' ban has ceased to operate'. Indeed, he believed that the general law of the Church against secret societies might 'well be invoked against the IRA as at present constituted'.[82]

The combined offensive by Church and State caused widespread panic among supporters of Republican radicalism. The mistake made by the organisers of Saor Éire was to move from the relatively secure position of advocating national rights into the exposed ground of social revolution.[83] The speed with which the movement yielded to clerical assaults on its supposedly godless and alien ideology suggests not only that there were 'clear ideological constraints on the agrarian

---

[80] The Pastoral Letter is reproduced in full in *ICD*, 1932, pp. 623–5.
[81] Fr T. McConnell to Professor John McCarthy, 28.10.42, Author's possession.
[82] Professor John McCarthy to Fr T. McConnell, 31.10.42, Author's possession.
[83] Seán Cronin, *Frank Ryan and the Search for the Republic* (Dublin, 1980), p. 36.

radicalism of which people like O'Donnell had such high hopes',[84] but that Republican radicalism had very shallow roots. The bishops' public association of their movement with atheistic communism, with the overthrow of Christian civilisation and the destruction of family life, caused many Republicans to dissociate themselves from the Saor Éire project and to take their stand on the safer and more congenial platform of Catholic Nationalism. Even before the bishops made their pronouncement, the official organ of Republicanism was proclaiming the soundly Catholic temper of Irish patriots. 'Our churches', it declared, 'are full to overflowing with fervent young men. They love their religion and next to it, liberty'.[85] In a response to the Bishops' Pastoral, Mary MacSwiney was able to assert, from first-hand experience, that its authors had been utterly mistaken in their judgment of the membership of Saor Éire. She did not approve of the movement, since, like the bishops, she considered it 'a bad national policy to divide the people of Ireland on a class basis'. She did, however, know the men who belonged to Saor Éire, whom the bishops had accused of wanting to banish religion from Ireland. 'Most of them', she asserted, 'are excellent practising Catholics and not one single one of my acquaintance would stand for an anti-Christian State or for a materialistic regime with its fanatical hatred of God'. They did, however, 'stand against the present iniquitous social system', and in this they had the moral support of the 'principles of social justice laid down in the encyclical of Pope Leo XIII', to the implementation of which the Irish bishops appeared somewhat indifferent.[86]

The more common view of Saor Éire, and the one the bishops shared and enforced on the public mind, was that expressed in a provincial newspaper which had supported the small farmer agitation organised by O'Donnell. The *Mayo News* was appalled that the organisers of Saor Éire claimed continuity with the 1916 Rising. Patrick Pearse, it declared, placed 'the cause of the Irish Republic under the protection of the Most High God' while 'the engineers of the new Workers' Republic at their first conference sent fraternal greetings to the Russian Soviets whose proclaimed policy is anti-God, who excel in obscene caricatures of the Blessed Virgin. The Proclamation on which Saor Éire takes its stand was drafted, not by Patrick Pearse, but by Mr Stalin in Moscow'. The *Mayo News* found the whole programme of Saor Éire 'foreign as well as anti-Christian . . . against every tradition and principle of Irish nationality'.[87] In the face of episcopal

[84] Patterson, *Politics of Illusion*, p. 52.
[85] *An Phoblacht*, 17.10.31.
[86] See MacSwiney Papers, UCDA, P 48a/404 (17); P 48a/47 (1).
[87] *Mayo News*, 10.10.31.

denunciation of radical Republicanism, people like Eamonn Corbett, an IRA veteran who had played a notable part in the agitation against annuities, felt it necessary to declare that 'many of us are indifferent or hostile to communistic ideas and propaganda but feel very strongly on the national question'.[88] De Valera did all he could to ensure that Fianna Fáil would not be tainted by suggestions of intimate links between Republicanism and Bolshevism; he argued that whatever revolutionary tendencies existed in Ireland were inspired by pressing social and economic problems. For these, Fianna Fáil would offer a solution 'having no reference whatever to any other country' but springing from 'our own traditional attitude towards life, a solution that is Irish and Catholic'.[89] The Saor Éire episode illustrated the determination of the bishops to deal vigorous and effective blows against forms of Republicanism which appeared to conflict with Catholic principles or to be at odds with native tradition. It is perhaps significant that when Seán MacBride, a leading member of Saor Éire, launched another Republican party, Cumann Poblachta na hÉireann, in 1936, he took care that the principles on which it was based would not attract the unfavourable notice of the bishops. The new Republic visualised by MacBride would not be socially divisive but socially inclusive. It would inaugurate 'a reign of social Justice based on Christian principles'.[90]

IV

The government strategy of inducing the bishops to believe, in 1931, that Church and State were menaced not merely by physical-force Republicans but by Communist Republicans acting in concert with them was bound to be an effective one, given the massive clerical preoccupation with the dangers posed to the Catholic faith by communism, and its suspicion of even relatively bland forms of socialism. Patrick O'Farrell explains 'the apparent clerical blindness to the violent revolutionary tendencies' of nationalist groups in the early years of the twentieth century by pointing out that 'clerical attention and concern were diverted by what appeared to be a much more dangerous threat elsewhere, the danger that all that was most valuable in Ireland, most notably religion, would be destroyed by socialist revolution'.[91] In the minds of clergymen who had observed its operation on the European continent, socialism had 'accumulated connotations

---

[88] Ibid., 24.10.31.
[89] Ibid., 10.10.31.
[90] The manifesto, constitution and rules of Cumann Poblachta na hÉireann are in the Coyle O'Donnell Papers, UCDA P 61/10 (1).
[91] O'Farrell, *Ireland's English Question*, p. 269.

of gross irreligion, violent revolution, expropriation and anarchic destruction of lawful authority and order'.[92] Bishops had been issuing anti-socialist pastorals since the early years of the century. In 1914, the archbishops and bishops of Ireland advised the faithful that the Pope, in sorrow, not in anger, was endeavouring 'to save men from following a will-o'-the-wisp into the quagmire of socialism'. The socialist creed, as a body of teaching, centred 'human existence on an impossible equality' and impelled victims of inequality 'to have recourse to the ruinous strikes and lock-outs which are becoming more frequent'.[93] Clerical horror of socialism was motivated by the fear that the socialist gospel preached by Larkin since 1907 would wean the mass of working-people away from the Church. O'Farrell quotes Bishop Donnelly's anxious comment to Bishop O'Dwyer: 'Larkin has got our entire working population in his hands and out of our hands and he is working hard to accentuate the separation of priest from people'. For decades afterwards, Catholic apologists endeavoured to assure the working class that its natural allies were not socialists or communists but priests. In 1931, the Rev. A.H. Ryan of Queen's University Belfast, in the course of a lecture on the wiles of communists, argued that 'as regards the interests of the workingman, no student of history will deny that the Catholic church is their greatest friend on earth' and that 'this was only natural, for its Founder, Our Divine Lord and Master, was a workingman'.[94]

The impression given by much clerical discourse is that bishops and priests regarded urban working people in particular as a group to be patronised, policed and controlled rather then to have their cause furthered with active Church support. This was partly explained by the constraints imposed on the clerical body by the social and geographical backgrounds of most of its membership. Arthur Mitchell points out that the Church in Ireland 'drew the great majority of its priests from the small farmer and lower middle classes; thus it had a bias towards the values and experiences of rural society'.[95] On the rare occasions

[92] Ibid. Much Irish clerical comment on radical political philosophies was of a piece with Leo XIII's denunciation of 'that sect of men who are known by the diverse and almost barbaric name of socialists, communists and nihilists'. G. Barraclough (ed.), *The Christian World* (Dublin, 1981, p. 306. The comment is from Pope Leo's encyclical, *Quod apostolici muneris* (1878).
[93] Pastoral Letter of the Archbishops and Bishops of Ireland, 11.2.1914. ELDA.
[94] *ICD*, 1932, p. 631.
[95] *Labour in Irish Politics, 1890–1930* (Dublin, 1974), p. 284. Emmet Larkin records that at a clerical conference in June 1912, M.J. O'Donnell, nephew of Archbishop O'Donnell, 'courageously pointed out that it was not the agitator who made the trouble in Ireland, but rather the agitator was the result of wretched Irish social conditions'. See Larkin's 'Socialism and Catholicism in Ireland', *Church History*, vol. xxxiii, December 1964.

during the period when priests addressed the membership of the Labour movement, it was to issue warnings against espousing anti-Catholic social and economic teachings. In this context it is significant that in the course of general election campaigns while numerous priests campaigned for Cumann na nGaedheal, Sinn Féin and Fianna Fáil, in the period from 1922 to 1937, there appears to be virtually no record of a clergyman appearing at a Labour Party meeting or indicating support for the Labour movement.[96] It is perhaps also significant that when Daniel Morrissey refused to vote with his Labour colleagues against Cosgrave's Public Safety legislation in 1931, he won the support of a number of Tipperary priests who denounced the Labour Party and applauded Morrissey for his services to religion. One of the priests, present for the launching of an Independent Labour Party which enjoyed 'the cooperation and benediction of the clergy', declared that if they had allowed things to drift in the direction favoured by official Labour, 'they would have awakened one morning to find their faith and religion attacked and people opposed to them in the saddle. They would be in the same position as they were in Spain and Mexico. Mr Morrissey voted to uphold his faith and country'.[97] It was the supposed socialist threat to faith as well as country that disposed many clergy favourably towards Catholic nationalism. O'Farrell points out that bishops and clergy were comforted by the notion that 'a proper Irish nationalism would kill socialism – an Irish nation would be a Catholic nation'.[98]

In many Pastoral letters, no distinction was made between socialism and other unapproved, but not necessarily related, ideologies. 'The Secularist and the Socialist', Bishop Coyne declared in 1920, 'who consider only the present life, are ever anxious to make the State supreme at the cost of individual freedom. They recognise no God in Heaven, and their religious instincts which cannot be silenced, prompt them to deify the State upon earth'.[99] Given this view of socialism, it is little wonder that the Synod of Maynooth in 1927, among its decisions affecting the Catholic laity, instructed the priests that 'particular care should be paid to the working class, lest, lured by the promises and deceived by the frauds of socialists, it lose its ancestral faith'.[100] With the approach of a General Election in 1923, Cardinal

---

[96] Ibid. In the 1923 General Election, the Labour candidate for Cavan was nominated by a priest. See p. 105, note 314.
[97] *Irish Press*, 2.11.31.
[98] O'Farrell, *Ireland's English Question*, p. 271.
[99] Pastoral Letter of Bishop Coyne for 1920. ELDA.
[100] *Synod of Maynooth 1927. Decrees which affect the Laity*. Translated with some notes by Rev. M.J. Browne, DD, DCL, p. 12.

Logue believed that it would be salutary for the working classes to abandon the Labour Party, for the latter to cease to function as the champion of a sectional interest and to place the cause of those it represented in the hands of Cumann na nGaedheal for the general good.[101] In the month before the same election, a writer in the *Irish Rosary* suggested that 'to keep Irish labour from becoming tainted by the influences that are distorting the democratic movement elsewhere will be an immediate necessity'. The writer did not say who should supervise this operation, but sensing that workers might have grievances, he was annoyed that 'socialists of the anti-Christian type' were exploiting these 'as a means of furthering their own designs'.[102]

According to the *Catholic Bulletin* in the year of the great lockout, these designs, if successful, would undermine the values, as well as the self-respect, of Irish Catholic workers. Larkin was imposing a materialist, alien creed on his followers, from which 'every idea of God, the soul, moral obligations and even intelligence was carefully eliminated'. A 'crowning shame' of the 1913 strike was that hungry Irish strikers had accepted food and money from English workers, so that 'the upright spiritualised Irishman for a time disappeared, and all of the brute that was in him was drawn out and fed'. The writer in the *Bulletin*, which at the time enjoyed official ecclesiastical approval, seemed to believe that the strikers should have preserved their pride and starved to death, like their grandfathers who 'gladly died on the roadside rather than accept the poorhouse taint, crunching the beggar's crust thrown by English Socialists'. These English Socialists, he believed, were using the bribes of food and money to enable them to fill 'the heads of Irish workmen with half-baked paganism'.[103] By 1931, Bishop Fogarty had evidently come to believe that a number had succumbed to the *Bulletin's* 'black devil of Socialism, hoof and horns'. It was plain to him that there was a group in Ireland 'which had adopted the methods, as well as the principles, of Soviet Russia, and who were preparing the ground by murder, intimidation and propaganda, sometimes open, sometimes disguised, so that an armed minority might rush the country when opportunity offered, and clap the harness of communism on Ireland's back before she realised the danger'. Some people were being attracted to this movement 'under specious pretext – like that of a republic'. They would get a Republic 'of the Russian type, which the Irish people knew to be anti-God,

[101] *The Irish Times*, 11.8.23. Logue believed that all other parties representing special interests should do the same.
[102] *Irish Rosary*, July 1923.
[103] *Catholic Bulletin*, November 1913.

anti-Christian, anti-social'.[104] A few months before the Eucharistic Congress, Cardinal MacRory appealed for 'a solid Irish Catholic front against the menace of Communism'. Like almost all clerical commentators, MacRory regarded communism as totally inappropriate to Irish circumstances. Its agents should be told 'that there is no room for them or their blasphemies among the children of St. Patrick'.[105]

Clerical interest in radical movements extended beyond mere public condemnation and warning. All political groups with even mildly socialist leanings were suspect, and underwent expert scrutiny with a view to establishing their conformity or otherwise to Catholic social principles. In this respect, the experience of the Labour Party is instructive. In 1934, efforts made by communists to enter the party were frustrated when the annual conference resolved to 'oppose any attempt to introduce anti-Christian communist doctrine into the movement'.[106] The bishops, however, do not appear to have been entirely satisfied that the party was sound from the Catholic point of view. At their June meeting in 1936, they commissioned a report from a committee of senior ecclesiastics on its Constitution. The investigating committee included one bishop, Jeremiah Kinane of Waterford, and two future ones: Michael Browne, bishop-elect of Galway, and Cornelius Lucey, who was to succeed Cohalan as Bishop of Cork. The committee reported to the bishops that the Labour Party Constitution contained a number of statements of principle and aim which were opposed to Catholic teaching, involving a denial of Catholic teachings 'on private and individual ownership' as well as 'a denial of the essential liberty and natural rights of every individual in the State'. The members of the Committee were particularly troubled by the party's statement of its first object: 'To establish in Ireland a Workers' Republic founded on the principles of social justice'. This, they held, must mean 'a Republic in which there are none but workers . . . a Socialist State in which all property is owned by the community, or, at least, a Republic in which only workers are recognised as having rights'. As the episcopal committee pointed out, the term 'Workers' Republic' had only a single meaning in the eyes of the world: it signified a republic 'of the type established in Soviet Russia'. Even if the Labour Party should argue that it understood the term in the sense propounded by James Connolly, the members of the Committee would retort that the Republic he desired to see

---

[104] *ICD*, 1932, p. 614.
[105] *ICD*, 1933, p. 591.
[106] E. Rumpf and A.C. Hepburn, *Nationalism and Socialism in Twentieth-Century Ireland* (Liverpool, 1977), p. 94.

established was 'of the Marxian–Socialist type'. Another aim of the Labour Party which concerned the Committee was 'to win for the people of Ireland, collectively, the ownership and control of the whole produce of their labour'. This appeared to imply 'the false Marxist principle that the products of industry are due to labour alone and belong by right entirely to the workers'. The members of the committee were further troubled by a statement made by Thomas Johnson, at the recent party conference at which the Workers' Republic was adopted as Labour's aim. 'The Labour Party', Johnson was reported to have said, 'in adopting the Republican faith of James Connolly, would henceforth be taking a line more to the left than it had. Connolly was a Socialist Revolutionary. The democratic principles proclaimed in Easter Week were not the Republican principles of James Connolly.'[107]

V

In the 1931 Pastoral, the IRA and Saor Éire were jointly depicted as enemies of civil and religious order. There is evidence, however, that for some time before the Pastoral was issued, some politically conscious clergymen entertained hopes that the bishops might be able to persuade the IRA membership that Saor Éire and other radical influences which had infiltrated the Republican ranks represented an aberration, and were leading the Republican movement in the wrong direction. There were some priests who hoped that the IRA might be converted into a force for good, and, with the approach of the Eucharistic Congress, ally itself with those who wanted to keep Ireland

---

[107] The 'Statement on the Constitution of the Irish Labour Party' signed by Kinane, Browne and Lucey is undated, but was composed in time for the October 1936 meeting of the Hierarchy. There is a copy in the Limerick Diocesan Archive. Thomas Johnson's statement was reported in the *Irish Independent*, 12.2.36. In February 1937, William Norton, leader of the Labour Party, felt obliged to write to Cardinal Pacelli, Vatican Secretary of State, to answer a charge made in the *Irish Catholic*, and repeated in *Osservatore Romano*, that 'the 204,000 Irish workers who are members of trade unions affiliated to the Irish Trade Union Congress and to the Irish Labour Party tacitly support Communism and that the Irish Trade Union Congress circulated an article in which the Catholic Church was described as an enemy of the workers'. Norton repudiated both statements 'as a Catholic', pointing out to Pacelli that the Labour Party had no contact with communists, and had made no secret of 'our determination that they shall have no contact with us'. He assured the Vatican that, as the 1934 Party Congress had resolved, 'the aim of the Irish Labour movement must continue to be the establishment of a just social order based on Christian teaching'. *ICD*, 1938, pp. 587–9. In June 1937, a leading member of the Labour Party, Ald. Corish of Wexford, gave a public assurance that 'if ever Communism showed its head, he would be the first to take the platform against it', Ibid., p. 602.

free from the contamination of alien social and economic doctrines. In some marginal notes he made on his copy of the 'Draft Constitution and Rules of Saor Éire', Bishop O'Brien of Kerry made clear his belief that the new organisation had taken control of the IRA. 'The present movement', he observed, 'is not a continuation of the IRA. The name alone remains. Under the guise of patriotism, new leaders have got hold of this organisation. They, the leaders, are in touch with Moscow from which they receive subsidies and are carrying on this insidious and poisonous propaganda among the unsuspecting young people.' O'Brien was especially concerned that Saor Éire was weakening the influence of the Church. Its agents in Kerry were 'organising night dances in defiance of all authority and thus bringing young people into conflict with the priests, whose authority and influence they hoped to undermine. It is thus hoped that on the one hand the young people will be demoralized, and on the other, the influence of the priests will be brought into contempt.'[108]

A number of priests, however, felt able to distinguish between the radical influences being brought to bear on the IRA and the more conventional religious and social attitudes of some of its members. One of these was John Hannon, a Jesuit at Milltown Park, who, on the basis of information he had received from concerned and well-informed Catholic laymen, believed that 'the position of religion in Ireland, especially in the Free State' was 'extremely perilous'. The reason, he told Bishop Mulhern of Dromore in September 1931, was 'the rapid dissemination of Communistic and anti-religious sentiments, especially in the ranks of the IRA'. Hannon was aware that this situation was known 'even by [some of] the leaders of the IRA

---

[108] Bishop O'Brien's copy of the Constitution and rules of Saor Éire, KYDA. O'Brien noted that 'two areas in Kerry which are affected particularly are: triangle Killarney, Castleisland, Rathmore; Listowel, Tarbert, Ballybunion – propaganda being extended throughout rest of diocese'. In 1931, similar recruiting drives were being undertaken in the diocese of Killaloe. In that year, an elderly woman, a member of a Republican family, died. Neither the Parish Priest nor the curate attended her burial service. The official reason was that she had not paid her Church dues for years. This was denied by her relatives, who wrote letters of complaint to the Papal Nuncio and Bishop Fogarty. The Parish Priest, by way of response to the complaints, identified the chief complainant as an IRA member who had tried to recruit young people of the parish. He employed 'porter dances' as a means of attracting youthful support, which caused demoralisation among the young. The family's resentment against the priest was, according to himself, fed by his success in suppressing the desire of the young people to join his 'army' and in putting an end to his porter dances. The priest told Fogarty that he did not confuse political and religious matters and seldom discussed politics, even *outside* the Church. Fogarty made it clear that he had a low opinion of the complainants, the main one especially. The correspondence is in the Killaloe Diocesan Archive.

themselves, who are perturbed by the views and utterances of many of their fellow-leaders and followers'. He feared that the growth of anti-religious and anti-clerical sentiment in the IRA would have extremely serious consequences for religion. If there were to be an IRA uprising, which seemed to him quite possible, it would be 'on behalf of a Workers' Republic on Communist lines', and 'attacks on Church property could not be warded off'. Hannon suggested a joint episcopal letter on Capital and Labour, in which 'the obligations of property-owners and employers should be given equal prominence with the obligations of the working man'. A second suggestion was more novel: 'a joint committee of representatives of every political party in Ireland, not excluding the IRA, similar to that formed in the anti-conscription days'. Hannon offered Mulhern a visionary project for Catholic Action in which the IRA would participate with 'practically the whole manhood and womanhood of the country for the defence of religion and the upholding of Catholic principles'.[109]

Another clerical correspondent, Professor P.J. McLaughlin of Maynooth, told Mulhern of the alarm felt by 'quite a number of prudent Catholic laymen in and around Dublin' at the extent of Soviet activities in the country. He mentioned a charity football match played at Kilrush for the benefit of the USSR, 'opprobrious allusions' to Irish priests by a Scottish communist agitator at Beresford Place, threats to sabotage the Eucharistic Congress, the 'uncombatted activities' of Russian societies in Ireland and disturbances at Cootehill, County Cavan, attributed to Soviet agents. McLaughlin believed that Soviet agents in Ireland were mostly 'disgruntled and dissatisfied ex-IRA men'. Like Hannon, McLaughlin hoped that the IRA might yet be induced to take up the cause of Catholic Ireland. He suggested to Mulhern that if the bishops 'took concerted action such as they did on the conscription occasion, and, say, through the priests in every parish put the people on their guard against the insidious propaganda of the Soviets, ex-IRA men etc. who are agents of the ROP[110] and similar companies would soon realise the disloyalty they are guilty of to faith and fatherland, and in view of the terrible consequences of a Soviet success, all classes and creeds, alive to the imminence of common danger, would unite and scotch it.'[111]

Bishop Mulhern took the comments of Hannon and McLaughlin seriously enough to submit them to Cardinal MacRory. Mulhern

---

[109] John Hannon, SJ to Bishop Mulhern, 30.9.31, DRDA.
[110] Russian Oil Products, 'essentially a propaganda agency, not an industrial company', according to Professor McLaughlin.
[111] Professor P.J. McLaughlin to Bishop Mulhern, 3.10.31, DRDA.

found Hannon's suggestions particularly good, even if 'some might be unpractical at the moment'. As an example, he mentioned the transformation of the IRA into an instrument of Catholic Action. 'It would seem strange', he observed, 'if the Bishops recognised the IRA and took them to their bosom'.[112] MacRory agreed. 'I'm astonished', he wrote to Mulhern, 'at the suggestion of having IRA representation on a joint committee'. What Hannon had suggested could only be done by 'a general appeal to all loyal Catholics to work together on religious grounds'. MacRory clearly believed, like Hannon and McLaughlin, that large elements of the IRA were not beyond redemption. If there were a general appeal to the better instincts of Catholic Ireland, MacRory acknowledged, 'of course great numbers of those who may be IRA men, but are not commonly known as such, could be included'. MacRory provided Mulhern with a shrewd assessment of the government's motives for approaching the bishops for help in dealing with threatened subversion. 'It is clear enough', he wrote, 'that there is trouble brewing but I'm inclined to think that there is a disposition to exaggerate with a view to more effectively moving the bishops to take action. The politicians feel that they could tighten the reins with better grace, and the hope of some support, after the bishops had spoken'. Just over two weeks before the Pastoral was read in all the churches, MacRory did not know 'to whom to turn for the bones of a pronouncement'. Bishop McKenna of Clogher came first to his mind, but would probably be reluctant to undertake the task. Fogarty 'would be inclined to be too fierce, and moreover he is no longer young'. In the circumstances, he felt that the Pastoral would have to be composed at the next episcopal meeting.[113]

The public positions taken by the IRA in the aftermath of the Church–State attack on Saor Éire must have confused clerical observers. An IRA convention held in March 1933 adopted a Governmental programme advocating radical social change: the new Republic the army hoped to create would be organised on communal lines. The nation's soil was to be 'the property of the people'; the

[112] Mulhern to MacRory, 30.10.31.
[113] MacRory to Mulhern, 2.10.31. The October Pastoral was greeted with dismay by Frank Aiken, who, on the day after it was read in the churches, wrote to MacRory to express his disapproval of the bishops' condemnation of the IRA. This, he believed, would do nothing to deal with the Northern problem. He thought MacRory might be better employed dealing with the causes of Irish problems than condemning their results. One of the 'active and fatherly steps' Aiken suggested MacRory might take was to agree to be chairman of a conference of all nationalist groups in Ireland, including Saor Éire and the IRA. Aiken to MacRory, 19.10.31. AAA.

State would encourage the cooperative organisation of the agricultural industry. Rivers, lakes and inland waterways would 'belong to the people', Irish industry was to be directed by the State, while distribution, credit, banking, marketing, exports and imports were to come under state control. The State was also to be responsible for the provision of adequate housing.[114] In June 1933, an Irish Communist Party was formed. Its aim was, according to Seán Murray, one of its founders, an independent Irish Republic under the rule of the Irish working-class and working farmers. The Party manifesto claimed that it would 'lead the toilers of Ireland to the goal of national freedom and to unify the North and South, to the overthrow of capitalism, to the emancipation of labour and to the dictatorship of the working-class'. It was decided to apply for affiliation to the Communist International and to send a special message to the IRA 'hailing their struggle for national freedom and urging Volunteers to become members of the Communist Party'. Although Bishop Collier of Ossory had pronounced at the beginning of the year that 'no Catholic can be a Communist; no Communist can be a Catholic', Seán Murray 'expressed the view that it was not inconsistent for a Catholic to be a communist'.[115] The leadership of the IRA made it clear that it did not approve of what the Communist Party stood for, or welcome its approaches. The IRA GHQ declared that no member of the army had authority to be present at the inaugural meeting of the Communist Party, and that 'there has not, and has never been, any connection between the Irish Republican Army and the Communist organisation'.[116] The IRA Army Council condemned the Communist Party for holding 'a dogma of atheism', while *An Phoblacht* affirmed that the IRA as a body did not support a policy of land nationalisation, a position that seemed to require explanation in the light of the programme adopted at the 1933 Convention.[117] At a Sinn Féin event held a few days after the launching of the Communist Party, Michael O'Flanagan declared that those wishing to honour Wolfe Tone 'should not join any organisation that had its headquarters outside Ireland. They might find themselves

---

[114] Óglaigh na hÉireann, Constitution and Governmental Programme for the Republic of Ireland: Adopted by a GAC of Óglaigh na hÉireann, March 1933. (1934). Coyle O'Donnell Papers, UCDA, P 61/11 (1)

[115] *Irish Independent*, 7.6.33. Seán Murray (1898–1961) was born on a small farm in Cushendall, Co. Antrim. He took part in the War of Independence as an IRA officer. He fought on the anti-Treaty side in the Civil War. In 1928–31 he was a student at the Lenin International School in Moscow. He was almost burned alive when Connolly House was set alight by religious activists in 1933.

[116] *An Phoblacht*, 10.6.33; 17.6.33.

[117] See Cronin, *Frank Ryan*, p. 52; *An Phoblacht*, 17.6.33.

dying in a cause that was not Ireland's cause. Instead, they should join the IRA[118]

The year 1933 was not a propitious one in which to found an Irish Communist Party. The anxiety of the IRA to be seen as free from Communist influence or involvement must be understood, in part at least, against the background of fear and hatred created by clerical forces and their lay auxiliaries. Throughout the year, episcopal pastorals and confirmation sermons were devoted in large measure to the menace of Communism. Bishop Fogarty warned 150 children at Borrisokane that it was 'the first principle' of communists to 'abolish the Catholic religion and to confiscate property'. He advised farmers to be very careful of what they were doing because 'they might wake up some morning and find that their land was gone'. There were, he declared 'two thousand Communists in Dublin alone, and they had their agents all over the country and even in the diocese of Killaloe'.[119] Catholic action against Communism was not merely rhetorical. When James Gralton, a Communist and former IRA member, prominent in workers' and small farmer movements in Leitrim, opened his Pearse–Connolly Hall for lectures and dances, the local curate, John O'Dowd, demanded his deportation and that of 13 other parishioners on the ground that they were Communists. In February 1933, his demand was partially met: the Minister for Justice, James Geoghegan, ordered Gralton's deportation.[120] Following a religious retreat in Dublin in March 1933, during which a priest had roused his congregation to anti-Communist frenzy, Connolly House, the headquarters of the Revolutionary Workers' Group, was attacked by a large crowd, windows were smashed and literature was burned. Two days later, another crowd, to the accompaniment of hymns, tried to set fire to the building.[121]

The formation of the Irish Republican Congress in 1934 marked the beginning of another acute phase in the struggle between the Church and radical Republicanism. At the 1934 Army Convention, Michael Price, whose views had become more radical since the Saor Éire episode, proposed that the IRA should adopt as its objective a Republic as visualised by James Connolly. The IRA leadership, now more than ever conscious of the consequences of alienating the Church, opposed

[118] *Irish Press*, 12.6.33.
[119] Ibid. 3.6.33. In 1935, Fogarty warned children he was confirming that Communism was cradled in Russia by the agents of the devil. He added that 'there was a communist agent in every parish in Ireland with a box of matches in his pocket to burn your church.' *Roscommon Messenger*, 18.5.35.
[120] *Irish Workers' Voice*, 18.2.33.
[121] *Irish Press*, 28.3.33; 30.3.33.

the adoption of a Workers' Republic as a policy aim. Then O'Donnell and George Gilmore proposed a resolution that the IRA should organise a campaign for a Republican Congress, a vehicle for radical Republican ideas which would 'wrest the leadership of the National Struggle from Irish Capitalism'. The IRA leadership ensured the defeat of this resolution, and Gilmore, O'Donnell and Frank Ryan, along with their supporters, resigned from the IRA and set about organising a Republican Congress in which these disaffected Socialist Republicans, the membership of the Communist Party and, according to O'Donnell, 'a very powerful section of the IRA', joined forces.[122] The first general assembly of the new movement was in Athlone on 7 and 8 April 1934. Its manifesto declared that 'a Republic of a united Ireland will never be achieved except through a struggle which uproots Capitalism on its way'. The inspiration for the Congress programme of action would be derived from the teaching of Connolly: 'a free Ireland could not be conceived which had a subject working class; nor could a subject Ireland be conceived with a free working-class'. The Republic, when established, would be 'a Republic of the workers and small farmers'.[123] A more detailed exposition of the outlook of the movement was provided in its weekly organ *Republican Congress*. The membership would take the lead in the 'mass struggle against fascism' which was a form of 'naked imperialism'. The big farmer was not only the enemy of the small farmer: he was also 'the enemy of the national struggle for freedom' and 'neither working class nor small farmer should give him any support'. One of the main organisers of the movement, Michael Price, argued that the only worthwhile Republican activity was to lead the rising of 'enslaved Ireland', the socially and economically oppressed. He saw the Congress as 'a great uprising of the Ireland of the poor', the voice of 'that Ireland which has borne all the burden of struggle across which careerists have climbed into office to serve not the poor but the enemies of the poor'.[124] Congress leaders complained that the IRA, having dropped Saor Éire and 'shed from its leadership those who had shouldered the organisation towards it', had shown its lack of interest in the cause of radical Republicanism. The lesson of Saor Éire was that 'the IRA may stagger, that working-class elements in it may even win a pull towards working-class ideals, but the power of anti-working-class forces within it will win the second pull'.[125]

[122] English, *Radicals and the Republic*, p. 188; Patterson, *Politics of Illusion*, p. 58.
[123] A good account of the genesis and character of the movement will be found in George Gilmore, *The Irish Republican Congress* (Cork, 1978).
[124] *Republican Congress*, 5.5.34.
[125] Ibid.

On 29 and 30 September 1934, the Congress met in Rathmines Town Hall.[126] Among the delegates was Frank Edwards, a teacher at a Christian Brothers' school in Waterford. Edwards, a student of the works of Marx and Lenin, had been a member of Saor Éire.[127] Although he was warned by the Parish Priest, Archdeacon Byrne, and by the Principal of his school, to desist from his left-wing activities, Edwards attended the September Congress. Soon afterwards, he received notice of his dismissal from his teaching post.[128] He was given three months in which to sever his connection with radical politics. At the beginning of 1935, he was still a member of the Republican Congress. When Bishop Kinane of Waterford tried to persuade him to sign a document dissociating himself from the Congress, he refused and was dismissed.[129] Attending the September Congress and being associated with the movement it represented were not, it appears, the only transgressions against Church doctrine and discipline of which Edwards had been guilty. His contribution to the programme of radical reform being promoted by the Congress had involved him in agitation against slum landlords and in supporting a lengthy strike by builders' labourers. The Parish Priest, Archdeacon Byrne, intervened on behalf of the employers during the strike. According to Edwards, this same priest was the trustee of some of the slum property he had investigated, though he did not know this at the time. Edwards recalled that when the strike was over, Byrne expressed his displeasure that 'certain people had intervened in it who had no right to do so. These people were attempting to set up in Ireland a state of affairs after the model of Moscow. Interference by these people in the affairs of Waterford must stop'. Edwards believed that his major sin was to have mentioned Byrne's slum property, however unwittingly.[130]

The dismissal of Edwards attracted considerable attention and comment, much of this unfavourable to the Church authorities. Edwards believed that the great majority of the people of Waterford were sympathetic to his cause. The local branch of the teachers' union to which he belonged demanded that its executive take up the issue.[131] The resentment generated was sufficient to provoke Bishop Kinane to deliver an address in Waterford Cathedral on 6 January 1935, justifying the dismissal. The bishop deplored Edwards's attendance at the Republican Congress which he described, accurately enough, as

[126] Gilmore, *Republican Congress*, p. 45.
[127] Mac Eoin, *Survivors*, p. 7.
[128] *Waterford News*, 11.1.35.
[129] Ibid.
[130] Mac Eoin, *Survivors*, p. 8.
[131] Ibid.

communistic and directed towards the establishment of a socialist republic. He declared that 'one who belongs to a movement of this kind is unfit to be a teacher of Catholic children', and that it was sinful for a Catholic to belong to the Republican Congress. Kinane extended the scope of his attack on Republican radicalism to include the IRA. From the published Constitution of the Republic promulgated at the 1933 IRA convention, it was clear to Kinane that 'this Republic was to be a socialist one in which . . . only one class in society is to be represented – the workers and working farmers'. He was convinced that 'the Republic at which the Irish Republican Army originally aimed has been abandoned and one based on the Russian model put in its place'. From this point of view, he could see no difference between the IRA and the Republican Congress. Its new radical orientation since 1931 had provided a more compelling reason than before for condemning the IRA, and for declaring emphatically that it was sinful to be a member or to cooperate with it in any significant way.[132] Kinane thus opened an acrimonious debate on the nature of the IRA in the 1930s, its purpose, motivation and conformity or otherwise to Catholic teaching.

Two days after the bishop's statement, the Army Council issued a long reply deploring the fact that he should have used the Edwards dismissal to 'launch a violent attack on the Irish separatist movement', particularly since his 'kinsmen in Tipperary have played a notable part in the fight for Irish independence'. Edwards, the statement pointed out, was not a member of the IRA, nor had the IRA any connection with the Republican Congress movement. At the same time, the IRA was 'behind Mr Edwards in his fight against the tyranny which has deprived him of his means of livelihood because of his membership of a political organisation'. The bishop, it was thus implied, was no better than a political tyrant. The members of the Army Council were surprised that the bishop should have considered the IRA 'Constitution and Programme for the Republic of Ireland' contrary to the teachings of the Church, suggesting that he should be aware that 'those who favour a Republic on the Russian model constantly attack the policy of the Irish Republican Army as reactionary and allege that it is the worst enemy of Communism in this country!' While the Army Council challenged Kinane to show in what respects its programme contravened Catholic social and economic doctrine, it made it clear that it regarded its policy of military force as

---

[132] *Waterford News*, 11.1.35. For an excellent account of the Edwards affair and other aspects of radical Republicanism, see M. Banta, 'The Red Scare in the Irish Free State, 1929–37', Unpublished MA thesis, University College Dublin, 1982.

morally legitimate. If, the Army Council argued, in stating that it was sinful to be a member of the IRA Kinane was defining the authoritative teaching of the Church, then this meant that 'according to the Church it is sinful to strive to assert national independence and unity and complete separation from the British Empire, by the only means by which history teaches that these national ideals can be achieved'.[133] Maurice Twomey, the IRA Chief of Staff, believed that Kinane's attack on the IRA might have been politically motivated. He found it significant that the *Irish Press* gave considerable prominence to the onslaught, and that 'His Lordship came out now when there is so much agitation in regard to ill-treatment of prisoners. He is supposed to be inclined politically to FF' Twomey believed that a reply to Kinane should draw attention to 'the silence of the bishops on the destructive campaign of the Blueshirts – the Bishop's own cousin had his house fired into a week or two ago'.[134]

In a detailed reply to the IRA statement, Kinane concentrated on trying to show that its 1933 Constitution did not properly safeguard the absolute right of the individual to private property. Catholic teaching laid it down that this right 'has been given to man by God's natural law'; the IRA programme implied that it derived solely from the State.[135] Soon afterwards, Archdeacon Byrne, with whom Edwards had been in conflict on the issue of slum landlords, issued a statement in support of his bishop in which he cast a wistful glance at the struggle for the Republic in pre-Congress days. That Republic, and the one Fianna Fáil had in mind, would, Byrne believed, 'safeguard the principle of private ownership, and live and breathe with the Christian spirit'.[136] Byrne's statement gave Frank Ryan an opportunity to rehearse some embarrassing features of ecclesiastical dealings with Republicanism since 1916, and to suggest to Byrne that in the light of his approval of pre-Congress Republicanism he might have to engage in a comprehensive revisionist project. 'Are we to take it', Ryan asked, 'that Mgr Byrne would repudiate ecclesiastical condemnation of the 1916 Rising? That he would repudiate Bishop Cohalan's 1920 Pastoral? That he would repudiate the Joint Pastoral of 1922 which condemned

[133] Statement by the Army Council. Irish Republican Army. Issued for Publication, 8 January 1935. MacSwiney Papers, UCDA, P 48a/208 (3). Mary MacSwiney suggested to Maurice Twomey, IRA Chief of Staff, that they should take Kinane's attack on the IRA 'up with the Pope'. Twomey felt that this would be 'sheer waste of time, so far as hoping to get an satisfaction or result is concerned'. Twomey to Mary MacSwiney, 11.1.35, MacSwiney Papers, UCDA, P 48a/199 (3).
[134] Twomey to Mary MacSwiney, 7.1.35, MacSwiney Papers, UCDA, P 48a/199 (4).
[135] *Cork Examiner*, 12.1.35.
[136] *Irish Independent*, 15.1.35.

those Republicans who were resisting in arms the forces which attacked the Republic? In short, are we to take it that the Monsignor takes his stand historically on the side of the Fenians?'[137]

At about this time, Mary MacSwiney observed that episcopal condemnation of the IRA was 'turning on the social programme, not the national'.[138] On 15 January 1935, the IRA issued what its Chief of Staff, Maurice Twomey, regarded as an effective statement, which concentrated on Kinane's charge that its social programme was modelled on that of Russia; it was, Twomey told Mary MacSwiney, who also admired it, 'the one that knocked the bottom out of the bishop's attack'.[139] This statement certainly made some effective debating points. Its object was to demonstrate that the social system for which the IRA stood, and which was outlined in its 1933 programme, was in conformity with Church teaching. 'We emphatically refute [sic] the allegations of Imperial propagandists', it declared, 'that our aim is to set up an anti-Christian social order. Our aim is rather to give practical application to the teachings of Christianity'. Indeed, the compilers of the statement were able to show that IRA policy 'dealing with State supervision of the nation's soil for the benefit of the community' should have commanded the warmest episcopal approval, since its proposals in this regard 'almost paraphrase the legislation enforced in the former Papal States to ensure the same results'. Kinane's fears that the IRA might not be sound on such issues as the control of wealth were addressed by pointing out that 'Republican economists' had benefited from the insights of 'many distinguished Catholic authorities' who insisted that such functions as banking and credit 'cannot be left in the control of private individuals'. The condemnatory words of Leo XIII in reference to the concentration in the hands of a few of accumulated wealth and 'immense power and despotic economic domination' were also invoked in support of the IRA policy on banking monopolies and the issue of credit. There was also the suggestion that Kinane's own commitment to Catholic principles of social justice might be less complete than that of the IRA. His emphasis on the rights of property-owners contrasted with the absence of any expression of concern for the large majority of the Irish people who 'are propertyless and have no assured means, or access to the means, of earning a livelihood; they either starve or exist

---

[137] Ibid., 16.1.35.
[138] Mary MacSwiney to Kathleen Brugha, 23.1.35, Kathleen Brugha Papers, UCDA A 5/8 (1).
[139] Maurice Twomey to Mary MacSwiney, 24.1.35, MacSwiney Papers, UCDA, P 48a,199 (5).

on doles or charity'.[140] Kinane might have done better to have concentrated on the more tractable issue of IRA militarism and to have left its social and economic policies alone.

Despite its protestations of loyalty to Catholic teaching, the IRA continued to be the subject of clerical denunciation as a communist-inspired grouping. It must be said that some of the public gestures condoned by its leadership left it extremely vulnerable to this kind of attack. A notable example was the rally it organised in Waterford on 27 January 1935 to protest against recent attacks by the local bishop and 'certain clerical elements', and to show support for Frank Edwards. Maurice Twomey knew that the Waterford meeting could be presented by enemies of the IRA as a token of its identification with Republican Congress Communism; he nevertheless felt that Edwards deserved public support because he was being victimised, 'not because he had done anything wrong as a teacher, but because he belongs to a particular group or party'.[141] Kinane responded to the announcement of the IRA meeting by asking Catholics not to attend it, declaring it 'gravely sinful for any Catholic, whether of this or any other diocese, to take part in it as a sympathiser and supporter'. He claimed that the meeting, 'in addition to other anti-Catholic and anti-Christian objects' had 'for its principal purpose to call in question my authority as spiritual teacher and ruler in the Diocese of Waterford and Lismore'.[142] Twomey's speech to the Waterford rally was, by contrast, moderate and conciliatory. The IRA, in common with all Catholic Republicans, was 'at all times, ready to obey the ecclesiastical authorities on questions of religion or morals or ethics'. They were interested in the Edwards case because they believed in 'the right of a citizen to his political beliefs and opinions'. Twomey used the meeting mainly to affirm that the IRA had nothing to do with organisations professing communist doctrines. 'This Congress Party', he pointed out, 'had its origin amidst a group of men in the Army who disagreed with its policy and left it, or were dismissed'.[143] Those who had remained in the IRA must have seemed to the people of Waterford more like a branch of Catholic Action than the communist cell depicted in clerical propaganda. The 800 IRA members from Waterford, Wexford, Cork Tipperary and Kilkenny marched through the streets behind banners, some of which were inscribed 'We Serve God and Country'.[144] Charles

[140] *Irish Independent*, 16.1.35.
[141] See note 139 above.
[142] *Irish Independent*, 28.1.35.
[143] Ibid.
[144] *Irish Press*, 28.1.35.

MacLogan, Nationalist MP for Armagh, told the meeting that 'as far as the IRA and kindred revolutionary organisations knew, the only real challenge to Catholic teaching here came through British imperialists'.[145] A letter was read from Patrick Kinane, 'stated to be a first cousin of the Bishop of Waterford', who was billed as a speaker, affirming that 'he stood firmly for the IRA and its policy as recently expressed'.[146]

At this period, leading Republicans were constantly asserting their sturdy Catholicism and particularly that of the IRA membership, while bishops were following the lead of Professor James Hogan of University College Cork in proclaiming that the IRA had been transformed from a purely separatist organisation into an actively communist one, and operated as recruiting agency for communism.[147] Some Lenten Pastorals for 1935 showed that the bishops believed that the IRA and Republican Congress were virtually indistinguishable. The Bishop of Kerry described Republican Congress as communistically orientated and declared that the IRA, 'as at present constituted, differs little from the Republican Congress movement as regards ultimate aims'.[148] Bishop O'Doherty of Galway condemned both groups for being communistic. He further developed this notion in a Confirmation sermon in May 1935, in which he described the IRA and Republican Congress as being 'under the ban of the Church', telling his congregation that 'it is a mortal sin to belong to these societies'.[149] Members of the IRA and Republican Congress came among the people in the guise of patriots; they were, in reality, 'agents of hell'.[150]

---

[145] Ibid.

[146] Ibid.

[147] See J. Hogan's tract, *Could Ireland Become Communist?* published in February 1935. This had been serialised in *United Ireland* the year before. See also Dermot Keogh, 'De Valera, the Catholic Church and the "Red Scare", 1931–1932', in J.P. O'Carroll and J.A. Murphy (eds), *De Valera and his Times* (Cork, 1980).

[148] *The Standard*, 8.3.35.

[149] Ibid.

[150] *Roscommon Messenger*, 25.5.35. Two years earlier, O'Doherty had delivered his celebrated assault on the Republican tradition at another Confirmation ceremony: 'Who fought in '98?' he asked. 'Was it the United Irishmen? It was not; it was the men of Meath and Wexford who fought. What about the men of '48? They hatched a cabbage-garden plot. What did Emmet do? He led a rabble through the streets of Dublin . . . What did cut-throat Tone do?' *The Irish Times*, 24.5.33. Monsignor John Rogers of San Francisco, who had arranged a meeting between de Valera and Mulcahy on 6.9.22 (See T. Ó Neill and Padraig Ó Fiannachta, *De Valera*, Vol. 2, p. 64) told Bishop Fogarty that 'the great mass' of American clergy, 'the men of Irish associations', were much perturbed by the exchanges coming from Ireland 'concerning the attitude of some of the hierarchy towards the national position'. O'Doherty, he wrote, 'has no defender, and those of us who are close to the intensely patriotic type of our countrymen wonder if His Lordship

In 1935, many leading Republicans tried to convince the bishops and the Catholic world in general that the members of Sinn Féin and the IRA were robustly Catholic in outlook. Mrs Buckley, a member of the Sinn Féin Executive, was astonished that the Bishop of Waterford had condemned the claim made in the IRA constitution that the soil of Ireland belonged to the people of Ireland, considering that this was a clause of the Proclamation of 1916, and 'the premise on which the Constitution of the Republic was built'. 'I am not a communist', Mrs Buckley declared, 'I am a Catholic, and have a great love and respect for my religion, the Church and its teachings and spiritual advisers as such. But I do not allow anybody, lay or clerical, to do my political thinking for me'. She found the IRA 'as fine a body of Catholics as can be got anywhere', and deemed it 'un-Christian, untrue, to libel them as anti-religious and anti-Catholic'.[151] In March 1935, at a Republican funeral at which a decade of the Rosary was recited in Irish, the editor of *An Phoblacht*, Donal Ó Donnchadha, dealt with the arguments of those who tried to associate the IRA with 'anti-religion and Communism' and who asserted that 'the mixing up of economic and social freedom with national freedom' was a departure from the earlier policy of the independence movement. 'We tell them', Ó Donnchadha proclaimed, 'that it is because we are Christians that we advocate such a policy. We are trying to put Christian principles into practice'.[152]

realises the evil that his words are calculated to do. His reference to Wolfe Tone has brought down universal condemnation. After all, he represents the very highest type of the men of the time'. When Rogers had last been in Ireland, he had begged the late Cardinal O'Donnell to consider what had happened in France and Italy, where the clergy had become divorced from national feeling. 'Heaven forbid', he wrote to Fogarty, 'that under provocation [from men like O'Doherty] our Irish people would ever drift into violent antagonism towards the religion of our fathers'. Rogers hoped that Fogarty himself might yet, by 'blessing and directing the real national forces in their proper channels and to their proper end', resume 'that old position of power and affection' he had once held. Mgr John Rogers to Bishop Fogarty, 3.9.33, KILLDA.

[151] *Irish Press*, 21.1.35.

[152] *Irish Press*, 25.3.35. A number of units of Fianna Fáil were represented at the funeral, that of George Fullerton, a veteran of the Citizen Army and the Civil War. In 1934, many people were ready to believe, on the slenderest of evidence, that a variety of foreign agencies of a Republican–Communist character were actively preparing to undermine Christian values in Ireland. In January, for example, circulars bearing the name of a fictitious organisation, the 'Irish Workers' Republican, Atheist, Birth Control, Civil and Industrial Alliance of New York', were widely circulated in Galway. The circulars announced the holding of a Communist congress in the city in July. On 19 January, Leitrim Board of Health called on the government to take immediate measures including jailing against those responsible for the circulars. (Banta, 'Red Scare', p. 181.) The Bishop of Galway denounced the imaginary project in his Lenten Pastoral, warning that

A letter from Mary MacSwiney to Kathleen Brugha on the eve of the Edwards demonstration in Waterford throws interesting light on attitudes within physical-force Republicanism in the mid-thirties. By the beginning of 1935, Sinn Féin had ceased to operate as a credible force for Republican action. For a public meeting to mark the anniversary of the First Dáil on 21 January, the party could find no speakers except Michael O'Flanagan and Mrs Buckley; J.J. O'Kelly did not bother to call a meeting of the surviving members of the Second Dáil to mark the occasion. Maurice Twomey had wanted no IRA representative on the platform for the Waterford meeting, but tried to persuade Brian O'Higgins, Professor Stockley[153] and Count Plunkett to represent Sinn Féin. O'Higgins was ill, Stockley was in England, and Plunkett refused to speak, saying he would visit the Papal Nuncio instead. 'I am very sad about Sinn Féin', MacSwiney wrote. 'It is a shame that after all these years it should go out like that – and it need not have happened'. She did not want to attend the Waterford meeting, fearing that it would be a Frank Edwards demonstration, not an IRA event. She was sure Edwards had been badly treated but had been told that he had been making 'most unwise statements – communistic in their nature'. MacSwiney's single preoccupation, at this stage, was to promote the welfare of the IRA by keeping it aloof from radical influence or exploitation and affirming its Catholic social outlook, a point of view shared by its Chief of Staff, as her correspondence with him makes clear.[154] Her concern, she told Kathleen

---

[153] cont. there was no room in Ireland 'for a blatant atheist'. (Standard, 16.2.34.) General O'Duffy told a UIP meeting that 'it is a terrible thing if the government permits that anti-God hosting of people from Russia, America and all over the world to come into the country' for an annual congress. 'I have some of their documents in my bag', he announced, 'but I could not read them on account of the young people here'. (Irish Press, 18.1.34.) Galway Urban Council debated a suggestion that resolutions be passed by every public body condemning the conference, and another that no hall be provided in Galway in which to hold it. One member deplored the fact that the Bishop of Galway had denounced the IRA and Communists, but had said nothing about the Blueshirts. Another member felt that public debate and protest would give the congress publicity its organisers would not be able to get for themselves. (Irish Press, 17.2.34.).

[153] W. F. P. Stockley, Professor of English at University College Cork, was returned unopposed as Sinn Féin TD for the National University of Ireland constituency in 1921 and as an anti-Treaty TD for the same constituency in 1922. He was defeated in 1923.

[154] Twomey had long been anxious to prevent the IRA from displaying unnecessary antagonism towards the clergy. In 1933, when a North Clare IRA member was criticised from the altar by a priest and had his Irish class attacked by a mob as a result, Twomey decided that the victim should ask for an ecclesiastical Court hearing from the Bishop and ruled out a public meeting 'which

Brugha, was 'for the IRA – not for Communism'. Peadar O'Donnell and Frank Ryan of the Republican Congress should 'have their heads knocked together until they learned sense'. She and the IRA in general agreed with much of the Congress programme, but thought its 'fundamental principles' wrong. She had 'absolutely no use for Seán Murray and Co. who are definitely communistic, and less for people in the Congress who only refrain from proclaiming Communism because it is bad policy'. She believed that the present IRA social programme, which, the bishops notwithstanding, was 'in accordance with Catholic principles' was 'quite good enough for anyone'. She suggested that it might, indeed, be excessively Christian for some Catholics, many of whom, 'including many Bishops and priests, would not care to see such [a programme] in operation'.[155]

VI

In 1936, it was not the social programme of the IRA that brought on its head the wrath of Church and State, but its violent criminal activity. The murder in March of Vice-Admiral Somerville, a retired

would be taken up as a challenge to the priests, as priests'. M. Twomey to Mary MacSwiney, 27.6.33. MacSwiney Papers, UCDA, P 48a/199 (1). The Waterford affair showed how challenges to ecclesiastical authority were met. Public bodies and societies throughout the diocese were encouraged to pass votes of loyalty to Bishop Kinane. Clonmel Corporation was one of these. J. Fennessy of Fianna Fáil moved a resolution 'of loyalty and confidence in the bishop as a guide and teacher in matters of faith and morals', declaring that 'in spite of slanderous statements that had been made there was no Communism in the Fianna Fáil party, and no party was stronger behind the bishop in matters of faith and morals'. On the other hand, the O'Brien-Mellows Fianna Fáil Cumann in Rialto condemned 'the victimisation of Mr Frank Edwards in his position as teacher in the Waterford schools' and considered it 'an outrage that he is denied the freedom of his opinions'. *Irish Press*, 30.1.35. Waterford Corporation declared its fidelity to Kinane as 'our divinely-appointed spiritual guide in faith and morals'. *Irish Press*, 22.1.35. Dungarvan Urban District Council, however, supported its Chairman in refusing to accept a resolution 'pledging allegiance' to the bishop. Ibid, 21.1.35. On the other hand, the Catholic Young Men's Society Holy Family Branch, at a meeting in Dublin, unanimously endorsed Kinane's action in 'removing from his position a person who, while a teacher in a Catholic school, was actively engaged in the work of an organisation known to be communistic'. Ibid. The Kilkenny Branch of the same society passed a resolution proposed by Bishop Collier 'affirming devoted loyalty and obedience to the Bishops' and the intent of members to 'oppose and resist any attacks made on the Bishops or clergy'. Ibid., 30.1.35. On 19.7.35, the *Irish Press* reported that a certificate that the applicant 'does not belong to any organisations opposed to the Church' was demanded in an advertisement published by the Manager of a Gaeltacht school for a Principal Teacher.
[155] Mary MacSwiney to Kathleen Brugha, 23.1.35. Kathleen Brugha Papers, UCDA, P 15/8 (1).

British naval officer in County Cork, and of an IRA 'traitor' in
Waterford in April, drew angry denunciations from the Church and
marked the termination of de Valera's policy of 'disarming the gunmen
by a peaceful process'.[156] The IRA was outlawed, and Maurice
Twomey its Chief of Staff jailed.[157] Twomey was replaced as Chief of
Staff first by Seán MacBride and then by Tom Barry, the most effective
IRA leader of the War of Independence, whose order, sanctioned by
GHQ in Dublin, to 'get' Vice-Admiral Somerville, had been over-
zealously interpreted by his murderers.[158] Against a background of
disarray and demoralisation in the main agency of physical-force
Republicanism, the outbreak of the Spanish Civil War in July 1936
provided radical Irish Republicans, mainly members of Republican
Congress, and their enemies, who included large and influential
clerical forces, with a new cause of conflict. Members of Republican
Congress saw the Spanish Civil War as a struggle between a demo-
cratically elected, lawfully established Republican régime and an
international fascist conspiracy to overthrow it.[159] The Irish supporters
of Franco's insurgents were numerous and powerful. They included the
episcopal body, many priests, Fine Gael, the Blueshirts, and the Irish
Christian Front, inaugurated on 31 August 1936 by Patrick Belton, a
former Fianna Fáil TD.This latter body organised a rally of 40,000
supporters in Cork in September to publicise atrocities said to have
been perpetrated by Spanish Republicans on priests and nuns.
Monsignor Sexton told the rally that 'in Barcelona, controlled by the
Red leader Caballero, they dragged out 24 Sisters of the Poor, stripped
them naked and crucified them'. Two men who questioned the
Monsignor's atrocity narratives were thrown into the Lee.[160] The Cork
promoters of the Christian Front told the receptive Bishop Fogarty that
'apart from the present purpose of voting sympathy with our brother
Catholics in Spain who are suffering, it is proposed that a permanent
organisation be established to combat Communism and communistic

---

[156] T. Ryle Dwyer, *De Valera: The Man and the Myths* (Dublin, 1991), p. 190. For
Somerville, see p. 300 above.
[157] Bowyer Bell, *Secret Army*, p. 156.
[158] Ibid.
[159] In the Election, held on 16.2.36, the parties of the Republican left (The
Popular Front) won 256 seats, those of the right, 143 seats, and those of the
centre, 54. The second round of voting gave the Popular Front 22 extra seats. A
correspondent for the London *Times* reported that the voting had been 'generally
exemplary'. See Hugh Thomas, *The Spanish Civil War* (London, 1961), pp. 132–4.
[160] Cronin, *Frank Ryan*, p. 75. Whatever the authenticity of Monsignor Sexton's
story, the truth was at least as appalling. Thomas records that 'several priests
were undoubtedly burned alive' while another 'was taken to a corral filled with
fighting bulls, where he was gored to unconsciousness'. *Spanish Civil War*, p. 230.

ideas in Ireland'.[161] In the mid-thirties, 'communistic ideas in Ireland' had a wide range of applications. They could include even token State intervention to alleviate the grosser forms of distress. When limited school meals were provided at State expense in late 1935, Canon Hegarty of Belmullet was concerned that the queueing up of children to avail of the scheme was 'engendering Communism'.[162]

In the Dáil in November 1936, Cosgrave asked the government to recognise Franco's insurgents, since 'a Christian democratic State such as ours should give a clean and clear lead in this matter which involves a life and death struggle against the enemies of our common civilisation'.[163] The leadership of the Catholic Church in Ireland had as decided a view of the Spanish war as the one Cosgrave expressed, and one quite similar to his. Bishop Doorly of Elphin was certain that 'everyone in Ireland' knew that it was not a war between royalists and republicans, or between rich and poor, but 'between Christ and anti-Christ'.[164] The bishops also had a clear policy for dealing with the Irish Republican radicals who publicly supported the Spanish Republican government. When Frank Ryan sent a cablegram of support to the Spanish Government, Cardinal MacRory, speaking in Drogheda, denounced the gesture, suggesting that the State should suppress movements such as the Republican Congress. MacRory told pilgrims at the shrine of Blessed Oliver Plunkett that the Spanish struggle was 'not a question of the army against the people, nor of the aristocracy plus the army and the church against labour. Not at all. It is a question of whether Spain will remain as she has been so long, a Christian and Catholic land, or a Bolshevist and anti-God one'.[165] MacRory went on to suggest that all Irish people should help Spain, by which he meant Franco's forces, 'from our purses, help her to obtain war supplies – what I should say is medical supplies for her sick and wounded. I do not want to say anything about any other kind of help'.[166] The other kind of help for Franco MacRory had in mind was General O'Duffy's Irish Brigade, whose formation he actively encouraged.[167] The Irish Brigade enjoyed the earnest good will of

---

[161] Irish Christian Front letter to Fogarty, 22.9.36, KILLDA.

[162] *The Irish Times*, 19.11.35.

[163] Banta, 'Red Scare', p. 234.

[164] *ICD*, 1938, p. 585.

[165] *Irish Independent*, 21.9.36.

[166] Ibid.

[167] See Eoin O'Duffy, *Crusade in Spain* (Dublin, 1938), pp. 12–15. MacRory contributed £10 to a fund for the supply of field-glasses for O'Duffy's Brigade. See F.F. MacCabe, Honorary Director, Medical Service, Irish Brigade, to Bishop Fogarty, 5.2.37, KILLDA.

other churchmen. Myles Ronan described it as the 'heroic legion' through which Ireland was repaying its debt to Spain;[168] Dean Innocent Ryan of Cashel believed that O'Duffy's men 'had gone to fight the battle of Christianity against Communism'.[169]

In their 1937 Pastorals, a number of bishops deplored the existence of Irish supporters of the Spanish government. 'We have', declared Bishop O'Kane of Derry, 'a group in our midst who are making every effort to draw off the sympathy of the people from the Insurgent forces and the Catholic Church . . . They appear to combine profession of the Catholic faith with Communism, a combination which Pius XI declares impossible'.[170] The group O'Kane had in mind included those members of the Republican Congress who invited a Basque priest, Ramon La Borda, to speak at a crowded meeting in the Gaiety Theatre, Dublin, in January 1937. The Spanish Civil War, La Borda asserted, was not religious: 'the left wing had beaten the right with votes, and now the right was trying to beat them with guns'. Franco was 'a blood-thirsty militarist', whose Spanish clerical allies had used churches and church services as 'an opportunity for pre-election political meetings',[171] a phenomenon long familiar to Irish Republicans.

In 1936, for churchmen as well as for radical Republicans, the Spanish Civil War carried telling echoes of the Irish struggle of 1922–23. In the new conflict, both bishops and Republican radicals played roles oddly at variance with the ones they had adopted in the twenties. Then the bishops were sternly defending the rights of what they deemed a freely elected government against a Republican insurgency; now they were promoting the cause of fascist insurgents bent on the overthrow of another freely elected government. Irish Civil War Republicans had, in episcopal and many other eyes, participated in unlawful rebellion against a legitimate government; now some of them were defending such a government against Irish bishops actively working for its overthrow. In October 1922, the bishops of Ireland had pronounced as a matter of Divine Law that 'no one is justified in rebelling against the legitimate government, whatever it is, set up by the nation and acting within its rights'. On 25 June 1940, the bishops were still reminding Irish Catholics that 'it is a sin against the law of God to conspire against the legitimate authority of the State'.[172] In 1936, the bishops clearly felt that the Spanish insurgents might be exempted from the application of this principle since, presumably,

[168] *Irish Press*, 18.12.36.
[169] See MacEoin, *Survivors*, p. 9.
[170] *ICD*, 1938, p. 585.
[171] *The Irish Times*, 18.1.37.
[172] Fanning, *Independent Ireland*, p. 133.

although the Popular Front might have been lawfully elected to govern, it had, as the *Irish Independent* put it, 'abandoned all the functions of government to a Communist junta bent upon the destruction of personal liberty, the eradication of religion, the burning of churches and the wholesale slaughter of the clergy'.[173] The latter claim was fully justified. An impartial historian of the war records that throughout Republican Spain, 'churches and convents were indiscriminately burned and looted . . . as the outposts of upper or middle-class morality and manners . . . These attacks were accompanied by a colossal onslaught on the lives of members of the Church . . . At no time in the history of Europe or perhaps even the world has so passionate a hatred of religion and all its works been shown.'[174]

In response to the righteous anger of the Irish bishops at such horrors, the best Frank Ryan could do was to assert his own Catholicism and his admiration for the Basque priests who were opposing Fascism and adhering to the Republican side in the face of condemnation by their own bishops.[175] Ryan told Cardinal MacRory that he found it as difficult to see 'the so-called Christian Front and Fascist General O'Duffy as custodians of Christianity' as to accept Franco's 'Mahommedan Moors and the Foreign Legion mercenaries as Christian crusaders in Spain'. MacRory's support for the forces of rebellion in Spain did not, Ryan hoped, imply that he applauded the massacre of 2,000 Catholics at Badajos.[176] Radicals could always exploit

[173] *Irish Independent*, 8.9.36.
[174] Thomas, *Spanish Civil War*, pp. 227ff. Thomas believes that 12 bishops, 283 nuns, 4,184 secular priests and 2,365 monks were murdered by Republicans, mainly between 18.7.36 and 1.9.36. These figures account for 12 per cent of Spanish monks, 13 per cent of secular priests and 20 per cent of bishops. Thomas argues that 'practically nowhere had the Church taken part in the Rising', and that 'nearly all the stories of firing by rebels from church towers' were untrue. Frank Ryan told his parents, in a letter dated 8.1.37, that churches wrecked by Republicans had been 'Fascist barracks'. Cronin, *Frank Ryan*, p. 89.
[175] Following the Pastoral Letter from the Bishops of Vitoria and Pamplona condemning the adhesion of the Basque Catholics to the Republican cause, the Basque priests consulted together and advised the Basque political leaders to continue to support the Republic. They justified this stand theologically by arguing that the Insurgents had not fulfilled the four conditions laid down by St Thomas Aquinas as justifying a rebellion, which were (*a*) that the common good (religion, justice and peace) must be severely compromised; (*b*) that the rebellion must be regarded as necessary by 'prudent men who represent the people'; (*c*) there must be a strong possibility of success, and the probable harm done by the rebellion must not be greater than the probable harm done by the absence of a revolt; (*d*) there must be no other remedy for the elimination of the danger to the common good. See Thomas, *Spanish Civil War*, pp. 261–2.
[176] *Irish Press*, 23.9.36.

the fact that the Irish Catholic crusade to prevent Spain from falling prey to irreligion had its absurd side, and its contradictions. The great majority of Spaniards whose Catholicism O'Duffy's 'heroic legion' was anxious to save, and for whose benefit more than £40,000 was collected at Masses on a single Sunday in October 1936, turned out, on closer inspection, not to be fully Catholic. The men of the Irish Brigade found themselves in a 'mental muddle' when they discovered that while women, girls, children and a few army officers might attend Mass, 'the ordinary Spanish male, in a 90 per cent majority, isn't interested in that sort of thing'. On the other hand, many Spaniards were disedified and disgusted by the drunkenness of their Irish saviours.[177]

Relatively few Irish Republicans, of whatever orientation, shared the enthusiasm of the Republican Congress group for the cause of the Popular Front in Spain; Maud Gonne MacBride, Dorothy Macardle and Michael O'Flanagan were exceptions. O'Flanagan undertook an American trip 'to link up with Irish people as supporters of democracy in Spain', without much success. Brian O'Higgins, a Franco supporter, was pleased to report to Mary MacSwiney that O'Flanagan had failed dismally to impress on American Catholics the merits of Republican Spain.[178] Tom Barry, who believed that Irish Republicans had no business interfering in foreign quarrels, issued an order providing that any member of the IRA attempting to join either of the two Irish groups 'about to intervene' in the Spanish war was to be 'automatically dismissed'.[179] De Valera's government resisted urgent requests from public bodies to sever diplomatic and trade links with what Tralee Urban District Council called the 'communistic government of Spain' and to recognise the 'Provisional Government' set up by Franco.[180] In taking this stand, de Valera could invoke the example of the Vatican which, in its tardiness to recognise Franco's regime and its reservations about it, had shown itself less enthusiastically 'Catholic' than the Irish hierarchy, Fine Gael or the Irish Christian Front.[181] He strengthened his non-interventionist position by introducing legislation making it a

---

[177] Dermot Keogh, 'An Eye-Witness to History: Fr Alexander J. McCabe and the Spanish Civil War, 1936–1939', *Breifne*, 1994, p. 479.
[178] Brian O'Higgins to Mary MacSwiney, 11.6.37, MacSwiney Papers, UCDA P 48a/252 (29). Some Northern Republicans supported Franco, as, apparently, did J.J. O'Kelly. Aodh de Blacam, a Republican Civil War veteran, was one of Franco's most ardent Irish publicists. He wrote a mass-circulation pamphlet in 1936 titled *For God and Spain*. For doubts about J.J. O'Kelly's attitude to the Spanish Civil War see Brian Murphy, *IHS*, vol. xxix, no. 115, May 1995, p. 420.
[179] Cronin, *Frank Ryan*, p. 108.
[180] Dermot Keogh, *Ireland and the Vatican: The Politics and Diplomacy of Church-State Relations, 1922–1960* (Cork, 1995), p. 128.
[181] Ibid., pp. 127–32.

criminal offence to go to Spain without governmental permission. In view of de Valera's insistence on a policy of neutrality in Spain, the many members of Fianna Fáil who sympathised with the Spanish Republicans were constrained to do so in silence.[182]

VII

In the late 1960s, George Gilmore, a central figure in Republican radical politics in the thirties, reflected on the failure of the movements with which he had been associated to convince the rural and urban working classes that their Republican ideals were being betrayed by 'the capitalist interests that dominated the Fianna Fáil party'. In a question-begging analysis, Gilmore suggested that the Republican Congress had enabled 'advanced members' of the IRA 'to bring about a meeting between a section of the Trades Union Movement and the militants of the countryside on terms that might have set the nation marching again under a leadership dominated by the political thought of working-class militancy'.[183] The radical Republican enterprise of the 1930s was based on two fundamental assumptions: that the Republican and working-class struggles were intimately linked, and that both were part of a worldwide struggle between 'advanced' and 'repressive' forces. The 'Nation' on whose behalf Gilmore and his fellow-radicals were agitating was not, on the whole, interested in the rhetoric of the class struggle: there is much evidence that the mass of rural and urban workers and small farmers were not convinced that socialist programmes of action answered to their circumstances, preferring the Republican rhetoric of Fianna Fáil which conformed to traditional pieties and did not attract ecclesiastical censure.

Reports of the Russian and Spanish experiences made it easy for a multitude of clerical voices to convince Catholics that political movements influenced by Communist and socialist ideas had as their aim the subversion of fundamental Christian values, and that such movements were thoroughly un-Irish. In 1933, Daniel Bourke, Secretary of the Ennis United Labourers' Association, was so impressed by Bishop Fogarty's attacks on Communism and radical Republicanism that he wrote to assure him that 'Communism will not enter our ranks and we will not be led astray by the empty promises of the Popular Front'. All Bourke's association wanted was to 'continue to work for better and more Christian homes for our Catholic working-men and their

---

[182] For evidence of Fianna Fáil support for the Spanish Republic, see J. Bowyer Bell, 'Ireland and the Spanish Civil War', *Studia Hibernica*, no. 9, 1969.
[183] Gilmore, *Republican Congress*, p. 63.

families'. He assured Fogarty that his members had no connection with 'Unions whose sympathies are with those whose object is to banish religion from society'[184] Other working-class groups appeared equally anxious to avoid the Communist taint. In 1934, de Valera claimed in the Dáil that 'the Able-Bodied Men's Association of Finglas savoured of Communism'.[185] Nicholas Russell, PP Finglas, in a vigorous reply, acknowledged that the members of the Association had made known 'their grievances and their desperate position', but asserted that there 'is not a man amongst them either a Communist or of Communistic tendencies'. He invited anyone who thought there was to come to Mass 'and see these working-men approaching the altar in their hundreds on their sodality morning'.[186] In 1936, Bishop Fogarty anxiously referred to Irish Trade Unionists 'being led by the nose by an Englishman'. His remarks met with the approval of the Secretary of the Federation of Irish Rail and Road Workers, a 'Catholic Trade Union', who had been doing his best to educate 'other workers in the railway world on the evils of belonging to a Trade Union [which] sends money to the Reds in Spain'. He was convinced, 'as an Irish Catholic and working railway man that the only way to stop the spread of communism in this country is to sever their connection with English unions'. He hoped that God would permit Fogarty to live long enough 'to see the last shreds of communism banished from the shores of our beloved Ireland as effectively as St Patrick banished the snakes'.[187] From the Church's point of view, the menace of international communism and the presence in Ireland of radical Republicans who could be identified as its agents had its positive side, reinforcing the faith of working-class Catholics, stimulating their ardour and determination to combine with the clergy to combat its influence, and generally contributing to the cohesiveness of the Church. Republican radicals did not enjoy corresponding benefits from ecclesiastical condemnation, and could do little to counteract it effectively, although since this made it difficult to operate at home, it may have stimulated some of them to promote the radical cause in Spain. The campaign of the Church against the radicals was all the more effective because, as Richard English remarks, 'its laity so widely considered socialist argument to be hostile to their worldly, economic interests'.[188]

---

[184] Daniel Bourke to Bishop Fogarty, 21.12.33, KILLDA.
[185] *Irish Press*, 2.3.34.
[186] Ibid., 5.3.34. A local Labour Councillor felt it necessary to 'state authoritatively that there is not one individual Communist in Finglas'. Ibid.
[187] Francis Hamill to Bishop Fogarty, 29.9.36, KILLDA.
[188] English, *Radicals and the Republic*, p. 212.

Non-radical Republicans in the thirties generally viewed radical ideas with distaste, and often because the Church did. At the beginning of the decade, when *An Phoblacht* permitted its readers to debate Republican ideology, several prominent ones indicated their preference for a Republic informed by Catholic principles rather than Marxist ones. It was enough for Tom Barry's wife, Leslie Bean de Barra, that the Church had made 'a worldwide declaration' against national ownership of resources; such ownership Mary MacSwiney found 'inconsistent with Christian ethics', and she rejected it because she judged such matters as a Catholic, 'first, last and all the time'. In answer to Seán MacBride's denunciation of 'private Capitalism in any form', Michael Price, who was to take a radical stand in 1934, argued that 'the Christian world must attach profound importance to encyclicals promulgated by Christ's vicar on earth'.[189] The depth of even Frank Ryan's radical convictions is open to doubt. Tom Barry believed that Ryan was no more a Communist than he himself was, but a patriotic Republican influenced by the social thought of Liam Mellows,[190] while Richard English rightly detects 'considerable irony' in Ryan's wartime emergence as 'a distinguished guest' in Germany following his struggle against 'international fascism' in Spain.[191] In the long run, Ryan's radical impulses proved less durable than his traditional Republican anti-British ones, which may help to explain why he could write from Germany on 6 November 1941 to Leopold Kerney, Irish Minister to Spain, suggesting that 'there might be a situation in which I might go as a liaison to your boss [de Valera]', and why he could imagine himself as a member of the next Irish government if Germany won the war.[192]

However angry their ideological conflicts with the Church in the twenties and thirties, and however often some of them might have been publicly numbered by Catholic publicists among the enemies of

---

[189] See *An Phoblacht*, 14.3.31; 21.2.31.

[190] See Cronin, *Frank Ryan*, p. 108. Ryan might also have been influenced by some of the social ideas of Pearse. In 'The Sovereign People', completed on 31.3.1916, Pearse argued that it was 'for the nation to determine to what extent private property may be held by its members, and in what items of the nation's material resources private property shall be allowed. A nation may, for instance, determine as the free Irish nation determined and enforced for many centuries, that private ownership shall not exist in land; that the whole of the nation's soil is the public property of the nation . . . A nation may go further and determine that all sources of wealth whatsoever are the property of the nation'. *Political Writings and Speeches of Pádraic H. Pearse* (Dublin, 1952), pp. 339–40.

[191] English, *Radicals and the Republic*, pp. 249–50.

[192] Ryan's letter to Kerney will be found in Secretary's Office Files, Dept of Foreign Affairs, NAI A 20/4.

religion,[193] few, if any, were fully lost to the institution. When Ryan's body was brought home to Ireland in 1979 from East Germany, representatives of 'all shades of Republicanism' were represented at his funeral Mass in the Carmelite Church, Whitefriars Street, 'where he attended Mass every Sunday when in Dublin in the 1920s and 1930s'.[194] Peadar O'Donnell might deplore the Catholic complexion of the 1937 constitution which seemed to him to have given 'the Roman Catholic Bishops of the South' a privileged position as 'the watch-dogs of the private property classes'. He might also object to any 'political privilege' accorded to the bishops 'except what devotion to the independence of the country and to the general democratic struggle may earn them'.[195] O'Donnell, like so many other Republicans, how-ever, could distinguish between the institution and its leadership. When he was asked by a small group of Republican priests, which included Michael O'Flanagan, to canvass support among Republicans for a 'National Church of Ireland' to cater specifically for the spiritual needs of Republicans, he was not interested.[196]

For the great majority of 'nationalist' anti-Treaty Republicans, Catholic allegiance was inseparable from Republicanism. The family of Count Plunkett had, since the Treaty, been at odds with various members of the Catholic hierarchy on fundamental issues of principle, but they strove to assert their point of view from within the Church rather than to attack it from without, betraying an extreme anxiety to win Church approval for their cause. A striking instance of this is found in 1940, when Josephine Mary Plunkett, wife of the Count and mother of the executed 1916 leader, was worried about the conditions being endured by her son on hunger-strike in Mountjoy where, she

[193] For a celebrated example, which led to a libel action by Peadar O'Donnell against the *Irish Rosary*, see the April 1932 issue of that periodical, where it was suggested that O'Donnell had gone to Moscow in 1929 to study 'anti-religious propaganda', the 'cornerstone of the Soviet technique of revolution'.

[194] Cronin, *Frank Ryan*, p. 234.

[195] *An Phoblacht*, 22.5.37. Donal Barrington points out that the 1937 Constitution 'places the rights of the Church and of religious orders in a very strong position. It protects Church property, even more strongly than that of ordinary citizens'. Barrington is referring to Article 44, Section 2, sub-section 6. *The Church, the State and the Constitution* (Dublin, 1959), p. 10.

[196] In 1974, O'Donnell recalled that 'Father O'Flanagan called for me one day and without a hint of what was afoot drove me to a hotel in Dun Laoghaire where six priests waited; it's likely each had got a crack from a crozier although I don't know for sure. My role was to report on what backing republicans could give them if they were to set up the National Church of Ireland. I had to pooh pooh the idea. There were enough of us in a towering rage with the bishops to give Father O'Flanagan a congregation but there was no coherence among us'. 'The Clergy and Me', *Doctrine and Life*, October 1974, pp. 542-3.

told Cardinal MacRory, 'sexual degenerates are also imprisoned'. It was to MacRory, as 'Supreme Pastor of God's flock in Ireland' that the Plunkett family looked for help in having Republicans transferred to 'non-criminal jails' with a view to ending 'their contamination, through association' by members of the 'criminal classes'. Countess Plunkett approached MacRory 'in absolute fealty to the Holy See and complete obedience to the Church', as the mother of one who had told a priest in 1916 that he was dying 'for the glory of God and the honour of Ireland'.[197] Nine years earlier, following the condemnation of Saor Éire by the bishops, the Pope was informed by the 'Executive Council of the Irish Republic' that a leading Irish 'Communist' member of the forbidden organisation had expressed the hope that 'a comprehensive National organisation' might be built on the basis of the social order outlined in the Pope's encyclical *Quadragesimo Anno*; the 'Republican Government' itself found fault with the Irish bishops for not having 'made the people familiar with the meaning of that Encyclical'.[198] Comments such as these, which are by no means isolated, underline the centrality of the Church and its teaching authority to the major elements of non-constitutional Republicanism, as well as the overwhelmingly confessional nature of the Republican vision.

[197] Josephine Mary Plunkett to Cardinal MacRory, 14.3.40, NAI S 11515.
[198] Executive Council of the Irish Republic to Pope Pius XI n.d. [late 1931].

CHAPTER SEVEN

===

THE NORTH

I

===

A little over a week after the Treaty was signed, Bishop Foley of Kildare and Leighlin was conscious of differences in attitude between Southern and Northern bishops on the value of the settlement. Commenting on the bishops whose dioceses were exclusively in the twenty-six counties, Foley told his Vicar-General that 'as individuals they favoured ratification'. The Northern bishops, on the other hand, were 'in a bad way about the Northern Parliament'. One of them, not identified by Foley, 'declared that in view of what is very likely to happen to their schools, convents etc. under the Treaty as it stands, he would much prefer to remain under the British Government'.[1] The Northern bishops whose dioceses were likely to be subject to the problems adverted to by Foley were Cardinal Logue of Armagh and Archbishop O'Donnell who became his co-adjutor in 1922; Bishops McKenna of Clogher, McHugh of Derry, MacRory of Down and Connor, Mulhern of Dromore and Finegan of Kilmore. Apart from MacRory, Mulhern was the only Northern bishop whose diocese was entirely within the six-county area. His initial enthusiasm for the Treaty was quickly tempered by his concern for the fate of Catholics under a Northern Parliament if a permanent partition of the country were to be the eventual outcome of the settlement. Like some of his Northern episcopal colleagues, he did not see this as inevitable. He believed that the suffering of Northern Catholics would be mitigated and shortened under an all-Ireland arrangement. 'The North-East question', he told Hagan, 'will be of short-lived duration if this happy, to my mind, consummation is reached'.[2] McKenna declared that 'the big blot on the Treaty to which no one in the Dáil seemed to give a thought is the uncertainty surrounding the position of Catholics in

[1] Foley to M.J. Murphy, 18.12.21, KLDA.
[2] Mulhern to Hagan, 6.1.22, Hagan Papers.

the North-East'.[3] McKenna, like Mulhern, trusted that 'everything may come right yet', but felt unable to rejoice in the meantime'.[4]

The uncertainty referred to by McKenna arose from the terms of three of the Articles of the Treaty. Article 14 outlined the arrangements to be made if Northern Ireland decided to incorporate itself with the twenty-six county state, in which case provision was made for a thirty-two county Free State with six counties under Home Rule, the reserved powers being passed from London to Dublin. Two of the Articles, 11 and 12, addressed the possibility that Northern Ireland might wish to exclude itself from incorporation with the South. In that event, Article 11 provided that the six-county entity could vote itself out of the all-Ireland settlement. On the other hand, if it did so its boundaries would, according to the terms of the Article 12, be subject to a revision by a Boundary Commission. This Article stipulated that the boundary was to be determined 'in accordance with the wishes of the inhabitants, as far as may be compatible with economic and geographic conditions'. The Irish signatories of the Treaty agreed to its terms on the understanding that Article 12 was designed to compel Sir James Craig and his Northern administration to choose between entering an all-Ireland settlement and acquiescing in a considerable reduction of the territory of Northern Ireland. On the Irish side, enthusiasm for the Boundary Commission was largely associated with the belief, 'not discouraged by Lloyd George, that it would recommend handing over to the South areas of such large extent that the Northern State must collapse'.[5]

It was soon evident that this was not a belief shared by Craig and the rest of the Unionist leadership, who were understandably angry that a settlement involving their fundamental interests should have been reached without their participation, particularly in the light of the strong claims, alluded to by R.F. Foster, that Lloyd George had guaranteed to Ulster Unionist leaders in 1920 'that their borders would remain impregnable'.[6] Against this, it must be borne in mind that the Treaty gave the Northern Ireland government, while not a party to it, effective control over the implementation of its most significant provisions in relation to the six counties. In January 1922, Craig was making it clear that he regarded the six-county area as immutable,

---

[3] Here McKenna was ignoring the contribution of Seán MacEntee, who devoted his speech against the Treaty to an examination of its function as a confirmation and perpetuation of Partition. See Dáil Éireann, Treaty Debates, 22 December 1921, pp. 152–7.

[4] McKenna to Hagan, 31.1.22.

[5] A.T.Q. Stewart, *The Narrow Ground* (London, 1977).

[6] R. F. Foster, *Modern Ireland, 1600–1972* (London 1988), p. 505.

and assuring Ulster Unionists that he would resist any attempt by a Boundary Commission to interfere with it. He told the Ulster Unionist Council that he would never agree to any rearrangements of the boundary 'that leaves our Ulster area less than it was under the Government of Ireland Act'.[7] A few months later, angered by the Collins–de Valera Pact, Craig promised the members of the Northern Parliament that they would 'hear no more about a commission coming to decide whether our boundaries shall be so and so. What we have now we hold, and we will hold against all combinations'.[8]

The fears of the Northern Catholic bishops and their senior clergy that the Treaty might have uniformly unfavourable consequences for their people were soon reflected in their urgent demands for reassurance from Southern political leaders. Before the Treaty was approved by the Dáil, Bishops O'Dea of Galway and McHugh of Derry called on Arthur Griffith for the purpose of arranging an episcopal delegation to discuss safeguards regarding education and patronage in the North. Griffith assured them that the safeguards in question would be inserted in the Treaty as 'necessary precautions' in case the Belfast Parliament rejected incorporation with the Free State. Even in the latter event, he told McHugh, Derry was bound to come into the Free State as a result of the deliberations of the Boundary Commission.[9] In January 1922, an influential deputation of Unionists from Newry was assured by Craig that Newry and the remainder of South Down would remain under the jurisdiction of the Northern Parliament.[10] Bishop Mulhern was sufficiently worried to write to Seán Milroy, a pro-Treaty TD for Cavan, who passed his letter to Michael Collins. The latter, basing his argument on 'obvious fairness', told Mulhern that the Provisional Government could not consent to the permanent inclusion of South Down in the Northern State. 'Quite clearly', Collins declared, 'the Irish government would have the allegiance of the people of such places as South and East Down and a great portion of Armagh. Newry is included in this territory. Therefore no action or no desire of the Northern Parliament could take this territory away from the Irish government.' Craig might well contemplate doing this, but 'whether he does or not the position remains unaltered, and it is for us to see that justice is done and that our ideas, which are unquestionably just, prevail'.[11] Mulhern immediately conveyed Collins's reassurance to John Tierney, PP Enniskillen, the clerical leader of Catholic opinion in

[7] *Freeman's Journal*, 28.1.22.
[8] Patrick Buckland, *James Craig* (Dublin, 1980), p. 76.
[9] McHugh to Byrne, 18.12.21, DAA; McHugh to Hagan, 7.2.22, Hagan Papers.
[10] Collins to Mulhern, 28.1.22, DRDA.
[11] Ibid.

Fermanagh.[12] Tierney interpreted Craig's rejection of boundary changes as a sign that 'the Six Counties are coming into the Free State, thus enabling Craig to retain his Parliament (subordinate) without the loss of an inch of territory'. Even with this relatively benign outcome, Tierney feared that Collins, who, he declared, 'does not know the Six Counties', would fail to obtain proper guarantees for the minority in regard to education and local government. He correctly predicted that the Unionists would ensure Nationalist loss of control of Fermanagh and Tyrone County Councils and Derry Corporation.[13]

Collins did not mention the Boundary Commission in his letter of assurance to Mulhern. On 21 January, a week before he wrote it, he and Craig had made the first of their two pacts, and agreed that the Boundary Commission arrangement in the Treaty should be changed and that the Dublin and Belfast governments would instead appoint one representative each to report back to Collins and Craig who would 'mutually agree on behalf of their respective governments on the future boundaries between the two'.[14] Craig interpreted this to involve 'an admission by the Free State' that Ulster was a separate entity.[15] Comments such as this provoked a vigorous response from clerics in strongly Catholic areas in Northern Ireland. In early February 1922, Michael Quinn, PP Dungannon, presiding at a rally of Catholic residents of the town, was concerned about the implications for Catholics of the Craig–Collins Pact. A resolution was passed 'protesting on principle against any attempt to include Tyrone, or any part of it, in the Belfast Parliament'. Quinn was determined, along with Catholic 'bishops, priests and laity' to resist Partition and what it would mean to Catholic schools 'under an unfriendly government'. He was also conscious of the likelihood of a new cultural conditioning which would represent a danger to nationality as well as to religion: whatever Irish history was allowed in the schools would be 'written by an unfriendly pen'.[16] John O'Doherty, PP Strabane, informed Griffith that 'the Catholic bishops of Ulster are very glad to know that the large areas of the Six Counties that are fully entitled to be included in the Free State are holding their meetings and are determined to vindicate their rights no matter who says nay'.[17]

---

[12] Cahir Healy, the Nationalist MP for the area described Tierney as 'by far the most influential and the ablest of the Northern clerics and the one who has a settlement at the back of his mind'. Healy to North Eastern Boundary Bureau, 18.9.24, NEBB Papers, Carton 9, NAI.
[13] Tierney to Mulhern, 31.1.22, DRDA.
[14] NAI S 1834 A.
[15] *Freeman's Journal*, 28.1.22.
[16] *Freeman's Journal*, 7.2.22.
[17] Ibid., 1.2.22.

In the immediate aftermath of the Treaty, the Catholic bishops and their clergy were acknowledged, both by the mass of Northern Catholics and by the Provisional Government in Dublin, as natural leaders of nationalist opinion in the North. This leadership role had been recognised by Southern politicians before the Treaty. In the negotiations leading up to the agreement, five bishops and eight priests from the North were among the 28 people whose views were sought by the Dáil Committee of Information on the Case of Ulster.[18] Patrick Keown, PP Carrickmacross, a member of the Clerical Managers' Association, outlined the case against Partition; Daniel Mageean, later Bishop of Down and Connor and John McShane, President of St Columb's College, Derry, helped to draft a memorandum on education, while John Tierney, PP Enniskillen made a case for the incorporation of Fermanagh with the Free State.[19] The title of the Northern clergy to this kind of political leadership was based on their close identification with the grievances of their people, their active involvement in campaigns to remedy these, and the notable absence of a significant number of lay politicians possessing the authority and expertise to rival that of the bishops and senior clerics. The parliamentary representatives chosen to represent the Northern minority in the 1921 election included Collins, who knew little of the North, as well as de Valera and Seán O'Mahony, whose opposition to the Treaty made it impossible for them to reflect the views of a Northern nationalist population overwhelmingly in favour of it. In 1922, the anti-Treaty movement was largely a Southern phenomenon; it had few followers among Northern supporters of Sinn Féin, in the northern divisions of the IRA or among the Ulster nationalists still loyal to the traditions of the Irish Parliamentary Party.[20]

Northern Catholic clerical leaders of the period had to contend with problems different from those which faced the bishops and priests of the South. The latter were deeply involved in the conflicting claims to the legitimacy of the Provisional government and the Republican leadership, and in the political and moral issues presented by the Civil War, on which a considerable number of them took a stand on one side or the other. Such issues were of much less immediate concern to Northern clerics. In March 1925, Cahir Healy the Nationalist MP spoke for them as well as other Northern Catholics when he pointed out, in response to Sinn Féin denunciations of the Free State during the Northern election campaign, that 'for the Nationalists of the

[18] Childers Papers TCD 7784/66/4.
[19] McGilligan Papers P35/6/90, UCDA; Childers Papers 7784/89.
[20] See E. Phoenix, *Northern Nationalism, Nationalist Politics, Partition and the Catholic Minority in* Northern Ireland, 1890–1940 (Belfast, 1994), p. 395.

North East it is not a question of Free State versus Republic: unfortunately they had neither'.[21] Up to November 1925 and the failure of the Boundary Commission to fulfil the political hopes of many Northern nationalists, particularly those living near the border, Church leaders in the North looked almost exclusively to the Free State government to secure their rights and protect their interests. They tended to regard the anti-Treaty minority in the South as a serious threat to the ultimate welfare of the Catholic people of the North; any attempt to undermine the Treaty necessarily involved jeopardising the Boundary Commission, on the promise of which many border Catholics placed their hopes for deliverance from the North to the South. Again, many northern churchmen, doing all they could to defend their beleaguered communities, particularly in Belfast, against militant Protestants, and the largely hostile, sometimes murderous, forces of law and order,[22] were understandably incensed at the part militant Southern Republicans were playing in fomenting and sustaining a civil war at the very time when the protection of Catholic lives, property and political and civil rights depended on the united efforts of Southern and Northern nationalists.

II

During the period between the signing of the Treaty in December 1921 and the Tripartite Agreement of 3 December 1925 between the governments of Great Britain, the Free State and Northern Ireland, the main provision of which was that the boundary was not to be altered,[23] the constitutional status as well as the territorial extent of the six-county state remained uncertain. In their earliest public statements, the Northern bishops and clergy accepted the Treaty as a *fait accompli* and gave no countenance to the Republican case for repudiating it. While MacRory, the least enthusiastic of the bishops, regarded it as 'a poor settlement for the Catholics of the six counties in the immediate future', he believed that 'things will come right before many years have passed'.[24] Collins had argued in the Dáil that the good will generated by the Treaty would 'lead very rapidly' to 'the entry of the North-East under the Irish Parliament'.[25] MacRory went further,

---

[21] *Irish News*, 31.3.25.
[22] For a first-hand account of the plight of Belfast Catholics in 1922, see Patrick J. Gannon, 'In the Catacombs of Belfast', *Studies*, June 1922.
[23] For details, see D. O'Sullivan, *The Irish Free State and its Senate* (London, 1940), pp. 178ff.
[24] MacRory to Hagan, 17.1.22, Hagan Papers.
[25] Dáil Éireann, Treaty Debates, 19.12.21, p. 35.

suggesting that 'Ulster would realise it could not flourish outside the Free State and would therefore be forced to accept inclusion'.[26] McHugh of Derry was hopeful that a convergence of self-interest and the national interest, North and South, would 'remove the obstacles in the way of a free and united Ireland'.[27] The clear preference of Northern Catholic church leaders was that the Belfast Parliament should choose inclusion in the Free State. MacRory spoke for all the bishops when he argued that there was no hope for peace 'if the North persisted in remaining outside the Free State' and dwelt on the injustice of 'subjecting Catholics . . . to a régime they did not want for the sake of Unionists who formed only 19% of the population of the island'.[28] In January 1922, MacRory hoped that the refusal of Catholics to recognise the Northern State might encourage Unionist leaders to seek union with the rest of Ireland. 'I take it', he told Mulhern, 'we shall ultimately have to recognise this [Northern] Parliament if it survive, and just at this time our refusal to recognise it might perhaps help towards union with the Free State. That is Mr Griffith's view, expressed to me last Thursday'. A central element of the non-recognition strategy was the refusal of the Catholic clerical school managers to sign teachers' salary forms. MacRory wondered whether it would be 'possible or wise' to ask the managers to 'abstain from signing for a month or so while the Ulster men are making up their minds as to whether they will throw in their lot with the South'.[29] The need to prevent the establishment of the Northern State and to do everything possible to undermine Craig's government soon appeared more urgent to northern episcopal minds as Belfast Catholics began to experience what Bishop McKenna called 'savage persecutions' at the hands of militant Protestants.[30]

The frequent atrocities perpetrated against Northern Catholics in the early months of 1922 encouraged prominent churchmen who feared for the lives and properties of those Catholics who might be forced to remain under the Belfast jurisdiction to support Provisional Government efforts to make it impossible for the Northern regime to function. In their joint pronouncement of 26 April 1922, the bishops, North and South, drew attention to the intolerable plight of Catholics in the North-East. 'Not only', they claimed, 'have Catholics been denied their natural right to earn their daily bread and thrown upon the charity of the world, but they are subjected to a savage

[26] *Irish Independent*, 10.1.22.
[27] Ibid., 4.2.22.
[28] Ibid., 17.3.22.
[29] MacRory to Mulhern, 26.1.22, DRDA.
[30] Lenten Pastoral for 1922, CLRDA.

persecution . . . Every kind of persecution, arson, destruction of property, systematic terrorism, deliberate assassination and indiscriminate
murder reigns supreme'.[31] Lacking faith in the will or the ability of the
Northern Government to alter this state of affairs, Catholic Church
leaders understandably believed that their people could be delivered
from persecution only through the collapse of the Northern State.
Members of the Dublin Government, most notably Collins, promoted
various strategies to bring this about, and involved Northern Catholic
Church leaders in their plans. On 28 January 1922, at a Government
meeting attended by MacRory, Collins declared that the 'non-
recognition of the Northern Parliament was essential – otherwise they
would have nothing to bargain with'.[32] MacRory was present at
another meeting, on 7 February, at which the Government decided to
pay the salaries of all Northern teachers who refused to recognise the
Belfast Ministry of Education.[33] This move was inspired by representations to Dublin from many Northern Catholic teachers and some
school managers who objected to placing their schools under the
control of the Belfast Parliament.

In early March 1922, the Provisional Government which, under
the influence of Collins, increasingly regarded itself as the protector of

[31] *Irish Ecclesiastical Record*, July 1922, p. 1. A Protestant response to the bishops'
indictment of the Northern authorities was issued under the signatures of the
Archbishop of Armagh, the Bishop of Down and Connor, the Moderator of the
Presbyterian General Assembly and the President of the Methodist Conference.
'It is not true', the Protestant leaders claimed, 'that Roman Catholics have been
denied their natural right to earn their daily bread. The [Protestant] shipyard
workers did not exclude any man because of his religion. A reign of terror was
organised by gangs of [Catholic] gunmen who encamped in certain quarters of
the city of Belfast, made war upon its people, throwing bombs into tramcars full
of workers and savagely shooting down men, women and children. This was an
attempt to intimidate the loyalists . . . The fact is that the trouble in Belfast is political and not religious. It is an effort to paralyse the Northern Government . . . It
is not an easy thing for a powerful majority to submit tamely to such treatment
at the hands of an aggressive minority . . . As to the Northern Government, it
has shown in many ways its earnest desire that Roman Catholics should have
their full share in the public and private life of Northern Ireland. It is eagerly
anxious that they should claim and enjoy equal rights with all others in the
citizenship of Northern Ireland'. See *Irish Ecclesiastical Record*, July 1922, p. 2 for a
copy of this statement, as well as a vigorous reply from Patrick J. Gannon, SJ,
who was unhappy with its account of events. Gannon pointed out that the 'vast
majority of the whole Catholic Community [in Belfast] were followers of Mr
Devlin, recruiter, constitutionalist and even, it would appear, convinced imperialist.
Yet all were indiscriminately driven from their work without any option of any
kind'. (Ibid. p. 3)
[32] Provisional Government Minutes, NAI G/1/1/45.
[33] Ibid., NAI S 1973 A.

Catholic rights in the North, set up a committee whose purpose, in the words of Collins, was 'to get the best possible advice from representative people in the North-East in order to help and direct its policy in regard to the whole [North-Eastern] question'. The duty of the Committee would be to advise and assist the Provisional Government 'on all questions affecting the 6-county area'. These included the formation of the Boundary Commission and its work, the Belfast pogrom and the possible reinstitution of the Belfast Boycott,[34] and 'all governmental functions as affected by or as affecting the Belfast Parliament'.[35] Provisional Government recognition of the central role of the Church in Northern political affairs was underlined by the composition of the North-Eastern Advisory Committee. Of the thirty-six pro-Treaty Northern nationalists invited by Collins to become members, thirteen were clerics. Three of these were bishops, MacRory, Mulhern and McKenna, while among the clergy were Sinn Féin priests from various parts of the North, including John Tierney of Enniskillen, Philip O'Doherty of Omagh and John Hassan of Belfast. The committee met for the first time on 11 April 1922. At the end of March, Craig and Collins had signed a second Pact, one clause of which proposed to reform the Belfast Special Constabulary.[36] Much of the discussion at the inaugural meeting of the North-Eastern Advisory Committee centred on a gross violation of this pact on 1 April, when, following the shooting of a Special Constable, several of his colleagues took part in the massacre at Arnon Street, Belfast, of five Catholics, including a seventy-year-old man and a boy of seven, whose father was beaten to death with a sledge-hammer.[37] In the course of a long discussion, it became clear that other members of the Provisional Government had serious reservations about the policy of non-recognition of the Northern Government so strongly urged by Collins and supported by Northern clergymen. Kevin O'Higgins spoke of the

[34] In July 1920, loyalists, following the assassination in Cork of an Ulster-born police commissioner, violently expelled thousands of Catholic workers from the Harland and Wolff shipyards in Belfast. In August, Bishop MacRory joined with a number of prominent Sinn Féin members including Seán MacEntee, Denis McCullough of the IRB, Frank Crummey of the IRA, and John Hassan, a Belfast curate, to launch a Belfast Boycott Committee. This committee petitioned Dáil Éireann to institute a boycott of Belfast goods and Belfast-oriented banks throughout the rest of Ireland in retaliation for the 'war of extermination' being waged against Catholics. See D. Macardle, *The Irish Republic*, 4th edn (Dublin, 1951), pp. 387 ff.

[35] Collins to Mulhern, 8.3.22, DRDA.

[36] M. Hopkinson, 'The Craig-Collins Pact of 1922: two attempted reforms of the Northern Ireland Government', *IHS*, vol. xxvii, November 1990, p. 151.

[37] For a full account of the meeting, see NAI S 1011.

futility of such a policy, while Griffith admitted that the government was unable to protect 'our people in Belfast'. MacRory urged that the pro-Treaty section of Sinn Féin in Belfast should 'come as a body into the Specials'.[38]

Whatever the views of his government colleagues on the wisdom of his Northern policy, Collins was not to be deterred from his efforts to embarrass and destabilise the Northern Government. On 4 May 1922, he sent a confidential circular to all his ministers asking them to institute schemes 'for non-cooperation in every possible way with the Northern Parliament' and, in addition 'a scheme making it impossible for them to carry on'.[39] In January 1922, Collins had, with the connivance of Richard Mulcahy, Minister for Defence in the Second Dáil Cabinet, and without the knowledge of other members of the Government, involved both pro- and anti-Treaty wings of the IRA in the preparation of an aggressive IRA policy against the North, which was to have its culmination in a joint IRA offensive on the Six Counties scheduled for May 1922 with the object of bringing down the Northern Government. February 1922 saw a wave of IRA attacks in the North which involved 'shooting a number of Northern Government officials and police; capturing a few barracks and destroying several thousand pounds worth of Northern Government property'.[40] These attacks were organised by the pro-Treaty IRA Chief of Staff, Eoin O'Duffy, with the authority of Collins and Mulcahy.[41] At a meeting in London with representatives of the British and Northern Ireland governments, Collins, in 'a truculently boastful mood, made no attempt to deny responsibility for outrages in the North and even claimed absolute control over the IRA'[42] His active involvement in this conspiracy strongly suggests that his peace policy, represented in his two pacts with Craig, was 'a mere public front'.[43] In the preparations for the May offensive, Collins had the cooperation of Liam Lynch, Chief of Staff of the anti-Treaty forces; recruits were to come from the anti-Treaty forces in the South, while resources for the operation were to be supplied by the pro-Treaty GHQ. Both Lynch and Collins

---

[38] Ibid.
[39] NAI S 1801 A, 4.5.22.
[40] Bryan A. Follis, *A State Under Siege, The Establishment of Northern Ireland* (Oxford, 1995), p. 91.
[41] Ibid.
[42] P. Buckland, *James Craig, Lord Craigavon* (Dublin, 1980), p. 76.
[43] Hopkinson, 'Craig–Collins Pacts'. J.M. Curran claims that although Collins was not directly involved, it is certain that 'his associates would not have embarked on such a dangerous enterprise without his blessing'. *The Birth of the Irish Free State, 1921–1923* (Birmingham, Alabama, 1980), p. 178.

presumably saw the Northern offensive as a significant element in the quest for IRA unity.[44]

The May offensive was a disastrous failure, placing the lives of some of those it was designed to help in even greater jeopardy. James Woods, the Belfast IRA leader, argued against IRA aggression in Belfast, where the Catholic minority had already been shown to be extremely vulnerable to wholesale reprisals. In Newry, the offensive had the effect of antagonising much of the Catholic population. Good relations had been maintained between Catholics and Protestants in the town until an attack was launched on the barracks, with the result that many Catholics had to endure the wrath of the Special Constabulary without the support of IRA units which had been compelled to cross the border into the South.[45] In late May and early June, when IRA volunteers and B Specials clashed on the Fermanagh–Donegal border, seven pro-Treaty IRA men were killed, six wounded and four taken prisoner. Collins felt compelled to deny pro-Treaty involvement. Decisions taken at a meeting of the Provisional Government on 3 June 1922 marked the end of Collins's aggressive Northern policy. Peaceful obstruction of the work of the Northern Government was now seen as the wiser course; the Government laid it down that no troops from the twenty-six counties 'either those under official control or attached to the Executive' should be recruited to invade the six-county area.[46] Collins's Northern policy and his clandestine activities on behalf of Northern Catholics were inspired by his deep hatred of loyalism and his belief that joint pro-Treaty and Republican activity against the North would help to restore IRA unity, which he appeared to value more highly than strict adherence to the terms of the Treaty. He was clearly violating these as early as February 1922 through his involvement in the kidnapping of leading loyalists and his arms exchange with the anti-Treaty IRA for the purpose of overthrowing the Belfast government.[47] By the end of June 1922, the manifest failure of his Northern policy had forced him to take a much less aggressive public position. He had come to realise that 'there can be no question of forcing Ulster into union with the twenty-six counties. If Ulster is to join us, it must be voluntarily.'[48]

---

[44] See M. Hopkinson, *Green Against Green. The Irish Civil War* (Dublin, 1988), p. 85; Macardle, *Irish Republic*, p. 899; C.S. Andrews, *Dublin Made Me* (Dublin, 1979), p. 222.
[45] Hopkinson, *Green Against Green*, pp. 85–6.
[46] Provisional Government Minutes, 3.6.22, NAI G1/2.
[47] For a detailed account of these matters, see T.P. Coogan, *Michael Collins* (Dublin, 1990), pp. 344 ff.
[48] *Belfast News Letter*, 30.6.22.

From the beginning, MacRory used his enormous influence in favour of the Treaty; his attitude helped to secure general Sinn Féin support for the agreement in Antrim and Down.[49] The pro-Treaty position taken by East Ulster Catholics was sustained by the optimistic expectation that the Belfast Parliament might, after all, choose inclusion in the Free State. Before the agreement was ratified, the *Irish News* expressed the hope that a united country might emerge, that a settlement would be made by common consent, 'under which the necessity for appointing a Boundaries Commission, of recognising any boundaries within Ireland . . . will not arise'.[50] It was inevitable that the Boundary Commission would not hold the same attraction for East Ulster Catholics as it did for those near the border. If it transferred large elements of the border population to the South, it would thereby convert the Catholics of East Ulster into a much smaller minority than they were at present and make their situation even more perilous. If the Boundary Commission could do nothing for them, some form of Irish unity, even one based on the Treaty provision for an all-Ireland Parliament, might yet secure their future. Whatever the outcome, MacRory could offer them no hope of 'complete freedom', by which he meant Irish unity, outside the terms of the Treaty. He considered de Valera's anti-Treaty attitude sterile.[51] Six months later, MacRory's attitude had not changed significantly. S.G. Tallents, Secretary to the Lord Lieutenant of Ireland, consulted him in an attempt to assess pro-Treaty Sinn Féin attitudes on the Northern question. MacRory was 'in close touch with Collins' and had 'great influence' on the Catholics of Belfast. He was not prepared to recognise the Belfast government 'unless it agreed to co-operate for large purposes with the Southern government'. He favoured 'an absolutely free Ireland' on principle but realised that this was not 'practical politics'. MacRory seems to have blamed de Valera for IRA violence in Belfast: he told Tallents that he had talked to de Valera 'at great length' in June to ask him 'if he had the power to call off the violent Catholic element in Belfast', but found him 'disoriented'.[52] In August 1922, according to an agent sent by Collins to the North, MacRory believed

---

[49] *Phoenix, Northern Nationalism*, p. 161.

[50] *Irish News*, 30.12.21.

[51] Ibid., 2.1.22.

[52] MacRory might have been better advised to have discussed the 'violent Catholic element in Belfast' with Collins, the main promoter of anti-Unionist disruption. During the Civil War, de Valera advocated only civil resistance in the North. He did not incite Republicans north of the border to involve themselves in military activities; he advised them to concentrate on 'civil organisation'. See J. Bowman, *De Valera and the Ulster Question, 1917–1973* (Oxford, 1982), p. 77.

that until the Northern Parliament 'entered wholeheartedly' into an all-Ireland Parliament, it should not be recognised, 'even if this meant unrest and bloodshed'.[53]

Enthusiastic support for the Treaty among Nationalists in the border areas was based largely on the hopes inspired by Article 12, the boundary clause of which they initially saw as a guarantee of their early deliverance from the Northern State. Pro-Treaty feeling was intense in Tyrone and Fermanagh, where the local TD, Seán O'Mahony, whose intention to vote against ratification was widely known, was the recipient of strongly worded appeals from Sinn Féin clubs, local bodies and clergymen to vote in accordance with the almost unanimous wishes of his constituents and not to gratify the wishes of 'the Orange and ascendancy party' who would welcome its rejection.[54] The Mayor of Derry, H.C. O'Doherty, was notably less enthusiastic about the settlement, telling Eoin MacNeill on the day after the Treaty was signed that if the Belfast Parliament contracted out of the all-Ireland arrangement, he was 'handing over manacled the lives and liberties of the Catholics who live in that area'.[55] In South Armagh and South Down, a local nationalist newspaper reported strong Catholic support for the Treaty; its editor believed that the Boundary Commission offered the prospect of 'complete freedom' for nationalists.[56]

The sanguine attitudes of border nationalists were soon to change under the impact of events in the South. The outbreak of full-scale civil war at the end of June 1922 had major consequences for Southern attitudes to the problems of Northern Catholics. On 12 July, Collins announced that 'he had arranged to take up duty as Commander-in-Chief of the Army and would not be able to act in his ministerial capacity until further notice'.[57] His preoccupation with military affairs meant that the direction of Northern policy fell largely into the hands of his colleagues in the Provisional Government, who soon decided on a radical departure from the courses of action hitherto pursued by him, mainly on his own initiative. In early August 1922, the Provisional Government set up a committee to formulate a Northern policy. A member of the Committee, Ernest Blythe, an Antrim-born Protestant and Minister for Local Government, wrote an influential memorandum implicitly criticising the Northern policy Collins had been pursuing. Blythe argued for recognition of the Belfast government, and urged that the Provisional Government should

[53] Phoenix, *Northern Nationalism*, pp. 237, 249.
[54] O'Mahony Papers, NLI.
[55] Phoenix, *Northern Nationalism*, pp. 156, 168.
[56] *Frontier Sentinel*, 31.12.21.
[57] Provisional Government Minutes NAI PG/57, 12.7.22.

encourage those within the six counties who looked to it for guidance to acknowledge the legitimacy of the Northern administration and refrain from attempts to prevent its functioning. Blythe took his stand on the obligations imposed by the Treaty on the Southern government and the rights it accorded to the Northern one. The Provisional Government was bound not to encourage 'any unconstitutional attacks' on the Northern Government, which, pending the boundary arbitration, was entitled to claim obedience in the whole of the six-county area. Blythe further argued that the payment of Northern teachers by the Provisional Government was indefensible and should be stopped forthwith, that border raids from the South should be prevented and the offenders handed over to the Northern authorities if flogging were dropped, that Northern Catholics should be urged to disarm, and that Catholic members of the Northern Parliament who had no conscientious objections to taking the Oath of Allegiance should be encouraged to take their seats and pursue the quest for Irish unity by means of propaganda.[58] On 19 August 1922, the Provisional Government formally adopted 'a peace policy . . . with North-East Ulster'.[59] On 26 August 1922, after the death of Collins, the Blythe memorandum was circulated to all the members of the Provisional Government, whose subsequent Northern policy was to be substantially in accord with its ideas. At the same meeting, the doctrine of collective Cabinet responsibility was enunciated with the purpose of preventing Cabinet members from pursuing the kind of individualistic role which Collins had adopted in relation to Northern policy.[60]

The death of Collins, which removed the only pro-Treaty leader who regarded Partition and the plight of Northern Catholics as pressing issues, and the intensification of the Civil War, led to the gradual abandonment of the policy of non-recognition which Blythe had falsely characterised as having been dictated by anti-Treaty groupings. Cosgrave, who had replaced Collins as chairman of the Provisional Government, let it be known that he had no objection to Northern Catholics making a declaration of loyalty to the King and to the Northern Government. By November 1922, the Provisional Government had stopped paying the salaries of Catholic schoolteachers in the North who refused to recognise the government there: 800 of these had been involved and had cost the Southern authorities over £170,000.[61] From August 1922 onwards, Northern Catholics had good

[58] There is a copy of the Blythe memorandum in the Blythe Papers, UCDA, P24/70.
[59] Provisional Government Minutes, 19.8.22, S 1801/A.
[60] See R. Fanning, *Independent Ireland* (Dublin, 1983), p. 36.
[61] D. Harkness, *Northern Ireland since 1920* (Dublin, 1983), p. 27.

reason to believe that Cosgrave and his colleagues had little inclination to involve themselves enthusiastically in Northern affairs, and that they would like to see all Catholic leaders following the example of Joseph Devlin the Belfast nationalist leader and adopting a more flexible attitude to the Northern Parliament. As early as 30 August 1922, Cahir Healy, the leading Nationalist politician in West Ulster, complained that Ulster nationalists had been 'abandoned to Craig's mercy'.[62]

III

Whatever lingering hopes there might have been that the Belfast Parliament might choose to be part of an all-Ireland settlement ended in December 1922. As early as March 1922, however, it was widely recognised that the Northern authorities were not going to pursue this course. On 13 March, the Northern Ireland Cabinet approved a draft motion prepared by the Parliamentary Draftsman, enabling Northern Ireland to vote itself out of the Free State.[63] The Treaty was given legal ratification on 6 December, the anniversary of its signature. Craig moved immediately to formalise the exclusion of the six counties from the jurisdiction of the Free State; on 7 December, both houses of the Northern Parliament presented the appropriate address to the King.[64] In order to vote itself out of the Free State, the Northern Parliament was obliged to avail of the first provision of Article 12 of the Treaty. At the same time, Craig was adamant in refusing to accept the constitutional consequences of doing this. During the short debate on the issue on 7 December, he 'stated emphatically that he would have nothing to do with the Boundary Commission' and added that 'there could be no boundary adjustments unless agreement existed between North and South and the border counties were satisfied'.[65] In February 1922, when Belfast Catholics and Protestants were being daily murdered in their houses and in the streets, Bishop McKenna of Clogher hoped that should the Belfast Parliament not choose to enter the Free State, 'the wishes of the people in all those large areas of the six counties which under the Treaty are fully entitled to remain in the Free State shall be respected and given effect to'.[66] Also in February 1922, it was decided at a conference between British and Provisional Government ministers, who anticipated Craig's

---

[62] Hopkinson, *Green Against Green*, p. 88.
[63] Follis, *State Under Siege*, p. 155.
[64] Harkness, *Northern Ireland*, p. 28.
[65] *Freeman's Journal*, 8.12.22.
[66] Lenten Pastoral 1922, CLRDA.

exclusionist intentions, that the Boundary Commission should meet once the North had rejected incorporation with the Free State.[67]

Following the decision of the Belfast Parliament to remain aloof from the Free State, the setting up of the Boundary Commission became an urgent issue for those Catholics who hoped for the incorporation of their areas with the South. Even before its formal rejection of Free State jurisdiction, the Northern government had embarked on a legislative programme which was bound to antagonise such Catholics and impel them to seek deliverance from its control. For the Catholic minority, the most significant part of this programme was the Local Government Act, passed on 5 July and granted royal assent on 11 September 1922, which provided for the abolition of Proportional Representation in local government elections, the creation of new county council and rural district areas by a commissioner who was appointed in October 1922, and the imposition of a declaration of allegiance and service to the monarch and 'to His government of Northern Ireland' upon members and officials of local authorities and those in receipt of payment from these bodies. The purpose of the latter measure was to penalise local authorities which had declared allegiance to Dáil Éireann. David Harkness points out that these measures assisted the effective domination of local government by unionists, 'but at the cost of much present and future resentment from nationalists who saw a real protection and symbol of good faith overturned with scant consideration for their viewpoint'.[68]

Many calls for a Provisional Government initiative on the boundary issue came from priests in the border areas. The result of such agitation was the establishment of the North-Eastern Boundary Bureau on 2 October 1922 under the direction of Kevin O'Shiel.[69] The main tasks of the Bureau provided scope for the kind of active clerical involvement which was to be a notable feature of its operations: collecting and compiling data for the Boundary Commission, enabling the Provisional Government to keep in touch with local nationalist opinion and preparing a case for the inclusion of relevant border areas in the Free State.[70] The Provisional Government considered clerical support for the work of the Bureau indispensable to its success. The Mayor of Derry, H.C. O'Doherty, was chosen as agent for his area because, as O'Shiel told Cosgrave, he 'possesses the

---

[67] Hopkinson, *Green Against Green*, p. 78.
[68] Harkness, *Northern Ireland*, p. 28.
[69] O'Shiel, a native of Omagh, was a lawyer and a friend of Collins. He played a significant part in drafting the Constitution of the Free State.
[70] Provisional Government Minutes, 2.10.22, NAI, G1/3.

bishop's conscience'.[71] There is evidence as early as December 1922 of Northern clerical misgiving about the enthusiasm of the Provisional Government for the implementation of Article 12 of the Treaty, in spite of official statements like that of O'Shiel on 7 December 1922 that a big effort was being made to complete the case for inclusion in the Free State of 'large areas in the six counties peopled by great pro-Free State majorities', and that he hoped to have the entire case for Tyrone, Fermanagh, South and East Down, Derry City and South Armagh, ready before Christmas.[72] Some of the priests who harboured misgivings about the reliability of such statements seem to have had little appreciation of the problems with which Cosgrave and his colleagues had to contend at the time. The senior clergyman in Omagh, Philip O'Doherty PP, was a typical case. On 15 December 1922, a week after the formal withdrawal of the Belfast government from the Free State and the Mountjoy executions of Mellows and his companions, O'Doherty wrote an anxious letter to Bishop Mulhern about the Free State government involvement in the preparations for the Boundary Commission. He had 'little confidence in the sincerity – or at any rate, the anxiety, of the Government to make a strong fight'. He was particularly troubled by the appointment of O'Shiel whom he unjustifiably regarded as incompetent, 'a purveyor of inanities' and, though an Omagh man, knowing 'nothing about Ulster'. As an illustration of 'what Dublin cares for Ulster', O'Doherty mentioned a promise by O'Shiel to send cars for the recent Westminster election. No cars were sent, with the result that the Nationalist poll was much lower than it might otherwise have been. Another worrying sign was the reluctance of the Free State government to pay for the legal work associated with the Boundary Commission and to have this funded through a public collection.[73]

In a further letter to Mulhern, O'Doherty found it ominous 'how silent, or when speaking, how lukewarm and insincere' the Dublin press was in its treatment of the plight of Ulster Catholics. He wanted every bishop in the affected areas 'to speak out plainly' to the Dublin Government.[74] In January 1923, O'Doherty reported that a meeting in Omagh of representatives 'lay and clerical from several parishes' wanted Cardinal Logue and other Northern bishops to press on the Free State Government 'the necessity for greater interest and a more intelligent and urgent supervision than seem to be taken or given in

[71] O'Shiel to Cosgrave, 21.10.22, NAI S 4743.
[72] *Freeman's Journal*, 8.12.22.
[73] O'Doherty to Mulhern, 15.12.22, DRDA.
[74] O'Doherty to Mulhern, 22.12.22, DRDA.

Dublin'. He himself could find nothing but 'incapacity and indifference' among Southern politicians.[75] The Free State Government's answer to such criticism was provided in a report by O'Shiel to Cosgrave in January 1923. O'Shiel argued reasonably enough that the government would place itself in 'a ridiculous position, both nationally and universally' were it to argue a claim for absorbing Northern population or territory 'when at our backs in our own jurisdiction is the perpetual racket of war', with its 'never-failing lists of our murdered citizens'.[76]

On 12 October 1923, the members of the hierarchy in the North collectively articulated Catholic grievances against the Belfast government under several headings. They protested against the recent abolition of PR which had been introduced in 1920 to protect the minority, argued that the constituencies had been 'shamelessly gerrymandered', that Catholics laboured under intolerable educational disabilities, that the government had trampled upon the feelings of those opposed to the partition of Ireland by imposing an oath of allegiance to the Northern Government as well as to the King. The bishops found the best illustration of the disregard for Catholic rights in the attitude of leading Northern ministers on the boundary question, specifically in regard to Tyrone and Fermanagh. They emphasised their role as leaders of Catholic opinion by calling on 'our people to organise openly on constitutional lines and resolve to lie down no longer under this degrading thraldom'.[77] The case made by the bishops was, in the main, a plausible one: the Government of Northern Ireland, instead of making what Patrick Buckland calls 'a sustained and imaginative effort to win over the minority and assuage their suspicions and fears', resorted to measures which reinforced Catholic hostility.[78]

It might, however, be argued that entrenched Catholic opposition to Partition, the spurious hopes of detachment from the Northern State offered by the Boundary Clause of the Treaty, and the non-recognition strategy initially encouraged by Church leaders and those of the Free State, inhibited Catholics from fighting for their rights under a Northern government. Archbishop O'Donnell's statement in Drogheda on 20 May 1922 was typical of many and reflected a general attitude. 'Surely', he declared, 'there was never anything so unnatural in political history as to sever six counties from the twenty-six. The sooner that dividing line is obliterated, the better for Ireland and the

[75] O'Doherty to Mulhern, 22.12.22, DRDA.
[76] See Cosgrave to Mulcahy, 25.1.23, Mulcahy Papers, UCDA, P7/B/101.
[77] *ICD*, 1924, pp. 606-8.
[78] P. Buckland, *The Factory of Grievances* (Dublin, 1979), p. 222.

better for Ulster.'[79] Almost a year after the Boundary Commission
had ended the hopes of border Catholics, Bernard O'Kane, McHugh's
successor as Bishop of Derry, was still rejecting the Northern State,
referring in his consecration address to the 'anomaly and absurdity' of
having one part of his diocese 'in one kingdom and the remainder in
another state', and pledging to work for a united Ireland.[80] The
bishops' argument that the minority had suffered from electoral boundary changes could be countered by pointing out that Catholics had
only themselves to blame for boycotting the Leech commission
appointed in October 1922 to determine the new County Council and
Rural District areas.[81] Similarly, one answer to the charge that
Catholics were labouring under educational disabilities was that the
Catholic hierarchy had refused to appoint a representative to the
Lynn Committee of enquiry into educational reform which had been
set up in September 1921. Cardinal Logue had offended the Minister
of Education, Lord Londonderry, by alleging that the Lynn Committee
would be used as a weapon for an attack on Catholic schools.[82] In
1922, a considerable number of Catholic secondary and elementary
schools refused to recognise the authority of the Northern Ministry of
Education as part of a clerical managerial stand against the Northern
Ireland government.

The call of the Northern bishops for a Catholic programme of
action against discrimination found a response in a representative
meeting of border nationalists in Omagh on 29 October 1923,
attended by senior clerics from Tyrone and Fermanagh, including
Philip O'Doherty of Omagh, Michael Quinn of Dungannon and John
Tierney of Enniskillen. Plans were made to hold further meetings at
Derry, Strabane, Enniskillen, Omagh, Cookstown, Armagh, Newry
and Dungannon, which would deal with electoral manipulation, oaths
of allegiance, policing, and Article 12 of the Treaty.[83] These meetings
were generally organised, presided over, or addressed by priests, many
of whom roundly denounced the Northern government for hating
Ireland 'with a malignant hate' as Philip O'Doherty put it, and for
planning to legislate Catholicism out of existence with a new penal
code.[84] The belief that the Belfast government was inaugurating a
return to the system which prevailed in the pre-Emancipation era was

[79] *ICD*, 1923, p. 569.
[80] *ICD*, 1927, p. 615.
[81] See Harkness, *Northern Ireland*, pp. 28ff.
[82] See Buckland, *Factory of Grievances*, p. 249.
[83] See M. Harris, *The Catholic Church and the Foundation of the Northern Irish State*
(Cork, 1993), pp. 157ff.
[84] *Irish Independent*, 6.11.23.

common at the time among priests. Michael Smith, CC Derry, claimed that before long, Catholics would be reduced to the state in which they found themselves in the penal days.[85] At Strabane, George Ryan claimed that the policy of the Belfast Parliament was to 'make Catholics poor, and keep them poor, to keep them a subordinate and inferior class'.[86] Michael Quinn, PP Dungannon, believed that it was also a part of that policy to employ such devices as the Oath of Allegiance to humiliate Catholics.[87] Clerical defence of Northern Catholics extended even to those whose activities incurred the displeasure of the generality of Irish bishops. Unlike the majority of Southern Church leaders who regarded the detention without trial and even the execution of Republicans as legitimate, senior Northern Churchmen publicly argued the case that Republicans detained in Northern Ireland were victims of official injustice. In late October 1922, when a Committee of Republicans and Nationalists organised a hunger-strike against the continuing detention of prisoners without trial, MacRory sought British press publicity for the hunger strikers, 'protesting against detention, in some cases for seventeen months, without any charge preferred against them'.[88] He and a number of priests issued a statement claiming that Northern Catholics regarded the detention of the prisoners as 'one more proof of the partisan and bigoted spirit' of Craig's government.[89] One priest argued the prisoners' only crime was 'loving their native land, and as far as he could see, the policy of the government was to exterminate all who loved Ireland'.[90]

The enthusiasm for action on Catholic grievances generated by the episcopal statement of 12 October 1923, led to an active clerical involvement in the Westminster election campaign in November and December of that year. There was a growing feeling among senior clergy that the abstentionist policy towards Westminster should end if only, as Philip O'Doherty of Strabane put it, because of the usefulness of having some members 'who would expose the intolerance and bigotry of the Belfast Parliament in the British House of Commons'.[91] The political activity of clerics in support of Nationalist candidates during the Westminster campaign was as intense as that of the Southern clergymen who acted as election agents for the Free State candidates in the South during the twenties. As in the South, priests

[85] Ibid.
[86] Ibid.
[87] Harris, *Catholic Church*, p. 157.
[88] *Irish Independent*, 6.11.23.
[89] Ibid., 15.11.23.
[90] Harris, *Catholic Church*, p. 158.
[91] *Irish News*, 23.11.23.

acted as chairmen and speakers at meetings, while bishops sent messages of good will. The clerical leadership considered it essential that Nationalist members be returned for Tyrone and Fermanagh, where they believed the results of the election were bound to have considerable significance for the deliberations of the Boundary Commission. A letter from Bishop McHugh of Derry, widely read at election meetings, emphasised the religious and national issues the election raised for Catholics. It was, he urged, 'probably the last opportunity we shall have before the Boundary Commission sits of publicly showing through the united voice of our people their right and determination to become embodied in the Free State'.[92] The Catholic electors of Tyrone and Fermanagh returned the Nationalist candidates Healy and Harbison with large majorities. The result was interpreted by Bishop McKenna of Clogher as a popular mandate for the transfer of the two counties to the Free State; in a congratulatory telegram he declared that the 'injustice constraining Tyrone and Fermanagh to remain in subjection to Belfast must now end'.[93]

It is, perhaps, difficult to blame Church leaders for their belief that the Boundary Commission would liberate many Catholics from what they regarded as an unjust and tyrannical regime and for their active encouragement of ideas and attitudes based on this belief. Their optimistic interpretation of Article 12 of the Treaty was shared and encouraged by Southern politicians, notably the two who were most intimately involved in the evolution of the agreement. Of these, Collins took the more hopeful view, assuming that Tyrone and Fermanagh would be detached as entire counties from the Northern area, along with parts of other counties. Griffith recognised that parts of Tyrone and Fermanagh would have to remain in Northern Ireland, but was confident that large parts of Down, Armagh and Derry would be transferred to the South.[94] This level of expectation survived the deaths of Collins and Griffith. In June 1923, O'Shiel told the members of the Executive Council that the 'minimum' Free State claim should include much of County Derry, including the city, almost all of Tyrone, all of Fermanagh, South Down, including Newry, and South Armagh.[95]

[92] *Irish Independent*, 3.12.23.
[93] Ibid., 12.12.23.
[94] D. Gwynn, *The History of Partition, 1912–25* (Dublin, 1950), p. 214.
[95] Executive Council Minutes, 5.6.23, NAI G2/2; C1/116. Nationalist expectations that the Boundary Commission would transfer Fermanagh and Tyrone to the Free State were based on the consideration that both counties had nationalist majorities. Against this, however, unionists advanced the argument that such numerical majorities should not be decisive. Follis points out that 'in an age when the rights of property were still regarded by conservatives as almost as

When, on 15 March 1924, the Governor-General, T.M. Healy, wrote
to the British Secretary of State for the Colonies asking on behalf of
the Free State Government for the setting up of the Boundary
Commission in accordance with Article 12, he reflected both the
Northern Nationalist impatience over tardiness in doing this and a
clear expectation of territorial adjustments. 'My ministers feel', he
wrote, 'that the effect of a further postponement would be to deprive
of the benefits of the Treaty those persons whose interest Clause 12,
without which the Treaty would never have been accepted, was
specially designed to protect'.[96]

Circumstances, however, were working against this kind of outcome.
The long delay in setting up the Commission was a significant factor.
This delay was partly occasioned by the Civil War in the South and
the task of reconstruction, partly by the collapse of the Lloyd George
Government only ten months after the signature of the Treaty with
consequent exceptional political instability in Great Britain, and partly
by the refusal of the Northern Ireland government to recognise that it
was bound by an Article in a Treaty to which it had not been a party.
The longer the delay, the less likely it was that the boundary changes
would be effected. There were times when the apparent irresolution of
the Free State Government troubled Northern clerical leaders. In
November 1923, when it was announced that Cosgrave had agreed to
confer with Craig on the boundary issue, John Tierney, PP Enniskillen
feared a 'broken treaty',[97] while Eugene Coyle, PP Devenish, told
Blythe that 'Nationalist Free Staters' were becoming 'tremendously
suspicious'.[98] In December 1923, Thomas Maguire, PP Newbliss,
presided at a farmers' meeting in Ballybay, Co. Monaghan where a
resolution was passed protesting against the delay in setting up the
Boundary Commission and calling on the Free State government 'to
cease attempts to befool our Northern Gaels or to barter their rights

---

important as the rights of man, it was inconceivable that the economic and
financial arguments used by the Ulster unionists should not strike a chord with
the Boundary Commission'. *State Under Siege*, p. 171. The Ulster Unionists insisted
that the Commission should balance their rights and wishes as the majority of
ratepayers and owners of property against those of the simple political Nationalist
majority. In Fermanagh, Unionists claimed that they paid over 75 per cent of
rates and over 90 per cent of income tax in the county, while in Tyrone their
research showed that against an annual Nationalist contribution of £25,090 to
rates, the figure for Unionists was £54,495, while Unionist-owned property was
worth twice that owned by Nationalists.

[96] F. Gallagher, *The Indivisible Island* (Dublin, 1957), p. 156.
[97] *Ulster Herald*, 10.11.23.
[98] Coyle to Blythe, 6.11.23, Blythe Papers, UCDA, P 24/204.

in a conference proposed by Britain'.[99] In October 1923, an agent sent by the Boundary Bureau to report on Belfast and Derry detected a drift to Republicanism among former supporters of the Treaty, mainly because these felt that the Free State Government 'took no interest in their position and the humiliation heaped upon them'.[100] One of the members of the Free State Government, J.J. Walsh, later expressed a similar point of view. He believed that the Northern issue had been 'badly bungled' in the South. Many within the Government party, he wrote, 'blamed Kevin O'Higgins for this unfortunate fiasco . . . It was his special duty to see that when Article 12 came up for determination, as it must some day, the groundwork had been fully prepared. As a matter of fact, a sub-committee of the Cabinet should have been working on this important task for a long time beforehand . . . It struck many of us at the time that had Mr O'Higgins and others of his colleagues devoted less of their brains to abuse of Mr de Valera and more to the vital matters of the Boundary Commission, better results might have accrued.'[101]

Within a year of the signing of the Treaty, influential British voices were being raised against altering the existing boundary in any significant way. In November 1922, Sir Robert Horne, the outgoing Chancellor of the Exchequer, dismissed as unthinkable 'any appreciable diminution' of Northern Ireland territory.[102] By 1924, these views had become louder and more insistent. Austen Chamberlain, one of the signatories of the Treaty, declared that what had been agreed on in Article 12 was 'in the opinion of the great lawyers who had advised them, the rectification of the existing boundary and not

---

[99] *Irish Independent*, 12.12.23. Father Maguire's suspicion that Cosgrave's government was less than fully committed to upholding the interests of Northern nationalists was not wholly baseless. In public, Cosgrave appeared determined to vindicate the right of border nationalists to become citizens of the Free State, telling the Dáil that he and his ministers 'cannot possibly ignore the discontent and dissatisfaction of those supporters of the Free State in the North who are kept against their will and wish out of the jurisdiction of the State to which they do not desire to belong'. (Dáil Debates, 20.7.23, Col. 1220). Ten days after making this public commitment to Northern nationalists, Cosgrave was writing privately to Craig in a totally opposite sense. He cynically remarked to the northern leader that as far as he (Cosgrave) was concerned, the only value the Boundary Commission had was that it provided 'a political cry, etc. . . . at the coming elections' in the South. Quoted in Paul Bew, Peter Gibbon and Henry Patterson, *Northern Ireland 1921–1944* (London, 1995), p. 46. I owe this reference to Paul Murray.
[100] H.A. MacCartan to K. O'Shiel, 30.10.23, NAI S 2027.
[101] J.J. Walsh, *Recollections of a Rebel* (Tralee, 1944), p. 68.
[102] Phoenix, *Northern Nationalism*, p. 265.

the creation of a new boundary'.[103] Another British signatory, Sir Laming Worthington-Evans, suggested that if the Boundary Commission transferred one Nationalist county to the Free State 'this would not be acceptable to the Ulster people', and the British Government 'would be guilty of the supreme folly of trying to enforce such a decision upon them'.[104] In the Dáil, Cosgrave betrayed his annoyance and disillusionment at comments like these. He had observed 'references by British politicians and British signatories to the Treaty and opinions which were carefully concealed when the negotiations which resulted in the Treaty were being undertaken'. Had these pronouncements been made at the time, he declared, 'there would not have been Irish signatories to the Treaty'.[105] A month before the Commission held its first meeting, Craig's inflexibility assumed a threatening aspect. He solemnly assured the Northern Parliament that if the report were unfavourable to Ulster, he would resign his office, and 'as leader of the people, not as Prime Minister, take all the steps that might become necessary to defend any territory that they thought had been unfairly wrested from them'.[106]

The Boundary Commission, consisting of Éoin MacNeill representing the Free State, J. R. Fisher, a Unionist nominated by the British Government to represent the interests of Northern Ireland, and Justice Richard Feetham of the South African Supreme Court, who acted as Chairman, began its work in November 1924. Throughout the affected areas, priests were involved in every major aspect of the Commission's activities. They furnished population returns, assembled economic and geographical data, and summoned meetings from the altar. Some priests, like Philip O'Doherty of Omagh, played a central role in the preparation of evidence, while almost thirty other priests presented oral or written testimony or both. Bishop Mulhern was the only member of the hierarchy to appear before the Commission. Basing his observations on information derived from the clergy, he confirmed that a large majority of the people of Newry favoured transfer to the Free State. Bishop MacNeely of Raphoe and John O'Doherty, Adm., Letterkenny, worked with E. M. Stephens, the representative of the North-Eastern Boundary Bureau [107] in the preparation of a case demonstrating the economic unity of Derry and Donegal. Most of the clerical witnesses placed their strongest emphasis

---

[103] *The Times*, London, 11.8.24.
[104] Ibid., 27.9.24.
[105] Dáil Debates, 15.10.24, Vol. XII, Col. 2502.
[106] St John Ervine, *Craigavon, Ulsterman* (London, 1949), p. 492.
[107] See p. 371, note 69.

on the argument that the majority of those they ministered to saw their future in the Free State, because they had no confidence in the even-handedness of the Northern Government.[108] While evidence was still being gathered, Craig called a General Election for 3 April 1925, campaigning on the slogan, 'Not an Inch'.[109] The Northern bishops and their clergy, having been made aware of the Free State government's view that the election be contested, determined that the campaign should have Partition as its central theme. The Nationalist candidates enjoyed impressive clerical support, eight of them being nominated by priests; many other clergymen campaigned actively in border constituencies. Patrick Convery, PP St Paul's, Belfast, expressed the hope in an open letter that Catholic voters would unite 'like a bar of steel all over the six counties'.[110] One Nationalist campaigner believed that the next election in Tyrone and Fermanagh would be for the Dáil; John Ward, PP Magharafelt declared that South Armagh was going into the Free State 'as safe as houses'.[111]

On 11 September 1925, the Chairman of the Boundary Commission, Justice Feetham, submitted his interpretation of Article 12 to his two colleagues in a lengthy memorandum. He made it clear that the Article did not give a warrant for revisions so drastic as to change the identity of Northern Ireland or to make it impossible for it to continue as a separate province of the United Kingdom. Again, to the detriment of the Free State and Northern Nationalist case, he decided that where the wishes of the inhabitants of a district were in conflict with economic and geographic considerations, the latter would be the decisive factor in any decision. His approach was typified in his judgment that Newry could not be separated from the rest of Northern Ireland because such separation, injurious as it would be to the economy of the town, would not be compatible with 'economic and geographic conditions', however obviously it might accord with the popular will. The case made by many border Catholic apologists, including leading clergymen, rested heavily on the assumption that the wishes of Catholic majorities would necessarily prevail. The essential point in Feetham's judgment was that this was not a correct interpretation of the relevant clause in Article 12. As he pointed out in his consideration of Newry, 'the two different sets of factors which the Commission is directed to take into account – the wishes of the inhabitants and economic and geographic conditions – are . . . found to be definitely in conflict with respect to

[108] For an excellent account of clerical involvement in the Boundary Commission hearings, see Harris, *Catholic Church*, pp. 164–9.
[109] See Harkness, *Northern Ireland*, p. 39.
[110] M. Farrell, *Northern Ireland: The Orange State* (Dublin, 1983), p. 103.
[111] *Irish Independent*, 31.3.25; 26.3.25.

this area, and under the terms of Article 12 economic and geographic considerations must prevail'.[112] Had the findings of the Commission been implemented, they would have transferred 183,290 acres and 31,319 persons to the Free State and 49,242 acres and 7,594 persons from the Free State to Northern Ireland.[113] The work of the Commission was, however, set at naught by the publication in the ultra-Tory *Morning Post* on 7 November 1925 of a substantially accurate 'forecast' of the terms of its report, accompanied by a map.[114] Éoin MacNeill, the Irish representative, finding his position 'impossible', resigned from the Commission on 20 November. [115] The Free State Government was now fearful for the potentially serious consequences for its own position. On Cosgrave's initiative, meetings were hastily arranged in London between British leaders and those of Northern Ireland and the Free State. On 3 December, Baldwin, Churchill, Cosgrave and Craig met Feetham and Fisher in a successful effort to secure suppression of the report.[116] Also on 3 December, a tripartite agreement

---

[112] G. Hand (ed.), *Report of the Irish Boundary Commission 1925* (Shannon, 1969), p. 137. Given the degree of assurance displayed by Feetham in his restrictive interpretation of the Boundary Clause in Article 12, it was inevitable that those disappointed with his findings should ask whether the Article had been so framed as to deceive the Irish signatories of the Treaty. A.J.P. Taylor argues that in 1921, 'probably no conscious swindle was intended . . . The British looked forward to friendly relations with the Free State and were willing to sacrifice Ulster'. Taylor acknowledges that the British signatories who in 1921 and 1922 had been telling the Irish delegates that the majority of Fermanagh and Tyrone 'would prefer being with their Southern neighbours' were expressing altered views in 1924, suggesting that only minor rectification of the existing boundary had been intended. He explains the change by suggesting that British statesmen were estranged by the Civil War in Ireland; he also points out that by 1924 there was a Conservative Government in Great Britain; Lloyd George was out of office and the others who had been involved in the Treaty negotiations 'were laboriously working their way back into the Conservative Party which they had deeply offended by their surrender to Ireland'. *English History 1914–1945* (Oxford, 1965), p. 162.

[113] Hand, *Boundary Commission*, p. 14.

[114] This map is reproduced in Hand.

[115] Ibid., p. xxi.

[116] Twenty copies of the report were run off and remained in obscurity until 1 January 1968 when they were made available to researchers. Hand, p. xxii. This meant that for over 40 years after it was compiled, the report, in effect Feetham's and Fisher's, could not be subjected to critical analysis. A close study of its argumentation, however, makes it difficult to avoid the impression that Feetham was determined to defend the status quo by making Article 12 conform to the Unionist position. This impression is suggested by his fundamental assumption, from which every conclusion in the report flows, that 'there could be no wholesale reconstruction of the map of Ireland based on the wishes of its inhabitants' (Report, p. 29). Feetham's arguments against nationalist claims in West Ulster are tendentious, as are the ones he advances against holding plebiscites, and in considering the smallest possible units of area in determining the wishes of the inhabitants. (Report, pp. 63–4, 96).

signed by Baldwin, Cosgrave and Craig confirmed the border as it stood, and 'friendly relations' and 'neighbourly comradeship' were pledged between the Free State and Northern Ireland.[117]

IV

Before the collapse of the Boundary Commission and the suppression of its findings, Article 12 of the Treaty, without which the agreement would not have been signed by the Irish negotiators, had been the one most deeply offensive to Northern Unionists, representing as it did a constant threat to the integrity of the six-county state and causing them to treat the Catholic minority with suspicion and intransigence. As Harkness puts it, 'so long as there was the threat of the Boundary Commission, so long was their state in mortal danger, their guard must be up and there must be no concession to minority wishes'.[118] But Article 12 was ultimately to prove even more inimical to the interests of the Northern Catholic minority, betrayed as they were into believing in its efficacy as the instrument of their wholesale deliverance from an alien jurisdiction. This belief led many of them to withhold cooperation from the new state and to conspire against its functioning, and this in turn compounded their disabilities by subjecting them to inevitably ungenerous treatment. The earliest consequence of the failure of the Boundary Commission and the tripartite agreement of December 1925 was the irrevocable alienation of the mass of border nationalists and their clerical leaders from the Free State administration. Their support for the pro-Treaty position since 1921 had been firmly grounded on their belief, fostered by a multiplicity of Free State representatives, that Article 12 offered the prospect of generous transfers of territory to the South. Their hostility to the anti-Treaty cause had its motivation in the belief that those who would put the Treaty in jeopardy might at the same time deprive them of the hope Article 12 offered. Now that the Free State Government was prepared to accept an agreement with Britain and Northern Ireland involving the maintenance of the border in return for financial concessions to the South, Northern nationalists were forced to the embarrassing conclusion that the Unionists and Republicans had been right all along, and that their own aspirations, which they had worked so hard to fulfil, had been founded on a baseless promise in a worthless document.

[117] Harkness, *Restless Dominion*, p. 40.
[118] *Northern Ireland*, p. 36.

Many of the priests who had played a leading part in preparing evidence for the Boundary Commission now took a lead in articulating the bitter disappointment and anger of their people at what they saw as their betrayal by the Free State government. In an indignant communication to Cosgrave, John Tierney, PP Enniskillen and two curates from Omagh, along with the members of Parliament for the Tyrone–Fermanagh area, claimed that since the Treaty had been signed by plenipotentiaries representing all Ireland, his government, representing only the twenty-six counties, had no right to deprive six-county nationalists of their birthright. Tierney and the others were appalled by Cosgrave's supposed Partitionist mentality. 'We are', they told him, 'thrown as unceremoniously to the wolves as if we were a people distinct from those of the twenty-six counties'. They accused the Free State ministers of having 'surrendered their trusteeship for the nationalists under Article 12'.[119] In this, they were not entirely unjust to Cosgrave's government. In many of his statements following his agreement with Craig, Cosgrave implicitly acknowledged the permanence of Partition. In the Dáil, in reply to the accusation that he had deserted the Northern nationalists, he suggested that their representatives enter the Northern Parliament and seek justice there; if this course proved fruitless, then it was time to admit that major changes had to be made.[120] When, in November 1927, Frank Aiken asked the government to compensate Northern nationalists whose property had been destroyed by British forces during and after the War of Independence, Cosgrave rejected the notion that the Northern nationalist community was its responsibility, declaring that the northern Parliament was the only place where Northern Catholics could insist on having their grievances dealt with. 'We have', he told Aiken, 'borne our own compensation here and it is no part of our business to bear the cost in another place'.[121]

Some northern nationalist priests who had most stoutly supported the Provisional Government in its fight for the Treaty now became its bitterest critics, and a number of them worked from 1926 onwards for its overthrow. Eugene Coyle, PP Garrison, a prolific letter-writer, speaker and publicist, was the most active of these, tireless in his articulation of minority grievances against the Free State.[122] On

[119] *Irish Independent*, 8.12.25.
[120] *Ulster Herald*, 19.12.25.
[121] Dáil Éireann Debates, 17.11.27, xxi, Col. 1624.
[122] Coyle was born *c.* 1874 in County Monaghan. In February 1922, he was appointed PP of Devenish West, Garrison, Co. Fermanagh, where he ministered until his death in 1955. Dr Patrick McCartan brought him into the IRB but did not ask him to take the oath. During the War of Independence, he was interned

7 December 1925, Coyle addressed an anti-Pact meeting in Dublin presided over by de Valera and sought, without success, to address the Dáil.[123] In September 1925, before the collapse of the Boundary Commission, Coyle had somehow become aware of Feetham's interpretation of Article 12, and communicated his forebodings in a challenging letter to Blythe, in which he made a remarkably accurate prediction of the outcome of the Commission's deliberations. He told Blythe that notwithstanding all the optimistic talk Northern Catholics had heard, their wishes were about to be overborne. A portion of Fermanagh was, he claimed, going to the Free State, while 'a section of the Free State in Donegal' was going to Derry. In the light of this, he advised the Free State government 'to revise its oft-repeated and unnecessarily repeated talk about the fairness of England'. What was to be the Magna Carta for border Catholics now meant 'a mere rectification of the frontier'. Coyle and John Tierney had observed that Justice Feetham had come to Fermanagh determined to give Enniskillen, with its Nationalist majority, to Northern Ireland, and when the evidence did not suit his preconceived view, 'he got more or less angry'.[124] All that Blythe felt able to say by way of reply was that he committed himself to doing the thing that seemed best in the national interest.[125]

Clerical anger that the Free State government had, as Lorcán Ó Ciarán, PP Magheramena, Co. Fermanagh, put it, given Nationalists 'over permanently to the Northern masters'[126] was soon conveyed forcefully to members of the Free State government and its agents. John Tierney wrote to Stephens of the North-Eastern Boundary Bureau, with whom he had worked on the preparation of evidence for the Commission, that the result of all their labours was 'a terrible fiasco'. Of the Free State Government he remarked that its members

[122] *cont.* by the Black and Tans, who later brought him to Crumlin Road, where, apparently, he had to direct them because they did not know the way (Clogher Diocesan Archives). For Coyle's activities on behalf of the Free State, see p. 39, notes 22 and 23. For his later support of Fianna Fáil and his opposition to Freemasonry, see p. 269, notes 92 and 93, p. 276, note 129 and p. 283, note 149.

[123] *Irish News*, 10.12.25.

[124] Coyle to Blythe, 15.9.25, Blythe Papers UCDA P 24/498. It was a common view among Nationalists that Feetham was, from the start, strongly prejudiced, or influenced, by the British view that only minimal rectification of the border should be engaged in. See for example, F. Gallagher, *The Indivisible Island*, pp. 175–6. Feetham's integrity has been strongly defended by Hand, who, however, acknowledges that his approach was marked by 'legalism and a remoteness from political realities'. *Boundary Commission*, p. xxi.

[125] Blythe to Coyle, 28.9.25, Blythe Papers, P24/498 UCDA.

[126] *An Phoblacht*, 11.12.25.

had done 'what no Irishman ever did before – they have signed away the unity of the country and made partition as permanent as anything in this world can be'.[127] The depth of Coyle's disillusionment with Cosgrave's government may be judged from the angry letters he addressed to newspapers and periodicals, North and South. In January 1926, he claimed that 'the Nationalists of Ulster, so far as Messrs Cosgrave, O'Higgins and Blythe can secure, belong permanently to . . . a province of England. They have no country, no nation; they are simply British helots living in the Six Counties'.[128] It would, he wrote to *An Phoblacht* soon afterwards, be a disgrace if Irish people of the present generation were to continue to tolerate a government that had agreed to partition their country permanently and sell their fellow-countrymen for a mess of pottage'.[129] He told the *Ulster Herald* that Cosgrave and his colleagues had practised deception on Ulster nationalists. The Dáil Ministers, who 'valued England's friendship and goodwill higher than they did the welfare of the Irish people', had allowed the boundary to remain unchanged 'contrary to all previous pledges of support for the nationalist minority'. If the Irish people did not immediately reject Cosgrave and his government they would be accepting 'permanent Partition and the continued slavery of Northern nationalists under an alien government'.[130]

The putative treachery and insincerity of Cosgrave's government quickly became a standard belief among border Catholics, lay as well as clerical. Cahir Healy, a responsible, level-headed politician, condemned the Baldwin–Craig–Cosgrave pact as 'a betrayal of the nationalists of the North and a denial of every statement put forward by the Free State in their alleged support of our cause since 1921'.[131] Clerical resentment of the pact persisted through the years. At an election meeting in Monaghan in 1927, Felix McKenna, PP Castleblaney declared that he was going to support an Independent and a Protestant Association candidate rather than Blythe, since there would be 'no decent government in Ireland until Blythe and Cosgrave were thrown out'. Their crime was to have 'signed away Tyrone and Fermanagh, two of the best counties in Ireland'.[132] The bitterness created by Cosgrave's dealings with the boundary issue engendered a strong animosity among the border clergy towards his government

---

[127] John Tierney to E.M. Stephens, 14.1.26, Boundary Papers, Carton 16, NAI.
[128] *An Phoblacht*, 8.1.26.
[129] Ibid., 22.1.26.
[130] Coyle to *Ulster Herald*, 23.1.26.
[131] P. Livingstone, *The Fermanagh Story* (Enniskillen, 1969), p. 317.
[132] *Roscommon Herald*, 14.5.27.
[133] A.T.Q. Stewart, *Narrow Ground*, p. 176.

and party. The forces of clerical nationalism could no longer show enthusiasm for the pro-Treaty cause. Like the generality of nationalists they were, as A.T.Q Stewart puts it, 'trapped in a Unionist State which would always regard them as second-class citizens'.[133] It was inevitable that growing numbers of them would abandon moderate pro-Treaty nationalism for the Republican versions represented first by Sinn Féin and very soon afterwards by Fianna Fáil. From the end of 1925 onwards, there were signs of a growing belief among Northern Nationalists that de Valera and his anti-Treaty followers might, after all, prove better protectors of their rights and liberties than the Free State Government had been.

V

The change in Catholic political attitudes which this represented is best appreciated when it is seen against the background of the extreme hostility inspired during the early 1920s by Republican opposition to the Treaty, the widespread feeling that Republicans were primarily to blame for the Civil War, and resentment at Republican attempts to make the anti-Treaty cause a central part of the Northern debate. The promise held out by Clause 12 was in itself sufficient to make border Catholics the natural allies of the pro-Treaty party, and the natural enemies of an anti-Treaty Republicanism which seemed bent on undermining a settlement on which their prospect of joining the Free State depended. This helps to explain the active involvement of border clergy in efforts to induce their representatives to vote for Dáil approval of the Treaty. It also explains why Fermanagh nationalists met on 6 April 1922 to renew their support for the Treaty, to organise a collection for the pro-Treaty candidates nominated to contest the 1922 General Election in the South, and to 'pledge our support to Messrs Griffith and Collins in the election campaign'.[134] The intensification of the conflict in the South and the increasing violence in word and deed there tended to be associated in Northern minds with Republicans. Nationalists in the North rightly saw the drift to Civil War as uniformly disastrous and destructive of their interests, since a full-scale conflict among Southern nationalists would inevitably strengthen the hands of the Ulster Unionists to the detriment of the Catholic minority. The increasing preoccupation of potential Southern allies of this minority with issues largely foreign to its immediate interests permitted Craig's government to consolidate

[134] Livingstone, *Fermanagh*, p. 298.
[135] T. Garvin, *1922: The Birth of Irish Democracy* (Dublin, 1996), p. 128.

its position. It is not surprising that leaders of Northern Catholic opinion in 1922 should have blamed de Valera and the Republican militants for betraying the beleaguered Northern nationalists for their own narrow and, to some minds, eccentric and unrealistic, political ends. The various strands of Northern nationalism, the clergy, the political moderates and the IRA, were at one in regarding the activities of the Southern Republicans with dismay. The Northern IRA, as Garvin points out, 'besieged as it was by a hostile majority' was pro-Treaty, and 'regarded the anti-Treaty stance represented by de Valera and Lynch as a threat to the cause of Northern nationalists'.[135]

A representative Northern Catholic view of anti-Treaty Republicanism was very frankly communicated by Bishop Mulhern to de Valera and his champion, Mgr John Hagan of the Irish College, Rome, in March and April 1922. In Belfast on 23 March, five men, some of them partly dressed in police uniforms, burst into the home of the McMahon family and murdered seven members of the household, one at a time. On the same day, de Valera sent Mulhern, who was staying in Dublin, a verbal message suggesting that the bishops issue a strong statement to the Pope and the Catholic world in general on the Belfast horrors, since the leaders of the divided nationalist forces could not do so 'without the risk of being charged with having sectional motives'.[136] An angry Mulhern, already distressed at the news of the McMahon murders, and writing less than a week after de Valera's 'rivers of blood' speech, confessed himself astounded at de Valera's message. 'My own opinion and that of my colleagues in the North and indeed of anyone I have met', he told de Valera, 'is that you, and you alone, are responsible for the recrudescence of the troubles in the North-East, and of all the disturbances elsewhere'. It was plain to everyone in the North-East, Mulhern claimed, that the relations between parties in the South were 'a perfect barometer of the Orange attitude towards the Catholics of the North-East', the Republicans, presumably, being the Southern counterparts of the Orangemen. Given the breach in Nationalist solidarity for which Mulhern thought de Valera culpable, he found the latter's notion of an episcopal plea for international action against Orangemen absurd. Such a plea, he suggested, 'would meet with the obvious answer that we Irish Catholics should close our ranks and present a united front to the Orange bigots of the North-East . . . This is genuine Sinn Féin'.[137] On the day after this letter was written, the

[136] Mulhern to Hagan, 7.4.22, DRDA.
[137] Mulhern to de Valera, 23.3.22, DRDA. By way of reply, de Valera wrote from Sinn Féin Headquarters, Suffolk Street: 'I received your letter of the 23rd.

officer board of the divided Sinn Féin party, de Valera presiding, passed a resolution, proposed by Kathleen Lynn, a Republican TD and seconded by Kevin O'Shiel, representing Collins, and assented to by both sides, appealing 'that common action be taken to bring the outrages committed in North-East Ulster before the public opinion of the world'.[138] Writing to Hagan two weeks later, Mulhern was appalled that 'men talk flippantly of wading through blood' in the cause of an illusory republic, and 'harp on the republic as if they had not abandoned the idea long before the Treaty was signed'. What angered Mulhern most was that Southern Republicans were disrupting national unity on what, in the light of circumstances prevailing in the North, were relatively trifling issues, when all the national energies should be directed toward helping the victims of Orange aggression. He could feel only contempt for Southern Republican militants. If, he claimed, 'some of the braves [the Republican IRA] who are out for further fight' were in Newry, 'far away as it is from Belfast, their ardour might quickly cool'. Even in Newry, 'men, young and old, women, even children, must leave their homes at night and seek shelter when they can manage it, many of them making their way to Omeath, which is Free State territory'.[139] Such people, he told Hagan, were understandably angry that those in the South who should be defending them were dissipating their energies in a pointless conflict of their own. All that was needed, he believed, to change the imperilled Catholic position into 'a position of security' was union in the South. Northern Catholics, he suggested, must be pardoned if they failed to see the Republican point of view, which was 'never brought nearer to them than the clouds of words in which it is mystified'.[140]

[137] *cont.* Though it is, perhaps, as you say, a time for plain speaking, I shall refrain from saying what I thought and felt as I read it'. De Valera to Mulhern, 25.3.22, DRDA. At least one Southern bishop, Thomas O'Dea of Galway, did not share Mulhern's view of the fundamental causes of Northern violence. The forthcoming episcopal statement, he told Mulhern, 'should insist that the British government is the cause of all the trouble in the North and is morally responsible for all the murders there'. O'Dea to Mulhern, 29.3.22, DRDA.

[138] *Freeman's Journal*, 25.3.22.

[139] Mulhern himself had to endure his share of Orange terrorism. In July 1922, he received a letter from 'Loyal Orange Lodge 777'. 'We heard tonight', the letter ran, 'you had come back to Newry. You had better clear out again as soon as you can. Neither de Valera nor priest again will save you bloody Shinners. The two of you [Mulhern and de Valera] have been tried in our lodge and death is the penalty. No matter where you go we will get you and plug you. You [will] never vote for de Valera again. (Mulhern had proposed de Valera as a candidate for Down in the 1921 election). To hell with you bloody papish bishop. No surrender. God save the King. We'll shoot you like a rat'. DRDA.

[140] Mulhern to Hagan, 7.4.22, DRDA.

The available evidence strongly suggests that the mass of Ulster nationalists shared Mulhern's view of anti-Treaty Republicanism as a threat to their welfare. Early in April 1922, when de Valera denounced the recent Craig–Collins Pact as merely giving Ulster Catholics 'the privilege of recognising the Northern Government if they wanted to', the editor of the Belfast *Irish News* warned nationalists that anti-Treaty groupings would engineer strife in the six counties to undermine the agreement. Denouncing de Valera, he argued that 'all the nationalists in the six counties have a vested interest in the success of the Irish Free State Government' and that if it were 'destroyed and driven to failure and ruin' by Republicans, Northern Catholics 'would be left helpless and hopeless'.[141] When de Valera intervened in Northern Nationalist politics during the December 1922 Westminster election campaign, it became clear that his intervention was unwelcome. Of the thirteen Westminster seats, Catholics had a chance of winning only two, both of these in the Fermanagh–Tyrone constituency. There was strong clerical support for contesting these seats, while the Provisional Government regarded the election as an opportunity for the nationalist people of the two counties to express their determination to free themselves from the control of the Belfast government. T. J. Harbison and Cahir Healy were proposed and supported by several priests,[142] one of whom urged that there should be no dissenting voices among Nationalists. When de Valera appealed for a boycott of the elections,[143] the nationalist electorate of the two counties largely ignored his advice, and Harbison and Healy won with large majorities.

A further Republican electoral intervention in the north was bitterly resented by clerical nationalists. Following the fall of MacDonald's government on 8 October 1924, an election to the Westminster Parliament was called for 24 October. Michael Quinn, PP Dungannon, expressed the general clerical and nationalist view when he told his congregation that the election was a 'Catholic' rather than a political matter: Nationalist unity was more than ever essential to give maximum force to the Free State case before the Boundary Commission.[144] On 11 October, de Valera announced his intention to run eight Sinn Féin abstentionist candidates in Northern constituencies, including Fermanagh–Tyrone.[145] Leading clerics in the latter constituency strongly opposed de Valera's intervention. Eugene Coyle, PP Garrison, soon to become one of de Valera's staunchest Northern allies, protested 'against

---

[141] *Irish News*, 3.4.22.
[142] Harris, *Catholic Church*, p. 153.
[143] *Irish News*, 18.11.22.
[144] *Irish Independent*, 13.10.24.
[145] *Irish News*, 13.10.24.

a crowd of Republicans who came here unasked by the masses of the people in Tyrone and Fermanagh from Dublin and other places. We forgive them but we cannot forget them, and we hope they will be wiser after their experience in the North.'[146] John Tierney, PP Enniskillen, articulated the common and justified fear among the border clergy that were the Fermanagh–Tyrone seats to be contested by Republicans as well as pro-Treaty nationalists, the split Catholic vote would mean the election of two Unionists.[147] This, as most border nationalists saw it, would be marginally preferable to the election of two Republicans, particularly in the light of de Valera's assertion that by relying on the Boundary Commission to detach themselves from the Northern Ireland state, the people of Tyrone and Fermanagh were displaying a selfish disregard for the welfare of Catholics elsewhere in Ulster.[148] Philip O'Doherty, PP Omagh, was appalled at the spectacle of 'Mr de Valera with a tongue of brass and a heart of lead sneering at the selfishness of Fermanagh and Tyrone'. O'Doherty's attack on de Valera and his followers featured some of the elements in the clerical case against them since the Treaty: he remembered 'de Valera's policy of wading through blood – a policy afterwards disastrously carried through' and expressed resentment that 'Republicans were now coming to Tyrone who had also presumed to instruct the hierarchy when moral issues were at stake, and the grievances of Catholics pressed lightly on them'.[149] The clergy of Tyrone and Fermanagh considered it best in the circumstances to advise their congregations to boycott the election, thus, as Tierney expressed it, placing the responsibility on de Valera 'for handing the seats to the Orange Party'.[150] This strategy was notably successful. Seán Lemass addressed an anti-Treaty meeting at Omagh and was greeted by two men, two women and five youths.[151] Only 15 per cent of Nationalists who normally voted cast their ballots for Republicans in Fermanagh–Tyrone, while about the same number seem to have voted Unionist, the remainder abstaining.[152] There can be little doubt

[146] Quoted by P.J. McLogan, MP in a letter to the *Irish Press*, 11.12.35.
[147] *Irish Catholic*, 18.10.24.
[148] *Irish Independent*, 20.10.24.
[149] Ibid.
[150] See *Irish Independent*, 20.10.24; Phoenix, *Northern Nationalism*, p. 309.
[151] Livingstone, *Fermanagh*, p. 299.
[152] See B.M. Walker, *Parliamentary Election Results in Ireland, 1918–92* (Dublin, 1992), p. 16. In the previous General Election, held on 6.12.23, with an electorate of 96,497, the two seats were filled by the Nationalists Harbison and Healy with 44,003 and 43,668 votes respectively. The Unionists Pringle and Falls polled 37,733 and 37,682. This represented a total poll of approximately 85 per cent. In 1924, the electorate was 97,044. The two seats were filled by the Unionists Falls

that de Valera's intervention in Northern politics in late 1924 greatly strengthened the Unionist position in West Ulster, and weakened the nationalist case for extensive changes by the Boundary Commission. It is not surprising that the Republicans were widely regarded in the area as traitors to the nationalist cause.[153]

VI

Following the collapse of the Boundary Commission, the Northern clergy were as divided as the Nationalist community in general in their responses to the new, and largely unwelcome, political situation. The main point at issue was whether Catholic members of the Belfast Parliament should maintain or abandon their long-standing abstentionist stance. Shortly after the London conference at which the boundary question was settled, Archbishop O'Donnell was created cardinal. His earliest pronouncements following his elevation were notably conciliatory and free from bitterness. They also gave a clear indication that O'Donnell was anxious that Catholics should participate fully in the Northern political system in pursuit of their interests in the hope that if they demonstrated goodwill towards the institutions of the State, this would inspire a more generous and accommodating Unionist attitude towards their grievances. Speaking in Armagh in February 1926, O'Donnell recognised that many Catholics were disappointed and frustrated at having to live in the Northern State, but hoped that such sentiments would be replaced by an early recognition of the new political circumstances. He seemed to regret that Catholics had not taken their seats in the Northern Parliament from the beginning: by not doing so they had left themselves open to the charge that they had failed 'to keep things right for themselves'. He himself had found the Marquess of Londonderry, the single member of the government with whom he had dealings, willing to make equitable arrangements for Catholic teacher-training. He was optimistic that a united Catholic parliamentary group could achieve much with

and Pringle with 44,716 and 44,711 votes respectively, the Republicans polling 6,812 and 6,685. Assuming that Nationalists and Unionists voted in equal proportions in 1923, the result of that election suggests that the former constituted 53.8 per cent of the electorate, and the latter 46.2 per cent. Assuming that approximately 85 per cent of Unionists voted again in 1924, and no non-Unionist electors voted for Unionist candidates, this would have given their candidates approximately 38,100 votes each. It therefore seems probable that the extra 6,600 votes they actually obtained came from people who had voted for nationalist candidates in the 1923 election.

[153] See J.B. Dooher, 'Tyrone Nationalism and the Question of Partition, 1910–1925', MPhil thesis, University of Ulster, 1986.

the help of a younger generation of Unionists who might be as well disposed to the alleviation of Catholic grievances as the Ulster Protestants of 1782 and 1798 had been.[154]

O'Donnell's commitment to full Catholic participation in Northern parliamentary politics was shared by a substantial number of the clergy of East Ulster. Already, in April 1925, two Catholic MPs, McAllister and Devlin, had taken their seats in the conviction that 'permanent abstention meant permanent disfranchisement'.[155] Two other Catholic MPs, Patrick O'Neill of South Down and George Leeke of Derry were prepared to maintain an abstentionist policy only as long as there was a chance that South Down and Derry City might be incorporated with the Free State. When O'Neill solicited the opinions of the Nationalists of County Down in January 1926, there was overwhelming support for an end to abstentionism. There was a considerable clerical involvement in a conference of nationalists at Castlewellan, County Down, on 7 February. Murtagh McPolin, Dean of the Dromore diocese, expressed the common view of senior clergy in the county when he wrote to the conference that 'a zealous and vigilant minority can perform much useful and necessary work, whilst remaining away [from Parliament] they are quite useless for any purpose'.[156] Frank O'Hare, PP Banbridge, told the delegates that Northern Catholics would henceforth have to look to themselves for redemption, 'not to the gymnasts of the Free State'.[157] At a Derry constituency convention on 7 March, 1926, where the clergy were also generously represented, the two Nationalist MPs, George Leeke and Basil McGuckin, were instructed to take their seats in the Belfast Parliament. There was a sharp contrast between the attitudes of the clergy of East Ulster and most of those in Fermanagh and Tyrone. While by March 1926, many nationalists in both counties had come to the conclusion that their members should attend Parliament, clerical opinion tended to the contrary view. On 4 March 1926, Cahir Healy told the veteran Home Rule politician, William O'Brien, that in the struggle between those who supported attendance and those anxious to remain abstentionist, the two contending parties were the Ancient Order of Hibernians, widely accused of having the interests of the licensed trade as their main motive in getting Nationalist MPs into Parliament [158] and the clergy of the two counties.[159] At separate

---

[154] *Irish Independent*, 15.2.26.
[155] This was Devlin's view. See Farrell, *Northern Ireland*, p. 103.
[156] Phoenix, *Northern Nationalism*, p. 339.
[157] Ibid., p. 340.
[158] See *Ulster Herald*, 27.2.26.
[159] See Phoenix, *Northern Nationalism*, pp. 341–2.

conventions of Fermanagh and Tyrone nationalists in March 1926, there were large majorities in favour of the policy advocated by the clergy: abstentionism was to remain the policy until such rights as PR for local government elections, which nationalists had enjoyed under the British, were restored.[160]

In 1927, the West Ulster MPs still boycotting the Belfast Parliament felt obliged to reconsider their position when Craig announced on 12 July that he intended to abolish PR for parliamentary elections. Since this would involve a reversion to single-member constituencies and a rearrangement of boundaries, nationalist fears of gerrymandering and even further legalised disfranchisement led to a widespread insistence that their abstentionist MPs enter Parliament to fight against discrimination.[161] These MPs made their first appearance in the Northern House of Commons on 3 November 1927.[162] An equally significant development was the decision of Fianna Fáil in August 1927 to abandon abstentionism and subscribe to the oath as an empty formula, a decision which resulted in substantially increased support for the party in the September 1927 General Election. Some of those nationalists, including priests, who had found de Valera's ventures into Northern politics in the early years of the decade distasteful, were now tempted to look at him and Fianna Fáil as new trustees of their rights and interests. The possibility that de Valera might be their effective champion was enhanced by the entry of his party to the Dáil. Eugene Coyle, one of his most outspoken critics in the aftermath of the Treaty, now gave him and his party unconditional allegiance, and, as a member of the Fianna Fáil National Executive, acted as intermediary between Northern nationalism and Southern Constitutional Republicanism in an effort to organise a united nationalist movement. Cahir Healy's draft for a new Northern Nationalist party, submitted to Coyle for Fianna Fáil approval in December 1927, marked a significant change in Northern Catholic attitudes to Southern Republicanism. Healy now saw de Valera as offering new possibilities for the revival of Nationalist fortunes and even as the agent to whom the Northern minority might entrust their political destiny. 'If Fianna Fáil', he told Coyle, 'can utilise such political machinery as Northern Nationalists possess for the furtherance of its national ideals, it would be a big stroke and a great work for the whole country'.[163] In January 1928, Seán Lemass and Gerald Boland told Coyle that their party would be

---

[160] *Ulster Herald*, 13.3.26.
[161] See Farrell, *Northern Ireland*, pp. 109–10.
[162] Harris, *Catholic Church*, p. 175.
[163] Ibid., p. 175.

willing to discuss cooperation with a new Ulster Nationalist party whose policy was not in conflict with that of Fianna Fáil. More significantly, such a new party would have to be 'thoroughly representative of Nationalist opinion within the six-county area'.[164]

The movement launched in St Mary's Hall, Belfast, on 28 May 1928, the National League of the North, under the leadership of Joseph Devlin, was not, however, fully representative of nationalist opinion. It proved unable to attract either the mass of pro-Treaty Sinn Féin elements or those Northern diehard Republicans who could not forgive or forget Devlin's association with the 'temporary Partition' proposals of 1916 and who were opposed on principle to a separate Northern nationalist party, believing as they did that 'the Ulster question must be kept national'.[165] Before making formal arrangements for the setting up of the National League, the nationalist MPs involved considered it essential that their ideas should first be explained to the Northern bishops with a view to soliciting their approval and help; Healy believed that to make their movement a success, the assistance of the clergy was 'quite essential'. Bishop Mulhern was found to be 'in complete sympathy and accord' with the objectives of the National League, while MacRory approved 'without qualification'.[166]

From the start, the National League had a distinctly clerical complexion. Its organisers were at pains to emphasise the impressive clerical support enjoyed by the party throughout the North. The Chairman of the inaugural meeting was John Tierney, PP; the formal proposal to establish the party came from Eugene Coyle, PP.[167] An Irish News editorial on the day after the League was launched drew attention to its intimate association with ecclesiastical structures, pointing out that it was to be organised on parish lines to facilitate the efficient registration of members. Newspaper reports of conventions of the League indicate a considerable clerical involvement in its affairs. At Strabane in 1928 two priests were elected to the local executive. There were eleven priests at the Castlewellan convention in 1929, five at that held in Armagh, while in Fermanagh, Tierney was elected chairman and five other priests were coopted. Senior clergy were involved in meetings in several districts to establish new branches.[168]

[164] Ibid., p. 176.
[165] This idea was expressed in a letter to Coyle from Eamon Donnelly, the Armagh absentionist MP, in March 1928. Donnelly, Republican Director of Elections in the Free State in 1923, when he was arrested, became a Fianna Fáil TD for Leix-Offaly in 1933. See Phoenix, Northern Nationalism, pp. 357–8, 352.
[166] Phoenix, Northern Nationalism, p. 356.
[167] Irish Independent, 29.5.28.
[168] Harris, Catholic Church, p. 177, 194.

The membership of the Central Council of the League included priests with differing political backgrounds and outlooks. Coyle had been a member of the IRB and was now a member of Fianna Fáil; he was, presumably, expected to attract the support of some extreme Republicans. Thomas McCotter, PP Antrim, had been a follower of Redmond and was a confidant of Devlin; he had supported the Partition proposals of 1916,[169] while Murtagh McPolin, PP Loughbrickland, had commented darkly in 1922 on the evils associated with Republican regimes.[170] In the eyes of many of its clerical members, including McPolin, the League, although its primary aim was 'the national unity of Ireland', was not a vehicle for advanced nationalist ideas, but a potential defender, through its parliamentary representatives, of Catholic education and the right of Catholics to fair treatment in a variety of fields. Although another of its aims was to 'foster a spirit of conciliation and co-operation amongst all creeds and classes', anti-Treaty Republicans, like the anonymous Ulster priest in *An Phoblacht*, insisted that it was a purely Catholic party and thus incapable of ever winning majority support for its policies in the six counties. Such Republicans also believed that parliamentarians would spend their time 'merely asking for justice from the tyrants in power', and by advising people 'to live and they'll get grass', would be committing 'crime against the country'.[171]

Officially, the National League was a non-sectarian grouping. It was, however, effectively a Catholic party, becoming more and more a defender of specifically Catholic interests. This was illustrated during the 1929 Parliamentary election campaign, fought on the straight vote system, when the Labour candidate, William McMullan, a Protestant, contested the new constituency of Falls, in the heart of the Belfast Catholic ghetto, with the National League candidate, Byrne, described by Farrell as 'a conservative Catholic publican and slum landlord'.[172] Campaigners for the National League in the Falls concentrated on Byrne's Catholic orthodoxy and on McMullan's Protestantism and Socialism. A leading member of the League thought it a conclusive

---

[169] Phoenix, *Northern Nationalism*, p. 29.
[170] On 20 May 1922, McPolin wrote to the *Irish Catholic*: 'If we compared the Republics of France and Portugal with the constitutional monarchies of Spain and Belgium in their political working and especially in the matter of liberty of conscience for Catholics and all others, Spain and Belgium stand much higher than France and Portugal. The Republics of France and Portugal were established, and have been administered, on a godless basis, and their fruits and results have been in keeping with the principles and practice of such a basis'.
[171] *An Phoblacht*, 11.2.28; 31.8.29.
[172] *Northern Ireland*, p. 115.

argument in Byrne's favour that he had been nominated by two senior Belfast priests.[173] On the eve of the election, a member of the Central Council of the League, Thomas McCotter, PP Antrim, wrote an article expressing astonishment at 'the spectacle of a non-Catholic Socialist seeking the votes of Catholics, who, if they obey the Church, cannot be Socialists, against a Catholic who is loyal to his Church'.[174] Farrell points out that McMullan was more nationalist that Byrne, whom he describes as a Tory; he also argues that the significance of the 1929 result in the Falls, where Byrne was elected, was that the abolition of PR had 'smashed the Labour–Nationalist alliance, stopped dead any trend towards secular radicalism in the Nationalists and forced them back into narrow Catholic sectarianism'.[175] In 1929, the League enjoyed considerable parliamentary success, returning two members to the Imperial Parliament, eleven to the Belfast House of Commons and three to the Senate. Success at the polls, however, was not matched by anything like a substantial record of achievement in the Belfast Parliament on behalf of the Catholic minority. Even Harbison, a committed constitutionalist, experienced nothing but frustration. 'No matter what we propose', he declared in August 1930, 'no matter how beneficial to the people, the mere fact that it is being proposed by our party is sufficient to bring it down'.[176] By 1932, even Devlin was commenting bitterly on 'the sham' and 'farce' of being a member of the Belfast Parliament.[177]

From the Unionist point of view, the measures which Catholics found discriminatory were acts of self-preservation. When, on 24 April 1934, frustrated nationalist MPs warned the Northern Government that Unionist policies would result in a boycott of Parliament by Catholic representatives, Sir Basil Brooke, Minister for Agriculture, explained to them that all Catholics were nationalists and all nationalists, from the most moderate to the most extreme, sought 'the destruction of Ulster as a unit and as a constitution'.[178] He might have added that up to the end of 1925, the primary ambition of many Catholics was to escape as soon as possible from the Northern jurisdiction. Such being the Unionist view, it is easy to understand the reluctance of the Northern administration to accommodate the

---

[173] *Irish News*, 13.5.29.
[174] Ibid., 21.5.29.
[175] Farrell, *Northern Ireland*, p. 116. In the 1925 General Election, McMullan, at the bottom of the poll on the first count, was elected on the distribution of Devlin's massive surplus.
[176] *Ulster Herald*, 23.8.30.
[177] Harkness, *Northern Ireland*, p. 76.
[178] Ibid., p. 62.

wishes of the many nationalists, including clergymen, who rejected the Northern state and all it stood for and at the same time complained about the injustices suffered by Catholics and urged radical reform. Unionists could point to the bitterness engendered in 1922 and afterwards when many Catholic priests, holding local government posts as chaplains to workhouses, lunatic asylums, prisons and military barracks, refused to declare allegiance to the monarch and 'His Government of Northern Ireland'. This refusal, which led to their temporary loss of their positions, publicly demonstrated their hostile attitude to the Northern State and prompted charges of disloyalty. A common Protestant view of the matter was expressed by the *Northern Whig* which wondered if it was the view of the Irish Catholic bishops 'that they are freed from any allegiance to a Protestant government'.[179] Some clerical objectors were prepared to take an oath of loyalty to the King but not to the Northern government unless it legislated 'for the common good, irrespective of creed or class'.[180]

The abolition of PR for both local government and parliamentary elections served a useful purpose in the Unionist scheme of things. It reinforced party divisions on traditional sectarian lines, and by largely eliminating all parties except Unionists and Nationalists, ensured that the major political issue would continue to be the very existence of the Northern State. As Buckland points out, Unionists felt that they had an incontestable case for demanding a system of local government that would increase their representation at the expense of Catholics, arguing that 'since they paid most of the rates, they should have had most of the representation, even when they were in a numerical minority'.[181] They also found it irksome to be in a minority on such bodies as Tyrone County Council, where one of them complained at having to 'sit there and listen to our King being insulted, to our government being derided'.[182] An obvious way to alleviate such distress was, for example, to allot one-third of the seats on Fermanagh County Council to the 56 per cent Catholic population and to reconstitute the wards of Derry so that 9,961 Nationalist electors returned eight councillors, while 7,444 Unionist voters returned 12.[183]

---

[179] *Northern Whig*, 15.10.23.

[180] *Freeman's Journal*, 15.1.23.

[181] *Factory of Grievances*, p. 230.

[182] Ibid.

[183] Ibid., p. 245. Harkness (*Northern Ireland*, p. 66) points out that in the Unionist bid for control, franchise conditions were crucial, and in 1923, legislation 'attempted to reduce the impact of impermanent and mountain and bogland voting claims in favour of more substantial property holders', generally Unionists. Another significant factor was the granting of additional voting rights to companies, which

By the early thirties it was becoming increasingly apparent to Northern Catholics that the Belfast Parliament was not an appropriate forum for the redress of their grievances. The 1931 Westminster election campaign for the Fermanagh and Tyrone constituency is instructive. Nationalist speakers, lay and clerical, tended to dismiss as futile the quest for justice at the hands of Unionists. A.E. Donnelly, the West Tyrone MP, thought of the Northern government as simply 'a Unionist clique' which had 'left nothing undone to deprive Catholics and Nationalists of their rights'. The full restoration of such rights, he suggested, could come only with the success of the policy of Devlin and Cahir Healy, which was to bring the six counties 'under the Free State government'.[184] The anti-Partition theme was central to the campaign. One of the clerical speakers believed that the return of Healy and Devlin would be a protest against 'the curse of Partition', while John Tierney, PP Enniskillen, was enthusiastic for a national government 'for the land to which he owed his sole allegiance, and that was Ireland'. The Treaty was now recognised not as an instrument of deliverance, but as the means by which Ulster Catholics 'were sold and consigned to the rank of an English shire'.[185]

The revival of Republican feeling North and South, de Valera's rise to power in 1932 with the help of Northern nationalists and fundamentalist Southern Republicans, the sense among Nationalists that the Northern political system was irreformable, and that pro-Treaty politicians in the South had betrayed and abandoned them, led to a growing militancy on the Nationalist side, and a new enthusiasm for de Valera and what he appeared to stand for. A striking symptom of the new mood was the withdrawal of Devlin and his followers from the Belfast Parliament on 11 May 1932. Devlin's last speech before his departure underlines the part played by Unionist intransigence in the growing tendency among Catholics to look once more to the South for deliverance, but this time through the agency of de Valera and his party. During the Catholic Emancipation centenary celebrations of 1929, Bishop Mulhern had pictured Northern Catholics as an enslaved people enduring the equivalent of the Babylonian Captivity, crying out with the Psalmist 'How can we sing the song of the Lord in a strange land!' as they lamented the disabilities under

---

[183] cont. meant that those with a stake in the community, 'deemed most likely to be Unionists', were given a greater chance to dominate. According to 1936 figures, this restriction and concentration of local government rights excluded 40 per cent of Parliamentary voters from local government voting. See also Gallagher, *Indivisible Island*, pp. 196ff.

[184] *Irish Press*, 20.10.31.

[185] Ibid.

which Catholics laboured, at the same time 'wholeheartedly rejoicing with Catholics in the Free State in their possession of full religious liberty'.[186] In his valedictory speech, Devlin told Unionist parliamentarians that they had rejected all 'friendly offers' of help, service and cooperation from nationalist members. They went on, he declared, 'on the old political lines, fostering hatreds, keeping one-third of the population as if they were pariahs', hoping 'to keep power in perpetuity by exacerbating the effects of religious differences and difficulties'.[187]

One reason for the new attractiveness of de Valera to Northern Catholics was given by Cahir Healy at a Fianna Fáil election rally in Belturbet in 1932. Healy declared that in his discussions with J.H. Thomas, the British Dominions Secretary, de Valera had, by raising what he called 'the question of the whole national position', done what no Free State minister had ever done; this robust attitude satisfied Healy that 'Mr de Valera would lead Ireland to national unity'.[188] In the campaign to end Partition, now at the centre of nationalist politics, even such former critics as J.H. Collins, MP for South Down, looked for inspiration to 'the great leader of the Irish people, Eamon de Valera'.[189] The 1933 election campaigns, North and South, provided an outlet for much anti-Partitionist and Republican energy. Many Northern priests and politicians campaigned in the Fianna Fáil interest in the border constituencies. The participating politicians included Cahir Healy, Joseph Stewart, MP for East Tyrone, and Joseph Connellan, MP for South Armagh. They and the Northern priests who addressed public meetings on behalf of Fianna Fáil candidates frequently denounced Cosgrave and Blythe in particular for what they saw as their callous disregard for the rights of Northern nationalists. Fianna Fáil, on the other hand, was seen as the party of promise, capable of solving the fundamental problems of the Northern nationalists by dealing firmly with the British government.[190] The Northern intervention in Southern electoral politics was reciprocated when de Valera acceded to the wishes of the nationalists of South Down that he represent their constituency as an abstentionist member.

Those northern nationalists who looked to Fianna Fáil for the kind of effective action on their behalf not forthcoming from Cumann na nGaedheal had long been encouraged by the speeches of Southern apologists for de Valera to believe that when Cosgrave's government

[186] *Irish Catholic*, 16.2.29.
[187] Phoenix, *Northern Nationalism*, p. 369.
[188] *Ulster Herald*, 28.1.33.
[189] Buckland, *Factory of Grievances*, p. 73.
[190] For an account of the part played by border priests in the 1933 Fianna Fáil campaign, see pp. 266–72 above.

was replaced by a Fianna Fáil one they would once again enjoy the active support of a southern administration. In 1929, the Fianna Fáil weekly, *The Nation*, could see no remedy for the misfortunes of Northern Catholics 'under present conditions'; before even a beginning could be made 'to lighten the daily aggravating burden of our compatriots in the six counties', the Cosgrave government, authors of such 'acts of treachery' as the boundary 'surrender' in 1925 would have to be 'driven from control'.[191] Also in 1929, the Fianna Fáil TD Thomas Derrig offered Northern Catholics the hope that the day was not far distant when a Fianna Fáil government, 'instead of bending the knee to Lord Craigavon', would stand up to him and demand for the nationalists of the six counties 'the same rights and privileges and fair play as the twenty-six county unionists were getting'.[192] Northern Catholics were to discover that de Valera's anti-Partitionist stand was essentially a rhetorical and opportunist one, and that Fianna Fáil policy on the North was indistinguishable in practical terms from that of its predecessors in office. This was soon made apparent to the leaders of Northern Catholic opinion when they sought to have one of de Valera's favourite anti-Partitionist ideas, canvassed by him during his days in opposition, put into effect. In 1924, de Valera had protested at the exclusion of six-county elected representatives from the Dáil.[193] In February 1933, Devlin and Healy approached de Valera and Seán T. O'Kelly with a proposal that Leinster House be opened to six-county MPs as an alternative to their attending Stormont. Not alone did de Valera refuse to entertain the proposal: he even declined to advise Devlin and Healy whether or not they should attend the Northern Parliament.[194]

Whenever the strong anti-Partitionist faction within Fianna Fáil urged the party leadership to match its rhetoric with practical moves on the direction of Irish unity, the response was invariably negative, defensive and even hostile. There was much enthusiasm among Northern anti-Partitionists and members of Fianna Fáil for a resolution proposed at the 1936 Ard Fheis of the party that the new constitution should make provision for 'elected representatives of North-East Ulster to sit, act and vote in Dáil Éireann'. De Valera, however, prevailed on the proposers to withdraw the resolution, asserting that it was premature.[195] He preferred symbolic gestures. The most notable of these, his agreement to be MP for South Down

[191] *The Nation*, 9.3.29.
[192] *Irish Independent*, 25.3.29.
[193] Minutes of Comhairle na dTeachtaí, 7.8.24, MacSwiney Papers, P 48/c/8.
[194] See Bowman, *De Valera*, pp. 133–4.
[195] *Irish Press*, 4.11.36.

in 1933, was of no benefit to the nationalists of the area; its only concrete effect, as Clare O'Halloran points out, was to deprive the people of South Down of their MP, since 'as Minister for External Affairs and President of the Irish Free State de Valera could hardly have had time to interest himself in their concerns'.[196] However, de Valera's Republican opponent in South Down, Thomas McGrath, had affirmed that if elected he would not take part in the proceedings of the Northern Parliament,[197] so that whatever the outcome of the election, South Down would have remained unrepresented. The contrast between energetic rhetorical commitment to Northern Catholic rights[198] and practical demonstrations of unconcern for these rights is neatly illustrated by the case of a Northern teacher who had endured financial loss as a result of his cooperation with the non-recognition strategy of the Southern government in 1922. Despite the teacher's pressing representations, de Valera refused to compensate him and others in his position, merely directing that the refusal be couched in 'sympathetic terms'.[199] Despite de Valera's habit of 'deflecting any unwelcome liaison with the northern nationalists'[200] since taking power, he still appears to have enjoyed their goodwill as late as October 1935 when Healy told him that 'the vast majority' among them 'would be supporters of Fianna Fáil'.[201]

The general hostility to the Northern parliament and government among Northern nationalists found expression in a growing militancy leading in turn to increasing support for the Republican abstentionist position. This militancy reciprocated that of the future Prime Minister Sir Basil Brooke, who in 1933 and 1934 was telling Protestants not to employ Catholics, almost all of whom were disloyal, and ready 'to cut their [Protestant] throats if opportunity arose'.[202] The generality of Northern priests, however, remained loyal to the moderate nationalist cause.[203] In November 1933, at the Fermanagh Nationalist Convention,

[196] Clare O'Halloran, *Partition and the Limits of Irish Nationalism* (Dublin, 1987), p. 154.
[197] *Irish Press*, 17.11.33.
[198] See, for example, the speech of de Valera's son Vivion in Rostrevor, in the course of which he asserted that 'every vote given for Mr de Valera would take a slice off the unnatural boundary'. *Irish Press*, 30.11.33.
[199] O'Halloran, *Partition*, pp.144–5.
[200] Bowman, *De Valera*, p. 136.
[201] Phoenix, *Northern Nationalism.*, p. 381.
[202] A.C. Hepburn, *Conflict and Nationality in Modern Ireland* (London, 1980), p. 164.
[203] A few exceptions come to light in newpaper reports. In 1928, Luke Donnellan, CC Crossmaglen was fined £20 for having an unlicensed gun. He refused to recognise the court, and declared that he had no intention of getting a licence. *Kerry Champion*, 24.1.28. An earlier example was Thomas McCann, C.C. Ballygawley, Co. Tyrone who, despite the widespread clerical determination to boycott the 1924 general election, advised the people to support the Republican candidate. *Irish Independent*, 24.10.24.

called under the auspices of the National League of the North to
select a candidate for the Belfast Parliament, priests played a leading
part. There was a significant clerical presence at other National League
conventions.[204] John Tierney, PP Enniskillen, presided at the Fermanagh
convention; Cahir Healy was proposed by Eugene McMahon, PP
Arney and seconded by Eugene Coyle, PP Devenish. The attendance
included twelve priests.[205] Healy described the Republican candidates
contesting the election as 'bands of comic-opera soldier-politicians'
and 'Dublin playboys' whose paper, *An Phoblacht*, had characterised
as 'infamous' the Bishops' Pastoral of 1931.[206]

In the mid-thirties, priestly rhetoric emphasised the need for
Catholics to pursue their nationalist aims by constitutional means,
however great a strain might be placed on this policy by incitements
such as those of Brooke and by such gerrymandering schemes as that
devised by the Unionist government for Omagh in 1935, where a
judicious manipulation of ward boundaries translated a Nationalist
majority of six into a Unionist majority of three, an arrangement
which prompted John McShane, the local PP to describe Stormont as
'a glorified Orange lodge'.[207] The Westminster election of November
1935 was called against the background of an intensification of
Catholic support for abstentionism, which forced the Nationalist
convention for Fermanagh and Tyrone to put the sitting MPs Healy
and Stewart forward as abstentionists and when even this failed to
satisfy the militants, alternative abstentionist candidates with strong
Republican backgrounds, Anthony Mulvey and Patrick Cunningham,
were chosen to represent the cause of 'Ireland's right to absolute
independence'.[208] The intervention of Southern Republican candidates
in the Northern electoral process was much resented by some leading
clerical supporters of the National League, among them Eugene
Coyle, who told the Fianna Fáil Ard Fheis in November 1935 that
nationalists like him did not want 'free-lance politicians coming among
our Nationalist people in the Six Counties from Dublin and the
twenty-six counties'. Northern Nationalists, he suggested, should 'stand
behind the national leader, Mr de Valera, the greatest national leader
since Hugh O'Neill'. Although Coyle resented the cross-border incur-
sion of twenty-six county Republicans, he was ready to offer comment
and guidance on the politics of the South. He was especially resentful
that 'one section of the people in the Free State were striving to hold

[204] *Irish Press*, 20.11.33.
[205] *Irish Press*, 15.11.33.
[206] *Irish Press*, 28.11.33.
[207] Phoenix, *Northern Nationalism*, p. 380.
[208] Ibid., p. 381.

one arm of the national leader as he fought the old enemy, and another section from the left tried to hold the other arm'.[209] Coyle was supported by Senator Connolly, de Valera's Minister for Lands, who, apparently unconscious of the ironic implications of his own words, spoken as they were in de Valera's presence, expressed resentment at 'the intervention of the type of politician who went up and made a fiery speech and exploited the position in the six counties and then returned to the Free State'.[210] The comments of Coyle and Connolly attracted the ridicule of Republicans and accusations that their anti-Partitionist discourse was at odds with the Partitionist mentality manifested in their dislike of Southern intervention in the North. A successful abstentionist, P.J. McLogan, MP for South Armagh, denounced Coyle and others in Fianna Fáil for giving 'a semblance of justification to Craigavon and Dawson Bates in issuing exclusion orders against Irishmen and Irishwomen because they assert the right of entering, and travelling in, any part of the country'.[211]

By the end of 1935, the forces of Nationalism, North and South, were hopelessly fragmented. Radical tendencies in the Republican movement, represented by the Republican Congress, disturbed moderate Nationalist clergymen like James McGlinchey, PP Draperstown, Co. Derry, who described the new policy as 'manifestly subversive of every traditional idea of Irish nationality' and who believed that the IRA had 'strayed from the true path, both of traditional Irish nationality and righteousness'.[212] The absence of a united political outlook among nationalist politicians meant that the Church continued to exert strong leadership at critical times. Priests were leaders of nationalist opposition to the Unionist gerrymander of Derry city in 1936. They were active in the establishment of the Irish Union Association on 26 July 1936, the aim of which was 'to consolidate the entire strength of the anti-partition elements in the six counties'.[213] Clerical anger at the gerrymander found an outlet in militant rhetoric. Patrick Devine, CC, Long Tower, Derry, declared that his part of Ireland 'belonged to our ancestors, not to planters' and that the treatment of the Abyssinians by Mussolini was 'kindness itself compared with the treatment meted out to our forefathers by their hireling forefathers'.[214] Peadar MacLoinsigh, CC Castlederg agreed with de Valera that there was 'no question of physical force' as a

[209] *Irish Press*, 5.12.35.
[210] Ibid.
[211] *Irish Press*, 11.12.35.
[212] Ibid., 10.4.35; 18.4.35.
[213] Ibid., 27.7.36.
[214] *Derry Journal*, 23.12.36.

solution to the problems of Northern Catholics, but believed that it might be morally justifiable.[215] The Irish Union Association did not long survive. It lacked the support of Belfast nationalists, two of whose leaders, Byrne and Campbell, had associated themselves with a loyal address to the King in 1936.[216]

De Valera's 1937 Constitution, as Clare O'Halloran has observed, marked the high point of official anti-Partitionist rhetoric, 'being the first official initiative by nationalists to register formally their opposition to Partition, seventeen years after the event'.[217] Senior Northern clergymen, in common with other Northern nationalists, responded enthusiastically to the Constitution through the medium of a new organisation which it inspired: the Northern Council for Unity.[218] Like many other initiatives, however, the relevant Articles in the Constitution could have no practical effect as remedies for the grievances which Catholics associated with Partition. Nor was it intended to, as de Valera was to demonstrate by his refusal to countenance the admission of Northern MPs to the Dáil as a first step towards the integration of the two states.[219] While Article 2, in its description of the national

[215] Ibid.

[216] Phoenix, *Northern Nationalism*, p. 384.

[217] O'Halloran, *Partition*, pp. 174, 177.

[218] See Phoenix, *Northern Nationalism*, pp. 382–98.

[219] De Valera would have regarded as unfair any suggestion that he did not do everything possible to end Partition. He was deeply sensitive to any attempts made by other Irish politicians to project themselves as unduly enthusiastic champions of a united Ireland, and tended to guard most jealously his sole proprietorship of the anti-Partition cause. Serious challenges to this proprietorship were presented by the Coalition Government of 1948–51, when he rightly divined that under Seán MacBride, Clann na Poblachta 'would try to steal his republican vestments' (Bowman, *De Valera*, p. 275). He felt obliged to respond with vigour to threats of this kind, and to the widespread feeling, North and South, that for all his multitudinous pronouncements on Partition, he had no serious commitment to finding a solution, that he was, essentially, a Partitionist. Following the suggestion from a Northern speaker at a meeting in Tuam in 1948, that his anti-Partition activity had amounted to little more than an annual message to the exiles in the USA (*Irish Press*, 9.8.48), he dictated a confidential memorandum on his fight against Partition to his Personal Secretary, Kathleen O'Connell. In this he claimed that he had joined the Volunteers in 1913 mainly because of Carsonism; that his conversations with Lloyd George in July 1921 were mainly on Partition; that one of his main objections to the Treaty was that it was likely to confirm Partition; that it was because of Partition that he had dissociated himself from the 1925 tripartite agreement; that during his sixteen years in office he had never met a British Minister without referring to Partition; that after the 1938 agreement with Britain he had tried to concentrate the whole weight of the influence of the Irish people at home and abroad against Partition. The full text of the memorandum is reproduced in the author's 'Voices of De Valera', MLitt thesis, TCD, 1995.

territory as 'the whole island of Ireland, its islands and the territorial seas' represented a formal rejection of Partition, Article 3 effectively recognised Partition in its acceptance of the fact that the Constitution applied only to the territory of the Free State, and thus appeared to render nugatory the claims made in Article 2. This situation, however, may not have proved unduly disturbing to some influential minds. While Catholic churchmen in the North and nationalist politicians in the South were prone to denounce Partition, it was not without its advantages to both groups. The Treaty settlement, confirmed in the 1925 pact, enabled Northern bishops, for example, to exercise, in common with their Southern colleagues, an influence on political and legislative developments in the South which was not open to them in the North,[220] and to advocate social and educational policies in the Free State which could not have been countenanced in a united Ireland having a large and articulate Protestant minority. In the same way, Free State administrations between 1922 and 1937 would have been severely limited in their freedom to enshrine in legislation the Catholic principles which the great majority of them found congenial.

[220] In early 1922, Northern bishops showed a deep interest in the ways in which Churchmen might influence the drafting of the Free State Constitution. In February of that year, O'Donnell submitted his ideas on the subject to Mulhern. He believed that 'we should have a recognition of God and Christianity on the face of the Constitution, and thought that there was a great deal to be said for a constitutional declaration that religion should be part of state education in the schools, primary, secondary and perhaps university. He did not think it wise to insist that Catholic marriage law should also be part of Constitutional law, being inclined to think that for the stability of marriage 'we had better depend on the law of the Church and the backing of a Catholic people'. (O'Donnell to Mulhern, 28.2.22, DRDA). Cardinal Logue believed that those engaged in drawing up the Constitution should remember that 'it is being drawn up for a Catholic country . . . Hence it must be submitted to the bishops, and a committee of theologians, aided by a lawyer, should examine it and see that it is in accordance with the principles of Christianity and with Catholic principles'. (Logue to McKenna, 22.3.22, AAA).

CHAPTER EIGHT

Epilogue

In the division on the Treaty, it is not surprising that the Church leadership upheld the more moderate point of view, which was also the majority one. There could never be any question of the Church using its authority in support of a political minority, or of denying legitimacy to those who expressed the national will.[1] Even before the Treaty was approved by the Dáil on 6 January 1922, it was clear that a substantial majority of people favoured this course.[2] Even those who led the opposition to the Treaty recognised that they did not reflect the popular view, and tended to fall back, as de Valera did, on the argument that there were 'rights which a minority may uphold, even by arms, against a majority'.[3] This kind of reasoning was rejected by the bishops as morally, and constitutionally, indefensible. In his 1923 Pastoral, for example, O'Doherty deplored what he called 'the novel and anarchical principle that a minority has the right to rule', when,

[1] See Emmet Larkin's valuable analysis of the Church's attitude to political authority in Ireland: 'When the Sinn Féin party . . . split on the question of whether the Irish State was to be a republic or a dominion, the Church threw the weight of its power and influence on the side of the constitutional majority. In doing so the Church was simply fulfilling the obligations it had contracted in 1884 when the Irish State was being born. As long as the party in the state fulfilled its part in the agreement and was the legitimate party sanctioned by the nation, the Church could in fact do no less'. The bishops, Larkin argues, declared against de Valera and the republicans, not because these 'posed any real threat to their own power and influence', but because de Valera, 'like Parnell thirty years before, no longer retained the confidence of the majority of the Party and was, therefore, no longer the legitimate leader'. 'Church, State and Nation in Modern Ireland', *American Historical Review*, 80, 1975, p.1273.

[2] On 3.1.22, the *Freeman's Journal* reported that 'hundreds of parish meetings have been held during the week-end all over the country, and without exception ratification was demanded'.

[3] *Chicago Tribune*, 15.5.22.

as he asserted, 'the plain and undisputed principles of Catholic teaching' prescribed majority rule.[4] In episcopal comment prior to the approval of the Treaty, there was considerable emphasis on the need to ensure that the national will, or what Fogarty called 'the considered judgment of the nation' [5] be taken into account by Dáil deputies when they voted. Fogarty argued that rejection of the Treaty by the Dáil in the face of the massive public demand for its ratification would be 'morally wrong' and 'a negation of representative government'.[6] Bishop Browne of Cloyne considered it the duty of those who favoured the Treaty to call on their representatives to 'obey the mandate of their constituents', while Harty, certain that 'the people of Ireland by a vast majority' supported the settlement, declared that 'in a democratic country the will of the people is the final court of appeal'.[7] When the anti-Treaty minority abandoned political methods and opposed the will of the majority in arms, it was only after months of warfare and the wholesale collapse of law and order that the bishops deployed their ultimate spiritual weapon against the insurgents. The episcopal view of these matters was explained by Archbishop Gilmartin in a letter of support to a Cumann na nGaedheal election meeting in August 1923. Gilmartin had little patience with the anti-Treaty argument that the Dáil had no power to ratify the Treaty and so disestablish the Republic. He wondered why, if the Dáil had no such power, the Republican minority had debated ratification. He could only conclude that by debating the Treaty issue the anti-Treaty party had, in effect, acknowledged the power of the Dáil to ratify the Treaty. That being so, he asked why the defeated minority did not form a constitutional opposition instead of organising an armed revolt, which, in the circumstances, was a crime. It was, as he saw it, now the 'duty of the people to make the repetition of such a crime impossible'.[8]

---

[4] Lenten Pastoral, 1923, CLDA. Pope Leo XIII would not have agreed with O'Doherty. In his encyclical *Diuturnum illud* (1881), the Pope does not regard majority consent as the only basis on which a legitimate government may be established. He recognises several others.

[5] *The Saturday Record*, Ennis, 31.12.21.

[6] Ibid.

[7] *ICD*, 1923, pp. 540, 542.

[8] *ICD*, 1924, p. 585. Gilmartin's argument was based on a misunderstanding of the provisions of Article 18 of the Treaty, which provided that the instrument should be submitted by the Irish signatories 'to a meeting summoned for the purpose of the members elected to sit in the House of Commons of Southern Ireland, and if approved shall be ratified by the necessary legislation'. The Dáil debate referred to by Gilmartin thus concerned approval, not ratification, of the Treaty. Gilmartin, however, might be pardoned for his imprecise use of terminology, since many of the deputies contributing to the Treaty debate appeared to

As Gilmartin's contribution suggests, moral considerations were central to episcopal pronouncements on the political issues of the day. Donal O'Sullivan interprets the outlook of the bishops on the problems raised by the division of national opinion over the Treaty in a sense which the great majority of them would no doubt have found accept-able. The Catholic hierarchy, he suggests, although unanimously in favour of accepting the Treaty, 'had no concern with politics as such, but they were, and are, the appointed custodians of Catholic faith and morals and they knew only too well that a continuance of the anarchic conditions of the past three years would result in a moral degeneration of their flocks from which it would take generations to recover'.[9] The moral degeneration which the bishops feared would be the inevitable consequence of a continuing war with Britain should the Treaty be rejected by the Dáil could be explained as a side-effect of the growing prestige of violence, particularly since 1919, as a means of dealing with political grievances. During the War of Independence this violence had confronted the bishops and their clergy with trouble-some ethical problems. These had been dealt with in a forthright uncompromising way by such bishops as Cohalan who, in December 1920, excommunicated those who organised ambushes or kidnappings, or shot policemen or members of the Crown forces, in the diocese of Cork, but who also condemned some of the activities of the Black and Tans. In his own diocese, Cohalan had to contend with an alternative moral code disseminated by such priests as the Capuchin Father Dominic, who encouraged members of the IRA in their prosecution of violent deeds against the British forces, on the ground that they were acting with the authority of the State, the Republic of Ireland, and therefore had a right and duty to protect 'the liberty of the state against the army of occupation of a foreign power unjustly present in the country'. This being the case, he argued, violent acts performed by the Volunteers were 'not only not sinful, but good and meritorious' and not subject to the censure of excommunication pronounced by Cohalan.[10] Many other bishops regarded Volunteer

---

[8] *cont.* believe that they were discussing ratification. Among these were Richard Mulcahy, Michael Hayes, Eoin MacNeill (the Speaker of the Dáil) and at times, de Valera. See Treaty Debates, pp. 10, 15, 16. On 20.12.21, however, de Valera asserted that Republicans had 'said from the start that there could be no question of ratification of this Treaty. It is altogether *ultra vires* in the sense of making it a legal instrument. We can pass approval or disapproval', Treaty Debates, p. 53. Despite this, we find Seán MacGarry 'supporting the motion for ratification of the Treaty' on 3.1.22, Treaty Debates, p. 209.

[9] D. O'Sullivan, *The Irish Free State and its Senate* (London, 1940), p. 49.

[10] See T. Ó Fiaich, 'The Catholic Clergy and the Independence Movement', *Capuchin Annual*, 1972, p. 486.

activity as Cohalan did. In December 1920, Bishop Finegan of Kilmore declared that to be just and lawful a war must be backed by a well-grounded hope of success; since there was no hope of success 'against the mighty forces of the British Empire', Volunteers who took lives in the course of the struggle were committing murder. In January 1921, Archbishop Gilmartin claimed that those who ambushed a company of Auxiliaries had 'incurred the guilt of murder', while in the following month Bishop Hoare of Ardagh and Clonmacnois denounced ambushes as 'contrary to the law of God'.[11] The fact that such pronouncements were largely ignored by those at whom they were directed and those who sustained them in their activities, and that even some of the clergy regarded them as theologically suspect, tended to call episcopal authority into question and undermine the status of bishops as infallible guardians of the moral law. There was the added problem that repeated condemnations tended to have a diminishing force.[12]

Against such a background of moral confusion and ambivalence among clergy and laity, the prospect of an indefinite extension of violent conditions was abhorrent to the bishops and many of the priests. Their willingness to champion the Treaty settlement arose in large measure from their conviction that it offered an honourable and just means of avoiding future conflict with its attendant threat of deepening moral anarchy. When civil war came, the old nightmare returned. A large number of priests were prepared to accord to the anti-Treaty cause the moral status of a war of independence and so pose a threat to Church authority and discipline, as well as to the credibility of Church teaching on political morality as this was interpreted by the hierarchy. From the point of view of the bishops, the moral issues presented by the Civil War were much clearer and less ambiguous than those which had confronted them during the War of Independence. They were no longer obliged to condemn the violent deeds of both sides impartially, or to give the impression of moral ambivalence. They had, however, as Bishop Foley told his Vicar General, to do all in their power to 'prevent their own priests from helping on the rebellion in every way they can'. Foley was troubled by a statement from the Bishop of Waterford and Lismore that 'orders had been given in one case known to the bishop that the Irregulars were not to mention in Confession such matters as murder, etc.', and feared that 'the same thing was done in the fight with the

[11] Quoted in E. O'Malley, *Raids and Rallies* (Tralee, 1982), pp. 96–7.
[12] O'Malley writes that 'pronouncements by the bishops did not, so far as I know, affect active members of the IRA in the Martial Law area nor our adherents who housed and fed us and the columns. In weak areas it may have had an effect and added to the worries of senior officers'. Ibid., p. 98.

British'. Foley was all too conscious of the widespread moral chaos which the bishops feared the rejection of the Treaty would bring. He had 'not the slightest hope that any of those who, by freely and habitually engaging in these detestable crimes, have seared their consciences, will pay the slightest attention to anything that priest, bishop or even the Pope himself may say on this painful subject'. Those who had grown up in a violent tradition had lost their moral bearings. 'Many of our young, unsophisticated people', Foley believed, 'fancy that so long as they have no direct part in these murderous attacks on human life by unauthorised persons,[13] in the looting or destruction of property, or in the raiding of houses, they need have no scruple of conscience about helping in other ways'.[14]

The churchmen who supported the Republican cause tended to take their stance on arguments similar to those advanced by the political opponents of the Treaty. Even moderate Republicans like Robert Egan, PP Mullahoran in the diocese of Ardagh and Clonmacnois, regarded the Treaty as a cynical exercise calculated to divide the Irish people, satisfying cowards, peace-lovers, bishops, Parish Priests and old men, but betraying those 'who ventured all, including life', for the cause of independence.[15] For most of the Republican clerical apologists, this sense of betrayal represented a strong motive for opposition to the Treaty and the Free State. The arguments advanced by 'A Western Priest' were typical. Dáil Éireann, he claimed, had in 1919 acted with the authority of the people in setting up a Republican government, a real and substantial thing and not the shadowy ideal of pro-Treaty propaganda. Those, including members of the Provisional Government, who had in 1919 assumed the responsibility of government in the name of the Republic 'and invited their countrymen to go out and kill and be killed in defence of the Republic, and yet did not believe themselves in the reality of the Republic, stood self-accused of complicity in murder'.[16] Others sought to undermine the position advanced by the bishops on the subject of majority rule. 'A Republican Priest' rehearsed the common Republican argument that 'when the majority are bent on compromising certain issues of transcendent importance,

[13] Foley's reference here to 'murderous attacks on human life by unauthorised persons' seems to suggest a temporary lapse of either clear thinking or moral judgment. The phrase anticipates the notorious reference to 'unauthorised murders' in the bishops' joint Pastoral of October 1922, suggesting perhaps that Foley may have had a part in the preparation of that document. See Appendix One.
[14] Foley to M.J. Murphy, 30.8.22. KLDA.
[15] Diary of Canon Robert Egan, PP Mullahoran. Copy made available to the author by Fr Owen Devanney.
[16] 'Who Betrayed the Republic?' By a Western Priest, n.d.

the minority can lawfully resist' [17], as if some form of compromise on the Republican issue had not been an inevitable outcome of the Treaty negotiations. Another Republican priest declared that the Plenipotentiaries 'had no right to take over from England anything except what we sent them for – a Republic'.[18] The oath of allegiance to the Constitution of the Free State and of fidelity to the British monarch as a replacement for the oath to the Republic incurred some clerical hostility. When T.M. Healy spoke to a Republican priest towards the end of the civil war, 'his great point was about the oath'. Healy suggested that the Republicans troubled by this 'could easily get one of their casuists to hold that an oath taken under duress was not binding and was worthless and that people who could commit crimes in defiance of the bishops' decision should not have such tender consciences as regards a verbal formula'.[19] The cynicism and hypocrisy imputed by Healy to Republicans are not reflected in the evidence available from the period. Their cause in the main was justified and sustained by unrealistic, other-worldly ideals and expectations which found their characteristic expression in the language of Catholic piety. It is difficult to believe that one of their clerical apologists was not in earnest when he proclaimed that 'the Irish Republic is not only the symbol of our independence. It is a Christian and a holy thing. It is the shrine wherein rise the sacred incense of Ireland's devotion and Ireland's holy aspirations . . . the road to that destiny which God has in mind for the children of the Gael.'[20] This mystical approach to the political problems of the day was one means by which Republicans could feel themselves immune from censure on merely ethical or doctrinal grounds.

Even at the level of constitutional and political theory, however, Republican casuists, lay and clerical, felt able to justify armed resistance to the Treaty by arguing that they were defending the lawfully constituted Republic against what de Valera called 'a usurping junta'.[21] Throughout the twenties, de Valera continued to insist that the

---

[17] 'An Appeal to the Irish Bishops'. By a Republican Priest, 1922.

[18] *Roscommon Herald*, 30.8.24.

[19] F. Callanan, *T.M. Healy* (Cork, 1996), p. 607. Healy was writing to his brother on 20.2.23. Healy's low estimate of the theology of the Republic is conveyed in a letter to Rev. Thomas Dawson, a clerical friend, dated 20.8.22. 'Both secular and religious teaching', he wrote, 'can be jettisoned to glut political passions. The demand from Mountjoy for absolution via hunger-strike reveals a phase of mind which treats the Sacrament as a superstitions or mechanical spell wrought by the priest irrespective of the state of the penitent's conscience'. p. 593.

[20] 'False Pastors'. By Columban na mBanban. 1922. The author of this pamphlet is the 'Republican Priest' who wrote the 'Appeal to the Irish Bishops'; see above, note 17.

ORACLES OF GOD

Provisional government had not come to power legitimately, telling the Dáil in 1929 that it had 'brought off a coup d'état in the Summer of 1922'.[22] It was not until 1936 that Michael Browne, Professor of Moral and Dogmatic Theology at Maynooth, and a consistent supporter of post-Treaty Sinn Féin and Fianna Fáil, fully, though perhaps unwittingly, exposed the weakness of the Republican case for the lawfulness of rebellion against the Provisional Government. In a paper read at a Maynooth Summer School in September of that year, Browne outlined in detail the fundamental principles of Catholic moral teaching, 'as it is summarised by theologians', on political authority. Browne's statement of these principles makes it clear that even if the validity of the Republican analysis of the constitutional position were acknowledged, and the Provisional Government were, indeed, a usurping junta, there was no right of rebellion against it. All Catholics agree, Browne argued, that 'a usurper who dislodges an existing Government by force has not, as such, any right, but if he maintains order, citizens are bound to obey him, for their first duty is to avoid anarchy'. The absolute need to avoid anarchy, whatever the merits of the constitutional arguments advanced by the contending sides, was a fundamental consideration for the bishops in 1922 and 1923, and this informed most of their pronouncements during the period. Another of Browne's judgments gave further retrospective validation to what many of the bishops had been saying. 'Where a revolution has, justly or unjustly, taken place', he declared, 'if only one government is possible, that is legitimate; if two or more governments are possible, that which has the consent of the people is legitimate'.[23]

The maintenance of discipline over clergy and laity was an even more serious consideration for the bishops in the post-Treaty period than it had been during the War of Independence. As F.S.L. Lyons pointed out, the Church leadership, 'by committing itself so

[21] See D. Macardle, *The Irish Republic*, 4th edn (Dublin, 1951), pp. 641–3.

[22] M. Moynihan, *Speeches and Statements by Eamon de Valera, 1917–1974* (Dublin, 1980), p. 162. For a defence of de Valera's position, see T. Ryle Dwyer, *De Valera, the Man and the Myths* (Dublin, 1991). p. 113.

[23] Browne's lecture was published under the title 'The Source and the Purpose of Political Authority', in *Studies*, September 1936, pp. 394ff. References are to p. 396. Browne was, of course, speaking at a time when de Valera was enthusiastically canvassing the benefits of majority rule. See, for example, the latter's New Ross speech of 14.8.36, published by Fianna Fáil in 'National Discipline and Majority Rule', 1936. The senior Republican cleric of the early twenties, Bishop Dignan of Clonfert, declared in 1924 that although he still stood where he had in 1918, and still believed 'as strongly as I did then in the right of Ireland to complete freedom and in the efficiency of the means then adopted to secure that right', he felt bound to obey the rule of the majority in the Free State. *Irish Press*, 13.4.53.

wholeheartedly to one side of an issue which had divided men so deeply . . . could be held to have threatened its own power-base in the country as a whole'.[24] In 1888, in order to maintain the goodwill of the mass of the people, the bishops were obliged to refrain from enforcing the Papal decree condemning the Plan of Campaign ,[25] an expedient necessary, as Bishop Gillooly of Elphin put it, 'to save the clergy of Ireland from the severeness and hostility of the people', to preserve the authority of the peaceful constitutional leadership and to prevent the people from falling into the hands of 'the lowest class of agitators and demagogues'.[26] In 1918, John Henry Bernard, Church of Ireland Archbishop of Dublin, believed that the dominant motive governing the populist stand by the Catholic bishops when they put themselves at the head of the anti-conscription campaign was 'the desire to keep control over their people'.[27] While the pro-Treaty party was undoubtedly the popular one in 1922, commanding the support of the overwhelming majority of lay and clerical Catholics in the North and that of perhaps three-quarters of those in the South,[28] the political and moral authority of the bishops was challenged by an articulate and determined minority of committed Republicans. The possible defection of at least some of these from the Church was a cause for concern to some bishops. Foley, for example, writing to his Vicar-General, had no doubt 'that a section, small or large, of the Republicans, have been alienated from the practice of their religion

[24] F.S.L. Lyons, *Culture and Anarchy in Ireland, 1880–1939* (Oxford, 1980), p. 150.
[25] The Vatican Decree of 20.4.1888 described the Plan of Campaign as 'foreign to natural justice and Christian charity'. The 'General Inquisitors against heretical error' pronounced that 'it cannot be held to be lawful that rent should be extorted from tenants and deposited with unknown persons, no account being taken of the landlord'. See E. Larkin, *The Roman Catholic Church and the Plan of Campaign, 1886-1888* (Cork, 1978), pp. 201–2.
[26] Larkin, *Roman Catholic Church*, pp. 309–10. Larkin points out that the bishops were compelled to give a lead in order not to forfeit their considerable influence in the political and agrarian agitation to their more militant lay colleagues'. Ibid., p. 203.
[27] D.W. Miller, *Church, State and Nation in Ireland 1898–1921* (Dublin, 1973), p. 408. Bernard suggested that Catholic bishops 'would have forfeited their influence years ago if they had not condoned the Plan of Campaign. They would have forfeited their influence with the Sinn Féiners (a growing body) if they had accepted the scheme of Home Rule which the constitutional Nationalists and Southern Unionists accepted in the Convention . . . And they would forfeit their influence now, if they did not fall in with the popular dislike of conscription'.
[28] Perhaps the best guide to the approximate level of Republican support in the immediate post-Treaty period is provided by the General Election results for 1923, which show a Republican vote of 27.4 per cent. C. O'Leary, *Irish Elections 1918–1977* (Dublin, 1979), p. 101.

and I fear from belief in it, if their words can be trusted. But as you remember, this occurred in the Parnell split and soon disappeared'.[29] One angry Republican, Dan Breen, claimed that the allegiance of Catholic Republicans to the Church was irreparably impaired by the conduct of the bishops in 1922 and 1923, and that the uncompromising severity of episcopal sanctions against Republicans had driven 'one half of the people against them with the result that they never regained the power they once had'.[30] This fails to take account of the enthusiasm with which a great number of Republicans, like their Fenian predecessors, could embrace Catholic spirituality and ecclesiastical authority on matters of faith while at the same time entertaining considerable scepticism about the competence of bishops to pronounce on political or constitutional issues.[31]

Had members of the hierarchy been regular readers of Republican journals in the immediate post-Treaty period, they would undoubtedly have been reassured, perhaps even edified, by the preoccupation of *Sinn Féin* and *An Phoblacht* with the minutiae of Catholic devotional practice, and their unfeigned concern for the welfare of the institutional church. Writers in these journals deplored the shortage of priests in Scotland and of Irish missionaries abroad, rejoiced at the increased number of seminaries in America, and treated reports of miracle cures at Knock with proper reverence.[32] Some contributors appropriated Catholic devotion to Republican purposes, and some even contrived to suggest that Catholicism was essentially, or even exclusively, a Republican faith. In 1924, one writer described the Feast of All Souls as the day on which 'the Republic enters into the spirit of sublime

---

[29] Foley to M.J. Murphy, 30.8.22 KLDA. Having contemplated the consequences for the church of episcopal severity towards Republicans, Foley appeared anxious not to antagonise them unduly. Having denounced recent ambushes in his diocese (See *Nationalist and Leinster Times*, 19.8.22), he admitted that had he known that his letter of condemnation was to be published, he would have 'omitted some of the adjectives and adverbs'.

[30] Quoted in Patrick O'Farrell, *Ireland's English Question* (London, 1971), pp. 296–7.

[31] The case of Stephen O'Mara, a leading Limerick Republican, is a typical one. O'Mara visited Hagan in Rome following his release from Mountjoy. The latter described him as 'a singularly clear-headed and fervent Catholic'. Hagan to Mannix, 5.10.23. Hagan Papers. De Valera, who accepted the practical consequences of episcopal excommunication of Civil War Republicans, nevertheless regarded himself and them as 'still spiritually and mystically' in communion with the Church. See the Earl of Longford and T.P. O'Neill, *Eamon de Valera* (Dublin, 1970), p. 220.

[32] See *An Phoblacht*, 26.6.25; 12.3.26; 14.8.25. For an excellent account of Republican journalism during the period, see J.P. Mc Hugh, 'Voices of the Rearguard: A Study of *An Phoblacht*. Irish Republican Thought in the Post-Revolutionary Era, 1923-1937', MA thesis, University College Dublin, 1983, p. 175.

ritual of the Christian Church'. In 1925, another described a Marian devotion as 'closely associated with the Republic and the protection of many of its faithful followers'. In 1928, the same journal recalled that over two hundred Republican prisoners at Ballykinlar internment camp had, during the Civil War, performed the same spiritual exercises as pilgrims at Lough Derg and hoped that all former internees of the Camp would participate in an annual pilgrimage to the shrine.[33] Some of the devotional material had a clear political import, as in the presentation of Joan of Arc as a sainted patriot who had fought the English, and Oliver Plunkett as a martyr to English injustice.[34] From time to time, republican journalists identified the Cumann na nGaedheal administration with what they supposed was a debasement of moral standards, a process inaugurated, according to Ruttledge, by the abandonment of 'sacred national principles' by those who supported the Treaty. This decline of morality could, he suggested, 'only be remedied by the functioning of the Republican government'.[35] Their emphasis on Church news and the pious and moralistic tone of their contributors made Republican journals as safe as official Catholic publications for potential clerical readers. When, in 1926, a contributor to *An Phoblacht* argued that the leaders of Freemasonry compared favourably with the bishops in their attitude to national and social questions, he was rebuked by another who, urging fidelity 'to Christ's Vicar in Rome', asserted that Republicans regarded 'the enemies of Christ's Church' as their own enemies.[36]

There is no evidence to suggest that what many Republicans saw as the partisan stand of the bishops against their cause diminished the loyalty to the Church of any but a small minority among them. Anti-clericalism was not a notable feature of the Republican response to episcopal condemnation. One of the most outspoken and uncompromising critics of post-Treaty Republicans and Republicanism was Cardinal Logue. The treatment of his death in the Republican press in instructive. *An Phoblacht* deplored 'the loss to our nation of a venerable and learned churchman and a kindly and simple prelate'. His opposition to the movement for Irish freedom was charitably attributed, not to 'any lack of love for liberty or disbelief in the honourable striving for a deathless ideal' but to 'a complete misunder-

---

[33] *Sinn Féin*, 1.11.24; *An Phoblacht*, 20.6.25; Ibid., 19.5.28.
[34] *Sinn Féin*, 7.6.24; *An Phoblacht*, 16.5.34.
[35] *Sinn Féin*, 12.4.24. Cosgrave's use of the word 'damn' inspired another Republican commentator to deplore the 'indecorous taste' he displayed in his use of 'language or epithets only too familiar to the man in the back streets'. Ibid., 13.8.23.
[36] *An Phoblacht*, 12.3.26.

standing based on misrepresentations and falsehoods of the daily press'. Republicans would mourn him as 'one whom the Lord had made a Prince'.[37] Far from being anti-clerical, Republicans, as one of their number ruefully observed, were only too ready to rejoice when any clerical voice was raised in their support. Redmond O'Hanlon remarked with much justification that 'if a priest or bishop comes out on our side, we placard the fact, as if the word of any priest on political matters was law'.[38] The prominence given in *An Phoblacht*, for example, to public approval of the kind mentioned by O'Hanlon suggests that Republicans were eager for the unique validity which clerical sanction could give their cause. Republican journalism exploited the benediction of Sinn Féin and the malediction of its political enemies by Archbishop Mannix in 1925. The approval of lesser clerical figures was also gratefully recorded, as in the case of the 'Patriot Priest' who sponsored Fianna Éireann or the American prelate who defended the IRA and described Republicanism as a movement 'born in the tradition of sanctity and patriotism of our Irish faith'.[39] Peadar O'Donnell's use of such fictional works as his 1930 novel *The Knife* to express violent anti-clerical feeling must be seen as an aberration from the norm.[40]

The great majority of the constitutional Republicans of Fianna Fáil, and those of a more militant temper like Count Plunkett, Mary MacSwiney, and Brian O'Higgins who persisted with Sinn Féin after de Valera had left it, were loyal Catholics, even ostentatiously so. In the 1930s, the remaining Republicans, the radicals associated with Saor Éire and Republican Congress, seemed to the Church authorities to present a serious challenge not only to ecclesiastical influence and discipline but to the Catholic faith. These became identified in many clerical minds as the active enemies of the Church in the universal struggle between Christ and anti-Christ. In many parts of Ireland, their proselytising activities met with a stern, effective and sometimes violent Catholic response, often led or inspired by priests. The air was

[37] Ibid., 19.2.26.
[38] Ibid., 17.9.27.
[39] *An Phoblacht*, 10.9.32; 28.7.34.
[40] The Knife of the title of O'Donnell's novel is a Republican leader who specialises in crude and savage abuse of his pro-Treaty priest. The novel may be read as an exercise in wish-fulfilment on O'Donnell's part. When the priest is about to condemn the Republican cause, the Knife threatens him: 'It might be a good thing to wreck this chapel; you have fouled it, you skunk. If you don't get down now and do it damn quick, I'll kick you off the altar'. O'Donnell's hero describes the bishops as 'a proper lot of anti-Christs' and 'a powerful parcel of blackguards'. P. O'Donnell, *The Knife* (London, 1930), pp. 177–8, 190, 252. In 1931, Cosgrave mentioned O'Donnell's novel as an illustration of the author's open anti-clericalism. See Cosgrave to Archbishop Byrne, 17.9.31. DAA.

filled with such exhortations as that of Bishop Cullen of Kildare and Leighlin, who saw no reason why 'anyone who propagates Communism should be allowed to do so with impunity', and encouraged those who valued their religion to 'fight the enemy who attacks it'.[41] Peadar O'Donnell, one of those most frequently attacked as a propagandist for Soviet irreligion, publicly proclaimed his Catholicism, and distinguished between radical Republicanism and hostility to the principles and practices of his faith, even acknowledging himself 'a very militant papist' when he found himself in foreign surroundings.[42] On the whole, even the most radical Irish Republicans showed little or no disposition to abandon their religious practice or embrace the militant anti-clericalism of the Continental left. Their fidelity was saluted in 1936 by Patrick Sexton, Dean of Cork when, proclaiming that 'Republicans are Christians', he simultaneously recruited James Connolly to the ranks of Catholic social thinkers. Connolly, he declared, was neither a Communist nor an atheist. Indeed, his 'social plan for Ireland was modelled on the Popes' Encyclicals' and 'he always laid it down that the country should be ruled on Catholic lines'.[43] Connolly's emergence as a Catholic activist must have appeared incongrous to those Republican radicals who, while thinking of themselves as his disciples, had earned the disapproval of so many clergymen for their supposedly unorthodox views.

II

In the Free State, the 1933 General Election, in which priests all over the country were enthusiastically engaged, marked the high point of this phase of clerical politics. By 1937, the Church had disengaged itself from active participation in the electoral process in the South: priests featured only to a minimal extent as platform speakers or public supporters of candidates. The period from 1922 to 1937 had seen wide and understandable differences between the political activity of Catholic churchmen in the North and that of their counterparts in the South. Even after 1925, when it became evident that the boundary between North and South was not going to change, most of the Catholic clergy who lived there afforded only a tentative and grudging recognition to the Northern State. In the immediate aftermath of the Treaty, when a solid majority of the Southern clergy were actively upholding the Provisional and Free State governments, clerical leaders

---

[41] *Irish Independent*, 6.3.33.
[42] See his non-fictional account of his Spanish experiences in P. O'Donnell, *Salud! An Irishman in Spain* (Dublin, 1937), p. 36.
[43] Dean Sexton's comments were reproduced in *An Phoblacht*, 16.5.36.

in the North, most of whom would have chosen continuing British rule in preference to a Unionist government as a means of defending such vital interests as Church control of Catholic education, were working through such mechanisms as the Boundary Bureau and the Boundary Commission in the hope of incorporating as many of their co-religionists as possible with the South. This inspired the further hope that substantial transfers of population would make the six-county state unviable. It is reasonable to speculate whether the Northern clergy would have been wiser to have accorded public assent to the six-county state from the beginning, and involved themselves actively in the political process as leaders of Catholic opinion, even in the face of widespread quasi-official persecution of Belfast Catholics. The evidence suggests that even the most extreme initial Catholic benevolence towards the Northern State would have been answered by the same kind of systematic discrimination and coercion which continued to prevail in the thirties in the face of conciliatory and helpful gestures from Nationalist parliamentarians.

Northern clerical views of Unionists and Unionism were mirrored in Southern clerical views of Republicans and Republicanism. In public at any rate, Southern episcopal political discourse was based on an almost unqualified acceptance of the official Free State view of itself and its enemies. Clerical depiction of Southern politics was coloured not only by an overwhelmingly anti-Republican bias, but by an accompanying sense that the politicians and institutions the Church was defending represented the best in Catholic democracy, indeed the only version of democracy available at the time. When lawlessness, anarchy and bad motives were chronicled by Church leaders, these were inevitably seen as characteristic of Republicans, indeed a Republican monopoly. There was also a tendency among bishops and senior clerics to attribute exclusive blame for the Civil War on Republican self-righteousness and intransigence, arising from an absolutist ideology. There is no record of official ecclesiastical censure of the civil and military personnel of the Free State who showed themselves capable of looting, commandeering, drunkenness, widespread breaches of civil and criminal law, and the perpetration of atrocities. Nor did any of the bishops take a public stand on some of the morally questionable courses followed by the Free State authorities in suppressing the Republican revolt: the virtual abrogation of the rule of law at the height of the struggle and the supererogatory intensification of executions in the spring of 1923 when the Republican cause was evidently lost. At this point at least, senior churchmen appeared to believe that killing even untried prisoners was not murder provided that it was performed by agents of the Free State, and

provided that a limited number of ruthless executions, legal or otherwise, offered the prospect of arresting the slide into anarchy apparent
during the Civil War.

When they exercised their fulminatory faculties, churchmen seemed
unconscious of the shared assumption of inerrancy on the part of the
Church itself and Republicans temporarily at odds with it. However,
just as the Church had found it possible to accommodate itself to
British rule and to the 'Godless constitution', of the Free State, it
eventually developed a mutually satisfactory relationship in the thirties
with those it condemned and made outcasts in the twenties. This last
accommodation was not difficult for either side because the great
body of anti-Treaty Republicans under de Valera were prepared to
compromise and live with much of what they had once condemned,
and to turn their fire on other Republicans who could not conscientiously do the same. That there was no permanent breach between
the Church and the post-Treaty Republican movement as a whole
was due largely to the profound Catholicism of the latter. However
anti-clerical some of them became in response to the unwelcome
political attitudes of churchmen, they showed no disposition to confuse
'errant' clergymen with the Church as a spiritual entity. Instead, they
incorporated their religion with their Republicanism, and evolved a
theology whose central tenet was that sacrifices endured in the
Republican cause were part of a twin service to God and country.
The highest ideal of the Republican faith was the offering of suffering,
and even life itself, to God for the Republic of Ireland. Once political
passions subsided, and the mass of Republicans tempered their
militancy and idealism with pragmatism, they could, to the satisfaction
and admiration of most churchmen, present themselves once more to
the world as model Catholics.

III

To focus narrowly on the Catholic Church as a power structure and a
political agency is, inevitably, to distort, however difficult it may be at
times to separate its pastoral, evangelical role from its political one. In
the nature of the case, these two roles are frequently inseparable. The
recurring political assertiveness of the Irish clerical church throughout
the period cannot be explained simply as a reflection of an impulse to
exert power for its own sake. Clerical political power was an essential
means to a greater end: to ensure that Irish society functioned in conformity with Catholic moral and social principles, which churchmen
could not but regard as fundamental to individual and communal
well-being.

The dealings of Catholic churchmen with politicians and with other religious denominations must be seen in the context of a doctrinal system vigorously expounded and sincerely held. The Catholic Church, believing itself to be the one authentic repository of the full Christian truth, with an exclusive mandate to teach and evangelise the nations, could not treat other Christian traditions as equals without betraying its identity. The most it could acknowledge was that there were vestiges of the true Church in other Christian bodies. Given what it saw as its divinely imposed duty to work for the concrete embodiment of Catholic truth in human affairs, it regarded itself as morally obliged to proclaim its doctrines to society and to the state. In societies where this was feasible, as it was in the Free State, the Church felt justified in enforcing its moral and social teaching through political action, since not to do so would suggest indifferentism, a betrayal of its duty actively to uphold and propagate truths of which it was the sole guardian and interpreter. In states with large Catholic majorities, the Church could see no reason why beliefs or practices in conflict with its teaching, divorce, for example, should be given sanction or even tolerance.[44]

For generations, Irish Catholic churchmen, largely through the medium of an educational system which they administered and controlled, had been singularly effective in inducing lay Catholics to regard these issues in the light of official Church teaching. It is therefore not surprising that the political leaders of the new state, who had been formed by such teaching, were happy to give churchmen a dominant voice in shaping those aspects of public policy, marriage, education and health being the most significant, in which they claimed a special competence and jurisdiction.

[44] Archbishop Sheehan, the most influential Irish Catholic apologist of the period, whose classic outline of traditional teaching was a standard school textbook from the twenties to the fifties, explained why active intolerance of points of view irreconcilable with Catholic ones was an essential defence against indifferentism. The Church, Sheehan declared, can never be unwilling to suppress erroneous doctrine, since like every lover of truth it must necessarily be intolerant of error. He believed that 'the so-called tolerance of the present age' was due 'either to the incapacity to persecute or to utter indifferentism in religious matters'. M. Sheehan, *Apologetics and Christian Doctrine*, 4th edn (Dublin, 1955), p. 197.

APPENDIX ONE

VERSIONS OF THE PASTORAL LETTER OF OCTOBER 1922

After their meeting in Maynooth on 10 October 1922, members of the Hierarchy handed copies of their Pastoral Letter on the condition of Ireland to representatives of the press. On the following day, the three National newspapers, *The Irish Times, Irish Independent,* and *Freeman's Journal* published identical versions of the Pastoral. The same text appeared in *The Irish Catholic* on 14 October and in the English Catholic journal, *The Tablet,* on the same day.

The version given by the bishops to the newspapers on 10 October suggested hasty composition and careless formulation to many of those who read it. Some readers seemed to find it difficult to believe that the newspaper version was an accurate representation of the document the bishops had drawn up. Mgr John Hagan, Rector of the Irish College, Rome, was one of these. Over a month after the Pastoral was issued to the Press, Hagan wrote to Mgr Borgongini Duca, the Vatican Under-Secretary of State, telling him that he had intended to send him, on behalf of the Irish bishops, an official copy of the document. 'I was all the more anxious to do so', Hagan wrote, 'because of certain inaccuracies which had crept into the version published by the Irish and English newspapers. In the interval, however, I have learned that an official copy has already reached the hands of the Holy Father and accordingly little remains for me to do in this connection, beyond pointing out that the newspaper version does not correspond to the original text'.[1] In this, Hagan, wittingly or not, was in error. The original text of the Pastoral was, in fact, accurately printed by the newspapers. The 'official copy' mentioned by Hagan was a thoroughly amended version, representing the embarrassed second thoughts of the bishops.

These matters were clarified exactly one year after the text of the Pastoral was issued to the Press at Maynooth. In October 1923, a

[1] Hagan to Borgongini Duca, 13.11.22, Hagan Papers.

Times Literary Supplement reviewer of *The Revolution in Ireland* by W.A. Phillips cited the notorious reference by the bishops in their original version to 'the many unauthorised murders recorded in the Press'.[2] In his book, Phillips had accurately quoted this phrase from the *The Irish Times* version of the Pastoral. The review prompted a reply from Archbishop Gilmartin of Tuam, who wondered where Phillips had got the word 'unauthorised'. 'If he got it in some newspaper', Gilmartin asserted, 'we think that a responsible writer would inquire further before attributing such a monstrous expression as "unauthorised murders" to a body of Bishops. As one who was present at the meeting I can say that the expression was not in the official version agreed upon by the Bishops and ordered to be printed.'.[3] Here, Gilmartin was being less than frank. His use of the term 'official version' is equivocal. The pressmen who received copies of the Pastoral with its reference to 'unauthorised murders' on the day of the Maynooth meeting understandably regarded what they received from the bishops as an authentic document supplied by an authoritative source. The 'official version' referred to by Gilmartin was printed in pamphlet form after extensive revision of the original. The odd reference to 'many unauthorised murders' was altered to 'the many murders' (footnote 42). Over forty other changes were made to the text of the 10 October version.

There is evidence to suggest that the revised pamphlet version of the Pastoral was not the one universally read in churches on Sunday 22 October, the date nominated by the bishops for this exercise. Many priests read from one or other of the newspaper versions. Edward O'Malley, CC, Doone, Clifden, read from the version published in the *Irish Independent*. A Republican priest in the area tried to persuade him that he was 'bound to repair the error by reading the document a second time' to his congregation from the revised version.[4] A correspondent signing himself 'A Catholic' wrote to the Dublin *Evening Mail* (20.10.23) that he had heard the newspaper version read three times in a Wexford church. The 'unauthorised murders' were mentioned the first time, but omitted from the second reading, 'the priest having apparently noticed what was wrong the first time'. The third reading was by a different priest who reverted to 'unauthorised murders'.

There was, it appears, considerable debate among puzzled Catholics about the significance of 'unauthorised murders'. The 'Catholic' who wrote to the *Evening Mail* remembered the Pastoral being criticised for

[2] *Times Literary Supplement*, 11.10.23.
[3] Ibid., 18.10.23.
[4] W. Kelly, CC Ballyconneeley, to M.J. Browne, 6.2.23, GDA.

the use of the word 'unauthorised'; he himself took it to mean that 'while the members of the IRA were murdering the RIC, murder was authorised, but when it came to murdering one another, it was unauthorised'. Another correspondent remembered talking over the matter with a Republican. Both agreed that 'the murder of a policeman or soldiers was legitimate because it was authorised by Dáil Éireann, but it would be immoral to murder a person out of spite because unauthorised'. W.A. Phillips, who dismissed Archbishop Gilmartin's assertions as contrary to the facts, believed that the use of 'unauthorised' was generally assumed to mean that the bishops, acting as a body, distinguished between murders 'authorised' since they were carried out or directed by those, including Collins, whom, since the elections of 1918, they had recognised as *de jure* rulers of Ireland, and 'unauthorised' murders committed by rebels against what the bishops regarded as lawful authority.

When the October Pastoral was issued, many Republicans were in jail. In drawing up the Pastoral, the bishops recognised that from the point of view of spiritual sanctions, prisoners were in a different position from Republicans still at liberty. This was their reason for the following formulation in the original document of 10 October: 'All those who in contravention of this teaching, participate in such crimes, are guilty of grievous sins, and may not be absolved in confession, nor admitted to Holy Communion, if they persist in such evil courses.' Bishop Foley of Kildare and Leighlin, in whose diocese many Republicans were incarcerated, explained the thinking of the bishops on this matter to his Vicar General two days after the Pastoral was issued. He pointed out that the bishops felt that the prisoners were not in quite the same position as 'those who, being outside, are free to continue, and do continue to take part in, or effectively to help, the terrible work that is going on in many parts of the country, and it was owing to the special circumstances of the prisons that the paragraph is so drawn as to leave room for the possibility, to say the least, of bona fides or invincible ignorance in the case of the prisoners'.[5] Foley also pointed out that the penal paragraph did not mention repentance in case there might have been bona fides.[6] On the face of it, then, the Pastoral seemed to impose a lesser burden on the consciences of the prisoners and of their confessors than it did on active-service Republicans. The revised version, however, significantly alters the paragraph discussed by Bishop Foley. The clause, 'if they persist in such evil courses' is changed to 'if they purpose to persevere in such

[5] Foley to M.J. Murphy, 12.10.22, KLDA.
[6] Ibid.

evil courses'. This new clause, if strictly interpreted by prison confessors, placed Republican prisoners in much the same spiritual position as their colleagues who were still at liberty.

The signature of O'Donnell, Bishop of Raphoe and Co-Adjutor to Logue, was absent from the copy published in the newspapers on 11 October, but included in the revised pamphlet version. A writer in the San Francisco *Leader* (20.1.23), most likely Fr Peter Yorke,[7] claimed that 'we have it on the very best authority that the bishops were not at all agreed' on what was to go into the document. He suggested that 'the form of the letter was drawn up in evident haste, and it is held that its argumentation was a concession demanded by the Bishop of Cork before he would sign'.

[7] See p. 220, note 350.

Text of October Pastoral

The version reproduced below is that printed in the Freeman's Journal *on 11 October 1922. The footnotes record the changes made in the pamphlet version later published by the Bishops. The changes in the later version are printed in italics.*

The present state of Ireland is a sorrow and humiliation[1] to its friends all over the world. To us, Irish Bishops, it is, because[2] of the moral and religious issues at stake, a source[3] of the most painful anxiety. Our country that but yesterday was so glorious is now a byeword before the nations for a domestic strife, as disgraceful as it is criminal and suicidal. A section of the community, refusing to acknowledge the Government set up by the nation have chosen to attack their own country as if she were a foreign Power. Forgetting, apparently, that a dead nation cannot be free, they have deliberately set out to make our Motherland, as far as they could, a heap of ruins.

They have wrecked Ireland from end to end, burning and destroying national property of enormous value, breaking roads, bridges and railways, seeking by this insensate[4] blockade to starve the people, or bury them in social stagnation. They have caused more damage to Ireland in three months than could be laid to the charge of British rule in so many decades.

They carry on what they call a war, but which, in the absence of any legitimate authority to justify it, is morally only a system of murder and assassination of the National forces – for it must not be forgotten that killing in an unjust war is as much murder before God as if there were no war. They ambush military lorries in the crowded streets thereby killing and wounding not only the soldiers of the Nation, but peaceful citizens. They have, to our horror, shot bands of these troops on their way to Mass on Sunday; and set mine traps in the public roads and blown to fragments some of the bravest Irishmen that ever lived.

Side by side with this woful destruction of life and property there is running a campaign of plunder, raiding banks and private houses, seizing the lands and property of others, burning mansions and country houses, destroying demesnes and slaying cattle.

But even worse and sadder than this physical ruin is the general demoralization created by this unhappy revolt – demoralization

[1] humiliation *a humiliation*
[2] it is, because *because*
[3] a source *it is a source*
[4] this insensate *an insensate*

especially of the young, whose minds are being poisoned by false principles, and their young lives utterly spoiled by early association with cruelty, robbery, falsehood and crime. Religion itself is not spared. We observe with deepest sorrow that a certain section is engaged in a campaign against the Bishops, whose pastoral office they would silence by calumny and intimidation; and they have done the priesthood of Ireland, whose services and sacrifices for their country will be historic, the insult of suggesting a cabal amongst them to brow-beat their bishops and revolt against their authority. And, in spite of all this sin and crime, they claim to be good Catholics and demand at the hands of the Church her most sacred privileges like the Sacraments reserved for her worthy members.[5] When we think of what these young men were only a few months ago, so many of them generous, kind-hearted and good, and see them now involved in this network of crime, our hearts are filled with bitterest anguish.

It is almost inconceivable how decent Irish boys could degenerate as tragically, and reconcile such a mass of criminality with their duties to God and to Ireland. The strain on our country for the last few years will account for much of it. Vanity, perhaps[6] self-conceit, may have blinded some who think that they, and not the nation, must dictate the national policy. Greed for land, love of loot and anarchy have affected others, and they we regret to say, are not a few; but the main cause of this demoralization is to be found in false notions on social morality.

The long struggle of centuries against foreign rule and misrule has weakened respect for civil authority in the national conscience. This is a great misfortune, a great drawback and a great peril to our young Government.[7] For no nation can live where the civic sense of obedience to authority and law is not firmly and religiously maintained. And if Ireland is ever to realize anything but a miserable destiny[8] of anarchy all classes of her citizens must cultivate respect for and obedience to the Government set up by the nation in whatever[9] shape it takes, while acting within the law of God. This difficulty[10] is now being cruelly exploited for the ruin, as we see, of Ireland. The claim is now made that a minority are entitled, when they think it right, to take arms and destroy the National Government. Last April, foreseeing the danger, we raised Our voices in the most solemn manner against

[5] for her worthy members *for worthy members alone*
[6] perhaps *and perhaps*
[7] our young Government *a young Government*
[8] destiny *record*
[9] in whatever *whatever*
[10] difficulty *defect*

this disruptive and immoral principle. We pointed out to our young men the conscientious difficulties in which it would involve them, and warned them against it. Disregard for[11] the Divine Law then laid down by the Bishops is the chief cause of all our present sorrows and calamities.

We now again authoritatively renew that teaching and warn our Catholic people that they are conscientiously bound to abide by it, subject of course to an appeal to the Holy See.

No one is justified in rebelling against the legitimate Government, whatever it is, set up by the nation and acting within its rights.

The opposite doctrine is false, contrary to Christian morals and opposed to the constant teaching of the Church. 'Let every soul', says St Paul, 'be subject to the higher powers' – that is to the legitimate authority of the State. From St Paul downwards the Church has inculcated obedience to authority as a divine duty as well as a social necessity; and has reprobated unauthorised rebellion as sinful in itself and destructive of social stability: as it manifestly is, for if one section of the community has that right, so have other sections the same right, until we end in general anarchy. No Republican[12] can evade this teaching[13] by asserting that the legitimate authority in Ireland[14] is not the present Dáil[15] or Provisional Government[16]. There is no other,[17] and cannot be, outside the body of the people. A Republic without popular recognition behind it is a contradiction in terms.

Such being Divine Law,[18] the guerilla warfare now being carried on by the Irregulars is without moral sanction, and therefore the killing of National soldiers in the course of it is murder before God. The seizing of public and private property is robbery. The breaking of roads, bridges and railways is criminal destruction, the invasion of homes and the molestation of citizens is a grievous crime. All those who in contravention of this teaching participate in such crimes, are guilty of grievous sins,[19] and may not be absolved in Confession, nor admitted to Holy Communion, if they persist[20] in such evil courses.

---

[11] for *of*
[12] No Republican *No one*
[13] this teaching *this teaching in our present case*
[14] in Ireland *in Ireland just now*
[15] the present Dáil *the Dáil*
[16] or Provisional Government. *or Provisional Government. That Government has been elected by the Nation, and is supported by the vast majority of public opinion.*
[17] no other, *no other Government,*
[18] Divine Law *the Divine Law*
[19] grievous sins *the gravest sins*
[20] they persist *if they purpose to persevere*

It is said that there are priests[21] who approve of this Irregular insurrection. If there be any such, they are false to their sacred office and are guilty of grievous[22] scandal, and will not be allowed to retain the faculties they hold from us.

Furthermore, we forbid[23] under pain of suspension, ipso facto, and reserve to the Ordinary[24] any priest who advocates such doctrine,[25] publicly or privately.

Our people will observe that in all this there is no question of mere politics, but of what is morally right or wrong according to the Divine Law in certain principles and in a certain series of acts, whether carried out for political purposes or otherwise. What we condemn is the armed campaign now being carried on against the Government set up by the nation.

If any section in the community have a grievance or disapprove of the National Government they have the elections to fall back upon; and such constitutional action as is recognised by God and civilised society. If their political views are founded on wisdom they will succeed sooner or later; but one thing is certain, the Hand of Providence will not be forced nor their cause advanced by irreligion and crime.

It may perhaps be said that in this our teaching we wound the strong feelings of many of our people; that we know and the thought is agony[26] to us. But we must teach Truth[27] in such a grave crisis[28] no matter what the consequences. It is not for want of sympathy with any part of our flock that we interfere, but from a deep and painful sense of our duty to God, to our people, and out of true charity to the young men themselves specially concerned.

Let it not be said that this our teaching is due to political bias and a desire to help one political party. If it[29] were true, we were unworthy of our sacred office. Our religion in such a supposition was[30] a mockery and a sham. We issue this Pastoral Letter under the grievous sense[31] of our responsibility, mindful of the charges[32] laid upon us by our Divine Master to preach His Doctrine and safeguard His sacred rule of faith

---

[21] priests *some priests*
[22] grievous *the gravest*
[23] we forbid *we, each for his own diocese, hereby forbid*
[24] and reserve to the Ordinary *reserved to the Ordinary*
[25] any priest who advocates such doctrine *any priest to advocate or encourage this revolt*
[26] agony *an agony*
[27] Truth *the Truth*
[28] such a grave crisis *this grave crisis*
[29] it *that*
[30] was *were*
[31] the grievous sense *the gravest sense*
[32] the charges *the charge*

and morals at any cost. We must, in the words of St Peter, 'Obey God rather than man[33]'.

With all earnestness we appeal to the leaders in[34] this saddest revolt to rise above their own feelings, to remember the claim of God and the sufferings of the people in their conscience, and to abandon methods which they now know beyond the shadow of a doubt[35] are un-Catholic and immoral, and look to the realisation of their ideals along lines[36] sanctioned by Divine Law and society.[37]

Let them not think we are insensible to their feelings – we think of them with compassion, carrying as they do on their shoulders a heavy[38] responsibility for what is now happening in Ireland. Once more we wish to appeal to[39] the young men in this[40] movement in the Name of God to return to their innocent homes and make, if necessary, the big sacrifice of their feelings[41] for the common good. And surely it is no humiliation, having done their best to abide by the verdict of Ireland.

We know that some of them are troubled and held back by the oath they took. A lawful oath is indeed a sacred bond between God and man; but no oath can bind any man to carry on a warfare against his own country in circumstances forbidden by the law of God. It would be an offence to God and to the very nature of an oath to say so.

We, therefore, hope and pray that they will take advantage of the Government's present offer and make peace with their own country, a peace which will bring both happiness and honour to themselves and joy to Ireland generally and to the friends of Ireland all over the world.

In this lamentable upheaval the moral sense of the people has, we fear, been badly shaken. We read with horror of the many unautho-rised murders[42] recorded in the Press. With feelings of shame we observe that when country houses and public buildings were destroyed the furniture and other fittings were seized and carried away by people in the neighbourhood. We remind them that all such property belongs in justice to the original owners, and now must be preserved for and restored to them by those who hold them.[43]

[33] man *men*

[34] in *of*

[35] a doubt *doubt*

[36] lines *the lines*

[37] and society *and the usages of well-ordered society*

[38] a heavy *the heavy*

[39] wish to appeal to *beg and implore*

[40] in this *of this*

[41] of their feelings *of their own feelings*

[42] the many unauthorised murders *the many murders*

[43] them *it*

We desire to impress on the people the duty of supporting the national Government, whatever it is, to set their faces resolutely against disorder, to pay their taxes, rents and annuities, and to assist the Government in every possible way to restore order and establish peace. Unless they learn to do so they can have no Government, and if they have no Government, they can have no nation.

As human effort is fruitless without God's blessing, we exhort our priests and people to continue the prayers already ordered, and we direct that the remaining October devotions be offered up for peace. We also direct that a Novena to the Irish saints for the same end be said in all public churches and oratories, and in semi-public oratories, to begin on the 28th day of October and end on November the 6th, the Feast of all the Irish Saints. These Novena devotions, in addition to the Rosary and Benediction, may include a special prayer for Ireland and the Litany of the Irish Saints.

POLITICAL ALLEGIANCE OF THE
ROMAN CATHOLIC CLERGY, 1922–37

This register incorporates the names of the Roman Catholic clergy whose political views and activities came to light during the course of my research.

Those whose names appear under the heading 'Pro-Treaty' were active in making a public case for the acceptance of the Treaty and worked in various ways for pro-Treaty political groups and their successors, particularly during election campaigns, from 1922 to 1937. The great majority of the clergy here described as anti-Treaty were supporters of the anti-Treaty cause in 1922 and later of Fianna Fáil. The anti-Treaty list contains three other groupings: those ordained from 1926 onwards whose allegiance was to Fianna Fáil, those who remained loyal to Sinn Féin after 1926, and those whose early allegiance had been to the Treaty settlement but who later supported Sinn Féin or Fianna Fáil or both. The names of the last group appear in both the anti-Treaty and pro-Treaty lists and are indicated by (*).

As my chapter on the Northern clergy makes clear, almost all of them might be classified as pro-Treaty until the end of 1925, after which an increasing number transferred their support to Fianna Fáil, particularly in areas close to the border. I have not listed the entire body of the northern clergy as putative supporters of the Treaty in 1922, instead giving only the names of those who made their views known.

Part One: Secular Clergy

ACHONRY – INCLUDES PARTS OF MAYO, SLIGO AND ROSCOMMON

Pro-Treaty	Rank	First Reported Declaration	Source
Morrisroe, Patrick	Bishop	1922	*Roscommon Messenger*, 22.7.22
Boland, Patrick	CC Achonry	1925	*Roscommon Herald*, 14.3.25
Burke, Felix	PP Straide	1922	*Connaught Tribune*, 28.1.33
Carney, Charles	PP Bunnenaddin	1923	*Roscommon Herald*, 25.8.23
Connington, Edward	PP Swinford	1925	*Western News*, 25.4.25
Connolly, Michael	PP Curry	1925	*Sligo Champion*, 21.2.25
Devine, Matthew	PP Achonry	1927	*Anglo Celt*, 10.9.27
Doyle, Michael	PP Collooney	1923	*Roscommon Herald* 25.8.23
Durcan, Michael	PP Killoran	1932	*Sligo Champion*, 13.2.32
Flynn, William	PP Bunnenaddin	1929	*Roscommon Herald*, 1.6.29
Gallagher, Thomas	CC Ballymote	1925	*Roscommon Herald*, 14.3.25
Henry, Edward	PP Keash	1925	*Roscommon Herald*, 14.3.25
Henry, Martin	PP Kilmovee	1922	U. MacEoin (ed.), *Survivors*, (Dublin, 1980), p. 289
Henry, Walter	PP Swinford	1925	*Irish Independent*, 2.3.25
Higgins, Patrick J.	CC Swinford	1925	*Western News*, 25.4.25
McKeon, John	PP Bonniconlon	1925	ditto
O'Connell, John	CC Kilmovee	1925	ditto
O'Connor, James	PP Gurteen	1929	*Roscommon Herald*, 1.6.29.
O'Donnell, Roger	PP Attymas	1925	*Western News*, 25.4.25.
Quinn, Thomas	PP Ballymote	1923	*Roscommon Herald*, 25.8.23.
Spelman, James	Adm. Ballaghdereen	1925	*Westmeath Independent*, 14.2.25.

Anti-Treaty			
Gildea, Denis	CC Achonry	1932	*Irish Press*, 9.2.32.
Mulligan, Philip	PP Carracastle	1922	*An Phoblacht*, 5.11.27.

ARDAGH AND CLONMACNOIS – INCLUDES ALMOST ALL OF LONGFORD, THE GREATER PART OF LEITRIM, AND PORTIONS OF OFFALY, WESTMEATH, ROSCOMMON, CAVAN AND SLIGO

Pro-Treaty			
Hoare, Joseph	Bishop	1922	*Roscommon Herald*, 1.3.22.
Burke, Michael	CC Drumcong	1922	*Roscommon Herald*, 25.3.22.
Clancy, Patrick	CC Mohill	1922	*Freeman's Journal*, 20.7.22.
Cosgrave, John	PP Drumsna	1933	*East Galway Democrat*, 11.3.33.
Dolan, Patrick	PP Bornacoola	1925	*Roscommon Herald*, 7.3.25.
Donlon, James	CC Ferbane	1927	*Leinster Reporter*, 10.9.27.
Donohoe, Patrick	PP Killenummery	1923	*Roscommon Herald*, 25.8.23.
Egan, James	CC Cortinty, Drumsna	1922	ditto 10.6.22.
Gilleran, Thomas	CC Kiltoghert	1933	*East Galway Democrat*, 11.3.33.
Goodwin, John	Adm. Athlone	1922	*Roscommon Herald*, 4.3.22.
Guinan, Joseph	PP Ardagh	1921	ditto 31.12.21.

Pro-Treaty	Rank	First Reported Declaration	Source
Higgins, Patrick	CC Ballintogher	1925	*Sligo Champion, 28.2.25.*
Kennedy, Michael J.	PP Shannonbridge	1922	*Westmeath Independent, 22.4.22.*
Keville, John	PP Drumlish	1928	*Roscommon Herald, 15.2.28.*
Kiernan, John	CC Drumcong	1925	*Irish Independent, 23.2.25.*
Langan, Thomas	PP Moate	1922	*Westmeath Independent, 21.3.22.*
Lynch, Hugh	PP Carrowerin	1925	*Sligo Champion, 28.2.25.*
Markey, Patrick	PP Clonbroney	1922	*Roscommon Herald, 7.1.22.*
Masterson, Michael J.	PP Mohill	1925	*Irish Independent, 16.2.25.*
Meehan, John	CC Moate	1922	*Offaly Independent, 25.3.22.*
Mulvin, Denis	CCTang, Ballymahon	1927	*Leinster Reporter, 10.9.27.*
McCabe, Matthew	PP Drumshanbo	1925	*Roscommon Herald, 28.2.25.*
McGaver, Anthony	PP Drumcong	1927	*Anglo-Celt, 10.9.27.*
McGivney, Joseph	PP Killoe	1932	*Westmeath Independent, 13.2.32.*
Newman, Patrick	PP Drumsna	1922	*Roscommon Herald, 25.3.22.*
O'Dowd, John	CC Gowel, Carrick-on-Shannon	1933	*Irish Workers' Voice, 18.2.33.*
O'Farrell, William	CC Gowel, Carrick-on-Shannon	1922	*Roscommon Herald, 25.3.22.*
O'Reilly, Edward	CC Ballingar, Dromahair	1922	ditto
O'Reilly, Patrick	CC Banagher	1923	*United Irishman, 30.6.23.*
O'Reilly, Thomas,	PP Kiltoghert	1922	*Leitrim Advertiser, 23.3.22.*
Pinkman, John	Adm. Athlone	1932	*Westmeath Independent, 13.3.32.*
Reynolds, Francis	CC Ballinahowen	1922	*Freeman's Journal, 20.7.22.*
Ryans, Edward	CC Aughavas	1922	*Roscommon Herald, 25.3.22.*
Wall, James	CC Athlone	1933	*Westmeath Independent, 14.1.33.*

Anti-Treaty

Butler, James	CC Drumshanbo	1933	*Irish Press, 15.1.33.*
Egan, Robert	PP Mullahoran	1922	Robert Egan's Diary, courtesy Rev. Owen Devanney, Mullahoran.
Kelly, Peter	Adm. Longford	1925	Information from Rev. Peadar Lavin, Boyle, 16.1.96.
Meehan, Terence	CC Aughavas	1933	*Irish Press, 15.1.33.*
O'Beirne, J.M.	CC Carrick-on-Shannon	1922	*Roscommon Herald, 10.6.22.*
O'Hara, Patrick	PP Edgeworthstown	1932	*Westmeath Independent, 13.2.32.*

ARMAGH – INCLUDES ALMOST ALL OF LOUTH AND ARMAGH, A LARGE PART OF TYRONE, AND PARTS OF DERRY AND MEATH

Pro-Treaty

Logue, Michael	Archbishop to 1925	1921	*Irish Independent, 10.12.21.*
O'Donnell, Patrick	Archbishop to 1927	1922	O'Donnell to Hagan, 10.4.22. Hagan papers.
MacRory, Joseph	Archbishop from 1928	1921	*Irish Independent, 27.12.21.*

Pro-Treaty	Rank	First Reported Declaration	Source
Donnellan, Bernard	PP Haggardstown	1927	*Anglo-Celt*, 10.9.27.
Lyons, Patrick	PP Ardee	1923	*Irish Independent*, 17.8.23.
McAleer, John	PP Riversdale	1922	*Freeman's Journal*, 5.8.22.
McKeown, James	Adm. Dundalk	1922	*Irish Independent*, 31.7.22.
Segrave, Patrick	PP Drogheda	1922	*Freeman's Journal*, 13.3.22.

Anti-Treaty

Carolan, Francis	PP Mellifont Drogheda	1933	*Dundalk Examiner*, 14.1.33.
Donnellan, Luke	CC Creggan Upper, Crossmaglen	1928	*Kerry Champion*, 24.11.28.
Downey, Patrick	CC Dundalk	1933	*Dundalk Examiner*, 21.1.33.
McCann, Thomas	CC Ballygawley Co. Tyrone	1924	*Irish Independent*, 24.10.24.
McCooey, James	CC Clogherhead Drogheda	1933	*Irish Press*, 12.1.33.
Murray, Laurence	Diocesan Inspector of schools	1928	*An Phoblacht*, 14.4.28.
Walsh, Louis	CC Dungannon	1933	*Irish Press*, 6.2.23.

CASHEL AND EMLY – INCLUDES THE GREATER PART OF TIPPERARY AND PART OF COUNTY LIMERICK

Pro-Treaty

Harty, John	Archbishop	1922	*ICD*, 6.1.22, p. 542.
Callanan, Cornelius	CC Caherconlish, Pallasgreen	1927	*Limerick Leader*, 10.9.27.
Cotter, Garrett	PP Tipperary	1922	*An Phoblacht*, 28.3.31.
Duggan, Dennis	CC Cashel	1922	*Freeman's Journal*, 1.9.22.
Finn, Michael	PP Drom, Thurles	1927	*Tipperaryman and Limerick Recorder*, 2.4.27.
Fitzgerald, William	CC Thurles	1927	*Tipperaryman and Limerick Recorder*, 2.4.27.
Hickey, Philip	CC Templemore	1927	*Midland Tribune*, 4.6.27.
Hourigan, Daniel	CC Pallasgreen	1927	*Limerick Leader*, 30.4.27.
Humphries, David	PP Killenaule	1922	*Freeman's Journal*, 18.3.22.
McCarthy, Joseph	PP Hospital Co. Limerick	1927	*Irish Independent*, 2.6.27.
McCarthy, Michael	PP Caherconlish	1927	*Limerick Echo*, 7.6.27.
Noonan, James	PP Ballyna & Boher	1923	*Irish Times*, 21.8.23.
O'Brien, Denis	PP Templemore	1927	*Midland Tribune*, 4.6.27.
O'Callaghan, John	CC Herbertstown	1927	*Limerick Leader*, 30.4.27.
Ryan, Innocent	PP Cashel	1922	W. Skehan, *Cashel and Emly Heritage* (Dublin, 1993), p. 93.
Ryan, James	The Hermitage, Thurles	1936	*Enniscorthy Guardian*, 25.7.36
Slattery, Joseph	PP Lattin	1927	*Tipperaryman and Limerick Recorder*, 28.5.27.

Anti-Treaty	Rank	First Reported Declaration	Source
Blake, Edward	CC Boherlahan, Cashel	1933	*Clonmel Chronicle*, 14.1.33
Byrne, Philip	PP Holycross	1933	ditto
Condon, William	PP Newport	1933	ditto
Mackey, Edmund	CC Gortnahoe	1922	W.Skehan, *Cashel and Emly*, p.39.
Meaney, Laurence	CC Cashel	1933	*Clonmel Chronicle*, 14.1.33
Murphy, John	CC New Inn	1922	ditto, 7.6.22.
Quinlan, Michael	CC Ballygarane	1933	ditto, 14.1.33.
Ryan, John	CC Kilenaule	1933	ditto
Ryan, Matthew	PP Knockavilla	1922	*Tipperaryman and Limerick Recorder*, 21.1.22.
Ryan, Michael	PP Lattin and Cullen	1922	W. Skehan, *Cashel and Emly*, pp. 285–6.
Walsh, John	PP Gortnahoe	1922	ditto, pp. 210–11

CLOGHER – INCLUDES MONAGHAN, ALMOST THE WHOLE OF FERMANAGH, A LARGE PART OF TYRONE, AND PARTS OF DONEGAL, LOUTH AND CAVAN

Pro-Treaty

McKenna, Patrick	Bishop	1921	*Freeman's Journal*, 8.12.21.
Boylan, A.H.	Adm. Monaghan	1923	*Derry People*, 4.2.23.
*Coyle, Eugene	CC Clontibret	1922	*Freeman's Journal*, 5.1.22.
Cullinan, Patrick	CC Maguiresbridge	1922	*Derry People*, 7.1.22
Duffy, James	Adm. Annyalla Castleblaney	1927	*Anglo Celt*, 10.9.27.
Keenan, Laurence	PP Ballybay	1927	*Irish Times*, 10.9.27.
McAdam, Eugene	PP Killeevan	1923	*Anglo Celt*, 4.8.23.
McGarvey, Bernard	CC Clontibret	1927	ditto, 28.5.27.
McHugh, Patrick	CC Scotshouse	1933	ditto, 13.2.33.
McKenna, Felix	PP Castleblaney	1927	ditto, 28.5.27.
McKenna, J.H.	CC Knockmoyle	1921	*Irish Independent*, 10.12.21
McNamee, James	Adm. Monaghan	1922	*Derry People*, 7.1.22.
Murphy, Patrick	CC Ballybay	1922	ditto
Mulligan, Philip	PP Tydvale	1923	*Irish Times*, 6.8.23.
Nolan, James	CC Annyalla	1927	ditto, 8.9.27.
O'Connor, Joseph	PP Aghavea, Brookborough	1922	O'Mahony Papers, NLI 24468
O'Daly, Bernard	CC Clones	1932	*Anglo Celt*, 16.4.32
O'Daly, James	CC Clones	1927	ditto, 28.5.27.
Tierney, John	PP V.G., Enniskillen	1922	NAI S 1011, 11.4.22.

Anti-Treaty

Caulfield, Terence	CC Scotshouse Clones	1921	*An Phoblacht*, 12.4.28.
Connolly, Michael	CC Threemilehouse	1933	*Dundalk Examiner*, 21.1.33

Anti-Treaty	Rank	First Reported Declaration	Source
*Coyle, Eugene	PP Garrison Co. Fermanagh	1925	*Irish News*, 9.12.25.
Dempsey, Patrick	CC Drumgosset	1933	*Dundalk Examiner*, 21.1.33
Donnelly, John	CC Carrickmacross	1933	ditto
Gormley, Daniel	PP Roslea, Co. Fermanagh	1933	*Derry People*, 21.1.33
Hackett, James	PP Donaghmoyne Carrickmacross	1922	Childers Diary, 26.4.22, TCD
Hackett, Francis	CC Lisdoonan Carrickmacross	1933	*Dundalk Examiner*, 21.1.33
McCarvill, Michael	PP Scotstown	1933	*Irish Press*, 14.1.33
McGarvey, Bernard	Adm. Clontibret	1933	*Dundalk Examiner*, 21.1.33
McHugh, Terence	CC Clontibret	1933	ditto
McKenna, John	CC Castleblaney	1933	ditto
McManus, James	CC Castleblaney	1933	ditto
McManus, Patrick	CC Pettigo, Co. Donegal	1933	*Derry People*, 22.1.33
Maguire, Thomas	PP Latnamard, Newbliss	1927	*Irish Independent*, 12.9.27.
Mulligan, Matthew	PP Trillick Co. Tyrone	1922	M. McCaughey, *Around Trillick Way*, Trillick Historical Society, n.d.
O'Kieran, Laurence	PP Pettigo	1933	*Irish Press*, 12.1.33.
Smyth, Peter	CC Roslea	1933	ditto, 20.1.33.
Ward, Edward	St Macartan's College, Monaghan	1933	*Dundalk Examiner*, 21.1.33.
Woods, Michael	CC Conduff Carrickmacross	1933	ditto

CLONFERT – INCLUDES PARTS OF GALWAY, ROSCOMMON AND OFFALY

Pro-Treaty			
O'Doherty, Thomas	Bishop to 1923	1921	*Irish Independent*, 10.12.21
Bowes, Bernard	PP Tynagh	1922	Canon Patrick K. Egan
Bowes, John P.	PP Woodford	1927	*Connaught Tribune*, 28.5.27
Brennan, Hubert	PP Killimor	1922	Canon Patrick K. Egan
Broderick, Martin	CC Ballymacward	1922	ditto
Callanan, Richard	PP Lusmagh, Banagher	1922	ditto
Clarke, John	CC Looscaun, Woodford	1922	*Connaught Tribune*, 7.1.22
Dunne, Thomas	PP Killtulla, Loughrea	1922	ditto
Fahy, Thomas	Professor of Classics Maynooth	1922	Canon Patrick K. Egan
*Fallon, John F.	PP Kellysgrove	1922	ditto
Harney, John	PP Kiltulla, Athenry	1922	ditto
Heagney, John	PP Abbey, Loughrea	1922	*Freeman's Journal*, 21.3.22
Heenan, J.P.	CC Ballinasloe	1927	*Irish Times*, 8.9.27.

Pro-Treaty	Rank	First Reported Declaration	Source
Hughes, Edward	CC Clonfert	1922	Canon Patrick K. Egan
Joyce. T.J.	PP Portumna	1922	ditto
Leahy, Martin	PP Eyrecourt	1922	ditto
Madden, John	Adm. Ballinasloe	1922	ditto
Mahon, Cornelius	PP Fahy, Eyrecourt	1922	ditto
Melvin, Thomas	CC Attymon	1922	ditto
Nagle, P.J.	PP Laurencetown	1922	ditto
O'Neill, J.K.	PP Cappataggle	1922	ditto
Pelly, Joseph	PP Ballymacward	1922	ditto
Porter, Thomas	PP Ballinakill, Loughrea	1922	ditto
Ryan, Michael	CC Killimor	1922	ditto
Spelman, James	PP Aughrim	1927	*Irish Independent*, 9.6.27.
Tuohy, Martin	PP New Inn	1922	Canon Patrick K. Egan.

Anti-Treaty

Dignan, John	Bishop from 1924	1922	*Connaught Tribune*, 10.6.22
Dempsey, Thomas	Garbally College, Ballinasloe	1922	ditto
Doyle, J.	CC Ballinasloe	1933	ditto, 21.1.33
Dunning, P.J.	CC Woodford	1927	*Irish Independent*, 13.9.27
Fahy, John	CC Eyrecourt	1922	Dr Brian S. Murphy
*Fallon, John F.	PP Kellysgrove	1927	*Connaught Tribune*, 23.4.27.
Hawkins, John	CC Woodford	1933	*Irish Press*, 15.1.33.
Larkin, Thomas	CC Portumna	1933	ditto
Moloney, Thomas	CC Ballinasloe	1922	Canon Patrick K. Egan
O'Connor, Michael	CC Kilmore Ballinasloe	1926	ditto
O'Connor, Thomas	PP Mullagh Loughrea	1922	ditto
O'Farrell, Martin	CC Kilrickle Loughrea	1922	ditto
O'Farrell, Patrick	PP Carrabane Athenry	1922	ditto
O'Loughlin, Patrick	CC Clostoken Loughrea	1922	ditto
O'Mahony, William	CC Looscann Woodford	1933	*Irish Press*, 15.1.33
O'Meara, Michael	CC Killoran Ballinasloe	1922	Canon Patrick K. Egan
Phair, Eric	Irish College, Rome	1922	Mgr. Daniel Long

CLOYNE – INCLUDES A LARGE PORTION OF CO. CORK

Pro-Treaty

Browne, Robert	Bishop to 1935	1921	*Irish Independent*, 10.12.21
Roche, James, J.	Bishop from 1935	1922	Tomás Ó Riordan, Cork, 10.1.96

Pro-Treaty	Rank	First Reported Declaration	Source
Browne, John	PP Rathcormack	1933	*Irish Press*, 27.11.33.
Burke, John	CC Charleville	1922	*Freeman's Journal*, 21.3.22
Cantillon, John	CC Kilmurray	1927	Canon Séamus Corkery
Corbett, C.W.	PP Mallow	1927	*Cork Weekly Examiner*, 3.9.27
Dinneen, David	CC Charleville	1923	*Irish Independent*, 10.8.23
Madigan, Thomas	PP Kanturk	1932	*Cork Weekly Examiner*, 23.1.32
Roche, Thomas	PP Charleville	1925	C. Kiernan, *Daniel Mannix and Ireland* (Dublin, 1984), p. 192.
Russell, Jeremiah	CC Cloyne	1933	*Irish Press*, 23.1.33.
Shinkwin, Thomas	PP Grenagh, Bantry	1922	MacSwiney Papers, P42/a 196 (25)

Anti-Treaty	Rank	First Reported Declaration	Source
Ahern, Jeremiah	CC Ballinspittle	1925	Canon Séamus Corkery
Ahern, John	Chaplain, Youghal	1932	ditto
Bowler, Michael	CC Mallow	1935	*Irish Press*, 16.11.35.
Brew, Cornelius	(ordained 1924)	1924	Canon Séamus Corkery
Cowhey, James	CC Doneraile	1926	*An Phoblacht*, 5.2.26.
Flannery, Francis	PP Castlemartyr	1922	Canon Séamus Corkery
Foley, Daniel	PP Liscarroll	1926	*An Phoblacht*, 5.2.26.
Gallagher, Thomas	PP Ballymacoda	1922	Canon Séamus Corkery
Harrington, Michael	CC Clondrohid	1922	ditto
Keating, John	CC Castletownroche	1922	ditto
Kelleher, Andrew	(ordained 1908)	1922	ditto
Leonard, James	CC Castletownroche	1922	ditto
Mortell, Philip	CC Aghinagh	1927	ditto
Morton, Patrick	CC Ballyhea Charleville	1926	*An Phoblacht*, 5.2.26.
O'Callaghan, John	PP Aghinagh	1922	Canon Séamus Corkery
O'Keeffe, Andrew	CC Clondrohid	1922	ditto
O'Keeffe, David	CC Cobh	1926	*An Phoblacht*, 16.7.26.
Roche, Denis	CC Aghinagh	1922	Canon Séamus Corkery
Roche, John	CC Churchtown, Buttevant	1926	*An Phoblacht*, 5.2.26.
Roche, Thomas	CC Kilnamartyra, Macroom	1922	Canon Séamus Corkery
Wilson, Thomas	CC Macroom	1922	ditto

CORK [AND ROSS] – CORK INCLUDES CORK CITY AND PARTS OF COUNTY CORK; ROSS INCLUDES PART OF COUNTY CORK

Pro-Treaty	Rank	First Reported Declaration	Source
Cohalan, Daniel	Bishop of Cork	1921	*Irish Independent*, 10.12.21
Kelly, Denis	Bishop of Ross	1922	ditto
Barrett, Thomas	PP St Finbarr's West	1923	*Irish Times*, 22.8.23.
Cahalane, Patrick	CC Skibbereen (Ross)	1922	*Skibbereen Eagle*, 25.2.22.
Cohalan, Jeremiah	PP Bandon	1922	ditto, 18.3.22.

Pro-Treaty	Rank	First Reported Declaration	Source
Collins, John	Adm. Union Hall (Ross)	1923	MacSwiney Papers, UCDA P42a/196(25)
Fitzgerald, Edward	CC Kinsale	1922	*Skibbereen Eagle*, 18.3.22
Lambe, Edward	CC Union Hall (Ross)	1923	MacSwiney Papers, UCDA P42a/197(25)
McCarthy, Timothy	PP Passage West	1923	ditto, P48a/196(7)
Murphy, Martin	PP Durrus, Bantry	1922	*Weekly Freeman*, 7.1.22
Murphy, Michael	CC Kinsale	1927	*Cork Weekly Examiner*, 3.9.27.
McSwiney, John	CC Bandon	1922	*Skibbereen Eagle*, 18.3.22
O'Connell, Patrick	CC Clonakilty (Ross)	1922	MacSwiney Papers UCDA P48a/213; *Éire*, 31.3.23
O'Dononvan, Patrick	PP Caheragh, Drimoleague	1922	*Weekly Freeman*, 7.1.22.
O'Leary, James	PP Dunmanway	1933	*Irish Press*, 23.1.33.
O'Leary, Patrick	CC Kilmurray	1927	Canon Séamus Corkery
O'Sullivan, Michael	Adm. St Mary's Cathedral	1923	*Éire*, 23.6.23.
Scannell, Joseph	St Finbarr's College, Cork	1922	MacSwiney Papers, UCDA P48a/196(21)
Tracy, Patrick	PP Kilmurray, Croakstown	1927	*Cork Examiner*, 14.9.27
Anti-Treaty			
Duggan, Thomas	St Finbarr's College	1922	Carthach McCarthy, *Archdeacon Tom Duggan, In Peace and in War*, 1994, p. 90.
Hurley, John V.	CC Bantry	1922	*Skibbereen Eagle*, 17.6.22
Long, William	PP St Michael's Macroom	1922	*Weekly Observer(Newcastle West)* 29.10.27
MacSwiney, Patrick	?	1923	*Éire*, 19.5.23;MacSwiney Papers, P48a/196(7).
Ó Murchú, Tadhg	?	1935	Canon Micheál Ó Dálaigh

DERRY – INCLUDES ALMOST ALL OF COUNTY DERRY, PART OF DONEGAL AND A LARGE PART OF TYRONE

Pro-Treaty			
McHugh, Charles	Bishop	1922	E. Phoenix, *Northern Nationalism*, (Belfast, 1994), p. 168
Byrne, Charles	CC Killygordon	1933	*People's Press*, Donegal, 7.1.33
Conway, Peter	CC Clonmany	1933	*Irish Times*, 11.1.33.
Elliott, William	CC Buncrana	1933	*People's Press*, Donegal, 14.1.33
Lagan, James	CC Moville	1933	ditto
Lagan, John	CC Desertegney	1933	ditto
McLaughlin, John	CC Moville	1933	ditto
McMenamin, Michael	CC Urney, Strabane	1927	*Irish Independent*, 9.6.27
Maguire, James	PP Clonmany Lifford	1923	*People's Press,* Donegal, 7.1.33

Pro-Treaty	Rank	First Reported Declaration	Source
Morris, James	PP Killygordon	1923	*Irish Times*, 10.8.23.
Murphy, William	CC Carndonagh	1923	*Irish Times*, 22.8.23
O'Doherty, John	PP Strabane	1927	*Irish Independent*, 13.9.27
O'Doherty, Philip	PP Omagh	1922	*Derry People*, 7.1.22
O'Neill, Anthony	CC Murlog, Lifford	1927	*Irish Independent*, 9.6.27
Sheerin, Michael	PP Moville	1933	*People's Press*, Sligo, 14.1.33
Treacy, Peter	CC Strabane	1922	O'Mahony Papers, NLI 24468

Anti-Treaty

Boyle, H.	PP Desertmartin	1933	*Irish Press*, 6.2.33.
Harkin, James	CC Castlefin, Lifford	1933	ditto, 10.1.33.
McCauley, Michael	CC Greencastle, Co. Tyrone	1933	ditto, 6.2.33.
McGlinchey, James	PP Ballinascreen	1933	ditto
McShane, John	St Columb's College Derry	1922	*Feasta*, October 1988, p.61
O'Mullin, Michael	PP Lifford	1932	*Kilkenny Journal*, 23.1.32

DOWN AND CONNOR – INCLUDES ANTRIM, THE GREATER PART OF DOWN AND PART OF DERRY

Pro-Treaty

MacRory, Joseph	Bishop to 1925	1922	See under Armagh
Hassan, John	Adm. St Mary's Belfast	1922	*Feasta*, October 1988, p. 61
Laverty, Bernard	PP Ormeau Road	1922	E. Phoenix, *Northern Nationalism* (Belfast, 1994)

Anti-Treaty

Mageean, Daniel	Bishop from 1929	1922	E. Phoenix, *Northern Nationalism*, p. 367
Ryan, Arthur	St Malachy's College Belfast	1928	Hagan to Dignan, 29.1.28, CLDA
Cahill, D.	CC Bloomfield Belfast	1929	*Kerry Champion*, 4.5.29.

DROMORE – INCLUDES PARTS OF COUNTIES DOWN, ARMAGH AND ANTRIM

Pro-Treaty

Mulhern, Edward	Bishop	1922	Mulhern to Hagan, 6.1.22, Hagan Papers
McPolin, Murtagh	PP Loughbrickland Co. Down	1922	*Irish Catholic*, 20.5.22.

Anti-Treaty

McEvoy, Peter	PP Dromara, Co. Down	1922	*Irish Press*, 8.7.35.

DUBLIN – INCLUDES DUBLIN, ALMOST ALL OF WICKLOW AND PARTS OF
KILDARE AND WEXFORD

Pro-Treaty	Rank	First Reported Declaration	Source
Byrne, Edward	Archbishop	1922	M.J. Curran to Hagan, 20.6.22, Hagan Papers.
Bowden, Richard	PP Bray	1927	*Irish Times*, 14.9.27.
Butler, Michael	PP Roundwood	1933	*Wicklow People*, 14.1.33.
Byrne, Thomas P.	PP St Patrick's Cambridge Road	1933	*Cork Weekly Examiner*, 14.1.33
Canton, P.J.	CC Westland Row	1936	*Enniscorthy Guardian*, 25.7.36
Cotter, Lewis	CC Dun Laoghaire	1933	*Irish Weekly Independent*,14.1.33
Dempsey, James	PP Clontarf	1927	*Irish Independent*, 2.6.27.
Dillon, John	CC Dunlavin Lower	1932	*Wicklow People*, 13.2.32
Dunlea, John	CC Monkstown	1927	ditto, 13.8.27.
Dunne, James	PP Donnybrook	1922	MacSwiney Papers, UCDA, P48a/205(1)
Farrell, Augustine	CC Donnybrook	1922	ditto
Fennelly, John	Clonliffe College	1923	NAI S 1859
Flanagan, John	Adm. Pro Cathedral	1922	*Poblacht na hÉireann*, War News, 12.7.22.
Flood, Christopher	PP Howth	1933	*Irish Times*, 12.1.33.
Flood, John	CC Marlboro Street	1923	*Éire*, 21.4.23.
Kavanagh, Patrick	CC Hollywood, Co. Wicklow	1927	*Wicklow People*, 10.9.27
Kelleher, John	CC Meath Street	1925	*Irish Independent*, 2.2.25.
Killeen, Joseph	PP Maynooth	1933	*Kildare Observer*, 14.1.33
Kinnane, Francis	CC Rathmines	1936	*Enniscorthy Guardian*, 25.7.36
McArdle, Joseph	CC Marlboro Street	1922	M.J. Curran to Hagan, 20.6.22
McCaffrey, James	President of St Patrick's College, Maynooth	1923	McCaffrey to Logue, 2.3.33, AAA
McDonald, Walter	CC Phibsboro	1925	*Irish Independent*, 2.2.25
McMahon, John	PP Lusk	1933	*Irish Weekly Independent*, 14.1.33
McMahon, M.	Chaplain Mountjoy Prison	1922	MacSwiney Papers, P48a/194(1)
Moriarty, Andrew	CC St Agatha's	1933	*Irish Times*, 12.1.33
Murphy, William J.	PP Dunlaoghaire	1933	*Irish Weekly Independent*, 14.1.33
Nolan, James P.	CC Fairview	1924	*Sinn Féin*, 1.3.24
O'Byrne, Patrick	PP Howth	1927	*Irish Weekly Examiner*, 4.6.27
O'Byrne, Thomas P.	PP Ringsend	1935	*Irish Press*, 25.3.35
O'Donnell, Pierce	PP Ashford	1927	*Wicklow People*, 10.9.27
O'Keeffe, Joseph	PP Rathfarnham	1922	*Skibbereen Eagle*, 13.5.22
O'Reilly, Thomas	CC Westland Row	1936	*Enniscorthy Guardian*, 25.7.36
Pigott, John	Chaplain, Wellington Barracks	1922	C.D. Greaves, *Liam Mellows and the Irish Revolution* (Dublin, 1971), p.388
Ryan, Patrick J.	CC Fairview	1924	*Sinn Féin*, 1.3.24
Ryan, Thomas	PP Sandymount	1937	*Irish Press*, 21.6.37

Pro-Treaty	Rank	First Reported Declaration	Source
Stafford, L.J.	PP Narraghmore Ballytore	1936	*Enniscorthy Guardian*, 25.7.36
Traynor, Eugene	CC Golden Bridge	1933	*Cork Weekly Examiner*, 14.1.33
Waters, John	PP Blackrock	1937	*Limerick Echo*, 22.6.37

Anti-Treaty

Browne, Michael J.	Professor Maynooth College	1922	W. Kelly to M.J. Browne, 12.11.22, GDA
Browne, Maurice	CC Athy	1922	T.P. O'Neill
Browne, Patrick	Professor Maynooth College	1922	Cosgrave to Archbishop Byrne, 21.7.22, DAA
Costello, John	CC St Michael's and John's	1922	ditto
Doyle, Eugene	Seconded from Australian Diocese to Dublin	1922	ditto
Fallon, Thomas	CC St Audeon's	1933	*Cork Weekly Examiner*, 14.1.33
Finegan, Charles	CC Ballymore Eustace	1922	T.P. O'Neill
Fitzgibbon, James	CC Glasnevin	1927	*The Nation*, 23.7.27; 1.10.27
Geraghty, Michael	CC High Street	1933	*Cork Weekly Examiner*, 14.1.33
Lillis, William	CC Castledermot	1929	*Kerry Champion*, 4.5.29
Lynch, J.	CC Rathdown	1932	*Wicklow People*, 13.2.32
Maguire, Francis	PP Blessington	1922	P. Ó Baoighill, *Óglach na Rosann* (Dublin, 1994)
O'Brien, Edward	All Hallows, Mallow	1922	Rev. Denis O'Callaghan, PP
O'Doherty, John	CC Rathdrum	1927	*Wicklow People*, 10.9.27
O'Keeffe, John	Castletown, Inch	1923	*Irish Times*, 14.8.23
O'Loughlin, Francis	Valleymount, Co. Wicklow	1932	*Wicklow People*, 13.2.32
O'Mahony, J.	CC Booterstown	1929	*Kerry Champion*, 4.5.29
O'Ryan, Thomas	PP Rolestown	1927	*Irish Weekly Independent*, 23.7.27
Pierse, Garrett	Professor, Maynooth College	1922	Curran to Hagan, 20.6.22, Hagan Papers
Troy Michael [Charles]	Maynooth Dunboyne	1922	Rev. Anthony Gaughan
Walsh Patrick	Valleymount	1922	*An Phoblacht*, 1.7.27

ELPHIN – INCLUDES A LARGE PART OF COUNTIES ROSCOMMON AND SLIGO, AND A SMALL PART OF GALWAY

Pro-Treaty

Coyne, Bernard	Bishop	1922	*Roscommon Messenger*, 22.7.22
Doorly, Edward	Bishop	1925	*Roscommon Journal*, 23.5.25
*Brennan, Malachy	CC Mantua	1922	*Roscommon Herald*, 7.1.22
Butler, P.A.	Adm. Sligo	1922	ditto, 6.5.22
Carney, D.	CC Strabane	1922	ditto, 10.6.22
Carney, Thomas J.	CC Kilteevan	1923	*Roscommon Messenger*, 25.8.23
Coleman, Peter	PP Tarmonbarry	1927	*Roscommon Herald*, 4.6.27

Pro-Treaty	Rank	First Reported Declaration	Source
Connellan, M.J.	CC Ballymore Castlerea	1932	*Roscommon Messenger*, 13.2.32
Crehan, Bernard	CC Kilbegnet	1922	Rev. Peadar Lavin
Crowe, John	Adm. Athlone	1922	*Roscommon Herald*, 4.3.22
Cummins, Thomas	PP Roscommon	1923	*Roscommon Journal*, 18.8.23
Curley, John	PP Riverstown	1925	*Sligo Champion*, 7.3.25
Currid, Bartholomew	PP Drumcliffe	1923	ditto, 25.8.23
Dignan, J.P.	CC Ardcarne, Boyle	1925	*Roscommon Herald*, 25.4.25
Feely, John	CC Athlone	1925	*Irish Independent*, 20.2.25
Finan, J.	CC Kilteevan	1922	Rev. Peadar Lavin
Flanagan, Patrick	PP Aughrim	1923	*Roscommon Messenger*, 25.8.23
Flanagan, Thomas	PP Cootehall, Boyle	1922	*Roscommon Herald*, 10.6.22
Flynn, P.J.	CC Curraghboy	1925	ditto, 28.3.25
Gearty, Roderick	PP Strokestown	1922	ditto, 7.1.22
Geiley, John J.	CC Boyle	1927	ditto, 10.9.27
Geraghty, Bernard	PP Loughglynn	1932	*Westmeath Independent*, 13.2.32
Gilmartin, Daniel	CC Glinsk, Ballymore	1925	*Roscommon Herald*, 10.6.22
Glynn, J.J.	CC Drumlion	1922	ditto
Harte, Michael	PP Kilkeevan Castlerea	1925	*Westmeath Independent*, 7.2.25
Heneghan, Michael	PP Balinameen, Boyle	1925	*Roscommon Herald*, 13.6.25
Hurley, Timothy	PP Ballinafad, Boyle	1922	ditto, 21.1.22
Keane, Bernard	CC Four Roads Roscommon	1925	*Roscommon Journal*, 28.2.25
Keane, J.	CC Bellanagar Castlerea	1925	*Roscommon Herald*, 28.2.25
Kelly, Bartholomew	PP Knockroghery	1932	*Westmeath Independent*, 13.2.32
Kelly, P.A.	CC Elphin	1925	*Roscommon Herald*, 11.4.25
Kielty, Martin	PP Ballygar	1923	*Roscommon Messenger*, 18.8.23
Kilmartin, Joseph	CC Fuerty	1933	*Westmeath Independent*, 14.1.33
Lavan, Thomas	PP Tulsk	1922	*Roscommon Herald*, 7.1.22
McDermott, John	PP Elphin	1922	ditto
McHugh, Cornelius	CC Ballyrush, Boyle	1925	*Sligo Champion*, 7.3.25
Murray, Patrick J.	CC Caltra	1927	*Irish Independent*, 14.9.27
Neary, Patrick J.	PP Dysart and Tissara	1925	*Westmeath Independent*, 10.2.25
Neary, James	CC Drum, Athlone	1925	ditto, 21.2.25
Neilan, B.J.	CC Rooskey, Strokestown	1927	*Roscommon Herald*, 4.6.27
Nunan, J.		1923	*Sligo Champion*, 25.8.23
O'Beirne, Michael	PP Fourmilehouse	1932	*Westmeath Independent*, 13.2.32
O'Beirne, P.	CC Strokestown	1923	*Roscommon Messenger*, 18.8.23
O'Beirne, P.J.	Adm. Sligo	1927	*Irish Weekly Independent*, 10.9.27
O'Donnell, M.	CC Castlerea	1923	*Westmeath Independent*, 11.8.23
O'Dowd, P.	CC Boyle	1922	*Freeman's Journal*, 29.8.22
O'Flynn, P.J.	PP Aughrim	1932	*Westmeath Independent*, 13.2.32
Roddy, James	CC Geevagh Ballyforan	1925	*Roscommon Herald*, 14.3.25
Smallhorne, John	PP Ballinameen, Boyle	1927	*Westmeath Independent*, 4.6.27

Pro-Treaty	Rank	First Reported Declaration	Source
Scott, Patrick	CC Kilnamanagh	1925	*Roscommon Herald, 28.2.25*
Sharkey, Timothy	PP Boyle	1927	*Westmeath Independent, 4.6.27*

Anti-Treaty

*Brennan, Malachy	CC Mantua	1927	*Roscommon Herald, 10.9.27*
Hannon, P.A.	CC Athleague	1923	*Éire, 10.3.23*
Keane, John	PP Cliffoney	1933	*Sligo Champion, 14.1.33*
Keane, Michael, J.	PP Cams Roscommon	1925	*Westmeath Independent, 28.2.25*
Kelly, Patrick A.	CC Castlerea	1932	*Roscommon Messenger, 13.2.32*
Neilan, B.	CC Rooskey	1933	*Westmeath Independent, 14.1.33*
O'Flanagan, Michael	CC Crosna	1922	*Poblacht na hÉireann, 29.6.22*
Quigley, Timothy	CC Castlerea	1933	*Westmeath Independent, 14.1.33*
Sharkey, Patrick	CC Highwood	1922	*Roscommon Herald, 11.2.22*

FERNS – INCLUDES ALMOST ALL OF WEXFORD AND PART OF WICKLOW

Pro-Treaty

Codd, William	Bishop	1922	*Freeman's Journal, 11.10.22*
Browne, John	PP Litter, Gorey	1933	*Enniscorthy Echo, 14.1.33*
Browne, Richard	CC Glenbrien	1925	*Enniscorthy Guardian, 11.3.25*
Cleary, Thomas	PP Marshallstown	1922	*Free Press Wexford, 8.4.22*
Crowe, Andrew	PP Mayglass	1927	ditto, 4.6.27
Cummins, Patrick	Adm. Enniscorthy	1925	*Enniscorthy Guardian, 11.3.25*
Darcy, Patrick	PP Kilrush, Ferns	1925	ditto
Doyle, Patrick	CC Wexford	1922	*Free Press Wexford, 8.4.22*
Dunne, John	PP Castlebridge	1925	*Enniscorthy Guardian, 11.3.25*
Fitzhenry, Robert	PP Our Lady's Island	1925	ditto
Forristal, Aidan	PP Newtownbarry	1922	*Free Press Wexford, 15.4.22*
Fortune, William	CC Kilanerin, Gorey	1927	*Irish Weekly Independent, 4.6.27.*
Furlong, James	CC Screen	1922	*Free Press Wexford, 10.6.22.*
Fortune, William	PP Taughmon	1922	*Free Press Wexford, 15.4.22*
Hickey, Michael	PP Clongeen	1933	*Enniscorthy Echo, 14.1.33*
Hore, David	PP Rathnore	1933	ditto
Jones, Laurence	PP Ballygarret	1933	*Free Press Wexford, 4.6.27*
Kavanagh, Owen	PP Ballygarret	1933	*Enniscorthy Echo, 14.1.33*
Kavanagh, Patrick	CC Rosslare	1927	*Irish Weekly Independent, 4.6.27*
Kinsella, Martin	CC Kilrane	1932	*Wexford People, 10.2.32*
Lambert, Henry	CC Mayglass	1927	*Free Press Wexford, 4.6.27*
Meehan, Thomas	PP Ballindaggin	1922	ditto, 15.4.22
Mernagh, Nicholas	PP Ballyoughter	1922	ditto
Moran, Nicholas	CC Castlerockhill	1927	*Wexford People, 10.9.27*
Murphy, Denis	PP Kilanerin	1936	*Enniscorthy Guardian, 25.7.36,*
Murphy, George	CC Wexford	1925	ditto, 11.3.25
Murphy, Martin	PP Ballymore	1933	*Enniscorthy Echo, 14.1.33*
Newcombe, Mark	PP Castlebridge	1933	*Enniscorthy Echo, 14.1.33*
O'Brien, Aidan	CC Castlebridge	1922	*Free Press Wexford, 15.4.22*
Quigley, John	PP Tagoat	1922	ditto

Pro-Treaty	Rank	First Reported Declaration	Source
Quigley, Thomas	PP Blackwater	1932	*Wexford People*,10.2.32
Rossiter, John	PP Gorey	1922	*Free Press Wexford*, 8.4.22
Rossiter, Walter	PP New Ross	1925	*Enniscorthy Guardian*, 11.3.25
Rowe, John	PP Oylegate, Enniscorthy	1933	*Enniscorthy Echo*, 14.1.33
Scallan, T.	CC Clearystown, Wexford	1922	*Free Press Wexford*, 15.4.22
Shiel, Patrick	PP Bree, Wexford	1927	ditto, 28.5.27
Wallace, Matthew	CC Caim, Enniscorthy	1927	ditto

Anti-Treaty			
Allen, Laurence	CC Wexford	1925	*Catholic Bulletin*, 1925, p. 1008
Browne, James	St Peter's College Wexford	1927	Hagan to de Valera, 7.7.27, FAK 1382
Butler, John	CC Wexford	1936	*Enniscorthy Guardian*, 6.6.36
Byrne, Mark	CC Askamore Carnew	1925	*Catholic Bulletin*, 1925, p. 1016
Byrne, Thomas	PP Piercetown	1925	ditto, p. 1008
Cardiff, Nicholas	CC Wexford	1925	ditto
Codd, John	Adm. Enniscorthy	1936	*Enniscorthy Guardian*, 6.6.36
Cullen, Sylvester	CC Gorey	1925	*Catholic Bulletin*, 1925, p. 1016
Darcy, James	CC Ferns	1922	*Free Press Wexford*, 10.6.22
Gaul, Richard	CC Coutnacuddy	1922	Canon John Gahan, Gorey
Harpur, William	CC Taughmon	1927	ditto, 4.6.27
Kehoe, Paul	PP Cloughbaun	1922	*Irish Press*, 24.10.31
Kavanagh, Patrick	CC Rosslare	1925	*Catholic Bulletin*, 1925, p. 1008
Keating, Matthew	House of Missions, Enniscorthy	1925	ditto
McCarthy, James	CC Galbally	1936	*Enniscorthy Guardian*, 15.8.36
Murphy, Michael	CC Galbally, Enniscorthy	1922	*Free Press Wexford*, 10.6.22
Murphy, Patrick	House of Missions, Enniscorthy	1925	*Catholic Bulletin*, 1925, p. 1016
Murphy, Patrick	PP Glynn	1936	*Enniscorthy Guardian*, 6.6.36
O'Brien, Aidan	CC Castlebridge	1925	ditto, p. 1008
O'Connor, John	CC Duncannon	1933	*Enniscorthy Echo*, 14.1.33
Parker, Patrick	PP Cushinstown	1932	*Wexford People*, 10.2.32
Ranson, Joseph	CC Enniscorthy	1936	*Enniscorthy Guardian*, 6.6.36
Ryan, Martin	CC Poulfur	1927	*Wicklow People*, 10.9.27
Wadding, Joseph	CC Enniscorthy	1936	*Enniscorthy Guardian*, 6.6.36

GALWAY, KILMACDUAGH AND KILFENORA – ALL THE PARISHES IN THE
DIOCESE OF GALWAY ARE IN COUNTY GALWAY, EXCEPT SHRULE, WHICH IS IN
COUNTY MAYO. ALL THE PARISHES IN KILMACDUAGH ARE IN COUNTY
GALWAY, WHILE THE PARISHES OF KILFENORA ARE ALL IN COUNTY CLARE.

Pro-Treaty	Rank	First Reported Declaration	Source
O'Dea, Thomas	Bishop to 1923	1922	Pastoral Letter, 1922, GDA
O'Doherty, Thomas	Bishop from 1923	1921	*Irish Independent*, 10.12.21
Cassidy, Joseph	PP Gort	1927	*Connaught Tribune*, 30.4.27
Connolly, J.	PP Moycullen	1922	*Freeman's Journal*, 5.8.22
Conroy, Marcus	PP Lisdoonvarna	1927	*Irish Independent*, 6.6.27
Craddock, James	PP Oughterard	1922	*Connaught Tribune*, 10.6.22
Davis, Peter	PP Rahoon	1927	*Irish Independent*, 2.6.27
Glennon, D.	St Mary's College, Galway	1936	*Galway Observer*, 6.6.36
Mullins, William	PP Killanin	1922	*Freeman's Journal*, 5.8.22
O'Dea, A.	CC Oughterard	1922	ditto
Walsh, Michael	PP Ballindreen	1927	*Connaught Tribune*, 23.4.27

Anti-Treaty			
Cawley, Thomas	PP Shanaglish, Gort	1922	*Connaught Tribune*, 10.6.22
Cloonan, John	College House	1935	*Irish Press*, 19.6.35
Considine, James	Adm. Carron Kilnaboy	1922	*Connaught Tribune*, 10.6.22
Considine, John	PP Ardrahan	1922	ditto
Curran, Michael	CC Gort	1933	*Irish Press*, 15.1.33
Donnelly, N.	PP Spiddal	1933	*Connaught Tribune*, 14.1.33
Feeney, Henry	CC Shrule	1922	ditto, 10.6.22
Glynn, Patrick	CC College House	1935	*Irish Press*, 19.6.35
Hehir, Denis	PP Bellharbour	1933	*Clare Champion*, 21.1.33
Hynes, John	University College Galway	1925	*An Phoblacht*, 15.6.25
Kenny, Matthew	PP Rosmuc	1933	*Irish Press*, 23.1.33
Larkin, James	CC Gort	1933	*Connaught Tribune*, 14.1.33
Lavin, James	CC St Joseph's Galway	1935	*Irish Press*, 10.6.35
O'Dea, James	Diocesan Secretary	1922	*Connaught Tribune*, 10.6.22
O'Dea, Patrick	PP Moycullen	1922	ditto
O'Fegan, N.	PP Castlegar	1927	*Irish Weekly Independent*, 4.6.27
O'Kelly, John	CC Kilbecanty, Gort	1922	*Connaught Tribune*, 10.6.22
O'Kelly, John	Adm. Liscannor	1933	*Clare Champion*, 21.1.33
O'Kelly, Thomas	U.C.G.	1922	*Connaught Tribune*, 10.6.22
Ó Móráin, Pádraig	PP Clargalway	1922	ditto
O'Reilly, Robert	CC Galway	1922	ditto

KERRY – INCLUDES KERRY AND PART OF COUNTY CORK

Pro-Treaty	Rank	First Reported Declaration	Source
O'Sullivan, Charles	Bishop	1922	Pastoral Letter 1922, KYDA
Barton, Patrick	PP Ardfert	1923	*Kerry People*, 28.7.23
Breen, David	CC Kilgarvin	1922	ditto, 29.4.22
Brennan, P.J.	PP Castlemaine	1922	ditto
Brosnan, Denis	St Brendan's Killarney	1922	*Skibbereen Eagle*, 29.4.22
Brosnan, Patrick	CC Kilcummin West	1927	*Irish Times*, 12.9.27
Browne, Patrick	PP Cahirciveen	1932	*Cork Weekly Examiner*, 23.1.32
Buckley, J.	CC Castleisland	1922	*Kerry People*, 29.4.22
Burke, James	PP Knocknagoshel	1927	*Kerryman*, 21.5.27
Byrne, William	PP Glenbeigh	1923	*Kerry People*, 18.8.23
Cahill, J.	CC Kilury, Causeway	1923	ditto, 28.7.23
Carmody, James	PP Kilcummin East	1923	ditto
Casey, Jeremiah	CC Killorglin	1922	ditto, 29.4.22
Casey, John	PP Castleisland	1927	*Kerryman*, 10.9.27
Costello, Maurice	CC Listowel	1923	*Éire*, 23.6.23
Curtayne, T.	CC Cahirciveen	1922	*Kerry People*, 29.7.22
Daly, Michael	PP Eyries, Co. Cork	1923	MacSwiney Papers P48a/196(6)
Dillon, Jeremiah	CC Ardfert	1922	*Kerry People*, 29.4.22
Ferris, William	CC Rathmore	1922	ditto
Fitzgerald, P.J.	Adm. Killarney	1922	ditto, 7.1.22
Fitzmaurice, Edmund	PP Tuogh, Beaufort	1932	*Irish Times*, 27.1.32
Galvin, M.	CC Tuosist	1922	*Kerry People*, 29.4.22
Keane, Michael	PP Newtownsandes	1922	T. O'Carroll to Bishop O'Sullivan, 3.11.22, KYDA
Lynch, John	CC Tralee	1922	*Kerry People*, 29.4.22
Lyne, T.J.	Adm. Aunascaul	1922	ditto
McDonnell, James	PP Abbeydorney	1927	*Kerryman*, 4.6.27
McDonnell, John	PP Dingle	1922	McDonnell to Bishop O'Sullivan, 28.12.22, KYDA
Marshall, Patrick	PP Aghadoe Kenmare	1922	*Kerry People*, 6.5.22
Meagher, P.	CC Rathmore	1927	*Kerryman*, 10.9.27
Moynihan, Denis	CC Killarney	1922	*Kerry People*, 29.4.22
O'Brien, Michael	Bishop after 1927	1927	*Kerryman*, 10.9.27
O'Callaghan, George	PP Causeway, Tralee	1927	ditto, 14.5.27
O'Connor, Denis	PP Listowel	1927	*Irish Independent*, 9.6.27
O'Connor Eugene	CC Kenmare	1922	*Kerry People*, 29.4.22
O'Connor, J.	PP Tarbert	1922	E. Dee to Bishop O'Sullivan, 25.4.22, KYDA
O'Connor, William	PP Glengariff	1922	*Weekly Freeman*, 7.1.22
O'Donoghue, J.	CC Killorglin	1923	*Kerry People*, 18.8.23
O'Donoghue, Michael	CC Killorglin	1923	ditto
O'Leary, David	PP St John's, Tralee	1922	*Skibbereen Eagle*, 29.4.22
O'Leary, Michael	CC Tralee	1927	*Kerryman*, 10.9.27
O'Riordan, W.	CC Brosna	1927	ditto, 21.5.27

Pro-Treaty	Rank	First Reported Declaration	Source
O'Shea, Timothy	CC Lixnaw	1933	*Irish Times*, 20.1.33
O'Sullivan, Alexander	CC Milltown	1922	*Freeman's Journal*, 8.9.22
O'Sullivan, Daniel	CC Listowel	1923	MacSwiney Papers, P 248a/213
O'Sullivan, James	PP Abbeydorney	1922	E. Neeson, *The Civil War in Ireland* (Cork, 1966), pp.282–3
Scanlan, Michael	PP The Spa, Tralee	1927	*Irish Times*, 8.9.27
Slattery, James	CC Annascaul	1922	*Kerry People*, 29.4.22
Supple, Thomas	St Brendan's, Killarney	1922	ditto
Trant, Timothy	PP Ballymacelligott	1927	ditto, 14.5.27

Anti-Treaty

Allmann, Myles	CC Tuosist	1922	*Kerry People*, 29.7.22
Behan, W.S.	CC Newtownsandes	1922	ditto, 26.3.22
Breen, John	St Brendan's Killarney	1922	*Freeman's Journal*, 4.8.22
Breen, Joseph	CC Millstreet	1922	*Kerry People*, 25.3.22
Brennan, Charles	CC Millstreet	1922	ditto
Collins, Michael	Tralee. Returned from American Mission 1922	1922	ditto, 27.5.22
Costello, Michael	CC Firies, Tralee	1935	*Irish Press*, 16.11.35
Galvin, Mortimer	CC Knocknagoshel	1927	*Limerick Leader*, 5.9.27
Lyne, James	PP Annascaul	1922	Mgr Daniel Long, Tralee
O'Connor, David	PP Castleisland	1922	ditto
O'Reilly, Robert	CC Glenbeigh	1922	ditto
Walsh, Robert	CC Knocknagoshel	1931	Rev. Kieran O'Shea, PP Knocknagoshel

KILDARE AND LEIGHLIN – INCLUDES THE COUNTY OF CARLOW, AND PART OF KILDARE, LAOIS, OFFALY, KILKENNY, WICKLOW AND WEXFORD

Pro-Treaty

Foley, Patrick	Bishop	1921	*Irish Independent*, 10.12.21
Bulger, Michael	PP Carlow, Graigue	1922	*Free Press Wexford*, 3.6.22
Breen, John	PP Abbeyleix	1922	*Freeman's Journal*, 3.1.22
Brennan, Edward	PP Mountrath	1922	ditto
Brophy, Martin	CC Baltinglass	1925	Rev. Thomas McDonnell Carlow
Coyne, Christopher	PP Raheen Mountrath	1923	Bishop Foley to M.J. Murphy, 10.1.23, KLDA
Dowling, Thomas	PP Myshall	1922	*Freeman's Journal*, 1.9.22
Doyle, Patrick	CC Maryborough	1923	*Offaly Independent*, 25.8.23
Kelly, William	CC Paulstown	1927	*Nationalist and Leinster Times*, 28.5.27
Keogh, Laurence	PP Clane	1933	*Kildare Observer*, 14.1.33

Pro-Treaty	Rank	First Reported Declaration	Source
Killian, John	Adm. Carlow	1927	*Nationalist and Leinster Times*, 3.9.27
Lalor, Matthew	PP Mountmellick	1923	M.J. Murphy to Bishop Foley, 2.2.23, KLDA
Lynam, Ambrose	PP Stradbally	1923	*Offaly Independent*, 25.8.23
Mahon, James	Adm. Tullow	1927	*Nationalist and Leinster Times*, 14.1.27
Mooney, John	PP Clonegal	1925	*Irish Independent*, 16.2.25
Murphy, Paul	PP Edenderry	1921	*Limerick Echo*, 31.12.21
Murphy, M.J.	PP Maryborough	1922	*Freeman's Journal*, 3.1.22
Norris, Thomas	PP Rhode, Offaly	1922	*Westmeath Independent*, 22.4.22
O'Neill, Laurence	CC Stradbally	1923	*Offaly Independent*, 25.8.23
Seale, Thomas	CC Bagenalstown	1933	*Kilkenny Journal*, 25.11.33
Wilson, William	CC Luggacurran	1923	*Offaly Independent*, 25.8.23

Anti-Treaty

Breen, James	CC Rosenallis	1923	M.J. Murphy to Bishop Foley, 2.2.23, KLDA
Burbage, Thomas	CC Geashill	1922	*Nationalist and Leinster Times*, 9.4.22
Byrne, Albert	CC Clonaslee	1923	M.J. Murphy to Bishop Foley, 2.2.23, KLDA
Campion, Edward	CC Clonegall	1922	T.P. O'Neill
Harris, Patrick	CC Portlaoise	1932	*Westmeath Independent*, 13.2.32
Hipwell, Patrick	PP Ballyadams	1933	*Kildare Observer*, 14.1.33
Kavanagh, Peter	CC Mountmellick	1922	*Nationalist and Leinster Times*, 9.4.22
Kelly, John C.	CC Rathoe, Tullow	1922	T.P. O'Neill
Kennedy, Michael	PP Killeigh	1932	O'Mahony Papers, NLI 24501
Lennon, John	CC Mountmellick	1922	*Irish Press*, 8.12.31
O'Brien, James	CC Carbury	1927	*Newcastle West Weekly Observer*, 8.9.27
Swayne, Peter	Knockbeg College, Carlow	1922	T.P. O'Neill

KILLALA – INCLUDES PARTS OF MAYO AND SLIGO

Pro-Treaty

Naughton, James	Bishop	1922	*Weekly Freeman*, 7.1.22
Davis, James	PP Templeboy	1925	*Sligo Champion*, 24.1.25
Dodd, Andrew	PP Binghamstown	1923	*Irish Times*, 24.8.23
Greany, William J.	Adm. Ballina	1922	*Weekly Freeman*, 7.1.22
Healy, William	PP Oghill	1925	*Roscommon Herald*, 29.8.25
Hegarty, John	PP Belmullet	1926	*An Phoblacht*, 26.3.26
Hegarty, Martin	PP Moygownagh	1934	*Irish Press*, 5.3.34
Heverin, William	PP Ballysokeary	1934	ditto, 12.2.34
Howley, Patrick	PP Kilcommon Erris	1923	*Irish Times*, 17.8.23
Kelly, John	PP Laherdane	1927	*Irish Independent*, 2.9.27

Pro-Treaty	Rank	First Reported Declaration	Source
Munnelly, Michael	PP Ballycastle	1933	*Connaught Tribune*, 14.1.33
O'Donnell, Michael	CC Crossmolina	1923	*Irish Times*, 24.8.23
O'Hara, Thomas	PP Ballycroy	1927	*Irish Weekly Independent*, 17.9.27
O'Reilly, Patrick	PP Killala	1925	*Western News*, 25.4.25
Timlin, Anthony	PP Skreen	1925	*Irish Independent*, 2.2.25
Tully, Michael	PP Easkey	1923	*Roscommon Herald*, 25.8.23

Anti-Treaty

Browne, Thomas	CC Dromore West	1922	E. O'Malley Papers UCDA, P 17b/136
Hewson, Patrick	PP Bangor Erris	1933	*Connaught Tribune*, 14.1.33

KILLALOE – INCLUDES PARTS OF CLARE, TIPPERARY, OFFALY, GALWAY, LIMERICK AND LAOIS

Pro-Treaty

Fogarty, Michael	Bishop	1921	*Irish Independent*, 10.12.21
Bourke, Peter	PP Clarecastle	1927	*Limerick Echo*, 10.5.27
Breen, Michael	PP Dysart	1922	*Clare Champion*, 6.1.22
Clancy, Anthony	PP Killaloe	1922	ditto, 14.4.22
Clancy, James	PP Kilballyowen	1922	ditto, 5.8.22
Considine, M.	P.P Caher, Feakle	1922	ditto
Crowe, M.J.	CC Doora, Ennis	1922	ditto
Culligan, C.	CC Kilkee	1922	ditto
Cunningham, John	PP Templederry	1922	*Freeman's Journal*, 18.3.22
D'Arcy, John	P.P Terryglan, Borrisokane	1922	*Clonmel Chronicle*, 4.1.22
Donnelly, P.J.	PP Corofin	1922	*Irish Independent*, 2.6.27
Enright, John F.	CC Birr	1927	*Leinster Reporter*, 10.9.27
Gavin, John	PP Kildysart	1932	*Saturday Record*, Ennis, 16.1.32
Gaynor, Patrick	CC Birr	1923	*Irish Independent*, 17.8.23
Gilsenan, P.J.	PP Birr	1927	ditto, 2.6.27
Glynn, John	PP Mullagh	1923	*Irish Times*, 6.8.23
Grace, M.J.	CC Roscrea	1927	*Midland Tribune*, 4.6.27
Hamilton, Michael	St Flannan's Ennis	1922	*Clare Champion*, 6.1.22
Hewitt, P.	CC Killard, Doonbeg	1927	*Limerick Echo*, 31.5.27
Houlihan, Joseph	CC Kinnitty	1923	*Westmeath Independent*, 7.7.23
McInerney, John	PP Kilrush	1927	*Irish Independent*, 12.9.27
Meehan, T.	CC Borrisokane	1922	*Freeman's Journal*, 12.7.22
Molloy, Thomas	CC Roscrea	1927	*Midland Tribune*, 4.6.27
Molony, Alfred J.	CC Kilrush	1922	*Freeman's Journal*, 6.1.22
Molony, Walter	CC Corofin	1922	*Clare Champion*, 5.8.22
Monaghan, James	PP Crusheen	1922	ditto
Murray, Martin	CC Nenagh	1931	*Irish Press*, 2.11.31
O'Connor, James	PP Shinrone	1927	*Westmeath Independent*, 3.9.27
O'Donoghue, John	CC Tulla	1922	*Clare Champion*, 5.8.22
O'Halloran, P.J.	CC Nenagh	1922	*Freeman's Journal*, 1.8.22
O'Kennedy, W.	St Flannan's, Ennis	1923	*Irish Independent*, 13.8.23

Pro-Treaty	Rank	First Reported Declaration	Source
O'Sullivan, P.J.	St Flannan's, Ennis	1922	*Clare Champion,* 5.8.22
Roche, John	CC Nenagh	1931	*Irish Press,* 2.11.31
Ryan, A.	CC Kilmaley, Ennis	1922	MacSwiney Papers, UCDA, P 48/a/202
Slattery, Stephen	PP Quin	1927	*Irish Times,* 6.9.27
Stuart, Patrick	St Flannan's, Ennis	1932	*Saturday Record Ennis,* 16.1.32
Vaughan, P.J.	St Flannan's, Ennis	1932	ditto
Vaughan, Thomas	PP Doonbeg	1932	ditto, 6.2.32
Vaughan, Michael	PP Whitegate, Limerick	1922	*Clare Champion,* 5.8.22
Walshe –	St Flannan's, Ennis	1927	*Irish Independent,* 7.9.27

Anti-Treaty

Galvin, M.J.	Chaplain, Ennis	1933	*Clare Champion,* 18.2.33
O'Dea, Daniel	CC Sixmilebridge	1922	Professor D. Fitzpatrick
O'Dea, John	CC Killaloe	1922	ditto
O'Flynn, D.	CC Clondegad, Ballynacally	1922	*Irish Weekly Independent,* 3.6.22

KILMORE – INCLUDES ALMOST ALL OF CAVAN, AND PARTS OF LEITRIM, FERMANAGH, MEATH AND SLIGO

Pro-Treaty

Finegan, Patrick	Bishop	1921	*Irish Independent,* 10.12.21
Brady, Bernard	PP Belturbet	1923	*Anglo-Celt,* 11.8.23
Brady, Hugh	Adm. Kellygarry	1923	*United Irishman,* 21.7.23
Brady, James	CC Kildoagh	1923	*Anglo-Celt,* 4.8.23
Comey, Charles	PP Carton Temple	1929	*Roscommon Herald,* 1.6.29
Comey, Martin	Adm. Cavan	1923	*Irish Independent,* 7.8.23
Farrelly, Bernard	CC Ballinamore	1923	*Roscommon Herald,* 21.1.25
Farrelly, James	PP Kill, Cootehill	1927	*Anglo-Celt,* 10.9.27
Flynn, Francis	PP Inishmagrath	1925	*Sligo Champion,* 21.2.25
Gaffney, Bernard	PP Virginia	1923	*Anglo-Celt,* 28.8.23
Galligan, Laurence	PP Drumreilly Lower	1925	*Roscommon Herald,* 28.2.25
Gilchrist, Patrick	PP Laragh	1933	*Anglo-Celt,* 7.1.33
Gilmartin, Francis	PP Killinagh Blacklion	1933	ditto
Gilmartin, Joseph	CC Dowra	1922	*Roscommon Herald,* 25.3.22
Judge, James	PP Killeshandra	1923	*Anglo-Celt,* 28.8.23
Keaney, John	PP Aughnasheelin	1922	*Roscommon Herald,* 29.4.22
Lynch, Peter	PP Crossdoney	1923	*Anglo-Celt,* 11.8.23
McCabe, James	CC Derrylin	1922	O'Mahony Papers, NLI
McDermott, John	CC Belturbet	1923	*Anglo-Celt,* 4.8.23
McGauran, John	PP Curlough	1923	ditto
McGauran, John	CC Ballintrillick	1925	*Irish Independent,* 2.3.25
McKiernan, Francis	PP Ballinamore	1922	Rev. D. Gallogley, PP Mullagh
McManus, Daniel	CC Killarga	1922	*Freeman's Journal,* 20.7.22

Pro-Treaty	**Rank**	**First Reported Declaration**	**Source**
Mallon, Patrick	PP Kinawley, Swanlinbar	1933	*Anglo-Celt,* 7.1.33
O'Connell, Patrick	PP Cootehill	1922	*Sligo Champion,* 15.4.22
O'Donoghue, Charles	CC Kinlough	1923	*Roscommon Herald,* 25.8.23
O'Donoghue, Patrick	CC Killeshandra	1923	*Anglo-Celt,* 28.8.23
O'Reilly, Bernard	PP Drung, Cavan	1927	ditto, 28.5.27
O'Reilly, John	CC Cavan	1923	ditto, 11.8.23
O'Reilly, Patrick	PP Swanlinbar	1923	ditto, 4.8.23
O'Reilly, Patrick	CC Baileborough	1923	*Irish Independent,* 8.8.23
O'Reilly, Peter	CC Lurgan, Virginia	1927	*Anglo-Celt,* 28.5.27
Osborne, Patrick	PP Mullagh	1923	ditto, 28.8.23
Prior, Francis	CC Dromahaire	1925	*Irish Independent,* 2.2.25
Sheridan, James	CC Swanlinbar	1923	*Anglo-Celt,* 4.8.23
Shiel, Francis	CC Carrigallen	1925	*Irish Times,* 2.3.25
Smith, Philip	PP Carrigallen	1922	*Roscommon Herald,* 10.6.22

Anti-Treaty

Lynch, E.	CC Glencar	1933	*Sligo Champion,* 14.1.33
Lynott, Francis	C.C. Glencar	1927	*Roscommon Herald,* 13.2.32
McPhillips, Patrick	PP Balaghameen, Garrison	1932	O'Mahony Papers, NLI 24501

LIMERICK − INCLUDES LIMERICK AND A SMALL PART OF CLARE

Pro-Treaty

Hallinan, Denis	Bishop to 1923	1921	*Irish Independent,* 10.12.21
Keane, David	Bishop from 1923	1927	ditto, 2.6.27
Breen, John	PP Rockhill	1927	*Limerick Leader,* 30.4.27
Carr, John	PP Mainstir, Croom	1927	ditto, 14.5.27
Carroll, James	CC St John's Cathedral	1923	*Irish Times,* 6.8.23
Coleman, Patrick	CC Athea	1927	*Limerick Leader,* 30.4.27
Connolly, Michael	Adm. Limerick	1923	*Limerick Herald,* 26.2.23
Cregan, J.M.	PP Abbeyfeale	1923	Cregan to Hallinan, 27.2.23, LKDA
Dwane, William	PP Newcastle West	1923	*Limerick Herald,* 26.2.23
Finn, Patrick	CC Coolcappa	1933	*Munster News,* 11.1.33
Fitzgerald, J.K.	PP Coolcappa	1927	*Limerick Leader,* 30.5.27
Hannan, Michael	PP St Mary's Limerick	1933	ditto, 11.1.33
Hartigan, Patrick	PP Tournafulla Newcastle West	1927	*Kerryman,* 7.5.27
Lee, John	PP Kilfinane	1923	*Irish Times,* 16.8.23
McNamara, T.J.	CC St John's Limerick	1927	*Limerick Leader,* 5.9.27
McNamara, Patrick	PP Ballyagran Charleville	1933	*Munster News,* 11.1.33
Murphy, Timothy	CC Rathkeale	1927	*Limerick Echo,* 7.6.27

Pro-Treaty	Rank	First Reported Declaration	Source
O'Carroll, J.	CC St John's Limerick	1927	*Irish Independent*,6.6.27
O'Connor, Jeremiah	PP St Mary's Limerick	1922	*Limerick Echo*, 16.5.22
O'Donnell, Michael	PP Rathkeale	1922	*Freeman's Journal*, 7.8.22
O'Driscoll, Daniel	PP St Munchin's	1923	*Limerick Herald*, 26.2.23
O'Dwyer, William	PP St Munchin's	1933	*Munster News*, 11.1.33
O'Gorman, J.	PP Feenagh and Kilmeedy	1934	O'Gorman to Bishop Keane, 18.6.34, LKDA
Ó h-Aodha, Mícheál	CC Newcastle West	1922	*Kerry People*, 29.4.22
O'Sullivan, C.	CC Askeaton	1927	*Limerick Echo*, 7.6.27
Reeves, John	PP Drumcollogher	1933	*Munster News*, 11.1.33
Thornhill, Patrick	CC St Michael's, Limerick	1922	*Limerick Echo*, 16.5.22
Treacy, Michael	CC Limerick	1923	*Limerick Herald*, 26.2.23
Woulfe, Patrick	CC Kilmallock	1922	Mannix Joyce

Anti-Treaty

Ambrose, Robert	PP Kilfinane, Glenroe	1922	*An Phoblacht*, 23.4.26
Hartnett, Edward	CC Kilfinane, Glenroe	1922	Mannix Joyce
Houlihan, John	CC Abbeyfeale	1925	*Catholic Bulletin*, 1925, p.1157
Murphy, Gerald	PP Abbeyfeale	1925	Mannix Joyce; Rev. G. Wall
O'Kelly, J.J.	PP Templeglantine	1927	*Limerick Leader*, 5.9.27
Ryan, Patrick	PP Monagea, Newcastle West	1927	ditto
Wall, Thomas	CC Foynes	1922	Canon G. Wall; Mannix Joyce

MEATH – INCLUDES THE GREATER PART OF MEATH, WESTMEATH AND OFFALY, AND SMALL PARTS OF COUNTIES LONGFORD, LOUTH, DUBLIN AND CAVAN

Pro-Treaty

Gaughran, Laurence	Bishop to 1929	1921	*Irish Independent*, 10.12.21
Mulvany, Thomas	Bishop from 1929	1927	ditto, 2.6.27
Bracken, Michael	PP Clara	1923	*Offaly Independent*, 25.8.23
Brett , ?	CC Mullingar	1922	*Freeman's Journal*, 18.3.22
Callery, Philip	PP Tullamore	1922	*Westmeath Independent*, 22.4.22
Clavin, Matthew	Military Chaplain, Gormanstown	1922	*Free Press Wexford*, 14.10.22
Cole, Dermot	PP Killucan	1927	*Westmeath Independent*, 4.6.27
Coyle, Patrick	Military Chaplain Gormanstown	1922	*Free Press Wexford*, 14.10.22
Dillon, Michael	PP Enfield	1927	*Irish Independent*,12.9.27
Donnellan, Thomas	PP Trim	1926	*An Phoblacht*, 14.5.26
Downes, Michael	PP Tyrrelspass	1923	*Éire*, 19.5.23
Kelly, Joseph	Adm. Mullingar	1922	Rev. Joseph Mooney
Lynam, James	PP Killina	1923	*Westmeath Independent*, 7.7.23
Macken, J.C.	CC Mullingar	1923	*Irish Times*, 23.8.23

Pro-Treaty	Rank	First Reported Declaration	Source
Magee, John L.	PP Tubber	1922	*Offaly Independent,* 25.3.22
Murphy, Patrick	CC Trim	1926	*An Phoblacht,* 14.5.26
Nulty, John	PP St Mary's Drogheda	1927	*Anglo-Celt,* 10.9.27
O'Farrell, Matthew	PP Athboy	1927	*Irish Times,* 13.9.27
O'Keeffe, T.	CC Tullamore	1927	*Leinster Reporter,* 10.9.27
O'Reilly, Edward	PP Kilcormac	1923	*Westmeath Independent,* 4.8.23
Rooney, William	PP Longwood	1932	*Irish Press,* 9.2.32

Anti-Treaty

Casey, Christopher	PP Ballymore	1922	Rev. Joseph Mooney
Clarke, Patrick	PP Drumraney	1922	ditto
Coyne, Denis	PP Clonmellon	1932	*Westmeath Independent,* 13.2.32
Flynn, Edward	PP Donore, Drogheda	1929	*Kerry Champion,* 4.5.29
Keappock, Thomas	CC Ballymore	1922	Rev. Joseph Mooney
Kilmartin, J.	CC Navan	1922	ditto
Smith, Patrick	CC Killina Tullamore	1922	*Westmeath Independent,* 22.4.22
Walsh, Paul	PP Multyfarnham	1932	Rev. Joseph Mooney

OSSORY – INCLUDES KILKENNY AND PARTS OF LAOIS AND OFFALY

Pro-Treaty

Brownrigg, Abraham	Bishop	1922	Jim Maher
Downey, James	Coadjutor Bishop	1925	Downey to Cosgrave, 19.9.25, NAI S 4127
Barry, Michael	PP Ballyragget	1923	*Irish Times,* 22.8.23
Bergin, John	CC Slieverue Waterford	1927	*Irish Weekly Independent,* 17.9.27
Brennan, Edward	PP Muckalee	1925	*Irish Independent,* 4.3.25
Brennan, Edward	PP Lisdowney, Ballyragget	1925	*Kilkenny Journal,* 13.6.25
Brennan, James	PP Windgap, Callan	1925	*Irish Independent,* 6.2.25
Carroll, John	Adm. St Patrick's, Kilkenny	1925	ditto, 9.3.25
Cavanagh, Charles	Adm. St John's Kilkenny	1925	*Kilkenny Journal,* 29.8.25
Coghlan, Laurence	PP Rosbercon, New Ross	1933	*Enniscorthy Echo,* 14.1.33
Crotty, Martin	PP Clough Castlecomer	1925	*Irish Independent,* 23.2.25
Dillon, James	PP Borris-in-Ossory	1927	*Leinster Reporter,* 10.9.27
Doyle, James	Adm. St Canice's, Kilkenny	1925	*Irish Independent,* 9.3.25
Drea, Michael	CC St Canice's	1925	ditto
Grace, William	CC Ballyhale	1925	ditto, 16.2.25
Henebery, Thomas	CC Dunamaggan, Callan	1922	Jim Maher

Pro-Treaty	Rank	First Reported Declaration	Source
Hughes, Daniel	CC Muckalee	1925	*Irish Independent*, 4.3.25
Loughrey, John	CC Thomastown	1925	ditto, 16.2.25
McNamara, Cornelius	PP Castlecomer	1923	*Irish Times*, 22.8.23
McNamara, Michael	CC Clough	1925	*Irish Independent*, 23.2.25
Madden, John	PP Mullinavat	1925	ditto, 2.3.25
Moore, Philip	CC The Rower Kilkenny	1925	ditto, 16.2.25
Murphy, William	CC Windgap Callan	1925	ditto, 23.2.25
O'Farrell, William	PP Urlingford	1925	*Kilkenny Journal*, 13.6.25
O'Keefe, Andrew	Adm. St Mary's, Kilkenny	1925	*Irish Independent*, 9.3.25
Phelan, James	CC St John's, Kilkenny	1925	ditto
Phelan, Thomas	PP Templeorum Piltown	1925	ditto, 2.3.25
Power, Michael	PP Kilmanagh Callan	1925	*Kilkenny Journal*, 13.6.25
Rowe, John	CC Callan	1925	*Irish Independent*, 2.2.25
Treacy, Patrick	PP Conahy Jenkinstown	1923	ditto, 8.8.23
Walsh, John	PP Gowran	1925	*Irish Independent*, 23.2.25
Walsh, Laurence	PP Johnstown	1923	ditto, 8.8.23
Walsh, Tobias	PP Freshford	1925	*Kilkenny Journal*, 13.6.25

Anti-Treaty

Delahunty, Patrick	CC Callan	1922	Jim Maher
Doody, John	PP Ferrybank Waterford	1932	*Kilkenny Journal*, 7.5.32

RAPHOE – INCLUDES ALMOST ALL OF COUNTY DONEGAL, WITH THE EXCEPTION OF INISHOWEN

Pro-Treaty

O'Donnell, Patrick	Bishop to 1923	1922	O'Donnell to Hagan, 10.4.22, Hagan Papers
Burns, James	PP Raphoe, Lifford	1927	*Irish Independent*, 2.9.27
McCafferty, John	PP Stranorlar	1933	*People's Press Donegal*, 14.1.33
McGinley, Teague	CC Dungloe	1933	*Derry People*, 14.1.33
McMullan, P.B.	F.S. Army Chaplain	1923	J. Quinn, *The Story of the Drumboe Martyrs*, Letterkenny, 1958, p. 27
Molloy, Thomas	Technical Institute, Glenties	1933	*Irish Press*, 27.11.33
Mullan, Alphonsus	CC Ballintra	1933	*Derry People*, 22.1.33
O'Donnell, James	CC Kilcar	1933	*People's Press Donegal*, 7.1.33
O'Doherty, John	PP Rathmullen	1933	*Irish Press*, 17.1.33
Scanlan, James	PP Dungloe	1933	*Derry People*, 14.1.33

Pro-Treaty	Rank	First Reported Declaration	Source
Sheridan, Francis	Adm. Letterkenny	1933	ditto
Sheridan, William, J.	CC Killybegs	1933	*People's Press Donegal*, 7.1.33
Walker, James	PP Donegal	1923	*Irish Independent*, 27.8.23
Anti-Treaty			
Gallagher, Thomas	CC Creeslough	1933	*Derry People*, 11.2.33
McDevitt, Charles	CC Glenvar	1933	ditto, 14.1.33
McNeely, William	Bishop from 1923	1933	ditto, 4.3.33
Maguire, Edward	PP Carrick	1927	*The Nation*, 1.10.27
O'Gara, Hugh	Adm. Glenswilly	1922	Rev. John Silke
Ward, Alphonsus C.	PP Carrick	1922	ditto

TUAM – INCLUDES HALF OF COUNTY MAYO, ALMOST HALF OF COUNTY GALWAY AND PART OF ROSCOMMON

Pro-Treaty	Rank	First Reported Declaration	Source
Gilmartin, Thomas	Archbishop	1921	*Irish Independent*, 10.12.21
Adams, Martin	PP Carna	1932	*Connaught Tribune*, 13.2.32
Campbell, J.	CC The Neale	1925	*Western News*, 25.4.25
Canavan, B.	PP Carnacon Ballyglass	1933	*Connaught Tribune*, 14.1.33
Colgan, Patrick	PP Kilkeerin	1927	ditto, 23.4.27
Colleran, Martin	PP Achill	1923	*United Irishman*, 27.10.23
Conroy, Michael J.	PP Kilmeena Westport	1923	*Éire*, 28.4.23
Cunningham, Charles	Adm. Tuam	1922	*Freeman's Journal*, 22.7.22
Curran, James	PP Dunmore	1923	*Roscommon Messenger*, 28.7.23
D'Alton, Edward	PP Ballinrobe	1926	*An Phoblacht*, 19.3.26
Diskin, Michael	PP Milltown, Tuam	1927	*Connaught Tribune*, 30.4.27
Diskin, W.	PP Letterfrack	1933	ditto, 14.1.33
Eaton, Alexander	St Jarlath's, Tuam	1922	*Freeman's Journal*, 21.3.22
Farragher, Murtagh	PP Athenry	1922	*Connaught Tribune*, 10.6.22
Egan, E.	CC The Neale	1933	ditto, 21.1.33
Fallon, John	PP Castlebar	1923	*Irish Independent*, 1.8.23
Flatley, John	PP Aughagower	1922	Rev. R. Horan, Ballydangan
Forde, Patrick	PP Claran	1927	*Irish Times*, 9.9.27.
Gibbons, John	CC Abbeyknockmoy	1927	*Connaught Tribune*, 21.5.27
Greally, John	PP Abbeyknockmoy	1927	ditto, 4.6.27
Hannon, Owen	PP Cummer	1932	ditto, 13.2.32
Healy, John	PP Killeen, Carraroe	1927	ditto, 4.6.27
Healy, Martin	PP Kilmaine	1922	U. MacEoin (ed.), *Survivors*, (Dublin, 1980), pp. 289–90
Healy, Michael	PP Kingsland South, Athenry	1922	*Connaught Tribune*, 10.6.22
Heaney, Thomas	PP Glenamaddy	1923	*Roscommon Messenger*, 28.6.23
Heaney, W.	PP Leenane	1933	*Connaught Tribune*, 14.1.33
Heavey, J.M.	CC Caherlistrane	1922	*Freeman's Journal*, 30.8.22
Hennelly, M.F.	CC Ballyconneely	1932	*Connaught Tribune*, 13.2.32

Pro-Treaty	Rank	First Reported Declaration	Source
Joyce, Patrick	CC Castlebar	1922	*Offaly Independent*, 7.4.22
Kelly, Peter	St Jarlath's, Tuam	1922	*Freeman's Journal*, 21.3.22
Kelly, Peter J.	Adm. Tuam	1932	*Connaught Tribune*, 13.2.32
Lavelle, E.	PP Clonbur	1932	ditto, 23.1.32
Loftus, Martin	CC Kilkeerin	1925	*Roscommon Herald*, 7.3.25
McAlpine, Patrick	PP Clifden	1927	*Irish Independent*, 10.9.27
McDermott, Francis	PP Ballinlough	1922	*Roscommon Herald*, 7.1.22
McDonald, Michael	CC Tully Cross	1932	*Connaught Tribune*, 13.2.32
MacGough, E.F.	PP Corrandulla	1932	ditto
McHugh, Michael J.	PP Ballyhaunis	1923	*Irish Times*, 2.7.23
McHugh, Patrick J.	CC Ballyconneely	1923	W. Kelly to M.J. Browne, 13.3.23, GDA
Macken, Thomas	PP Claremorris	1923	*Irish Independent*, 1.8.23
Madden, P.	Adm. Williamstown	1923	*Roscommon Messenger*, 28.7.23
Malone, Michael	CC Cashel Co. Galway	1923	*Irish Times*, 21.8.23
Moran, James	St Jarlath's, Tuam	1922	*Freeman's Journal*, 21.3.22
Mylotte, John	PP Claran	1932	*Irish Press*, 16.2.32
Nicholson, Patrick	PP Menlough	1933	*Connaught Tribune*, 14.1.33
Noone, John	CC Carnacon	1925	*Western News*, 25.4.25
O'Connor, M.	CC Irishtown Ballindine	1925	ditto
O'Grady, J.	CC Athenry	1933	*Connaught Tribune*, 14.1.33
O'Malley, Edward	CC Doone, Clifden	1922	W. Kelly to M.J. Browne, 12.11.22, GDA
O'Malley, John	PP Bekan	1923	*United Irishman*, 27.10.23
O'Malley, John	PP Turloughmore	1923	*Irish Times*, 21.8.23
O'Malley, Thomas	PP Partry, Ballinrobe	1925	*Western News*, 25.4.25
Prendergast, Geoffrey	CC Castlebar	1925	ditto
Reidy, Thomas	PP Balla and Manulla	1922	C. Younger, *Ireland's Civil War* (London, 1979), p. 291
Varden, Peter	CC Belclare, Tuam	1927	*Connaught Tribune*, 21.5.27
Waldron, John	PP Keelogues	1925	*Western News*, 25.4.25
Waldron, P.	PP Kilkeerin	1933	*Connaught Tribune*, 21.1.33
Walsh, J.S.	President, St Jarlath's, Tuam	1932	ditto, 23.1.32
*White, Charles	PP Bekan Ballyhaunis	1933	*Irish Press*, 12.1.33

Anti-Treaty			
Brett, Thomas	CC Kilmaine	1925	*Western News*, 25.4.25
Burke, Thomas	CC Garbally Menlough	1933	*Irish Press*, 15.1.33
Joyce, Patrick	CC Belclare	1933	ditto
Kelly, William	CC Errismore Clifden	1922	Kelly to M.J. Browne, 12.11.22, GDA
King, Patrick	CC Hollymount	1933	*Irish Press*, 15.1.33
Lavelle, Michael	CC Annaghdown	1933	*Connaught Tribune*, 14.1.33
McEvilly, Michael	CC Ballyhaunis	1922	*Feasta*, October, 1988, p. 19

Anti-Treaty	Rank	First Reported Declaration	Source
Moran, Andrew	CC Headford	1932	*Connaught Tribune*, 13.2.32
O'Grady, J.	CC Athenry	1933	*Irish Press*, 15.1.33
O'Kelly, James	PP Spiddal	1927	*Irish Independent*, 2.6.27
Ryder, Denis	St Jarlath's, Tuam	1926	*An Phoblacht*, 22.1.26
Walsh, John	PP Williamstown	1933	*Connaught Tribune*, 4.2.33
*White, Charles	PP Bekan, Ballyhaunis	1933	*Irish Press*, 21.1.33

WATERFORD AND LISMORE – INCLUDES WATERFORD AND PARTS OF TIPPERARY AND CORK

Pro-Treaty

Hackett, Bernard	Bishop	1922	*Freeman's Journal*, 17.8.22
Byrne, William	PP Convent Hill, Waterford	1935	*Irish Independent*, 28.1.35
Conway, Henry	CC Ring	1922	*Skibbereen Eagle*, 1.4.22
Fitzgerald, Patrick	PP Clogheen	1927	*Irish Independent*, 12.9.27
Fitzgerald, Thomas	CC Ninemilehouse, Callan	1927	*Tipperary Star*, 11.6.27
Furlong, Thomas	PP Dungarvan	1925	*Irish Independent*, 18.2.25
Gleeson, John	PP Cappoquin	1922	*Skibbereen Eagle*, 1.4.22
Hearne, Pierse	CC Cahir	1923	*Irish Times*, 27.8.23
Keating, Patrick	PP Ballyporeen	1927	*Tipperaryman and Limerick Recorder*, 28.5.27
Meskel, Peter	CC Cappoquin	1927	*Irish Independent*, 7.6.27
Morrissey, Daniel	CC Ballyporeen	1927	*Tipperaryman and Limerick Recorder*, 28.5.27
O'Donnell, John	PP Newtown, Kilmacthomas	1923	*Irish Times*, 21.8.23
O'Donnell, William	PP Cahir	1932	*Irish Press*, 9.2.32
Prendergast, Edward	PP Trinity Without, Waterford	1922	*Freeman's Journal*, 22.8.22
Rea, Joseph	CC Dungarvan	1922	*Skibbereen Eagle*, 1.4.22
Sheehy, William	PP Carrick-on-Suir	1927	*Kerryman*, 4.6.27
Synott, Henry	CC Ardmore, Youghal	1933	*Irish Press*, 14.1.33

Anti-Treaty

Kinane, Jeremiah	Bishop from 1933	1935	M. Twomey to M. MacSwiney, 7.1.35., MacSwiney Papers, P48a/199(4)
Aherne, Thomas	CC Kilmacthomas	1934	*Irish Press*, 2.4.34
Harty, James	CC Kilrossanty	1934	ditto
Henebry, James	CC Portlaw	1926	Kathleen O'Connell Diary, 2.6.26
Power, Thomas	CC Kilgobinet	1922	T.P. O'Neill
Prendergast, Matthew	Ballinlee, Cappoquin	1933	*Irish Press*, 17.1.33
Shine, Philip	Manor Hill, Waterford	1922	Seán Murphy, Kilmacthomas
Skally, Bernard	CC Ardfinnan, Cahir	1927	*Tipperary Star*, 4.6.27

Part Two: Regular Clergy in Ireland

Augustinian Order

Anti-Treaty	Diocese	First Reported Declaration	Source
Mansfield, E.A.	Galway	1922	S. Murphy, *The Comeraghs, Refuge of Rebels*, n.d., p. 74

Capuchin Order

Pro-Treaty

Ignatius	Ossory	1923	*Éire*, 16.10.23
Stanislaus	Dublin	1925	*Enniscorthy Guardian*, 11.3.25

Anti-Treaty

Albert	Dublin	1922	Cosgrave to Byrne, 21.7.22, DAA
Aloysius	Dublin	1922	Marie O'Kelly
Augustine	Dublin	1922	*Roscommon Herald*, 21.3.25
Canice	Dublin	1922	A. de Blacam to Fr Canice, 27.7.22, Desmond FitzGerald Papers, UCDA
Dominic	Dublin	1922	Cosgrave to Byrne, 21.7.22, DAA
James	Cork	1937	Kathleen O'Connell Diary, 11.7.37
Michael	Cork	1937	ditto
Sebastian	Dublin	1922	*Irish Press*, 14.9.31
Senan	Dublin	1937	Kathleen O'Connell, 18.7.37

Carmelite Order (Calced)

Pro-Treaty

Maher, P.A.	Ardagh	1922	*Offaly Independent*, 25.3.22

Carmelite Order (Discalced)

Pro-Treaty

Barry Francis	Clonfert	1922	*Connaught Tribune*, 10.6.22

Anti-Treaty

Benedict	Dublin	1922	Marie O'Kelly
Meleady, Berthold	Dublin	1922	MacSwiney Papers, UCDA P 48a/215
Murphy, Laurence	Dublin	1932	O'Mahony Papers, NLI 2450
O'Brien, Fintan	Dublin	1927	*Irish Weekly Independent*, 4.6.27

CONGREGATION OF THE HOLY GHOST

Anti-Treaty	Diocese	First Reported Declaration	Source
Byrne, John	Cashel and Emly	1922	S.P. Farragher, *Dev and his Alma Mater* (Dublin, 1984)
Byrne Joseph	Dublin	1922	Ibid.
Crehan, E.A.	Cashel and Emly	1926	De Valera to E. Cahill, S.J. 17.2.36, Jesuit Archives
Farrell, Herbert	Dublin	1925	T.P. O'Neill
Healy, Laurence	Dublin	1922	Farragher, *Dev*
Kingston, John	Cashel and Emly	1922	Ibid.
O'Mahony, Martin	Cashel and Emly	1933	*Clonmel Chronicle*, 14.1.33
Walshe, Patrick	Dublin	1922	T.P. O'Neill

CONGREGATION OF THE MISSION (VINCENTIANS)

Anti-Treaty			
Walsh, Daniel	Cork	1926	*An Phoblacht*, 16.7.26

DOMINICAN ORDER

Pro-Treaty			
Brosnahan, Henry	Limerick	1923	*Limerick Herald*, 26.2.23
Fogarty, Albert	Kildare and Leighlin	1927	*Nationalist and Leinster Times*
McInerny, M.H.	Dublin	1927	*An Phoblacht*, 12.8.27
O'Reilly, Alphonsus	Sligo	1922	*Roscommon Journal*, 4.11.22

Anti-Treaty			
Ayres, Raphael	Kerry	1922	Rev. Henry Peel, o.p.
Heuston, John	Dublin	1927	*The Nation*, 23.7.27
Houlihan, J.D.	Kerry	1922	*Kerry People*, 15.7.22
McKenna, Paul	Armagh	1929	*Kerry Champion*, 4.5.29
Noonan, J.	Dublin	1922	*Kerry People*, 27.5.22
O'Donoghue, T.	Dublin	1929	*Kerry Champion*, 4.5.29
Power, J.H.	Dublin	1929	ditto
Ryan, Vincent	Dublin	1927	*The Nation*, 23.7.27
Smyth, F.J.	Armagh	1925	*Catholic Bulletin*, 1925, p. 1018
Walsh, Thomas	Dublin	1929	Rev. Henry Peel, o.p.

FRANCISCAN ORDER

Pro-Treaty			
Leonard Begley	Limerick	1923	*Limerick Herald*, 26.2.23
Peter Begley	Ferns	1922	*Westmeath Independent*, 28.10.22
Mark Connaughton	Kerry	1922	*Skibbereen Eagle*, 29.4.22
Nicholas Dillon	Armagh	1922	Rev. Patrick Conlan, o.f.m.
Francis Donnelly	Limerick	1923	*Limerick Herald*, 26.2.23
Chrysostom Dore	Ardagh	1922	*Roscommon Herald*, 4.3.22

Pro-Treaty	Diocese	First Reported Declaration	Source
Fidelis Griffin	Kerry	1922	*Skibbereen Eagle*, 29.4.22
Columba Hanrahan	Ardagh	1922	*Skibbereen Eagle*, 15.4.22
Barnabas McGahan	Ardagh	1922	*Roscommon Herald*, 4.3.22
Albert McLoughlin	Limerick	1923	*Limerick Herald*, 26.2.23
Jarlath Mangan	Kerry	1922	Vergil Mannion, *A Life Recalled*, n.d. p. 60
Hubert Quinn	Dublin	1922	Rev. Patrick Conlan, o.f.m.
Leo Sheehan	Dublin	1922	*Freeman's Journal*, 17.8.22
Peter Sheehan	Ferns	1923	*Irish Independent*, 20.8.23
Bonaventure Slattery	Limerick	1923	*Limerick Herald*, 26.2.23
Edmund Walsh	Killaloe	1932	*Saturday Record Ennis*, 16.1.32

Anti-Treaty			
Alfred Clarke	Galway	1935	*Irish Press*, 19.6.35
Gregory Cleary	Dublin	1927	*Irish Weekly Independent*, 23.7.27
Michael Connolly	Wexford	1925	*Catholic Bulletin*, 1925, p. 1008
Antoine Kelly	Dublin	1927	*The Nation*, 23.7.27
Vergil Mannion	Kerry	1922	V. Mannion, *A Life Recalled*, (Dublin, n.d.) p. 40
Ferdinand O'Leary	Armagh	1922	P.Conlan, *The Franciscans in Drogheda* (Dublin, 1987), p. 50
Leopold O'Neill	Killaloe	1922	*Clare Champion*, 26.2.22
Ephrem O'Shea	Kerry	1933	ditto
Declan Ryan	Kerry	1933	*Kerry Champion*, 4.2.33
Francis Ryan	Drogheda	1925	*Catholic Bulletin*, 1925, p. 1018

OBLATES

Pro-Treaty			
Dawson, Thomas	Dublin	1922	T.M. Healy to Dawson, 20.8.22 NLI MS 18516

REDEMPTORISTS

Pro-Treaty			
Fitzgerald, John	Limerick	1923	*Limerick Herald*, 26.2.23
Hartigan, Patrick	Limerick	1923	*Limerick Herald*, 26.2.23
Jones, Edward	Limerick	1923	Jones to Hallinan, 27.2.23, LKDA
Maguire, Patrick	Limerick	1923	ditto
Robinson, Thomas	Limerick	1923	ditto

Anti-Treaty			
Coyle, J.B.	Clonfert	1937	Coyle to Kathleen O'Connell, 14.1.38, Kathleen O'Connell Papers

PASSIONISTS

Anti-Treaty	Diocese	First Reported Declaration	Source
Keegan, Brendan	Clogher	1922	MacSwiney Papers, P 48a/196(9)
Smith, Joseph	Dublin	1922	Kevin O'Higgins to Archbishop Byrne, 20.12.22, DAA

MARIST FATHERS

Anti-Treaty

Leonard, J.V.	Dublin	1935	*Irish Press*, 19.6.35

SOCIETY OF JESUS

Pro-Treaty

Connolly, Patrick	Dublin	1922	*Studies*, September 1922, p. 337
Dinneen, Patrick	Dublin	1922	D. Ó Ceileachair agus P. Ó Cónlúin, *An Duinníneach*, 1958, p. 236
Downing, Edmund	Galway	1922	*Freeman's Journal*, 18.3.22
Fahy, John	Dublin	1923	Fahy to Fr E. Cahill, S.J. 5.1.23, Jesuit Archives
Finlay, Peter	Dublin	1922	*Freeman's Journal*, 12.10.22
Finlay, Thomas	Dublin	1922	F. Callanan, *T.M. Healy* (Cork, 1996), p. 627
Gannon, P.J.	Dublin	1922	*Freeman's Journal*, 14.10.22
Gleeson, William	Dublin	1922	Teresa O'Connell
Healy, Paul	Dublin	1922	Callanan, *Healy*, p. 739
O'Reilly, William	Limerick	1923	*Limerick Herald*, 26.2.23
Potter, Henry	Limerick	1923	ditto

Anti-Treaty

Boyd-Barrett, S.	Limerick	1923	*Éire*, 3.11.23
Cahill, Edward	Dublin	1923	John Fahy, S.J. to Edward Cahill, 5.1.23, Jesuit Archives
Corcoran, Timothy	Dublin	1922	T.P. O'Neill
Flynn, Joseph	Dublin	1932	O'Mahony Papers, NLI, 24501
Gallagher, Richard	Galway	1922	T.P. O'Neill

Part Three: Monastic Clergy

BENEDICTINES

Pro-Treaty	Diocese	First Reported Declaration	Source
Nolan, Patrick	Ferns	1922	Article on Dom Francis Sweetman in W.J. Shiels and D. Wood (eds), *The Churches, Ireland and the Irish* (Dublin, 1989), pp. 409–10

Anti-Treaty			
Sweetman, John [Dom Francis]	Ferns	1922	*Free Press Wexford*, 10.6.22

CISTERCIANS

Pro-Treaty			
McCarthy, Justin	Killaloe	1933	*Leinster Reporter*, 10.9.33

Anti-Treaty			
Luddy, Ailbe	Waterford and Lismore	1922	S.J. Moloney, *The History of Mount Melleray*, Cork, n.d.

Part Four: Prominent Clergy Abroad

Pro-Treaty	Diocese	First Reported Declaration	Source
Curley, Michael	Archbishop of Baltimore	1922	*Irish Times*, 19.7.23
Duhig, James	Archbishop of Brisbane	1922	Cosgrave to Duhig, 27.12.23, NAI S 1369/21
Kelly, Michael	Archbishop of Sydney	1922	D. Carroll, *They Have Fooled You Again* (Dublin, 1993), p.144
O'Gorman, Canice	Augustinian Provincial-General	1924	Hagan to O'Donnell, 10.1.24
O'Reilly, M.	President, St John's College, University of Sydney	1922	Proceedings of Irish Race Congress, Paris, 1922, n.d., p. 187
Turner, William	Bishop of Buffalo	1922	J. O'Dea to M.J. Browne, 15.12.22, GDA

Anti-Treaty			
Curran, Michael J.	Vice-Rector Irish College, Rome	1922	Curran to Hagan, 20.6.22
Gallagher, M.J.	Bishop of Detroit	1921	*Irish World*, 17.12.21
Hagan, John	Rector Irish College Rome	1921	Hagan to Mulhern, 14.1.21, DRDA

Anti-Treaty	Diocese	First Reported Declaration	Source
Mannix, Daniel	Archbishop of Melbourne	1922	De Valera to Mannix, 6.11.22, M. Moynihan, *Speeches and Statements by Eamon de Valera* (Dublin, 1980), p. 109
Magennis, Peter	General of Calced Carmelites, Rome	1922	Magennis to Hagan, 8.12.22, Hagan Papers
O'Connor, D.F.	Carmelite Prior, New York	1922	T.P. O'Neill
O'Doherty, D.J.	Rector, Irish College, Salamanaca	1922	Curran to Hagan, 21.1.22, Hagan Papers
Rogers, John	Monsignor, San Francisco	1933	Rogers to Fogarty, 3.9.33, KILLDA
Ronayne, C.F.	Assistant General Calced Carmelites, Rome	1927	*Irish Weekly Independent*, 23.7.27
Yorke, Peter	Rector, St Peter's, San Francisco	1922	J.S. Brusher, *Consecrated Thunderbolt* (New Jersey, 1973)

THE CIVIL WAR IN MINIATURE

Letter from: Rev. William Kelly, CC, Ballyconneely.
To: Rev. Dr Michael Browne, St Patrick's College, Maynooth,
  12.11.22, GDA.

As there is a possibility that letters may go out tomorrow – a fortnight's mail to the tune of 85 bags having come in last night, I took the notion of writing to you ———how Clifden was captured by the IRA with the Mallaranny Hotel boiler for an armoured car, how the victors and vanquished fraternised, shook hands and developed into a mutual admiration society after the shock of the battle was over, how Mrs Moran with her good man and eight hopefuls spent ten hours in the coal shed, and like the Miller when the mill stopped, cannot sleep now for want of the sweet rifle music; how the five prisoners escaped – as everyone knew they would – in real comic-opera style——— how the officers of the Marconi station garrison signed the surrender and with characteristic fidelity scooted off before the IRA came to disarm them; how there was scarcely a nerve or a pane of glass left in the town after the terrific bombardment, how Fr McHugh (Aughagower) produced his best malt and most excellent mutton for the IRA (when on their way here) thinking them to be some of the People's Army, and so on ad infinitum.

Well seriously it was a fierce fight and no opera bouffé work either. The mine explosion rattled the delf and startled the cocks over at Slyne Head. The morning was beautifully calm and I slept till ten minutes past eight without any forebodings of trouble. The car man was the first to acquaint me of the news and as we neared Ballinaboy and faced for the school on the hill-top, the fact that operations were afoot was pretty obvious. Small Congregation. A mine explosion rocks the chalice on the altar. The IRA are in position around the place. Firing ceases till Mass is finished, the people dispersed, and the priest safely crouched behind a stone wall on the roadside. The troops from the Marconi Station under cover of the returning Mass-goers have made their way down near their opponents and now the duel begins. I smoke a cigarette to soothe the nerves but don't get time to finish it. A yell of pain from the Free State position, then a cry of agony. I hoist a dirty handkerchief and repair to the spot. He is lying in the swamp, weltering in blood, his rifle beside him, death in his face. His four companions, rather stupefied-looking, are obviously relieved by my advent. He is in shocking agony, fully conscious, can take Holy Communion, and talks Irish. I have finished – and now what to do with him? He cannot be left alone to die in the marsh; he is too heavy for me even to turn. 'We cannot do anything Father. If the Irregulars see our uniforms they will snipe us all. There's a house 40 yards away.' I look for assistance. Yes, they will go with the priest – the old man too.

We bring a sort of bed with us, lift in the wounded man, plaster ourselves all over with blood, and stagger and plough our way through the bog knee deep in water. 'Won't you come back and hear our confessions Father' is shouted after me. We put him before the fire: the woman of the house does all that can be done but his heart's blood is pumping out. The pity of it. Back I go to the others, and lying flat on our bellies, I shrive them one by one. My heart goes out to them and I bid them goodbye, and hie to Ballyconneely. I begin 11 o'clock Mass at 12.15, thinking strange and sad thoughts.

I hasten to the scene of battle after Mass. 'For God's sake hurry Father: there are two dead Republicans on the hill up near the school. They (the Free Staters) shot them with their hands up, Father. I saw the whole thing.' I ran till the froth was thick on my lips, and the pounding of my heart vieing with the rifle cracks. Ah, here is one of them, warm but just dead, his mouth open, the eyeballs staring wildly, a pierced bicycle-pump in his breast pocket, brain-matter bedaubing the wild heather, his head half-buried in a clump of furze – his companion (both from the same village near Ballina) is alive. A dozen people are around him. After six hours of heavy firing they appear to have got quite accustomed to the sensation, and heed not the splutter, bang, ping and crack that goes merrily on a quarter of a mile away, not to speak of the terrific bombardment in the town. They have beads,holy water, Sacred Heart pictures etc., some of them chanting the prayers for the dying, all of them ardent Free Staters. One of them wonders has her son been blown to bits in the Clifden barracks.

Such a handsome boy, so young, and boyish, so clean of limb, so proudly resigned – just twenty, his long black unruly hair tossing about on his pale brow. He knows there's no hope for him. He is lead all over, two fingers blown away, a bullet in the forearm, one in the shoulder, one in the thigh, one through the small of the back. Yes, he thanks God for having got the rites of the church. How is Tom (the dead companion)? Did I get him in time? Yes, they missed the main body and lost their way on the hill. Seven Free Staters came on them ———the people crowd around him. 'They shot me lying down, Yes, they did. I am going before my God soon but I want you all to know that they did that, and one of them used horse-language to me. But I forgive them, I forgive them'. They bear him to a house nearby. Everybody is kind to him: somehow they can't help it. He is in agonies, but offers all his sufferings for the souls in Purgatory, thanks God for the Sacraments, repeatedly calls the Holy Name, never murmurs or complains, but is so sorry that poor Tom hadn't the priest in time. So he lingered for twenty-four hours.

And now a man appears on the road – two civilians wounded out near the town – calling for a priest. Death to attempt going into Clifden – won't I come. Yes, through very shame at what he risked to acquaint me. We get in without mishap, although the rifles are busy all around . . . There's a fierce explosion, a cloud of thick, murky smoke, a shout, a cheer, one last wild crescendo of rifle and machine-gun fire, and all is over. . . . The hill barrack is still standing, but though consumed with curiosity I must repair to Ballyconneely for the Novena. Devotions at five-thirty and it's now five o'clock. Late at night a messenger reaches me to say that no one was killed in the town. The news is incredible, though the best I've heard for a long time. I expected anything up to 50 casualties, and yet the only deaths – three – were all in Ballinaboy.

I went there the next day. A boat was ready. The Free State troops, all a bit shaken, got on board, with their four wounded and one dead. A feeble cheer from their dazed townspeople and they are off – 110 strong, seven having run away from the Marconi station. I don't know if you'll wade through this long-winded, egotistical narrative, but you will understand that as life is very uneventful down here, it looms large as an experience. Peter McDonnell was in charge of the [Republican Military] operation, [General Michael] Kilroy being away at the [Anti-Treaty] Conference in the South.

BIBLIOGRAPHY

Primary Sources

Manuscript Material

1. Franciscan Archives, Killiney
   De Valera papers. Now in Archives Department, University College Dublin

2. Irish College Rome Archive
   Monsignor John Hagan Papers

3. National Archives of Ireland
   Executive Council Minutes
   Taoiseach's Department Files
   Department of Justice Files
   North-Eastern Boundary Bureau Papers

4. National Library of Ireland
   Frank Gallagher Papers
   Count Plunkett Papers
   Séan O'Mahony Papers
   Joseph McGarrity Papers

5. University College Dublin Archives
   Richard Mulcahy Papers
   Ernest Blythe Papers
   Mary MacSwiney papers
   Todd [C.S.] Andrews Papers
   James Ryan papers
   Patrick McGilligan Papers
   Caitlín Brugha Papers
   T.M. Healy Papers
   Desmond FitzGerald Papers
   Ernie O'Malley Papers
   Moss Twomey Papers
   Coyle O'Donnell Papers

6. Trinity College Dublin Archives
   Erskine Childers Papers
   Frank Gallagher Papers

7. Fianna Fáil Headquarters Dublin
   Fianna Fáil Archives

8. Masonic Order Archives
   Records of membership of the Masonic Order

9. Private Possession
   Kathleen O'Connell papers (now in Archives Department, University
   College Dublin). Diary of Robert Egan, PP Mullahoran.

10. Jesuit Archives Dublin
    Edward Cahill Papers.

11. Ardagh and Clonmacnois Diocesan Archive
    Joseph Hoare Papers

12. Armagh Archdiocesan Archive
    Michael Logue Papers
    Patrick O'Donnell Papers
    Joseph MacRory Papers

13. Clogher Diocesan Archive
    Patrick McKenna Papers
    Records of Clergy of the diocese of Clogher

14. Clonfert Diocesan Archive
    John Dignan Papers

15. Dromore Diocesan Archive
    Edward Mulhern papers

16. Dublin Archdiocesan Archive
    Edward Byrne Papers

17. Galway Diocesan Archive
    Thomas O'Dea Papers
    Thomas O'Doherty Papers
    Michael J. Browne Papers

18. Kerry Diocesan Archive
    Charles O'Sullivan Papers
    Michael O'Brien Papers.

19. Kildare and Leighlin Diocesan Archive
    Patrick Foley Papers

20. Killaloe Diocesan Archive
    Michael Fogarty Papers

21. Limerick Diocesan Archive
    Denis Hallinan Papers
    David Keane Papers

22. Tuam Archdiocesan Archive
    Papers of Thomas Gilmartin
    Papers of Pádraig Ó Móráin.

Published Material

1. Dáil Debates

    Dáil Éireann. *Official Report for the period 16 August 1921 to 26 August 1921 and 28 February 1922 to 8 June 1922.*
    Dáil Éireann. *Official Report – Debate on the Treaty between Great Britain and Ireland signed in London on 6 December 1921.*
    Dáil Éireann. *Private Sessions of the Second Dáil, 1921–2.*

2. Government Publications

    Correspondence of Mr. Eamon de Valera and others. Published by the Stationery Office for Dáil Éireann, (Parlimint Sealadach), 1922.

3. Newspapers and Periodicals

Anglo-Celt	*Freedom (Saoirse na h-Éireann)*
Catholic Bulletin	*Freeman's Journal*
Capuchin Annual	*Free Press Wexford*
Clare Champion	*Irish Catholic*
Clonmel Chronicle	*Irish Catholic Directory and Almanac*
Connaught Sentinel	*Irish Historical Studies*
Connaught Tribune	*Irish Ecclesiastical Record*
Cork Examiner	*Irish Press*
Derry Journal	*Irish Independent*
Derry People	*Irish News*
Donegal Democrat	*Irish Rosary*
Dundalk Examiner	*Irish Weekly Independent*
East Galway Democrat	*Irish World*
Éire	*The Irish Times*
Enniscorthy Echo	*Kerry Champion*
Feasta	*Kerryman*
Fermanagh Herald	*Kerry People*

Kildare Observer
Kilkenny Journal
Leader (Dublin)
Leader (San Francisco)
Leinster Reporter (Birr)
Leitrim Advertiser
Leitrim Observer
Limerick Echo
Limerick Herald
Limerick Leader
Limerick Weekly and District
  Advertiser
Longford Leader
Mayo News
Meath Chronicle and Cavan and
  Westmeath Herald
Midland Tribune
Munster News
The Nation
Nationalist and Leinster Times
Nenagh Guardian
Offaly Independent
People's Press, Donegal

An Phoblacht
Republican Congress
Roscommon Journal
Roscommon Herald
Roscommon Messenger
Saturday Record and Clare Journal
  (Ennis)
Sinn Féin
Sligo Champion
Standard
Strokestown Democrat
Tablet (London)
Times Literary Supplement
Tipperaryman and Limerick Recorder
Tuam Herald
United Irishman
Weekly Freeman
Western News (Ballina)
Western People
Westmeath Independent
Wicklow People
Wexford People
Wolfe Tone Annual

Interviews and/or Correspondence with the following:

Tony Benn, MP; Martin Browne, Ennis; Sr M. Cabrini, Cobh; Rev. Patrick Conlan, o.f.m. Cork; Rev. Professor Thomas Corbett, Maynooth; Rev. Séamus Corkery, Charleville; Rev. Professor Patrick J. Corish, Maynooth; Rev. Owen Devanney, Mullahoran; Rev. Dr Joseph Duffy, Bishop of Clogher; Rev. Dr P.K. Egan, Portumna; Michael Farry, Trim; William Fraher, Dungarvan; Rev. J. Anthony Gaughan, Dublin; Rev. Daniel Gallogley, Mullagh, Co. Cavan; Mgr John Hanly, Irish College Rome; Mannix Joyce, Limerick; Rev. Professor Donal Kerr, Maynooth; Rev. Brendan Kilcoyne, Tuam; Professor Emmet Larkin, Chicago; Rev. Peader Lavin, Boyle; Professor J.J. Lee, Cork; Mgr Daniel Long, Tralee; Rev. Professor John Mc Areavy, Maynooth; Jim Maher, Kilkenny; John Mansfield, Dungarvan; Dr Patrick Maume, The Queen's University, Belfast; Rev. Joseph Mooney, Tullamore; Aubrey Murphy, Wexford; Dr Brian P. Murphy, Glenstal Abbey; Dr Brian S. Murphy, Dublin; Seán Murphy, Kilmacthomas; Fr Nessan, o.f.m. Cap., Cork; Canon Michéal Ó Dálaigh, Cork; Rev. Pádraig Ó Fiannachta, Dingle; Rev. Denis O'Callaghan, Mallow; T.P. O'Neill; Máire Ní Cheallaigh; Rev. Ciarán Ó Sabhaois, Roscrea; Rev. Kieran O'Shea, Knocknagoshel; Sr Philomena, Poor Clare Convent, Kenmare; Rev. Stephen Redmond, SJ; Mr Richard Roche, Dublin; Rev. John Silke, Portnablagh, Donegal; Rev. Dr Michael Smith, Bishop of Meath;

Rev. Mark Tierney, Glenstal Abbey; Rev. Henry Tonra, Cootehall, Boyle; Brother Linus Walker, Carlow; Rev. Michael Wall, Limerick; Miss Alex Ward, Dublin; Rev. Ian Waters, Melbourne Diocesan Historical Commission.

Secondary Sources

Akenson, D.H. 'Was de Valera a Republican?' *Review of Politics*, vol. 33, no. 2, 1972.

Akenson, D.H. and J.F. Fallin, 'The Irish Civil War and the Drafting of the Free State Constitution', *Éire-Ireland*, Summer, 1970 and Winter, 1970.

Anderson, W.K., *James Connolly and the Irish Left* (Dublin, 1994).

Andrews, C.S., *Dublin Made Me* (Dublin, 1979).

Andrews, C.S., *Man of No Property* (Dublin, 1979).

Anon, *The Story of Fianna Fáil: First Phase* (Dublin, 1960).

Bane, Liam, 'The Irish Catholic Secular Clergy, 1850–1900', PhD thesis, TCD, 1994.

Banta, Mary, 'The Red Scare in the Irish Free State, 1929-37', Unpublished MA Thesis, UCD, 1982.

Barrington, Donal, *The Church, the State and the Constitution* (Dublin, 1959).

Bell, J. Bowyer, 'Ireland and the Spanish Civil War' *Studia Hibernica*, no. 9, 1969.

Bell, J. Bowyer, *The Secret Army* (London 1970).

Bellenger, D.A. 'An Irish Benedictine Adventure: Dom Francis Sweetman (1872–1953) and Mount St Benedict Gorey' in W.J. Shiels and D. Wood (eds), *The Churches, Ireland and the Irish* (London, 1989).

Bew, Paul, Gibbon, Peter and Patterson, Henry, *Northern Ireland 1921–1994. Political Forces and Social Classes* (London, 1995).

Blythe, Ernest [de Blaghad Earnan] *Gael á Múscailt* (Dublin, 1973).

Blythe, Ernest, *Slán le Ultaibh* (Dublin, 1970).

Bolster, Evelyn, *The Knights of St Columbanus* (Dublin, 1979).

Bourke, Marcus, *John O'Leary. A Study in Irish Separatism* (Tralee, 1967).

Bowman, John, *De Valera and the Ulster Question, 1917–1973* (Oxford, 1982).

Boyce, D.G. (ed.), *The Revolution in Ireland, 1879–1923* (Dublin, 1988).

Breen, Dan, *My Fight for Irish Freedom* (Tralee, 1964).

Brennan, Robert, *Allegiance* (Dublin, 1950).

Browne, Kevin J. *Eamon de Valera and the Banner County* (Dublin, 1987).

Browne, M.J. 'The Source and Purpose of Political Authority', *Studies*, September, 1936.

Browne, M.J. (ed.), *The Synod of Maynooth, 1927. Decrees which Affect the Catholic Laity* (Dublin, 1930).

Brusher, J.S. *Consecrated Thunderbolt. Father Yorke of San Francisco* (New Jersey, 1973).

Buckland, Patrick, *A History of Northern Ireland* (Dublin, 1980).

Buckland, Patrick, *James Craig, Lord Craigavon* (Dublin, 1980).

Buckland, Patrick, *The Factory of Grievances. Devolved Government in Northern Ireland 1921–39* (Dublin, 1979).

Buckley, Margaret, *The Jangle of the Keys* (Dublin, 1938).

Cahill, Edward, *Freemasonry and the Anti-Christian Movement* (Dublin, 1929).

Callanan, F. *T.M. Healy* (Cork, 1996).

Canning, B.J., *Bishops of Ireland* (Donegal, 1987).

Canning, Paul, *British Policy Towards Ireland, 1921–1941* (Oxford 1985).

Carroll, Denis, *They have fooled you again. Michael O'Flanagan (1876–1942). Priest, Republican, Social Critic* (Dublin, 1993).

Clarke, Kathleen, *Revolutionary Woman* (Dublin, 1991).

Columban na Banban, *False Pastors*, n.d. [*c*.1924]

Conlan, Patrick, *St. Isidore's College, Rome* (Rome 1982).

Conlan, Patrick, *The Franciscans in Drogheda* (Dublin, 1987).

Coogan, T.P., *The I.R.A.* (London, 1970).

Coogan, T.P. *Michael Collins* (London, 1989).

Coogan, T.P. *De Valera. Long Fellow, Long Shadow* (London, 1993).

Corish, P.J. (ed.), *A History of Irish Catholicism*, vol. 5. *The Church Since Emancipation* (Dublin, 1970).

Corish, P.J. *Maynooth College, 1795–1995.* (Dublin, 1995).

Coyle, Eugene, *Freemasonry in Ireland* (Dublin, 1928).

Cronin, S. (ed.), *The McGarrity Papers* (Tralee, 1972).

Cronin, S. *Frank Ryan and The Search for the Republic* (Dublin, 1980).

Crozier, F.P., *Ireland for Ever* (Dublin, 1963).

De Valera, Eamon, *National Discipline and Majority Rule* (Dublin, 1936).

De Valera, Eamon, *The Way to Peace* (Dublin, 1934).

Devoy, John, *Recollections of an Irish Rebel* (New York, 1929).

Donnelly, P. 'Violence and Catholic Theology', *Studies*, Autumn 1994, pp. 331–40.

Dooher, J.B., 'Tyrone Nationalism and the Question of Partition, 1910–25', MPhil thesis, University of Ulster, 1986

Dunphy, Richard, *The Making of Fianna Fáil Power in Ireland, 1923–1948* (Oxford, 1995).

Dwyer, T. Ryle, *De Valera: The Man and the Myths* (Dublin, 1991).

Edwards, Ruth Dudley, *Patrick Pearse: The Triumph of Failure* (London, 1977).

Elliott, Marianne, *Wolfe Tone. Prophet of Irish Independence* (Yale, 1989).

English, Richard, *Radicals and the Republic. Socialist Republicanism in the Irish Free State, 1925–1937* (Oxford, 1994).

English, Richard and O'Malley, Cormac (eds), *Prisoners* (Dublin, 1993).

English, Richard and O'Malley, Cormac (eds), *The Civil War Letters of Ernie O'Malley* (Dublin, 1991).

English, Richard, *Ernie O'Malley, I.R.A. Intellectual* (Dublin, 1998).

Fallin, C.H., *A Soul of Fire. A Biography of Mary MacSwiney* (Cork, 1986).

Fanning, Ronan, *Independent Ireland* (Dublin, 1983).

Farragher, S.P. *Dev and his Alma Mater. Eamon de Valera's long association with Blackrock College, 1898–1975* (Dublin, 1984).

Farrell, Brian (ed.), *De Valera's Constitution and Ours* (Dublin,1988).

Farrell, Michael, *Arming the Protestants. The Formation of the Ulster Special Constabulary, 1920–27* (London, 1983).

Farrell, Michael, *Northern Ireland. The Orange State* (Dublin, 1983).

Faughnan, S., 'The Jesuits and the drafting of the Irish Constitution of 1937', *IHS*, vol. xxvi, no. 101, May, 1988, pp. 79–102.

Fitzgerald, W.G. (ed.), *The Voice of Ireland. Glór na hÉireann. A Survey of the Race and Nation from all Angles* (Dublin, 1933).

Fitzpatrick, David, *Politics and Irish Life 1913–1921. Provincial Experience of War and Revolution* (Dublin, 1977).

Fitzpatrick, David, 'Divorce and Separation in Modern Irish History', *Past and Present*, no. 14, February 1987, pp. 172–96.

Fitzpatrick, David, 'The Undoing of the Easter Rising', in J. P. Carroll and J.A. Murphy (eds), *De Valera and His Time* (Cork, 1983).

Fitzpatrick, David (ed.), *Revolution? Ireland 1917–23* (Dublin, 1990).

Fitzpatrick, David, *The Two Irelands, 1912–1939* (Oxford, 1998)

Follis, Bryan, A., *A State Under Siege, The Establishment of Northern Ireland*, (Oxford, 1995).

Foster, R.F., *Modern Ireland, 1600–1972* (London, 1988).

Freyer, Grattan, *Peadar O'Donnell* (Lewisburg, 1973).

Gallagher, Frank, *The Indivisible Island. The History of the Partition of Ireland* (London, 1957).

Gallagher, Frank, *A Prisoner's Letter to His Grace the Archbishop of Dublin* (Dublin, 1922).

Gallagher, Michael, *Electoral Support for Irish Political Parties, 1927–1973* (London, 1976).

Gallagher, Michael, *Political Parties in the Republic of Ireland* (Dublin, 1985).

Gannon, Patrick J., 'In the Catacombs of Belfast', *Studies*, June, 1922.

Garvin, Tom, *The Evolution of Irish Nationalist Politics* (Dublin, 1981).

Garvin, Tom, *Nationalist Revolutionaries in Ireland* (Oxford, 1987).

Garvin, Tom, *1922. The Birth of Irish Democracy* (Dublin, 1996).

Gaughan, J.A. *Austin Stack: Portrait of a Separatist* (Dublin, 1977).

Gaughan, J.A. (ed.), *The Memoirs of James G. Douglas: Concerned Citizen* (Dublin, 1998).

Gilmore, George, *The Republican Congress* (Cork, 1978).

Golden, Peter, *Impressions of Ireland*, n.d.

Greaves, C.D., *Liam Mellows and the Irish Revolution* (London, 1971).

Griffin, James, 'Daniel Mannix and the Cult of Personality' in O. MacDonagh and W.E. Mandle (eds), *Ireland and Irish Australia: Studies in Cultural and Political History* (London, 1986).

Gwynn, Denis, *The History of Partition, 1912–1925* (Dublin, 1950).

Hamell, Patrick, *Maynooth Students and Ordinations* (Dublin, 1982, 1984)

Hand, G. (ed.), *Report of the Irish Boundary Commission 1925* (Shannon, 1969).

Harkness, D.W., *The Restless Dominion: The Irish Free State in the British Commonwealth of Nations, 1921–31* (London, 1969).

Harkness, D.W., *Northern Ireland since 1920* (Dublin, 1983).

Harrington, N.C., *Kerry Landing, August 1922* (Dublin, 1992).

Harris, Mary, *The Catholic Church and the Foundation of the Northern Irish State* (Cork 1993).

Hopkinson, M., 'The Craig–Collins Pact of 1922: two attempted reforms of the Northern Ireland Government', *IHS*, vol. xxvii, no. 106, November, 1990.

Hopkinson, M., *Green Against Green. The Irish Civil War* (Dublin, 1988).

Inglis, T., *Moral Monopoly: The Rise and Fall of the Catholic Church in Modern Ireland*, 2nd edn (Dublin, 1998).

Irish Race Congress, *Proceedings of the Irish Race Congress in Paris. January 1922.* Issued by Fine Ghaedheal. Central Secretariat, Dublin, n.d.

Isaacson, Alfred (ed.), *Irish Letters in the New York Carmelites' Archives* (Baton Rouge, 1988).

Kearney, Richard (ed.), *The Irish Mind* (Dublin, 1984).

Kennedy, D., *The Widening Gulf. Northern Attitudes to the Independent Irish State* (Belfast 1988).

Keogh, Dermot, *The Vatican, the Bishops and Irish Politics 1919–39* (Cambridge 1986).

Keogh, Dermot, 'The Jesuits and the 1937 Constitution', *Studies*, vol. 78, Spring, 1989, pp. 82–95

Keogh, Dermot, *Ireland and Europe, 1919–1989. A Diplomatic and Political History* (Dublin, 1989).

Keogh, Dermot, 'Fr Alexander J. McCabe and the Spanish Civil War, 1936–1939', *Breifne*, 1994.

Keogh, Dermot, *Twentieth Century Ireland. Nation and State* (Dublin, 1994).

Keogh, Dermot, *Ireland and the Vatican. The Politics and Diplomacy of Church–State Relations, 1922–1960* (Cork, 1995).

Kiernan, Colm, *Daniel Mannix and Ireland* (Dublin, 1984).

Laffan, Michael, *The Partition of Ireland, 1911–1925* (Dundalk, 1983).

Larkin, Emmet, *The Roman Catholic Church and the Plan of Campaign, 1886–1888* (Cork, 1978).

Larkin, Emmet, 'Socialism and Catholicism in Ireland', *Church History*, vol. xxiii, December 1964, pp. 464–83

Larkin, Emmet, 'Church, State and Nation in Modern Ireland', *American Historical Review*, vol. 80, 1975

Lee, J.J., *Ireland 1912–1985. Politics and Society* (Cambridge, 1989).

Lee, J.J. and Ó Tuathaigh, G. *The Age of de Valera* (Dublin, 1982).

Lindsay, Patrick, *Memories* (Dublin, 1993)

Livingstone, Peter, *The Fermanagh Story*, Clogher Historical Society (Enniskillen, 1969).

Livingstone, Peter, *The Monaghan Story*, Clogher Historical Society (Enniskillen, 1980).

The Earl of Longford and T.P. O'Neill, *Eamon de Valera* (Dublin, 1970).

Lyons, F.S.L., *Ireland Since the Famine* (London, 1971)

Lyons, F.S.L., *Culture and Anarchy in Ireland 1880–1939* (Oxford 1980).

Lyons, F. S. L., *Charles Stewart Parnell* (London, 1977).

MacBride, Seán, 'Rome Rule?', *Irish Press*, 12.4.86.

MacCarthy, Carthach, *Archdeacon Tom Duggan. In Peace and in War* (Dublin, 1994).

McCaughey, Michael, *Around Trillick Way* (Trillick Historical Society, n.d.).

McCoole, Sinéad, *Hazel, A Life of Lady Lavery, 1880–1935* (Dublin, 1996).

McDonagh, Oliver, *States of Mind. A Study of Anglo-Irish Conflict 1780–1980* (London, 1983).

McDonald, Walter, *Some Ethical Questions of Peace and War with special reference to Ireland* (London, 1920).

McDowell, R.B. and Webb, D.A., *Trinity College Dublin, 1592–1952, An Academic History* (Cambridge, 1982).

McDowell, R.B., 'Trinity College Dublin and Politics', *Hermathena*, 1997

MacEoin, Uinseann, *Survivors* (Dublin, 1980).

Mac Gabhann, Gearóid, 'Portráid Sean-Chara', *Feasta*, Deire Fomhair, 1988

Mac Ghiolle Chiolle, B. (ed.), *Chief Secretary's Intelligence Notes* (Dublin, 1966).

McGowan, Joe, *In the Shadow of Ben Bulben* (Manorhamilton, n.d.).

McHugh, J.P., 'Voices of the Rearguard: A Study of *An Phoblacht*. Irish Republican thought in the post-Revolutionary Era 1923–1937', MA thesis, UCD, 1983.

McInerny, M.H., *A History of the Irish Dominicans* (Dublin, 1916).

McInerney, Michael, *Peadar O'Donnell. Irish Social Rebel* (Dublin, 1974).

McMahon, Deirdre, *Republicans and Imperialists: Anglo-Irish Relations in the 1930s* (London, 1984).

McRedmond, Louis, *To the Greater Glory. A History of the Irish Jesuits* (Dublin, 1991).

Macardle, Dorothy, *The Irish Republic*, 4th edn (Dublin, 1951).

Macardle, Dorothy, *Tragedies of Kerry* (Dublin, 1924).

Maguire, G.E., 'The Political and Military Causes of the Division in the Nationalist Movement. January 1921 to August 1923', DPhil thesis, Oxford, 1985.

Maher, Jim, *The Flying Column – West Kilkenny 1916–1921* (Dublin, 1987).

Mannion, Vergil, *A Life Recalled. Experiences of an Irish Franciscan* (Dublin n.d.).

Mannix, Daniel, *Speeches of the Most Rev. Dr Mannix, Archbishop of Melbourne in the Rotunda, Dublin, October 22nd and 29th 1925*. Published by Sinn Féin n.d. [1925].

Martin, F.X. 'The 1916 Rising: A Coup d'État or a "Bloody Protest"', *Studia Hibernica*, vol. viii, 1968, pp. 106–37.

Maume, Patrick, *D.P. Moran* (Dublin, 1995).

Miller, D.W., *Church, State and Nation in Ireland, 1898–1921* (Dublin, 1973).

Mitchell, Arthur, *Labour in Irish Politics, 1890–1930* (Dublin, 1974).

Moran, Gerard, *Patrick Lavalle: A Radical Priest in Mayo* (Dublin, 1994).

Moran, Gerard (ed.), *Radical Irish Priests 1660–1970* (Dublin 1998).

Morrissey, T.J., *Towards a National University: William Delany, SJ, 1835–1924* (Dublin, 1979).

Moss, W., *Political Parties in the Irish Free State* (New York, 1933).

Moynihan, Maurice (ed.), *Speeches and Statements by Eamon de Valera, 1917–1973* (Dublin, 1980).

Murphy, Brian, P. 'J.J. O'Kelly ("Sceilg") and the *Catholic Bulletin*: Cultural Considerations – Gaelic, Religious and National, *c*.1898–1929', PhD thesis, UCD, 1986.

Murphy, Brian, P., *Patrick Pearse and the Lost Republican Ideal* (Dublin, 1991).

Murphy, J.A., 'Priests and People in Modern Irish History', *Christus Rex*, vol. xxiii, no. 4, October, 1969, pp. 235–59

Murphy, Seán and Sighle, *The Comeraghs. Refuge of Rebels. The Story of the Deise Brigade IRA 1914–24*, n.d.

Murray, Patrick, 'Voices of de Valera', MLitt thesis, TCD, 1995.

Neeson, Eoin, *The Civil War in Ireland, 1922–23* (Cork, 1966).

Newsinger, J., 'I bring not peace but a sword: The religious motif in the Irish War of Independence'. *Journal of Contemporary History*, vol.13, no. 3, July 1978, pp. 609–28

Ó Baoighill, Pádraig, *Niall Pluincéad Ó Baoighill. Óglach na Rosann* (Dublin, 1994).

O'Brien, C.C., *Passion and Cunning* (New York, 1988).

O'Brien, C.C., *Ancestral Voices. Religion and Nationalism in Ireland* (Dublin, 1994).

O'Brien, J. and Travers, P., *The Irish Emigrant Experience in Australia* (Dublin, 1991).

O'Callaghan, Margaret, 'Language, Nationality and Cultural Identity in the Irish Free State, 1922–7', *IHS*, vol. xxiv, no. 94, November 1984, pp. 226–45.

O'Carroll, J.P. and Murphy, J.A. (eds), *De Valera and His Times* (Cork, 1983).

O'Casey, Sean, *Autobiographies* (Dublin, 1963).

Ó Ceallaigh, Seán T., *Seán T. In eagar ag P. Ó Fiannachta* (Dublin, 1972).

O'Connor, Séamus, *To-morrow Was Another Day* (Tralee, 1970).

O'Doherty, K., *Assignment America* (New York, 1957).

O'Donnell, Peadar, *The Knife* (London, 1930).

O'Donnell, Peadar, *Salud! An Irishman in Spain* (London, 1937).

O'Donnell, Peadar, *There Will Be Another Day* (Dublin, 1963).

O'Duffy, Eoin, *Crusade in Spain* (Dublin, 1938).

O'Dwyer, Peter, *Peter Magennis. Priest and Patriot, 1886–1937* (Dublin, 1975).

Ó Faoláin, Seán, *Vive Moi* (London, 1965).

O'Farrell, Patrick, *Ireland's English Question. Anglo-Irish Relations 1534–1970* (New York, 1971).

Ó Fiaich, Tomás, 'The Clergy and Fenianism 1860–70', *Irish Ecclesiastical Record*, February 1968.

Ó Fiaich, Tomás, 'The Irish Bishops and the Conscription Issue 1918', *Capuchin Annual*, 1968.

Ó Fiaich, Tomás, 'The Catholic Clergy and the Independence Movement', *Capuchin Annual*, 1970.

Ó Fiaich, Tomás, *Magh Nuad* (Dublin, 1972).

O'Halloran, Clare, *Partition and the Limits of Irish Nationalism, An Ideology Under Stress* (Dublin, 1987).

O'Higgins, Brian (ed.), *Wolfe Tone Annual*, 1916 number, 1935.

O'Kelly, J.J., *A Trinity of Martyrs* (Dublin, 1947).

O'Leary, John, *Recollections of Fenians and Fenianism* (London, 1896).

Ó Loinsigh, Pádraig, *Gobnait Ní Bhruadair, The Hon. Albinia Brodrick* (Dublin, 1997).

O'Malley, Ernie, *The Singing Flame* (Tralee, 1978).

Ó Maoiléidigh, B., *Reply to the Pastoral Address by the Irish Hierarchy*, October 1922.

O'Neill, T.P., 'In Search of a Political Path: Irish Republicanism 1922–1927', *IHS*, vol. x, pp. 147–71.

O'Neill, T.P., 'Dr J.C. McQuaid and Eamon de Valera: Insights on Church and State', *Breifne*, 1993.

O'Neill, T.P. agus Ó Fiannachta, P., *De Valera* (Dublin, 1970).

O'Reilly, Noel, 'Pro fide et patria?: The Catholic Church and Republicanism in Ireland, 1912–23', PhD. thesis, Queen's University of Belfast, 1994.

O'Riordan, Michael, *Connolly Column* (Dublin, 1979).

O'Shea, J., *Priests, Politics and Society in Post-Famine Ireland* (Dublin, 1983).

O'Sullivan, Donal, *The Irish Free State and its Senate. A Study in Contemporary Politics* (London, 1940).

Patterson, Henry, *The Politics of Illusion. Republicanism and Socialism in Modern Ireland* (London, 1989).

Pearse, Pádraic H., *Political Writings and Speeches* (Dublin, 1952).

Phillips, W.A., *The Revolution in Ireland 1906–1923*, 2nd edn (London, 1926).

Phoenix, Eamon, *Northern Nationalism: Nationalist Politics, Partition and the Catholic Minority in Northern Ireland, 1890–1940* (Belfast 1994).

Plunkett, Horace, *Ireland in the New Century* (London, 1904).

Quinn, James, *The Story of the Drumboe Martyrs* (Letterkenny, 1958).

Rafferty, O., *Catholicism in Ulster, 1603–1983* (Dublin, 1994).

Rumpf, E. and Hepburn, A.C., *Nationalism and Socialism in Twentieth-Century Ireland* (Liverpool, 1977).

Ryan, Desmond, *Socialism and Nationalism* (Dublin, 1948).

Ryan, Desmond, *Unique Dictator* (Dublin, 1936).

Shaw, Nessan (ed.), *The Irish Capuchins. Record of a Century 1885–1985* (Dublin, 1985).

Sheedy, K., *The Clare Elections* (Dublin, 1993).

Sherry, R. (ed.), *Holy Cross College, Clonliffe Dublin. College History and Centenary Record* (Dublin, 1959)

Skehan, W.G., *Cashel and Emly Heritage* (Dublin, 1993).

Stewart, A.T.Q. *The Narrow Ground* (Belfast, 1977).

Tansill, T.D., *America and the Fight for Irish Freedom 1886–1923* (New York, 1957).

Taylor, A.J.P., *English History, 1914–45* (Oxford, 1965).

Thomas, Hugh, *The Spanish Civil War* (London, 1961).

Tierney, Mark, *Croke of Cashel: The Life of Archbishop Thomas William Croke, 1823–1902* (Dublin, 1976).

Towey, T., 'The Reaction of the British Government to the 1922 Collins–de Valera Pact', *IHS*, vol. xxii, 1985, pp. 65–76.

Townshend, Charles, *Political Violence in Ireland* (Oxford, 1983).

Walker, Brian M., *Parliamentary Election Results in Ireland, 1918–92* (Dublin, 1992).

White, Terence de Vere, *Kevin O'Higgins* (Dublin, 1966).

Whyte, J.H., *Church and State in Modern Ireland, 1923–1979*, 2nd edn (Dublin, 1980).

Williams, T.D. (ed.), *Secret Societies in Ireland* (Dublin, 1973).

Yorke, Peter, *Irish Bishops Usurp Papal Rights* (Glasgow 1923).

INDEX

War of Independence, 6, 12, 13, 20, 48, 408–9
Ward, Rev. John, 380
Westmeath, 51, 78
Wexford, 64, 105, 260
White, Rev. Charles, 251, 283
Whyte, J.H., 108–9, 274, 292
Wicklow, Earl of, 142

Wilson, Sir Henry, 66
Wolfe, Jasper Travers, TD, 279
Woods, James, 366
Worthington-Evans, Sir Laming, 379

Yorke, Rev. Peter, 17, 220, 221, 424
Young Irelanders, 5